Volume 1

D1490086

Artificial Intelligence at MIT

Volume 1

Artificial Intelligence at MIT
Expanding Frontiers

edited by Patrick Henry Winston
with Sarah Alexandra Shellard

The MIT Press
Cambridge, Massachusetts
London, England

This book was printed and bound in the United States of America.

Library of Congress Cataloging-in-Publication Data

Artificial intelligence at MIT: expanding frontiers/edited by Patrick Henry Winston with Sarah Alexandra Shellard.

     p.   cm. — (Artificial intelligence series)
     ISBN 978-0-262-23150-3 (hc.:alk. paper)
     ISBN 978-0-262-52640-1 (pb.)

    1. Artificial intelligence. I. Winston, Patrick Henry. II. Shellard, Sarah Alexandra. III. Series: Artificial intelligence series (London, England)
Q335.A78713   1990
006.3—dc20   90-5540
                                              CIP

Contents: Volume 1

23

Series Foreword

Artificial intelligence is the study of intelligence using the ideas and methods of computation. Unfortunately a definition of intelligence seems impossible at the moment because intelligence appears to be an amalgam of so many information-processing and information-representation abilities.

Of course psychology, philosophy, linguistics, and related disciplines offer various perspectives and methodologies for studying intelligence. For the most part, however, the theories proposed in these fields are too incomplete and too vaguely stated to be realized in computational terms. Something more is needed, even though valuable ideas, relationships, and constraints can be gleaned from traditional studies of what are, after all, impressive existence proofs that intelligence is in fact possible.

Artificial intelligence offers a new perspective and a new methodology. Its central goal is to make computers intelligent, both to make them more useful and to understand the principles that make intelligence possible. That intelligent computers will be extremely useful is obvious. The more profound point is that artificial intelligence aims to understand intelligence using the ideas and methods of computation, thus offering a radically new and different basis for theory formation. Most of the people doing work in artificial intelligence believe that these theories will apply to any intelligent information processor, whether biological or solid state.

There are side effects that deserve attention, too. Any program that will successfully model even a small part of intelligence will be inherently massive and complex. Consequently artificial intelligence continually confronts the limits of computer-science technology. The problems encountered have been hard enough and interesting enough to seduce artificial intelligence people into working on them with enthusiasm. It is natural, then, that there has been a steady flow of ideas from artificial intelligence to computer science, and the flow shows no sign of abating.

The purpose of this series in artificial intelligence is to provide people in many areas, both professionals and students, with timely, detailed information about what is happening on the frontiers in research centers all over the world.

J. Michael Brady
Daniel G. Bobrow
Randall Davis

Preface cum Introduction

Patrick Henry Winston
Sarah Alexandra Shellard

Thirty years ago, Marvin Minsky published *Semantic Information Processing*, a collection of his students' theses, because there were no journals devoted to Artificial Intelligence. Today, we face the opposite problem: research results are scattered widely among highly specialized journals, conference proceedings, and monographs, making it almost impossible to see the general trends emerging from myriad research and development centers. To help address this problem, we are publishing these volumes, which provide an overview of current work in Artificial Intelligence from the perspective of the students, staff, and faculty of the MIT Artificial Intelligence Laboratory.

Fighting Fragmentation

We believe that such an overview is needed because the expansion of the field has led to narrowness and fragmentation. Until recently, people from different subfields attended the same meetings, and ideas moved quickly. Today, however, the once-small AI community has grown large, and people in one subfield are slow to learn about the exciting new results emerging in other subfields.

Yet historically, cross fertilization has been of great value in Artificial Intelligence. The idea of constraint propagation, for example, emerged in formal logic, became popular through Waltz's work on line-drawing analysis, and then settled in as a dominant paradigm in model-based problem solving. Similarly, the notion of frame became part of the AI vernacular in a paper by Minsky that concentrated on the visual world, but subsequently became mostly associated with expert systems that have nothing to do with vision. And the Connection Machine, which was conceived in our laboratory as a machine for searching semantic nets, has become a dominant vehicle for executing early vision procedures, for computing paths for manipulators, and for brute-force database mining. Elsewhere, the Connection Machine is being used for a host of other unrelated applications ranging from weather modeling to lattice gauge theory in high energy nuclear physics.

Who Should Read these Volumes

We believe that cross fertilization should be as common today as it was in the early days. Accordingly, we have assembled these two volumes to stimulate and provoke a new generation of students, researchers, and those who strive to solve practical problems using cutting-edge technology. If you are among them, read these volumes to learn about emerging trends in Artificial Intelligence and to equip yourself with a host of innovative, reusable ideas.

How To Read these Volumes

We do not expect many readers to devour every chapter in these two volumes. After all, forty-three chapters and more than 1200 pages are too many to digest in a day or two.

Consequently, we have written a short vignette to introduce each chapter. Collectively, these vignettes provide historical perspective, explain the key ideas, describe exciting results, and suggest practical consequences. We recommend that you start with these vignettes so as to determine which chapters best suit your own needs and interests.

Expanding Frontiers

Our title, *Expanding Frontiers*, is meant to be a *double entendre*. One reading is that the traditional AI subfields are advancing, as indeed they are, for there has been great progress in the past decade on everything from model-based reasoning to image understanding. Another reading is that Artificial Intelligence is expanding through the addition of new subfields, such as subsumption-based control and neural-net learning, which have joined the traditional subfields.

It would be wrong to suppose that the subfields of Artificial Intelligence are moving further apart. In the following paragraphs, we outline what we believe to be unifying challenges and unifying approaches to those challenges.

Scalable Solutions

In the early days of Artificial Intelligence, nearly all AI work involved a toy problem. Image understanding programs analyzed line drawings of blocks. Learning programs learned about structures made of blocks. And natural language programs attempted to unravel questions about blocks.

Fifteen years ago, some practical programs had emerged, but for the most part, toy problems still filled the literature.

Today, however, it is increasingly hard to attract attention unless your idea seems robust enough to be scaled up to the level demanded by real-world complexities. You do not necessarily need to exhibit a real-world prototype, but it should be clear that the gap between what you have done and what real technology consumers need can be bridged without another breakthrough.

Throughout these volumes, there are many examples of programs that are manifestly scalable because they have already met the challenge of the real world. For example, Sussman, Abelson, and their students have helped oceanographers solve problems in wave dynamics. Lathrop has helped biologists find new patterns for recognizing proteins in the reverse transcriptase class. Katz has helped journalists access information about Voyager 2's Neptune encounter with a program that reads text and answers questions in English. And Grimson has helped production engineers write vision programs for recognition and testing.

Unmodelable and Chaotic Worlds

Most of today's builders of applied AI systems assume that everything can be modeled and that the world behaves according to model-based predictions. Yet some situations, like desk clutter, defy detailed symbolic description because there is just too much to be described. And some dynamic systems, like robot arms or national economies, seem chaotic in that predictions based on models diverge quickly from reality.

Accordingly, many AI researchers have begun to concentrate on unmodelable and chaotic worlds. Some believe that such worlds cannot be handled with the traditional symbolic systems, arguing instead for neural nets and a variety of other nonsymbolic approaches.†

Within our laboratory, many of us believe that symbolic and nonsymbolic systems are both important. As Marvin Minsky said recently, "The trouble with symbolic systems is that they are too fragile, and the trouble

---

†Some critics of Artificial Intelligence even seem to have succumbed to a nonsequitur: there are some kinds of intelligence that cannot be modeled by symbolic reasoning, therefore symbolic reasoning cannot have anything to do with intelligence.

with neural nets is that they are too stupid." One of the great challenges ahead is to learn how to design systems that are partly symbolic and partly nonsymbolic so that they are neither fragile nor stupid.

But what can be meant by *nonsymbolic*? Some researchers work on neural nets because they believe that the road to intelligent machines must travel through biology. Others disagree. But everyone agrees that we need better theories that show what neural nets can and cannot do. Along these lines, Poggio and Girosi have contributed considerably to our understanding of neural net capabilities and limits by exploiting the mathematics of interpolation and approximation.

Other critics of traditional symbolic computation believe that neural nets are not the right thing either. Brooks, for example, advocates his subsumption architecture, which is based on layers of finite state machines and the principle that the world must be its own model.

Learning and Regularity Recognition

Learning is another approach to dealing with the unmodelable and chaotic in particular and the unspeakably complicated in general. As Artificial Intelligence faces harder challenges, it is natural for more AI researchers to include some aspect of learning in their research agendas. Atkeson, for example, not only wants to make robots agile, he insists that robots learn to be agile. Lee not only wants programs to help decision makers, he insists that programs use knowledge from past decisions. Lathrop not only wants programs to help biologists, he insists that programs dig regularity out of big biology databases. And Davis not only wants programs to debug malfunctioning hardware, he insists that programs learn to handle more difficult debugging problems.

Massive Parallelism

We can now process data like bulldozers process gravel, using parallel machines with thousands of processors. Increasingly, this changes the way we think. Minimally, we can do what we have always wanted to do but could not because of computing limitations; more dramatically, we can have thoughts that we could not have had before because our thinking was shackled by what seemed like realistic hardware expectations. Much of the learning work done at MIT would not have been done were there no massively parallel hardware. Similarly, much of computer vision research would be stifled without experiments enabled by massively parallel hardware.

Today, *massively parallel* means the Connection Machine, which, like the Lisp Machine, is part of a long tradition of innovative hardware and software system invention and development in our laboratory. In that tradition, we continue to expand the frontiers of computer hardware and software, especially those frontiers with obvious impact on AI research. Knight, for example, is working on a medium-grain machine that enables ordinary symbolic programs to be run largely in parallel, without the tedium of removing side effects. Dally is working on a fine-grain machine that supports many models of parallel computation, including those that concentrate on message passing. And in the software dimension, Hewitt continues to develop the theoretical and practical aspects of his Actor model.

Content of these Volumes

Many of the chapters are points of intersection with respect to these emerging challenges and approaches. One way to be certain a solution scales up is to put the solution in harness with a learning idea. One way to learn is to do massive computation enabled by parallelism. And massive parallelism offers one approach to dealing with unmodelable and chaotic worlds.

Consequently, ideas about scalable solutions, unstructured environments, learning, and massive parallelism are pervasive throughout our laboratory, just as they are pervasive throughout the six parts of these volumes:

Volume 1:

- Scalable Solutions for Real-World Problems
- Fueling the Next Generation
- Creating Software and Hardware Revolutions

Volume 2:

- Conquering Unstructured Environments
- Jumping through Hoops and Manipulating Objects
- Recognizing Objects and Understanding Images

To be sure, understanding the computations that enable what we call intelligence remains an extreme challenge. Nevertheless, the ideas and results presented in these volumes demonstrate that the frontiers are expanding at an ever increasing rate. We hope that you find these volumes to be stimulating and provocative, and we hope that you share our excitement about the present and our optimism about the future.

Acknowledgments

Funding and Support

Many government agencies, foundations, and companies have sponsored work in the Artificial Intelligence Laboratory. The Defense Advanced Research Projects Agency, in particular, has taken a visionary position with respect to the impact of Artificial Intelligence for many years, along with the System Development Foundation, National Science Foundation, Office of Naval Research, and the Air Force Office of Scientific Research.

Other sponsors who have made it possible to do essential work include: Analog Devices, Apple Computer, Bear Stearns Company, Dana Farber, Digital Equipment Corporation, Draper Laboratory, E.I. duPont de Nemours, Exxon Research and Development Company, Fujitsu, General Dynamics, General Motors Research Laboratories, Hughes Research Laboratories, International Business Machines, ISX Corporation, Kapor Family Foundation, Lockheed Missiles and Space Company, Lotus Development Corporation, Martin Marietta, Mazda, MCC Corporation, McDonnell Douglas, NASA, NATO, NYNEX, Olivetti, Sandia National Laboratory, Sharp, Siemens, Sloan Foundation, Smithsonian, Sperry, and Wang Laboratories.

Preparation of the Manuscript

We are particularly grateful to all the students, staff, and faculty of the MIT Artificial Intelligence Laboratory who contributed to these volumes. Their enthusiastic cooperation and support were invaluable.

Boris Katz helped enormously with the preface and chapter introductions. The manuscript was typeset in ɣTEX, a local version of TEX written by Daniel Brotsky. Book design evolved gradually during production, which took a full year.

Several people assisted in producing the camera-ready copy: Berthold Horn and Jerry Roylance helped with Postscript; Roger Gilson's *prestissimo* typing was called upon for those manuscripts not available in electronic form and for the index; Joe Snowdon and Gary Bisbee of Chiron Inc. worked around the clock to print the 1300 pages on a Linotronic 300P imagesetter. And, finally, SAS would particularly like to acknowledge E.P.S. Shellard for his TEXnical advice and continual encouragement throughout the project.

Volume 1

Artificial Intelligence at MIT

Part I

Scalable Solutions for Real–World Problems

Increasingly, researchers in Artificial Intelligence aim to produce exciting, AI-enabled tools for scientists, engineers, biologists, decision makers, data analysts, and programmers. Their work has led to research systems like those described in Part I, many of which have already demonstrated impressive, helpful competence. All of them have sufficient scope that they seem unlikely to break down as they are scaled up:

- In the opening chapter, Abelson et al. explain how they are creating symbolic and numeric computing tools that help scientists and engineers to solve long-standing problems.
- Halfant and Sussman illustrate how modern symbolic computing enables the modular, highly-productive construction of numeric subroutine libraries for scientists and engineers.
- Ulrich explains his vision of how computation should help mechanical designers to specify what they need, to design what they specify, and to test what they design.
- Lathrop et al. show how classical learning heuristics, combined with massive parallelism, can mine protein databases for regularity, helping biologists to create class-recognizing patterns that are more sensitive and selective than those that biologists can create alone.
- Lee describes his approach to providing decision makers with qualitative analysis tools that enable sophisticated what-if scenarios to be computed and that enable previous decisions to be reused.
- Katz discusses his system for putting information in the hands of data analysts by way of a natural language system that reads sentences, indexes the facts they convey, and retrieves those facts in response to English questions.
- Rich and Waters describe how to represent programming knowledge and how to put that knowledge to work via their Programmer's Apprentice to help good programmers become even more productive.
- Finally, Rich and Wills show how ideas in the Programmer's Apprentice can be deployed to help programmers understand old code.

How do scientists and engineers think as they work through a mathematical analysis? Thirty years ago, Slagle addressed this question when he wrote his symbolic integration program which performed like first-year calculus students. Today, the authors of this paper also study how scientists and engineers think, but on a much more sophisticated level, writing programs that analyze complicated dynamic systems and that produce journal-quality, humanlike reports.

Importantly, such programs cannot be mere symbol crunchers because they must help to decide what symbol crunching to do. One such program, for example, decides what to do by deploying simple image-understanding techniques on its internal equivalents to drawings and sketches. Working with this program helped solve a wave-instability problem that had held respected ocean engineers at bay for nearly a year.

Occasionally, such a mathematical associate may suggest that you build a fast, special-purpose computer to solve a problem. Even without today's emerging tools, Sussman championed the idea that hardware construction can be easy by building a digital orrery to compute the path Pluto will take for the next 850 million years or so. The results demonstrate that Pluto's orbit is chaotic and imply that there can be no proof that the solar system is stable. One day, the Sun and Jupiter may well be all that remains.

Intelligence in Scientific Computing

Harold Abelson

Michael Eisenberg

Matthew Halfant

Jacob Katzenelson

Elisha Sacks

Gerald Jay Sussman

Jack Wisdom

Kenneth Yip

Combining numerical techniques with ideas from symbolic computation and with methods incorporating knowledge of science and mathematics leads to a new category of intelligent computational tools for scientists and engineers. These tools autonomously prepare simulation experiments from high-level specifications of physical models. For computationally intensive experiments, they automatically design special-purpose numerical engines optimized to perform the necessary computations. They actively monitor numerical and physical experiments. They interpret experimental data and formulate numerical results in qualitative terms. They enable their human users to control computational experiments in terms of high-level behavioral descriptions.

As an example of such a tool, imagine an ocean engineer designing an offshore mooring tower for large ships. When standing free, such a tower can be modeled in a straightforward way as an inverted pendulum anchored to the sea bed, driven by wave motion, and restored to vertical position by its buoyancy in sea water. However, a massive ship attached to the mooring structure vastly complicates the dynamics: when the mooring line is slack, the restoring force is the same as before; but when the line is taut, the ship also exerts a force through tension in the line. Numerical simulations of such systems have shown that the effect of even small waves can lead to potentially dangerous resonances that can make the structure fail [Thompson 1986]. The goal of the engineer is to design a structure that can withstand the worst conditions that can be expected to occur in the environment without making the structure excessively expensive.

The following excerpt of a dialogue shows how we imagine an intelligent computer assistant aiding an ocean engineer in the design of such a structure. Assume that the engineer has already proposed a particular structure, either by drawing it or by combining previously defined structures.

:

Computer: The dynamical equations for this model are: *(displays a very large set of equations)*.

Engineer: Call that the `full model`. Try to find a simpler approximate model.

Computer: The time constants for the bending moments and torsional stresses in equations 1 through 25 are very small compared with the period of lowest mode of the structure seen as a pendulum and with the periods of the largest components in our standard wave spectrum for this region of the gulf coast. Because the deflections of the structure are small we can use the following approximate model: *(displays a much smaller number of equations)*.

Engineer: Call that the `simplified model`.

Engineer: Characterize the response of the `simplified model` to the standard wave spectrum.

Computer: State-space analysis shows that the response of this system can be broken into three regions. For very small deflection angles (smaller than 2 degrees) there are stable oscillations, damped with time constants similar to the oscillation frequencies. Significant deflections toward the `boat` show trajectories with competing domains of attraction. There are large subharmonic responses. For deflections larger than about 10 degrees we find complex chaotic motions, but such large deflections violate the assumptions of the model.

Engineer: Characterize the response to the dominant frequency in the spectrum as the amplitude varies from one foot to twenty feet seas.

Computer: There are two families of periodic motions here, A and B. Family A is present at the start of the parameter range $s = 1$, with a periodic motion of order 1. At $s = 5.2$ this motion undergoes a symmetry-breaking bifurcation and splits into a pair of motions A_1 and A_2. As s increases, both A_1 and A_2 undergo period-doubling cascades: order 2 ($s = 6.5$), order 4 ($s = 9.8$), order 8 ($s = 10.7$), and order 16 ($s = 10.9$) The cascade was not traced past the order 16 motions. Chaotic motions were observed at $s = 12$. Family B begins with a motion of order 1 arising from a fold bifurcation at $s = 8$. This motion persists through the end of the parameter range $s = 20$.

Engineer: How do the maximum stresses affect the structure?

Computer: Family A motions are within the safe operating region for structures of type UG/751 construction, but the family B motions can easily exceed the safe operating region in a 50-year storm.

Engineer: Perform the same analysis, assuming that we triple the buoyancy of the float.

Computer: The qualitative behavior in the two situations differs slightly in the initial phase of growth of oscillations. Once oscillations are established the behavior is approximately the same. The maximum deflections differ by less than 10% between the two situations, but the frequencies are very different.

Engineer: Begin design of an `active stabilizer` to damp the family B motions. Assume we install thrusters at positions halfway up the structure and at 90% of the height of the structure. Expand the `full model` to include drives from these thrusters. ...

⋮

No systems as sophisticated as this engineer's assistant yet exist. However, computer programs incorporating important pieces of it are already in place. Generating stylized natural language is not too hard, although understanding unstructured English text is still difficult, and we will not address that problem in this chapter. Additionally, our discussion is not really about ocean engineering; the scenario above is not intended to illustrate good design practice in that domain. Rather, our concern here is with the development of intelligent techniques appropriate for the automatic preparation, execution, and control of numerical experiments, and with the automatic interpretation of their results.

- Our envisioned engineer's assistant begins with a description of a mechanism and automatically generates efficient numerical programs that predict its dynamical behavior. This may require more than just straightforward simulation. A stability-analysis task such as "characterize the response to the dominant frequency in the spectrum" requires compiling procedures that evolve, in addition to the state, the variations with respect to changes in initial conditions and the sensitivities with respect to changes in parameters.

- The engineer's assistant automatically prepares high-performance numerical experiments. It has extensive knowledge of numerical methods and it can compose appropriate and correct numerical procedures tailored to the specific application. For critical applications, this compilation can be targeted to the automatic synthesis of special-purpose hardware.

- The engineer's assistant interprets the results of numerical experiments in high-level qualitative terms. This interpretation is based on general mathematical and physical knowledge that constrains the kind of behavior to expect. The interpretation is used to prepare a report to the user, but it is also used in the experimental protocol. The summary of behavior produced from observations of the results of previous experiments is used to automatically select critical values of experimental parameters for subsequent experiments, thus efficiently uncovering the salient phenomena.

The first section of this chapter demonstrates significant portions of these capabilities. These include the automatic preparation and monitoring of numerical simulations, the automatic generation of qualitative interpretations of numerical results, and the achievement of breakthrough performance on computationally-demanding problems with the aid of specially-designed computers. (Our special-purpose engine for computing planetary motions has produced the first solid numerical evidence that the solar-system's long-term dynamics is chaotic, thereby answering the famous question of the stability of the solar system.)

The section under "Intelligent Numerical Computing" takes a closer look at the technology behind these demonstration results. We explain how algorithms from computer vision are applied to interpret phase-space diagrams in dynamics. We illustrate how knowledge about dynamical systems can be encoded using constraints and symbolic rules. We show how to formulate numerical algorithms at appropriate levels of abstraction with higher-order procedures and how to combine these with symbolic algebra to automatically generate numerical programs.

The section under "Intelligent tools" sketches some next steps required to realize the vision of systems like the engineer's assistant.

Numerical Modeling can be Automated

In a typical numerical modeling study, an investigator repeatedly prepares and runs a series of computations and examines the results at each step to select interesting new values for parameters and initial conditions. When enough values have been tried, the investigator classifies and interprets the results. Even with powerful numerical computers, this process requires substantial human effort to prepare simulations, and it relies upon significant human judgment to choose interesting values for parameters, to determine when a simulation run is complete, and to interpret numerical results in qualitative terms.

This section exhibits three programs that automate much of the above process. The *Bifurcation Interpreter* investigates the steady-state orbits in parameterized families of dynamical systems, classifying the types of orbits and the bifurcations through which they change as parameters vary. The KAM program autonomously explores nonlinear conservative systems and produces qualitative descriptions of phase-space portraits and bifurcations. Both programs automatically generate summary reports similar to those appearing in published papers in the experimental dynamics literature and in engineering studies of artifacts that have complex dynamics, such as airfoils, ship hulls, and mooring structures. In addition, the capabilities demonstrated by these programs have application in the design of intelligent automatic control systems. The breadth of applicability is illustrated by the *Kineticist's Workbench*, a program that models how chemists understand complex chemical reactions. It combines numerical and symbolic methods to characterize reaction mechanisms in qualitative terms that are useful for the working chemist.

We also discuss the place of special-purpose numerical engines as scientific instruments and survey significant results in planetary dynamics obtained using the *Digital Orrery*.

Programs can discover and interpret qualitative behavior

In a nonlinear dynamical system with a periodic drive, motion starting from any set of initial conditions will typically evolve to a steady-state orbit.[1] For a parameterized family of dynamical systems, tracing the changes in steady-state orbits as the parameters vary provides a valuable summary of the family's qualitative behavior. Much research in nonlinear dynamics is devoted to studying these *bifurcations*, or changes in type, of steady-state orbits. For one-parameter families at least, the bifurcations generically encountered have been classified and are well-understood. Some examples are the *fold* bifurcation, at which a stable orbit can appear or vanish, the *flip* bifurcation, at which the period of an orbit doubles, and the *pitchfork* bifurcation, at which an orbit splits into two orbits of the same period. There are also commonly-observed bifurcation sequences that occur as the parameter varies. An example is the *period-doubling cascade*, where the order of an orbit successively doubles via a sequence of increasingly closely spaced flip bifurcations, producing chaos.[2]

---

[1]Possible types of steady-state orbits are periodic orbits, quasi-periodic orbits (which have discrete-frequency spectra, but not at rational multiples of the drive period), and chaotic orbits (which, loosely speaking, are steady-state orbits that are neither periodic nor quasi-periodic).

[2]Various authors use different, and sometimes incompatible terminology to refer to these bifurcation types. For example, the flip is sometimes called a cusp or a pitchfork. We have adopted the terminology used in the book by Thompson

Dynamicists commonly gain insight into the qualitative behavior of nonlinear systems by developing summary descriptions of steady-state orbits and bifurcations. Figure 1 reproduced here from Franceschini [1983] shows a schematic summary drawn by a physicist based on numerical studies of the two-dimensional Navier-Stokes equation for an incompressible fluid. As the Reynolds number of the fluid increases, the steady-state orbits evolve through a sequence of bifurcations. The diagram summarizes how the evolving orbits can be grouped into four distinct families.

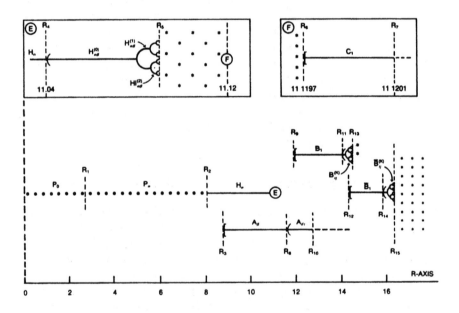

Figure 1. This diagram, reproduced from a published paper in fluid mechanics, is a physicist's schematic summary description of an approximation to the two-dimensional Navier-Stokes equation for an incompressible fluid. The varying parameter here is the Reynolds number.

The *Bifurcation Interpreter*, a computer program being developed at MIT by Hal Abelson, automatically generates such summary descriptions for one-parameter families of periodically driven dynamical systems. The dynamical system can be specified by differential equations to be integrated, by a period map that directly computes successive states at multiples of the drive period, or by a description of a physical model such as an electrical network. Given a dynamical system, a parameter range to explore, and

and Stewart [1986], which provides an introduction to the methods of nonlinear dynamics together with an extensive bibliography.

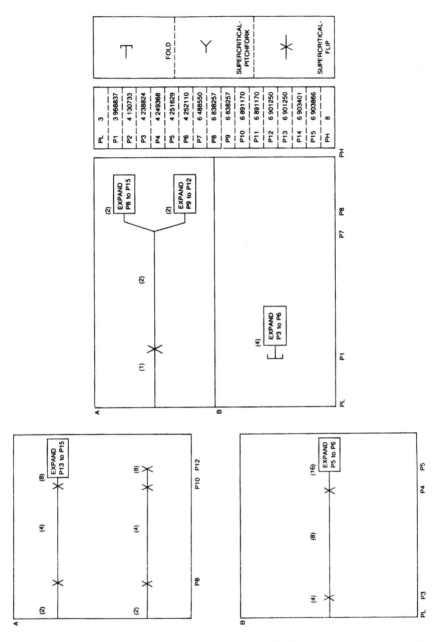

Figure 2. The Bifurcation Interpreter automatically generates summary descriptions of dynamical systems similar to those appearing in published papers. This diagram describes the behavior of a periodically impacted hinged beam as the load varies, exhibiting the evolution of two different families of steady-state motions.

a domain in state-space, the interpreter discovers periodic orbits, tracks their evolution as the parameter varies, and locates and classifies bifurcations. Using this information, the program categorizes the orbits into families and produces a summary report that describes each family and its evolution through bifurcations.

Here is a sample input to the interpreter:

Period map
$$x \mapsto x - \frac{1-e^{-2m}}{2m} a \sin x + \frac{1-e^{-2m}}{2m} y$$
$$y \mapsto -e^{-2m} a \sin x + e^{-2m} y$$

Values for fixed parameters

m	0.1π

Range for varying parameter

a	1 to 7

Bounds on state variables

x	$-\pi$ to π (periodic)
y	-4 to 4

The system to be investigated models the vibration of a hinged bar with viscous damping subjected to a fixed-direction periodic impact load at the free end. This problem is discussed in Hsu et $al.$ [1977], which derives the period map for this motion. Here x is the angular displacement and y is the angular velocity, a specifies magnitude of the load and m specifies the damping factor. The interpreter is asked to explore the system as the load ranges from 1 to 7. With this specification, the interpreter analyzes the system and generates the following report:

There are 2 distinct families of periodic orbits, A and B.

Family A is already present at the start of the parameter range $a = 1$ as a periodic orbit A_0 of order 1. At $a = 4.130$ there is a supercritical flip bifurcation at which A_0 undergoes period doubling to produce a periodic orbit A_1 of order 2. At $a = 6.489$ there is a supercritical pitchfork bifurcation at which the family A splits into subfamilies $A(1)$ and $A(2)$, beginning with A_1 splitting into two periodic orbits of order 2. As the parameter a increases, each subfamily undergoes a period-doubling cascade via a sequence of supercritical flip bifurcations to order 4 at $a = 6.838$, order 8 at

$a = 6.891$, order 16 at $a = 6.901$, order 32 at $a = 6.903$. The period-doubling cascade was not traced past the order 32 orbit, which apparently period doubles again at $a = 6.904$.

Family B first appears at $a = 3.969$ with an orbit B_0 of order 4 appearing at a fold bifurcation. As the parameter a increases, B undergoes a period-doubling cascade via a sequence of supercritical flip bifurcations to order 8 at $a = 4.239$, order 16 at $a = 4.239$, order 32 at $a = 4.251$. The period-doubling cascade was not traced past the order 32 orbit, which apparently period doubles again at $a = 4.252$.

The program can display this same information as a diagram (see figure 2) that is similar in style to manually developed Navier-Stokes analysis in figure 1.[3]

Smart programs can see what not to compute

Dynamical behavior is complex, but it is not arbitrary. There is structure on phase space that restricts the classes of legal trajectories and provides a grammar of legal phase portraits. For example, trajectories of autonomous systems cannot intersect, and as we vary the initial conditions, the trajectories vary smoothly except at isolated places where the behavior changes. As we vary parameters, the phase portrait changes qualitatively only at bifurcations. In Hamiltonian systems the evolution of the phase space is area-preserving, which greatly restricts the classes of possible structures that can occur in the phase space. This kind of knowledge enables dynamicists to infer a good understanding of a physical system from only a small, but well-chosen, set of experiments.

The phase portrait in figure 3, taken from a historically important paper in dynamics by Hénon [1969], describes how adding a simple quadratic nonlinearity to a linear rotation can lead to dramatic changes in dynamical behavior. Observe how the figure characterizes the dynamics by showing only a few orbits. Presumably, Hénon was able to generate this figure after performing only a few judiciously chosen numerical experiments.

The KAM program developed by Yip at MIT [1987, 1988] can analyze systems in the same way. It knows enough about the constraints on the structure of phase space to choose initial conditions and parameters as cleverly as an expert dynamicist. KAM's summary description of Hénon's map is shown in figure 4. Observe that this is almost identical to the summary presented by Hénon. Moreover, KAM was able to deduce this description after trying only ten initial conditions.

---

[3]The diagram-generation program illustrated in figure 2 was developed by Ognen Nastov.

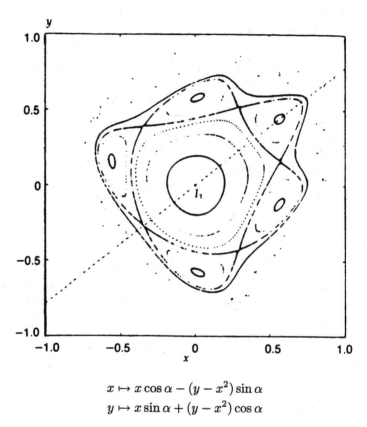

$$x \mapsto x \cos \alpha - (y - x^2) \sin \alpha$$
$$y \mapsto x \sin \alpha + (y - x^2) \cos \alpha$$

Figure 3. This phase portrait is Hénon's summary of the dynamics of the map for $\cos \alpha = 0.24$.

KAM's ability to control numerical experiments arises from the fact that it not only produces pictures for us to see—it also *looks at* the pictures it draws, visually recognizing and classifying different orbit types as they numerically evolve. By combining techniques from computer vision with sophisticated dynamical invariants, KAM is able to exploit mathematical knowledge, represented in terms of a "grammar" that dictates consistency constraints on the structure of phase space. When it chooses new initial conditions to explore, it does so in an attempt to make the picture consistent with these constraints. In addition to drawing the picture, KAM generates a textual analysis that explains what the program "sees." Here is KAM's description of the picture it generates for Hénon's map.

The portrait has an elliptic fixed point at $(0, 0)$. Surrounding the fixed point is a regular region bounded by a KAM curve with rota-

tion number between 1/5 and 1/4. Outside the regular region lies
a chain of 5 islands. The island chain is bounded by a KAM curve
with rotation number between 4/21 and 5/26. The outermost
region is occupied by chaotic orbits that eventually escape.

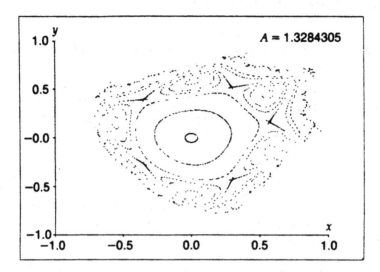

Figure 4. The KAM program generates this summary picture of Hénon's map.

Programs can construct and analyze approximations

A powerful strategy for analyzing a complicated dynamical system is to approximate it with a simpler system, analyze the approximation, and map
the results back to the original system. The approximations must be accurate enough to reproduce the essential properties of the original system,
yet simple enough to be analyzed efficiently. Human experts have found
that piecewise linear approximations satisfy both criteria for a wide class
of models. The PLR program, developed by Sacks at MIT [1987b, 1988],
exploits this fact to automate the analysis of second-order autonomous
ordinary differential equations. It derives the qualitative behavior of intractable equations by approximating them with piecewise linear equations
and constructing phase diagrams of the approximations.

PLR constructs a composite phase diagram for a piecewise-linear system by combining the local phase diagrams of its linear regions. It employs the standard theory of linear equations to ascertain the local phase

diagrams. Linear systems have simple well-understood dynamics. Either all trajectories are periodic, all approach a fixed point, or all approach infinity. PLR pastes together the local phase diagrams by determining which sequences of regions trajectories can traverse. It summarizes the results by a *transition graph* whose nodes and links represent regions and transitions. Each path through the transition graph of a piecewise-linear system indicates that trajectories traverse the corresponding regions in the prescribed order. Loops denote trajectories that remain in one region forever, whereas longer cycles denote trajectories that continually shift between a sequence of regions.

As a simple example, PLR can qualitatively analyze the behavior of an undriven van der Pol oscillator, a simple nonlinear circuit consisting of a capacitor, an inductor, and a nonlinear resistor connected in series. The current through the circuit obeys the equation

$$i'' + \frac{k}{L}(i^2 - 1)i' + \frac{1}{LC}i = 0, \tag{1}$$

with C the capacitance, L the inductance, and k a scaling factor. PLR approximates this equation with a piecewise linear equation and constructs the phase diagram and transition graph shown in figure 5. It deduces that the system oscillates from the fact that tracing edges starting from any node in the graph leads to a cycle. Intuitively, the system oscillates because the nonlinear resistor adds energy to the circuit at low currents and drains energy at high currents.

Domain knowledge can guide numerical modeling

Eisenberg's *Kineticist's Workbench*, also being developed at MIT, is a program that combines general knowledge of dynamics with specific knowledge about chemical reactions in the analysis, understanding, and simulation of complex chemical reaction mechanisms.

Chemists, in trying to model reactions, typically hypothesize a set of elementary reaction steps (corresponding to molecular collisions) that constitute a proposed pathway for the overall reaction. This collection of elementary steps may be large. It usually gives rise to a mathematical model consisting of many tightly coupled nonlinear differential equations. The problem of simulating such a system can be formidable, but a simulation merely provides numerical results. Even more important to the chemist is to achieve some sort of *qualitative* understanding of the reaction mechanism. The Kineticist's Workbench combines numerical simulation with a variety of symbolic methods in order to characterize reaction mechanisms in terms that are meaningful to the working chemist such as "equilibrium," "steady states," and "oscillations."

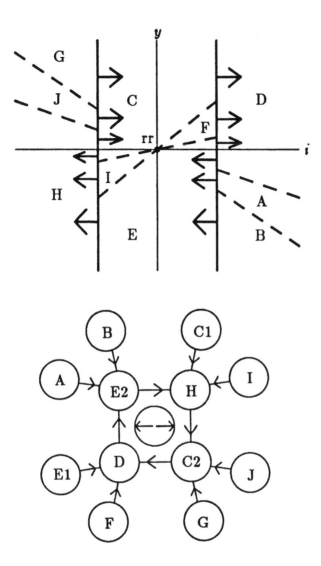

Figure 5. PLR's phase diagram and transition graph for its piecewise linear van der Pol approximation. Arrows indicate boundaries that trajectories cross.

The Workbench also suggests ways to simplify complex mechanisms. The key idea here is that the program can use its qualitative characterization of a given mechanism's behavior to determine which steps within the mechanism have an important behavioral effect, and which are superfluous and may therefore be dropped from the chemist's model.

The following scenario shows how the Workbench is intended to interact with a user in the analysis of a chemical process. The initial information is specified as follows:

Step no.	Step	Rate Constant
(1)	$C \rightarrow B$	300
(2)	$B \rightarrow C$	100
(3)	$A \rightarrow X$	1
(4)	$B + X \rightarrow Y + D$	1
(5)	$2X + Y \rightarrow 3X$	0.333
(6)	$X \rightarrow E$	1
(7)	$C \rightarrow F$	100

External sources for species C (rate of addition: 100 mmol/liter-sec). Concentration of A assumed constant at 1 mmol/liter. Initial concentrations of all species besides A are 0 mmol/liter.

With this specification, the Workbench responds:

The mechanism may be decomposed into two submechanisms. The first may be written as follows:[4]

$$(1.1) \quad [External] \leftrightarrow C \leftrightarrow B \rightarrow [External]$$

This submechanism results in a rapid equilibrium between C and B; the final concentrations of both C and B (1 and 3 mmol/liter, respectively) are independent of their initial concentrations.[5]

The second submechanism may be written as follows:

$$(2.1) \quad [External] \leftrightarrow X$$
$$(2.2) \quad B + X \rightarrow Y$$
$$(2.3) \quad 2X + Y \rightarrow 3X$$

---

[4]The notation [External] used in this example is a catchall used to indicate the presence of external sources or sinks for some species. The notation corresponds roughly to the "zero complex" notation of Feinberg [1980].

[5]In performing this simplification, the Workbench has treated the original reaction (7) as the presence of an external sink for species C, because the concentration of species F merely grows with time and does not affect any other species. Similarly, reaction (4), being slow compared to all the reactions included in (1.1), may be treated as a slow (but time-varying) sink for species B. This reasoning could be exposed at the user's request.

$$(2.1') \quad [External] \leftrightarrow X \to Y$$
$$(2.2') \quad 2X + Y \to 3X$$

Because the concentration of B in the first submechanism is constant at 3 mmol/liter, the second submechanism may be further simplified as follows:

Simulation of this second mechanism reveals that the concentrations of X and Y oscillate over time. Each oscillation consists of five phases:

1   Slow growth in the concentrations of X and Y.

2   More rapid growth in X.

3   Large jump in X and decline in Y.

4   Large decline in X and increase in Y.

5   Slower decline in X and slow increase in Y.

The time between oscillation peaks is approximately 17.8 seconds.

The chemist now asks the program to compare the results of the approximate mechanism $(2.1'-2.2')$ with the numerically exact results of mechanism $(1-7)$, comparing the qualitative behavior of the two mechanisms as reflected in species X and Y. The workbench responds:

> The qualitative behavior of the two mechanisms differs slightly during the initial phase of slow growth in X and Y. Once oscillations begin, the exact mechanism $(1-7)$ displays the same qualitative structure as the approximate mechanism $(2.1'-2.2')$, and the period is still approximately 17.8 seconds. The concentrations of X and Y at comparable points in the oscillations differ by less than 2 percent between the two mechanisms.

The chemist now tries a different variation on the original reaction, and alters the original mechanism so that the concentration of A is not constant over time, but is rather an explicit function of time, as given by the equation $[A] = 1 + \sin t$. The workbench responds:

> The decomposition into submechanisms is not affected; nor is the constant concentration of B. Again, the concentrations of X and Y appear to be oscillating, but each oscillation now consists of eight phases, instead of five, as before.

It is worth noting some of the key features of this example. First, the Workbench is able to decompose the original mechanism into two submechanisms, each of which is capable of independent simulation; this simplifies both the analysis and simulation of the larger mechanism. Second, the Workbench is able to decompose the first of the two submechanisms in terms of a dichotomy between fast and slow steps; this allows the program to approximate the submechanism as a system in equilibrium. Third, the program uses numerical simulation to derive equilibrium concentrations for this submechanism. Finally, the Workbench is able to describe the results of simulating the second submechanism in terms of a succession of qualitative episodes characterized by changing growth rates of the species X and Y.

Fast computers need not be large or expensive

Numerical modeling often requires substantial resources. Scientists and engineers have traditionally obtained these resources either by acquiring large-scale computers or renting time on them. However, a specialized computer can be simple and physically small. Indeed, it may be just as easy to design, build, and program a special-purpose computer as to develop software for general-purpose supercomputers. Moreover, the specialized computer can become an ordinary experimental instrument belonging to the research group that made it, thus avoiding the administrative burden and the scheduling problems associated with expensive, shared resources.

The question of the stability of the solar system is probably the most famous longstanding problem in astrodynamics. In fact, it was investigations into precisely this problem that inspired Poincaré to develop the modern qualitative theory of dynamical systems. Sussman and Wisdom [1988] completed a series of numerical experiments at MIT demonstrating that the long-term motion of the planet Pluto, and by implication the dynamics of the Solar System, is chaotic.

The stability question was settled using the Digital Orrery [Applegate 1985], a special-purpose numerical engine optimized for high-precision numerical integrations of the equations of motion of small numbers of gravitationally interacting bodies. Using 1980 technology, the device is about 1 cubic foot of electronics, dissipating 150 watts. On the problem it was designed to solve, it is measured to be 60 times faster than a VAX 11/780 with FPA, or 1/3 the speed of a Cray 1.

Figure 6 shows the exponential divergence of nearby Pluto trajectories over 400 million years. This data is taken from an 845-million-year integration performed with the Orrery. Before the Orrery, high-precision integrations over simulated times of millions of years were prohibitively expensive. The longest previous integration of the outer planets was for five million years, performed on a Japanese supercomputer [Kinoshita 1984]. Even though the Orrery is not as fast as the fastest supercomputer, its small scale and relative low cost mean that it can be dedicated to long computations in ways that a conventional supercomputer could not. To

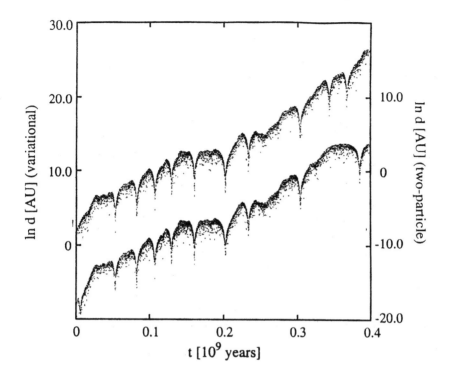

Figure 6. The exponential divergence of nearby trajectories is indicated by the average linear growth of the logarithms of the distance measures as a function of time. In the upper trace we see the growth of the variational distance around a reference trajectory. In the lower trace we see how two Plutos diverge with time. The distance saturates near 45AU; note that the semimajor axis of Pluto's orbit is about 40AU. The variational method of studying neighboring trajectories does not have the problem of saturation. Note that the two methods are in excellent agreement until the two-trajectory method has nearly saturated.

perform the integration that established Pluto's chaotic behavior, the Orrery ran continually for five months.

The Orrery was designed and built by six people in only nine months. This was possible only because of novel software support for the design process. The simulator for the Orrery is partially symbolic—simulated registers hold symbolic values and simulated arithmetic parts combine these to produce algebraic expressions (in addition to checking timing and electrical constraints). This means that a successful simulation yields a simulated memory containing algebraic expressions that can be checked for correctness.

Intelligent Numerical Computing Rests on AI Technology

The illustrations above achieve their impressive results by bringing symbolic methods to bear on the problems of numerical computation. Some of these techniques are traditional AI methods, which achieve new power when they are combined with deep knowledge of dynamical systems. The KAM program, for example, uses techniques from machine vision to recognize and classify the relevant geometrical properties of the trajectories. The Bifurcation Interpreter uses algebraic manipulation and knowledge about the local geometry of bifurcations to automatically generate numerical procedures that track periodic orbits. The key to automatically generating high-performance numerical algorithms is to express knowledge of numerical analysis at an appropriate level of abstraction. This is supported by a library of numerical methods that is organized around the liberal use of higher-order procedural abstractions. With this organization, one constructs sophisticated numerical methods by mixing and matching standard components in well-understood ways. The resulting programs are both more perspicuous and more robust than conventional numerical methods.

The KAM program exploits techniques from computer vision

Yip's KAM program is notable because it applies judgment, similar to that of an expert dynamicist, in directing the course of its numerical experiments. In making judicious choices of what to try next, KAM must interpret what it sees. This process occurs in three phases: aggregation, clustering, and classification. The images of an initial point produced by iterating the map forms a set of isolated points. This orbit must be classified. In Hamiltonian systems there are three types of orbits to distinguish. In a surface of section, periodic orbits appear as isolated points, quasiperiodic orbits appear as closed curves or island chains, and chaotic orbits appear to take up regions of 2-dimensional space. KAM must also aggregate the components of an orbit so that it can be further classified. It must be able to determine the number of islands in an island chain, as this number gives the period of the enclosed periodic point. KAM must be able to estimate the centroid and area enclosed by a curve and to recognize the shape of a curve. KAM implements these abilities with techniques from computational geometry and computer vision.

KAM classifies orbits using methods based on the Euclidean minimal spanning tree—the tree that interconnects all the points with minimal total edge length—which it constructs by means of the Prim-Dijkstra algorithm [Baase 1978]. For each sub-tree of the spanning tree, KAM examines the degree of each of its nodes, where the degree of a node is the number of nodes connected to it in the sub-tree. For a smooth curve, the spanning

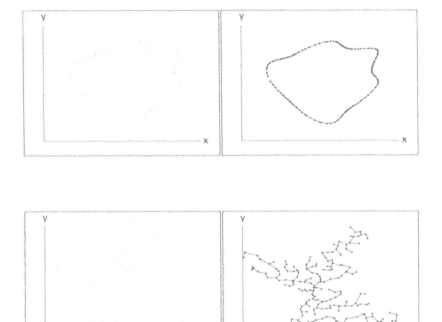

Figure 7. Starting with the successive iterates of a point, KAM classifies orbits using algorithms from machine vision. As shown above, a quasiperiodic orbit can be distinguished from a chaotic orbit by examining the branching factor in the Euclidean minimal spanning tree.

tree consists of two terminal nodes of degree one and other nodes of degree two. For a point set that fills an area, its corresponding spanning tree consists of many nodes having degree three or higher (see figure 8).

To aggregate points, KAM deletes from the tree edges that are significantly longer than nearby edges, following an aggregation algorithm suggested by Zahn [1971]. This divides the tree into connected components. Figure 9 shows how the program aggregates points of a quasiperiodic orbit and recognizes it as an island chain.

To compute the area and centroid of the region bounded by a curve, KAM generates an ordered sequence of points from the spanning tree, and spline-interpolates the sequence to obtain a smooth curve. Straightforward algorithms are then applied to compute the area and centroid. Shape recognition is accomplished using scale-space methods pioneered by Witkin [1983].

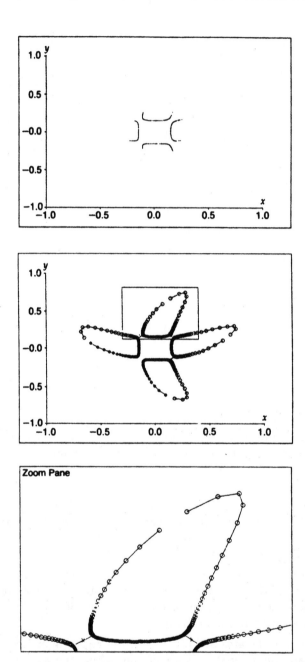

Figure 8. KAM uses the minimal spanning tree to cluster orbits into components. The components of an island chain can be isolated by detecting long edges in the spanning tree and deleting these from the graph.

AI techniques can implement deep mathematical knowledge

Viewed as abstract examples of AI technology, our demonstration programs
are hardly novel. The uniqueness of these programs, and the source of
their power, is that they use classic AI methods to exploit specific domain
knowledge based on rigorous mathematical results.

PLR, for instance, combines geometric reasoning, symbolic algebra,
and inequality reasoning to test whether trajectories of a piecewise linear
system cross between adjacent regions in phase space. For a trajectory to
cross from region R to S via boundary u, its tangent t at the intersection
point with u must form an acute angle with the normal n, as shown in
figure 9. This geometric condition is equivalent to the algebraic condition
that the inner product $t \cdot n$ be positive. Hence, a transition exists from R
to S unless $t \cdot n \leq 0$ everywhere on u. PLR resolves the inequality $t \cdot n \leq 0$
on u with the BOUNDER inequality reasoner [Sacks 1987a].

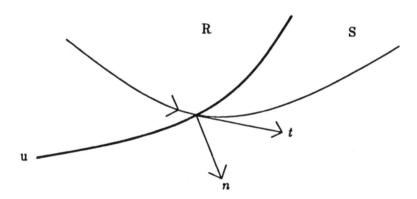

Figure 9. Trajectory crossing from R to S via u: the tangent t at the crossing
point must form an acute angle with n, the normal to u that points into S.

PLR combines symbolic reasoning with deep knowledge about dynamical
systems to interpret the transition graphs that it constructs. For example,
the transition graph for the van der Pol equation shows that all trajectories
spiral around the origin, but tells nothing of whether they move inward,
move outward, or wobble around. PLR invokes a difficult theorem to prove
that all trajectories converge to a unique limit cycle. It tests the preconditions of the theorem by proving inequalities and manipulating symbolic
expressions.

The KAM program limits the number of phase-space trajectories it
must explore by drawing upon constraint analysis, as pioneered by Waltz
[1985]. As in any constraint analysis, KAM relies upon "grammar" that expresses the consistent ways in which primitive elements can be combined.

In KAM's case, the primitive elements incorporate sophisticated mathematical invariants, and the grammatical rules embody deep theorems about the behavior of dynamical systems.

One such invariant, for example, is the *rotation number* of an orbit, a quantity that measures the asymptotic average of the angular distances between any two successive iterates in units of 2π-radians. A rule in KAM's grammar embodies a theorem that the rotation numbers of nearby orbits must change continuously [MacKay 1982]. As an example of how this is used, suppose that KAM has located two nearby almost-periodic orbits having rotation numbers ρ_1 and ρ_2 respectively. Suppose ρ_1 is slightly smaller than 1/5, and ρ_2 slightly larger. With only these two orbits, KAM's evolving phase-space picture cannot be complete. By continuity, KAM expects to find a third, nearby orbit with rotation number exactly equal to 1/5, that is, a periodic orbit of period 5, which KAM proceeds to search for and classify.

In a similar manner, Abelson's Bifurcation Interpreter draws upon knowledge of the geometry of typical changes in the steady-state orbits of one-parameter families of dynamical systems. Periodic orbits of a periodically driven oscillator can be identified as fixed-points of the *period map*, which maps a state to the end-point of the trajectory starting from that state and evolving for one period of the drive. Stability of an orbit is determined by the stability of the corresponding fixed point. If the interpreter notices that a stable orbit suddenly becomes unstable as the family parameter increases, it attempts to explain this change as the result of a bifurcation. The type of bifurcation can be conjectured by examining the eigenvalues of the period map at the fixed point, and the conjecture can be verified by a search that is tailored to the local geometry for that bifurcation type.

For example, for a stable orbit, the complex eigenvalues of the corresponding fixed point of the period map must lie within the unit circle. If stability is lost with an eigenvalue apparently crossing the unit circle at -1, a classification theorem for bifurcations [Guckenheimer & Holmes 1983] tells the interpreter to expect that this is a supercritical-flip bifurcation, which corresponds to a period doubling of the orbit. Near the bifurcation one should expect to see a stable orbit just before the critical parameter value and, just after the critical value, an unstable orbit together with a stable orbit of double the period. For this type of bifurcation, the interpreter attempts to locate the new expected orbits using a search technique that detects fixed points by computing the *Poincaré index* of the period map [Hsu *et al.* 1980]. If these orbits are located, the bifurcation is probably a flip. If a different local geometry is found, the apparent bifurcation may be the result of numerical error, or the interaction of two nearby bifurcations, or it may be a bifurcation of non-standard type. In any case, the result of the search is passed to a critic that attempts to reconcile the local results for all bifurcations detected and produce a consistent description.

Going beyond general knowledge of dynamical systems, the Kineticist's Workbench program employs a number of techniques specific to the domain of chemical kinetics. For example, the program examines the qualitative history of a reaction simulation, attempting to find periods of time during which concentrations of some species may be treated as constant; this is an automation of the kind of steady-state analysis that is a staple of kinetic investigation [Laidler 1987]. Another portion of the program—that portion devoted to spotting fast equilibria within a mechanism—makes extensive use of the *reaction network* formalism developed by Feinberg, Horn, Jackson, and coworkers at the University of Rochester [Feinberg 1980]. An especially fruitful result of their work is the *zero-deficiency theorem*, which provides a simple algorithmic test for determining whether a reaction mechanism gives rise to stable equilibria. Finally, the portion of the Workbench program devoted to decomposing mechanisms according to mutual influence between species may be used to identify transient species, and to drop those species from a particular simulation as soon as their concentrations are deemed too low to affect the remainder of the simulation.

Numerical experiments can be prepared automatically

Translating high-level specifications into high-quality numerical routines can be a tedious and error-prone process whose difficulty limits the utility of even the most powerful numerical computers. A program by Abelson and Sussman [1987] draws upon a spectrum of computational tools—numerical methods, symbolic algebra, and semantic constraints (such as dimensions)—to automate the preparation and execution of numerical simulations. These tools are designed so that combined methods, tailored to particular problems, can be constructed on the fly. One can use symbolic algebra to automatically generate numerical procedures, and one can use domain-specific constraints to guide algebraic derivations and to avoid complexity.

Figure 10 shows the wiring diagram for a simple nonlinear circuit, a driven van der Pol oscillator consisting of voltage source, a capacitor, an inductor, and a nonlinear resistor with the cube-law characteristic $v = ai^3 - bi$. The figure also shows a description of this wiring diagram in a language formulated for describing electrical networks. This description specifies circuit's parameters, its primitive parts, and how the parts are interconnected.

Given this description, the program combines models of the primitive elements to form equations that are then algebraically solved to produce state equations for the van der Pol oscillator. The state equations are com-

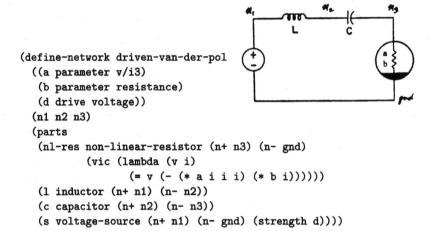

```
(define-network driven-van-der-pol
  ((a parameter v/i3)
   (b parameter resistance)
   (d drive voltage))
  (n1 n2 n3)
  (parts
   (nl-res non-linear-resistor (n+ n3) (n- gnd)
           (vic (lambda (v i)
                  (= v (- (* a i i i) (* b i))))))
   (l inductor (n+ n1) (n- n2))
   (c capacitor (n+ n2) (n- n3))
   (s voltage-source (n+ n1) (n- gnd) (strength d))))
```

Figure 10. The wiring diagram of a simple nonlinear circuit is described by means of a special-purpose language of electrical networks. This description can be automatically compiled into numerical procedures that evolve the state of the system.

piled into a procedure (the system derivative) that will evolve the system numerically when combined with an appropriate numerical integrator.

These operations can involve a considerable amount of algebraic manipulation. Even for systems that are specified in closed form, most nonlinear systems cannot be algebraically solved to produce explicit state equations. In the general case, the program recognizes variables that cannot be eliminated from the state equations and compiles an iterative scheme for approximating these variables. This requires symbolic differentiation to produce a Jacobian that is incorporated into a Newton-Raphson search and to augment the system state so that it will evolve good starting points for Newton's method at each step of the integration.

For applications such as the Bifurcation Interpreter, one must also compile numerical routines that find period orbits and track them as the system parameters vary. Finding and tracking periodic orbits rests upon determining the sensitivity of trajectories to variations in initial state and parameters. This can be done by evolving the variational system, obtained by symbolic manipulation of the state equations, and by evolving various derived systems obtained by differentiating the state equations with respect to parameters. Figure 11 shows a numerical routine, automatically generated from the circuit description in figure 10, that can be combined with a numerical integrator to evolve the states and the variational states of the driven van der Pol oscillator.

The result of the physical modeling, algebraic manipulation, and fancy compilation shown above in figure 11 is a higher-order procedure—a *system-*

```
(lambda (c.c 1.1 d b a)
  (lambda (*varstate*)
    (let ((t (vector-ref *varstate* 0))
          (v.c (vector-ref *varstate* 1))
          (i.1 (vector-ref *varstate* 2))
          (v.c.del.v.c (vector-ref *varstate* 3))
          (v.c.del.i.1 (vector-ref *varstate* 4))
          (i.1.del.v.c (vector-ref *varstate* 5))
          (i.1.del.i.1 (vector-ref *varstate* 6)))
      (let ((g27 (* a i.1 i.1)))
        (let ((g28 (* -3 g27)))
          (vector 1
                  (/ i.1 c.c)
                  (/ (+ (* -1 g27 i.1) (* -1 v.c) (* b i.1) (d t))
                     1.1)
                  (/ v.c.del.i.1 c.c)
                  (/ (+ (* -1 v.c.del.v.c)
                        (* b v.c.del.i.1)
                        (* g28 v.c.del.i.1))
                     1.1)
                  (/ i.1.del.i.1 c.c)
                  (/ (+ (* -1 i.1.del.v.c)
                        (* b i.1.del.i.1)
                        (* g28 i.1.del.i.1))
                     1.1)))))))
```

Figure 11. This numerical procedure is the augmented system derivative generator for evolving variational states for the driven van der Pol oscillator. The procedure was automatically generated from the circuit description shown above.

derivative generator for the dynamical system under study. The generator takes as arguments numerical values for the system parameters and produces a *system-derivative* procedure, which takes a system state vector as argument and produces a differential state (a vector that when multiplied by an increment of time is an increment of state). This system-derivative procedure is passed to an *integration driver* that returns a procedure which, given an initial state, evolves the system numerically.

Because all system derivative procedures are constructed to respect the same conventional interfaces, we may choose from a variety of integration methods. Moreover, the integration methods themselves can be automatically constructed from a library of procedures that can be used as interchangeable components in the construction of traditional applications. Going further, we believe that it is not difficult to automatically implement these numerical procedures as special-purpose hardware, like the Orrery.

To support the automatic construction of numerical procedures, we are

```
(define (romberg f a b tolerance)
  (stream-limit
    (richardson-sequence (trapezoid-sums f a b)
                          2
                          2)
    tolerance))
(define (trapezoid-sums f a b)
  (define (next-S S n)
    (let* ((h (/ (- b a) 2 n))
            (fx (lambda(i) (f (+ a (* (+ i i -1) h))))))
      (+ (/ S 2) (* h (sigma fx 1 n)))))
  (define (S-and-n-stream S n)
    (cons-stream (list S n)
                  (S-and-n-stream (next-S S n) (* n 2))))
  (let* ((h (- b a))
          (S (* (/ h 2) (+ (f a) (f b)))))
    (map-stream car (S-and-n-stream S 1))))
(define (richardson-sequence seq start-index inc-index)
  (define (sequences seq order)
    (cons-stream seq
      (sequences
        (let* ((2p (expt 2 order)) (2p-1 (- 2p 1)))
          (map-streams (lambda (Rh Rh/2)
                          (/ (- (* 2p Rh/2) Rh) 2p-1))
                        seq
                        (tail seq)))
        (+ order inc-index))))
  (map-streams head (sequences seq start-index)))
```

Figure 12. Romberg's method of quadrature can be built by combining a primitive trapezoidal integrator with an accelerator that speeds convergence of sequences by Richardson extrapolation. The result is an infinite sequence (stream) of increasingly accurate approximations to the definite integral. The same Richardson accelerator can be combined with other sequence generators to build other classical numerical routines.

developing a kernel numerical library that is organized around the liberal use of high-order procedural abstractions. For example, figure 12 illustrates this mix-and-match construction of numerical routines, expressing Romberg's method of quadrature as a combination of trapezoidal integration and Richardson extrapolation, following the exposition given by Halfant and Sussman [1988]. Such a formulation is valuable in that it separates the ideas into several independent pieces. Clever ideas need to be coded and debugged only once, in a context independent of the particular application, thus enhancing the reliability of software built in this way.

For instance, Roylance [1988] shows how to construct high-performance implementations of special functions, abstracting recurrent themes such as Chebyshev economization. His automatically constructed procedure for computing Bessel functions is 40 times more accurate, for the same number of terms, than the approximation specified in the National Bureau of Standards tables [Abramowitz & Stegun 1965]. More significantly, Roylance's formulation clearly exposes the underlying approximation methods so that parameters, such as the required precision of the routines, can be changed at will.

Besides providing a convenient target for automatic construction of numerical procedures, powerful abstraction mechanisms help us to express some of the vocabulary and methods of numerical analysis in a form that is close to the mathematical theory, and is thus easy to understand and check. A program is a communication, not just between programmers and computers, but also between programmers and human readers of the program; quite often, between the programmer and him/herself. One power of programming is that it allows one to make the knowledge of methods explicit, so that methods can be studied as theoretical entities. Traditional numerical programs are hand-crafted for each application. The traditional style does not admit such explicit decomposition and naming of methods, thus forfeiting much of the power and joy of programming.

Intelligent Tools are Feasible

The work described in the preceding sections demonstrates much of the technology required to produce programs that can serve scientists and engineers as intelligent problem-solving partners, programs such as the engineer's assistant that we envisioned at the beginning of this chapter.

We have used symbolic algebra to compile high-level descriptions such as circuit diagrams directly into numerical modeling and simulation programs whose elements can be automatically generated from a library of mix-and-match numerical subroutines expressed at appropriate levels of abstraction. Our experience with the Digital Orrery proves that such numerical programs can be run at supercomputer speeds, without the cost of a general-purpose supercomputer. The Bifurcation Interpreter, KAM, and PLR demonstrate that intelligent programs incorporating knowledge of dynamical systems can automatically control and monitor numerical experiments and interpret the results in qualitative terms. The Kineticist's Workbench illustrates how these capabilities can be combined with knowledge about a particular domain to produce a sophisticated tool for modeling and analysis.

Higher-dimensional systems are hard

Most systems of interest have more than two degrees of freedom, yet the KAM and PLR programs and the Bifurcation Interpreter depend upon special properties of low-dimensional systems. The grammar of possible phase portraits and the catalog of generic bifurcations embodied in these programs cannot be extended to higher dimensional systems easily. On the other hand, there are qualitative features of such systems that can be usefully extracted and used to guide numerical experiments.

Exploring the qualitative behavior of high-dimensional systems requires a combination of analytic and numeric methods. Analytic methods can provide clear definitive information, but are often hard to apply or unavailable. There are well-established methods for deriving the local behavior of trajectories in the neighborhood of fixed points, but few tools exist for determining global behavior. On the other hand, a program could detect a saddle analytically, calculate its stable and unstable manifolds numerically, determine whether the manifolds intersect each other, and draw conclusions about global behavior.

Moreover, even in high-dimensional spaces, it is still possible to use clustering techniques to examine the set of iterates of a map or the flow of a differential equation and determine if a trajectory is confined to a lower dimensional submanifold of the formal state space. Each reduction in dimension is evidence of an integral of motion, such as conservation of energy. One can also (as people do) apply visual recognition techniques to low-dimensional sections and projections of the full space. Despite the fact that orbit types and bifurcations in high-dimensional spaces have not been completely classified, it is still possible to recognize qualitatively different regions of behavior, and to map out these regions in state space and parameter space.

Computers, like people, need imagistic reasoning

In observing professional physicists and engineers, we are often struck by how an expert's "intuitive grasp" of a field is hard to articulate verbally. This is perhaps indicative of the use of non-verbal reasoning processes as part of the process of solving otherwise verbally presented problems. We observe scientists, mathematicians, and engineers continually using graphical representations to organize their thoughts about a problem. The programs we are developing use numerical methods as a means of shifting back and forth between symbolic and geometric methods of reasoning. The programs not only draw graphs and state-space diagrams, but they look at these diagrams and hold them in their "mind's eye" so that powerful visual mechanisms can be brought to bear on what otherwise would be purely symbolic problems.

The idea that problem solvers employing visual, analogue, or diagrammatic representations can be more effective than those relying on linguistic representations alone is not new. Even before 1960, Gelernter's Geometry-Theorem Proving Machine [Gelernter 1959] used diagrams to filter goals generated by backward chaining. Nevins's [1974] forward-chaining theorem prover focused its forward deduction of facts on those lines explicitly drawn in a diagram. Sussman and Stallman's EL [1975] program performed antecedent deductions in circuit analysis by exploiting the finite connectivity of devices.

What is provocative, however, is the suggestion that our thought processes are importantly imagistic, and that visual thinking may play a crucial role in problem solving. In scientific computation there has been tremendous emphasis on visualization, but this has mostly meant the development of computer-graphics technology to aid *human* visualization [McCormick *et al.* 1987]. We believe that imagistic reasoning is a very general class of problem-solving strategies, each with its own appropriate representations and technical support. The programs discussed above suggest that it may be at least as important for scientific computation to develop visualization aids for programs as well as for people.

References

Abelson, H., M. Halfant, J. Katzenelson, and G. J. Sussman [1988], "The Lisp Experience," *Annual Review of Computer Science*, vol 3., Annual Reviews, Palo Alto, pp. 167–195.

Abelson, H., and G. J. Sussman [1987], "The Dynamicist's Workbench I: Automatic Preparation of Numerical Experiments," Report AIM–955, Artificial Intelligence Laboratory, Massachusetts Institute of Technology, Cambridge, MA.

Abramowitz, M., and I. Stegun [1965], *Handbook of Mathematical Functions*, Dover Publications.

Applegate, J., M. Douglas, Y. Gürsel, P. Hunter, C. Seitz, G. J. Sussman [1985], "A digital orrery," *IEEE Trans. on Computers*.

Baase, S. [1978], *Computer Algorithms*, Addison-Wesley.

Feinberg, M. [1980], "Chemical oscillations, multiple equilibria, and reaction network structure," in *Dynamics and Modelling of Reactive Systems*, edited by W. Stewart, W. H. Ray and C. Conley, Academic Press, New York, pp. 59–130.

Franceschini, V. [1983], "Two models of truncated Navier-Stokes equations on a two-dimensional torus," *Phys. Fluids*, vol. 26, no. 2, pp. 433–447.

Halfant, M., and G. J. Sussman [1988], "Abstraction in Numerical Methods," Report AIM–997, 1987. To appear in proceedings of *ACM Conference on Lisp and Functional Programming*.

Hénon, M. [1969], "Numerical Study of Quadratic Area-Preserving Mappings," *Quarterly Journal of Applied Mathematics*, vol. 27.

Gelernter, H. [1963], "Realization of a geometry theorem proving machine," *Proc. Int. Conf. on Information Processing*, Paris: Unesco House, pp. 273–282, 1959; also in *Computers and Thought*, edited by E. Feigenbaum, and J. Feldman, McGraw-Hill, New York, pp. 134–152.

Guckenheimer, J., and P. Holmes [1983], *Nonlinear Oscillations, Dynamical Systems, and Bifurcations of Vector Fields*, Springer-Verlag.

Hsu, C. S. [1980], "A theory of index for point mapping dynamical systems," *Journal of Applied Mechanics*, vol. 47, pp. 185–190.

Hsu, C. S., W. H. Cheng, and H. C. Yee [1977], "Steady-state response of a nonlinear system under impulsive parametric excitation," *Journal of Sound and Vibration*, vol. 50, no. 1, pp. 95–116.

Kinoshita, H., and H. Nakai [1984], "Motions of the Perihelions of Neptune and Pluto," *Celestial Mechanics*, vol. 34.

Laidler, K. [1987], *Chemical Kinetics* (3rd edition), Harper and Row, New York.

MacKay, R. [1982], *Renormalization in Area-Preserving Maps*, Ph.D. thesis, Princeton University.

McCormick, B., T. Desanti, and M. Brown (editors) [1987], "Visualization in Scientific Computing," *Computer Graphics*, vol. 21, no. 6.

Nevins, A. J. [1974], "Plane Geometry theorem Proving using Forward Chaining," Report AIM–303, Artificial Intelligence Laboratory, Massachusetts Institute of Technology, Cambridge, MA.

Novak, G. [1977], "Representations of Knowledge in a Program for Solving Physics Problems," *Proc. 5th IJCAI*, Cambridge, MA, pp. 286–291.

Roylance, G. L. [1988], "Expressing mathematical subroutines constructively," Report AIM–999, 1987. To appear in proceedings of *ACM Conference on Lisp and Functional Programming*.

Sacks, E. P. [1987a], "Hierarchical reasoning about inequalities," AAAI, pp. 649–654.

Sacks, E. P. [1987b], "Piecewise linear reasoning," AAAI, pp. 655–659.

Sacks, E. P. [1988], "Automatic Qualitative Analysis of Ordinary Differential Equations Using Piecewise Linear Approximations," Report TR–416, Laboratory for Computer Science.

Sussman, G. J., and R. M. Stallman [1975], "Heuristic techniques in computer-aided circuit analysis," *IEEE Trans. on Circuits and Systems*, **CAS-22**, pp. 857–865.

Sussman, G. J., and J. Wisdom [1988], "Numerical evidence that the motion of Pluto is chaotic," *Science*, (to appear). Also available as Report AIM–1039, Artificial Intelligence Laboratory, Massachusetts Institute of Technology, Cambridge, MA.

Thompson, J. M. T. [1983], "Complex dynamics of compliant offshore structures," *Proc. Royal Soc. London A*, vol. 387, pp. 407–427.

Thompson, J. M. T., and H. B. Stewart [1986], *Nonlinear Dynamics and Chaos*, Wiley.

Waltz, David A. [1985], "Generating semantic descriptions from drawings of scenes with shadows," in *The Psychology of Computer Vision*, edited by P. H. Winston, McGraw-Hill, New York.

Witkin, Andrew P. [1983], "Scale-Space Filtering", *IJCAI*.

Yip, K. [1987], "Extracting qualitative dynamics from numerical experiments," AAAI.

Yip, K. [1988], "Generating global behaviors using deep knowledge of local dynamics," AAAI.

Zahn, C. T. [1971], "Graph-theoretical methods for detecting and describing Gestalt clusters", IEEE, *Trans. on Computers*, vol. C-20.

Zhao, F. [1987], *An O(N) Algorithm for three-dimensional N-body Simulations*, Report TR–995, Artificial Intelligence Laboratory, Massachusetts Institute of Technology, Cambridge, MA.

2

Computer scientists and engineers often champion their favorite programming language like single-minded religious zealots. These days, most AI people remain effusive about Lisp; many commercial in-house software organizations are waxing enthusiastic about C; most programmers working on military and government projects are trying to wax enthusiastic about Ada; and many scientists remain locked to Fortran scientific libraries written years ago. And no matter how rigid a programming-language bigot may be, he is probably paid by a Cobol program.

One reason for this unsuppressible diversity is that the space of all programs to be written is far too big to be covered efficiently by one particular programming language. All popular programming languages are, of course, Turing equivalent, but for any given problem, programming productivity in one language may be enormously greater than programming productivity in another.

The obvious reason for productivity differences lies in the primitives offered, shared, and instantly recognized by all programmers in that language. Lisp, for example, offers a handy set of primitives for working with lists; C does not even have the concept of list built in. A less obvious, but perhaps more important reason for productivity differences lies in the degree to which a programming language encourages abstraction and procedure reuse. The point of this chapter is that Scheme, a variant of Lisp, encourages just the right kind abstraction to revolutionize the construction of numerical-method libraries. In particular, Halfant and Sussman show how a procedure for Richardson extrapolation, a technique for dramatically accelerating series convergence, can be reused over and over.

Abstraction in Numerical Methods

Matthew Halfant
Gerald Jay Sussman

A numerical analyst uses powerful ideas such as Richardson extrapolation for organizing programs, but numerical programs rarely exhibit the structure implied by the abstractions used in their design. It is traditional practice in the domain of numerical methods for each program to be hand crafted, in detail, for the particular application, rather than to be constructed by mixing and matching from a set of interchangeable parts. Such numerical programs are often difficult to write and even more difficult to read.

In this chapter we illustrate how the liberal use of high-order procedural abstractions and infinite streams helps us to express some of the vocabulary and methods of numerical analysis. We develop a software toolbox encapsulating the technique of Richardson extrapolation, and we apply these tools to the problems of numerical integration and differentiation. By separating the idea of Richardson extrapolation from its use in particular circumstances we indicate how numerical programs can be written that exhibit the structure of the ideas from which they are formed.

A First Example: Archimedean Computation of π

We begin with a playful example: approximating the value of π by the method of Archimedes. Let S_n be the length of one side of a regular n-sided polygon inscribed in a unit circle. As n approaches infinity, the semi-perimeter $P_n = nS_n/2$ approaches π. Applying the Pythagorean Theorem to right triangles ACD and ADO from figure 1 we derive the relation:

$$S_{2n} = \sqrt{2 - \sqrt{4 - S_n^2}}\,.$$

Equivalently,

$$S_{2n} = \frac{S_n}{\sqrt{2 + \sqrt{4 - S_n^2}}}\,,$$

the latter form being preferred because it avoids the subtraction of nearly equal quantities as $S_n \to 0$. In Scheme [Rees & Clinger et al. 1986] (the dialect of Lisp we use) we can write the transformation from S_n to S_{2n} as:

```
(define (refine-by-doubling s)              ; s is a side
   (/ s (sqrt (+ 2 (sqrt (- 4 (* s s)))))))
```

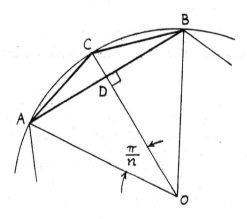

Figure 1. $|AB| = S_n$, $|AC| = |CB| = S_{2n}$.

Starting with a square (S_4 is simply $\sqrt{2}$), we want to form the sequence of side lengths $S_4, S_8, S_{16}, \cdots$. Such sequences are naturally represented with *streams*—effectively infinite lists whose terms are evaluated only on demand (for a discussion of streams see Abelson and Sussman [1985]). We use a stream generator to produce the orbit of a starting **value** under repeated application of a transformation **next**:

```
(define (stream-of-iterates next value)
   (cons-stream value
                (stream-of-iterates next (next value))))
```

Now we can define the stream of side lengths:

```
(define side-lengths
         (stream-of-iterates refine-by-doubling (sqrt 2)))
```

and the corresponding stream of numbers of sides:

```
(define side-numbers
         (stream-of-iterates (lambda (n) (* 2 n)) 4))
```

Combining these termwise using `map-streams` lets us form the sequence of semi-perimeters $P_4, P_8, P_{16}, \cdots$, whose limit is π:

```
(define (semi-perimeter length-of-side number-of-sides)
  (* (/ number-of-sides 2) length-of-side))
(define archimedean-pi-sequence
  (map-streams semi-perimeter side-lengths side-numbers))
```

We can look at the results:

```
(print-stream archimedean-pi-sequence)
   ==>     2.82842712474619
           3.06146745892072
           3.12144515225805
           3.13654849054594
           3.14033115695475
           3.14127725093277      ; term 6
           ...
           3.14159265358862      ; term 20
           3.14159265358950
           3.14159265358972
           3.14159265358977
           3.14159265358979
           3.14159265358979
           3.14159265358979
           ...
```

As expected, the sequence converges to π, but it takes 24 terms to reach the full machine precision. Imagine poor Archimedes doing the arithmetic by hand: square roots without even the benefit of our place value system! He would be interested in knowing that full precision can be reached on the fifth term, by forming linear combinations of the early terms that allow the limit to be seized by extrapolation.

To understand how this is done, rewrite the expression for the semi-perimeter P_n by using the Taylor series for $S_n = 2 \sin (\pi/n)$ (see figure 1):

$$P_n = (n/2)S_n$$
$$= (n/2)(2 \sin (\pi/n))$$
$$= \pi + A/n^2 + B/n^4 + \cdots$$

where A and B are constants whose values are not important here. As n gets larger, it is the A/n^2 term that dominates the *truncation error*— the difference between π and P_n for finite n. Whenever we double n, this principal component of the truncation error is reduced by a factor of 4; that knowledge allows us to combine successive terms of the sequence $\cdots P_n, P_{2n}, \cdots$ to eliminate entirely the effect of this quadratic term.

Specifically: multiply P_{2n} by 4, so that its $1/n^2$ term matches that of P_n; then subtract P_n to eliminate this term; after some slight rearrangement we get

$$4P_{2n} - P_n 3 = \pi - \frac{B}{4n^4} + \cdots .$$

The accelerated sequence P_n' is defined by the expression on the left; it approximates π with a truncation error that goes to 0 like $1/n^4$, which is much faster than before.

We could revise our program to compute the sequence $P_4', P_8', P_{16}', \cdots$, and demonstrate that its convergence is more rapid than that of $P_4, P_8, P_{16}, \cdots$. However, this acceleration scheme is quite general, and we prefer to develop it away from the present context. Afterwards, we can apply it to this and other pursuits.

The Method of Richardson Extrapolation

Instead of phrasing our argument in terms of a parameter n that gets larger through successive doubling, we will follow the convention of using a positive quantity h that approaches 0 through successive divisions by 2. In the example above, we need only make the identification $h = 1/n$. Sometimes n, sometimes h, will be the more natural, and we can formulate the problem however we prefer. Typically h will arise as a step size.

Now imagine that we seek the limit, as $h \to 0$, of some function $R(h)$, and that we pursue it by constructing the sequence $R(h), R(h/2), R(h/4), \cdots$. We suppose that each expression $R(h)$ represents the limiting value A with a truncation error that is analytic at $h = 0$:

$$R(h) = A + Bh^{p_1} + Ch^{p_2} + Dh^{p_3} + \cdots .$$

The exponents $p_1, p_2, p_3, \cdots$ may well be just the natural numbers $1, 2, 3, \cdots$; but they might represent a subsequence—for example, the even numbers, as they did in the Archimedean example above. We assume this sequence is known. On the other hand, we need not know in advance the values of $A, B, C, \cdots$; indeed, our whole purpose is to determine A.

Knowing the truncation error as a power series in h allows us to eliminate the effect of the dominant term: we do this by subtracting the appropriate multiple of $R(h/2)$ from $R(h)$:

$$R(h) - 2^{p_1} R(h/2) = (1 - 2^{p_1})A + C_1 h^{p_2} + D_1 h^{p_3} + \cdots$$

or

$$R'(h) = \frac{2^{p_1} R(h/2) - R(h)}{2^{p_1} - 1}$$
$$= A + C_2 h^{p_2} + D_2 h^{p_3} + \cdots .$$

We view this as a transformation applied to (adjacent terms of) the sequence

$$R(h), R(h/2), R(h/4), \cdots$$

to produce a new sequence

$$R'(h), R'(h/2), R'(h/4), \cdots$$

whose truncation error is now dominated by the term containing h^{p_2}. That is, the R' sequence converges faster than the original.

Now we come to Richardson's great idea: because R' has a truncation error dominated by $C_2 h^{p_2}$, we can apply the same idea again

$$R''(h) = \frac{2^{p_2} R'(h/2) - R'(h)}{2^{p_2} - 1}$$

$$= A + D_3 h^{p_3} + \cdots$$

yielding a sequence $R''(h), R''(h/2), R''(h/4), \cdots$ whose truncation error now has the dominant term $D_3 h^{p_3}$. And so on. Given the sequence $p_1, p_2, p_3, \cdots$, one can form a tableau (see figure 2) in which the original sequence appears as the vertical s column at the left; to the right is the derived t column; the u column is derived from t as t is from s, and so on. All columns converge to the same limit, $R(0+)$, but each converges faster than its predecessor. Thus, s converges with an error term $O(h^{p_1})$—that is, of *order* h^{p_1}; t converges with error term $O(h^{p_2})$; u has error term $O(h^{p_3})$, and so on.

If the sequence $p_1, p_2, p_3, \cdots$ is *not* known in advance, one can take the conservative approach of assuming it to be the natural number sequence $1, 2, 3, \cdots$; this leads at worst to the inefficiency of creating adjacent columns with the same error order. Alternatively, the appropriate exponent p for a given column can be inferred numerically from the early terms of that column; we have done that in our library, but do not pursue it here.

s1					
s2	t1				
s3	t2	u1			
s4	t3	u2	v1		
s5	t4	u3	v2	w1	
...	...	...	...	...	...

Figure 2. The Richardson Tableau.

The Richardson Toolbox

Having sketched the basic ideas, we develop Richardson extrapolation as a set of tools that can be applied in diverse contexts. First, if we do not already have the sequence $R(h), R(h/2), R(h/4), \cdots$ we need to be able to make it, given R and h. The name `make-zeno-sequence` derives from

the suggestive connection to successive halving in the statement of Zeno's
paradox.

```
(define (make-zeno-sequence R h)
  (cons-stream (R h) (make-zeno-sequence R (/ h 2))))
```

The basic operation of accelerating the sequence requires that we know the
order of the dominant error term. Accelerate-zeno-sequence takes this
order as an explicit argument.

```
(define (accelerate-zeno-sequence seq p)
  (let* ((2p (expt 2 p)) (2p-1 (- 2p 1)))
    (map-streams (lambda (Rh Rh/2)
                   (/ (- (* 2p Rh/2) Rh)
                      2p-1))
                 seq
                 (tail seq))))
```

In the case of the full tableau we iterate the application of accelerate-
zeno-sequence to make an infinite sequence of accelerated sequences. In
forming the full tableau, we make the simplifying assumption that the
exponent sequence is arithmetic:

$$\{p_1,\ p_2,\ p_3, \cdots\} = \{p,\ p+q,\ p+2q,\ p+3q, \cdots\}.$$

Hence it can be specified by the initial order p and an increment q. In
typical cases, q is 1 or 2.

The procedure make-zeno-tableau accepts as arguments the original
Zeno sequence along with the characterizing order p and increment q; it
returns the sequence of accelerated sequences.

```
(define (make-zeno-tableau seq p q)
  (define (sequences seq order)
    (cons-stream seq
                 (sequences (accelerate-zeno-sequence seq order)
                            (+ order q))))
  (sequences seq p))
```

Finally, the procedure first-terms-of-zeno-tableau produces a sequence s1, t1, u1, v1, w1, ... of the first terms taken from each of the
accelerated sequences. The sequence of first terms converges at a remarkable rate: not only are the first n terms of the original truncation-error
series removed, but the remainder is effectively divided by $2^{n^2 q/2}$ (see the
Appendix for details).

```
(define (first-terms-of-zeno-tableau tableau)
  (map-streams head tableau))
(define (richardson-sequence seq p q)
  (first-terms-of-zeno-tableau (make-zeno-tableau seq p q)))
```

Archimedes Revisited

Before proceeding any further, let us see how well this does on our original example. We apply richardson-sequence to the archimedean-pi-

`sequence` previously computed and examine the result:

```
(print-stream (richardson-sequence archimedean-pi-sequence 2 2))
  ==>     2.82842712474619
          3.13914757031223
          3.14159039312994
          3.14159265328605
          3.14159265358979
          3.14159265358979
          3.14159265358979
            . . .
```

As indicated earlier, full precision is reached on the 5th term (although we need to compute the 6th to know that we have reached it, and may want to compute the 7th just to be sure). What remains now is to establish some algorithmic means for ascertaining when a limit has been reached.

Completing and Applying the Richardson Toolbox

Now that we have the idea under control, we must fill in our Richardson toolbox to allow its application in a variety of situations. We need ways of extracting our best estimate of the limit from a sequence. One simple criterion that may be used is this: We declare convergence when two consecutive terms are sufficiently close.

Alas, the notion of sufficient closeness is slightly sticky: relative accuracy is what is generally wanted, but that fails in the case of a sequence with limit 0. One way around the difficulty is to use the metric

$$\frac{|h_1 - h_2|}{(|h_1| + |h_2|)/2 + 1}$$

to measure the distance between two numbers h_1 and h_2:

```
(define (close-enuf? h1 h2 tolerance)
  (<= (abs (- h1 h2))
      (* .5
         tolerance
         (+ (abs h1) (abs h2) 2))))
```

This criterion amounts to relative closeness when the numbers to be compared are large, but makes a graceful transition to absolute closeness when the numbers are much smaller (in magnitude) than 1.

Using this or any similar predicate, we construct our limit detector:

```
(define (stream-limit s tolerance)
  (let loop ((s s))
    (let* ((h1 (head s)) (t (tail s)) (h2 (head t)))
      (if (close-enuf? h1 h2 tolerance)
          h2
          (loop t)))))
```

A more cautious version of the limit detector would require close agreement for three or more successive terms (we have been bitten ourselves by accidental equality of the first two terms of a sequence). Actually, there is another modification we will be forced to make very shortly: we will need an optional final argument m that forbids stream-limit from examining more than the first m terms of the sequence before returning an answer.

Given stream-limit, the following combination proves useful for finding the Richardson limit of a function. The arguments ord and inc are our previous p and q.

```
(define (richardson-limit f start-h ord inc tolerance)
  (stream-limit
    (richardson-sequence (make-zeno-sequence f start-h)
                         ord
                         inc)
    tolerance))
```

We are ready now to apply our tools to a significant example.

Numerical Computation of Derivatives

The following higher-order procedure takes a procedure that computes a numerical function and returns a procedure that calculates an approximation to the derivative of that function:

```
(define (make-derivative-function f)
  (lambda (x)
    (let ((h .00001))
      (/ (- (f (+ x h)) (f (- x h)))
         2 h))))
```

Note the ad hoc definition of h. We are walking the line between truncation error (not having h small enough for the difference quotient to adequately approximate the derivative) and roundoff error (having h so small that the subtraction of nearly equal quantities loses all accuracy in the answer). The optimal h depends both on x and on the number of digits carried by the machine, but even with this h we will generally lose about a third of our significant digits (we would lose half of our digits had we used the forward, rather than the centered difference quotient). Of course we are hoping that Richardson will allow us to do better.

It is instructive to experiment with letting h go to 0. Given f, x, and h, we produce a stream of difference quotients in which h is successively reduced by a factor of 2.

```
(define (diff-quot-stream f x h)
  (cons-stream (/ (- (f (+ x h)) (f (- x h))) 2 h)
               (diff-quot-stream f x (/ h 2))))
```

We apply this to the estimation of the derivative of the square root at 1 (exact answer is 0.5).

```
(print-stream (diff-quot-stream sqrt 1 .1))
```

```
==>     0.500627750598189
        0.500156421150633
        0.500039073185090
        0.500009766292631
        0.500002441447984
        0.500000610354192
        0.500000152587994
        0.500000038146951
        0.500000009536734
        0.500000002384411
        0.500000000595833
        0.500000000148475
        0.500000000038199
        0.500000000010914        ; 14th term
        0.500000000010914
        0.499999999974534
        0.499999999992724
        0.500000000029104
        0.499999999883585
        . . .
        0.500183105468750        ; 40th term
        0.500488281250000
        0.499267578125000
        0.498046875000000
        0.502929687500000
        0.507812500000000
        0.488281250000000
        0.468750000000000
        0.546875000000000
        0.625000000000000
        0.312500000000000        ; 50th term
        0.
        0.
        0.
        . . .
```

We observe that the error diminishes steadily until the 14th term is reached; after this, the error builds back up in a somewhat erratic manner until, after the 50th term, we are left with a steady parade of zeros. This problem results from the subtraction of nearly equal quantities in the numerator of the difference quotient: we lose more and more significant figures until h becomes so small that $x + h$ and $x - h$ are equal to full working precision, after which only 0 quotients can be returned.

Hence we are in a race between truncation error, which starts out large and gets smaller, and roundoff error, which starts small and gets larger. Richardson helps the situation by creating new sequences in which the truncation error diminishes more rapidly, which is just what we need. To be more precise, we need to look at how the roundoff error works in this example.

Any real number x, represented in the machine, is rounded to a value $x(1+e)$, where e is effectively a random variable whose absolute value is on the order of the *machine epsilon*, ϵ: that smallest positive number for which 1.0 and $1.0 + \epsilon$ can be distinguished. For IEEE double precision (as used, for example, by the 8087 numeric coprocessor), $\epsilon = 2^{-53} = 1.11 \times 10^{-16}$. Now if h is small, both $f(x+h)$ and $f(x-h)$ have machine representations in error by around $f(x)\epsilon$; their difference suffers an absolute error of this same order. Because the difference $f(x+h) - f(x-h)$ *should* equal around $f'(x)2h$, the relative error is of the order

$$\epsilon \left| \frac{f(x)}{2hf'(x)} \right| .$$

The relative error of the difference quotient is essentially the same as that of its numerator, the denominator being just $2h$ which is known to full precision.

From the above expression, we see that the relative error due to round-off basically doubles each time h is halved—a result that is easy to see directly in terms of the binary representation of $x + h$: dividing h by 2 shifts the binary representation of h one position to the right; but the presence of x nails down the high order bits of $x + h$, whence the low order bits of h fall off the end, one per iteration.

Suppose we want to compute the derivative of the square root at 1 with a relative error of at most 10^{-13}, and starting with $h = 0.1$. We need to estimate the initial relative roundoff error; the preceding formula must be modified slightly for this purpose. First, the denominator is actually $f(x + h) - f(x - h)$, which is what we must use (it was written above as $2hf'(x)$ only to show the trend as h gets small). Second, we want to ensure that the predicted relative roundoff error is at least a positive multiple of the machine epsilon; hence we take the *next-highest-integer* of the absolute-value subexpression:

$$1 + floor \left(\left| \frac{\sqrt{1}}{\sqrt{1.1} - \sqrt{0.9}} \right| \right) = 10 .$$

Thus, the initial relative roundoff error is 10 *roundoff units*, or $10\epsilon = 1.1 \times 10^{-15}$. Because the roundoff error roughly doubles at each iteration, we ask: How many times can 1.1×10^{-15} be doubled before reaching 10^{-13}?

$$1.1 \times 10^{-15}2^n \leq 10^{-13}$$

so

$$n \leq \frac{\log\left(10^{-13}/1.1 \times 10^{-15}\right)}{\log 2} = 6.5 .$$

Hence if we restrict ourselves to at most 6 terms past the first (for a total of 7 terms), we can be reasonably sure our data is uncontaminated by noise at the level of interest. This makes accelerated convergence really crucial: we have to reach our limit quickly or not at all.

Here is a modified version of stream-limit that accepts an optional final parameter m, designating the maximum number of stream terms to examine in the search for the limit. If m is reached without convergence, we just return the final term as a best guess; a more professional approach would be to return some kind of an error code, along with the best guess and an estimate of its truncation error.

```
(define (stream-limit s tolerance . opts)  ;opts = optional args
  (let ((M (if (null? opts) 'nomax (car opts))))
    (let loop ((s s) (count 2))
      (let* ((h1 (head s)) (t (tail s)) (h2 (head t)))
        (if (close-enuf? h1 h2 tolerance)
            h2
            (if (and (number? M) (>= count M))
                h2
                (loop t (+ count 1))))))))))
```

The revised version of richardson-limit is simply:

```
(define (richardson-limit f start-h ord inc tolerance . opts)
  (stream-limit
    (richardson-sequence (make-zeno-sequence f start-h)
                         ord
                         inc)
    tolerance
    (if (null? opts) 'nomax (car opts))))
```

We can now define our derivative estimator in the following natural way. (In practice, the routine as shown admits of several pitfalls: h becomes 0 if x is; delta might end up as 0 by chance; and possibly some other bad things we have not thought of. It will serve for purposes of illustration here.)

```
(define rderiv
  (lambda (f tolerance)
    (lambda (x)
      (let* ((h (* 0.1 (abs x)))
             (delta (- (f (+ x h)) (f (- x h))))
             (roundoff (* *machine-epsilon*
                          (+ 1 (floor (abs (/ (f x) delta))))))
             (n (floor (/ (log (/ tolerance roundoff))
                          (log 2)))))
```

```
(richardson-limit (lambda (dx)
                    (/ (- (f (+ x dx))
                          (f (- x dx)))
                       (* 2 dx)))
                  h
                  2
                  2
                  tolerance
                  (+ n 1))))))
```

Note that the ord and inc arguments are both 2: the truncation error involves only even powers of h. Had we used the forward difference quotient, $(f(x + h) - f(x))/h$, then all powers of h would arise, and ord and inc would both be 1. These results follow easily from the Taylor expansion of f.

Applied to the square root example, we find:

```
((rderiv sqrt 1e-13) 1) ==> 0.500000000000016
```

which shows a relative error of 0.32×10^{-13}. Further testing shows that the relative error of 10^{-13} is generally met.

We pass now to another significant application, in which roundoff error is happily not an issue.

Numerical Integration by Romberg's Method

Given a function f that behaves nicely (that is, has two continuous derivatives) on a finite interval $[a, b]$, we seek numerical approximations to the definite integral of f from a to b. The plan of attack is to divide $[a, b]$ into some number, n, of subintervals each of length $h = (b - a)/n$. We apply the trapezoidal rule to compute an approximating sum S_n; we then form a sequence of approximations by repeatedly doubling n (equivalently, halving h) and use Richardson extrapolation on the result.

We get the ball rolling with the following procedure. It takes f, a, and b, and returns a procedure that, given n, computes S_n:

```
(define (trapezoid f a b)
  (lambda (n)
    (let ((h (/ (- b a) n)))
      (let loop ((i 1) (sum (/ (+ (f a) (f b)) 2)))
        (let ((x (+ a (* i h))))
          (if (< i n)
              (loop (+ i 1) (+ sum (f x)))
              (* sum h)))))))
```

We use this to estimate π:

```
(define (f x) (/ 4 (+ 1 (* x x))))
(define pi-estimator (trapezoid f 0 1))
(pi-estimator 10)     ==> 3.13992598890716
(pi-estimator 10000) ==> 3.14159265192314
```

It is shown in standard texts (for example Dahlquist and Bjork [1974] or Press *et al.* [1986]) that, for f in $C^2[a, b]$ as we have assumed, the truncation error involves only even powers of h. Hence we proceed:

```
(define (pi-estimator-sequence n)
  (cons-stream (pi-estimator n)
               (pi-estimator-sequence (* 2 n))))
(print-stream
  (richardson-sequence
    (pi-estimator-sequence 10) 2 2))
==>     3.13992598890716
        3.14159265296979
        3.14159265362079
        3.14159265358979
        . . .
```

The convergence rate is very encouraging—we get full machine accuracy in only 80 evaluations of the original function f—but there is considerable redundant computation here. Every time we double the number of points we reevaluate the integrand at the old grid points; this is a lamentable inefficiency in cases where f is expensive to compute. Romberg's method of quadrature, to which we now proceed, is a variation of the above that avoids unnecessary recomputation of f.

We begin with a utility procedure that computes a sum of terms $f(i)$, where i takes unit steps from a to (not-greater-than) b:

```
(define (sigma f a b)
  (let loop ((sum 0) (x a))
    (if (> x b)
        sum
        (loop (+ sum (f x)) (+ x 1)))))
```

We examine how the sum S_{2n} is related to S_n. In the former, we employ a partition of $[a, b]$ into $2n$ equal parts, having grid points at $x_i = a + ih$, with $h = (b - a)/2n$, and i going from 0 to $2n$. The even-index terms of this point sequence comprise the entire point sequence for S_n; in computing S_{2n}, we need only evaluate f at the odd indices, the others being already incorporated into S_n:

$$S_{2n} = \frac{1}{2}S_n + h\sum_{i=1}^{n} f(x_{2i-1}).$$

This recursion is the basis of the following procedure, which generates the sequence $S_1, S_2, S_4, \cdots$:

```
(define (trapezoid-sums f a b)
  (define (next-S S n)
    (let* ((h (/ (- b a) 2 n))
           (fx (lambda(i) (f (+ a (* (+ i i -1) h))))))
      (+ (/ S 2) (* h (sigma fx 1 n)))))
  (define (S-and-n-stream S n)
    (cons-stream (list S n)
                 (S-and-n-stream (next-S S n) (* n 2))))
  (let* ((h (- b a))
         (S (* (/ h 2) (+ (f a) (f b)))))
    (map-stream car (S-and-n-stream S 1))))
```

We arrive at the more economical version of our previous method:

```
(define (romberg f a b tolerance)
  (stream-limit
    (richardson-sequence (trapezoid-sums f a b)
                         2
                         2)
    tolerance))
```

Conclusion

We have shown how a classical numerical analysis method, Richardson extrapolation, can be formulated as a package of procedures that can be used as interchangeable components in the construction of traditional applications such as the estimation of a derivative and Romberg quadrature. Such a formulation is valuable in that it separates out the ideas into several independent pieces, allowing one to mix and match combinations of components in a flexible way to facilitate attacking new problems. Clever ideas, such as Richardson extrapolation, need be coded and debugged only once, in a context independent of the particular application, thus enhancing the reliability of software built in this way. Roylance [1987] has similar goals. He constructs high-performance implementations of special functions, abstracting out recurrent themes such as Chebyshev economization.

The decompositions we displayed have used powerful abstraction mechanisms built on high-order procedures, interconnected with interfaces organized around streams. The programs were implemented functionally—there were no assignments or other side-effects in any of our example programs. Because functional programs have no side effects they have no required order of execution. This makes it exceptionally easy to execute them in parallel.

A program is a communication, not just between programmers and computers, but also between programmers and human readers of the program; quite often, between the programmer and him/herself. A program describes, more or less clearly, an idea for how to obtain some desired results. One power of programs is that they allow one to make the knowledge of methods explicit, so that methods can be studied as theoretical entities. Traditional numerical programs are hand crafted for each application. The traditional style does not admit such explicit decomposition and naming of methods, thus losing a great part of the power and joy of programming.

References

Abelson, H., and G. J. Sussman, with J. Sussman [1985], *Structure and Interpretation of Computer Programs*, MIT Press, Cambridge, MA.

Dahlquist, G., and A. Bjork [1974], *Numerical Methods*, Prentice-Hall.

Press, W. H., B. P. Flannery, S. A. Teukolsky [1986], and W. T. Vetterling, *Numerical Recipes: The Art of Scientific Computing*, Cambridge University Press.

Rees, J., and W. Clinger *et al.* 1986], *Revised³ Report on the Algorithmic Language Scheme*, ACM SIGPLAN Notices, vol. 21, no. 12, pp. 37-79, 1986; also, Report AIM-848a, Artificial Intelligence Laboratory, Massachusetts Institute of Technology, Cambridge, MA.

Roylance, G. L. [1987], *Expressing Mathematical Subroutines Constructively*. Report AIM-999, Artificial Intelligence Laboratory, Massachusetts Institute of Technology, Cambridge, MA.

Appendix: Convergence Rate of the First-Terms Sequence

We offer here the mathematical justification for claims made earlier about the rate of convergence of the sequence of first terms returned by the procedure `richardson-sequence`.

As for hypotheses, we suppose that R is a function analytic in a disk that contains h as an interior point; thus we have an expansion

$$R(h) = A + \sum_{i=1}^{\infty} E_i h^{p_i} ,$$

where $\{p_1, p_2, \cdots\}$ is an increasing sequence of positive integers. We assume the p_i are chosen so that no E_i is 0. Let us identify R with $R^{[1]}$; the sequence of first terms is given by

$$S = \{R^{[1]}(h), R^{[2]}(h), \cdots, R^{[n]}(h), \cdots\}$$

where for all $n > 0$,

$$R^{[n+1]}(h) = \frac{2^{p_n} R^{[n]}(\frac{h}{2}) - R^{[n]}(h)}{2^{p_n} - 1} .$$

This is the operation concocted to remove the dominant error term at each stage; thus we know

$$S_n = R^{[n]}(h) = A + \sum_{i=n}^{\infty} E_i^{[n]} h^{p_i} .$$

Because it is possible that the coefficients $E_i^{[n]}$ grow large as $n \to \infty$, we cannot immediately conclude that S_n converges to A or even converges at all. We settle this question by a straight-forward computation. To begin with, we have

$$S_2 = A + \frac{1}{2^{p_1} - 1} \sum_{i=2}^{\infty} E_i \left(\frac{1}{2^{p_i - p_1}} - 1 \right) h^{p_i}$$

and

$$S_3 = A + \frac{1}{(2^{p_1} - 1)(2^{p_2} - 1)} \sum_{i=3}^{\infty} E_i \left(\frac{1}{2^{p_i - p_1}} - 1 \right) \left(\frac{1}{2^{p_i - p_2}} - 1 \right) h^{p_i} ;$$

the general case is seen to be

$$S_{n+1} = A + \left(\prod_{i=1}^{n} \frac{1}{2^{p_i} - 1} \right) \sum_{i=n+1}^{\infty} E_i \left\{ \prod_{j=1}^{n} \left(\frac{1}{2^{p_i - p_j}} - 1 \right) \right\} h^{p_i} .$$

The term appearing in braces is less than 1 in magnitude; this gives us the estimate

$$|S_{n+1} - A| \leq \left(\prod_{i=1}^{n} \frac{1}{2^{p_i} - 1} \right) \sum_{i=n+1}^{\infty} |E_i h^{p_i}| .$$

Because R is analytic at h, the summation part

$$\mu_n = \sum_{i=n+1}^{\infty} |E_i h^{p_i}|$$

converges monotonically to 0 as $n \to \infty$. The product appearing in parentheses is estimated as follows. Let $\sigma_n = \sum_{i=1}^{n} p_i$; then

$$\prod_{i=1}^{n} \frac{1}{2^{p_i} - 1} = \frac{1}{2^{\sigma_n}} \prod_{i=1}^{n} \left(\frac{1}{1 - 2^{-p_i}} \right) .$$

Using the inequality, valid for $x \in [0, \frac{1}{2}]$,

$$\frac{1}{1 - x} \leq 1 + 2x ,$$

we see that the product above is dominated, in magnitude, by

$$\frac{1}{2^{\sigma_n}} \prod_{i=1}^{n} \left(1 + \frac{2}{2^{p_i}} \right) < \frac{1}{2^{\sigma_n}} \prod_{i=1}^{\infty} \left(1 + \frac{2}{2^{p_i}} \right) \leq \frac{1}{2^{\sigma_n}} \prod_{i=0}^{\infty} \left(1 + \frac{1}{2^i} \right) = \frac{K}{2^{\sigma_n}} .$$

where $K = \prod_{i=0}^{\infty}(1 + 2^{-i})$ is an absolute constant.

Thus we have shown that the absolute error with which S_{n+1} approximates the limit A is less than

$$\frac{K\mu_n}{2^{\sigma_n}}.$$

In the cases cited in our discussion, $\{p_i\}$ is an arithmetic progression $\{p + (i-1)q\}$; hence

$$\sigma_n = \sum_{i=1}^{n}(p + (i-1)q) = np + \frac{n(n-1)}{2}q.$$

This justifies our earlier claim.

3

A wise person once said that success is not a matter of how hard you work, but rather how smart you work. Today, mechanical designers do not have any productivity-improving, work-smart help from computers. Computer-aided design systems help with drafting and some kinds of analysis, but little else. To improve productivity, mechanical designers need better interfaces so that they can tell computers what they want; mechanical designers need smarter synthesis programs so that the computer can do what they are told to do; and mechanical designers need better simulation methods so that the computer can test what they have done.

Suppose, for example, that you could tell a computer about shape by bending an instrumented strip of flexible material with your hands. Suppose that you could tell a computer where you want a shaft supported such that the computer itself decides what the necessary bracket should look like. And suppose that you could tell the computer to decide if a part buckles, not by solving plate and beam equations, but by breaking the part up into a three-dimensional array of tiny cubes, each of which is simulated in real-time by its own processor.

In this chapter, Ulrich explains his work on such interface tools, synthesis tools, and simulation tools. His ultimate aim is to create total environments in which design engineers develop high-quality products better, faster, and much more competitively.

Intelligent Tools for Mechanical Design

Karl T. Ulrich

In the most general sense, design is a transformation from a functional description of an artifact to a structural description of an artifact. Although this definition includes landscape architecture as well as bridge design, this chapter focuses more narrowly on the design of discrete manufactured products like automobiles, photocopiers, disk drives, and home appliances. My primary interest is in computer tools to support the design of the mechanical systems in these devices. Further, I am most interested in design as it is practiced within the business context of the firms that manufacture these products. This chapter outlines my vision for the future of computer tools for mechanical design, describing some initial efforts in four different research areas that are aimed at realizing this vision.

The importance of design

Manufacturing is often viewed as the activities that occur in factories to transform engineering documentation into physical artifacts. I view manufacturing in a broader way as the entire process of delivering an artifact in response to a customer need. Product design plays the central role within this broader view of manufacturing. Many researchers believe that, particularly in discrete goods manufacturing, up to 85 percent of the manufacturing cost of a product is established through decisions made during the product's design stage [Whitney 1988]. For example, NCR claims that the elimination of several screws in their 2760 cash register design resulted in manufacturing cost savings of over $12,000 per screw over the life of the product [Port 1989]. The implication of this ability to influence overall product cost during product design is that improvements in the way that products are designed will have a large impact on the effectiveness of the complete manufacturing system.

Characteristics of design problems and design practice

Unfortunately, design as practiced in an industrial setting often appears to proceed without guidance from any kind of principles, theory, or organizing tools. The difficulty in systematically approaching design problems with an arsenal of productivity-enhancing tools stems from some inherent characteristics of design problems as well as some practical realities of the size, scope, and nature of most industrial design projects: design problems are ill defined; there is a dearth of formal methods for solving design problems; design projects are amazingly complex and resource consuming; and there has been little research in design outside of several narrow problem domains.

Design specifications occur at many different levels of detail. The specification for a new automobile might be in terms of a target market segment, while the specification for a new alternator on an existing model might give detailed requirements on dimensions, materials, and performance parameters. Even in the case of the alternator, however, there are many functional characteristics that are left unspecified: Should the housing have a dull or shiny finish? Should the shape of the alternator be aesthetically consistent with the engine? Should the input shaft be designed to be adaptable to future models? Some of these issues are left to the design team to resolve internally, some of them require further information gathering, experimentation, or negotiation with other groups within the firm. Design problems are rarely completely specified and the specifications that are given often evolve as the project progresses.

There are very few formal methods for solving design problems. In most cases this is because the problems are very difficult to completely and formally specify, and because the combinatorial complexity of design problems is severe. There are some exceptional cases in which limited kinds of problems have associated formal methods. One example is Karnough mapping for simple digital circuits whose function is specified by a truth table. Another exception is single-input, single-output dynamic systems consisting of lumped parameter networks [Ulrich 1989]. This is not to say that the development of design methods is not possible. Rather, there are thousands of different problem domains in design, each posing apparently diverse representation problems and involving formidable combinatorial complexity.

In practice, design is a costly, time consuming, and complex activity. As an example, consider the case of automobile design. Out of a sample of 29 auto projects in Japan, the United States, and Europe between 1980 and

1987, Clark found that the average engineering time expended for a new automobile project from concept generation through product engineering (but excluding process engineering) is 2.6 million hours over an average development lead time of 54 months [Clark 1987]. A project like this may cost half a billion dollars, and at peak intensity may involve one thousand engineers working on hundreds of subsystems. This daunting project scope is not confined to automobiles; even a relatively small product like a personal computer printer may involve 300,000 hours of engineering effort and 100 engineers.

There has been relatively little research on tools for mechanical design outside of the areas of computer-aided drafting, computer graphics, computer-controlled machining, and finite-element analysis. Voelcker *et al.* [1988] have written a good survey of the progress made in these areas. Although as early as 1965 [Mann] some researchers identified the potential for extensive computational assistance for design, a real focus of attention did not develop until the early 1980s. In the past 10 years, there has been a swelling of interest in computer methods for many aspects of the design process from concept generation through detailed design. Some examples of this research are formal synthesis methods for well-defined design domains, the representation of design knowledge, and theories of innovative design. Finger and Dixon [1989] have written a good survey of this work.

Vision for the future

When these attributes of design problems and design research are viewed in light of trends in industrial practice, several important future research areas emerge. Product design is an intensely competitive global activity. Companies now compete on the basis of development time, product variety, product cost, and product quality. Consider the following supporting examples for each of these trends. Auto companies have been shrinking the development time for a new model from 60 months to 30 months. On a recent trip to Japan, I counted over 70 different variations on walkman-type tape players in one shop, all made by Sony. Some firms can manufacture videocassette recorders, highly complex electromechanical devices, for less than $100. A new car buyer can now expect to have the first three or so years of ownership to be repair free. These trends are part of an increasingly competitive global business environment. In this marketplace product development has become a critical competitive tool for successful manufacturing firms.

There are several approaches to maintaining a competitive advantage in product development. One important action is to improve education and management practices. Some of these issues are discussed at length in Dertouzos [1989], Hayes [1988], and Eppinger [1989]. An equally important

long-term strategy is design automation. Although there are many fruitful
areas for design automation research, I see four critical problems at the
intersection of computing technology and the demands of design practice.
These are:

1   Better human-computer interfaces for the rapid description of design
    geometry.

2   Synthesis tools for engineering structures.

3   Simulation tools for mechanical behavior.

4   Accurate production cost estimation.

Put together, I believe that the results of this research program will lead
to a new computational environment for design.

In this environment, engineers will be able to rapidly enter geometrical concepts into their design system with intuitive and efficient human-
computer interface devices. Certain design operations, like component selection and simple part detailing, will be highly automated. Device performance simulation will be readily available, skirting the need for resource-
consuming prototypes. Production cost information will be provided as
a result of the specification of the design attributes, the production process, and the production management policies. This cost information will
be used to evaluate design-for-production decisions. Together these tools
will allow design teams to generate new products faster and better than
ever before, allowing the associated firms to compete on the dimensions of
product variety and new product frequency as well as on cost and product
performance.

It is not surprising that my research agenda coincides with this view
of the central challenges in applying computation to design problems. In
the balance of this chapter I present the research approach we[1] are taking
at the MIT Artificial Intelligence Laboratory to each of these challenges.
This research program is quite young, and so these descriptions of research
problems and approaches are meant to be an indication of the direction and
approach that we are taking rather than reports on finished projects. All
of these projects are problem-driven; they arise from a real industrial need.
The basic philosophy of the research program is inductive we believe that
immersion in real problems with real constraints will force us to confront
the critical theoretical and practical issues in design automation. On the
other hand, we have targeted problems that we do not believe will be
immediately addressed within industrial research groups. We are building
the foundation for a generation of tools that will be developed over the
next 10 or 15 years.

---

[1]Most of the ideas in this chapter were developed in collaboration with my
graduate students Marc Filerman, Peter Graham, and Jin Oh.

Interfaces

There has been some progress made towards the development of computer-aided design systems that allow mechanical engineers to conceptualize, modify and prototype designs Cutkosky [1987], Pentland [1988]. Despite successes in some areas, most of these systems are conspicuously unequipped with intuitive methods for entering part geometry. In fact, we assert that the primary reason many of the current systems serve more as design verification tools than as true design synthesis tools is that the human interfaces are too awkward. Most conventional CAD systems have as input devices a stylus, mouse, and keyboard. These input devices have evolved from an assumption that CAD representations are either textual or two-dimensional. We believe that new interfaces are needed that are based on an assumption that the objects being designed are three-dimensional.

Our claim is that input devices for CAD should exploit human abilities to reason spatially and tactilely. We hypothesize that if a mechanical designer could physically manipulate an input device in much the same way as an artist or designer would work with clay, then he or she could rapidly conceptualize a design and easily iterate through many design options to produce the best final geometry.

In its most general form, this input device is a kind of intelligent modeling clay in which the spatial and tactile inputs from the designer's hands are transformed into operations on a geometric representation and graphic display of the object being created. This concept offers the advantage of allowing a designer to quickly sketch a design simply by molding the part with his or her hands. Our vision is of a sketching tool for three-dimensional part geometry that provides the same kinds of flexibility as a pencil and paper provides for two-dimensional images.

There are at least three research issues which must be resolved before this vision can be realized. They are:

1   The completeness of the input language.
2   The physical properties of the input device.
3   The nature of the correspondence between hand operations and system modeling operations.

The completeness issue resonates with representation problems in artificial intelligence. The central problem is devising a set of primitive operations that will provide an adequate covering of the space of possible design shapes while being both efficient and intuitive. The physical properties issue is a problem of human perception and action. Here the question is what the look and feel of the device should be to provide the best coupling between the motions of a designer's hands and the primitive operations of the geometry modeler. The issue of the correspondence between human actions and modeling operations relates to the appropriate application of constraints:

how can the designer's intent to create a set of perfectly orthogonal planes be extracted from a real input signal that can never be specified perfectly?

Because of the high degree of complexity associated with developing the first prototype of the complete many-degree-of-freedom input device, we have begun with a smaller, more tractable part of the problem. We are building a system for designing sheet metal parts. Sheet metal processing, along with injection molding and machining, accounts for a large fraction of the fabrication processes for engineered artifacts. So we feel that the solution to the problem of effectively providing a human interface for computer-aided sheet metal part design is intrinsically important as well as being a tractable first step towards our broader vision. The primary advantage of beginning with the sheet metal problem is that the range of relevant design operations is relatively small. One only need consider cutting and bending operations on sheets of flat material (initially we are ignoring drawing and extruding operations).

Our initial system design presents the engineer with two separate views of the part being created, and allows him or her to alter the geometry of the part from either view. To use the system, the designer first specifies the outline of the part using the two-dimensional, unfolded view of the part, and will then change the three-dimensional geometry by physically manipulating a flexible strip of material. The actual bending of the strip in the designer's hands will induce bending of the part displayed on the screen. To establish a relationship between the input device and the part, the designer highlights a specific region of the part on the two dimensional image with a mouse, making those regions active. With the active areas specified, the designer may then bend the flexible strip in any fashion to produce the desired part geometry. In this scheme, the designer has two degrees of freedom with the flexible strip: the location and magnitude of a bend (see figure 1.)

We have completed construction of the first experimental prototype of the system which allows only a single bend in a given flat metal sheet. A single potentiometer provides the voltage signal from a two segment input strip to an input signal processor which is in turn connected to an engineering workstation. The resulting data is converted to an angle measurement and is used to update the screen image. Based on our experience with the first prototype we are constructing a second device that will allow for the selection of the position of the bend along the length of the strip.

Synthesis of Engineering Structures

The task of automatically synthesizing an arbitrary mechanical part from a specification of its behavior is quite difficult. This is largely because of the problems associated with representing the part specifications. Engineering

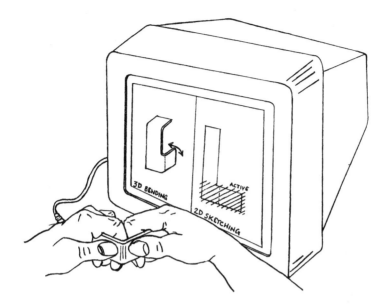

Figure 1. Sheet metal spatial-tactile input device.

structures,[2] in contrast, are ubiquitous mechanical parts whose function can be easily specified. This section describes a project focused on the automatic synthesis of these structures.

Most of the design effort in a product development project is spent deciding upon a geometric configuration for parts and specifying their dimensions and tolerances. The primary function of many of these parts is simply to maintain a geometric relationship between critical surfaces. One of the initiatives we are taking is to develop ways of synthesizing these structural parts given a specification of their associated critical surfaces. In order to describe a design problem, an engineer must specify:

- Any arbitrary part geometry required by the situation.
- Mating or interconnecting surfaces of a part.
- Obstacles.
- Part loadings.
- Geometric restrictions on the size of a part.

A valid design can be thought of as a path that connects the interface surfaces while avoiding all obstacles and supporting all part loadings. The

---

[2]Structure in this context refers to a part that supports a load while preventing relative motion of the parts to which it is connected. In this context, structure takes on a slightly more specific meaning than when used in the AI literature, as in the phrase *function and structure*.

structure synthesis task can be thought of as a kind of generalized connect-the-dots problem where the key measure of part quality is production cost. Our aim is to generate a collection of design alternatives based on production cost that will be presented to the design engineer for final evaluation. We have chosen not to attempt to completely automate the optimal design of an engineering structure. Rather, we aim to present the designer with several alternative structures synthesized automatically from a description of the key part interfaces.

As a starting point for this research we have tackled the problem of sheet metal part design. Sheet metal parts are fabricated by cutting and bending flat sheets of metal. Although parts as diverse as aluminum beverage cans, automobile fenders, and computer cabinets are considered to be sheet metal parts, we only consider parts with straight edges involving right angles made by blanking (a process like cookie-cutting) and orthogonal bending operations. Although we have begun this work by looking at the design of sheet metal parts, we expect the ideas from this exercise to be useful in other synthesis applications, like those associated with injection molded parts, cast parts, machined parts, and forged parts.

Our fundamental approach to the synthesis task is to first generate a set of initial design candidates that each represent a family of topologically distinct designs, and then to improve these initial designs iteratively. The guidance for the iteration is provided by an estimate of the part manufacturing cost. The appeal of this scheme is that by first generating distinct families of parts, the design space is partitioned into several well-behaved regions. Further, by incorporating manufacturability directly into the synthesis procedure, the resulting parts will be inexpensive to produce.

Generating distinct families of designs

The first step in our approach to structural synthesis is to generate a set of candidate designs each representing a family of topologically similar parts. The definitions of these families can be thought of in terms of a graph in which the nodes are the faces of the part and the edges are the types of bends that can connect different faces. For example the two parts shown in figure 2 represent two different part topologies because the sequence of connections between faces is different for the two parts. In this illustration both of the designs meet the basic functional requirement of connecting points A and B. The two parts shown in the figure are members of two different families of designs whose members are parametric modifications to the two basic topologies. Our current approach is to exhaustively generate the different topologies from the specification of the critical part interfaces. This task is tractable because of the practical limitation that few sheet metal structural parts contain more than three or four bends.

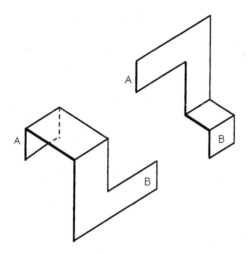

Figure 2. Two topologically distinct parts, both connecting A and B.

Iteratively improving a design

Once a set of candidate designs representing each possible structure topology is generated, the next step is to iteratively improve the designs based on part functionality and production cost. This iterative improvement is done for each topology, under the assumption that this partitioning of the solution space creates several well-behaved search regions. The improvement scheme we are currently employing is a kind of focused hill-climbing. The steps (or moves) in the design space are generated by a set of myopic design modification operators whose only purpose is to improve the design along one of the dimensions of the design quality metric. This approach, described in Ulrich [1989], allows for modular program organization, while providing a more effective means of improvement than a random step in the design space. As a metric on part manufacturing cost, we are using a guide to sheet metal stamping die cost estimation that is based on a formula involving the length of the part edges and the number of part bends [Harig 1976].

We have prototyped the approach we propose for a two dimensional problem that we feel is roughly analogous to the three-dimensional sheet metal synthesis problem. We have devised a representation for the problem specification and for the parts for the three-dimensional case and are currently focusing our attention on generating the distinct families of designs for the three dimensional case.

Simulation

One of the most imposing handicaps for designers is the lack of engineering tools for rapid simulation of materials. Some simulation tools exist: skilled engineers can develop very accurate finite element models for simulating specific kinds of device behavior like deformation and heat conduction [Bathe 1982; Crandall 1986]. Commercial software packages exist for simulating systems described with differential equations or systems that can be characterized by the language of kinematics. In each of these cases, the tools are most useful for examining the implications of relatively small design changes on the details of a solution that is already roughly known.

For a design simulation tool to be effective, simulations must run fast enough to grant engineers immediate feedback on their design changes. Conventional methods of simulating mechanical behaviors are slow and require significant expertise. For example, simulation of the crash performance of a new automobile design requires on the order of 10 hours of computation on a Cray-2 supercomputer.

Our vision is of a simulation tool that is able to model many of the diverse behaviors that a device might exhibit, so that the model could be used to develop a novel process or to explore unanticipated consequences of a design decision. We have as a goal the ability to simulate diverse behaviors such as the crushing of thin-walled cylinders, the fracture of armor due to impacts from projectiles, and the deformation of landing gear under complicated loading. A tool for performing these simulations should have the following properties.

- *Speed:* The system must be interactive and allow immediate feedback at rates of the same order as the real time experiment.
- *Modeling assumptions:* The simulation should involve very few assumptions about the form of behavior that one expects to see.
- *Graphics:* The user must be able to see a vivid graphical representation of the physical object being simulated.
- *Object descriptions:* The user should only be required to specify the material properties and geometry of the objects to be simulated, as well as the initial state of the objects and any sources or sinks of energy or material.

Designers must be able to see and understand the changing states of their design objects as deformations occur. They must be notified if certain loadings are not safe. Increasing the speed and ease with which designers can simulate mechanical devices will increase the likelihood that tools for addressing these needs will be used. Current improvements in simulation technology have been confined to increases in the processing speed of supercomputers. We do not believe that tools meeting our specifications will evolve from this trend. Rather, a qualitatively different approach must be taken.

We propose a scheme we call Fine-Grained Parallel Simulation (FGPS). FGPS uses thousands of processors to compute the local behavior of thousands of finite regions of the object to be simulated. The idea is to mirror physics with computers, using a single computer processor for each of thousands of finite regions in the object to be simulated. In this scheme, the behavior of each processor is programmed to simulate the behavior of a finite region of the object. The advantage of this approach is that modeling assumptions can be made at a physical particle level rather than at a macroscopic continuum mechanics level, and that within certain bounds the resulting simulation runs in constant time, independent of the size of the problem.

In most simulation programming, physical systems are modeled, and governing equations are derived. Next these equations are solved by manipulating large matrices to numerically solve simultaneous equations. In FGPS, we discretize continuous domains into a crystalline structure of point masses with programmable elastic-plastic connections. The important difference between this approach and traditional finite element methods is that we use simple second-order particle models in parallel rather than higher order governing equations (like those for beams and plates) in series to determine element displacements. Our aim is to push the modeling assumptions down to a fine particle level. In this scheme, buckling, for example, follows from the assumption that particles are connected to each other in a grid with elastic-plastic connections. Particle interactions are computed at a fine level to give a macroscopic result. The validity of this basic approach has been verified by other researchers who have successfully used the idea on serial machines to simulate elastic and plastic bodies [Pentland 1989]. Central to our efforts, however, is the idea of using a large number of computational units in a one-to-one mapping with a large number of individual particles (see figure 3). Because a single processor is assigned to each particle in the model, and because the behavior of a particle is based on local information, the simulation machine can run in time proportional only to the desired length of the simulation; as long as there are enough physical processors to simulate each particle in the model.

We have prototyped the FGPS concepts on the Connection Machine (CM), a computer containing up to 65,236 parallel processors in a cube with 1.5 M sides (manufactured by Thinking Machines Corporation). The CM is a single instruction/multiple data (SIMD) computer. Because of the large number of processors and their ability to operate simultaneously, the CM is capable of performance of up to 4 gigaflops for appropriately mapped computations such as the ones we are doing. These qualities make the CM a versatile tool for our prototyping needs. In the future we hope to build a special purpose parallel computer with up to one million processors to simulate physical systems. The argument for building special-purpose machines for simulation has been articulated quite well by others [Feynman

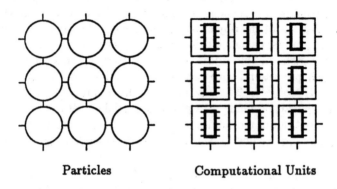

Particles   Computational Units

Figure 3. One-to-one mapping of particles to computational units.

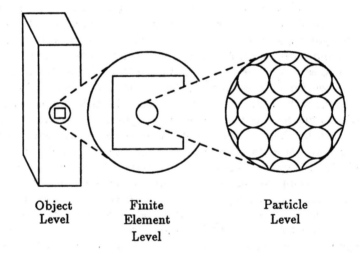

Object   Finite   Particle
Level   Element   Level
                Level

Figure 4. Break-down of an object into particles.

1982; Fox 1987; Hut 1987]. Our strategy is to use the CM to expand our understanding of the kinds of properties we will need in a special-purpose machine that implements this long-term vision. The properties in question include: hardware architecture, number of processors, kinds of required computations, and the human interface. The flexibility of the CM allows us to learn how to solve problems involving multiple bodies, elasticity, plasticity, collisions, vibrations, thermal behaviors, and wave propagation. This learning is important before we commit to a particular hardware strategy for a special purpose machine.

During each cycle of our simulation program, all particles obtain status information from neighboring particles and compute their net resultant forces. Then, using a fourth-order Runge-Kutta integration, they update their new positions and velocities. In essence the program numerically integrates a second order differential equation for each particle connection. It is important to note that this cycle runs simultaneously for all particles, as all processors execute given instructions at once. Although FGPS is in a preliminary state of development, it is still extremely fast. With the CM hardware, the program operates at about five complete cycles per second using 16,000 processors to simulate a 16,000 particle system. We have run the same program on a serial machine (a Symbolics 3640) and if we were to let it run to completion, each cycle would take about two hours.

Cost Modeling

We believe that the best way to generate production-worthy designs is to give designers production cost information. After all, cost is the most important metric of manufacturability, as long as the cost information available to the engineer is an accurate reflection of the true costs to the firm of making the product. This approach is inherently superior to the heuristic approach that is current industrial practice. Heuristics or design guidelines can at best prescribe trends that are valid in the aggregate; they do not always prescribe the best course of action in any particular design situation. As an example of the kind of product cost distortions that are possible with current cost estimation techniques consider the case of a switch from an industrial electromechanical product we have studied [Munster 1989]. In this case the apparent component cost was $1.46 per unit yet, primarily due to the fact that this part was the only part ordered from a particular vendor, there were additional purchasing costs associated with the switch amounting to over $2.50 per unit. This kind of information would be extremely valuable to a design engineer trying to evaluate two different switch options.

The central premise of this work is that humans are capable of good iterative search control and that the trade-offs between product cost and product functionality are sufficiently imprecise that the human engineer should remain in control of most of the design-for-production decisions. In order to exploit the human capacity to control the search process, we believe that a cost estimation tool must give immediate feedback on product costs corresponding to a particular set of design attributes and that the relationships between the cost figures and the design attributes must be made explicit. Displaying the link between product attributes and production costs provides the feedback to the designer that is necessary for learning and will guide the designer in making further product improvements.

The product cost estimation challenge is large. We are making the research task tractable by focusing the project in such a way as to maximize the impact of the work while limiting the number of difficult subproblems that must be solved before important results can be achieved. The three focusing assumptions we make are to:

- Consider only discrete assembled products.
- Focus on the detailed design stage of the product development process.
- Assume the existence of a process plan for manufacturing the product.

The design-for-production tool we are developing is based on a decision model that is adaptable to a wide variety of production facilities. It should give cost information in such a way that the dependencies between design attributes and costs are clear. It should give cost information over a specified time horizon. And it should be based on the minimum set of design attributes necessary to compute accurate product costs.

The basic framework of our solution to the estimation task is to make the product in simulation while allowing the simulated production process to place simulated demands on various factory services. As the demands are posted, the services respond according to a specified management policy. By monitoring the simulated costs of operating these services over time, the engineer can infer product cost information. A simplified version of this conceptual framework is shown in figure 5. In this scheme the engineer specifies the design attributes which include a bill of materials, the required process steps, and the expected production schedule. The production schedule is then followed in simulated time. Each process step is executed the specified number of times in each time period. These process steps cause demands for factory overhead services (in addition to incurring material costs and direct labor costs). The simulated departments corresponding to each overhead service respond to demands according to a management policy. This response incurs costs which are displayed back to the engineer.

Consider the following simple example to clarify the proposed framework. Imagine that a product consists of a housing and two subassemblies. The engineer specifies the vendors for the parts in the bill of materials, the process plan for the assembly operations, and the expected demand for the product over time. In simulation, the product is made. In fact, a computational procedure is executed for each of the process steps involved in making the product. One of these steps might be to supply a bin of each part to the assembly area. This step has the side effect of creating a demand for certain parts. In simulation, a computational module corresponding to the purchasing function of the plant must respond to this demand according to some specified policy. It may follow an economic order quantity or just in time model [Schmenner 1987], depending on the management policy of the plant. In following this policy to meet the demand for parts, the

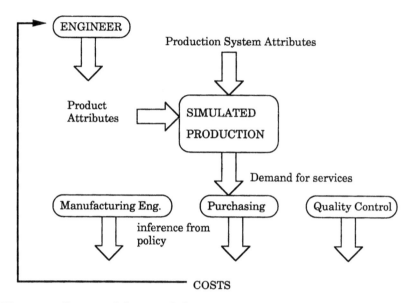

Figure 5. Conceptual framework for cost estimation.

purchasing module incurs certain costs. These costs may include salaries of the personnel in the purchasing department, telephone expenses, and document processing expenses. Given this simulation, the engineer can see that if both of the two subassemblies are supplied by the same vendor, then the purchasing costs may be reduced substantially. This insight would be overlooked by a traditional product cost estimation approach in which the design engineer is driven to only consider materials cost and direct labor.

Obviously we will not be able to simulate every detail of a production facility. But we can gain insight and improved program performance by developing a program architecture that mirrors the architecture of the production facility. By running the production facility in simulation, costs can be observed as they are incurred over time. The focus of our research is to devise the program architecture, to identify a relevant set of product attributes, and to establish a way of specifying management policies for each of the functional groups in the production system. Although the simulation task is complicated, the resulting model has the advantage of being a principled foundation upon which design decisions can be made. One key advantage to this approach is the ability to use the solution framework for a variety of purposes. Not only can a design engineer evaluate a range of product options for a given production facility, manufacturing engineers can evaluate a variety of management policies for a particular product. This capability would be useful for evaluating decisions such as whether to use temporary labor or to pay overtime for example, or to evaluate make-buy decisions for specific product components.

Conclusion

I have argued that good design is critically important to the success of a manufacturing enterprise. There are many hard problems associated with improving the performance of product development systems in industrial practice. Some of these problems are managerial, political, organizational, and educational. But some of the problems can be addressed with better tools. My vision is of a work environment in which groups of engineers attack design problems with tools for rapidly communicating geometrical concepts to one another and to computer programs; in which special-purpose computing hardware runs rapid simulation of the physical properties of proposed parts; in which much of the detail work of generating part geometries is automated; and in which engineers can explore the cost implications of a design within a virtual factory created in their workstations. The four projects I have outlined are the first steps towards this vision.

The goals that I have outlined are both centrally important and intellectually challenging. Design research is rich with problems in physical reasoning, mathematical problem solving, understanding device function, search, and learning. Design problem solving involves the use of knowledge, analogy, precedents, and planning. I argue that a part of the hope for better design practice lies with the development of new ways of thinking about design automation. Our tools in the next century can not represent incremental improvement to the tools we have now. Rather, we must extend our thinking about the kinds of tools that are possible. Fortunately, the research questions that come out of this kind of thinking are not just important, they are also interesting.

References

Bathe, K. [1982], *Finite Element Procedures in Engineering Analysis*, Prentice Hall.

The research described in this chapter was performed at the MIT Artificial Intelligence Laboratory and at the MIT Sloan School of Management. Support for the laboratory's research is provided in part by the Advanced Research Projects Agency of the Department of Defense under Office of Naval Research contract N00014-85-K-0124. Additional support for this research was provided by the MIT Leaders for Manufacturing Program.

Clark, K. B., W. B. Chew, and T. Fujimoto [1987], "Product Development in the World Auto Industry: Strategy, Organization and Performance," Working Paper, Harvard Business School 1987.

Crandall, S. H. [1986], *Engineering Analysis*, Robert E. Krieger Publishing Co.

Cutkosky, M. R., and J. M. Tenenbaum [1987], "CAD/CAM Integration Through Concurrent Product and Process Design," *Proceedings of the ASME Winter Annual Meeting*, PED vol. 25.

Dertouzos, M. L., R. K. Lester, and R. M. Solow [1989], *Made in America*, MIT Press Cambridge, MA.

Eppinger, S. D., C. F. Fine, and K. T. Ulrich [1989], *Interdisciplinary Product Design Education*, Working Paper 3013-89-MS, Sloan School of Management, Massachusetts Institute of Technology, Cambridge, MA.

Finger, Susan, and John Dixon [1989], "A Review of Research in Mechanical Engineering Design," *Research in Engineering Design*, vol. 1, no. 1.

Feynman, R. [1982], "Simulating Physics with Computers," *International Journal of Theoretical Physics*, vol. 21, pp. 468-488.

Fox, G. C., and P. C. Messina [1987], "Advanced Computer Architectures," *Scientific American*, vol. 267 no. 4.

Hayes, R. H., S. C. Wheelwright, and K. B. Clark [1988], *Dynamic Manufacturing*, The Free Press, New York.

Hut, P., and G. J. Sussman [1987], "Advanced Computing for Science," *Scientific American*, vol. 257, no. 4.

Harig, Herbert [1976], *Estimating Stamping Dies*, Harig Educational Systems, Philadelphia, PA.

Mann, R. W., and S. A. Coons [1965], "Computer-Aided Design," *McGraw-Hill Yearbook Science and Technology*, McGraw-Hill.

Munster, Gregory A. [1989], *Analyzing the Costs of Product Quality*, M.S. Thesis, Sloan School of Management, Massachusetts Institute of Technology, Cambridge, MA.

Pentland, A., and J. Kuo [1989], "The Artist at the Interface," *Media Lab Vision Science Technical Report*, vol. 114, Massachusetts Institute of Technology, Cambridge, MA.

Port, Otis [1989], "The Best-Engineered Part is No Part at All," *Business Week*.

Schmenner, Roger W. [1987], *Production/Operations Management: Concepts and Situations*, Science Research Associates, Chicago.

Ulrich, K. T. [1989], "Achieving Multiple Goals in Conceptual Design," in *Intelligent CAD* edited by Yoshikawa and Gossard, North-Holland.

Voelcker, H. B., A. A. G. Requicha, and R. W. Conway [1988], "Computer Applications in Manufacturing," *Ann. Rev. Comput. Sci.* vol. 3, pp. 349-87.

Whitney, Daniel E. [1988], "Manufacturing by Design," *Harvard Business Review*.

In this chapter, the authors exhibit a method for mining large databases. The particular database they mine, which happens to contain protein data, is representative of many databases that hide useful, but unknown regularity.

Why proteins? Today it is relatively easy to work out a protein's amino-acid sequence, but it remains impossible to determine a protein's function-specifying, three-dimensional shape from that amino-acid sequence. Nevertheless, it is possible, in many cases, to finesse the shape problem by separating proteins into functional classes by recognizing important embedded amino-acid sequences and their structural correlates. All you need is an appropriate sequence-based pattern.

But finding the appropriate sequence-based pattern is itself a major challenge. Here the authors show how to improve on sequence patterns devised by people for the proteins that catalyze DNA synthesis. Their program uses a combination of heuristic search, classical induction heuristics (like climb tree and drop link), and prodigious amounts of computation (a Connection Machine with four-thousand processors). With the Connection Machine, many derivative patterns can be tried on many examples and near misses in parallel, reducing the time of individual experiments from tens of hours to minutes.

ARIEL: A Massively Parallel Symbolic Learning Assistant for Protein Structure and Function

Richard H. Lathrop   Temple F. Smith[†]
Teresa A. Webster[†‡]   Patrick H. Winston

The research described in this chapter focuses on the development and implementation of efficient algorithms for several symbolic machine learning induction operators on a massively parallel computer[1] (see figure 1). We invoke these operators as hardware induction subroutines under the control of a higher-level front-end LISP program. Together, they function as an "Induction Assistant" (ARIEL[2]) that helps a domain expert construct structural patterns for functionally defined concepts from positive and negative examples of functional assignments of proteins. The time complexity of the induction algorithms is essentially independent of the total size of the instance data pool. Everything described below has been implemented in Common LISP [Steele 1984] or PARIS [Thinking Machines 1988]. The PARIS portion runs on a CM-2 Connection Machine[3] [Hillis 1986].

[†] Molecular Biology Computer Research Resource, Dana Farber Cancer Institute, Harvard School of Public Health.

[‡] Currently at Arris Pharmaceutical Corp., Cambridge, MA, USA.

[1] The term "massively parallel" is generally used to refer to computers with 1K or more processors, to distinguish them from smaller multi-processor systems in which many of the communication and coordination issues take on a different flavor. Future generations will smile at this distinction.

[2] A combination of ARI-adne and parall-EL, and also a pleasing character from Shakespeare's *The Tempest*.

[3] PARIS and CM-2 are trademarks, and Connection Machine is a registered trademark, of Thinking Machines Corporation.

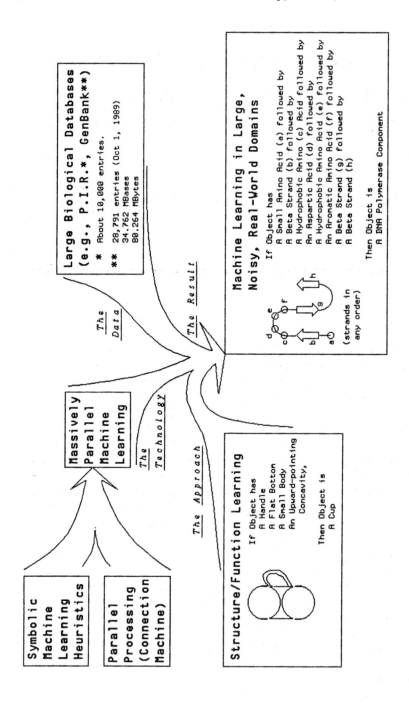

Figure 1. An overview.

Introduction

A similar molecular function is often (but not always) implemented by a similar molecular structure. We look for similar patterns within functionally related families of proteins, across multiple weakly informative sources of structural knowledge. From these we hypothesize tentative structural assignments corresponding to functional sites in proteins. Because these patterns are based on structural correlates computable only from the protein sequence, this is of interest in the empirical domain for:

- Suggesting targets for genetic manipulation in known molecules.
- Suggesting functional identification and confirmatory tests in unknown or newly discovered molecules.
- Increasing general scientific knowledge by suggesting essential structural elements of the molecular function.

This work was done in collaboration with a larger ongoing effort to associate symbolic structural patterns with functionally defined classes of proteins [Bradley *et al.* 1987; Figge *et al.* 1988; Figge & Smith 1988; Lathrop *et al.* 1987; Webster *et al.* 1987, 1988, 1989a, 1989b].

This chapter has been written to be comprehensible to the computer scientist with no biological knowledge whatsoever.[4] For our purposes, both DNA and proteins are sequences that may be thought of as strings: the DNA alphabet has four letters (deoxynucleotides), the protein alphabet has twenty letters (amino acids). The protein sequence folds up into a complicated three-dimensional shape that determines its function, which is often to catalyze a particular chemical reaction critical to life. Unfortunately, its shape is usually unknown. Typically, all that is known about a protein of interest is its sequence (its string of letters). The problem of predicting three-dimensional shape from sequence is currently unsolved. Many important advances have been made nonetheless by string similarity approaches, as when the sequence of an oncogene (cancer related gene) was found to be similar to sequences for human growth hormones [Doolittle *et al.* 1983], clearly relating cancerous growth to defective normal cell growth. Unfortunately, many important structural elements do not often exhibit recognizable string patterns. However, a number of clues (weak structural correlates) about the lower levels of structural organization are computable (with varying degrees of noise and reliability) from the sequence, and this gives us another source of knowledge to exploit. We are interested in finding the common patterns that occur in sets of protein strings annotated with computable structural correlates.

---

[4]Consequently, where terminology conflicts, it is used in the computer science, not the biological, sense. For example, *domain* refers to a micro-world, and not to a unit of protein organization; *structure* refers to the interrelation of elements or parts of an entity, and not to the three-dimensional placement of atoms; *domain expert* refers to a molecular biologist.

The task

In general, we would like to be able to inductively construct such patterns from sets of positive and negative examples. One methodology for pattern construction by a domain expert is described by Webster *et al.* [1988]. An initial seed pattern is refined in an iterative loop consisting of:

1   Matching the pattern against the instances.
2   Evaluating the performance of the pattern.
3   Modifying the pattern and repeating.

This methodology has successfully constructed several such structure/function patterns [Bradley *et al.* 1987, Figge *et al.* 1988, Figge & Smith 1988, Webster *et al.* 1987, 1988, 1989a, 1989b]. The work described in this chapter is one step in the direction of automating pattern construction. The task currently performed by the system is to function as an "Induction Assistant" for domain experts. Work is ongoing to increasingly automate the remaining role of the domain expert.

Domain interest

The function of many proteins is unknown, and this will increasingly be the case as the sequence of the entire human genome becomes known over the next few decades [Alberts *et al.* 1988]. This generates a great deal of domain interest in the possibility of predictive patterns. These may motivate or guide experimental work. For example, Figge and Smith [1988] proposed a structural pattern for cell-division regulation based on Figge *et al.* [1988]. The pattern proved to be nearly 100% diagnostic for cotransformation with *ras* (a cancer causing gene involved with abnormal cell division), and motivated experimental investigation and sequencing of a number of other cancer related genes [Goldsborough *et al.* 1989]. The experimental work showed that the pattern was diagnostic of which Papilloma virus strains were carcinogenic, thus contributing to the underlying structural molecular basis for understanding these cancers.

Chapter organization

The first section, "Structural Patterns for Functional Concepts," describes examples from two different domains. The second section, "Machine Learning Formalism," describes machine learning details of our learning model, instances, their selection, noise, instance and description languages, and pattern evaluation. The third section, "An Illustration from the Domain," gives an example showing how this work is instantiated in the domain. The next section, "Fast, Efficient, Parallel Matching," discusses matching patterns against instances. The fifth section, "Efficient Induction Operators," treats induction as a search for patterns with useful discrimination between positive and negative instances. Finally we discuss limitations and future work, then related work, and conclude with a summary.

Structural Patterns for Functional Concepts

A structural pattern

We often wish to learn a structural pattern that discriminates instances of a functionally defined concept. For example, in figure 1 the functionally defined concept of a cup (something from which to drink liquids, especially hot ones) is associated with a pattern phrased in structural terms such as handle, concavity, and so forth.[5]

Recognition/identification. Imagine a robot passing through a city with the cup structural pattern from figure 1, looking for matches. In general, it will do fairly well but not perfectly. It will have errors of under-prediction (false negatives), where it fails to recognize a styrofoam cup. It will have errors of over-prediction (false positives), when the erroneous match to a small maple syrup pitcher. If perception is imperfect (noisy), it may fail to match a perfectly good cup because it fails to perceive the handle. But generally, if perception is not too noisy, it will find most of the cups and it will exclude most of the non-cups (items such as sofas, automobiles, and fire hydrants will present little confusion).

Structure/function insight. Besides giving us a recognition tool for cups, such a pattern yields further insight into the structure/function relationships involved. For example, if we have *a priori* knowledge about what handles are used for, a successful match to the cup pattern from figure 1 tells us where to pick the object up. Some quite crucial structural properties, like "non-porous," do not appear in the pattern at all. Nonetheless the pattern gives us hints about the structurally important components—for example, the upward-pointing concavity. It also suggests tests and experiments to confirm or refute these initially weak hints—for example, delete (or mutate) the concavity property in a positive instance, perhaps by filling it with cement, to see whether the cup function is retained.

Another structural pattern

The protein pattern in figure 1 is another such structural pattern. The functionally defined concept of a DNA polymerase molecule (something which attaches the next deoxynucleotide—that is, the next letter of DNA—onto the end of a growing DNA string, thereby duplicating genetic information)

---

[5]The cup example is taken from Winston *et al.* [1983].

is associated with a pattern phrased in structural terms such as β-strand, aromatic residue, and so forth. The pattern was partially constructed using the parallel induction techniques described in this chapter.[7]

Recognition/identification.   When we pass this pattern through a database of protein sequences, looking for matches, it identifies most of the DNA polymerase molecules (80% of 24 clusters comprising 53 sequences), and excludes most of the molecules without this function (98% of 10,421 sequences). This pattern is useful as a recognition tool for tentative identification of the DNA polymerase function in uncharacterized instances, such as will flow from the Human Genome Project [Alberts *et al.* 1988]. Like the cup pattern, such identification will have errors of over- and under-prediction, and it remains tentative until confirmed by experiment. While domain experts have experimental tests for such functions, the space of possibilities is very large, and remains tentative. Characterization of an unknown helps them to apply the most likely tests first.

Structure/function insight.   A successful match to the protein pattern from figure 1 also gives us hints about relating function to explicit pieces of structure. This is useful if we wish to do genetic engineering, for example, by telling us where to modify the gene, much as a match to the cup pattern told us where to pick up the object. Some crucial properties, like strand order or the detailed spatial placement of atoms, do not appear in the pattern at all. The pattern gives us hints about the structurally important elements—probably the aspartic amino acid, but probably not the amino acids separating the last two β-strands. It suggests tests and experiments to confirm these hints—for example, modify the aspartic acid, or disrupt one of the predicted β-strands.[8]

Machine Learning Formalism

In this section we describe machine learning details of our learning model, including instances, their selection, noise, instance and description languages, and pattern evaluation.

---

[7]The DNA polymerase example is taken from Webster *et al.* [1989b].

[8]The analogy to the cup example is imperfect. We can explain how the parts of a cup work by appeal to known precedents (for example, we can explain (or predict) that the handle of the cup is for grasping, by appeal to the handle of a suitcase) and this is, in fact, how the cup example was originally introduced [Winston *et al.* 1983]. This subsequent explanatory (or predictive) step is more difficult in molecular biology, because the domain is less well understood. It is possible only in some cases (for example, the orienting effect of the dipole moment in an α-helix, or the catalytic effect of key residues in loop regions), and generally depends on other, situation-specific, knowledge.

Learning model

We are working in the empirical machine learning symbolic concept acquisition framework (a survey of machine learning appears in Michalski *et al.* [1983]). System input consists of one set of positive instances and another set of negative instances, plus one or more initial seed patterns. The positive instances are known *a priori* to share a common function, for example catalyzing similar reactions on similar chemicals. The negative instances are known to possess a different function. The system operates as an "Induction Assistant," performing low-level induction tasks under the high-level control of a domain expert. Desired system output will be a symbolic structural pattern that discriminates the positive from the negative instances. Due to several sources of noise in the domain, perfect discrimination will rarely be possible. Pattern evaluation is based on performance on *both* the positive and the negative instance sets. Throughout the chapter, we use "match against" to refer to comparing a pattern with an instance, and "match to" or "successful match" to indicate that the comparison resulted in an admissible correspondence (see the match cut-off score later in this chapter).

Instances, their selection, and noise

Instances are protein sequences. They are annotated with various structural correlates computable from the sequence, for example secondary structure predictions (weakly inferred areas of local three-dimensional structural organization), hydropathy and amphipathy peaks and valleys (correlated with interior and exterior regions), or special constructions devised by a domain researcher (for example, "acid-faced helix"). We use existing domain programs in a pre-processing step for this. Figure 2 shows graphically a protein sequence, annotated with secondary structure predictions, from the reverse transcriptase protein of an HIV virus (Human Immunodeficiency Virus, causing AIDS), an RNA-directed DNA polymerase molecule.

Instances are characterized as positive or negative on the basis of biochemical tests. Assembling the positive and negative sets requires extensive searches of available databases and the scientific literature. Instances are positive if they are explicitly known to possess the function under study. Instances explicitly known to possess a different function are assumed to be negative instances, a heuristic that is usually but not always correct (because some proteins are multi-functional, and due to occasional mistaken characterization by domain experts).

Although errors in functional assignment introduce some noise, there are much more important sources of noise in this domain. Significantly more noise arises from inherent inaccuracies in the secondary structure predictions and other weak structural correlates. In some cases nearly

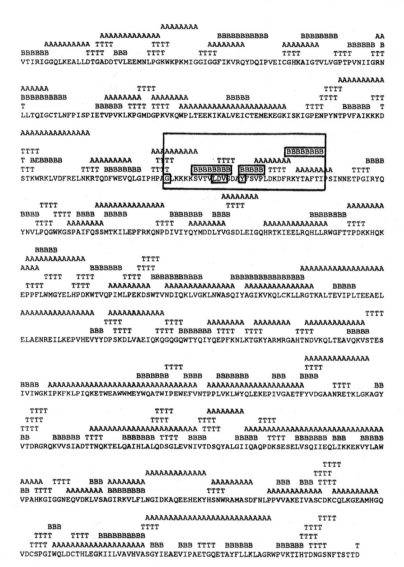

Figure 2. An instance, GNVWA2 [Sanchez-Pescador *et al.* 1985], the reverse transcriptase protein of an HIV virus (causing AIDS), an RNA-directed DNA polymerase. The long strings of letters at the bottom of each layer (beginning "VTIRIG..." in the upper-left corner) denote the amino acid sequence. Each letter represents one amino acid. The computable structural correlates here are secondary structure predictions [Ralph *et al.* 1987] (AAAA = α-helix, BBBB = β-strand, TTTT = β-turn). These are denoted by long repeated strings of the same letter (for example, the "BBBBBB" over the "VTIRIG" in the upper-left corner means a β-strand prediction extends from the first "V" to the first "G"). Prediction weights are not shown. The boxed section refers to figure 7.

identical structures may be encoded by very different amino acid strings, while in other cases very different structures may be encoded by nearly identical amino acid strings. More noise is supplied by nature. This takes the form of natural variation arising through compatible mutations and other genetic rearrangements.

In practice, we typically work with all the known positive instances (usually a few dozen) and one or two hundred negative instances. We control for amino acid sequence similarity. Initially the negative instances are carefully selected to approximate a uniform sampling of instance space (the extant databases represent a biased sampling). After initial pattern development produces a stable interim pattern, a new set of negative instances is constructed consisting of the pattern's *near misses*. These are negative instances that match, or nearly match, the robust core features of the interim pattern (see Webster *et al.* [1989b]), and serve to focus the final pattern refinement steps.

Instance language

Although the sequences are inherently strings, we use a graph-based instance representation. We do this because it facilitates representation of the annotated structural correlates (overlapping features of the same type lose their individual identity, hence individual boundaries, if represented as type properties marked on the string characters), and to demonstrate that the techniques we have developed apply more widely than to strings alone.

Nodes in our graph representation represent the amino acids in the protein sequence. There is one node type for each of the twenty amino acid types. Nodes participate in a class generalization hierarchy depending on amino acid physico-chemical properties (volume, charge, hydropathy, etc.).

One arc type is distinguished as the *successor-of* relation, and encodes the sequential relationship between nodes. The other arc types are used to encode structural correlate features. They are represented by an arc from the node at the start of the predicted feature to the node at its end. For example, the first β-strand prediction in figure 2 would be represented as an arc of type β from the node representing the first "V" to the node representing the first "G." These arcs tend to be mostly local with respect to the successor-of relation (typically no more than one or two dozen nodes long, though occasionally much longer). The number of arc types is not fixed and depends on the particular structural correlates chosen, though typically a given study will use no more than half a dozen. Each arc has an individual weight, which may reflect the strength of the predicted feature or the degree of confidence in the prediction.

Pattern description language

ARIEL currently implements a restricted sub-set of the generality provided by ARIADNE [Lathrop *et al.* 1987]. Only the most commonly used language terms are currently included. ARIEL's description language permits description of nodes and their generalization classes, arcs, weights, match cut-off scores, and interval relationships. A pattern consists of a series of *terms* separated by *intervals*. A *cut-off score* governs the overall match quality required to qualify as a successful match.

Each term specifies either a node class, or an arc type. The semantics of a term specifying a node class are to match to a node belonging to the class. The semantics of a term specifying an arc type are to match to and traverse an arc of that type. Terms carry an associated *score-if-missing* and *score-if-present* (having both is redundant but convenient). These govern how the pattern term matched against instance features contributes to the overall match score, and may indicate either a numeric score associated with a pattern term, minus infinity, or the weight attached to the instance feature. Arc type terms carry a *length-if-missing* field, usually set to the average length of arcs of that type, which indicates the number of successor arcs to traverse in case the arc type cannot be successfully matched in the instance (presumably due to noise or error in the predicted feature).

Intervals separate adjacent pattern terms, and govern where to look for the next term after having been matched against the previous one. Each interval specifies the minimum and maximum number of nodes to skip (following successor arcs) from the previous term, before commencing to look for the next. It is possible to allow matches to terms slightly outside this interval, but the further outside the interval the more the match score is penalized (this allows the match process to be more robust).

Pattern evaluation

During induction, evaluation of a pattern's performance is based on its *sensitivity* and *specificity,* terms used in medical clinical trials. *Sensitivity* is the fraction of the *positive* instances that it correctly classifies (that is, how sensitive is the pattern at picking out the population of interest). *Specificity* is the fraction of the *negative* instances that it correctly classifies (that is, how specific is the pattern for the population of interest and no others). Both are required, because virtually all instances are negative, so an extremely low overall error rate could be attained simply by guessing "no" on each instance. The 2×2 *correlation coefficient* measures the linear correlation between reality and a pattern's predictions. It is a rough heuristic indicator of discrimination quality, though *it cannot be used as a statistical measure of significance because the assumption of independent trials is violated by the incremental refinement methodology.* A perfect pattern will have sensitivity, specificity, and 2×2 correlation coefficient all equal to 1.0, although this ideal state is rarely realized in this domain due to the presence of noise and incomplete knowledge.

The domain constrains which patterns expressible in the description language are consistent with reality. For example, unrealistic intervals between pattern terms may correspond to superimposing inferred structures that are physically incompatible. We eliminate (or never generate) these procedurally. When the pattern is integrated into the larger scientific knowledge structure, pattern evaluation also includes its relationship to other scientific studies in the literature, especially experimental results.

An Illustration from the Domain

The RNA-directed DNA polymerase molecules are found in the retroviruses, a class of viruses that carry their genetic information as RNA instead of DNA. They include viruses that cause AIDS, hepatitis B, human T-cell leukemia I and II, and a number of animal diseases. When the virus enters a cell, these polymerase molecules copy the viral RNA (the viral genetic information) into the host cell's DNA, and the host cell machinery begins assembling more viruses from the new DNA template. In contrast, the DNA-directed DNA polymerases are found in all cellular life. These molecules make possible the genetic basis of life, duplicating strands of DNA so that cells can divide and life can propagate. Both these polymerase families share the (sub-)function of polymerizing DNA (that is, attaching the next letter of DNA to the end of a growing DNA chain).

Here, the domain expert explores the hypothesis that a structural pattern, previously published for the RNA-directed DNA polymerases [Webster *et al.* 1989a] could be modified to include the DNA-directed DNA polymerases as well. A common structural pattern could unite (on a structural basis) these two ancient classes of molecules, which share at least one common (sub-)function. This in turn would suggest to which structural elements the encoding of this function may be assigned.

The initial seed pattern

The domain expert generated an initial seed pattern, a modification of the RNA-directed DNA polymerase pattern given by Webster *et al.* [1989a].[9] The pattern that the domain expert brought to ARIEL, and its discriminatory performance, is shown in figure 3.

---

[9]This project was initiated while ARIEL was still being written, so the domain expert had first partially refined the seed pattern (manually) using ARIADNE (a serial matcher with no induction facilities).

(a)

min	*max*	*term*	*present*	*missing*
—	—	b-strand	arc weight	−1.5
−4	1	hydrophobe	0.0	−∞
0	0	aspartic-acid	0.0	−∞
0	0	hydrophobe	0.0	−∞
3	3	aromatic	0.0	−∞
−2	3	b-strand	arc weight	−1.5
2	6	b-strand	arc weight	−1.5

Pattern RDDD1B, cut-off-score −1.3

(b)

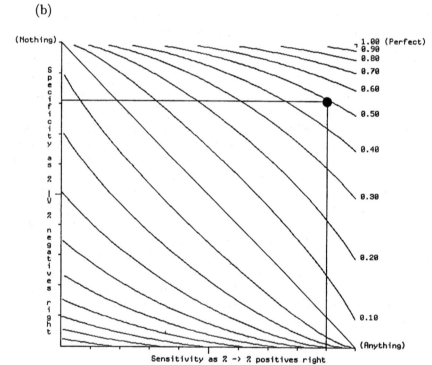

Figure 3. The initial seed pattern. (a) The pattern in schematic: *min* and *max* refer to the interval separating adjacent terms; *present* and *missing* refer to the term scores. (b) The large black dot is its performance on the positive and negative sets. Every other pattern falling into its lower-left quadrant (outlined in black) exhibits inferior discrimination. The x-axis represents *sensitivity* (fraction of positives correct), the y-axis represents *specificity* (fraction of negatives correct). Curved lines are equipotentials of the 2×2 correlation coefficient (unsymmetric because there are unequal numbers of positive and negative instances).

Example of an induction script

The basic task performed by the system is to apply an induction operator to a pattern, thereby creating and evaluating new patterns. In practice it is usually more convenient to use scripts, which are formed by alternating several induction operators with filters that prune unpromising intermediate candidates.

For example, figure 4 illustrates ADD-TERM-AND-REFINE. This script explores adding a term between two existing terms or at the end of the pattern. First, tentative terms to add are explored by the operator ADD-TERM (all operators are defined below). If the added term resides in a generalization hierarchy then the operator REFINE-CLASS is applied to explore possible classes. Unpromising candidates are pruned by filters (this happens between each step). Because adding a term probably changes the spacing, the intervals between the new term and each of its neighbors are next refined by the operator REFINE-INTERVAL. Finally, the term scores are refined and the cut-off score for a successful match is adjusted by REFINE-TERM-SCORE.

Figure 5 illustrates the effect of applying ADD-TERM-AND-REFINE to the initial seed pattern shown in figure 3. A number of child patterns are generated and evaluated (the multiple quadrants outlined in figure 5b). This script discovers the conserved SMALL amino acid (matching to amino acids A, G, or S) previously unknown to the domain expert (in domain terms, the extra alignment information afforded by the secondary structure predictions exposed the conservation of the amino acid class). This is not a big discovery,[10] but it does illustrate that the system is capable of discovering regularities in the domain.

Further pursuit with ARIEL

Figure 6 shows a trace near the end of the domain expert's session with ARIEL. At this stage of refinement the negative instances are the near misses. As more patterns are explored, a *frontier* demarking attainable pattern discrimination pushes toward the upper-right corner of figure 6. The resulting display is similar to a Relative Operating Curve (ROC) from signal detection theory [Swets 1986a, 1986b]. It indicates the spectrum of sensitivity/specificity trade-offs possible by selecting patterns with different discriminatory power. We maintain a corresponding internal data structure, with patterns falling into each point on the frontier which is organized into a Version Space concept lattice [Mitchell 1977]. The final pattern was selected from the patterns falling on the frontier of figure 6, based on domain considerations.

---

[10]Because it is a SMALL amino acid.

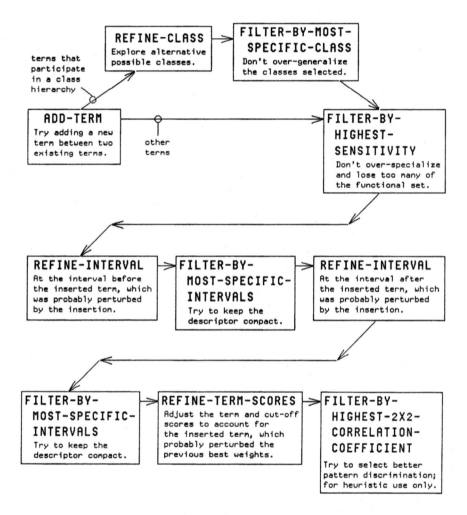

Figure 4. An induction script example of ADD-TERM-AND-REFINE.

The pattern matched to an instance

Figure 7 shows the protein pattern from figure 1 matched to the instance from figure 2 (a viral RNA-directed DNA polymerase) along the bottom line, and matched to human DNA polymerase (DNA-directed) along the top. The corresponding area is boxed in figure 2. Terms in the pattern denoting secondary structures are matched to secondary structure arcs of the corresponding type, and terms in the pattern denoting amino acid types or classes are matched to amino acid nodes. The successful match localizes a putative enzymatic site on these DNA polymerase molecules.

(a)

min	max	term	present	missing
—	—	small	1.3	−1.35
2	5	b-strand	arc weight	−1.5
−4	1	hydrophobe	0.0	−∞
0	0	aspartic-acid	0.0	−∞
0	0	hydrophobe	0.0	−∞
3	3	aromatic	0.0	−∞
−2	3	b-strand	arc weight	−1.5
2	6	b-strand	arc weight	−1.5

Pattern #:0-1903-SCORES-AT-0$0-2478, cut-off-score 2.2

(b)

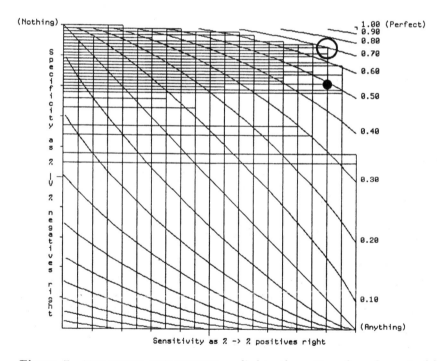

Figure 5. ADD-TERM-AND-REFINE applied to the pattern from figure 3. (a) One pattern created by ARIEL. A SMALL term (matching to amino acids A, G, or S) has been added, the spacing to the B-STRAND term adjusted, its term score adjusted, and the overall match cut-off score raised from −1.3 to 2.2. (b) Discriminatory performance. The performance of the pattern shown is circled on the graph. Outlined lower-left quadrants represent other patterns explored. Markings are described in the caption of figure 3.

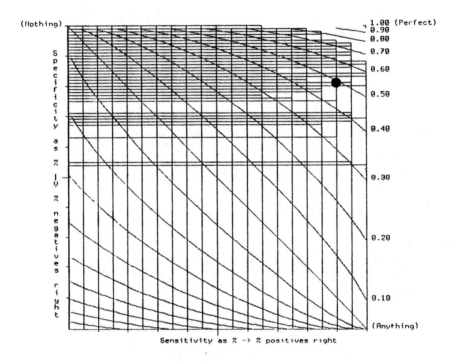

Figure 6. A trace near the end of the domain expert's session with ARIEL. The *frontier* converging to the upper-right corner shows the discriminatory power of the current best candidates (see the ROC discussion in the text). Markings are described in the caption to figure 3.

Fast, Efficient, Parallel Matching

In this section we discuss matching patterns against instances. First we state our underlying machine model. Then we describe how instances are stored in the machine, and how patterns can be matched against them. Finally, we discuss holding multiple copies of the complete functional and control sets (multiple *full instance sets*) in the machine and evaluating multiple descriptors against them concurrently.

Machine model

Our abstract parallel machine architecture is a SIMD (Single Instruction Multiple Data) machine, attached to a front-end host. It has a large number

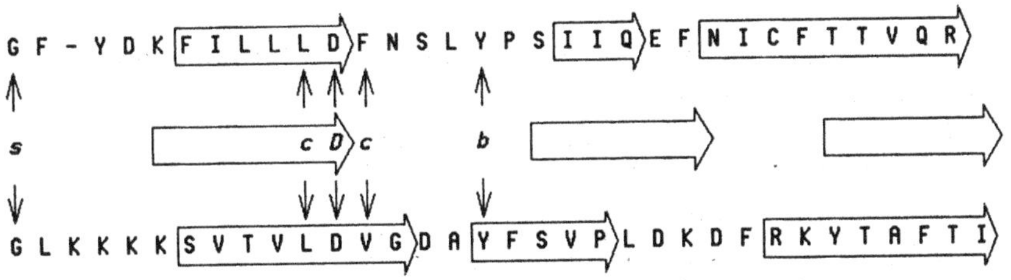

Figure 7. The pattern from figure 1 matched to the instance from figure 2 and huPol. The top line is from human DNA polymerase (DNA-directed) [Wong *et al.* 1988]. The bottom line is from the reverse transcriptase molecule (RNA-directed) of the HIV virus (causing AIDS) [Sanchez-Pescador *et al.* 1985]. The pattern schematic is between them. Arrows represent β-strands, **s**, a SMALL amino acid (matching to A, G, or S), **c**, a HYDROPHOBE (matching to C, F, I, L, M, V, W, or Y), **b**, an AROMATIC (matching to F, W, or Y), **D**, an aspartic acid. The matched subsequence is boxed in figure 2.

of processors, each with a private memory. Inter-processor communication occurs by message-passing between physically adjacent processors. There is a mechanism for computing the global inclusive OR, and the global MAX, of a data field across a subset of the processors (if available, a global router significantly increases the efficiency of these steps). We used a 4K CM-2 Connection Machine.

Virtually all processors (over 97%) are of type *match,* and they receive a pattern to test and an instance segment to match against it. A few processors are of type *collection,* and they collect the global results of the match. A few processors are of type *induction,* and they are used to combine the results of the induction operators as described in the next section.

Embedding instances in the machine

Both the pattern, and the instance data against which it is matched, are stored in the private data of a processor (see figure 8). Once loaded, the instance data is permanently resident in the processor. New patterns are broadcast to the processors each match cycle. No more than one instance is placed in each match processor. Each instance is assigned a unique bit position in a global bit vector, also cached in the processor. If the instance is too large to fit into one processor it is divided into segments, and adjacent segments are placed in adjacent processors. Since the underlying domain structure is linear (inherited from the *successor-of* relation between nodes)

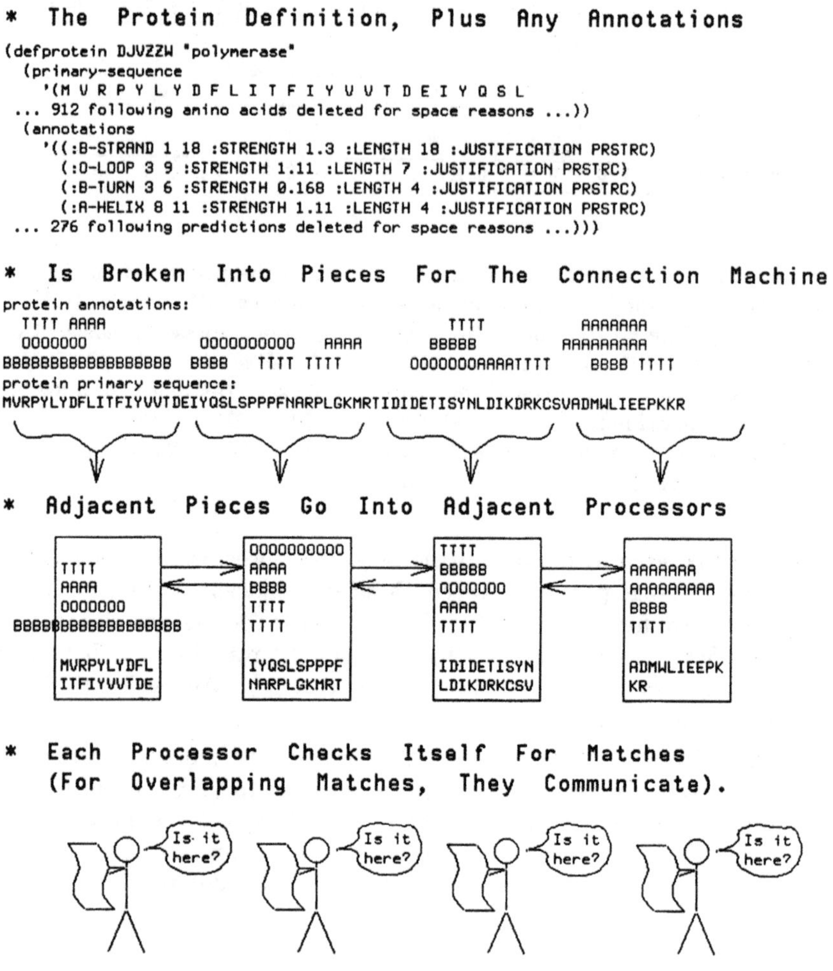

* **The Protein Definition, Plus Any Annotations**

```
(defprotein DJVZZW "polymerase"
  (primary-sequence
    '(M V R P Y L Y D F L I T F I Y V V T D E I Y Q S L
    ... 912 following amino acids deleted for space reasons ...))
  (annotations
    '(((:B-STRAND 1 18 :STRENGTH 1.3 :LENGTH 18 :JUSTIFICATION PRSTRC)
       (:O-LOOP 3 9 :STRENGTH 1.11 :LENGTH 7 :JUSTIFICATION PRSTRC)
       (:B-TURN 3 6 :STRENGTH 0.168 :LENGTH 4 :JUSTIFICATION PRSTRC)
       (:A-HELIX 8 11 :STRENGTH 1.11 :LENGTH 4 :JUSTIFICATION PRSTRC)
    ... 276 following predictions deleted for space reasons ...)))
```

* **Is Broken Into Pieces For The Connection Machine**

```
protein annotations:
  TTTT AAAA                                 TTTT        AAAAAAA
  OOOOOOO           OOOOOOOOOO   AAAA        BBBBB       AAAAAAAAA
BBBBBBBBBBBBBBBBBBBB BBBB   TTTT TTTT        OOOOOOOAAAATTTT   BBBB TTTT
protein primary sequence:
MVRPYLYDFLITFIYVVTDEIYQSLSPPPFNARPLGKMRTIDIDETISYNLDIKDRKCSVADMWLIEEPKKR
```

* **Adjacent Pieces Go Into Adjacent Processors**

* **Each Processor Checks Itself For Matches (For Overlapping Matches, They Communicate).**

Figure 8. Embedding and matching instances in the machine.

a linear processor geometry is used,[11] so adjacent instance segments are always in physically adjacent processors.

---

[11]Other domains might use other geometries, for example, VLSI structure/function studies [Lathrop *et al.* 1987] might use a planar embedding, while ARIEL, if it were adapted to protein crystal structures, would use a three-dimensional embedding.

Performing the match

Matching one pattern against one instance is independent of matching another pattern against a different instance, and so it can be done in parallel (see figure 9). A large instance may span several processors, but matching a pattern against a segment of the instance held in one processor can be made nearly independent of matching it against a second segment in a different processor, provided that matches spanning several processors are handled properly. Thus, allowing adjustment of the segment size to achieve nearly 100% processor utilization, as well as a number of other attractive match properties.

The pattern which it is being matched against is resident in each match processor's memory. The match process consists of iterating through the terms of the pattern, at each step matching against the next term. A communication protocol handles cases in which a successful match spans more than one processor. When the match process is complete, each processor which successfully matched to its pattern sends its instance bit (with logical inclusive OR) to a global collection processor. Thus, the collection processor winds up with a global bit-vector of exactly the successfully matched instances.

Full sets of instances

Most of our instance sequences can fit into one or two processors (though some take five, or seven, or more). Because we usually use no more than one or two hundred instances in the working set, but we do have thousands of processors, it is possible to hold many duplicate copies of the complete sets of positive and negative instances in the parallel hardware. Each complete copy of the positive and negative instances is called a *full instance set,* and the processors holding them is called a *full processor set.* We put different patterns in each full processor set, but each processor in the same full set receives the same pattern (see figure 9). By matching against all of these concurrently, we obtain the result of matching many different patterns exhaustively against all the positive and negative instances, essentially, in the real time taken to match one pattern against one segment of one instance.

Attractive match properties

For the domain studied here, this yields the following attractive match properties:

- **Constant time in instance size.** An instance is segmented and split over several processors and any one processor looks only at a

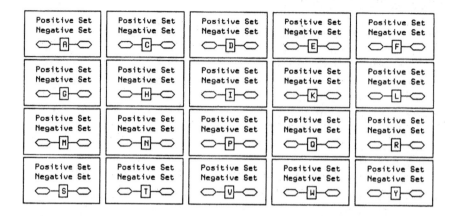

Figure 9. Many copies of the positive and negative instances. We show twenty
full processor sets (defined in the text), each matching against a different pattern
(shown schematically as two lozenges flanking the different terms, see figure 11).

constant-length segment regardless of the total length of the instance.
Because the domain has high locality and the algorithms and data
structures preserve this, communication costs for following arcs from
one processor to another are constant in instance size.

- **Near-constant time in number of instances.** The match against
  each instance is independent and concurrent. The only time dependency on number of instances occurs in transmitting the bit vector
  to the global collection processor, an operation that consumes a tiny
  fraction of the time of the match.

- **Space linear in total instance pool size.** We need only one processor per segment.

- **Space constant adjustable to available hardware, for nearly
  100% processor utilization.** We can vary the length of the segment
  we put in each processor, decreasing the length uses more processors,
  increasing it uses fewer. We can vary the length to fill the machine.

- **Most communication local for domains with high locality.** If
  the domain is sufficiently local, most communication except the global
  bit-vector OR can use local (NEWS) communication with adjacent processors.

- **Nearly all non-local communication evenly distributed in both source and destination (no bottlenecks or collisions).** Except for the global bit-vector OR, all non-local communication has
  unique source and unique destination.

- **Fast on real problems using real hardware.** The DNA polymerase pattern from Webster *et al.* [1989b], for example, was run on a 4K CM-2.

Efficient Induction Operators

In this section we treat induction as a search for patterns with useful discrimination between positive and negative instances (but, see Hunter [1989] for a discussion of learning as planning). We review the induction operators we have currently implemented, and conclude by looking at one example in more detail.

Searching pattern space

For us, an induction operator transforms one initial pattern (parent) into a set of related patterns (children), and evaluates their performance on the positive and negative instances. It is not necessary to exhaustively test every possible child against the instances to obtain its discriminatory performance. It is usually possible to test only a subset of the children spawned by an operator, then to use those results to construct the performance of the remaining children. Hence, the operators may be used to efficiently search pattern space for useful discriminating patterns. The parent is usually drawn from the ROC frontier (see figure 6), thereby implementing a beam search [Winston 1984]. It is usually most convenient to form scripts by sequencing several induction operators, separated by filters to prune unpromising candidates.

The matcher is invoked as a subroutine by the individual induction operators. The induction operators, in turn, are invoked by induction scripts. Finally, a domain expert invokes the scripts (see figure 10).

Figure 10. A logical system architecture.

Currently implemented operators

The operators currently implemented are summarized as follows:

- DROP-TERM. This removes a specified term, or each term in turn, from the pattern. (The Near Miss version(s) may be constructed by XORing the returned match bit-vector with that of the original pattern, here and below.)

- ADD-TERM. This adds a term to the pattern at a specified position.

- REFINE-CLASS. This explores optimizations attainable by replacing a specified (generalization class) term in the pattern by some other term from the generalization hierarchy that the term resides in.[12]

- REFINE-TERM-SCORE. This explores optimizations attainable by replacing a score attached to a term (that is, the *score-if-missing* or the *score-if-present*) by some other score, and simultaneously changing the overall match cut-off score.

- DROP-INTERVAL. This explores removing the restrictions imposed by a specified interval relation between two adjacent terms, or each interval in turn, by replacing it with a very large interval.

- REFINE-INTERVAL. This explores optimizations attainable by replacing a specified interval between terms by some other interval.

Example of an induction operator

For many operators, it is possible to evaluate all of the children much more efficiently than by exhaustively matching each child against the instances. This is possible if a selected subset of children can be matched against the instances, and then combined to give the effect of matching any other child to the instances. We find that the time and space consumption of the subsetting and combining steps is miniscule (a few percent or less) compared to the match step. Consequently the attractive match properties are inherited by the induction operators.

An example induction operator, REFINE-CLASS, is shown in figure 11. It shows a parent pattern and one term in it, HYDROPHOBE, that denotes a node class and so resides in a class generalization hierarchy. The HYDROPHOBE term is surrounded by other terms in the pattern that precede and follow it (shown schematically as flanking lozenges). The REFINE-CLASS operator will explore patterns constructible by replacing HYDROPHOBE with a different class.

First we copy the candidate pattern once for each *leaf* in the generalization hierarchy, creating a subset of variant children by substituting each leaf for HYDROPHOBE in the parent (it is not actually necessary to start at the leaves, but the presentation has been simplified).

Each variant child is then loaded into a different full processor set (see figure 9). All the variant children are matched against all the positive and

---

[12]This corresponds to Climb-Tree in the machine learning literature, but we use the more general term here because it explores more classes than those accessible by climbing.

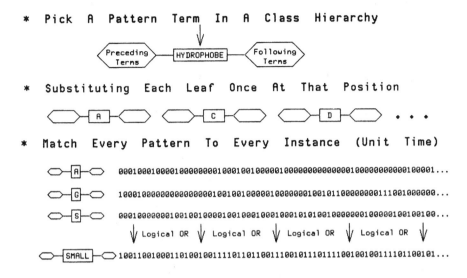

* Pick A Pattern Term In A Class Hierarchy

* Substituting Each Leaf Once At That Position

* Match Every Pattern To Every Instance (Unit Time)

* The Matches Of Any Class At That Term
  Are The Logical 'OR' Of Its Constituents.

The class SMALL is the union of A, G, and S.

Consequently, the matches to the pattern if SMALL were to be substituted there, are exactly the union of the matches to the descriptors with A, G, and S substituted.

* These Logical 'OR's Are Computed In Parallel

So we return the result of substituting every possible class at that position, then matching each resulting descriptor against the positive and negative sets, in the time for one processor to match its own protein segment to one pattern.

Figure 11. Induction operator example of REFINE-CLASS.

negative instances in one step. The bit-vectors describing the match results are collected as described in the previous section.

Next, every full processor set sends its match bit-vectors to every induction processor (one induction processor for each class in the generalization hierarchy). Figure 11 illustrates the bit-vectors that would be used by an induction processor for the SMALL class composed of the leaves A, G, and S. Every class from the generalization hierarchy is processed by a different processor. Each induction processor computes (concurrently) the logical OR of the match bit-vectors corresponding to the leaves subsumed by its class. This OR is the match bit-vector which would be generated if its class (SMALL, in figure 11) were to be substituted into the original

pattern for the original term (HYDROPHOBE, in figure 11). In little more
than the time taken to match one pattern against one instance segment,
we have evaluated (against all the instances) all of the patterns formable
from the parent, by substituting any generalization class for the specified
term.

Limitations, Future Work, and Open Questions

The approach as implemented is limited to domains having a mostly local
embedding of features and relations. While domains exhibiting a planar or
three-dimensional embedding might be acceptable, the approach is probably inapplicable to embeddings with a very high dimensionality.

Currently our basic control strategy is hill-climbing, beam search and
succumbs to its well-known perils [Winston 1984]. Especially interacting or
conjoined effects are not handled well. We are identifying the most common
of these and will implement scripts for them, a utilitarian but incomplete
approach. A better beam search control mechanism than the ROC frontier would be desirable. The Version Space concept lattice [Mitchell 1977]
which has already been inplemented on the [ROC frontier as data structures, should be more fully integrated. A planning component should be
added as well, possibly along the lines suggested by Hunter [1989].

Using arcs in a graph-based instance language to represent structural
correlates (such as secondary structure predictions) is an improvement over
marking features on the amino acids (this is done in some string-based approaches), because it preserves the individual identities and boundaries of
overlapping but distinct features of the same type. However, it makes it
more difficult to verify whether a given amino acid is contained within a
certain feature type. A hybrid representation would be more useful (as,
for example, in the full ARIDANE). The implementation of arcs in the parallel machine would be much more efficient if an efficient hardware array
reference instruction were available on an individual processor basis.

We currently have no rigorous basis for establishing the statistical significance of pattern discriminatory performance. We have explored various
statistical, probabilistic, information-theoretic [Smith & Smith 1990], and
minimal descriptor length approaches. Complicating statistical analysis,
varying but unknown degrees of shared evolutionary history across species
ensure the instances are not statistically independent (for example, human
DNA and chimpanzee DNA are identical to within a few percent). The
available databases represent an intentionally non-random sampling of instance space by domain experts pursuing specific research areas. Many
statistical tests of significance (for example, the chi squared statistic) are
inapplicable because the iterative pattern refinement process violates assumptions about a single independent test. Jack-knife or leave-one-out

methods are infeasible until the role of the domain expert is fully automated.

Along similar lines, we would like to relate the complexity of the pattern to its discriminatory power [Pearl 1978]. If the description language has an arbitrarily large expressive power, any arbitrary partitioning of the set of instances may be possible. By admitting graph structure into the instance language and corresponding terms into the description language, we have greatly increased the expressive power of our language relative to string-based approaches. This may limit the reliability of these patterns for prediction, analysis and interpretation. Conversely, many important structural features do not often exhibit recognizable string patterns, which limits the applicability of string-based approaches for complex structural patterns. By admitting new types of computable structural correlates as they are proposed by a domain researcher (for example, "acid-faced helix"), we increase the expressive power of the language. However, the best indicators of protein structure are not yet known. In such circumstances, a domain researcher should seek reliability by first ensuring that any puported pattern (or model) is robust when translated across different description languages; and also by relating it directly to experimental work in the literature.

The term match scores are not assigned on a rigorous basis. The approach described here optimizes them on discriminatory performance. This works well for pattern discovery (in practice pattern discrimination tends to be robust in this respect anyway), but has no clear tie to domain semantics. We have also explored probabilistic and specificity-based approaches.

We expect to extend the description language to include hierarchical patterns (as in ARIADNE), as well as more flexibility in the terms provided. The domain reality constraints on admissibility of patterns expressible in the description language (for example, constraints on realistic spacing) should be represented as declarative knowledge rather than in a procedural filter.

The role of the domain expert should be increasingly automated. We expect to explore the use of PLSEARCH family consensus sequences [Smith & Smith 1990] to obtain initial seed patterns. Other points to automate include search guidance, and construction of the sets of positive and negative examples. Our scripts currently have no conditionalization, and currently, there is no convenient way for the domain expert to create new scripts other than in LISP.

ARIEL performs parameter estimation, where the parameters are both numeric (for example, intervals) and symbolic (for example, generalization classes). Neural networks also do parameter estimation. Although our parameters are directly interpretable in a symbolic framework, perhaps some adaptation of neural network back-propagation machinery might be useful here. Conversely, perhaps some of our induction operators might be adaptable to neural networks. Hybrid systems, combining massively parallel implementations of both symbolic an distributed induction, potentially appear to have an immensely powerful future.

It is clear that we have barely scratched the surface of the inductive power potentially available. We expect that more and better parallel induction operators will be devised (we can envisage several ourselves), and that other approaches to parallel induction, both symbolic and non-symbolic, will continue to be explored (several have already been proposed or implemented). Parallel techniques for constructive symbolic induction would be especially useful. This work should be regarded as an initial foray into parallel inductive processes, not a definitive final statement.

Related Work

Theoretical treatment of massively parallel induction appears in Minsky [1986]. Neural networks and genetic algorithms have also been proposed for massively parallel induction. Neural networks and related structures have been used to predict secondary structure [Qian & Sejnowski 1988; Holley & Karplus 1989] and tertiary structure [Friedrichs & Wolynes 1989]. Genetic algorithms (classifier systems) [Holland et al. 1986] have been used to model the immune system response [Farmer & Packard 1986]. Massively parallel implementations of the Smith and Waterman [1981] sequence comparison algorithm have been reported by Collins and Coulson [1984] and by Lander et al. [1988]. Zhang et al. [1989] reported a massively parallel implementation for an attempt to predict protein ϕ–ψ angles based on an associative memory (N-nearest-neighbors) approach. A parallel implementation of the matching procedure in the SOAR learning system was reported by Tambe et al. [1988]. Drescher [1989] implemented a massively parallel induction system modeling Piagetian early childhood learning. With several massively parallel learning and induction systems now current, it is possible to envision hybrid systems with several different massively parallel induction modes available.

Some machine learning techniques useful elsewhere are difficult to apply because of the nature of the domain. Explanation-based learning is difficult to use because there is little predictive domain theory. The Version Space algorithm [Mitchell 1977] is difficult to apply because the domain is very noisy, therefore, S and G collapse (although the Version Space concept lattice is quite useful as a means of organizing patterns). Grammar induction techniques (for example, Maryanski and Booth [1977]) may not apply because typically only a very small fraction of the total sequence (or string) is used in the concept, the remainder is essentially unconstrained. The requirement to do well but not perfectly on both the positive and negative examples simultaneously is in distinction to Probably Approximately

Correct (PAC) learning models in which every positive example must be correct (for example, Valiant [1984]), or in which only the overall error rate is considered, however, PAC learning can approximate this model by adjusting the distribution of positive and negative instances.

A discussion of the general connection between artificial intelligence and molecular biology appears in Friedland and Kedes [1985]. A quite lucid exposition of basic protein structure is given by Richardson [1981]. The general problem of inferring protein structure from amino acid sequence is summarized by Kolata [1986]. Methods which compare amino acid sequences as strings include finite-state grammars, regular expression matching, measures of "edit distance," exact string matches, and metric similarity measures are reviewed by Sankoff and Kruskal [1983] and by Waterman [1984]. Searls [1988] proposed a formal grammar for genetic information. Important early work in symbolic patterns for protein structure was pioneered by Abarbanel [1984] and applied to turn prediction by Cohen *et al.* [1986], recent work is reviewed by Cohen and Kuntz [1989]. Hayes-Roth *et al.* [1986] used a constraint-based method to elucidate three-dimensional protein structure. Gascuel and Danchin [1986] used the machine learning system PLAGE to discriminate bacterial protein leader sequences. Taylor [1987] used empirical inductive techniques to infer amino acid classes. Qualitative symbolic functional simulation from structure of molecular systems was reported by Koile and Overton [1989] and Karp and Friedland [1989].

Summary and Discussion

We have described a running system that embodies efficient parallel implementations of several symbolic machine learning induction operators. It functions as an "Induction Assistant" to a domain expert. First we developed an efficient, noise-tolerant, similarity-based parallel matching algorithm. This should apply to other graph-based representations of domains possessing an embedding in which the low-level features (relations or groupings) are mostly local. It was used as infrastructure to construct efficient parallel implementations of several symbolic machine learning induction operators. Finally, the induction operators were sandwiched together with sets of filters (both syntactic and empirical) to compose a crude form of induction scripts, which are invoked by a domain expert. The matching algorithm has very attractive scaling properties as the size of the problem and/or the number of processors increases. Hardware usage is efficient. The results reported in this chapter were obtained on a 4K Connection Machine. The implemented system was used to discover something previously unknown to the domain expert [Webster *et al.* 1989b]. Details of the parallel implementation appear in Lathrop [1990].

We find that the level of abstraction at which the search planning process is carried out has been raised. The plans formulated by the domain expert have approximately the same relative depth and bushiness as before ARIEL was available, but the level at which plans are formulated has been raised because the previous lower levels are now handled automatically by the induction assistant.

As suggested in figure 1, this research stands at the confluence of two emerging themes in computer science and artificial intelligence. These are machine learning and parallel processing. One goal of this research is to contribute to the effort to integrate them. There are many reasons to seek parallel methods for machine learning, these include:

- The potential speedup immediately available.

- General intrinsic interest in developing new algorithms and intuitions for the next generation of parallel computing hardware.

- Scalability, to let us move beyond initially necessary toy domains into larger real world problems, because parallel algorithms usually scale much differently from serial ones. This is particularly important if learning systems are to serve as an enabling component of other artificial intelligence systems.

- Flexibility, to have efficient algorithms for both parallel and serial implementations in our artificial intelligence armory, so that our systems can most effectively map the structure of a problem to the structure of a solution, and take advantage of all hardware advances, parallel or serial.

For us, the key contribution of this work is its demonstration of the *scalability* of the algorithms involved: *The time complexity of every algorithm reported here is essentially independent of the size of the data,* provided that sufficient parallel hardware is available.

A million-processor Connection Machine, now in development, would permit us to perform induction over multiple copies of every instance in the domain (tens of thousands), with little or no increase in the real elapsed time. The amount of domain data is approximately doubling every two years, and is expected to continue to increase. This parallels Moore's Law, which asserts that the performance/price ratio of computing hardware roughly doubles every two years. The algorithms described here can be expected to accommodate both the increase in the domain data and the increase in computing power, again with little or no increase in real elapsed time, in the foreseeable future.

Although we have chosen molecular biology as a domain, we expect that other application areas will benefit from symbolic induction techniques whose time complexity is, essentially, independent of the size of the instance pool. For example, every complex manufacturing operation (say, a large steel plant) generates vast amounts of data about process control (for example, melt temperatures, roller pressures) and structural qualities (for example, elemental composition). These are all more or less obscurely related to the final functional qualities of the product (for example, ductility, hardness). Inductive techniques that scale to handle vast quantities of data might allow construction of empirical relationships between manufacturing processes and functional qualities (for example, a process-based discriminator for "high ductility"). This could potentially allow fine-tuning the process parameters to optimize specific desired final qualities, thereby increasing the quality and productivity of a whole industrial sector. Because there are other domains with regularities hidden in vast quantities of data, we expect that these algorithms, and related ones that improve on these first steps, will be increasingly useful as the future of computation unfolds.

References

Abarbanel, R. M. [1984], "Protein Structural Knowledge Engineering," Ph.D. Thesis, University of California, San Francisco.

Alberts, B. M. (chairman) [1988], *Report of the Committee on Mapping and Sequencing the Human Genome,* Natl. Research Council for Natl./Academy of Sciences, Natl. Acad. Press, Washington, DC.

Bradley, M., T. Smith, R. Lathrop, D. Livingston, and T. Webster [1987], "Consensus Topography in the ATP Binding Site of the Simian Virus 40 and Polyomavirus Large Tumor Antigens," *Proc. Natl. Acad. Sciences USA,* vol. 84, pp. 4026–4030.

Cohen, F. E., R. M. Abarbanel, I. D. Kuntz, and R. J. Fletterick [1986], "Turn Prediction in Proteins Using a Pattern-Matching Approach," *Biochemistry,* vol. 25, pp. 266–275.

We thank Marvin Minsky and Ron Rivest for discussion and suggestions. Helpful suggestions were received from Jeremy Wertheimer and Randy Smith.

Personal support for the first author has been provided in part by a National Science Foundation Graduate Fellowship and an IBM Graduate Fellowship. This research was performed at the Artificial Intelligence Laboratory of the Massachusetts Institute of Technology, in consortium with the Molecular Biology Computer Research Resource of the Harvard School of Public Health at the Dana Farber Cancer Institute. Support for the consortium research is provided in part by the National Science Foundation under grant DIR8715633. Support for the Artificial Intelligence Laboratory's research is provided in part by the Advanced Research Projects Agency of the Department of Defense under Office of Naval Research contract N00014-85-K-0124. Support for the Molecular Biology Computer Research Resource's research is provided in part by the National Institutes of Health under grant RR02275-05.

Cohen, F. E., and I. D. Kuntz [1989], "Tertiary Structure Predictions," in *Prediction of Protein Structure and the Principles of Protein Conformation*, edited by G. D. Fasman, Plenum Press, New York, pp. 647-706.

Collins, J. F., and A. F. Coulson [1984], "Applications of Parallel Processing Algorithms for DNA Sequence Analysis," *Nucl. Acids Res.*, vol. 12, pp. 181–192.

Doolittle, R. F., M. W. Hunkapillar, L. E. Hood, S. G. Devare, K. C. Robbins, S. A. Aaronson, and H. N. Antoniades [1983], "Simian Sarcoma Virus *onc* Gene, v-*sis*, Is Derived from the Gene (or Genes) Encoding a Platelet-Derived Growth Factor," *Science*, vol. 221, pp. 275–277.

Drescher, G. L. [1989], "A Mechanism for Early Piagetian Learning," Ph.D. Thesis, Massachusetts Institute of Technology, Cambridge.

Farmer, J., and N. Packard [1986], "The Immune System, Adaptation, and Machine Learning," *Physica*, vol. 22D, pp. 187–204.

Figge, J., T. Webster, T. Smith, and E. Paucha [1988], "Prediction of Similar Transforming Region in Simian Virus 40 Large T, Adenovirus E1A, and myc Oncoproteins," *J. Virology*, vol. 62, no. 5, pp. 1814–1818.

Figge, J., and T. Smith [1988], "Cell-Division Sequence Motif," *Nature*, vol. 334, p. 109.

Friedland, P., and L. Kedes [1985], "Discovering the Secrets of DNA," *Computer*, vol. 18, no. 11, pp. 49–69.

Friedrichs, M., and P. Wolynes [1989], "Toward Protein Tertiary Structure Recognition by Means of Associative Memory Hamiltonians," *Science*, vol. 246, pp. 371–373.

Gascuel, O., and A. Danchin [1986], "Protein Export in Prokaryotes and Eukaryotes: Indications of a Difference in the Mechanism of Exportation," *J. Mol. Evol.*, vol. 24, pp. 130-142.

Goldsborough, M. D., D. DiSilvestre, G. F. Temple, A. T. Lorincz [1989], "Nucleotide Sequence of Human Papilloma Virus Type 31: A Cervical Neoplasia-Associated Virus," *J. Virology*, vol. 171, pp. 306–311.

Hayes-Roth, B., *et al.* [1986], "PROTEAN: Deriving Protein Structure from Constraints," in *Proc. Fifth Natl. Conf. on Artificial Intelligence*, pp. 904–909.

Hillis, W. D. [1986], *The Connection Machine*, MIT Press, Cambridge, MA.

Holland, J., K. Holyoak, R. Nisbett, and P. Thagard [1986], *Induction: Processes of Inference, Learning, and Discovery*, MIT Press, Cambridge, MA, USA.

Holley, L. H., and M. Karplus [1989], "Protein Structure Prediction With a Neural Network," *Proc. Natl. Acad. Sciences USA*, vol. 86, pp. 152–156.

Hunter, L. E. [1989], *Knowledge Acquisition Planning: Gaining Expertise Through Experience*, Ph.D. Thesis, Yale University.

Karp, P., and P. Friedland [1989], "Coordinating the Use of Qualitative and Quantitative Knowledge in Declarative Device Modeling," in *Artificial Intelligence, Modeling and Simulation,* edited by, Widman, L. E., D. H. Helman, and K. Loparo, John Wiley and Sons, 1988.

Koile, K., and C. Overton [1989], "A Qualitative Model for Gene Expression," *Proc. 1989 Summer Computer Simulation Conf.,* Soc. for Computer Simulation.

Kolata, G. [1986], "Trying to Crack the Second Half of the Genetic Code," *Science,* vol. 233, pp. 1037-1039.

Lander, E., J. Mesirov, and W. Taylor [1988], "Study of Protein Sequence Comparison Metrics on the Connection Machine CM-2," *Proc. Supercomputing 1988.*

Lathrop, R. H., T. A. Webster, and T. F. Smith [1987], "ARIADNE: Pattern-Directed Inference and Hierarchical Abstraction in Protein Structure Recognition," *Comm. of the ACM,* vol. 30, no. 11, pp. 909–921.

Lathrop, R. H., R. J. Hall, and R. S. Kirk [1987], "Functional Abstraction From Structure in VLSI Simulation Models," in *Proc. 24th Design Automation Conf.,* Miami Beach, FL, pp. 822–828.

Lathrop, R. H. [1990], *Efficient Methods For Massively Parallel Symbolic Induction: Algorithms and Implementation,* Ph.D. Thesis, Massachusetts Institute of Technology, Cambridge (in preparation).

Maryanski, F. J., and T. L. Booth [1977], "Inference of Finite-State Probabilistic Grammars," *IEEE Trans. on Computers,* C-26, no. 6, pp. 521–536.

Michalski, R. S., J. G. Carbonell, and T. M. Mitchell [1983], (editors), *Machine Learning: An Artificial Intelligence Approach,* (first in a series), Tioga Press, Palo Alto, CA.

Minsky [1986], *The Society of Mind,* Simon and Schuster.

Mitchell, T. M. [1977], "Version Spaces: A Candidate Elimination Approach to Rule Learning," *Proc. Fifth Intl. Joint Conf. on Artificial Intelligence,* Cambridge, MA, pp. 305–310.

Pearl, J. [1978], "On the Connection between the complexity and Credibility of Inferred Models," *Int. J. General Systems,* vol. 4, pp. 255-264.

Qian, N., and T. Sejnowski [1988], "Predicting the Secondary Structure of Globular Proteins Using Neural Network Models," *J. Mol. Biol.,* vol. 202, pp. 865–884.

Ralph,‘W., T. Webster, and T. Smith [1987], "A Modified Chou and Fasman Protein Structure Algorithm," *CABIOS,* vol. 3, pp. 211-216. *PRSTRC* program available from MBCRR, Dana Farber Cancer Institute, 44 Binney St., Boston, MA.

Richardson, J. [1981], "The Anatomy and Taxonomy of Protein Structure," *Advances in Protein Chemistry,* vol. 34, pp. 167–339.

Sanchez-Pescador, R., M. Power, P. Barr K. Steimer, M. Stempien, S. Brown-Shimer, W. Gee, A. Renard, A. Randolph, J. Levy, D. Dina, and P. Lucie

[1985], "Nucleotide Sequence and Expression of an AIDS-Associated Retrovirus (ARV-2)," *Science*, vol. 227, pp. 484–492.

Sankoff, D., and J. B. Kruskal [1983], (editors) *Time Warps, String Edits, and Macromolecules: The Theory and Practice of Sequence Comparison*, Addison–Wesley, Reading, MA.

Searls, D. B. [1988], "Representing Genetic Information with Formal Grammars," in *Proc. of the Seventh Natl. Conf. on Artificial Intelligence*, pp. 386–391.

Smith, R. F., and T. F. Smith [1990], "Automatic Generation of Primary Sequence Patterns from Sets of Related Protein Sequences," *Proc. Natl. Acad. Sci. USA*, in press.

Smith, T. F., and M. S. Waterman [1981], "Identification of Common Molecular Subsequences," *J. Mol. Biol.*, vol. 147, pp. 195–197.

Steele, G. L. [1984], *Common LISP: The Manual*, Digital Press, Billerica, MA.

Swets, J. A. [1986a], "Indices of Discrimination or Diagnostic Accuracy: Their ROCs and Implied Models," *Psychological Bull.*, vol. 99, no. 1, pp. 100–117.

Swets, J. A. [1986b], "Form of Empirical ROCs in Discrimination and Diagnostic Tasks: Implications for Theory and Measurement of Performance," *Psychological Bull.*, vol. 99, no. 2.

Tambe, M., D. Kapl, A. Gupta, C. Forgy, B. Milnes, A. Newell [1988], "Soar/PSM-E: Investigating Match Parallelism in a Learning Production System," *Proc. Parallel Programming Environments Applications Languages and Systems*.

Taylor, W. [1987], "Identification of Protein Sequence Homology by Consensus Template Alignment," *J. Mol. Biol.*, vol. 188, pp. 233-258.

Thinking Machines Corp. [1988], *Paris Reference Manual*, Cambridge, MA.

Valiant, L. G. [1984], "A Theory of the Learnable," *Comm. of the ACM*, vol. 27, no. 11, pp. 1134–1142.

Waterman, M. S. [1984], "General Methods of Sequence Comparison," *Bull. of Math. Biol.*, vol. 46, pp. 473-500.

Webster, T. A., R. H. Lathrop, and T. F. Smith [1987], "Prediction of a Common Structural Domain in Aminoacyl-tRNA Synthetases Through Use of a New Pattern-Directed Inference System," *Biochemistry*, vol. 26, pp. 6950–6957.

Webster, T. A., R. H. Lathrop, and T. F. Smith [1988], "Pattern Descriptors and the Unidentified Reading Frame 6 Human mtDNA Dinucleotide-Binding Site" *Proteins*, vol. 3, no. 2, pp. 97–101.

Webster, T. A., R. Patarca R. H. Lathrop, and T. F. Smith [1989a], "Potential Structural Motifs in Reverse Transcriptases," *Mol. Biol. Evol.*, vol. 6, no. 3, pp. 317-320.

Webster, T. A., R. H. Lathrop P. H. Winston, and T. F. Smith [1989b], "Predicted Common Structural Motif in DNA-directed and RNA-directed DNA Polymerases," (submitted).

Winston, P. H., T. O. Binford, B. Katz, and M. Lowry [1983], "Learning Physical Descriptions from Functional Descriptions, Examples, and Precedents," in *Proc. of the Natl. Conf. on Artificial Intelligence,* (Washington, DC., Aug. 22-26, 1983), William Kaufman, Los Altos, CA, 1983, pp. 433-439.

Winston, P. H. [1984], *Artificial Intelligence, 2nd edition,* Addison-Wesley, Reading, MA.

Wong, S., A. Wahl, P. Yuan, N. Arai B. Pearson, K. Arai, D. Korn, M. Hunkapillar, T. Wang [1988], "Human DNA Polymerase α Gene Expression is Cell Proliferation Dependent and its Primary Sequence is Similar to Both Prokaryotic and Eukaryotic Replicative DNA Polymerases," *EMBO J.,* vol. 7, pp. 37–47.

Zhang, X., D. Waltz, and J. Mesirov [1989], "Protein Structure Prediction by a Data-level Parallel Algorithm," *Proc. Supercomputing 1989,* Nov. 13–17, Reno, NV, USA, pp. 215–223.

5

What should you buy? From whom? Each time questions like these are decided, the decision-making effort should become a piece of history that others can benefit from later on. Yet decisions of essentially the same kind are made over and over and the participants in the decision making go over the same tedious ground already plowed by thousands of others.

In this chapter, Lee shows that what we need is a language for describing how decisions are made in terms that make goals and arguments explicit. With such a language, all sorts of questions can be answered that traditional decision science can deal with only obliquely. To what extent, for example, can a past decision serve as a precedent for a current decision? How would a particular decision turn out if cost were not important? What would person X decide to do? What are the risks involved in choice Y? What would be the effect of product Z, if announced?

Thus Lee's language makes a new kind of what-if exercise possible for decision makers. Importantly, Lee's language also makes what-happened exercises vastly easier too. Just keeping track of what happened in big government system-integration contracts, so as to provide an audit trail later on, can consume half of the total cost. Were decisions made in the way envisioned by Lee, the audit trail would be a byproduct of decision making, not an add-on activity.

SIBYL:
A Qualitative Decision
Management System

Jintae Lee

In this chapter, we describe a Qualitative Decision Management System, called SIBYL.[1] The goal of a Qualitative Decision Management System is to help users represent and manage the qualitative aspects of the decision making process—such as the alternatives being considered, the goals to satisfy, and the arguments evaluating alternatives with respect to the goals. For this purpose, SIBYL provides a language for representing decision making processes and also provides a set of services that help to manage the dependencies represented in the language.

We proceed as follows. We first present a scenario that illustrates the kinds of services that a qualitative decision management system should provide. In the remainder of the chapter, we describe how SIBYL provides these services. First we describe the Decision Representation Language (DRL) that SIBYL uses to represent the qualitative aspects of decision making processes. In the section, "An Example," we show an example decision graph—that is, the representation in DRL of a particular decision making process. In the section, "Services," we discuss the major types of services that we have identified—the management of dependency, plausibility, viewpoints, and precedents. We illustrate these services with the example in the section, "An Example." In the section, "Related Work," we discuss how our approach is related to similar attempts to support qualitative decision making. Finally, we conclude with topics for future research.

---

[1] A sibyl was one of a number of prophetesses in Greek mythology who gave wise counsel by mediating with the Gods on behalf of human supplicants.

Scenario

Imagine you are trying to decide which knowledge representation language to use for your project called ZEUS. You ask your project members to use a qualitative decision management system to enter thoughts relevant to this decision. These include all the alternatives that should be considered, the constraints an ideal alternative should satisfy, the relevant facts and claims for evaluating the alternatives, and the dependencies that hold among these claims. The system provides a language and a user-interface for using the language, such as object editors, menus, and graphic displays. Also, the system is distributed so that users can examine what has already been entered and then can enter additional opinions incrementally. Suppose users have given their initial inputs; the following scenario illustrates a session with a hypothetical qualitative decision management system. Here, it assumes natural language input for the purpose of exposition, but the interface can be graphical and mouse-based, as it is implemented in SIBYL.

User: Show me the current status.

System: *The system displays the decision matrix shown in figure 1.*

Status of the Decision: Find an Optimal Knowledge Representation Language for Zeus			
Goals **Importance** Alternatives	**Support Zeus Requirements** H+	**Minimize Cost** H	**Customizability** L
STROBE	H	H	H- *
KEE	H-	L	M
LOOPS	H	unresolved	H

Figure 1. An overall evaluation of the alternatives for the decision problem of finding an optimal knowledge representation language for ZEUS.

In the figure, each row represents an alternative, each column represents a desirable property or a goal, and each cell represents the evaluation of the alternative with respect to the goal. Although the evaluation is shown in terms of H (high), M (medium), and L (low), the evaluation measure can be numerical or defined by the user. An evaluation measure marked with a '*' means that there is some qualification on the measure.

User: What is the qualification on the evaluation of STROBE with respect to customizability?

System: The evaluation of STROBE is 'H-' with respect to Customizability, provided that we can get the source code.

When this qualifying assumption turns out to be wrong, the system updates all the objects that depended on this assumption and reevaluates the alternatives.

User: Why is LOOPS' evaluation unresolved with respect to Minimize Cost?

System: The following questions need to be answered for evaluation.

  Q1 Which hardware platform should be used for
    the project?
  Q2 Would ENVOS give us a free copy of LOOPS?

User: What are the possible answers to Q1?

System: Sun, Symbolics, or Dandetiger. By the way, there is a decision record associated with this question. See Decision Problem, Hardware Platform, if you want to look at it.

User: What are the current overall evaluations for the hardware alternatives?

The system retrieves the decision record associated with this question and shows the overall evaluation of the alternatives.

System: Sun (very good)
      Symbolics (very good)
      Dandetiger (poor)

This overall evaluation is computed by merging the evaluation measures, like the ones shown in figure 1, but for this hardware decision problem, properly weighted by the importance of the different goals. The system can use a default merging procedure or one that the user specifies. The user can now examine how the evaluation was arrived at by asking the system to display the decision matrices for this hardware platform decision. But, instead, she goes back to the current decision problem, and wants to make an assumption to see its consequences.

User: Assume that we use Symbolics. How would it affect the evaluations?

System: STROBE (very good)
      KEE (good)
      LOOPS is not an alternative any more because it
      is incompatible with the hardware choice.

LOOPS *does not run on Symbolics. This dependency information has been entered earlier, so the system knows that* LOOPS *should no longer be an alternative. Other arguments that depend on this new knowledge get updated and the alternatives are reevaluated.*

User: Tell me how you arrived at the evaluation of STROBE with respect to Minimize Cost?

System: *The system displays the matrix shown in figure 2. The matrix shown is like the matrix in figure 1 except that the columns now show the subgoals of the goal, Minimize Cost.*

Status of the Subgoals of: the Goal: Minimize Cost		
Goals Importance Alternatives	Minimize Development Cost M	Get One Cheaper L
STROBE	H-	H
KEE	H-	L
LOOPS	M	H

Figure 2. Evaluation of the alternatives with respect to the subgoals of the goal, Minimize Cost.

User: Tell me how you arrived at the evaluation of STROBE with respect to Minimize Development Cost?

System: *The system displays the the argument graph in figure 3. The argument graph shows the arguments evaluating STROBE with respect to the goal of Minimizing Development Cost.*

User: Suppose we do not consider the goal, Minimize Cost. How would that change the evaluation?

System: KEE (very good)
                      STROBE (good)

The user can ask to see the matrix responsible for these evaluations but, instead, the user wants to freeze the current state so that she can come back to it later or compare it to other states that have also been frozen.

User: Create a viewpoint with the current assumptions and call it "Not Considering Development Cost."

System: The current assumptions that have been introduced since last time are:

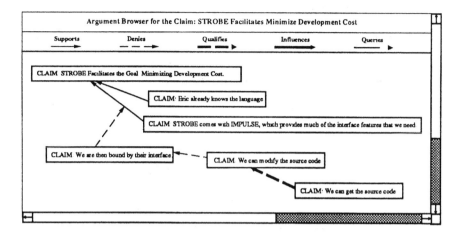

Figure 3. Arguments evaluating STROBE with respect to the goal, Minimize Development Cost.

1   We use Symbolics as the hardware.
2   "Get One Cheaper" is no longer a goal. Do you still want to create the viewpoint?

User: Yes

System: The viewpoint, "Not Considering Development Cost" has been saved.

Having created a viewpoint, the user can add further arguments under this viewpoint. Alternatively, she could switch to another viewpoint, and add arguments in that viewpoint.

The user would like to know if there have been any decisions in the past that would be worth examining.

User: Retrieve useful past decisions.

System: The following are the past decisions that might be relevant in the order of similarity to the current decision problem.

Choose an optimal knowledge representation language for the project XANADU. (Decision 140)
Choose a programming language for the project, ZEUS. (Decision 245)
Choose an operating system for the project, ZEUS. (Decision 247)

After the user examines these past decisions, she decides to transfer some of the relevant knowledge from these earlier decisions.

User: Show me the relevant information from DP 140.

System: *The system displays the folder shown in figure 4. The folder contains all the alternatives, the desirable properties, and the arguments that the system judged to be relevant. The user examines each of these objects in more detail and selects those that she judges to be relevant.*

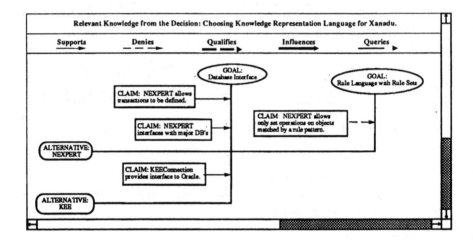

Figure 4. Knowledge judged relevant from a past decision.

User: Transfer all the objects that I selected to the current decision problem.

System: Done

User: Show me the current overall evaluation of the alternatives with the new knowledge.

System: STROBE (very good)
NEXPERT (very good)
KEE (good)
KNOWLEDGE CRAFT (unresolved)

The user explores these alternatives and examines relevant arguments in the ways described. She then goes on to add further issues and arguments, saves them, and calls it a day.

The above scenario illustrates the features desirable for a qualitative decision management system. The rest of the chapter shows how they are realized in SIBYL, our implemented system.

Decision Representation Language (DRL)

The services of SIBYL, revolve around decision graphs—the records of the pros and cons evaluating alternatives with respect to the goals. In this section, we briefly describe the language used for constructing these decision graphs, which we call the Decision Representation Language.

Figure 5 shows the objects and relations that form the vocabulary of DRL. Figure 6 presents them graphically. The fundamental objects of DRL are **Alternatives**, **Goals**, and **Claims**. Other objects in DRL are no less essential in decision making, but they are either special cases of the above three, or they are objects useful beyond the context of decision making, as we discuss below.

```
Alternative
Goal
  Decision Problem
Claim
  DRL Relation
    Is-A-Sub-Decision-Of (Dec. Prob., Dec. Prob.)
    Is-A-Subgoal-Of (Goal, Goal)
    Facilitates (Alternative, Goal)
      Is-An-Alternative-For (Alternative, Dec. Prob.)
    Supports (Claim, Claim)
    Denies (Claim, Claim)
    Qualifies (Claim, Claim)
    Queries (Question, Claim)
    Influences (Question, Claim)
    Are-Arguments-For (Group of Claims, Claim)
    Is-An-Answering-Procedure-For (Procedure, Question)
    Is-A-Result-Of (Claim, Procedure)
    Answers (Claim, Question)
    Are-Possible-Answers-To (Group of Claims, Question)
    Is-A-Sub-Procedure-Of (Procedure, Procedure)
    Is-A-Kind-Of (Object, Object)
Question
Procedure
  Procedure Description
  Executable Procedure
Group
Viewpoint
```

Figure 5. The DRL Vocabulary.

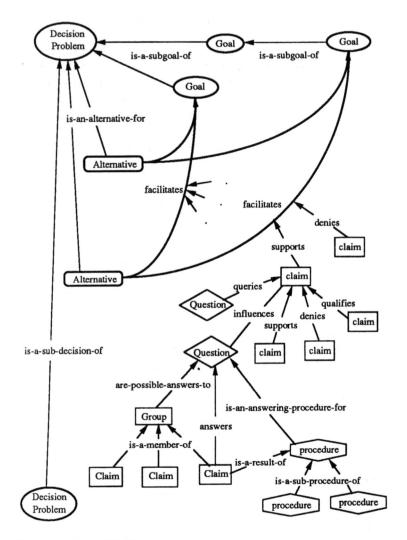

Figure 6. The DRL Model.

Alternatives represent the options to choose from. **Goals** specify the properties that an ideal option should have. A **Goal** G1 may be related to another **Goal** G2 through an **Is-A-Subgoal-Of** relation, meaning that satisfying G1 facilitates satisfying G2. A special subtype of **Goal** is **Decision Problem**, representing the topmost goal of the form "Choose X optimal for Y." Hence, all the goals are subgoals of the decision problem because they elaborate ways of satisfying this top level goal. A **Decision Problem** DP1 is related to another **Decision Problem** DP2 through an

`Is-A-Sub-Decision-Of` relation if DP2 requires solving DP1. For example, choosing the best computer environment for one's project has among its subdecisions choosing the hardware, choosing the operating system, and choosing the programming language. When this is the case, the alternatives of the parent decision consist of combinations of the alternatives from its subdecisions.

`Claims` are used to represent arguments relevant for choosing among the alternatives. DRL makes no distinction between facts and claims. Any statement is defensible, that is, it can be denied in DRL. A `Claim` can be related to another `Claim` through `Supports`, `Denies`, or `Qualifies` relations. A `Claim` C1 `Supports` another `Claim` C2 if the plausibility of C2 becomes higher (or lower) when that of C1 goes up (or down). A `Claim` C1 `Denies` another `Claim` C2 if the plausibility of C2 becomes lower (or higher) when that of C1 goes up (or down). Exactly how the plausibilities get updated is discussed in the section, "Plausibility Management." A `Claim` C1 `Qualifies` another `Claim` C2 if the plausibility of C2 becomes null when that of C1 becomes low enough. As long as the plausibility of C1 remains high, it has no effect on the plausibility of C2. All DRL relations are subtypes of `Claim`. For example, `Supports` (C1,C2) is itself a claim that the claim C1 supports the claim C2. Hence, the relation itself can be supported, denied, or qualified—for example, when a person agrees with C1 and C2 but does not agree that C1 *supports C2*. The `Is-A-Kind-Of` relation is a claim asserting a specialization relation between two objects. For example, `Is-A-Kind-Of` (A1, A2) holds when A1 is the alternative "Use Sun" and A2 is the alternative "Use Sun 4." All the claims that influence the plausibility of a claim can be grouped and related to it through an `Are-Arguments-For` relation.

`Facilitates` (A, G) is the `Claim` that the alternative A facilitates satisfying the goal G. The plausibility of this `Facilitates` claim is the measure of how satisfactory the alternative is with respect to the goal in question. `Is-An-Alternative-For` (A, DP) is the claim that the alternative A represents an option for solving the decision problem, DP, that is, that A facilitates satisfying the top level goal represented by D. Hence, the `Is-An-Alternative-For` relation is a subtype of the `Facilitates` relation.

A `Question` represents an uncertain state which requires more information to determine its outcome uniquely. There are two kinds of `Questions`. A `Question` might be a simple request for an explanation—for example, Why do we need an email interface? Alternatively, it may represent a major uncertainty whose different potential outcomes might lead the decision in different ways. The first kind of `Question` can be linked to any object through a `Queries` relation. The second kind of `Question` is linked to a claim through an `Influences` relation. A `Question` Q `Influences` a `Claim` C if the plausibility of C depends on the answer to Q. A `Claim` C `Answers` a `Question` Q if C represents a possible answer to Q. All the possible answers to a `Question` can be grouped and related to the `Question` through an `Are-Possible-Answers-To` relation.

A `Procedure` represents either an actual executable procedure (`Executable Procedure`) or a textual description of a procedure (`Procedure Description`). A `Procedure` object can be related to a `Question` through an `Is-An-Answering-Procedure-For` if it is believed that the procedure can be used to answer the `Question`. A `Claim` C `Is-A-Result-Of` a Procedure P if C is the information obtained as a result of executing P. A `Procedure` may be related to other `Procedures` through an `Is-A-Sub-Procedure-Of` or an `Is-A-kind-of` relation. The `Is-A-Sub-Procedure-Of` relation describes the part/whole relationship among procedures, and it is used when one wants to describe a procedure in terms of the component procedures that implement it. For example, "Get Simulation Software" is a sub-procedure of "Run Simulation." The `Is-A-Kind-Of` relation mentioned above can be used to specify the specialization relationship among procedures. For example, "Run System Dynamics Simulation" `Is-A-Kind-Of` "Run Simulation."

A `Group` represents a set of objects of the same type, among which we want to indicate some relationship. A `Group` object has the following attributes: Members and Member-Relationship. The Members attribute points to all the objects that belong to the group. The Member Relationship attribute takes as values such relationships as Conjunctive, Disjunctive, Mutually Exclusive, and Exhaustive. A `Viewpoint` is an object that represents a collection of objects sharing a given constraint. For example, all the alternatives, goals, and the claims that were created under the assumption that the hardware platform is Symbolics form a viewpoint. As such, a `Viewpoint` is a generalized `Group`, where the members are not just a set of objects of one type, but objects of different types related to one another through various relations. `Viewpoints` are discussed in more detail in the section, "Viewpoint Management."

An Example

Figure 7 shows an example decision graph constructed using DRL. This graph is a small portion of the decision graph constructed in the course of an actual decision process using SIBYL, slightly modified for the purpose of presentation. SIBYL has been implemented in Object Lens [Lai *et al.* 1989], which is a general tool for computer supported cooperative work and information management that provides many of the features needed for SIBYL. These include a friendly user interface, a knowledge base interface, hypertext capability, and an email interface. SIBYL has been actually used in several decision making processes—such as choosing an optimal computer environment for different projects, and cooperatively designing a

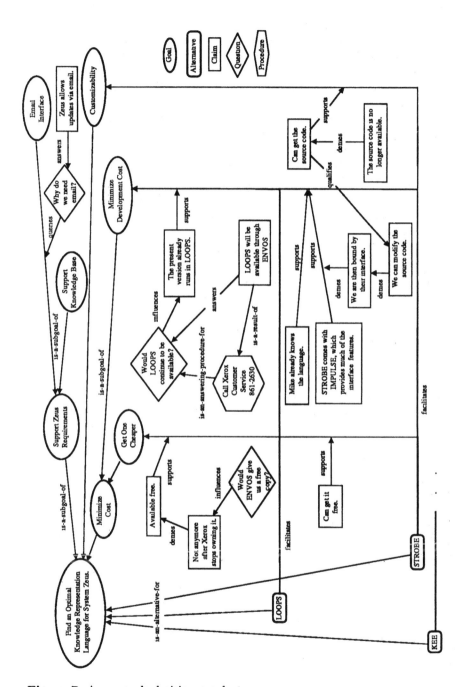

Figure 7. An example decision graph.

floor space. The example in this section will be used later to illustrate the services that SIBYL provides.

The decision problem is that of choosing an optimal knowledge representation language for implementing the system called ZEUS. Three alternatives (LOOPS, STROBE, and KEE) are considered, although all the arguments concerning KEE have been omitted. The desirable properties of the knowledge representation language are represented as goals. The arguments evaluating the alternatives are represented as claims about the Facilitates relations between the alternative and the relevant goals. For example, the claim that the present version already runs in LOOPS is an argument in favor of the claim that the alternative LOOPS facilitates satisfying the goal of minimizing development time, represented by the Facilitates relation between them. Hence, the plausibility of the Facilitates relation represents the evaluation measure of LOOPS with respect to the goal in question.

As noted above, all the relations in DRL are claims. Hence, they can be supported, denied, or qualified. For example, if one accepts the claim, "STROBE comes with IMPULSE, which provides much of the interface functionalities" but one does not agree that this claim supports the claim that "STROBE facilitates minimizing development time," then one denies the Supports relation between the claim and the Facilitates relation in question (see figure 7).

It is important to emphasize that the decision graph is only a graphical rendering of the knowledge base, and that the user does not see it in the form presented in figure 7. The system selectively displays portions of the decision graph or relevant attributes of selective objects in different formats (for example, a table, a graph, or a matrix) appropriate to different contexts. It also provides a template-based editor for easily creating and linking objects. Hence, the implemented user interface is much more friendly, but it is not the topic of this chapter.

To reduce the complexity, figure 7 omits the group objects that convey the information about the relations among a set of claims or goals; an example of a group is shown in figure 8.

Services

Dependency Management

Dependency Management is responsible for maintaining a consistent state of the knowledge base when a change is introduced. In decision making, objects or their attribute values depend on others. For example, in figure 7, the fact that LOOPS is an alternative depends on which hardware is chosen for implementing ZEUS. If Symbolics is the chosen hardware, LOOPS is no longer an alternative because it does not run on Symbolics. We should be able to represent such dependency as well as representing what should be done when we acquire the information.

Figure 8a shows how such a dependency is represented in DRL. Any uncertainty involved in a dependency is represented as a `Question`. Hence, we create a `Question` object, "Which hardware is chosen for implementing ZEUS," and link it to the `Is-An-Alternative-For` relation through an `Influences` relation. The possible outcomes of the `Question` are claims of the form, We use X, which are linked to the `Question` through the `Answers` relation. Alternatively, if we wanted to specify a relationship among these outcomes (for example, disjunctive or mutual exclusive relations), we would group these claims via a Group object as shown in figure 8b.

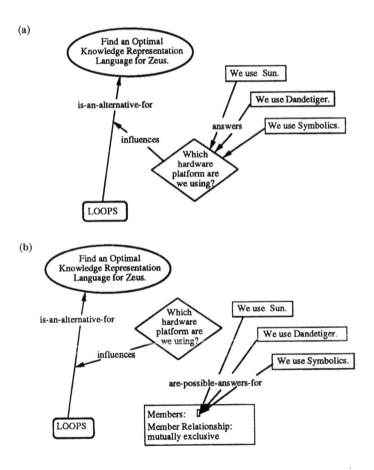

Figure 8. A representation of dependency in DRL.

Each of these claims has an attribute called `UpdateProcedure`, which provides the following information: a predicate on the plausibility of the claim, and the action to perform when the predicate is true. The predicate can be, for example, (> 30) if the plausibility measure used is numerical, or (> Very-High) if the measure is categorical. The system provides a set of standard plausibility measures and the appropriate predicates, but the user is free to invent her own. A typical action that one can specify is that of updating the plausibility of the influenced claim. Thus, we can specify the following pair, ((> Very-High), Set-Plausibility(0)) as the value of the `UpdateProcedure` attribute of the claim, "We use Symbolics" so that when Symbolics becomes the most likely hardware of choice, LOOPS would no longer be considered as an alternative. Figure 9 shows the updated decision graph. The alternative, LOOPS, and the relevant claims, do not get deleted, however; they only become invisible and have no effect on the decision. They become visible again if their importance or plausibility becomes non-zero. Other kinds of actions that can be performed include creating new objects and linking them to existing objects via specified relations. We plan to provide a high level language for specifying such actions. With such a language, the action can be an arbitrary procedure written in the language.

Other relations among claims, such as `Qualifies`, `Supports`, `Denies`, are special cases of `Influences`, and represent more specialized kinds of dependency. The action of a `Qualifies` relation is to set the plausibility of the qualified claim to zero when the plausibility of the qualifying claim becomes low. That is, the `UpdateProcedure` of the qualified claim is of the form, ((< Threshold), Set-Plausibility(0)), where the value of Threshold is set either globally or locally. Above the threshold, the qualifying claim has no effect on the plausibility of the claim qualified. For example, in figure 10, the claim, "Can get the source code" had no effect on the claim it qualifies. However, when it is denied by the claim, "The source code is no longer available" and if its plausibility becomes low enough, the plausibility of the claim it qualifies, "We can modify the source code," is set to zero. A consequence is that this change propagates so as to make the evaluation of STROBE with respect to the goal of Minimize Development Cost less strong. The action of a `Supports` relation is to raise (or lower) the plausibility of the supported claim when the plausibility of the supporting claim goes up (or down). The action of a `Denies` relation is to lower (or raise) the plausibility of the denied claim when the plausibility of the denying claim goes up (or down).

Plausibility Management

Plausibility Management is a special case of Dependency Management. It is responsible for maintaining consistency among the plausibilities of related

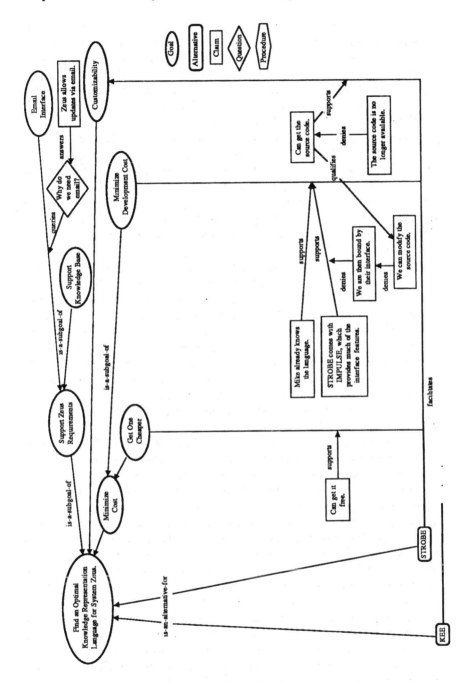

Figure 9. The example decision graph with Symbolics chosen as the hardware platform.

claims. Suppose, in figure 7, we want to know how good STROBE is overall, given the arguments produced so far. In DRL, the overall evaluation of an alternative is the plausibility of the `Is-An-Alternative-For` relation between the alternative and the top level goal (that is, the decision problem). This plausibility is in turn a function of the plausibility of the `Facilitates` relations between the alternative and the associated subgoals as well as a function of the importance of these goals. The plausibility of a claim, in particular a `Facilitates` relation, is a function of the plausibility of the claims that support, deny, or qualify it, as well as the claims answering a question influencing the claim. Hence, to see how good STROBE is as an alternative, we need to propagate plausibilities across the links and merge them into one. This merging should not only depend on the component plausibilities but also on the type of link that they have been propagated across. Plausibility Management is responsible for such propagation and merging of the plausibilities.

Going back to our example, evaluating STROBE overall requires, among other things, knowing how good STROBE is with respect to the goal of Minimize Development Cost—that is, the plausibility of the `Facilitates` relation between the alternative, STROBE, and the goal, Minimize Development Cost. This knowledge in turn requires knowing the plausibility of the claims supporting, refuting, and qualifying the `Facilitates` claim. Each claim has *a prior* plausibility initially given by its author, reflecting the measure of how confident she is about the claim. The plausibility of a claim is a function of this *a priori* plausibility and the plausibilities of the claims that are related to it via one of the relations such as `Supports`, `Denies`, and `Qualifies`. When we view a claim as a hypothesis and the supporting or denying claims as pieces of evidence, the problem of computing the plausibility of a claim is the classical problem in belief management. And there are many existing theories of confirmation, such as Bayesian or Dempster-Shafer's which have their own requirements, such as independence or exhaustiveness assumptions.

Rather than being committed to a particular theory or proposing a new confirmation theory, SIBYL provides an interface for any confirmation theory and lets the user choose one that suits her best. Such an interface requires the following information: the merging procedure, the arguments the procedure takes, and the information about the way that the pieces of evidence are related to one another. The system provides some of the well-known procedures such as Bayes or Dempster-Shafer so that the user can choose one of them. However, she can also write her own procedure. Furthermore, because SIBYL allows the user to specify a merging procedure for a claim, she can specify one procedure as the default globally, yet locally override this procedure by specifying a different one for a given claim or a type of claim.

There are two kinds of knowledge that a confirmation procedure needs

at each step. One is the plausibility values of the component claims that
are being merged. In the case of Dempster-Shafer, each piece of evidence (a
claim C) needs to supply an information pair, (Belief(C), Plausibility(C)).
In one version of the Bayesian procedure [Duda *et al.* 1979], each claim
needs to supply $Pr(C)$, and each relational claim that links two claims,
C1 and C2, needs to supply a pair $(Pr(C2|C1), Pr(C2|\neg C1))$. The pa-
rameters that the chosen procedure needs as input is to be found in the
Plausibility attribute of the claims involved. Thus, if the user is supplying
her own procedure, then she needs to ensure that the Plausibility attribute
of claims supply appropriate arguments for the procedure. The other kind
of information that a procedure needs is how the component claims are
related—for example, whether they are independent, mutually exclusive,
and/or conjunctive. As discussed above, this knowledge is contained in
the Member Relationship attribute of the group object which groups the
claims related to a given claim.

Once we compute the plausibility of all the Facilitates relations
between STROBE and all of the goals, we need to propagate them across
the Is-A-Subgoal-Of relations and merge them properly to produce the
overall evaluation of STROBE. Given that G2 and G3 are subgoals of G1,
that we have the evaluation measures of STROBE with respect to G2 and G3,
and that we have the importance measures for G2 and G3, how should they
be reflected in the evaluation of STROBE with respect to G1? For example,
what is the evaluation of STROBE with respect to "Minimize Cost" when
we have computed its evaluations with respect to the subgoals, "Get One
Cheaper" and "Minimize Development Cost"?

The answer to the above question requires a careful analysis of the
relations that can hold among goals. The Is-A-Subgoal-Of relation is
not sufficient to capture these relations. For example, subgoals can be
independent or have tradeoffs; they may exhaust their parent goal; or they
can be mutually exclusive or overlapping. Also, subgoals may interact in
various ways, as planning research has discovered [Sussman 1975; Sacerdoti
1977; Chapman 1985]. How the evaluation measures propagate and merge
across the goals will depend on the kinds of relations that hold among
them. We are still working out the taxonomy of these relations, based on
Quinlan's work [1983]. Depending on what kind of relation holds among
the subgoals, we may be able to use a simple algorithm such as the weighted
average of the plausibilities by the importance. Again, rather than being
committed to a particular algorithm we provide an interface for a merging
procedure so that the user has control over how the merging should be
done.

Another issue that we have not yet resolved satisfactorily is how to
represent and reflect the degree of consensus. If more users agree with
a claim, the plausibility of that claim should go up. On the other hand,
the mere number of users should not be an indication of the plausibility

because, for instance, users might not endorse a claim even when they agree with it, judging it to be obvious. Hence, the number of users who happen to endorse a claim explicitly is somewhat accidental. In the present version of SIBYL, when a user makes a claim, she is associated with the claim as its creator. Then, if users want to express approval of the claim, they do so by associating themselves with the claim as its co-creators. This scheme allows the decision maker to assign plausibility to the claim by considering not only the number but also other factors such as the credibility and the expertise of the users associated with the claim. We are not completely satisfied with this scheme, and we would like to find one that places less burden on the decision maker. We plan to find a better measure of consensus by studying other work, for example, Lowe [1986].

Viewpoint Management

Viewpoint Management is responsible for creating, storing, retrieving, mapping, and merging Viewpoints. A Viewpoint is an object that represents a collection of objects that share certain assumptions. Multiple Viewpoints on a decision record represent multiple perspectives on the given decision problem. Figure 10 shows a viewpoint which evaluates alternatives without considering a particular goal. The importance of the goal of getting a cheaper language (and its subgoals if there were any) has been set to null so that it no longer shows; nor do the the claims that were relevant to these goals.

There are at least five types of cases where we want to create multiple Viewpoints in SIBYL. We need viewpoints with:

- Different assignments of importance to goals.
- Different assignments of plausibilities to claims.
- Different subset of objects such as goals and alternatives.
- Different, hypothetical, answers to a question.
- Objects at different time points.

The first two cases are obvious. They are needed when we want to see what happens if we place different weights on goals or claims. A typical example of the third case is found when one wants to consider only goals or claims whose importance or plausibility measure is beyond certain threshold. Another example, mentioned earlier, is the one where all the goals of minimizing cost have been deactivated. In the fourth case, a viewpoint corresponds to a state in a truth-maintenance system. When faced with uncertainty, one makes different assumptions and pursues their consequences from different viewpoints. In the fifth case, Viewpoints provide a version mechanism. One should be able to freeze the states into viewpoints at different times so that one can see the way that the decision making unfolded at a later time, or even revert back to a previous viewpoint if necessary.

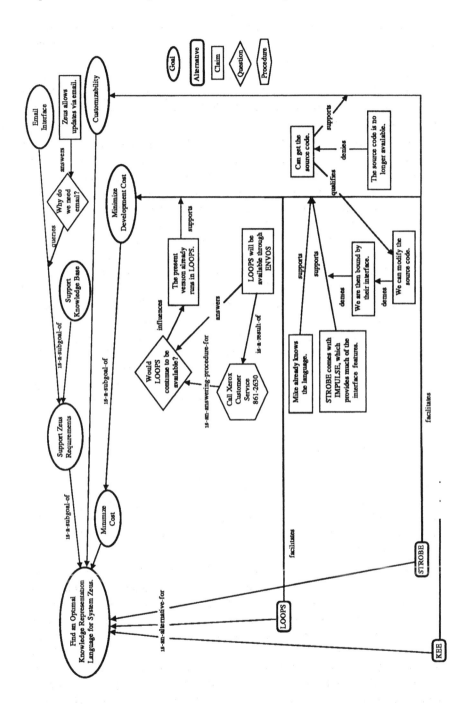

Figure 10. A viewpoint not considering the goal, "Get One Cheaper."

Viewpoints are first-class objects in DRL. As such, they can appear as alternatives in a meta-decision problem such as whether we should stop exploring additional alternatives. Also, Viewpoints can be related to one another in more ways than chronologically. The following relations have not yet made their way into DRL, but they will in the future: `Is-A-Next-Version-Of, Elaborates, Restricts, Has-Different-Importance, Has-Different-Plausibilities`.

It is also important to be able to establish mappings between objects in different viewpoints. Such mappings would show how the problem representation has evolved in the course of a decision making process. For example, a claim may differentiate into more specific claims; or several alternatives may be merged into one if their differences prove unimportant for a given purpose. We would represent this evolution as mapping between viewpoints representing different time slices. It is also useful to be able to merge viewpoints. For example, if the marketing group and the design group were both evaluating alternatives for a computer environment, it is natural that they make their evaluations within their own viewpoints and then later merge these viewpoints for an overall evaluation. We are still working out this aspect of Viewpoint Management. Relevant literature includes: studies on view and schema integrations in database research [Battini *et al.* 1986; Lee & Malone 1988], work on versions [Katz *et al.* 1984; Goldstein & Bobrow 1981; Bobrow *et al.* 1987], and work on viewpoints [Attardi 1981; Barber 1982; Kornfeld 1982]. We would like to incorporate some of these ideas in our next version of Viewpoint Management.

Precedent Management

Precedent Management is responsible for indexing past decisions and retrieving ones that are useful for the current decision problem. Once they are retrieved, the precedent manager extracts from them the pieces of the knowledge that are relevant for the present problem and places them in the present decision graph.

SIBYL uses goals to index past decisions. Two decision problems are judged to be similar and potentially useful to the extent that they share goals. Using goals as the index also allows the system to determine which parts of the retrieved decision graph are actually relevant. It is those objects—the claims and the alternatives—that are linked to the shared goals and their subgoals. We can, so to speak, lift out the shared goals and the subgoals and take with them all the objects that are linked to them. We place this structure in the current decision graph by overlaying the shared goals. Figure 11 shows a new decision problem, to which the shared goals have been overlaid. Using precedents this way is also useful because

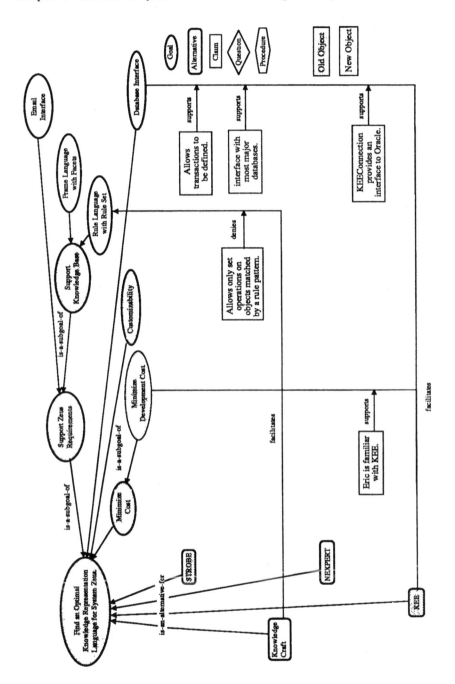

Figure 11. The example decision graph augmented by knowledge from a past decision.

it allows the new decision maker to become aware of other alternatives or of different ways of achieving a given goal.

The following problems are still to be solved. First, some of the goals and claims that have been transferred in this way would not be relevant after all, due to context dependency. What is represented in a decision graph usually leaves out many things that were assumed in that context. For example, the claim, "Eric already knows the language" was a supporting claim for the claim that KEE facilitates minimize development time, because in that context Eric was the person who was going to develop the system. This fact is probably not true any more, especially if it is a different group that is retrieving this decision graph. The present solution is to let users filter out irrelevant facts from the ones that the system suggests. We will, undoubtedly, try to improve the algorithm for determining the relevance so that the user has less to filter out. However, we do not think that such an algorithm can entirely eliminate the need for the user to check the result without, at the same time, requiring her to supply details that would otherwise be unnecessary.

Another problem is to determine which goals are shared across decision problems. Certainly, matching names would not be appropriate as names can be arbitrary strings. A solution is to provide a taxonomy of goals, from which users can create instances. Then, we would have a basis for judging the similarity among goals. We have partially developed such a taxonomy, but more work needs to be done. Yet another problem is that of credit assignment. One would not want to make a decision based on the knowledge used for past decisions that turned out to be disasters. Nevertheless, some pieces of the knowledge in such decisions may still be useful. We would like to associate the failure or the success of a decision with the pieces of knowledge responsible for the result. The present solution in SIBYL is to represent this information in the following attributes of decision problem object: Outcome and Responsible-Objects. This way, SIBYL at least allows users to represent and examine the needed information. However, at the moment, these attributes have no computational significance. We want to explore ways to make these attributes computationally useful. Obviously, there is room here for applying the ideas from learning and case-based reasoning research [Michalski et al. 1986; Kolodner 1988; Winston 1986]. It would be a challenge to incorporate some of the ideas from this research into Precedent Management.

Related Work

Studies on decision making abound. There are quantitative decision theories, psychological studies on human decision making, organizational theories, political decision making, decision support systems, and studies on qualitative decision making. Many of these studies are relevant to the work described in this chapter. For example, a qualitative decision management system like SIBYL can be viewed as complementing classical maximum expected utility theory. In the classical decision theory, only the alternatives and possible consequences are represented explicitly; goals are merged into the utility function and the arguments disappear into the probability distribution over the consequences. In this sense, a qualitative decision management system provides a means for retrieving and, when necessary, changing the intuitions behind the utility and probability assignments. However, it should be clear that a qualitative decision management system and the classical decision theory are quite different in both their goals and structures.

In the rest of this section, we discuss the relation of SIBYL to various computational studies on qualitative decision making because they share the goal of a qualitative decision management system; namely the representation and management of the qualitative aspects of decision making processes. This category includes work such as Toulmin's [1969] theory of arguments, gIBIS [Conklin & Begeman 1988], and Doyle's [1980] model of deliberation. We include Toulmin's work, though it is not computational, because his work has been adopted widely as a model of argument in many computational studies [Birnbaum *et al.* 1980; Lowe 1986] as well as in other fields. Below, we give a brief comparison of these studies to SIBYL.

A British philosopher, Stephen Toulmin, proposed a model of argument in 1969. Figure 12 shows Toulmin's model and an example. A *Claim* is the main assertion being made; a *Datum* supports the claim; a *Warrant* is the basis on which the Datum is said to support the claim, a *Backing*, in turn, supports the Warrant; a *Qualifier* qualifies the extent to which the Datum supports the claim, and a *Rebuttal* gives a reason for the Qualifier.

We decided not to use Toulmin's model for representing arguments because Toulmin's object types do not support the uniformity and extendibility of representation. For example, Toulmin's model allows a Claim to be backed up, qualified, or rebutted but not a Datum or a Warrant. It is not clear what to do if one wants to argue about the validity of a Datum or disagrees with a Warrant. Also, one can deny an existing claim only in a round-about way by supporting its negation. One can qualify a claim, but it is not clear whether that qualification is due to some uncertainty over situations, less than perfect plausibility of data, or the weak relation between data and claim.

gIBIS (graphical Issue Based Information System) is a "hypertext tool for exploratory policy discussion" that is being developed by Conklin and Begeman [1988]. The goal of gIBIS is to capture the design rationale: the design problems, alternative resolutions, tradeoff analysis among these alternatives, and the tentative and firm commitments that were made during

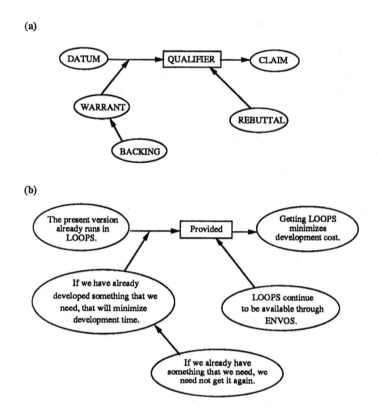

Figure 12. (a) Toulmin's model of argument and (b) an example.

the decision making process. gIBIS is similar to SIBYL in its goal and also in that it is a system designed to *support* human decision making.

The difference between SIBYL and gIBIS comes from the structures provided in achieving this goal and the types of services they provide using these structures . Figure 13 shows the ontology of gIBIS. *Issue* corresponds to Decision Problem in DRL, *Position* corresponds to Alternative, and *Argument* corresponds to Claim. Notably lacking in gIBIS is the explicit representation of Goal. In Lee [1989a], we point out the importance of making goals explicit: they allow modular representation of arguments; they force users to articulate evaluation criteria; they let users argue about them, and they provide a basis for precedent management as well as multiple viewpoints. Another general difference between gIBIS and SIBYL is that gIBIS is mainly a hypertext system whose services focus on the *presentation* of objects in such a way that it is easy to enter arguments and easy to see the structure of what has been represented. On the other hand, SIBYL is

(a)

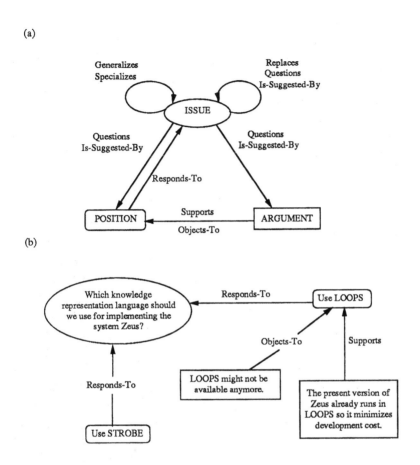

Figure 13. (a) The gIBIS model of argument and (b) an example.

a knowledge-based system whose services focus on the *management of the dependency* among the objects.

Doyle [1980] proposed "a model for deliberation, action, and introspection." It is worth relating the model underlying SIBYL to his model because his is the most comprehensive and detailed model of defeasible reasoning that we have seen so far, that is, where the assertions are nonmonotonic. As Doyle points out, this provides an important framework for dialectical reasoning, that is, reasoning based on arguments, Doyle's theory is very comprehensive and we could not do it justice here. However, Doyle's work is described in Lee [1989a]. Here, we note that the goal of Doyle's model is to control or direct the reasoning and actions of a *computer program* by explicitly representing and justifying the reasoning process itself. SIBYL has a less ambitious goal than Doyle's. SIBYL provides a model for decision making sufficient to support *users* making decisions. Furthermore, the scope of SIBYL is restricted to the kind of decision making which involves evaluating well-defined alternatives against a set of goals. That restriction in scope lets SIBYL provide task-specific constructs such as the Facilitates relations, which allows more modular representation of the arguments evaluating alternatives, as well as allowing one to argue about such relations.

We would like to view SIBYL as a system that is compatible with Doyle's model but is non-committal about some of its aspects. Thus, the model underlying DRL is not as explicit as Doyle's, however, it does not have to do things like making assertions, the way Doyle prescribed. What SIBYL requires is that claims are produced and linked to other claims through the relations that DRL provides. The claims could have been produced in a manner consistent with Doyle's model or otherwise. Also, one may decide, for computational tractability, not to keep justifications for every step in the reasoning process. In that sense, SIBYL can be viewed as a higher level interface to something like Doyle's model, but not bound to it.

Future Work

We mentioned above many of the specific problems that we are still tackling. Here, we discuss more general topics of future research.

Earlier we discussed four major types of services—dependency, plausibility, viewpoint, and precedent management. As we apply SIBYL to more complex decision making processes, we expect to identify more types of services that prove useful. For example, the importance of risk management has been pointed out by Boehm [1988]. Risk management would be responsible for identifying the significant sources of risk, evaluating the risk associated with each alternative, and helping users to allocate the resources based on the evaluation. Given that risk is the uncertainty of achieving important goals and that uncertainty is represented in DRL by an Influences relation, SIBYL can help identify risks by finding, for example, the important goals whose associated Facilitates relation is influenced by a Question, directly or indirectly. The technique used to resolve the risk can also be represented as a Procedure and linked to the Question through Is-An-Answering-Procedure-For so that the knowledge can be used by others later. We plan to explore this and further potential types of services that are useful in complex decision making.

We also plan to study the process of qualitative decision management as a computational problem solving paradigm based on arguments. So far, we have discussed SIBYL in the context of providing support for human decision making. However, the importance of human-like decision analysis—

in the sense of involving arguments, evaluating alternatives, compromising and negotiating—is also important in automated reasoning. Hewitt [1986], for example, pointed out the features of open systems, such as incompleteness and inconsistency, which makes a purely deductive approach unrealistic. What happens in real systems and what needs to be included in artificial systems is the complexity of the dialectical processes involving the interactions among agents with different goals, shared resources, and different expertise. A Qualitative Decision Management System is an attempt to identify and articulate the objects and the processes involved in such decision making processes. As such, we feel that there is no reason why the same language and the same services could not be used in making decisions by computational agents, provided that the attribute values of the objects are themselves computational objects. Doing this requires much more work, including a careful analysis of the relation between SIBYL and those in other systems such as Doyle's.

References

Attardi, G., and M. Simi [1981], "Semantics of Inheritance and Attributions in the Description System Omega," *Proceedings of IJCAI 81*, Vancouver, BC, Canada.

Barber, G. [1982], "Office Semantics," Ph.D. Thesis, Artificial Intelligence Laboratory, Massachusetts Institute of Technology, Cambridge, MA.

Battini, C., M. Lenzerini, and S. B. Navathe [1986], "A Comparative Analysis of Methodologies for Database Schema Integration," *ACM Computing Survey* vol. 18, no. 4, pp. 323-364.

Birnbaum, L., M. Flowers, R. McGuire [1980], "Towards an AI Model of Argumentation," in *Proceedings of AAAI*, pp. 313-315, Stanford, CA.

Bobrow, D., D. Fogelsong, and M. Miller [1987], "Definition Groups: Making Sources into First-Class Objects," in [Wegner & Shriver 1987] pp. 129-146.

An extended version of this chapter can be found in Lee [1989a].

I would like to thank Patrick Winston, Rick Lathrop, Jonathan Amsterdam, Gary Borchardt, and others in the learning group at the Artificial Intelligence Laboratory for keeping my enthusiasm alive as well as many useful comments. The author is also affiliated with the Center for Coordination Science at MIT Sloan School of Management. I appreciate the comments and the encouragements from those at the Center—especially Thomas Malone, Kevin Crowston, and most of all Kum-Yew Lai. Many others have contributed in various ways to the work reported here: Franklyn Turbak, Paul Resnick, John Mallery, Carl Hewitt, Marvin Minsky, David McAllester, and Jon Doyle from the Artificial Intelligence Laboratory; Frank Manola, Mike Brodie, and the members of the Intelligent Database Management Systems group at GTE Labs. I thank them all.

Boehm, B. W. [1988], "A Spiral Model of Software Development and Enhancement," *IEEE Computer*, pp. 61-72.

Brodie, M., and J. Mylopoulos [1986], *On Knowledge Base Management Systems*, Springer-Verlag, New York.

Chapman, D. [1985], "Planning for Conjunctive Goals," Report AI-TR-802, Artificial Intelligence Laboratory, Massachusetts Institute of Technology, Cambridge, MA.

Conklin, J., and M. L. Begeman [1988], "gIBIS: A Hypertext Tool for Exploratory Policy Discussion," *Proceedings of Computer Supported Cooperative Work*, Portland, Oregon.

Doyle, J. [1980], *A Model for Deliberation, Action, and Introspection*, Report AI-TR-581, Artificial Intelligence Laboratory, Massachusetts Institute of Technology, Cambridge, MA.

Duda, R. O., P. E. Hart, and N. Nilsson [1976], "Subjective Bayesian Methods for Rule-based Inference System," in [Webber & Nilsson 1981], pp. 192-199.

Goldstein, I., and D. Bobrow [1981], "Layered Networks as a Tool for Software Development," *Proceedings of 7th IJCAI*, University of British Columbia, Vancouver, BC, Canada, pp. 913-919.

Hewitt, C. [1986], "Offices Are Open Systems," *Proceedings of ACM Conference on Office Information Systems*, Providence, RI.

Katz, R. H., M. Anwarrudin, and E. Chang [1986], "Organizaing a Design Data/-base Across Time," in [Brodie & Mylopoulos 1986].

Kolodner, J. [1988], (Editor) *Proceedings of a Workship on Case-Based Reasoning*, Clearwater Beach, FL.

Kornfeld, B. [1982], "Concepts in Parallel Problem Solving," Ph.D. Thesis Artificial Intelligence Laboratory, Massachusetts Institute of Technology, Cambridge, MA.

Lai, K., T. Malone, and K. C. Yu [1989], "Object Lens: A Spreadsheet for Cooperative Work," *ACM Transaction on Office Information Systems*, vol. 6, pp. 332-353.

Lee, J. [1989a], "A Qualitative Decision Management System: An Overview," Report AIM–1191, Artificial Intelligence Laboratory, Massachusetts Institute of Technology, Cambridge, MA (to appear).

Lee, J. [1989b], "Task-Embedded Knowledge Acquisition through a Task-Specific Language," *Proceedings of IJCAI Knowledge Acquisition Workshop*, Detroit, MI.

Lee, J., and T. Malone [1988], "How Can Groups Communicate When They Use Different Languages?" *Proceedings of ACM Conference on Office Information Systems*, Palo Alto, CA.

Lowe, D. [1986], "SYNVIEW: The Design of a System for Cooperative Structuring of Information," *Proceedings of Computer Supported Cooperative Work*, Austin, TX.

Malone, T., K. C. Yu, and J. Lee [1989], "What Good Are Semi-Structured Objects?" Sloan Working Paper, 3064-89-MS, Massachusetts Institute of Technology, Cambridge, MA.

Michalski, R. S., J. G. Carbonell, and T. Mitchell (editors) [1986], *Machine Learning* vol 2, Morgan Kauffman, Los Altos, CA.

Quinlan, J. R. [1983], "Inferno: A Cautious Appropach to Uncertain Inference," *The Computer Journal*, vol. 26, no. 3, pp. 255-267.

Sacerdoti, E. [1975], *A Structure for Plans and Behavior*, American Elsevier, New York, NY.

Shafer, G. [1976], *A Mathematical Theory of Evidence*, Princeton University Press, Princeton, NJ.

Shafer, G., and Logan, R. [1987], "Implementing Dempster's rule for hierarchical Evidence," *Artificial Intelligence* vol. 33, no. 3, pp. 271-98

Shriver, B., and P. Wegner [1987], *Research Directions in Object-Oriented Programming*, MIT Press, Cambridge, MA.

Sussman, G. [1975], *A Computational Model of Skill Acquisition*, American Elsevier, New York, NY.

Toulmin, S. [1969], *The Uses of Argument*, Cambridge University Press, Cambridge, England.

Webber, B., and N. Nilsson [1981], *Readings in Artificial Intelligence,* Tioga Publishing Company, Palo Alto, CA.

Winston, P. [1986], "Learning by Augmenting Rules and Accumulating Censors," in Michalski *et al.* [1986].

6

Most language theorists study one or two stimulating and provocative problems without concern for the practical problems that have to be solved before computers can read text usefully. Katz stands apart from such theorists, however, because his objective is to build a practical system that reads sentences, indexes the facts they convey, and retrieves those facts when asked. Accordingly, his work on his START system is always directed at solving problems so as to produce the maximal improvement in practical language competence.

In this chapter, Katz explains some of his solutions. In particular, he shows how START handles noun-phrase referents; he shows how START indexes and retrieves using subject-relation-object triples, decorated with what he calls a history; he shows how START handles alternate ways of saying essentially the same thing by using semantic rules; and he shows how START assigns truth values—true, false or unknown—to deeply embedded phrases.

Bringing these solutions together makes it possible for START to handle an extraordinary range of language. In one experiment, START digests, indexes, and retrieves material of the sort used in Graduate Record Examinations to test reading skills. In another experiment, START read text from space publications and other sources about the Voyager 2 mission and then answered questions as they were posed by journalists who were at the Jet Propulsion Laboratory during the 1989 Neptune encounter.

Using English for Indexing and Retrieving

Boris Katz

This chapter describes a natural language system START (SynTactic Analysis using Reversible Transformations). The system analyzes English text and automatically transforms it into an appropriate representation, the *knowledge base*, which incorporates the information found in the text. The user gains access to information stored in the knowledge base by querying it in English. The system analyzes the query and decides through a matching process what information in the knowledge base is relevant to the question. Then it retrieves this information and formulates its response also in English.

Researchers at MIT, Stanford University, and the Jet Propulsion Laboratory, have used the START system for creating knowledge bases from English text and for information retrieval in domains as diverse as medicine, politics, space, vision, and common sense physics. (See, for instance, Winston [1982, 1984], Winston *et al.* [1983], Doyle [1984], Katz and Brooks [1987], McLaughlin [1987, 1988], and Frank, Katz and Palmucci [1989]). In the last few sections of this chapter we present examples of actual dialogs with START in several different domains.

Understanding Language

Before we provide a detailed description of the START system we should make clear what we mean by *understanding*. What does it mean for a machine to understand language?

Let us consider a situation where a mother gives instructions or tells a story to her daughter Jill. Hopefully, this child has "stored" the new information/knowledge in her memory. In this case, we say that the child understood her mother.

How can this be verified?

- If Jill heard a story, her mother can ask questions relevant to the story. If after searching her memory, Jill is able to utilize the acquired knowledge and answer the questions correctly, then she understood the story.

- Suppose instead of a story Jill heard a set of instructions for a task she is supposed to perform. If Jill is able to retrieve the knowledge given by the instructions and accomplish the task, then she understood the instructions.

We will use these two criteria as "Turing tests" to help us define what it means for a computer to understand English:

1 English text is typed into the computer and on the basis of this text a knowledge base is created. The user queries the knowledge base in English. If the computer's responses are correct, then we can say the computer understood the text.

2 A sequence of English commands or instructions is entered in the computer. If the computer carries out appropriate actions in response to them, then we can say the computer understood the instructions.

Remarkably, START passes these two tests in a variety of situations although it possesses no explicit theory of meaning.

As suggested by these two criteria, knowledge bases created by START can either be used in question-answering situations or they can provide input data for other computer systems. The START knowledge base is employed by both the language understanding and generating modules. These two modules also share the same Grammar (see Katz [1980] and Katz and Winston [1982] for a detailed description of the Grammar). Moreover, most of the definitions, techniques, and constructs of START may be discussed in both the understanding and the generating mode. As it seems appropriate, we will use either of the two modes to explain how START works.

Kernel Sentences

Most English sentences break up into units that we will call *kernel sentences*. For instance, the following aphorism can be broken up into five smaller units:

(1) If the orator wants to persuade people, he must speak the things people wish to hear.

(S1) The orator$_i$ wants S2.

(S2) The orator$_i$ persuades people.

(S3) He$_i$ must speak the things$_j$.

(S4) People$_k$ wish S5.

(S5) People$_k$ hear the things$_j$.

One of the goals of the START system is to identify these smaller units and to determine how they assemble together in a larger sentence.

Before we can formally define kernel sentences let us examine how START represents sentence elements internally. The system uses three types of building blocks for constructing a kernel sentence, the *noun-template*, the *verb-template*, and the *adverb-template*:

noun-template (NT) = [prep det mod adj* noun]

verb-template (VT) = [aux1 neg aux2 aux3 verb]

adverb-template (AT) = [mod adverb]

Here *prep, det, mod, adj, aux,* and *neg* are, respectively, abbreviations for preposition, determiner, modifier, adjective, auxiliary, and negation. The superscript * indicates that a string of one or more symbols or their conjunction is allowed. All the elements in the templates are optional. Noun phrases and prepositional phrases in English can be constructed by reading off the slot values in instantiated noun-templates. In a similar way, verbs and their auxiliaries can be obtained by reading off slot values in verb-templates. For example, the well-formed instantiation of the noun-template, NT = [(noun **Mary**)], where most elements of the NT are omitted, produces a simple noun phrase *Mary*, but the same template with all its elements filled,

NT = [(prep **after**) (det **a**) (mod **very**) (adj **long**) (noun **flight**)]

generates a full-fledged prepositional phrase *after a very long flight* . Similarly, the verb-template may produce either one main verb, *launch*, when using VT = [(verb **launch**)], or a more complex string like *could have been watching*:

VT = [(aux1 **could**) (aux2 **have**) (aux3 **been**) (verb **watching**)]

Templates can be combined to represent a conjunction, for instance, *Jessica, Gabriella and Miriam*.

Note that in our grammar the noun-templates are used for constructing both noun phrases and prepositional phrases. The existence of languages with nominal case marking, like Russian, indicates that the idea of having a prepositional element within a noun-template is not as far-fetched as it may seem (see Katz and Winston [1982])

Now let us define a *kernel structure* as the following sequence of templates:

(2) $NT^{initial}$ $NT^{subject}$ VT NT^{object} NT^{final}

Here $NT^{subject}$ and NT^{object} are noun-templates that represent the subject and the object in the sentence; $NT^{initial}$ and NT^{final} represent its initial and final prepositional phrases; VT is a verb-template.

We should point out that most of the elements in the kernel structure are optional. Also for simplicity the adverb-templates have been omitted although they may appear in (2) in a number of places. In addition, transformational rules, introduced in the section on Transformations, are allowed to modify the kernel structure and change the order of templates.

A *kernel sentence* is an English sentence obtained by reading off from left to right all slot values in all templates in (2). Note that the kernel structure contains only one verb-template and can therefore represent only a limited class of English sentences, without any embedded clauses. However, as we will see in subsequent sections, kernel structures can be recursively combined in several different ways to account for a large variety of English sentences, including complex sentences involving embedding.

We define *parsing* as a process of syntactic analysis which, given an English kernel sentence as input, produces the corresponding kernel structure as output.[1] For example, given the sentence below:

(3) After the launch the commander will give additional instructions to the astronaut.

The *parser* produces the following instantiated kernel structure where the order of templates follows that of (2):

$NT^{initial}$	[(prep **after**) (det **the**) (noun **launch**)]
$NT^{subject}$	[(det **the**) (noun **commander**)]
VT	[(aux1 **will**) (verb **give**)]
NT^{object}	[(adj **additional**) (noun **instructions**)]
NT^{final}	[(prep **to**) (det **the**) (noun **astronaut**)]

Many natural language understanding systems restrict themselves to the parsing process just defined and stop there. However, this is clearly not enough to satisfy our definition of understanding. It is not enough to teach the computer to recognize different syntactic categories and fill in the slots in the kernel structure. Our goal is to enable the computer to use the knowledge encoded in the kernel structure; in other words, to *index* and *retrieve* this knowledge efficiently.

From Kernel Structures to T-expressions

Recall that in order to understand her mother, Jill had to perform two important operations. When listening to the story, Jill had to store (or *index*) the new knowledge in her memory. When answering the questions,

---

[1]In the sections on Transformations and Relative Clauses this notion of parsing is extended to a wider class of English sentences. See also last sections of this chapter for examples from the "real world".

she had to search her memory and *retrieve* the knowledge. These two operations, indexing and retrieving, are crucial in our model of understanding language. In this section we will describe the indexing procedure of START. The retrieval task is carried out by a matching procedure described in the section on Questions.

Suppose we type the following English sentence on a computer terminal:

(4) Jane will meet Paul tomorrow.

and the parsing procedure constructs the appropriate kernel structure. Now, there are many things about this sentence that the computer should remember: that *Jane* is the subject of the sentence, *Paul* is the object, that *meet* is the relation between them. There is more to remember: the tense and the aspect of the sentence, its auxiliaries, its adverbs. Was this sentence embedded in a larger sentence? Does it have a relative clause? Was the verb in the active or passive form? We certainly want all this information about the sentence to be stored in the computer's memory. However, we also want to be able to retrieve this information efficiently.

We could store all these sentence features in one long list. This approach, however, would not account for the fact that some of the features in a sentence seem more salient than others. A simple list of features in sentence (4) would also fail to capture its structural affinity with the following two sentences:

(5) Yesterday Jane could have met Paul.

(6) Paul wasn't met by Jane.

And finally, this approach would turn the matching/retrieval task into a computational nightmare.

We could try to emphasize the hierarchical nature of the English sentence by using the kernel structure representation. However, because most elements of the kernel structure are optional, its shape is too unpredictable to allow the system to match the kernel structures efficiently.

Our system, START, rearranges the elements of the kernel structure by tying together the three most salient parameters of a sentence: the subject, the object, and the relation between them. These are combined into *ternary expressions (T-expressions)* of the form **<subject relation object>**. For example, sentence (4) will yield the *T*-expression

(7) **<Jane meet Paul>**

Note that the relation of this *T*-expression is the infinitive form of the main verb in the sentence.

Certain other parameters are used to create additional *T*-expressions in which prepositions and several special words serve as relations. The remaining parameters, adverbs and their position, tense, auxiliaries, voice, negation, *etc.*, are recorded in a representational structure called *history*. The history has a *page* pertaining to each sentence which yields the given

T-expression. When we index the T-expression in the knowledge base, we cross-reference its three components and attach the history H to it: **<subject relation object>**$_H$.

For example, suppose START is analyzing a text containing sentence (5) and later sentence (6). The system would produce the T-expression
(8)   **<Jane meet Paul>**$_H$
with a two-page history. One page would contain additional information about the first sentence, such as the fact that sentence (5) used perfective "have" and the modal "could", and that it starts with an adverb "yesterday". The second page would show the use of passive form and negation in sentence (6). One can thus think of a T-expression as a "digested summary" of the syntactic structure of a proposition and of its use within an English text.

The T-expression is the cornerstone of the representational hierarchy of the START system. It is the level of the hierarchy where several START modules meet. The understanding module analyzes English sentences and creates a set of T-expressions stored in the knowledge base. If a question is asked, the resulting T-expressions serve as a pattern used by the matching module to query the knowledge base. Given a set of T-expressions returned by the matcher, the generating module produces English text.

Referents for Noun Phrases

The subject and the object of T-expression **<Jane meet Paul>** are proper names which are taken directly from sentence (4). However, the process is more complex if, for example, the subject of a sentence is not a proper name but a complex noun phrase:
(9)   Jane's good friend from Boston met Paul.
In sentence (9) the system needs to establish the referent for the head noun, *friend*. The system has to come up with a *unique name* for this noun in case a different instance of *friend* appears later in the analyzed text. In order to do this, START computes the *name environment* E_1 for this occurrence of *friend*. We define E_1 as a list of adjectives (in this case, *good*), possessive nouns (*Jane's*), prepositional phrases (*from Boston*), etc. modifying that noun in the present sentence. Then START associates with this environment a unique name, say *friend-1*, which we will call a *referent*[2] for the noun *friend* in the environment E_1. The main T-expression for sentence (9) will therefore take the form **<friend-1 meet Paul>**.[3]

The analyzed noun, *friend*, its name environment E_1, and its referent, *friend-1* are then recorded in the computer's memory. This bookkeeping

---

[2]In calling a unique name a referent we deviate from standard usage, which reserves the term for an object in the world.

[3]The analysis of the subject noun-phrase in sentence (9) will produce three additional T-expressions (see the section on Relative Clauses).

gives the system the ability to compute efficiently the referent of a noun given its name environment. If, for instance, the same noun phrase,

(10) Jane's good friend from Boston

occurs again in a different sentence later in the text, then its name environment would coincide with E_1 and hence the same referent, *friend-1*, would be retrieved and utilized in the T-expressions constructed for this sentence.

Suppose now that START encounters a new sentence where the noun *friend* appears in a slightly different noun phrase like:

(11) Tracy's good friend from Pasadena.

The environment E_2 associated with the new noun phrase is different from E_1 and is not to be found in the computer memory. This means that there is no referent readily available for the noun *friend* in this sentence and the system needs to generate a new unique name, *friend-2*, to be associated with E_2.

START recursively employs the procedure just described to find a referent for *every* noun in the sentence. Thus, given the noun phrase

(12) The young woman's good friend from the big city.

the system first determines the referents of the nouns *woman* and *city*. Only after that, once the computation of its name environment becomes possible, does the head noun, *friend*, get its referent.[4]

Sometimes, however, the information in the name environment is not sufficient to find referents for noun phrases. For instance, if a noun phrase is modified by a relative clause, the entire knowledge base has to be consulted in order to determine the appropriate referent.

Transformational Rules

The standard kernel structure introduced earlier in this chapter,

(2) $NT^{initial} \; NT^{subject} \; VT \; NT^{object} \; NT^{final}$

allows the system to generate or parse only a limited variety of English sentences. To account for other kinds of sentences, START employs commutative *transformational rules* (see Chomsky [1957] and Katz [1980]). For instance, consider how the kernel sentence:

(13) The probe reached Venus.

is modified by several transformational rules, where each transformation is applied to the outcome of the previous one:

---

[4]In the remainder of this chapter, for reasons of simplicity, we will use the nouns themselves in T-expressions rather than their referents.

Transformation	Sentence
	Voyager discovered a new moon.
Question	Did Voyager discover a new moon?
Negation	Didn't Voyager discover a new moon?
Passive	Wasn't a new moon discovered by Voyager?
There Insertion	Wasn't there a new moon discovered by Voyager?

When the START system analyzes an English sentence, its goal is to recognize which transformations were applied. In some cases, for instance, *Negation*, START simply makes the appropriate additions to the histories of the resulting *T*-expressions. In other cases, the system must actually *reverse* the effect of the transformation.

START uses a set of commutative transformational rules (two transformations are said to commute if they can be applied in either order and both orderings produce the same result). The fact of their commutativity is proved in Katz [1980]. Apart from its theoretical interest, the commutativity of the transformations provides the system with considerable computational advantages because no attention needs to be paid to the ordering of the transformations or to the so-called interactions between them (compare with Akmajian and Heny [1975]).

All the examples of English sentences considered so far have been very simple. We can make them a little more complex by allowing simpler sentences to be embedded in larger sentences, as shown below:

(14) Jessica wanted the computer to print the message.

(15) For Miriam to ignore the request would anger Jessica.

The transformational rules responsible for sentence embedding form a special class called *connective transformations* (see Katz [1980]). Each connective transformation takes two kernel sentences as input; these correspond to the *matrix* clause and the *embedded* clause in the resulting English sentence. For example, sentence (14) above consists of a matrix clause, *Jessica wanted it*, and an embedded clause, *the computer printed the message*: We assume that one of the noun-templates in the kernel structure of the matrix clause always contains *it* as a *joining point* for gluing the two kernels together.

A connective transformation is fully determined by the values of three parameters, each referring to a position in the kernel structure of the embedded clause: *COMP, NP,* and *INFL*. A different set of values for these parameters results in a different final shape of the English sentence generated using connective transformations. The complementizer *COMP* introduces the embedded clause; the binary parameter *NP* indicates whether the subject of the matrix clause is coreferent with the subject of the embedded clause; the inflectional element *INFL* specifies how the verb in the embedded clause should be inflected. For instance, in sentence (14) the value of *COMP* is *null* (while in (15) its value is *for*) and the value of *INFL* is *to*. The value of the parameter *NP* is set to indicate that the subject of the matrix clause, *Jessica*, is different from the subject of the embedded clause, *the computer*.

The positions of these three parameters in the kernel structure and their actual values are described in Katz [1980]. Table 1 shows examples illustrating the application of several different connective transformations.[5]

Matrix clause	Embedded clause	Resulting Sentence
It angered Kirk	The computer ignored the message	That the computer ignored the message angered Kirk
Spock suggests it	McCoy is silent	Spock suggests that McCoy be silent
Spock watched it	Kirk read the message	Spock watched Kirk read the message
Kirk asked it	The computer repeated the message	Kirk asked the computer to repeat the message
Spock claims it	Spock has written the message	Spock claims to have written the message
It shocked Kirk	Spock ignored the command	Spock's ignoring the command shocked Kirk
Spock saw it	McCoy read the message	Spock saw McCoy reading the message
It angered Kirk	Kirk read the message	Reading the message angered Kirk
Kirk knew it	The computer ignored the message	Kirk knew whether the computer ignored the message

Table 1. Examples of applications of connective transformations.

Note that in each example the element *it* in the matrix clause indicates the location where the embedded clause is inserted. The embedded clause is adjusted according to the values of the parameters *COMP, NP*, and *INFL*.

The main verb of the matrix clause plays an important role in both the execution and recognition of connective transformations. It determines the shape which its embedded clause may take and specifies the kinds of connective transformations that may be applied in each particular case. It is imperative, therefore, that the dictionary entry for any verb which may appear in a matrix clause (that is, can take a sentential complement) contain a list of permissible connective transformations.

---

[5]Because this family of transformations is completely defined by the values of parameters *COMP, NP*, and *INFL*, it can be considered a single *connective transformation* whose surface manifestation has several different forms depending on the values of these parameters.

Now let us examine how START analyzes embedded sentences. Recall that earlier we defined *parsing* only for kernel sentences. Connective transformations allow us to extend this notion to a wider class of English sentences which includes embedded sentences. The process consists of four steps:

1   The system determines the connective transformation involved.

2   The system reverses the connective transformation and splits the sentence into kernel sentences.

3   The system parses each kernel sentence separately and produces kernel structures.

4   The indexing procedure utilizes the lexical material provided by kernel structures to construct and index corresponding T-expressions.

In order to handle embedded sentences, START allows any T-expression to take another T-expression as its subject or object. Thus, sentence (16) leads to *right embedding*:

(16) Jessica wanted the computer to print the message.

(17) **<Jessica want <computer print message>>**

while sentence (18) leads to *left embedding*:

(18) For Miriam to ignore the request would anger Jessica.

(19) **<<Miriam ignore request> anger Jessica>**

Connective transformations may be recursively applied without any restrictions on the depth of embedding. This means that START can analyze and generate sentences with arbitrarily complex embedded structures.

Complex Noun Phrases and Relative Clauses

We have seen how START analyzes a sentence and produces a T-expression which "summarizes" the syntactic structure of the sentence. In this section we examine sentences with complex noun phrases and show how such noun phrases result in the construction of several additional T-expressions. Consider sentence (20):

(20) Jane's good friend from Boston met Paul.

A complex noun phrase in English consists of three components: the *head* around which the other components cluster, the *premodification* which includes all the adjectives and possessive nouns placed before the head, and the *postmodification* which includes all the items placed after the head, including prepositional phrases, non-finite clauses, and relative clauses (see Quirk *et al.* [1985]). In our example, the head of the noun phrase, *friend*, is premodified by *Jane's* and *good* and postmodified by the prepositional phrase *from Boston*. As a result, along with the main T-expression, **<friend-1 meet Paul>**, the system will construct three additional T-expressions: **<friend-1 is good>**, **<friend-1 related-to Jane>**, and **<friend-1**

from Boston>. In fact, every adjective or possessive noun in the sentence, as well as every prepositional phrase or relative clause, will cause new T-expressions to be built and stored in the knowledge base.

START can handle different types of relative clauses:

(21) The girl *who wants to become an astronaut* is young.

(22) The planet *which Voyager photographed yesterday* was shrouded in clouds.

(23) The man *we admire* walked on the Moon.

(24) The planet *the spacecraft flew behind* has a strong magnetic field.

(25) The satellite *to which the antennas were pointing* had an impact crater.

(26) The spacecraft *orbiting the Earth* photographed its surface.

(27) The satellite *launched by NASA* handles telecommunications.

(28) The space shuttle *whose protective tiles were damaged* underwent repairs.

These examples show sentences with full relative clauses, as in (21) or (25), with reduced relative clauses (26, 27), with subject relative pronoun (21), object relative pronoun (22), or even without it (23). The relative pronoun may be governed by case (28) or by a preposition (25). The preposition may precede (25) or follow (24) its complement. Let us analyze sentence (22), which involves a full relative clause with an object relative pronoun. First, the system has to find the relative clause boundaries and identify the location of the *gap* (denoted by e) which is coreferent to the head noun phrase:

(29) The planet$_i$ [which Voyager photographed e_i yesterday] was shrouded in clouds.

Then the relative clause is "removed" from the sentence, the gap is filled with its antecedent and the modified clause is processed independently. As a result, sentence (22) will be split into the following two sentences:

(30) Voyager photographed the planet$_i$ yesterday.

(31) The planet$_i$ was shrouded in clouds.

To indicate that these two sentences go together in a relative clause relationship (compare with Woods [1985]), the history of the T-expression of main clause (31) is provided with a pointer to the T-expression of relative clause (30).

Relative clauses do not need to be simple kernel sentences (see example (21), for instance). In fact, any two sentences that may be analyzed by START, with arbitrarily complex embedded structures, can be combined into main and relative clauses of a larger sentence as long as they have a common noun phrase (see the GRE sample passage at the end of this chapter). Moreover, several relative clauses may be recursively embedded inside one another.

Lexical Ambiguity

Every word in the sample sentences discussed so far was assumed to belong
to a unique part of speech. Thus, *Jill, friend*, and *man* are nouns, *read,
write*, and *tell* are verbs, and *old* and *good* are adjectives. This assumption
however is not always correct. Most words in English can receive several
alternative category assignments (that is, can serve as different parts of
speech); the particular choice depends on the context. Consider, for instance, the following sentence from a detective story:

(32) The gangsters *can supply uniform* alibis.

The word *can* is used here as a modal auxiliary, but it could also serve as a
noun; the word *supply* is a verb, but it could also be a noun or a modifier
in a noun-noun modification sequence; the word *uniform* is an adjective
that could be used as a noun in a different context. Sentence (32) will be
analyzed correctly only if the system selects the right category assignments
for each word; any other assignment will result in an error.

Lexical entries in START (see the Lexicon section) are allowed to specify more than one category assignment. The system is equipped with a
mechanism for category disambiguation which uses error feedback from
the parser (including context information and type of error) to efficiently
resolve ambiguities. As a result, along with sentence (32), START is able to
process successfully another sentence from the same detective story:

(33) But the policeman found the *uniform* in the *supply can*.

Note that each of the three ambiguous words in sentence (33) is a different
part of speech from what it was in (32).

Forward and Backward S-rules

In the previous sections we showed how START builds *T*-expressions using
the pattern <**subject relation object**> at every level of embedding. As a
consequence, *T*-expressions closely follow the syntax of analyzed sentences.
This property incidentally is one reason why the language generator is frequently able to reconstruct the original English sentence almost verbatim.
Unfortunately, this property also implies that sentences which have different surface syntax but are close in meaning will not be considered similar
by the system.

An example will clarify this point. Given as input sentence (34) START
will create an embedded *T*-expression (35):

(34) Miriam presented Gabriella with a gift.

(35) <<**Miriam present Gabriella**> **with gift**>

whereas a near paraphrase, sentence (36), will generate T-expression (37):

(36) Miriam presented a gift to Gabriella.

(37) **<<Miriam present gift> to Gabriella>**

Speakers of English know that sentences (34) and (36) both describe a transfer of possession. In both sentences, *the gift* is the transferred object, *Gabriella* is the recipient of this object, and *Miriam* is the agent of the transfer, despite different syntactic realizations of some of these arguments. It seem natural that this kind of knowledge be available to a natural language system. However, the START system, as described so far, does not consider T-expressions (35) and (37), which are associated with these sentences, to be similar.

The difference in the T-expressions becomes particularly problematic when START is asked a question. Suppose, for example, that the input text contains only one *present* sentence, (38), and the knowledge base contains only the corresponding T-expression, (39):

(38) Miriam presented Gabriella with a gift.

(39) **<<Miriam present Gabriella> with gift>**

Now suppose the user asked the following question:

(40) To whom did Miriam present a gift?

Although a speaker of English could easily answer this question after being told sentence (38), the START system, as described so far, would not be able to answer it. This question presents a problem for START because T-expression (41) produced by question (40) will not match T-expression (39).

(41) **<<Miriam present gift> to** *whom***>**

START is unable to answer such questions because it is unaware of the interactions between the syntactic and semantic properties of verbs. This limitation is a serious drawback because interactions similar to the one just described pervade the English language and, therefore, cannot be ignored in the construction of a natural language system.

The *present* example illustrates that START needs information that allows it to deduce the relationship between alternate realizations of the arguments of verbs. In this instance, we want START to know that whenever A presents B with C, then A presents C to B. We do this by introducing rules that make explicit the relationship between alternate realizations of the arguments of verbs. We call such rules *S-rules* (where S stands for both *S*yntax and *S*emantics). Here is the *S*-rule that solves the problem caused by the verb *present*:

(42) *Present S*-rule

> **If**   <<subject **present** object1> **with** object2>
> **Then** <<subject **present** object2> **to** object1>

S-rules are implemented as a rule-based system. Each *S*-rule is made up of two parts, an antecedent (the IF-clause) and a consequent (the THEN-clause). Each clause consists of a set of templates for *T*-expressions, where the template elements are filled by variables or constants. For example, the *Present S*-rule contains three variables, *subject, object1, object2*, which are used to represent the noun phrases in the *T*-expressions. This rule also contains three constants, **present, with,** and **to**, shown in boldface. The *Present S*-rule will apply only to *T*-expressions which involve the verb *present* and which meet the additional structural constraints.

S-rules operate in two modes: *forward* and *backward*. When triggered by certain conditions, *S*-rules in the forward mode allow the system to intercept *T*-expressions produced by the understanding module, transform or augment them in a way specified by the rule, and then incorporate the result into the knowledge base. For instance, if the *Present S*-rule is used in the forward mode, as soon as its antecedent matches *T*-expression (43) produced by the understanding module, it creates a new *T*-expression (44) and then adds it to the knowledge base:

(43) <<**Miriam present Gabriella> with gift**>

(44) <<**Miriam present gift> to Gabriella**>

Now question (40) can be answered because *T*-expression (41) associated with this question matches against *T*-expression (44). The generating module of START responds:

(45) Miriam presented a gift to Gabriella.

All additional facts produced by the forward *S*-rules are instantly entered in the knowledge base. The forward mode is especially useful when the information processed by START is put into use by another computer system because in such a situation START ought to provide the interfacing system with as much data as possible.

In contrast, the backward mode is employed when the user queries the knowledge base. Often for reasons of computational efficiency, it is advantageous not to incorporate all inferred knowledge into the knowledge base immediately. *S*-rules in the backward mode trigger only when a request comes in which cannot be answered directly, initiating a search in the knowledge base to determine if the answer can be deduced from the available information. For example, the *Present S*-rule used in the backward mode does *not* trigger when sentence (38) is read and *T*-expression (39) is produced by START. The *S*-rule triggers only when question (40) is asked because this question cannot be answered directly.

In a more complex situation, S-rules are allowed to trigger each other and to ask each other for help. At any given moment hundreds of rules may be hidden in the computer's memory examining the output flow generated by START and waiting for their turn to participate in the deduction process. S-rules fundamentally expand the power of our language understanding system; they open a window into the intricate world of syntax-semantic interactions.

The Lexical Component

In order to understand an English sentence, the system needs to have morphological, syntactic, and semantic information about the words in the sentence. All the words that the system is aware of, along with information about their part of speech, inflection, gender, number, *etc.* are stored in the *Lexicon*. Virtually every branch of our system resorts to the Lexicon to accomplish its task. In the understanding mode, the Lexicon is used to recognize embedded clauses, to construct kernel structures, to build T-expressions. In the generating mode, the Lexicon is consulted when a noun or verb phrase is built, when a connective transformation is applied, when a question is answered.

The Lexicon extends the system's abilities for semantic interpretation. Consider two sentences:

(46) The man wipes the table clean.

and

(47) The man eats the fish raw.

We use START's T-expressions to show that although these sentences seem to have apparently identical surface syntactic structure, their semantic interpretations are quite different. The first sentence (46) has a causative interpretation:

(48) **<<man wipe table> effect <table is clean>>**

while the second sentence (47) is depictive:

(49) **<<man eat fish> when <fish is raw>>**

In order to determine the appropriate interpretation (causative or depictive) for each sentence the system needs to examine lexical entries of verbs and adjectives involved in sentences like (46) or (47). The additional information required to make this decision must be provided by the Lexicon.

Let us examine how lexical information about verbs and verb classes may be utilized by the S-rules. A verb denotes an action, state, or process involving one or more participants, which we refer to as the *arguments* of the verb. Some verbs may express their arguments in more than one way, sometimes with slightly different semantic interpretations. Such verbs participate in *argument alternations*. (See Atkins, Kegl and Levin [1986], Hale and Keyser [1986], and Levin [1985] for a description of various alternations.) In this section, we introduce the *property-factoring* alternation [Van Oosten 1980]. Suppose we typed the following sentence into the computer:

(50) Paul surprised the audience with his performance.

An English speaker knows that sentence (50) can be paraphrased as:

(51) Paul's performance surprised the audience.

Note that in (50), the subject brings about the emotional reaction (*surprise*) by means of some property expressed in the *with* phrase. Sentence (51) describes the same emotional reaction as in (50) but in (51) the property and its possessor are collapsed into a single noun phrase.

Suppose that after sentence (50) is typed into the computer, we ask:

(52) Did Paul's performance surprise the audience?

While a speaker of English would know that the answer to this question is *Yes*, this reply is not obvious to START because T-expressions related to sentence (50) and question (52) are very different:[6]

(53) <<**Paul surprise audience> with performance>**

(54) <**performance surprise audience>**

Extending the approach taken to the example with the verb *present* in the section on S-rules, we could formulate a simple *S*-rule that could be used to answer question (52). The *Surprise S*-rule (55), like the *Present S*-rule, makes explicit the relationship between the alternate realizations of the arguments of the verb *surprise*:

(55) *Surprise* S-rule

> **If**   <<subject **surprise** object1> **with** object2>
> **Then**   <object2 **surprise** object1>

Formulating a special purpose *S*-rule which applies only to the verb *surprise* does not seem, however, to be the best solution to the problem. *Surprise* is only one of many verbs which exhibit the property-factoring alternation. This alternation holds for a large class consisting of over one hundred verbs, among them:

(56) amuse, anger, annoy, disappoint, embarrass, frighten, please, worry ...

These verbs share a certain semantic property as well: they all denote *emotional reactions*. For this reason we identify a class of *emotional-reaction* verbs and say that the syntactic property of the verb *surprise* responsible for the alternations shown in (50) and (51) holds for all verbs that comprise

---

[6]To simplify the exposition we do not show the T-expression describing the relation between the property (*performance*) and its possessor (*Paul*).

the *emotional-reaction* class.[7]

Now instead of writing a number of verb-specific S-rules, we can write a single general S-rule which triggers not only on the verb *surprise*, but on any verb from the emotional-reaction class:

(57) *Property-factoring* S-rule

> **If**　　　 <<subject verb object1> **with** object2>
> **Then**　　 <object2 verb object1>
> **Provided**　verb ∈ *emotional-reaction* class

The revised S-rule contains a PROVIDED-clause which specifies the class of verbs to which the rule applies, ensuring that it applies to the emotional-reaction verbs.

When question (52) is asked, the Property-factoring S-rule (used in the backward mode) will trigger, because the T-expression

(58) **<performance surprise audience>**

produced by the question matches the THEN-part of the rule, and furthermore, the verb *surprise* belongs to the emotional-reaction class. The correct answer to question (52) is deduced when the appropriately instantiated IF-part of the rule is matched to T-expression (53) found in the knowledge base. Here is how START responds:

(59) Yes, Paul's performance surprised the audience.

This example shows how the transparent syntax of the S-rules coupled with the information about verb class membership provided by the Lexicon facilitates fluent and flexible dialog between the user and the language understanding system. (See Katz and Levin [1988] for additional examples.)

Our current Lexicon contains several thousand entries. However, the process of *lexical acquisition* (adding new words to the Lexicon, with all relevant information about them) is very simple. In fact, introducing a new lexical item in START amounts to little more than appending it to a list of similar words, adding a few idiosyncratic features when necessary. Acquisition of S-rules is equally simple. Adding a new S-rule to the system requires typing in a set of English sentences (such as sentences (50) and (51)) which capture a specific instance of the rule. START will analyze the sentences, query the user for additional information regarding elements of corresponding T-expressions (ascertaining whether they are matching variables, constants, or predicates), and then build and generalize the S

---

[7]These verbs have been the subject of extensive study in the linguistic literature because of these and other characteristic properties that set this class apart. (See Postal [1971], Pesetsky [1987], Belletti and Rizzi [1988], Grimshaw [1990], and many others.)

-rule automatically. All this makes the system *transportable*, that is, easily adaptable to new domains.

Answering Questions

In this section we will concentrate on the question-answering machinery in START. Suppose the system has analyzed and indexed a text containing sentence (60). As a result, the knowledge base contains T-expression (61):

(60) Jessica wanted the computer to print the message.

(61) **<Jessica want <computer print message>>**$_H$

Suppose now that a user asks:

(62) What did Jessica want the computer to print?

The first step in answering this question is to reverse the effect of the *wh*-movement transformation that is used to create English *wh*-questions. In order to accomplish this, START must find the place in sentence (62) that the *wh*-word *what* came from and then insert the *wh*-word in this position:[8]

(63) Jessica wanted [the computer to print *what*].

Next, the START system leads sentence (63) through the same flow of control as any other declarative sentence and produces the following T-expression which serves as a pattern used by the matching module to query the knowledge base:

(64) **<Jessica want <computer print *what*>>**

Treating *what* as a matching variable, the system attempts to determine whether there is anything in the knowledge base that matches (64). In this case, it finds the T-expression

(61) **<Jessica want <computer print message>>**$_H$

The language generation module then takes this T-expression with its associated history and produces the English response to question (62):

(65) Jessica wanted the computer to print the message.

The matching process treats other types of English questions, including *Yes/No*-questions, *when*-questions, *where*-questions, *why*-questions, *etc.* in a similar fashion.

In this example we implicitly assumed that the tense and the aspect of question (62) were identical to the tense and aspect of sentence (60) in the text. We also assumed that sentence (60) was used in the text only once and that it was not embedded in another sentence. All these assumptions

---

[8]This situation is very similar to the treatment of *relative clauses* discussed earlier. In fact, the same computational machinery is used to handle these two phenomena.

need not necessarily hold, however. For instance, one might ask:

(66) Does Jessica want the computer to print the message?

or

(67) Did the computer print the message?

A person answering these questions in the context of (60) would probably say "I don't know" because sentence (60) just states that Jessica wanted a certain action to happen at one time in the past. Sentence (60) does not imply that Jessica wants this action to happen in the present nor does it imply that this action actually happened.

To illustrate a different case, suppose that it is known from the text that

(68) The telescope is orbiting the Earth.

Now someone may ask the following questions:

(69) Has the telescope been orbiting the Earth?

(70) Can the telescope orbit the Earth?

In spite of the fact that in the original sentence (68) the auxiliaries and the form of the main verb are different from those in questions (69) and (70), a person would most likely answer *Yes* in both cases. Somehow people know when they can or cannot answer such questions.

What about computers, then? Although clearly world knowledge plays an important role here, the text itself may often provide sufficient data to determine whether the information in the system's knowledge base implies a definitive answer to the question. Matching the embedded T-expressions described earlier is only a "rough" first step in answering a question; some further reasoning is required in order to determine the proper response.

One way of thinking about the problem is to divide the question-answering task into two parts:

1   Finding relevant information within the knowledge base, and

2   Determining the implications of this information.

Finding relevant information in this case means retrieving the appropriate T-expression, either through matching alone or with the help of S-rules. The second subtask requires a more subtle analysis of the histories attached to the T-expressions returned by the matcher. Given a question and a matching T-expression, the system must use the information contained in the histories to calculate the most accurate, helpful response possible.

Let us consider an example. Suppose that the analyzed text contains sentence (71) and later sentence (72):

(71) Miriam will be reading the book.

(72) Miriam was reading the book.

The T-expression

(73) **<Miriam read book>**

will thus have a two-page history. Now we ask:

(74) Has Miriam been reading the book?

Recall that when START analyzes a question, it reverses the effect of the movement transformation that is used to create English questions and converts it into T-expression form, like any other sentence. We will call the question in the assertional form the *Q-assertion*, so that

(75) Miriam has been reading the book.

is the Q-assertion for question (74). The task for the system is then to determine whether the known statements, (71) and (72), individually, imply Q-assertion (75).

The information from histories that START must use to calculate the implications falls roughly into three categories. Ties to embedded or embedding T-expressions (if any) give the proposition's *intrasentential context*. Tense and aspect place the proposition in a certain *time frame*. Modals, including negation as a special instance, show the *mood* of the proposition.

Accordingly, START employs an ordered set of filters, one for each type of information. A kernel sentence may receive one of three labels, YES, NO, or UNKNOWN, as it passes through the filter set. The UNKNOWN label is further broken down to show which filter assigned it, so that this information can be used in responding to the question in the most helpful way.

The embedding filter must be applied first. Thus, the sentence "Miriam read the book" which is embedded in (76) is labeled UNKNOWN *(embedding)*:

(76) Gabriella thinks that Miriam read the book.

A sentence that is not labeled UNKNOWN by the embedding filter is passed to the tense-aspect filter. This filter determines whether the time interval referred to by the kernel sentence overlaps with that given by the question. If they do not overlap, the sentence is labeled UNKNOWN *(time)*. For example, in attempting to answer the question "Has Miriam been reading the book," this filter would label the sentence "Miriam will be reading the book" UNKNOWN *(time)*. The sentence "Miriam was reading the book" would pass through the time-aspect filter, to be considered by the modal filter. The modal filter compares the modals (including negation) used in the kernel sentence and in the question. Each combination results in one of the three labels YES, NO, or UNKNOWN *(modals)*. (In Gaulding and Katz [1989] the operation of the tense-aspect and modal filters is discussed in more detail.)

If a sentence has internal embeddings, the reasoning process is repeated for each T-expression involved, producing a decision at each level of embedding. These decisions are then arbitrated in the following manner. If at any point the time frame referred to is inappropriate, or the modal combination is inconclusive, the entire sentence is labeled UNKNOWN *(time)* or UNKNOWN *(modals)*. Otherwise the "logical combination" of affirmative and negative responses is calculated, and the overall sentence is labeled with the result. For example, suppose the system had indexed the sentence

(77) Gabriella wishes that Miriam had read the book.

and were asked

(78) Does Gabriella wish that Miriam will be reading the book?

The outer clause would receive the label YES but the inner clause would not pass the tense-aspect filter, and as a result the entire sentence would be relabeled UNKNOWN *(time)*. Although this solution gives correct answers for many internal-embedding situations, it seems that the general case requires more complex reasoning (see Gaulding and Katz [1989] for possible approaches).

Once a final label has been calculated for each sentence contained in the history, START arbitrates the resulting combination of YES's, NO's, or UNKNOWN's and decides upon the final response. Because the overall goal is to be as informative as possible, the response does not consist merely of a "yes", "no", or "unknown". All the sentences corresponding to the matching T-expression are generated for the user, and the explanations are given when necessary.

The following interaction illustrates that the system's final responses, made on the basis of this analysis, echo people's judgments in answering such questions. Note that inputs to START are given to the prompt "==>".

==> Ed expects to like rock music, but he does not like it now.
==> Mom hopes Ed will not like it.
==> Will Ed like rock music?

I don't know. However, I do have some information:

Ed expects to like rock music.

Mom hopes that Ed will not like rock music.
(*The proposition* 'Ed likes rock music' *was embedded within these sentences.*)

Ed doesn't like rock music now.
(*This sentence did not refer to the time interval about which you asked.*)

A Dialogue with START

The following is a slightly shortened and modified passage from the *Testing Reading Skills* chapter of the book *How to Prepare for the Graduate Record Examination* [Brownstein & Weiner 1985] as entered into the computer:

> *The establishment of the Third Reich influenced events in American history by starting a chain of events which culminated in war. The complete destruction of democracy, the persecution of Jews, the cruelty of the Nazis, and the plans of Germany for the conquest of the world caused great indignation in the United States. While speaking out against Hitler's atrocities, the American people generally favored isolationist policies and neutrality. The Neutrality Act of 1935 prohibited trade with any belligerent nation. In 1937 the President was empowered to declare an arms embargo in wars between nations at his discretion.*
>
> *American opinion changed after President Roosevelt's speech at Chicago in which he severely criticized Hitler's policies. Germany's seizure of Austria and the Munich Pact also aroused the American people. The conquest of Czechoslovakia in 1939 was another rude awakening to the menace of the Third Reich. The United States attempted to maintain neutrality in spite of sympathy for the European democracies. The Neutrality Act of 1939 repealed the arms embargo and permitted exports of arms to belligerent nations. In 1940 a strong national defense program was begun and a draft act was passed to strengthen the military services. In 1941 Japan launched the unprovoked attack on the United States at Pearl Harbor. Immediately thereafter, Germany declared war on the United States.*

The understanding module of START analyzes this text and indexes the knowledge contained within it into a knowledge base. The user is then able to interact with the system in English. Shown below is an actual dialogue with START. The user asks questions and the computer answers them. Note that the English sentences generated by START may differ from the original text. Any stylistic deficiencies are the responsibility of START and not of this author.

The astute reader will observe that in addition to syntactic analysis, indexing, matching, retrieving the information, and generating English sentences, the START system was quietly performing additional tasks, such as: resolving lexical ambiguities (for example, the word *attack* was used as a verb and as a noun); working with synonyms (*begin-start, permit-allow, etc.*); employing *S*-rules (for example, in answering the question about Japan attacking the USA); and providing further information (in parentheses) when the correct answer could not be found due to embedding, or disagreements in time intervals or modality.

Querying the GRE Knowledge Base

What did Germany's plans cause?

> Germany's plans for the world's conquest caused great indignation in the United States.

Did the American people favor neutrality?

> Yes—The American people generally favored neutrality while speaking out against Hitler's atrocities.

What did the Neutrality Acts do?

> The Neutrality Act of 1935 prohibited the trade with any belligerent nation.
> The Neutrality Act of 1939 repealed the arms embargo.
> The Neutrality Act of 1939 permitted the arms' exports to the belligerent nations.

When was the Arms embargo declared?

> *Well, all I know is the following:*
>
> The President was empowered to declare the arms embargo in the wars between the nations at his discretion in 1937.

Who criticized Hitler's policies?

> President Roosevelt severely criticized Hitler's policies in his speech.

When did the American opinion change?

> The American opinion changed after President Roosevelt's speech at Chicago in which President Roosevelt severely criticized Hitler's policies.

Who maintained neutrality?

> *Well, I know that:*
>
> The United States attempted to maintain neutrality in spite of the sympathy for the European democracies.

To which nations did the Neutrality Act allow exports?

> The Neutrality Act of 1939 permitted the arms' exports to the belligerent nations.

Why was the Draft Act passed?

> The Draft Act was passed in order to strengthen the military services.

Will a national defense program be started?

> *I don't know. However, I do have this information:*

The strong national defense program was begun in 1940.

(This sentence did not refer to the time interval about which you asked.)

Did Japan attack the USA?

Yes—Japan launched the unprovoked attack on the United States at Pearl Harbor in 1941.

The Voyager Neptune Encounter

In August 1989 the Voyager 2 spacecraft concluded its twelve-year Grand Tour of the outer planets: from Earth, past Jupiter, Saturn, and Uranus, to Neptune. It sent back spectacular images of Neptune and its largest moon, Triton, and discovered new moons and rings around the planet. In cooperation with researchers from the Jet Propulsion Laboratory (JPL), we conducted our own experiment during this encounter in order to assess the viability and robustness of the START system in an open setting. Members of the press in the JPL press room and attendees of the Second International Conference on Solar system exploration at the California Institute of Technology were invited to use START to ask about the encounter, the Voyager spacecraft, and the Solar system.

For this experiment, the knowledge that the system utilized in answering questions was pulled from a variety of different sources. These sources include English text taken from various space publications, distance tables from the Voyager navigation team, timeline information from the sequencing group, etc. The resulting knowledge base contained several thousand objects and T-expressions.

The experiment was a success. During the encounter week, START was able to answer a wide variety of questions about the "Voyager world." The robustness and adaptivity of the system to a new and large domain leads us to believe that computer natural language interfaces, in a limited capacity at least, are becoming a reasonable option and not a source of endless frustration.

The following are fragments of actual sessions with START, recorded at the Jet Propulsion Laboratory during the Voyager Neptune encounter.

Querying the Voyager Knowledge Base

When was Voyager launched?

The Voyager Spacecraft was launched in Florida on August 20 1977.

Where is Voyager?

At 8/26/89 17:29:56, the Voyager II is:

2,161,314 (two million one hundred sixty thousand) kilometers from Neptune,
4,521,386,190 (four billion five hundred twenty-one million four hundred thousand)
kilometers from the Sun, and
4,429,958,949 (four billion four hundred thirty million) kilometers from the Earth.

How far is Voyager from Neptune now?

The Voyager II is 2,162,126 (two million one hundred sixty thousand) kilometers
from Neptune at 8/26/89 17:30:44.

How fast is it going?

At 8/26/89 17:33:26, Voyager is traveling 60,896 kilometers per hour away from
Neptune.

At what time will Voyager lose contact with Earth?

The Voyager Spacecraft will lose the contact with the Earth around 2014.

What does the abbreviation CCS stand for?

Voyager's CCS means its main computer command subsystem.

When will the next picture be taken?

Voyager takes 21 pictures of Triton from 8/27/89 02:58:00 to 8/27/89 04:58:00.

How long is the year on Neptune?

Neptune's period of revolution is about 165 earth years.

Why is Neptune blue?[9]

When you look at a photograph of Neptune, you see the planet's atmosphere and
the tops of clouds. Neptune looks bluish because the methane in its atmosphere
reflects blue and green frequencies of light. The methane absorbs red and yellow
frequencies of sunlight.

How does Voyager talk to Earth?

Commands are sent from the Earth to one of two receivers on the Voyager spacecraft. Engineering data and scientific information are sent to the Earth over two
channels. One channel is on all the time but both channels are on during encounters with the planets. The radio transmitter on the Voyager transmits with about
25 watts of power, or with about the same power as a refrigerator light bulb. These
faint signals are picked up on Earth by ultra-sensitive receivers known as the Deep
Space Network.

When are the best pictures of Triton taken?

Voyager takes Triton's best pictures on Aug 25 1989.

Whom was Triton named after?

Triton was named after the mythical son of the sea.

Which planet has the smallest moon?

---

[9]For this and the next question START did not attempt to generate its response
directly from T-expressions in the knowledge base but instead used previously
composed text which it determined to be relevant.

Mars has the smallest moon, Deimos.

Whose moon is Miranda?

Miranda is a moon of Uranus.

Is any moon of Jupiter larger than our moon?

Yes, Jupiter's moon, Ganymede, Jupiter's moon, Io, and Jupiter's moon, Callisto, are larger than the moon of the Earth because:

Callisto's diameter is 4,800 kilometers.
Io's diameter is 3,630 kilometers.
Ganymede's diameter is 5,262 kilometers.
The moon of the Earth's diameter is 3,476 kilometers.

Spacecraft Sequencing

In this section we demonstrate the application of the START system in a real-world situation: interplanetary exploration. The scientists and engineers who plan to perform experiments aboard an interplanetary spacecraft compete for a limited amount of time and resources. Their requests are coordinated and integrated into a sequence of activities for the spacecraft through a *spacecraft sequencing* process. This process involves designing, scheduling and programming the onboard activities, as well as controlling its functions. It is a complex, tedious, and time consuming process which is carried out by a team of experts called the *Sequence Team*. In order to perform this task, the Sequence Team uses a set of computer programs, the *Mission Sequence Software (MSS)*. These programs do everything from simulating the geometry of the encounter to detailed constraint checking of the proposed sequence and actual command simulation and generation. Unfortunately, this software is very difficult to use. Producing MSS which is more "user friendly" could reduce the cost of a mission dramatically.

In Katz and Brooks [1987] we have identified several possible roles that START could play in improving the MSS performance. The long-range goal is to develop a system that scientists and engineers can employ in planning future space missions. The Mars Observer Mission, scheduled for launch in 1992, provided a testbed for our first attempt towards this goal. The Mission plans to use small modular sequence components called Sequence Segments. These segments, which are based on the geography of Mars, will be used during mission operations to build the sequences of activities to be executed onboard. Shown below is a sample of the types of observations which will be specified in a typical segment. This document is automatically transformed by the START system into a knowledge base which incorporates the information found in the text. Following that, we show how the user obtains the information about the events which are taking place in the sequence by querying the knowledge base in English.

In the sample segment below, MOC, VIMS, TES, and PMIRR are all scientific instruments on the Mars Observer spacecraft (MO). IR is an abbreviation for Infra-red. All other capitalized words (ALBA PATERA, ASCRAEUS MONS, TANTALUS FOSSAE, etc.) are names of targets on the planet's surface.

Mars Observer Sequence Segment
(as entered in the computer)

00:04:20 ASCRAEUS MONS is at Nadir.
00:04:35 MOC takes 5 pictures of ASCRAEUS MONS.
00:04:35 TES performs experiment number 16 on ASCRAEUS MONS.
00:04:35 PMIRR performs IR study of ASCRAEUS MONS.
00:04:35 VIMS takes 1 picture of ASCRAEUS MONS.
00:08:20 Entering CERAUNIUS FOSSAE region from south side.
00:10:25 PMIRR performs IR study of CERAUNIUS FOSSAE.
00:12:30 Exiting CERAUNIUS FOSSAE region from north side.
00:14:30 Entering TANTALUS FOSSAE region from south side.
00:14:35 MOC takes 4 pictures of TANTALUS FOSSAE.
00:16:40 +40-deg latitude crossing pulse occurs northbound.
00:17:00 Entering ALBA PATERA region from south-east side.
00:17:00 Exiting TANTALUS FOSSAE region from north side.
00:18:40 Entering ALBA FOSSAE region from south side.
00:18:40 Exiting ALBA PATERA region from north-east side.
00:18:45 Take 5 pictures of ALBA FOSSAE with MOC.
00:20:40 Entering VASTITAS BOREALIS region from south side.
00:20:40 Exiting ALBA FOSSAE region from north side.
00:22:55 Take 2 pictures of VASTITAS BOREALIS with MOC.
00:22:55 VIMS takes 1 picture of VASTITAS BOREALIS region.
00:27:05 +65-deg latitude crossing pulse occurs northbound.
00:29:10 MOC takes 3 pictures of the north-polar region.
00:29:10 Take 1 picture of north-polar region using VIMS.
00:31:15 PMIRR begins continuous IR study of north-polar region.
00:33:20 TES begins study of north-polar region.
00:34:10 Entering north-polar region.
00:37:30 +90-deg latitude crossing pulse occurs.
00:37:30 MOC takes 6 pictures of the North Pole.
00:37:30 PMIRR performs internal experiment # 21 on North Pole.
00:37:30 TES does internal experiment #11 on North Pole.
00:37:30 VIMS executes internal experiment number 1 on North Pole.
00:41:40 TES ends study of north-polar region.
00:43:45 Exiting VASTITAS BOREALIS region from north side.
00:43:45 Exiting north-polar region.
00:43:45 PMIRR ends study of north-polar region.
00:47:55 +65-deg latitude crossing pulse occurs southbound.
00:52:05 Entering UTOPIA PLANITIA from north side.
00:54:10 Use MOC to take 2 pictures of VASTITAS BOREALIS.
00:54:10 VIMS takes 1 picture of VASTITAS BOREALIS.
00:58:20 +40-deg latitude crossing pulse occurs southbound.

01:00:25 Entering NILOSYRTIS MENSAE from north side.
01:00:25 Exiting UTOPIA PLANITIA from south side.
01:01:15 Take 1 picture of NILOSYRTIS MENSAE using MOC.
01:01:15 Take 1 picture of NILOSYRTIS MENSAE with VIMS.
01:04:35 Entering NILI FOSSAE region from north side.
01:04:35 Exiting NILOSYRTIS MENSAE from south side.
01:06:40 Entering SYRTIS MAJOR PLANITIA region from north side.
01:06:40 Exiting NILI FOSSAE region from south side.
01:06:40 PMIRR begins IR study of SYRTIS MAJOR PLANITIA.
01:06:40 VIMS takes 1 picture of NILI FOSSAE.

Querying the Mars Observer Knowledge Base

How many pictures of ASCRAEUS MONS does MOC take?

     At 00:04:35, MOC takes 5 pictures of ASCRAEUS MONS.

When does PMIRR begin continuous IR study of north-polar region?

     At 00:31:15, PMIRR begins the north-polar region's continuous IR study.

When does VIMS take pictures of VASTITAS BOREALIS region?

     At 00:54:10, VIMS takes 1 picture of VASTITAS BOREALIS.
     At 00:22:55, VIMS takes 1 picture of VASTITAS BOREALIS.

Which instruments take pictures of ASCRAEUS MONS?

     At 00:04:35, MOC takes 5 pictures of ASCRAEUS MONS.
     At 00:04:35, VIMS takes 1 picture of ASCRAEUS MONS.

When does PMIRR execute the experiment #21 on North Pole?

     At 00:37:30, PMIRR performs experiment21 on North Pole.

What does PMIRR do between 00:10:00 and 00:50:00?

     At 00:10:25, PMIRR performs CERAUNIUS FOSSAE'S IR study.
     At 00:31:15, PMIRR begins the north-polar region's continuous IR study.
     At 00:37:30, PMIRR performs experiment21.
     At 00:43:45, PMIRR ends the north-polar region's continuous IR study.

When do latitude crossing pulses occur?

     At 00:58:20, the +40-deg latitude crossing pulse occurs southbound.
     At 00:16:40, the +40-deg latitude crossing pulse occurs northbound.
     At 00:47:55, the +65-deg latitude crossing pulse occurs southbound.
     At 00:27:05, the +65-deg latitude crossing pulse occurs northbound.
     At 00:37:30, the +90-deg latitude crossing pulse occurs.

Does Mars Observer enter the NILI FOSSAE region?

Yes—At 01:04:35, spacecraft enters NILI FOSSAE from the north side.

From which side does MO exit the regions?

At 00:12:30, spacecraft exits CERAUNIUS FOSSAE from the north side.
At 00:17:00, spacecraft exits TANTALUS FOSSAE from the north side.
At 00:18:40, spacecraft exits ALBA PATERA from the north-east side.
At 00:20:40, spacecraft exits ALBA FOSSAE from the north side.
At 00:43:45, spacecraft exits VASTITAS BOREALIS from the north side.
At 01:00:25, spacecraft exits UTOPIA PLANITIA from the south side.
At 01:04:35, spacecraft exits NILOSYRTIS MENSAE from the south side.
At 01:06:40, spacecraft exits NILI FOSSAE from the south side.

Which targets does VIMS look at?

At 01:06:40, VIMS takes 1 picture of NILI FOSSAE.
At 01:01:15, VIMS takes 1 picture of NILOSYRTIS MENSAE.
At 00:29:10, VIMS takes 1 picture of the north-polar region.
At 00:54:10, VIMS takes 1 picture of VASTITAS BOREALIS.
At 00:22:55, VIMS takes 1 picture of VASTITAS BOREALIS.
At 00:04:35, VIMS takes 1 picture of ASCRAEUS MONS.

How many pictures does MOC take after 00:20:00?

At 00:22:55, MOC takes 2 pictures of VASTITAS BOREALIS.
At 00:29:10, MOC takes 3 pictures of the north-polar region.
At 00:37:30, MOC takes 6 pictures of North Pole.
At 00:54:10, MOC takes 2 pictures of VASTITAS BOREALIS.
At 01:01:15, MOC takes 1 picture of NILOSYRTIS MENSAE.

Total number of pictures is 14.

A number of students have participated in the project, in particular, David Chanen, Robert Frank, Jill Gaulding, and Jeff Palmucci contributed significantly to various parts of the system. I am grateful to Mikhail Katz and Beth Levin for their time and numerous helpful suggestions concerning this chapter. The idea to use START in the space domain came from William McLaughlin. Robert Brooks developed the data for the Mars Observer mission and supplied the principal interface with the Voyager project.

This chapter describes research done at the Artificial Intelligence Laboratory of the Massachusetts Institute of Technology. Support for the Laboratory's Artificial Intelligence research is provided in part by the Advanced Research Projects Agency under Office of Naval Research contract N0014-85-K-0124.

References

Akmajian A., and F. Heny [1975], *An Introduction to the Principles of Transformational SyntaxF*, MIT Press, Cambridge, MA.

Atkins, B. T., J. Kegl, and B. Levin [1986], "Explicit and Implicit Information in Dictionaries," Lexicon Project Working Papers 12, Center for Cognitive Science, MIT, Cambridge, MA.

Belletti, A., and L. Rizzi [1988], "Psych-Verbs and Θ-Theory," *Natural Language and Linguistic Theory*, vol. 6, pp. 291-352.

Brownstein, S. C., and M. Weiner [1985], "How to Prepare for the Graduate Record Examination," Barron's Educational Series, Inc., Woodbury, N.Y.

Chomsky, N. [1957], *A Theory of Syntactic Structures,* Moulton & Co.

Doyle, R. J. [1984], "Hypothesizing and Refining Causal Models," Report AIM-811, Massachusetts Institute of Technology, Artificial Intelligence Laboratory, Cambridge, MA.

Frank, B., B. Katz, and J. Palmucci [1989], "Reviewing the Voyager Information System," Technical Report, Jet Propulsion Laboratory, Pasadena, CA.

Gaulding, J., and B. Katz [1989], "Using Word-Knowledge Reasoning for Question Answering," in *The Society of Text*, edited by E. Barrett, MIT Press, Cambridge, MA.

Grimshaw, J. [1990], *Argument Structure*, MIT Press, Cambridge, MA.

Hale, K. L., and S. J. Keyser [1986], "Some Transitivity Alternations in English," Lexicon Project Working Papers 7, Center for Cognitive Science, MIT, Cambridge, MA.

Katz, B. [1980], "A Three-step Procedure for Language Generation," Report AIM-599, Massachusetts Institute of Technology, Artificial Intelligence Laboratory, Cambridge, MA.

Katz, B., and R. Brooks [1987], "Understanding Natural Language for Spacecraft Sequencing," *JBIS*, vol. 40, no. 10.

Katz, B., and B. Levin [1988], "Exploiting Lexical Regularities in Designing Natural Language Systems," *Proceedings of the 12th International Conference on Computational Linguistics, COLING '88*, Budapest. A version of this paper also appears as Lexicon Project Working Papers 22, MIT Center for Cognitive Science, and as Report AIM-1041, Artificial Intelligence Laboratory, Massachusetts Institute of Technology, Cambridge, MA, 1988.

Katz, B., and P. H. Winston [1982], "A Two-way Natural Language Interface," in *Integrated Interactive Computing Systems*, edited by P. Degano and E. Sandewall, North-Holland, Amsterdam.

Levin, B. [1985], "Introduction," in *Lexical Semantics in Review*, edited by B. Levin, Lexicon Project Working Papers 1, Center for Cognitive Science, MIT, Cambridge, MA.

McLaughlin, W. I. [1987], "Automated Sequencing," *Spaceflight*, vol. 29, no. 1.

McLaughlin, W. I. [1988], "Computers and Language," *Spaceflight*, vol. 30, no. 8.

Pesetsky, D. [1987], "Binding Problems with Experiencer Verbs," *Linguistic Inquiry* vol. 18, pp. 126-140.

Postal, P. [1971], *Cross-Over Phenomena*, Holt, Rinehart, and Winston, NY.

Quirk, R., S. Greenbaum, G. Leech, and J. Svartvik [1985], *A Comprehensive Grammar of the English Language*, Longman, London.

Van Oosten, J. [1980], "Subjects, Topics and Agents: Evidence from Property-factoring," *Proceedings of the Berkeley Linguistics Society* 6, Berkeley, CA.

Winston, P. H. [1984], *Artificial Intelligence*, Addison-Wesley, Reading MA.

Winston, P. H. [1982], "Learning New Principles from Precedents and Exercises," *Artificial Intelligence*, vol. 19, no. 3.

Winston, P. H., T. O. Binford, B. Katz, and M. R. Lowry [1983], "Learning Physical Descriptions from Functional Definitions, Examples, and Precedents," *National Conference on Artificial Intelligence*, Washington, DC.

Woods, W. A. [1985], "What's in a Link: Foundations for Semantic Networks," in *Readings in Knowledge Representation*, edited by R. J. Brachman and H. J. Levesque, Morgan Kaufmann Publishers, Los Altos. (Originally published in *Representation and Understanding: Studies in Cognitive Science*, Academic Press, 1975.)

The history of programming languages is a history of movement from what-to-do descriptions to what-I-want descriptions. When computers were first introduced, they were programed in octal, and each programmer had to be intimate with his machine's architecture and instruction set. Now programmers work at a much higher level, telling their machines what to do using language primitives that are translated into hundreds or thousands of machine instructions.

In this chapter, Rich and Waters describe their way of moving even further away from the what-to-do style of interaction toward the what-I-want style. Their vision is of an environment that serves the same role that an apprentice serves to a craftsman, performing routine tasks with less and less direction.

A fundamental enabling idea is that programmers accumulate personal libraries of standard, templatelike arrangements of primitives and lower-level arrangements. These arrangements, which Rich and Waters call clichés, enable experienced programmers to do common things quickly. Their programmer's apprentice also has a cliché library and knows how to help human users to find clichés, combine them, and fill them in.

The Programmer's Apprentice

Charles Rich
Richard C. Waters

The long-term goal of the Programmer's Apprentice project is to develop a theory of how expert programmers analyze, synthesize, modify, explain, specify, verify and document programs. This is basic research at the intersection of artificial intelligence and software engineering. From the perspective of artificial intelligence, we are using programming as a domain in which to study fundamental issues in knowledge representation and reasoning. From the perspective of software engineering, we are applying techniques from artificial intelligence to automate the programming process. Other work in this intersection area is reviewed in IEEE [1988].

Recognizing that it will be a long time before it is possible to fully duplicate human programming abilities, the near-term goal of the project is to develop a system, called the Programmer's Apprentice, that provides intelligent assistance in all phases of the programming task.

The goals of this chapter are to lay out our vision of the Programmer's Apprentice, the principles and techniques underlying it, and our progress towards it. The primary vehicle for this exposition is three scenarios illustrating the use of the Apprentice in three phases of the programming task: implementation, design, and requirements. The first of these scenarios is taken from a completed working prototype. The second and third scenarios are the targets for prototype systems currently under construction.

Before the scenarios, we discuss below the two basic principles underlying this chapter, namely, the assistant approach and inspection methods (clichés), and our two main technical advances, namely the Plan Calculus and a hybrid reasoning system (CAKE).

The Assistant Approach

One approach to solving current software problems is to totally eliminate programmers through *automatic programming*. As typically conceived, automatic programming calls for an end user to write a complete specification for what he wants; a completely automatic system then generates a program satisfying this specification. Program generators of this type have been successfully developed for a number of narrow applications. However, completely automatic programming for a broad range of applications is not a realistic near-term goal [Rich & Waters 1988].

A fundamental difficulty with the completely automatic approach is the trade-off between, on the one hand, the generality of a specification language, and on the other hand, its ease of use and compilation (implementation). Specification languages have been developed that are easy to use and relatively easy to compile, but only for narrow applications. The situation with general-purpose specification languages, however, is much less satisfactory. Writing a complete specification in a general-purpose specification language (for example, first-order logic) is seldom easier—and often incredibly harder—than writing a program. Furthermore, there has been little success in developing automatic systems that compile efficient programs from such specifications.

An alternate approach is to assist programmers, rather than replace them. A provocative example of the assistant approach was proposed by IBM's Harlan Mills in the early 1970's. He suggested creating "chief programmer teams" by surrounding expert programmers with support staffs of human assistants, including junior programmers, documentation writers, program librarians, and so on. The productivity of the chief programmer was thereby increased, because he could apply his full effort to the most difficult parts of a given software task without getting bogged down in the routine details that currently use up most of every programmer's time. Experience has shown that this division of labor can be very successful. Our goal is to provide *every* programmer with a support team in the form of an intelligent computer program, called the Programmer's Apprentice.

We think of the Apprentice as a new *agent* in the software process (see figure 1), rather than a tool. It should interact with the programmer like a human assistant. Furthermore, both the programmer and the Apprentice have access to all the facilities of the existing programming environment. The key to making this approach work is the communication between the programmer and the Apprentice: it must be based on a substantial body of shared knowledge of programming technique. If the programmer had to explain everything to the Apprentice from first principles, it would be easier to do it himself.

The assistant approach lends itself to incremental progress. Initially, the Apprentice will be able to take over only the simplest and most routine

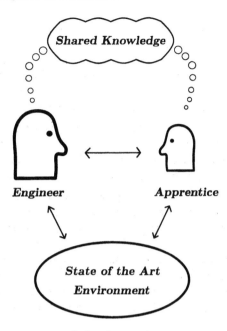

Figure 1. The Programmer and the Apprentice are two cooperating agents in the software process. Both of them use tools in the programming environment through the existing interfaces. The scenarios in this chapter illustrate how the Programmer and the Apprentice communicate with each other and the shared programming knowledge which makes this communication possible.

parts of the programming task (as illustrated in the first scenario below). As technology advances, however, the proportion of the task handled by the Apprentice will increase—we don't have to wait until some subtask can be totally automated. Note that some parts of a given program may always have to be hand-coded due, for example, to extremely strict performance requirements. However, especially in large systems, there is always plenty of routine work to be done.

Inspection Methods

Human programmers seldom think only in terms of primitive elements, such as assignments and tests. Rather, like engineers in other disciplines, they mostly think in terms of commonly used combinations of elements with familiar names. We call these familiar combinations *clichés*. *Successive approximation*, *device driver*, and *information system*, are examples of programming clichés spanning the range from low-level implementation ideas to high-level specification concepts. (For evidence of the psychological reality of programming clichés, see Soloway and Ehrlich [1984]).

In general, a cliché consists of *roles* and *constraints*. The roles of a cliché are the parts that vary from one occurrence of the cliché to the next. The constraints are used to specify fixed elements of structure (parts that are present in every occurrence), to check that the parts that fill the roles in a particular occurrence are consistent, and to compute how to fill empty roles in a partially specified occurrence of a cliché.

An essential property of clichés is their relationship to one another. For example, a cliché may be a special case or an extension of another cliché. Algorithmic and data structure clichés may be related as possible implementations of specification clichés.

Given a library of clichés, it is possible to perform many programming tasks *by inspection*, rather than by reasoning from first principles. For example, in analysis by inspection, properties of a program are deduced by recognizing occurrences of clichés and referring to their known properties. In synthesis by inspection, implementation decisions are made by recognizing clichés in specifications, and then choosing among various implementation clichés. (An intelligent assistant that makes use of a library of clichés about the *process* of programming is described by Huff and Lesser [1988]).

The Programmer's Apprentice focuses on the use of inspection methods to automate programming, as opposed to more general, but harder to control methods, such as deductive synthesis or program transformations. In human programming, inspection methods are the most effective approach to use whenever they are applicable. However, because inspection methods are ultimately based on experience, they are applicable only to the routine parts of programming problems. This is compatible with the intended division of labor between the programmer and the Apprentice.

Codifying clichés is a central activity in the Programmer's Apprentice project. The upcoming scenarios show parts of the libraries we are building in the areas of program implementation, design, and requirements. The scenarios also illustrate how a shared vocabulary of clichés serves as the language of communication between the programmer and the Apprentice.

The Plan Calculus

Clichés and inspection methods are theoretical (and perhaps psychological) concepts. To apply these ideas, clichés need to be represented in a concrete, machine-usable form. A cornerstone of the Programmer's Apprentice is a formal representation for programs and programming clichés, called the *Plan Calculus*. This formalism was developed early in the project. We will summarize only its key properties here (for more details see Rich [1981] and Rich and Waters [1990]).

To a first approximation, the Plan Calculus can be thought of as combining the representation properties of flowcharts, data flow schemas, and abstract data types. A *plan* is essentially a hierarchical graph structure made up of different kinds of boxes (denoting operations and tests) and arrows (denoting control and data flow). The representation has both a graphical notation (see the Plan Calculus Example) and a formal semantics used for reasoning (see the next section).

The Plan Calculus gives the Apprentice a "mental language" that abstracts away from the details of algorithms and data structures that are a result only of their expression in a particular programming language. For example, data flow between two operations can be achieved either by setting a variable and then using it, or (if the language allows) by nesting the invocation of the producing operation inside the invocation of the consuming operation. Similarly, the same net control flow between operations and tests can be achieved by many different combinations of conditional primitives available in different languages. The explicit representation of control and data flow in the Plan Calculus greatly simplifies all of the manipulations that need to be performed to support the programming task, as well as making most of the internals of the Apprentice programming-language independent.

In the architecture of the Programmer's Apprentice, program text (for example, in Lisp or Ada), is considered only a *presentation* of program structure for communication between the programmer and the Apprentice or between the Apprentice and other parts of the programming environment (for example, the compiler). Other presentations, such as graphics, may also be appropriate in certain circumstances, though this is not a research direction we are pursuing at the moment.

The Plan Calculus is also a wide-spectrum formalism. Each operation and test in a plan has associated with it a set of preconditions and postconditions specified in a logical language. A plan in which all of the operations and tests are specified to be the primitives of some programming language is equivalent to a concrete program. However, the Plan Calculus is also used to represent partially designed programs and programming clichés, in which case the operations and tests in a plan may have abstract or incomplete specifications, and there may be arbitrary logical constraints, as well as data and control flow.

Taxonomic relationships between clichés, such as specialization, are handled by special-purpose mechanisms in the cliché library. The relationship between a specification and an implementation is represented in the Plan Calculus by an *overlay* (see figure 2). Formally, an overlay defines a mapping from the set of instances of the implementation plan to the set of instances of the specification. (This is a generalization of the *abstraction function* in the abstract data type methodology). A cliché library may contain different overlays with the same domain and/or range, corresponding to different ways of abstracting the same implementation and/or different ways of implementing the same specification.

A key feature of overlays is that they can be used for both analysis and synthesis by inspection. The scenarios in this chapter concentrate on program synthesis; examples of the use of the Plan Calculus in program analysis can be be found in the following chapter in this volume, Wills [1990], and in Rich and Waters [1990].

A Plan Calculus example

An example of the graphical notation for an overlay in the Plan Calculus is shown in figure 2. The name of the overlay is *bump-and-update-as-push*. In general, an overlay diagram has a plan diagram on each side, with a set of hooked lines, called *correspondences*, between them. The plan diagram on the left side defines the implementation, which is the domain of the mapping defined by the overlay; the plan diagram on the right side defines the specification, which is the range of the mapping; the correspondences define the mapping.

In this example, the right side of the overlay is a degenerate plan diagram with only a single box: the specification being implemented in this overlay is the *push* operation on a *list*. (List is a data abstraction having a *head* of any type and a *tail*, which is a list or empty). The diagram shows that *push* has two inputs, the *old* list and the *input* (of any type), and one output, the *new* list. The postcondition of push (logical specifications are usually not shown in diagrams), specifies that the head of the new list is equal to the input and that the tail of the new list is equal to the old list.

The left side of this overlay is a plan diagram representing a clichéd combination of operations on an *indexed sequence* (a *base* sequence with an associated *index* integer), in which the index is decremented and a new term is stored. The name of this plan is *bump-and-update*. It has four roles: *old* (an indexed sequence), *bump* (an operation that adds one), *update* (an operation that stores a new term in a sequence), and *new* (an indexed sequence). Data flow constraints between these roles are indicated by solid arrows. (Because this plan has no conditional structure, there are no control flow arrows—control flow is indicated in plan diagrams by cross-hatched arrows).

There are three correspondences in this overlay. Two of these correspondences are annotated with the name of another overlay called *indexed-sequence-as-list*. This means that the old indexed sequence of bump-and-update, viewed as a list according to indexed-sequence-as-list, corresponds to the old input of push, and similarly for the new roles. Indexed-sequence-as-list is a data abstraction function defined as follows: the head of the list corresponds to the term of the base indexed by the index; the tail of the

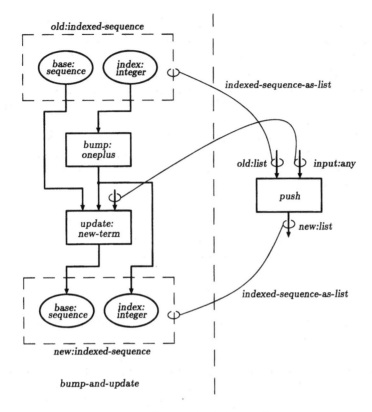

Figure 2. An overlay in the Plan Calculus.

list is recursively defined as the list implemented by the indexed sequence with the same base and one minus the index; the empty list corresponds to the indexed sequence with index zero. The third correspondence in the diagram indicates that the new term input of the update operation in bump-and-update (the other two inputs are the sequence and the index) corresponds to the object being pushed onto the list.

A Hybrid Reasoning System

The degree of automation that the Apprentice can provide ultimately depends on its ability to reason about structured objects (programs, specifications, requirements) and their properties. Our approach to this reasoning task is to use a combination of special-purpose techniques and general-purpose logical reasoning.

Special-purpose representations and algorithms are essential to avoid the combinatorial explosions that typically occur in general-purpose logical reasoning systems. On the other hand, logic-based reasoning is very valuable when used, under tight control, as the "glue" between inferences made in different special-purpose representations.

This section describes a hybrid knowledge representation and reasoning system, called CAKE [Rich 1985], that we have developed and are using for all current work in the project. Figure 3 shows the architecture of CAKE. Note that CAKE combines special-purpose representations, such as frames and the Plan Calculus, with general-purpose logical and mathematical reasoning. Each layer of CAKE builds on facilities provided by the layers below.

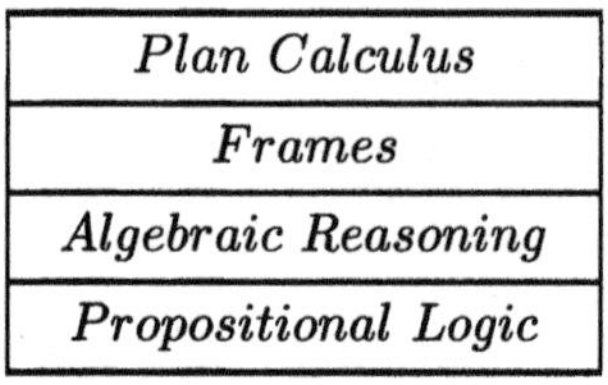

| *Plan Calculus* |
| *Frames* |
| *Algebraic Reasoning* |
| *Propositional Logic* |

Figure 3. The hybrid knowledge representation and reasoning system (CAKE) has a layered architecture.

A short transcript from the currently running version of CAKE, illustrating some of the facilities provided in the propositional, algebraic, and frame layers is shown in figure 4. (Line numbers in the following discussion refer to those in the figure). These facilities are motivated in general by the desired characteristics of the Apprentice; we will later point out specific examples of their use in the scenarios.

The propositional layer of CAKE provides three principal facilities. First, it automatically performs simple "one-step" deductions (lines 1–3) (technically, unit propositional resolution). The use of this very limited form of logical deduction is a kind of tight control essential to the hybrid architecture.

Second, the propositional layer acts as a recording medium for dependencies (what is often called a truth-maintenance system), and thus supports explanation (line 3) and retraction (lines 4–5). These facilities are motivated by the observation that when you delegate work to an assistant, you also need to have accountability and the ability to recover from mistakes, in case it doesn't do what you expected.

Third, the propositional layer detects contradictions (lines 6–7). Furthermore, contradictions are represented explicitly in such a way that reasoning can continue with other information not involved in the contradiction. This feature is motivated by the desire for the Apprentice to support an evolutionary programming process. In this kind of process, the pro-

```
1>  (Assertq P)
2>  (Assertq (Implies P Q))
3>  (Whyq Q)
        Q is TRUE by Modus Ponens from:
            1. (IMPLIES P Q) is TRUE as a premise.
            2. P is TRUE as a premise.
4>  (Retractq P)
5>  (Whyq Q)
        I don't know whether or not Q is true.
6>  (Assertq (And P (Not Q)))
        **Contradiction: There is a conflict between the premises:
            1. (AND P (NOT Q)) is TRUE.
            2. (IMPLIES P Q) is TRUE.
        Type cr to postpone dealing with this contradiction.
        Type premise number to retract one of the premises.
7>  1
        Retracting (AND P (NOT Q)) being TRUE...
        #<Node (AND P (NOT Q)): False>
8>  (Assertq (= I J))
9>  (Whyq (= (F I) (F J)))
        (= (F I) (F J)) is TRUE by Equality from:
            1. (= I J) is TRUE as a premise.
10> (Assertq (Transitive R))
11> (Assertq (R W X))
12> (Assertq (R X Y))
13> (Assertq (R Y Z))
14> (Whyq (R W Z))
        (R W Z) is TRUE by Transitivity from:
            1. (R W X) is TRUE as a premise.
            2. (R X Y) is TRUE as a premise.
            3. (R Y Z) is TRUE as a premise.
            4. (TRANSITIVE R) is TRUE as a premise.
15> (Assertq (Subset A B))
16> (Assertq (Member X A))
17> (Whyq (Member X B))
        (MEMBER X B) is TRUE by Subsumption from:
            1. (SUBSET A B) is TRUE as a premise.
            2. (MEMBER X A) is TRUE as a premise.
18> (Deftype Address (:Specializes Number))
19> (Deframe Interrupt
        (:Roles (Location Address) Program))
20> (Deframe Device
        (:Roles (Transmit Address) (Receive Address)))
21> (Deframe Interface
        (:Roles (Target Device) (From Interrupt) (To Interrupt))
        (:Constraints (= (Location ?From) (Receive ?Target))
                      (= (Location ?To) (Transmit ?Target))))
22> (FInstantiate 'Interface :Name 'K7)
23> (FPut (>> 'K7 'Target 'Receive) 777777)
24> (FGet (>> 'K7 'From 'Location))
        777777
25> (Why ...)
        (= 777777 (LOCATION (FROM K7))) is TRUE by Equality from:
            1. (= (LOCATION (FROM K7))
                  (RECEIVE (TARGET K7))) is TRUE.
            2. (= (RECEIVE (TARGET K7)) 777777) is TRUE as a premise.
```

Figure 4. A transcript illustrating the capabilities of CAKE.

grammer's knowledge is very often in an inconsistent state, particularly during the requirements acquisition and analysis phase.

The algebraic layer of CAKE contains special-purpose decision procedures for congruence closure, common algebraic properties of operators (such as commutativity, associativity, and transitivity), partial functions, and the algebra of sets. The congruence closure algorithm in this layer determines whether or not terms are equal by substitution of equal subterms (lines 8–9). The decision procedure for transitivity (lines 10–14) determines when elements of a binary relation follow by transitivity from other elements. The algebra of sets (lines 15–17) involves the theory of membership, subset, union, intersection and complements.

Equality reasoning is very important for the Apprentice, because the formal semantics of the Plan Calculus makes heavy use of equality. Data flow arrows in plans imply equalities between terms representing the source and destination points; correspondences in overlays are also equalities. Other algebraic properties, such as transitivity, commutativity, etc., come up everywhere in the formal modeling of data structures.

The frames layer of CAKE supports the standard frame notions of inheritance (:Specializes in line 18), slots (:Rôles in lines 19–21), and instantiation (line 22). The organization of the Apprentice's cliché library is based on frame inheritance.

A notable feature of CAKE's frame system is that constraints are implemented in a general way. For example, the definition of the *interface* frame (line 21) has constraints between the roles of the instances filling its roles. When an instance of an interface is created (line 22) and a particular value ("777777") is put into one of its "second level" roles (line 23), the same value can be retrieved from the other constrained role (line 24). This propagation is not achieved by *ad hoc* procedures, but by the operation of the underlying logical reasoning system, including dependencies (line 25). Constraint propagation is intended to support the ability of the Apprentice to incrementally acquire information in any order.

The Plan Calculus layer of CAKE supports graph-theoretic manipulations of plan diagrams and overlay diagrams, such as following arcs. It also implements the formal semantics of the Plan Calculus, so that hybrid reasoning can take place involving both structure (as expressed by the diagrams) and function (as expressed in the preconditions, postconditions, and other logical annotations). In the semantics of the Plan Calculus, names of plans become predicate symbols, names of roles and overlays become function symbols, correspondences become equalities, data flow becomes a combination of equalities and a partial order, and control flow becomes a combination of an equivalence relation and a partial order.

Programmer's Apprentice Scenarios

Viewed most simply, the software development process has, at one end, the desires of an end user and, at the other end, a program that can be executed on a machine. The part of the software process closest to the user is typically called requirements acquisition; the part of the process nearest the machine is typically called implementation; the area in the middle can be generally described as design. In order to achieve dramatic productivity improvements, the Programmer's Apprentice must eventually span the entire process between these boundaries. However, because this is a very large undertaking, we have begun by building prototypes of parts of the Apprentice.

Rather than trying to define the boundaries between requirements acquisition, design, and implementation *a priori* (as for example, in the traditional waterfall model), we have adopted the strategy of working inward from the two external boundaries, as shown in figure 5. This strategy allows us to explore and discover the appropriate internal boundaries as we proceed. We want to emphasize, however, that this division into two efforts is a research strategy. We plan to eventually connect the two prototypes as a first demonstration of a complete Apprentice. We then expect to need to rebuild significantly based on what is learned.

Figure 5. Prototypes of the Programmer's Apprentice are being built working inward from the two boundaries of the software development process.

There are three scenarios following. The first two scenarios illustrate a progression of capabilities of the Apprentice in the areas of implementation and design; the third scenario illustrates capabilities in the requirements area. The first scenario is the actual output of a completed running system, called KBEmacs. The second and third scenarios are *target* scenarios, which are guiding work in progress on what we are calling the Design Apprentice and the Requirements Apprentice.

KBEmacs

Knowledge-Based Editor in Emacs (KBEmacs) is a prototype of a part of the Programmer's Apprentice completed several years ago to demonstrate the utility of the assistant approach and clichés in the implementation part of the software process. Figure 6 shows an example of using KBEmacs to implement a 55 line Ada program. (We have omitted the intermediate states of the editing session after each command. See Waters [1985] and Rich and Waters [1990] for the full scenario).

The implementation clichés used in this scenario are: *simple report* (which is defined in the next section), *chain enumeration*, and *query user for key*. Note that *enumerator, main file key, title*, and *summary* are the names of roles in these clichés. Our current library of implementation clichés is similar in scope and level to earlier machine-usable codifications, such as Green and Barstow [1978]; however, as discussed above, we have developed an improved formal representation.

In essence, KBEmacs adds a new, higher level of editing commands to the existing text and syntax-based commands of Emacs (consistent with the assistant approach, the text and syntax-based commands are still available). Using KBEmacs, changes in the algorithmic structure of a program can be achieved by a single command, even when they correspond to widespread textual changes in the program.

Two important capabilities of KBEmacs that are not illustrated in figure 6, but appear in the full scenario, are the automatic generation of program documentation (that is, explaining the program in terms of the clichés used), and programming-language independence. KBEmacs was originally constructed to operate on Lisp programs; relatively little effort was required to extend it to operate on Ada programs as well.

The major deficiencies of KBEmacs are related to the fact that it was completed before CAKE was available. (In fact, many of the features of CAKE are motivated in part by the deficiencies of KBEmacs). The implementation of the Plan Calculus used in KBEmacs is essentially the graph formalism, without the associated logical reasoning. This means, for example, that KBEmacs cannot reason about side-effects in any general way. Also, constraints in KBEmacs (see the next section) are implemented by *ad hoc* procedures rather than using a general-purpose scheme.

Defining an implementation cliché

Figure 7 illustrates the facility in KBEmacs for defining clichés using an extension of Ada syntax. KBEmacs automatically analyzes this text to extract the underlying plan for the cliché. This plan may then be combined with the plans for other clichés, using KBEmacs commands, to make new programs. Figure 7 defines the cliché *simple report*, which is used in the scenario of figure 6. The only extensions to the syntax of Ada in cliché definitions are the new defining form "`cliche ... is ...`," and the use of braces for role names and other annotation. Note, however, that this provides a more general form of parameterization than supported by the Ada package facility.

Define a simple_report procedure UNIT_REPAIR_REPORT.
Fill the enumerator with a chain_enumeration of UNITS and REPAIRS.
Fill the main_file_key with a query_user_for_key of UNITS.
Fill the title with ("Report of Repairs on Unit" & UNIT_KEY).
Remove the summary.

⇓

```
with CALENDAR, FUNCTIONS, MAINTENANCE_FILES, TEXT_IO;
use CALENDAR, FUNCTIONS, MAINTENANCE_FILES, TEXT_IO;
procedure UNIT_REPAIR_REPORT is
   use DEFECT_IO, REPAIR_IO, UNIT_IO, INT_IO;
   CURRENT_DATE: constant STRING := FORMAT_DATE(CLOCK);
   DEFECT: DEFECT_TYPE;
   REPAIR: REPAIR_TYPE;
   REPAIR_INDEX: REPAIR_INDEX_TYPE;
   REPORT: TEXT_IO.FILE_TYPE;
   TITLE: STRING(1..33);
   UNIT: UNIT_TYPE;
   UNIT_KEY: UNIT_KEY_TYPE;
   procedure CLEAN_UP is
      begin
       SET_OUTPUT(STANDARD_OUTPUT);
       CLOSE(DEFECTS); CLOSE(REPAIRS); CLOSE(UNITS); CLOSE(REPORT);
      exception
       when STATUS_ERROR return; =>
      end CLEAN_UP;
begin
   OPEN(DEFECTS, IN_FILE, DEFECTS_NAME);
   OPEN(REPAIRS, IN_FILE, REPAIRS_NAME);
   OPEN(UNITS, IN_FILE, UNITS_NAME);
   CREATE(REPORT, OUT_FILE, "report.txt");
   loop
      begin
         NEW_LINE; PUT ("Enter UNIT Key: "); GET(UNIT_KEY);
         READ(UNITS, UNIT, UNIT_KEY);
         exit;
      exception
         when END_ERROR => PUT("Invalid UNIT Key"); NEW_LINE;
      end;
   end loop;
   TITLE := "Report of Repairs on Unit" & UNIT_KEY;
   SET_OUTPUT(REPORT);
   NEW_LINE(4); SET_COL(20); PUT(CURRENT_DATE);
   NEW_LINE(2); SET_COL(13); PUT(TITLE); NEW_LINE(60);
   READ(UNITS, UNIT, UNIT_KEY); REPAIR_INDEX := UNIT.REPAIR;
   while not NULL_INDEX(REPAIR_INDEX) loop
      READ(REPAIRS, REPAIR, REPAIR_INDEX);
      if LINE > 64 then
         NEW_PAGE; NEW_LINE; PUT("Page: "); PUT(INTEGER(PAGE-1), 3);
         SET_COL(13); PUT(TITLE); SET_COL(61); PUT(CURRENT_DATE);
         NEW_LINE(2); PUT("   Date      Defect     Description/Comment");
         NEW_LINE(2);
      end if;
      READ(DEFECTS, DEFECT, REPAIR.DEFECT);
      PUT(FORMAT_DATE(REPAIR.DATE)); SET_COL(13); PUT(REPAIR.DEFECT);
      SET_COL(20); PUT(DEFECT.NAME); NEW_LINE;
      SET_COL(22); PUT(REPAIR.COMMENT); NEW_LINE;
      REPAIR_INDEX := REPAIR.NEXT;
   end loop;
   CLEAN_UP;
exception
when DEVICE_ERROR | END_ERROR | NAME_ERROR | STATUS_ERROR =>
   CLEAN_UP; PUT("Data Base Inconsistent");
when others => CLEAN_UP; raise;
end UNIT_REPAIR_REPORT;
```

Figure 6. A verbatim transcript from KBEmacs. Given the five commands above, it produced these 55 lines of Ada code.

We envisage two levels of cliché definition activity using the Apprentice. First, the language-oriented interface makes it easy for a programmer to quickly define a cliché for his own (perhaps short-term) use. A second, much more intellectually demanding task, is to define a "suite" of clichés to be used by a large group of people over a long period of time.

Like most clichés, simple report includes some standard computation (for example, the printing of the title page), some roles to be filled in (for example, the title itself), and the data flow and control flow between them. This cliché has seven roles.

- The *file name* is the name of the file that will contain the report being produced.
- The *title* is printed on a title page and (along with the page number) at the top of each succeeding page.
- The *enumerator* enumerates the elements of some aggregate data structure.
- The *print item* is used to print out information about each of the enumerated elements.
- The *line limit* is used to determine when a page break should be inserted.
- The *column headings* are printed at the top of each page of the report to explain the output of the print item.
- The *summary* prints out some summary information at the end of the report.

The enumerator is a compound role with four sub-roles: the *input data*, the *empty test*, the *accessor*, and the *step*. These sub-roles can be filled individually, or they can be filled as a unit with an enumeration cliché (such as *chain enumeration* in figure 6).

The simple report cliché also includes four constraints, which are specified at the beginning of the cliché definition. The first constraint specifies "report.txt" as the default name for the file containing the report. This name will be used unless the programmer specifies some other name.

The second constraint specifies that the line limit should be 65 minus the number of lines printed by the print item and the number of lines printed by the summary. Because the line limit role is computed by this constraint, the programmer never has to fill it explicitly; the role will automatically be updated if the print item or summary are changed. For example, the line limit is computed to be 64 in figure 6.

The remaining two constraints provide default formats for printing items in the report and the column headings. If clichés have been defined for how to print a given type of object in a report and the corresponding headings, then the functions CORRESPONDING_PRINTING and CORRESPONDING_HEADINGS retrieve the appropriate clichés; otherwise, these functions are simple program generators that construct appropriate code based on

```
with CALENDAR, FUNCTIONS, TEXT_IO;
use CALENDAR, FUNCTIONS, TEXT_IO;
cliche SIMPLE_REPORT is
  primary roles ENUMERATOR, PRINT_ITEM, SUMMARY;
  described roles FILE_NAME, TITLE, ENUMERATOR, COLUMN_HEADINGS,
                  PRINT_ITEM, SUMMARY;
  comment "prints a report of the input data of the enumerator";
  constraints
    DEFAULT(the file_name, "report.txt");
    DERIVED(the line_limit,
              66-SIZE_IN_LINES(the print_item)
                -SIZE_IN_LINES(the summary));
    DEFAULT(the print_item,
              CORRESPONDING_PRINTING(the enumerator));
    DEFAULT(the column_headings,
              CORRESPONDING_HEADINGS(the print_item));
  end constraints;
  use INT_IO;
  CURRENT_DATE: constant STRING := FORMAT_DATE(CLOCK);
  DATA: {};
  REPORT: TEXT_IO.FILE_TYPE;
  TITLE: STRING(1..{});
  procedure CLEAN_UP is
  begin
    SET_OUTPUT(STANDARD_OUTPUT); CLOSE(REPORT);
  exception when STATUS_ERROR => return;
  end CLEAN_UP;
begin
  CREATE(REPORT, OUT_FILE, {the file_name});
  DATA := {the input data of the enumerator};
  SET_OUTPUT(REPORT);
  TITLE := {the title};
  NEW_LINE(4); SET_COL(20); PUT(CURRENT_DATE); NEW_LINE(2);
  SET_COL(13); PUT(TITLE); NEW_LINE(60);
  while not {the empty_test of the enumerator}(DATA) loop
    if LINE > {the line_limit} then
       NEW_PAGE; NEW_LINE; PUT("Page: "); PUT(INTEGER(PAGE-1), 3);
       SET_COL(13); PUT(TITLE);
       SET_COL(61); PUT(CURRENT_DATE); NEW_LINE(2);
       {the column_headings}({CURRENT_OUTPUT, modified});
    end if;
    {the print_item}({CURRENT_OUTPUT, modified},
                     {the accessor of the enumerator}(DATA));
    DATA := {the step of the enumerator}(DATA);
  end loop;
  {the summary}({CURRENT_OUTPUT, modified});
  CLEAN_UP;
exception
  when DEVICE_ERROR | END_ERROR | NAME_ERROR | STATUS_ERROR =>
    CLEAN_UP; PUT("Data Base Inconsistent");
  when others => CLEAN_UP; raise;
end SIMPLE_REPORT;
```

Figure 7. An Ada presentation of the simple report cliché. This program text is analyzed by KBEmacs to extract the underlying plan, which is stored and can then be referred to in KBEmacs commands, as in figure 6.

the definitions of the types of objects involved. As mentioned earlier, one of the deficiencies of KBEmacs is that the collection of functions used in constraints, such as SIZE_IN_LINES, CORRESPONDING_PRINTING, and COR-RESPONDING_HEADINGS, is not easy for the programmer to extend.

General issues in the target scenarios

Before presenting the following two target scenarios, it is important to set the scene by discussing what the Apprentice knows. In each case, the Apprentice is assumed to have an "intermediate" level of prior knowledge.

If it were possible for the Apprentice to know everything about what the user was going to do, then it would be preferable to have a program generator that constructed the desired programs completely automatically. However, this kind of complete knowledge is possible only in very restricted applications. The Apprentice is intended to be usable in a broad range of programming applications.

Alternatively, if the Apprentice knew much less than what is illustrated in the scenarios, the user would have to say too much. In particular, the user would either have to define the missing clichés or make do without them. In either case, the productivity and reliability benefits of the Apprentice would be significantly eroded. A major focus of this research is, therefore, to make sure that the Apprentice knows enough to be useful.

A second general issue in the two target scenarios is the user interface. Because the interface has not been fully designed, the interactions in the scenarios are intended to illustrate its major features, without being overly specific about details.

For example, input typed by the user is shown in simple English. The Apprentice will not, however, support arbitrary English input. The most important feature of the interface language shown in the scenarios is not the degree of syntactic flexibility, but the use of a large vocabulary of clichés. Because the Apprentice is currently targeted at expert programmers (we can also imagine applications of the technology to computer-aided education of novice programmers), we can assume that the user is conceptually familiar with the appropriate clichés. We expect that some combination of training, familiarization, synonyms, spelling correction, and browsing the cliché library will get around the problem of needed to know the exact names of the clichés.

Finally, note that several errors have intentionally been introduced into what the user says in each scenario. The particular errors chosen may not appear plausible to all readers. However, large numbers of errors *are* made during the programming process—many of which look obvious with hindsight. The errors introduced here were chosen to illustrate the capabilities of the Apprentice to detect and help correct errors in general.

The Design Apprentice

We are currently building a prototype of a part of the Programmer's Apprentice, called the Design Apprentice, which extends the capabilities of KBEmacs into the realm of design. The target scenario in this section represents our goals in this area. In comparison with KBEmacs, the Design Apprentice will demonstrate the following three major new capabilities of the Programmer's Apprentice.

- A declarative (specification-like) input language.
- Detection and explanation of errors made by the programmer.
- Automatic selection of reasonable implementation choices.

Work on the Design Apprentice began a short while ago with a small programming example, similar to figure 6, but emphasizing the use of CAKE to detect and explain errors made by the programmer.

The target scenario for the Design Apprentice concerns the detailed design of a device driver program. This type of program was chosen as a domain for two reasons. First, device drivers are of significant practical importance. Second, they are a good example of the kind of domain in which the Apprentice approach is most appropriate—namely domains in which there are many similar programs, but in which each program is likely to have some unanticipated idiosyncrasy.

Design clichés

The Design Apprentice's knowledge is embodied in clichés for typical specifications, typical designs, and typical hardware (see figure 8). Examples of specification clichés in the device driver domain include *initializing*, *reading*, *writing*, *opening*, and *closing* a device. Each of these clichés is annotated with information about what roles and constraints are mandatory, likely, or possible.

Examples of design clichés in the device driver domain include *device driver* and its specializations, such as *printer driver* and *interactive display driver*. The device driver cliché is a very abstract cliché, containing information that is common to all drivers. The printer driver cliché specifies, for example, that printer drivers only support writing operations and that complex output padding is sometimes required after characters that cause large movements of the print head. Examples of low-level algorithm clichés in the device driver domain include *semaphores*, *busy-wait*, and *watermark processing*.

Examples of hardware clichés that the Design Apprentice knows include *serial line unit*, *printer*, and *interactive display device*. A serial line unit is a standard bus interface used by many different kinds of hardware

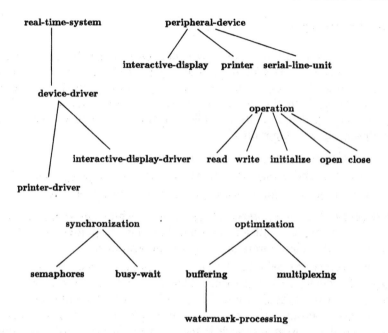

Figure 8. Part of a cliché library for the design of device drivers.

devices. It specifies a standard cluster of four buffer and control registers, which are used to operate the device.

Target scenario for program design

Figure 9 shows an interaction between a programmer and the Apprentice at the level of detailed program design. This is the first part of a much longer target scenario [Rich & Waters 1987], in which this initial design of the program is further elaborated and changed by the programmer, with assistance from the Apprentice.

Figure 9 begins with the programmer providing a specification. This could be done interactively or prepared with a text editor and submitted to the Apprentice all at once. The specification consists of two parts. The first part describes the hardware (here an imaginary device called the K7). The second part describes a driver program for the K7.

The specification of the K7 uses the cliché interactive display device. The K7 specification contains both positive information, which describes how particular roles of this cliché are filled in (for example, the screen height), and negative information, which states that some aspects of the cliché are not relevant (for example, the K7 does not support direct cursor positioning).

> The "K7" is an interactive display device where:
  The screen height is 4 lines.
  The screen width is 40 characters.
  The character mode is ASCII.
  Direct cursor positioning is not supported.
  The keyboard has three keys.

key	character	
ACKNOWLEDGE	ACK	#O006
YES	Y	#O131
NO	N	#O116

  The bus interface is a standard SLU except that:
  Writing a 1 in Bit 1 of the XCSR initializes the device.
  Initializing the device blanks the screen and homes up the cursor.
  Sending characters to the K7 and initializing the K7 cannot be
    done at the same time.
> The K7 driver is an interactive display driver where:
  Echoing is not supported
  Rubout handling is not supported.
  The basic software functions are:
  Supported: PUTC, WRITE & GETC.
  Ignored: OPEN & CLOSE.
  Not supported: READ & SEEK.
  The control codes are:
    :CLEAR - blanks the screen.
    :RESET - does a :CLEAR and flushes pending input.
    :LINE-NUMBER - returns the cursor line.
  The implementation guidelines are:
  1- Do no consing.
  2- Favor space efficiency.
  3- Defer error checking.
> Write code for the K7 driver.
  Request for Advice: I do not know how to support :CLEAR.
  Note:
  (1) :CLEAR blanks the screen.
  (2) The only K7 operation that blanks the screen is initialization.
  Unfortunately:
  (3) Initializing the K7 homes up the cursor.
  (4) A device should not be initialized except by the INIT function.
> :CLEAR should home up the cursor.
> Support :CLEAR by initializing the device.
  Request for Advice: I do not know how to support :LINE-NUMBER.
  Note:
  (1) :LINE-NUMBER returns the cursor line.
  (2) No K7 operation returns the cursor line.
> Postpone.
  Constraint Violation: There should be a lookahead operation.
  Note: The following standard operations provide lookahead:
  (1) :ARE-CHARS-WAITING returns T if there are
      pending input characters.
  (2) :NUMBER-CHARS-WAITING returns the number of pending
      input characters.
  (3) :PEEK returns the next pending input character (without
      removing it from buffer) or NIL if none.
  NIL *if there are no pending*
      input characters and returns the next character
      (without removing it from the input buffer) if a
      character is pending.
> Use (2).

Figure 9. Hypothetical dialog between a programmer and the Design Apprentice. Programmer input follows the > prompt. Response from Apprentice is in italics.

The last five lines of the K7 specification make use of the serial line unit (SLU) cliché. The phrase "except that" indicates that the programmer is modifying the SLU cliché rather than just filling in its roles. The exception description makes use of a number of technical terms (that is, "XCSR," "initialize the device," "blank the screen," etc.), which are defined for SLU's. This vocabulary makes it possible for the programmer to describe the exception succinctly.

The second part of the specification in figure 9 concerns the driver program. As with the K7 specification, most of the specification says how various roles of the relevant cliché are filled in (the cliché in this case is interactive display driver).

A particularly interesting part of the driver specification is the implementation guidelines section at the end. The Apprentice uses these guidelines to decide which algorithms to pick when implementing the driver. For example, the first two guidelines cause the Apprentice to select algorithms with no dynamic storage allocation and which trade time for space. The third guideline instructs the Apprentice to defer inclusion of error checking code until after the prototype version of the driver is written and tested. The key benefit of this postponement is not that it saves the Apprentice coding time, but that it saves the programmer thinking time.

The remainder of the interaction in figure 9 illustrates the Design Apprentice's ability to detect and explain errors made by the programmer. These errors can be roughly divided into errors of omission (incompleteness) and errors of commission (inconsistency).

Incompleteness can be of two kinds. First, the specification may be missing some expected information, which if provided, would allow the Apprentice to finish the implementation. In this case, the Apprentice requests the needed information and proceeds (for example, the interaction concerning :CLEAR in figure 9). Second, the Apprentice may simply not have enough knowledge to implement a given specification. In this case, the programmer is asked to provide specific implementation instructions (for example, the interaction concerning :LINE-NUMBER in figure 9). Note that the programmer may postpone answering such a question. This enables the programmer to control the interaction.

Inconsistency can also be of two kinds. First, there may be inconsistency between different things the programmer says explicitly. Second, there may be inconsistency between what the programmer says and the knowledge contained in the clichés he invokes (for example, the last interaction in figure 9).

After the problems with :CLEAR and :LINE-NUMBER have been resolved, the Apprentice generates executable code for the K7 driver, as requested. To do so, the Apprentice needs to automatically make a number of low-level implementation decisions. For example, the Apprentice chooses watermark processing to increase the throughput of the small output buffers. It also makes a number of reasonable decisions regarding the implementation of the various queues and semaphores in the driver. For more details, see Rich and Waters [1987].

The Requirements Apprentice

This section describes a prototype of a part of the Programmer's Apprentice, called the Requirements Apprentice, that we are currently building to support the earliest part of the programming process, namely requirements acquisition and analysis (see Reubenstein and Waters [1989]). The target scenario in this section represents our goals in this area for a three-year effort that began approximately two years ago. Like the Design Apprentice, this prototype uses CAKE as the underlying knowledge representation and reasoning system.

Research on requirements acquisition is important for two reasons. From the perspective of artificial intelligence, it is a good domain in which to pursue fundamental issues in knowledge acquisition. From the perspective of software engineering, studies have indicated that errors in requirements are more costly than any other kind of error. Furthermore, requirements acquisition is not well supported by current software tools.

From informal to formal descriptions

It is useful to distinguish several phases in the requirements acquisition process. The earliest phase usually takes the form of a "skull session," whose goal is to achieve consensus among a group of end users about what they want. The requirements analyst's main role in this phase relies on his interpersonal skills. The end product of this phase is typically an *informal* description of the requirements.

Informal descriptions are characterized by, among other things, incompleteness, ambiguity, contradiction, misordering of information, and the use of undefined terms. These characteristics are not usually due to laziness or incompetence, rather, informality is an essential characteristic of the human thought process. It is part of a powerful debugging strategy for dealing with complexity, which shows up in many problem solving domains: start with an almost-right description and then incrementally modify it until it is acceptable. Thus, dealing with informality in software requirements is not just a matter of being user-friendly—it is a fundamental requisite.

Most current work on software requirements tools focuses on validating *formal* descriptions (that is, descriptions that obey a strict set of mathematical rules of form and content). The main goal of formal validation is to increase the user's confidence that a given formal description actually corresponds to his desires by applying simulation, symbolic execution, and various kinds of mathematical analysis. This does not, however, address the key question of how an informal description becomes a formal description in the first place.

The focus of the Requirements Apprentice is on the transition from informal to formal descriptions. For example, one of the goals of our research is to elaborate the initial characterization of informality given above, and to develop strategies and heuristics for removing these features from informal descriptions.

Requirements clichés

As part of our research on the Requirements Apprentice, we are codifying clichés in the area of software requirements (see figure 10). Compared to implementation and design clichés, the range of clichés involved in software requirements is much more open-ended. In principle, any part of the real world may be relevant to specifying a requirement. The Apprentice will be more or less useful in a given application to the extent that the relevant clichés have been codified.

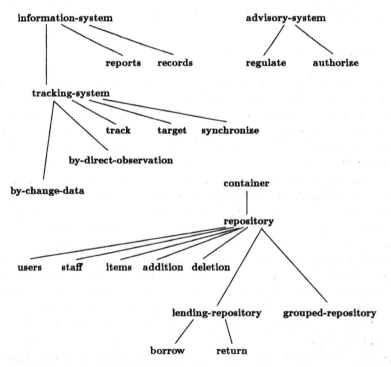

Figure 10. Part of a cliché library for software requirements.

The target scenario for the Requirements Apprentice concerns the requirements for a hypothetical library system (see Wing [1988]) for a comparison with other approaches to the same example). Three examples of clichés in this area are: *repository, information system,* and *tracking system.*

A repository is an entity in the physical world. The basic function of a repository is to ensure that items entering the repository will be available for later removal. There are a variety of physical constraints that apply to repositories. For example, because each item has a physical existence, it can only be in one place at a time and therefore must either be in the repository or not.

There are several kinds of repositories. Simple repositories merely take in items and then give them out. A more complex kind of repository supports the lending of items, which are expected to be returned. Another dimension of variation concerns the items themselves. The items may be unrelated or they may be grouped into classes. Example repositories include: a storage warehouse (simple repository for unrelated items), a grocery store (simple repository for items grouped in classes), and a rental car agency (lending repository for items grouped in classes).

In contrast to the repository cliché, the information system cliché describes a class of software systems rather than a class of physical objects. The intent of the information system cliché is to capture the commonality between programs such as personnel systems, bibliographic data bases, and inventory control systems. Roles of an information system include an *information schema*, a set of *transactions* which can create/modify/delete the data, a set of *reports* which display parts of the data, *integrity constraints* on the data, a *staff* which manage the information system, and *users* which utilize the information system.

A tracking system is a specialized kind of information system which keeps track of the state of a physical object (called the *target*). The target object is assumed to have a (possibly complex) state and to be subject to various physical operations that can modify this state. The information in the tracking system describes the state of the target object. The transactions modify this information to reflect changes in the target's state.

There are several kinds of tracking systems. A tracking system may follow several targets instead of just one. A tracking system may keep a history of past states of the target. A tracking system may operate based on direct observations of the state of the target or based on observations of operations on the target. Finally, a tracking system may participate in controlling the operations on the target, rather than merely observing them. Example tracking systems include: aircraft tracking systems (tracking multiple targets based on direct observations of their position) and inventory control systems (tracking a repository based on observations of operations that modify its contents).

Target scenario for requirements

The scenario in figure 11 shows an analyst interacting with the Requirements Apprentice. It is important to emphasize that we are not trying to build a system to be used directly by the end user. We are relying on the interpersonal skills of the analyst to facilitate the knowledge acquisition process.

The first four commands in figure 11 begin the process of building a requirement by introducing the new terms *library* and *book*. Based on these four commands and the contents of the tracking system and repository clichés, the Apprentice augments its internal model of the evolving requirement in a number of ways.

For example, because the state of a repository is the collection of items it contains (in this case, books), the Apprentice uses the constraints in the tracking system cliché to derive an information schema that provides fields for the three properties listed for books. Also based on the constraints in the tracking system cliché, an expectation is created within the Apprentice that a set of transactions will be defined corresponding to the typical operations on a repository.

Note that the new terms are far from fully defined at this point. They are incomplete because many roles remain to be filled in. They are ambiguous because it is not yet clear which kind of tracking system is intended, or which kind of repository a library is. Because incompleteness and ambiguity are inevitable during the early stages of constructing a requirement, the Apprentice refrains from complaining at this point. It accepts information and performs inferences on a "catch as catch can" basis. However, if requested, the Apprentice can provide a list of currently unresolved issues (see figure 12) to guide the analyst in finishing the requirement.

The next four commands in figure 11 begin the definition of the transactions to be supported by the database. The key terms in these commands are *addition* and *removal*: these are two of the standard operations supported by a repository.

The first command to trigger a response from the Apprentice is the analyst's attempt to define the *return* transaction. The Apprentice complains that, as currently defined, returning a book is identical to acquiring a book. (The equality reasoning facilities in CAKE can make this deduction). This contradicts the Apprentice's expectation that new terms should not be synonymous with old terms unless explicitly declared to be so. The analyst does not have to deal with this problem immediately—he could go on to other things leaving the problem pending. In this case, however, he decides to deal with the problem right away.

Studying the explanation generated by the Apprentice at his request (using the dependency facilities of CAKE) the analyst realizes that he made

> Begin a requirement for a system called "LIBDB."
> LIBDB is a tracking system which tracks a "library."
> A library is a repository for "books."
> A book has the properties:
>   title - a text string,
>   author - a person's name,
>   ISBN - a unique alphanumeric key.
> Display the transactions subsection.
> The "acquire" transaction tracks the addition of a book.
> The "checkout" transaction tracks the removal of a book.
> The "return" transaction is the inverse of checkout.
Problem: The return transaction is identical to the acquire transaction.
> Explain.
(1) The return transaction is identical to the acquire transaction.
Because:
(2) The acquire transaction tracks the addition of a book.
(3) The return transaction tracks the addition of a book.
Because:
(4) The checkout transaction tracks the removal of a book.
(5) The return transaction is the inverse of the checkout transaction.
> Retract (4).
> The checkout transaction tracks the borrowing of a book.
Note: Assuming a library is a lending repository.
> The "retire" transaction tracks the removal of a book.
The "purge" transaction tracks the removal of every copy of a book.
Note: The term every suggests that book is a class. If this is not the
*   case, then the retire transaction is identical to the purge*
*   transaction.*
> Redefine "book" to be a class.
Book is a class with properties:
*   title - a text string,*
*   author - a person's name,*
*   ISBN - a unique alphanumeric key.*
> A "copy" is an instance of a book.
> A copy has the property:
>   copy number - a number unique within the class.
> Redefine transactions on a book to apply to a copy.
Redefining acquire, retire, checkout, and return.

Figure 11. Hypothetical dialog between an analyst and the Requirements Apprentice. Programmer input follows the > prompts; responses from Apprentice are in italics.

3.1.1.1 Checkout

The "checkout" transaction tracks the borrowing of a copy of a book
from the library.

INPUTS: ISBN number and copy number.

OUTPUTS: none.

PRECONDITIONS: The copy of the book uniquely identified by the
inputs must be in the roster of copies of books, which are
in the library.

EFFECT ON THE INFORMATION STORE: The input is borrowed
from the roster of copies of books which are in the library.

UNUSUAL EVENTS: If the input is not in the roster of copies of
books which are in the library, then the information system is
inconsistent with the state of the repository. A notation is made
in the error log.

USAGE RESTRICTIONS: none.

Unresolved issues:

Should historical record keeping be added?

Should checking of user validity be added?

Should checking of staff member validity be added?

Figure 12. Portion of a hypothetical requirements document to be produced by
the Requirements Apprentice at the end of the dialog in figure 11.

an error earlier in the definition of checkout. He corrects the error by
redefining the checkout transaction in terms of borrowing.

The remaining portion of the scenario illustrates the Apprentice detecting what turns out to be a fundamental epistemological confusion on
the part of the analyst—between book as a class and book as instances.
The analyst decides that title, author and ISBN are better thought of as
properties of a class of books, with each copy as an instance. This conceptual reorganization is propagated by the Apprentice throughout the
requirement.

The essential product of interacting with the Requirements Apprentice
is its internal representation of the requirements as frames and plans in
CAKE. This representation will eventually feed into the Design Apprentice.
In the meantime, however, this representation can be used to answer queries
and to generate various documents for the requirements analyst, the end
user, and the system designer.

An example of the kind of document the Apprentice will be able to
generate is shown in figure 12. As in the case of natural language input
to the Apprentice, the syntactic aspects of good English are not the key
concern here. What is important is deciding *what* to say by, for example,
choosing the appropriate level of detail.

Conclusion

The goal of the prototypes described above is to demonstrate the feasibility of the cliché-based assistant approach to automatic programming, using the technology of the Plan Calculus and CAKE. We plan to eventually connect the Design Apprentice and Requirements Apprentice as a first demonstration of a complete Apprentice.

In addition to these prototypes, the Programmer's Apprentice project also includes a number of other investigations based on the same approach and underlying technology. For example, an intelligent debugging assistant [Kuper 1988] has been built, which uses the Plan Calculus and the dependency-directed reasoning capabilities of CAKE to help a programmer localize bugs. A reverse engineering system [Wills 1986] has been demonstrated which, given a program and a library of clichés, applies graph-parsing techniques to the Plan Calculus to construct a plausible design of the program in terms of the clichés. An experiment in program translation has been performed [Waters 1988] using reverse engineering and the Plan Calculus. A new programming language construct [Waters 1988] has been developed embodying the clichéd forms of iteration. Finally, the propositional, algebraic, and frame layers of CAKE have been packaged into a separate utility, which could be used to build assistants in other engineering domains.

The Programmer's Apprentice is a basic research project. However, some of the principles and technology described here are now beginning to move into practical application. Frame-based knowledge representations and dependency-directed reasoning are beginning to appear in the repertoire of techniques for Computer-Aided Software Engineering (CASE). For example, Bachman Information Systems, with consultation from the authors, has developed and is marketing an intelligent assistant for data base design based in part on the Programmer's Apprentice. Sanders Associates, also with consultation from the Programmer's Apprentice project, has developed a Knowledge-Based Requirements Assistant [Czuchry & Harris 1988]. We hope that these efforts are just the leading edge of the transfer of this research into commercial practice.

The Programmer's Apprentice project is a collaboration involving students, faculty, and staff over a number of years. In connection with the work described in this chapter, we would in particular like to acknowledge Yishai Feldman, who has been responsible for the development of CAKE for the past several years, Howard Reubenstein, who is working on the Requirements Assistant, and Yang Meng Tan, who is working on the Design Apprentice.

This chapter describes research done at the Artificial Intelligence Laboratory of the Massachusetts Institute of Technology. Support for the laboratory's

References

Czuchry, A. J., and D. R. Harris [1988], "KBRA: A New Paradigm for Requirements Engineering," *IEEE Expert*, vol. 3, no. 4, pp. 21-35.

Green, C., and D. R. Barstow [1978], "On program synthesis knowledge," *Artificial Intelligence*, vol. 10, no. 3, pp. 241–279, 1978. Reprinted in Rich and Waters [1986].

Huff, K. E., and V. R. Lesser [1988], "A plan-based intelligent assistant that supports the process of programming," *ACM SIGSOFT Software Engineering Notes*, vol. 13, no. 5, pp. 97-106; also *Proc. ACM SIGSOFT 3rd Symp. on Software Development Environments*, Boston, MA.

IEEE [1988], Special issues on expert-system software, *IEEE Software*, vol. 5, no. 6, and *IEEE Expert*, vol. 3, no. 4.

Kuper, R. I. [1988], "Automated techniques for the localization of software bugs," M.S. Thesis Report AIM-1053, Artificial Intelligence Laboratory, Massachusetts Institute of Technology, Cambridge, MA.

Reubenstein, H. B., and R. C. Waters [1989], "The Requirements Apprentice: An Initial Scenario" *Proc. 5th Int. Workshop on Software Specs. and Design.*

Rich, C. [1981], "A formal representation for plans in the Programmer's Apprentice," *Proc. 7th Int. Joint Conf. Artificial Intelligence*, pp. 1044–1052, Vancouver, BC, Canada. Reprinted in Rich and Waters [1986].

Rich, C. [1985], "The layered architecture of a system for reasoning about programs," *Proc. 9th Int. Joint Conf. Artificial Intelligence*, pp. 540–546, Los Angeles, CA.

Rich, C., and R. C. Waters [1986], editors, *Readings in Artificial Intelligence and Software Engineering*. Morgan Kaufmann, Los Altos, CA.

Rich, C., and R. C. Waters [1987], "The Programmer's Apprentice: A program design scenario," AIM-933A, Artificial Intelligence Laboratory, Massachusetts Institute of Technology, Cambridge, MA.

Rich, C., and R. C. Waters [1988], "Automatic programming: Myths and prospects," *IEEE Computer*, vol. 21, no. 8, pp. 40–51.

Rich, C., and R. C. Waters [1990], *The Programmer's Apprentice*, Addison-Wesley, Reading, MA; also ACM Press, Baltimore, MD.

---

artificial intelligence research has been provided in part by the National Science Foundation under grant IRI-8616644, in part by the IBM Corporation, in part by the NYNEX Corporation, in part by the Siemens Corporation, and in part by the Advanced Research Projects Agency of the Department of Defense under Office of Naval Research contract N00014-85-K-0124. The views and conclusions contained in this chapter are those of the authors, and should not be interpreted as representing the policies, neither expressed nor implied, of the National Science Foundation, of the IBM Corporation, of the NYNEX Corporation, of the Siemens Corporation, or of the Department of Defense.

Soloway, E., and K. Ehrlich [1984], "Empirical studies of programming knowledge," *IEEE Trans. on Software Engineering*, vol. 10, no. 5, pp. 595–609. Reprinted in Rich and Waters [1986].

Waters, R. C. [1985], "The Programmer's Apprentice: A session with KBEmacs, *IEEE Trans. on Software Engineering*, vol. 11, no. 11, pp. 1296–1320. Reprinted in Rich and Waters [1986].

Waters, R. C. [1988], "Program translation via abstraction and reimplementation," *IEEE Trans. on Software Engineering*, vol. 14, no. 8.

Waters, R. C. [1988], "Using obviously Synchronizable series expressions instead of loops," *Proc. 1988 IEEE Int. Conf. on Computer Languages*, Miami, FL.

Wills, L. M. [1990], "Automated program recognition: A Feasibility Demonstration," *Artificial Intelligence*, North-Holland, Amsterdam, (to appear).

Wing, J. M. [1988], "A study of 12 specifications of the library problem," *IEEE Software*, pp. 66–76.

8

In the previous chapter, Rich and Waters introduce the notion of programming and requirements clichés, which are standard, templatelike arrangements of lower-level primitives and smaller clichés. In this chapter, Rich and Wills argue that clichés are useful not only for program synthesis, but also for program analysis. After automatically translating a program into a description in a language-independent representation called the plan calculus, cliché recognition becomes a matter of graph matching. Once component clichés are recognized, they can be used as a foundation for translating the program into another programming language or for explaining the program to a human programmer.

Recognizing a Program's Design

Charles Rich
Linda M. Wills

An experienced programmer can often reconstruct much of the design of a program simply by recognizing commonly used data structures and algorithms. Knowing how these programming structures are typically used to implement higher-level abstractions, the programmer is able to construct a hierarchical description of the program's design.

Clichés

We call commonly used programming structures *clichés*. Examples of algorithmic clichés include: list enumeration, binary search, and successive approximation loop. Examples of data structure clichés include: sorted list, balanced binary tree, and hash table.

Psychological experiments [Soloway & Ehrlich 1984] support the view that programmers make heavy use of clichés in many programming tasks. Rather than reasoning from first principles, programmers—like other problem solvers—tend to rely as much as possible on their accumulated experience.

In general, a cliché contains both fixed parts and parts that vary from one occurrence of the cliché to the next. For example, every occurrence of the binary search cliché must include computations to apply the search predicate and divide the remaining search space in half; however, the specific search predicate will vary. A cliché may also include constraints that restrict the varying parts. For example, the operation that computes the next approximation in a successive approximation loop must reduce the error term.

This chapter describes a prototype system, called the Recognizer, that automatically finds all occurrences of a given set of clichés in a given program and builds a hierarchical description of the program in terms of the clichés found. Thus far, the Recognizer has only been demonstrated on small Lisp programs. However, the underlying technology is essentially programming-language independent.

There are both practical and theoretical motivations for automating cliché recognition. On the practical side, cliché recognition is a prominent activity in many software engineering tasks, including maintenance, documentation, enhancement, optimization, and debugging. Automated cliché recognition will facilitate these tasks. From a theoretical standpoint, automated cliché recognition is an ideal problem for studying how programming knowledge and experience can be represented and used.

Difficulties in Automating Cliché Recognition

Our goal is not to mimic the human *process* of cliché recognition, but rather to use human experiential knowledge (in the form of clichés) to achieve a similar result. This is difficult due to the following factors.

- *Syntactic variation*—The same net flow of data and control can typically be achieved in many different ways.
- *Non-contiguousness*—The parts of a cliché may be scattered throughout the text of a program, rather than appearing in adjacent lines or expressions.
- *Implementation variation*—A given abstraction can typically be implemented in many different ways. For example, the buckets of a hash table may or may not be sorted.
- *Overlapping implementations*—Program optimization often merges the implementations of two or more distinct abstractions. Therefore, portions of a program may need to be recognized as part of more than one cliché.
- *Unrecognizable code*—Not all programs are constructed completely of known clichés. The recognition process must be able to ignore an indeterminate amount of idiosyncratic code.

An Example

The performance of the Recognizer on a simple program that retrieves entries from a hash table is demonstrated in figure 1. The Recognizer's main output is a design tree (see figure 2). The documentation shown in figure 1 is produced by combining schematized textual fragments associated with clichés, filling in slots in the text with identifiers taken from the program

```
(DEFUN TABLE-LOOKUP (TABLE KEY)
  (LET ((BUCKET (AREF TABLE (HASH KEY TABLE))))
    (LOOP
      (IF (NULL BUCKET) (RETURN NIL))
      (LET ((ENTRY (CAR BUCKET)))
        (IF (EQUAL (KEY ENTRY) KEY) (RETURN ENTRY)))
      (SETQ BUCKET (CDR BUCKET)))))
```

⇓

TABLE-LOOKUP is an associative retrieval operation.
  If there is an element of the set TABLE with key KEY,
  then that element is returned; otherwise NIL
  is returned.
  The key function is KEY.
The set TABLE is implemented as a hash table.
  The hashing function is HASH.
A bucket BUCKET of the hash table TABLE is implemented
as a list.
  The elements of the list BUCKET are enumerated.
  Linear search is used to find the first element of the
  list BUCKET whose key is equal to KEY.

Figure 1. Given the Common Lisp program above (and an appropriate cliché library), the Recognizer automatically produces the documentation shown. Upper case words in the documentation, for example, KEY, indicate relevant identifiers in the program.

(for example, TABLE, BUCKET, and KEY). The documentation that results sounds stilted, but describes the important design decisions in the program and can help a programmer locate relevant objects in the code (via the identifiers).

Three clichés used in this example program are: *hash table* (a data structure cliché typically used to implement associative retrieval), *cdr enumeration* (the pattern of CAR, CDR, and NULL typically used in Lisp to visit each element of a list), and *linear search* (an algorithmic cliché which applies a given predicate to a sequence of elements until either an element is found that satisfies the predicate, or there are no more elements).

One way to evaluate the potential practical benefit of automated cliché recognition is to imagine using automatically produced documentation, such as shown in figure 1, for the maintenance of poorly documented or undocumented programs. An advantage of automatically produced documentation is that it can be automatically updated whenever the corresponding source code is changed, thereby avoiding the pernicious problem of misleading, out-of-date documentation.

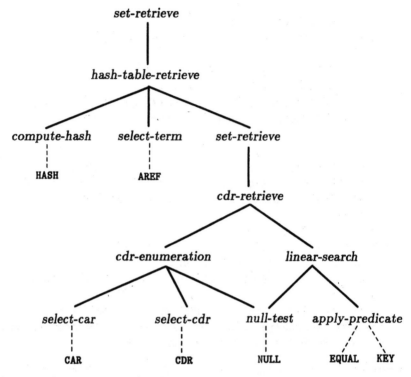

Figure 2. Design tree produced by the Recognizer for the program in figure 1. Each nonterminal in the tree is the name of a cliché that has been recognized in the program. The dashed lines at the fringe of the tree are links to identifiers in the source code to facilitate documentation generation.

Representation Shift

The key to the Recognizer's approach to cliché recognition is a representation shift. Rather than looking for patterns directly in the source code for a program, the Recognizer first translates the program into a language-independent, graphical representation, called the Plan Calculus. Part of the motivation for using the Plan Calculus comes from the Recognizer being a component of the Programmer's Apprentice (for an overview see Rich and Waters [1988]). However, as we will see later, the Plan Calculus also helps solve several of the specific difficulties in automating cliché recognition.

Plan Calculus

To a first approximation, the Plan Calculus can be thought of as combining the representation properties of flowcharts, data flow schemas, and abstract data types. A *plan* is essentially a hierarchical graph structure made up of different kinds of boxes (denoting operations and tests) and arrows (denoting control and data flow).

For example, the plan on the left side of figure 3a represents a clichéd combination of operations used to retrieve an entry from a hash table. The name of this plan is *hash-table-retrieve*. It has three parts: *hash* (compute the index of the table corresponding to a input key), *select* (select the indexed bucket of the table), *retrieve* (apply associative retrieval to the set of entries in the bucket). Data flow constraints between these parts are indicated by solid arrows. Because this plan has no conditional structure, there are no control flow arrows—control flow is indicated in plan diagrams by cross-hatched arrows.

Cliché library

In the Programmer's Apprentice, the Plan Calculus is used to represent both individual programs and the library of clichés out of which they can be constructed. Relationships between library clichés are represented by *overlays*. An overlay is composed of two plans and a set of correspondences between their parts. Formally, an overlay defines a mapping from instances of the plan on the left to instances of the plan on the right. For more details on the syntax and semantics of plans and overlays see Rich [1981] and Rich and Waters [1990].

Figure 3a is an example of an overlay representing the relationship between a specification and an implementation. The specification on the right side of the overlay is called *set-retrieve*. If the operation succeeds, its output is an element of the given set whose key is equal to the input key; if there is no such element, the operation fails. Preconditions and post-conditions are specified in a separate logical language that annotates the diagrams. The left side of the overlay in figure 3a is the hash-table-retrieve plan described above. The hooked lines in the figure denote correspondences: the set is implemented as a hash table. The input to the hash computation is the input key. The key function of the bucket retrieval is the key function of the overall retrieval. The output of the bucket retrieval is the output of the overall retrieval.

A cliché library may contain several overlays sharing the same left and/or right sides. Each such overlay represents a different way of abstracting the same implementation or implementing the same specification.

Overlays in the cliché library can be used for both synthesis (design) and analysis (cliché recognition) of programs. In program synthesis, occurrences of the right side of the overlay (the specification) are replaced by occurrences of the left side (the implementation). In program analysis, occurrences of the left side are replaced by occurrences of the right side.

(a)

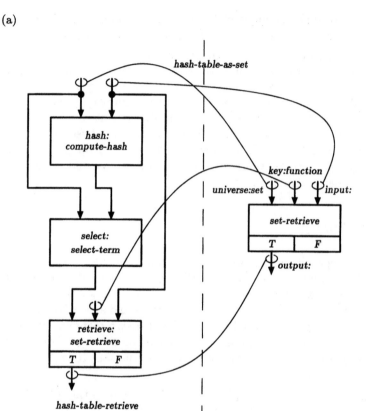

(b)

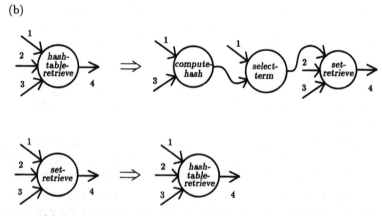

Figure 3. (a) Representation in the Plan Calculus of how associative retrieval can be implemented using a hash table. This overlay is part of the cliché library used to recognize the program in figure 1. (b) Part of the encoding of (a) into graph grammar rules (the constraints are not shown).

As part of the Programmer's Apprentice, an initial library of several hundred plans and overlays has been compiled in the area of basic programming techniques, such as manipulating arrays, vectors, lists, and sets. Approximately a dozen of these are used in the analysis of the hash table example given in figure 1.

Flow graphs and grammars

Because plans are essentially directed graphs, and cliché recognition involves identifying subgraphs and replacing them by more abstract operations, it is natural to view cliché recognition as a flow graph parsing problem.

A *flow graph* is a labeled, directed, acyclic graph in which edges connect labeled input and output ports of nodes. Node labels identify node types; each node type has a fixed 'arity' of input and output ports. Fan-in and fan-out are allowed.

A flow graph is derived from a context-free flow graph grammar much the same as a string is derived from a context-free string grammar. A context-free flow graph grammar (see figure 4) is a set of rewrite rules, each specifying how a node in a graph may be replaced by a subgraph. The left side of each rule is a nonterminal node; the graph on the right side may contain both terminal and nonterminal nodes. Note that, unlike string grammars, each rule in a flow graph grammar specifies a mapping (shown by numbering) between the unconnected input and output ports on the left side and unconnected input and output ports on the right side. This mapping determines how the subgraph is connected to the surrounding nodes when it replaces a nonterminal node in a derivation. For more information on graph grammars in general see Ehrig *et al.* [1986].

As with string grammars, it is convenient to abstract a graph derivation sequence as a tree that shows how each nonterminal is expanded (see figure 4).

Flow graph grammars are a natural formalism for encoding various kinds of engineering diagrams, such as electrical circuits or data flow. Furthermore, polynomial-time algorithms have been implemented for parsing flow graphs based on generalizations of existing string parsing algorithms [Brotsky 1984; Lutz 1989].

Using graph parsing

The heart of the Recognizer is a flow graph parser developed by Brotsky [1984]. As shown in figure 5, the source code for a program is translated into the Plan Calculus, encoded as a flow graph, and parsed against the grammar derived from the cliché library. If the grammar is ambiguous, as is

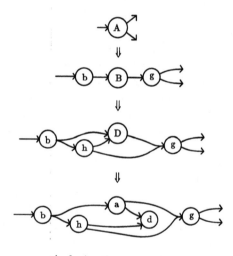

A flow graph grammar

A derivation sequence

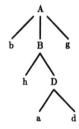

A derivation tree

Figure 4. Example of flow graph grammar and derivation.

typically the case, the parser produces all possible derivations. Constraint checking is interleaved with parsing for efficiency. The primary output of the recognition process is a derivation tree (see example in figure 2), which reconstructs a design for the program. This design tree can then be used by a documentation generator or other tools.

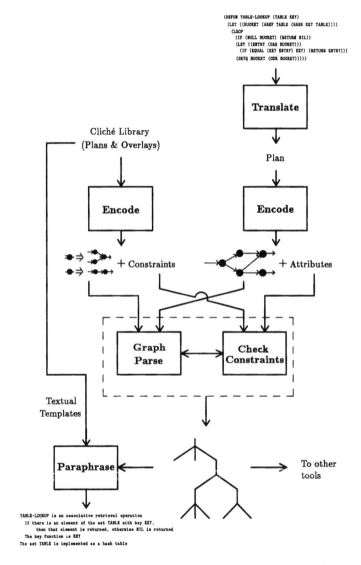

Figure 5. Architecture of the Recognizer. Note that only the module that translates source code into the Plan Calculus is programming-language dependent. As part of the Programmer's Apprentice, translators have been written for subsets of Lisp, Fortran, Cobol, and Ada.

Plans are encoded as flow graphs as follows: the boxes of a plan become the nodes of the flow graph. The data flow arrows of a plan become the edges of the flow graph. All the other information in a plan, such as control flow, preconditions, and postconditions, is encoded in the attributes of the flow graph. The resulting graphs are acyclic because iteration is modelled in the Plan Calculus by tail-recursion.

The cliché library is similarly encoded as an attribute graph grammar (a straightforward generalization of attribute string grammars [Knuth 1968]). Each plan definition in the library gives rise to a grammar rule, where the left side of the rule is a node with the plan name as its type, and the right side of the rule is the plan's translation into a flow graph (the additional information in the plan definition becomes the constraints of the grammar rule).

For example, the first rule in figure 3b is the encoding of the hash-table-retrieve plan in figure 3a. Using this rule when parsing a flow graph amounts to recognizing the hash-table-retrieve cliché in a program.

In addition, each overlay in the cliché library gives rise to a simple grammar rule with single nodes on both the left and right sides. The left and right sides are reversed in comparison with the way overlay diagrams are drawn. The mapping between the input and output ports of the nodes on the two sides of the grammar rule is derived from the overlay's correspondences.

For example, the second rule in figure 3b is the encoding of the overlay in Figure 3a. Using this rule when parsing a flow graph amounts to reconstructing a design decision in a program.

Plan definitions are encoded as individual grammar rules (instead of having a single rule for each overlay) for two reasons. First, there can be plans in the library that are not used in any overlay. Second, some overlays have plans on both sides, whereas a grammar rule must have a single node on the left side. The Recognizer handles such overlays by interleaving expansion steps with reduction steps during the parsing process (for details see Wills [1987, 1990]).

Difficulties Revisited

Syntactic variation

The Recognizer's ability to deal with syntactic variation in the input program is illustrated in figure 6. A detailed comparison of the program in this figure with the original TABLE-LOOKUP program in figure 1 shows many syntactic differences, such as different variable names (L versus TABLE), different control primitives (PROG and GO versus LOOP), and radically different syntactic trees. However, both of these programs have the same plan.

```
(DEFUN R (L X &AUX B)
  (SETQ B (AREF L (H X L)))
  (PROG (E)
 LP (WHEN (NULL B) (RETURN NIL))
    (SETQ E (CAR B))
    (COND ((EQUAL (K E) X) (RETURN E))
          (T (SETQ B (CDR B))
             (GO LP)))))
```

$$\Downarrow$$

```
R is an associative retrieval operation.
  If there is an element of the set L with key X,
  then that element is returned; otherwise NIL
  is returned.
  The key function is K.
The set L is implemented as a hash table.
  The hashing function is H.
A bucket B of the hash table L is implemented as a list.
  The elements of the list B are enumerated.
  Linear search is used to find the first element of the
  list B whose key is equal to X.
```

Figure 6. A syntactic variation of the program in figure 1 and the corresponding documentation produced by the Recognizer. Note that the documentation is identical to figure 1, except for the names of the identifiers.

Therefore the Recognizer produces the identical design tree (figure 2) and the identical documentation (except identifiers) for both.

This example emphasizes that the Recognizer identifies clichés using only structural information in the code (that is, the flow of data and control and the types of the primitive operations); it does not rely upon (or make use of) any information in the names of variables or procedures. As will be discussed later, this is both a strength and a limitation of the system.

Non-contiguousness

The use of the Plan Calculus in the Recognizer also addresses the difficulty of non-contiguousness, that is, the problem that parts of a cliché may be scattered throughout the text of a program. For example, even though the CAR, CDR, and NULL steps of the cdr-enumeration cliché are separated by unrelated expressions in the source code of the example programs, they become neighboring nodes in the flow graph representation.

Implementation variation

Figure 7 illustrates the Recognizer's ability to deal with implementation variation in the input program. Given the same grammar as used in figure 2, with additional rules describing the implementation of set-retrieve on sorted Lisp lists, the Recognizer produces a design tree (not shown here) that has the same top three levels as figure 2, but differs below.

```
(DEFUN TABLE-LOOKUP (TABLE KEY)
  (LET ((BUCKET (AREF TABLE (HASH KEY TABLE))))
    (LOOP
      (IF (NULL BUCKET) (RETURN NIL))
      (LET* ((ENTRY (CAR BUCKET)))
            ((Y (KEY ENTRY))))
        (COND ((STRING> Y KEY) (RETURN NIL))
              ((EQUAL Y KEY) (RETURN ENTRY)))
        (SETQ BUCKET (CDR BUCKET)))))
```

⇓

```
TABLE-LOOKUP is an associative retrieval operation.
  If there is an element of the set TABLE with key KEY,
    then that element is returned; otherwise NIL
    is returned.
  The key function is KEY.
The set TABLE is implemented as a hash table.
  The hashing function is HASH.
A bucket BUCKET of the hash table TABLE is implemented
  as a sorted list.
  The elements of the sorted list BUCKET are enumerated.
  The iteration is terminated when an element of the
    sorted list BUCKET is found whose key Y is greater
    than KEY.
  Linear search is used to find the first element of the
    sorted list BUCKET whose key Y is equal to KEY.
  The sorting relation on keys is STRING>.
```

Figure 7. An implementation variation of the program in figure 1, in which the buckets of the hash table are sorted lists. Note that the first seven lines of the documentation are the same as in figure 1.

Overlapping implementations

Figures 8 and 9 illustrate the Recognizer's ability to deal with overlapping implementations in the input program. The grammar for this example includes rules for implementing the *list-min* specification (find the minimum element of a list) by enumerating the elements of the list and accumulating the maximum element seen thus far; and similarly for *list-max* (find the maximum element of a list).

```
(DEFUN MAX-MIN (L)
  (VALUES (LIST-MAX L) (LIST-MIN L)))

(DEFUN LIST-MAX (L)
  (LET ((MAX MOST-NEGATIVE-FIXNUM))
    (LOOP
      (IF (NULL L) (RETURN MAX))
      (LET ((N (CAR L)))
        (IF (> N MAX) (SETQ MAX N)))
      (SETQ L (CDR L)))))

(DEFUN LIST-MIN (L)
  (LET ((MIN MOST-POSITIVE-FIXNUM))
    (LOOP
      (IF (NULL L) (RETURN MIN))
      (LET ((N (CAR L)))
        (IF (< N MIN) (SETQ MIN N)))
      (SETQ L (CDR L)))))
```

Figure 8. Unoptimized Common Lisp program that computes the maximum and minimum elements of a non-empty list of integers.

The MAX-MIN program in figure 8 is the simple, inefficient program for computing both the maximum and minimum elements of a given list, which could be straightforwardly generated from the cliché library by implementing the list-max and list-min specifications separately. It is inefficient because it enumerates the list twice.

The optimized version of this program in figure 9 only enumerates the list once, that is, there is an overlap between the implementations of list-max and list-min. This overlap is evident in the design tree produced by the Recognizer for this program, wherein the cdr-enumeration nonterminal is shared between the two subtrees below list-max and list-min. The Recognizer has in effect "undone" the optimization.

```
(DEFUN MAX-MIN (L)
  (LET ((MAX MOST-NEGATIVE-FIXNUM)
        (MIN MOST-POSITIVE-FIXNUM))
    (LOOP
      (IF (NULL L) (RETURN (VALUES MAX MIN)))
      (LET ((N (CAR L)))
        (IF (> N MAX) (SETQ MAX N))
        (IF (< N MIN) (SETQ MIN N)))
      (SETQ L (CDR L)))))
```

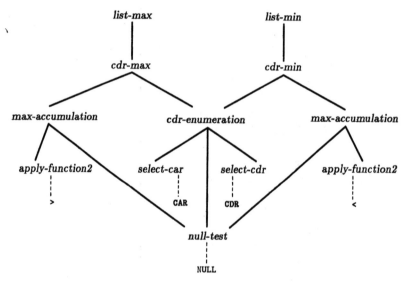

Figure 9. Optimized version of program in figure 8 with design tree produced by the Recognizer. Note the shared occurrence of the cdr-enumeration cliché.

Unrecognizable code

The basic parsing algorithm used in the Recognizer is polynomial in the size of the input and the grammar. If we could guarantee that the input graph would always be completely derivable from the given grammar, then cliché recognition could be performed in polynomial time. Of course, most programs are only partially constructed of clichés. Brotsky's algorithm was therefore extended in two ways to facilitate partial recognition. Because subgraph isomorphism is known to be NP-complete, it comes as no surprise that these changes result in the loss of polynomial time behavior in the worst case.

First, to recognize clichés in the midst of unrecognizable code, the parser must be able to ignore indeterminate amounts of both leading and trailing input that is unparsable. To allow for unparsable leading input, the parser's "read head" is started not only at the leftmost edge of the input graph, but at every possible intermediate position in the graph. Unparsable trailing input is trivially handled by allowing parses to complete before the input graph is totally scanned.

Second, every nonterminal in the grammar is considered as a possible starting type for a derivation. This allows for the possibility of partially reconstructing the design of a program, that is, recognizing only the lower-level clichés, but not how they are being used together. This kind of partial recognition is illustrated in the design tree in figure 9. Because there is no single specification in the cliché library for computing both the maximum and minimum elements of a given list, there is no nonterminal in the grammar that can be the root of the tree. It seems reasonable in this example that the library need not include such trivial combinations of specifications. In general, a tree with multiple roots indicates either that the top-level structure of the program is idiosyncratic or just that the relevant cliché is not in the library.

Other Recognition Systems

The feasibility of automated cliché recognition has been demonstrated by a number of other researchers using different program representations, kinds of knowledge, and computational approaches. All of these factors affect how well these systems deal with the difficulties in automating recognition.

Most current systems (for example, Johnson's PROUST [1986] and Lukey's PUDSY [1980]) operate directly on source code. This limits the variability and complexity of the clichés that can be recognized. Too much of these systems' effort is expended applying source-to-source transformations to deal with syntactic variation. In addition, non-contiguous clichés pose a serious problem.

Letovsky's CPU [1988] uses a lambda-calculus representation for programs which, like the use of flow graph grammars in the Recognizer, provides a firm mathematical foundation for the system. For a cliché to be recognized by CPU, it must be localized as a single lambda expression. In practice, this requires applying many transformations to copy subexpressions, leading to an exponential increase in the size of the program representation.

Many recognition systems (unlike the Recognizer) are given some independent description of the purpose of the input program. This purpose description generates expectations about the design of the input program, which are then checked against the code. For example, PROUST is given a set of "goals" the input program is supposed to achieve, Murray's Talus [1985] is given a "model program" that performs the same task as the input program, and PUDSY is given a formal program specification. Most of these systems are intended to be used for intelligent tutoring, such as correcting programming class assignments. In this application, the complete specification of the input program is easily known. However, in most other applications, especially software maintenance, this kind of information is rarely complete, accurate, or formal. On the other hand, any available partial knowledge about a program can be useful input to the recognition process, if used in a defeasible manner.

Biggerstaff's DESIRE [1989] is an example of a recognition system that tries to take advantage of informal knowledge. DESIRE is organized around a "domain model," which contains elaborate cross-indexing between words and concepts that are likely to appear in programs in a given domain. The goal of DESIRE's recognition is to identify regions in a program listing where certain concepts are used, based on a statistical analysis of the words appearing in the text and documentation. A virtue of this technique is that it can focus attention on particular sections of a large program. DESIRE could in principle be used together with the Recognizer in a hybrid approach (see discussion of future work).

The Recognizer's computational approach is exhaustive. The graph parser is guaranteed to find all possible derivations of the input graph from the graph grammar. Other systems use heuristics to prune away alternate analyses during the recognition process. For example, one heuristic PROUST uses is to prefer the cliché with greatest number of currently recognized parts. In general, the use of heuristics can lead to missing a useful way of understanding the input program.

Future Work

The Recognizer is still under development. To make it a practical aid for software maintenance, it will need to be improved and extended in a number of ways.

Extensions

The Recognizer has been developed in parallel with—and lagging slightly behind—the evolution of the Plan Calculus. In particular, the Recognizer does not currently handle data plans or data overlays (these are the facilities in the Plan Calculus for language-independent modelling of data structures and data abstraction). Also, the Recognizer's handling of destructive operations (such as modifying an array) is not adequate. These deficiencies should be relatively straightforward to correct. We also plan to connect the Recognizer with a new logical reasoning system developed as part of the Programmer's Apprentice, for use in checking constraints and reasoning about attributes in the grammar.

Hybrid approach

It is already clear from our experiments with small programs that the exhaustive, purely structural approach used by the Recognizer will not scale up directly to programs of commercial size and complexity. An exhaustive algorithmic search for clichés is too expensive.

A possible source of guidance to reduce this search is the many forms of existing documentation, such as comments and the mnemonic identifiers used for variables and procedures. This kind of information is not currently used by the Recognizer, because it is often incomplete and inaccurate. However, it could provide an important independent source of expectations about the purpose of a program and how it was designed. These expectations could then be confirmed, amended, and completed by checking them against the code.

In addition to a program and the cliché library, many other recognition systems are given a third input in the form of a specification, a set of goals, or a "model program" that performs the same task. We envisage a hybrid approach to cliché recognition in the future, with two complementary processes: one documentation- and/or specification-driven ("top-down") and the other code-driven ("bottom-up"). The heuristic top-down process will use the available documentation information (or user guidance) to guide the code-driven process by generating expectations. The algorithmic bottom-up process will fill in the gaps in the documentation and verify or reject the expectations.

To design such a hybrid recognition system, we first need to conduct additional theoretical and empirical analyses of complexity of the Recognizer. We are currently attempting to apply the Recognizer to programs at least an order of magnitude larger than the examples in this chapter.

Learning clichés

Finally, and more long range, we hope to explore how the Recognizer can be used to help automate the task of knowledge acquisition in the Programmer's Apprentice; in particular, how the system might automatically learn new clichés.

One idea is to look at programs that implement familiar specifications using some parts that are unfamiliar. First, the Recognizer would be used to identify what specifications are being implemented by those parts of the program that are familiar. Working generatively from the given top-level specification of the program, it should also be possible to identify some lower-level specifications that are not accounted for by the recognized parts of the program. A learning procedure could then reasonably hypothesize that the unrecognizable part of the program is a new cliché for implementing the remaining specifications. Hall [1988] has demonstrated a similar learning scheme in the domains of digital circuits and mechanical gears.

References

Biggerstaff, T. [1989], "Design recovery for maintenance and reuse," *IEEE Computer*, vol. 22, no. 7, pp. 36–49.

Brotsky, D. C. [1984], "An algorithm for parsing flow graphs," M.S. Thesis, Report AI-TR-704, Artificial Intelligence Laboratory, Massachusetts Institute of Technology, Cambridge, MA.

Ehrig, H., M. Nagl, G. Rozenberg, and A. Rosenfeld, (editors) [1986], *Graph-Grammars and Their Application to Computer Science*, Springer-Verlag, New York. Lecture Notes In Computer Science Series, vol. 291.

Hall, R. J. [1988], "Learning by Failing to Explain: Using Partial Explanations to Learn in Incomplete or Intractable Domains," *Machine Learning*, vol. 3, pp. 45–77.

Johnson, W. L. [1986], *Intention-Based Diagnosis of Novice Programming Errors*, Morgan Kaufmann, Los Altos, CA.

Knuth, D. E. [1968], "Semantics of context-free languages," *Mathematical Systems Theory*, vol. 2, no. 2, pp. 127–145.

Letovsky, S. [1988], "Plan analysis of programs," Ph.D. Thesis, Research report, Yale University, Computer Science Deptment.

Lukey, F. J. [1980], "Understanding and debugging programs," *International Journal of Man-Machine Studies*, vol. 12, pp. 189–202.

We are grateful for discussions with Elliot Chikofsky, Richard Waters, Dilip Soni, Howard Reubenstein, Yang Meng Tan, and Scott Wills for their suggestions on improving this chapter.

This chapter describes research done at the Artificial Intelligence Laboratory of the Massachusetts Institute of Technology. Support for the laboratory's artificial intelligence research has been provided in part by the following organizations: National Science Foundation under grant IRI-8616644, Advanced Research Projects Agency of the Department of Defense under Naval Research contract N00014-88-K-0487, IBM Corporation, NYNEX Corporation, and Siemens Corporation. The views and conclusions contained in this chapter are those of the authors and should not be interpreted as representing the policies, expressed or implied, of these organizations.

Lutz, R. [1989], "Chart parsing of flowgraphs," *Proceedings 11th Int. Joint Conf. Artificial Intelligence*, pp. 116–121, Detroit, MI.

Murray, W. R. [1985], "Heuristic and formal methods in automatic program debugging," *Proceedings 9th Int. Joint Conf. Artificial Intelligence*, pp. 15–19, Los Angeles, CA.

Rich, C. [1981], "A formal representation for plans in the Programmer's Apprentice," *Proceedings 7th Int. Joint Conf. Artificial Intelligence*, pp. 1044–1052, Vancouver, British Columbia, Canada. Reprinted in *Readings in Artificial Intelligence and Software Engineering*, edited by C. Rich and R. C. Waters, Morgan Kaufmann, 1986.

Rich, C., and R. C. Waters, [1988], "The Programmer's Apprentice: A research overview," *IEEE Computer*, vol. 21, no. 11, pp. 10–25. Reprinted in *Artificial Intelligence and Software Engineering*, edited by D. Partridge, Ablex, Norwood, NJ, 1989.

Rich, C., and R. C. Waters, [1990], *The Programmer's Apprentice*, Addison-Wesley, Reading, MA; and ACM Press, Baltimore, MD.

Soloway, E., and K. Ehrlich [1984], "Empirical studies of programming knowledge," *IEEE Trans. on Software Engineering*, vol. 10, no. 5, pp. 595–609. Reprinted in *Readings in Artificial Intelligence and Software Engineering*, edited by C. Rich and R. C. Waters, Morgan Kaufmann, 1986.

Wills, L. M. [1987], "Automated program recognition," M.S. Thesis, Report AI-TR-904, Artificial Intelligence Laboratory, Massachusetts Institute of Technology, Cambridge, MA.

Wills, L. M. [1990], "Automated Program Recognition: A Feasibility Demonstration," *Artificial Intelligence*, North-Holland, Amsterdam, (to appear).

Part II

Fueling the
Next Generation

No doubt about it, computers are not smart enough. To make them smarter, there is a great need for basic advances in connectionist-style computation, regularity recognition, language understanding, knowledge repair, reasoning, discovery, and invention.

- *In the two opening chapters, Minsky argues that we should not be debating whether the symbolic approach to Artificial Intelligence is better or worse than the connectionist approach; instead, we should study how to use both together to best advantage.*
- *Poggio and Girosi introduce a new way of looking at neural nets, arguing that the mathematics of interpolation and approximation leads to key conclusions about how many layers neural nets should have and what the individual neurons should compute.*
- *Berwick and Fong show how sentence parsing can be done by a few principled modules, harnessed together, which do the work that previously required thousands of not-particularly-principled rules.*
- *Dorr explains how principle-based parsing, modern theories of sentence semantics, and language-specific concept structures combine to produce natural-sounding sentence-level language translations.*
- *Winston and Rao describe how rulelike knowledge, once learned, can be repaired by using experience to explain failures.*
- *Davis and Hamscher champion the merits of model-based reasoning, as distinguished from rule-based reasoning, and introduce several important new problem-solving paradigms.*
- *Williams explains a program that invents fundamentally new devices by assembling networks of constraint-enforcing elements and by looking for new paths through those networks.*
- *Finally, in the last two chapters of Part II, McAllester looks at fundamental issues in mathematics, asking, among other things, why conclusions that are obvious to people are so obscure to most theorem-proving programs.*

9

Engineering and scientific education conditions us to expect everything, including intelligence, to have a simple, compact explanation. Accordingly, when people new to AI ask "What's AI all about," they seem to expect an answer that defines AI in terms of a few basic mathematical laws.

Today, some researchers who seek a simple, compact explanation hope that systems modeled on neural nets or some other connectionist idea will quickly overtake more traditional systems based on symbol manipulation. Others believe that symbol manipulation, with a history that goes back millennia, remains the only viable approach.

Minsky subscribes to neither of these extremist views. Instead, he argues that Artificial Intelligence must employ many approaches. Artificial Intelligence is not like circuit theory and electromagnetism. There is nothing wonderfully unifying like Kirchhoff's laws are to circuit theory or Maxwell's equations are to electromagnetism. Instead of looking for a Right Way, Minsky believes that the time has come to build systems out of diverse components, some connectionist and some symbolic, each with its own diverse justification.

Minsky, whose seminal contributions in Artificial Intelligence are established worldwide, is one of the 1990 recipients of the prestigious Japan Prize—a prize recognizing original and outstanding achievements in science and technology.

Logical vs. Analogical or Symbolic vs. Connectionist or Neat vs. Scruffy

Marvin Minsky
1990 Japan Prize Laureate

Why is there so much excitement about Neural Networks today, and how is this related to research on Artificial Intelligence? Much has been said, in the popular press, as though these were conflicting activities. This seems exceedingly strange to me, because both are parts of the very same enterprise. What caused this misconception?

The symbol-oriented community in AI has brought this rift upon itself, by supporting models in research that are far too rigid and specialized. This focus on well-defined problems produced many successful applications, no matter that the underlying systems were too inflexible to function well outside the domains for which they were designed. (It seems to me that this happened because of the researchers' excessive concern with logical consistency and provability. Ultimately, that would be a proper concern, but not in the subject's present state of immaturity.) Thus, contemporary symbolic AI systems are now too constrained to be able to deal with exceptions to rules, or to exploit fuzzy, approximate, or heuristic fragments of knowledge. Partly in reaction to this, the connectionist movement initially tried to develop more flexible systems, but soon came to be imprisoned in its own peculiar ideology—of trying to build learning systems endowed with as little architectural structure as possible, hoping to create machines that could serve all masters equally well. The trouble with this is that even a seemingly neutral architecture still embodies an implicit assumption about which things are presumed to be "similar."

The field called Artificial Intelligence includes many different aspirations. Some researchers simply want machines to do the various sorts of things that people call intelligent. Others hope to understand what enables people to do such things. Yet other researchers want to simplify programming; why can't we build, once and for all, machines that grow and improve themselves by learning from experience? Why can't we simply explain what we want, and then let our machines do experiments, or read some books, or go to school—the sorts of things that people do. Our machines today do no such things: Connectionist networks learn a bit, but show few signs of becoming "smart;" symbolic systems are shrewd from the start, but don't yet show any "common sense." How strange that our most advanced systems can compete with human specialists, yet be unable to do many things that seem easy to children. I suggest that this stems from the nature of what we call *specialties*—for the the very act of naming a specialty amounts to celebrating the discovery of some model of some aspect of reality, which is useful despite being isolated from most of our other concerns. These models have rules which reliably work—so long as we stay in that special domain. But when we return to the commonsense world, we rarely find rules that precisely apply. Instead, we must know how to adapt each fragment of 'knowledge' to particular contexts and circumstances, and we must expect to need more and different kinds of knowledge as our concerns broaden. Inside such simple "toy" domains, a rule may seem to be quite "general," but whenever we broaden those domains, we find more and more exceptions—and the early advantage of context-free rules then mutates into strong limitations.

AI research must now move from its traditional focus on particular schemes. There is no one best way to represent knowledge, or to solve problems, and limitations of present-day machine intelligence stem largely from seeking "unified theories," or trying to repair the deficiencies of theoretically neat, but conceptually impoverished ideological positions. Our purely numerical connectionist networks are inherently deficient in abilities to reason well; our purely symbolic logical systems are inherently deficient in abilities to represent the all-important *heuristic connections* between things—the uncertain, approximate, and analogical linkages that we need for making new hypotheses. The versatility that we need can be found only in larger-scale architectures that can exploit and manage the advantages of several types of representations at the same time. Then, each can be used to overcome the deficiencies of the others. To do this, each formally neat type of knowledge representation or inference must be complemented with some "scruffier" kind of machinery that can embody the heuristic connections between the knowledge itself and what we hope to do with it.

Top-Down vs. Bottom-Up

While different workers have diverse goals, all AI researchers seek to make machines that solve problems. One popular way to pursue that quest is to start with a "top-down" strategy: begin at the level of commonsense psychology and try to imagine processes that could play a certain game, solve a certain kind of puzzle, or recognize a certain kind of object. If you can't do this in a single step, then keep breaking things down into simpler parts until you can actually embody them in hardware or software.

This basically reductionist technique is typical of the approach to AI called heuristic programming. These techniques have developed productively for several decades and, today, heuristic programs based on top-down analysis have found many successful applications in technical, specialized areas. This progress is largely due to the maturation of many techniques for representing knowledge. But the same techniques have seen less success when applied to "commonsense" problem solving. Why can we build robots that compete with highly trained workers to assemble intricate machinery in factories—but not robots that can help with ordinary housework? It is because the conditions in factories are constrained, while the objects and activities of everyday life are too endlessly varied to be described by precise, logical definitions and deductions. Commonsense reality is too disorderly to represent in terms of universally valid "axioms." To deal with such variety and novelty, we need more flexible styles of thought, such as those we see in human commonsense reasoning, which is based more on analogies and approximations than on precise formal procedures. Nonetheless, top-down procedures have important advantages in being able to perform efficient, systematic search procedures, to manipulate and rearrange the elements of complex situations, and to supervise the management of intricately interacting subgoals—all functions that seem beyond the capabilities of connectionist systems with weak architectures.

Short-sighted critics have always complained that progress in top-down symbolic AI research is slowing down. In one way this is natural: in the early phases of any field, it becomes ever harder to make important new advances as we put the easier problems behind us—and new workers must face a "squared" challenge, because there is so much more to learn. But the slowdown of progress in symbolic AI is not just a matter of laziness. Those top-down systems are inherently poor at solving problems which involve large numbers of weaker kinds of interactions, such as occur in many areas of pattern recognition and knowledge retrieval. Hence, there has been a mounting clamor for finding another, new, more flexible approach—and this is one reason for the recent popular turn toward connectionist models.

The bottom-up approach goes the opposite way. We begin with simpler elements—they might be small computer programs, elementary logical principles, or simplified models of what brain cells do—and then move upwards in complexity by finding ways to interconnect those units to produce larger scale phenomena. The currently popular form of this, the connectionist neural network approach, developed more sporadically than did heuristic programming. In part, this was because heuristic programming developed so rapidly in the 1960s that connectionist networks were swiftly outclassed. Also, the networks need computation and memory resources that were too prodigious for that period. Now that faster computers are available, bottom-up connectionist research has shown considerable promise in mimicking some of what we admire in the behavior of lower animals, particularly in the areas of pattern recognition, automatic optimization, clustering, and knowledge retrieval. But their performance has been far weaker in the very areas in which symbolic systems have successfully mimicked much of what we admire in high-level human thinking—for example, in goal-based reasoning, parsing, and causal analysis. These weakly structured connectionist networks cannot deal with the sorts of tree-search explorations, and complex, composite knowledge structures required for parsing, recursion, complex scene analysis, or other sorts of problems that involve *functional parallelism*. It is an amusing paradox that connectionists frequently boast about the massive parallelism of their computations, yet the homogeneity and interconnectedness of those structures make them virtually unable to do more than one thing at a time—at least, at levels above that of their basic associative functionality. This is essentially because they lack the architecture needed to maintain adequate short-term memories.

Thus, the present-day systems of both types show serious limitations. The top-down systems are handicapped by inflexible mechanisms for retrieving knowledge and reasoning about it, while the bottom-up systems are crippled by inflexible architectures and organizational schemes. Neither type of system has been developed so as to be able to exploit multiple, diverse varieties of knowledge.

Which approach is best to pursue? That is simply a wrong question. Each has virtues and deficiencies, and we need integrated systems that can exploit the advantages of both. In favor of the top-down side, research in Artificial Intelligence has told us a little—but only a little—about how to solve problems by using methods that resemble reasoning. If we understood more about this, perhaps we could more easily work down toward finding out how brain cells do such things. In favor of the bottom-up approach, the brain sciences have told us something—but again, only a little—about the workings of brain cells and their connections. More research on this might help us discover how the activities of brain-cell networks support our higher level processes. But right now we're caught in the middle; neither purely connectionist nor purely symbolic systems seem able to support the sorts of intellectual performances we take for granted even in young children. This essay aims at understanding why both types of AI systems have developed to become so inflexible. I'll argue that the solution lies somewhere between these two extremes, and our problem will be to find out how to build a suitable bridge. We already have plenty of ideas at either extreme. On the connectionist side we can extend our efforts to design neural networks that can learn various ways to represent knowledge. On the symbolic side, we can extend our research on knowledge representations, and on designing systems that can effectively exploit the knowledge thus represented. But above all, at the present time, we need more research on how to combine both types of ideas.

Representation and Retrieval: Structure and Function

In order for a machine to learn, it must represent what it will learn. The knowledge must be embodied in some form of mechanism, data-structure, or *representation*. Researchers in Artificial Intelligence have devised many ways to do this, for example, in the forms of:

- Rule-based systems.
- Frames with default assignments.
- Predicate calculus.
- Procedural representations.
- Associative data bases.
- Semantic networks.
- Object oriented programming.
- Conceptual dependency.
- Action scripts.
- Neural networks
- Natural language.

In the 1960s and 1970s, students frequently asked, "Which kind of representation is best," and I usually replied that we'd need more research before answering that. But now I would give a different reply: "To solve really hard problems, we'll have to use several different representations." This is because each particular kind of data-structure has its own virtues and deficiencies, and none by itself seems adequate for all the different functions involved with what we call "common sense." Each have domains of competence and efficiency, so that one may work where another fails. Furthermore, if we rely only on any single "unified" scheme, then we'll have no way to recover from failure. As suggested in section 6.9 of *The Society of Mind*, "The secret of what something means lies in how it connects to other things we know. That's why it's almost always wrong to seek the *real meaning* of anything. A thing with just one meaning has scarcely any meaning at all."

In order to get around these constraints, we must develop systems that combine the expressiveness and procedural versatility of symbolic systems with the fuzziness and adaptiveness of connectionist representations. Why has there been so little work on synthesizing these techniques? I suspect that it is because both of these AI communities suffer from a common cultural-philosophical disposition: they would like to explain intelligence in the image of what was successful in Physics—by minimizing the amount and variety of its assumptions. But this seems to be a wrong ideal; instead, we should take our cue from biology rather than from physics. This is because what we call "thinking" does not emerge directly from a few fundamental principles of wave-function symmetry and exclusion rules. Mental activities are not the sorts of unitary or "elementary" phenomenon that can be described by a few mathematical operations on logical axioms. Instead, the functions performed by the brain are the products of the work of thousands of different, specialized sub-systems, the intricate product of hundreds of millions of years of biological evolution. We cannot hope to understand such an organization by emulating the techniques of those particle physicists search in the simplest possible unifying conceptions. Constructing a mind is simply a different kind of problem—of how to synthesize organizational systems that can support a large enough diversity of different schemes, yet enable them to work together to exploit one another's abilities.

To solve typical real-world commonsense problems, a mind must have at least several different kinds of knowledge. First, we need to represent goals: what is the problem to be solved. Then the system must also possess adequate knowledge about the domain or context in which that problem occurs. Finally, the system must know what kinds of reasoning are applicable in that area. Superimposed on all of this, our systems must have management schemes that can operate different representations and procedures in parallel, so that when any particular method breaks down or gets stuck, the system can quickly shift over to analogous operations in other realms that may be able to continue the work. For example, when you hear a natural language expression like

"Mary gave Jack the book"

this will produce in you, albeit unconsciously, many different kinds of thoughts (see *The Society of Mind*, section 29.2)—that is, mental activities in such different realms as:

- A visual representation of the scene.
- Postural and tactile representations of the experience.
- A script-sequence of a typical script-sequence for "giving."
- Representation of the participants' roles.
- Representations of their social motivations.
- Default assumptions about Jack, Mary, and the book.
- Other assumptions about past and future expectations.

How could a brain possibly coordinate the use of such different kinds of processes and representations? Our conjecture is that our brains construct and maintain them in different brain-agencies. (The corresponding neural structures need not, of course, be entirely separate in their spatial extents inside the brain.) But it is not enough to maintain separate processes inside separate agencies; we also need additional mechanisms to enable each of them to support the activities of the others—or, at least, to provide alternative operations in case of failures. Chapters 19 through 23 of *The Society of Mind* sketch some ideas about how the representations in different agencies could be coordinated. These sections introduce the concepts of:

- *Polyneme*—a hypothetical neuronal mechanism for activating corresponding slots in different representations.

- *Microneme*—a context-representing mechanism which similarly biases all the agencies to activate knowledge related to the current situation and goal.

- *Paranome*—yet another mechanism that can apply corresponding processes or operations simultaneously to the short-term memory agents' *pronomes* of those various agencies.

It is impossible to summarize briefly how all these mechanisms are imagined to work, but section 29.3 of *The Society of Mind* gives some of the flavor of our theory. What controls those paranomes? I suspect that, in human minds, this control comes from mutual exploitation between:

- A long-range planning agency (whose scripts are influenced by various strong goals and ideals; this agency resembles the Freudian superego, and is based on early imprinting).

- Another supervisory agency capable of using semi-formal inferences and natural-language reformulations.

- A Freudian-like censorship agency that incorporates massive records of previous failures of various sorts.

Relevance and Similarity

Problem-solvers must find relevant data. How does the human mind retrieve what it needs from among so many millions of knowledge items? Different AI systems have attempted to use a variety of different methods for this. Some assign keywords, attributes, or descriptors to each item and then locate data by feature-matching or by using more sophisticated associative data-base methods. Others use graph-matching or analogical case-based adaptation. Yet others try to find relevant information by threading their

ways through systematic, usually hierarchical classifications of knowledge—
sometimes called *ontologies*. But, to me, all such ideas seem deficient because it is not enough to classify items of information simply in terms of
the features or structures of those items themselves. This is because we
rarely use a representation in an intentional vacuum, but we always have
goals—and two objects may seem similar for one purpose but different for
another purpose. Consequently, we must also take into account the functional aspects of what we know, and therefore we must classify things (and
ideas) according to what they can be used for, or which goals they can help
us achieve. Two armchairs of identical shape may seem equally comfortable
as objects for sitting in, but those same chairs may seem very different for
other purposes, for example, if they differ much in weight, fragility, cost,
or appearance. The further a feature or difference lies from the surface of
the chosen representation, the harder it will be to respond to, exploit, or
adapt to it—and this is why the choice of representation is so important.
In each functional context we need to represent particularly well the heuristic connections between each object's internal features and relationships,
and the possible functions of those objects. That is, we must be able to
easily relate the structural features of each object's representation to how
that object might behave in regard to achieving our present goals. This is
further discussed in sections 12.4, 12.5, 12.12, and 12.13 of *The Society of
Mind*.

New problems, by definition, are different from those we have already
encountered; so we cannot always depend on using records of past experience. Yet, to do better than random search, we must still use what we have
learned from the past, no matter that it may not match perfectly. Which
records should we retrieve as likely to be the most relevant?

Explanations of "relevance," in traditional theories, abound with synonyms for nearness and similarity. If a certain item gives bad results, it
makes sense to try something different. But when something we try turns
out to be good, then a similar one may be better. We see this idea in myriad forms, and whenever we solve problems we find ourselves employing
metrical metaphors: we're "getting close" or "on the right track;" using
words that express proximity. But what do we mean by "close" or "near."
Decades of research on different forms of that question have produced theories and procedures for use in signal processing, pattern recognition, induction, classification, clustering, generalization, etc., and each of these
methods has been found useful for certain applications, but ineffective for
others. Recent connectionist research has considerably enlarged our resources in these areas. Each method has its advocates—but I contend that
it is now time to move to another stage of research. For, although each such
concept or method may have merit in certain domains, none of them seem
powerful enough alone to make our machines more intelligent. It is time to
stop arguing over which type of pattern classification technique is best—

because that depends on our context and goal. Instead, we should work at a higher level of organization, discover how to build managerial systems to exploit the different virtues, and to evade the different limitations, of each of these ways of comparing things. Different types of problems, and representations, may require different concepts of similarity. Within each realm of discourse, some representation will make certain problems and concepts appear to be more closely related than others. To make matters worse, even within the same problem domain, we may need different notions of similarity for:

• Descriptions of problems and goals.
• Descriptions of knowledge about the subject domain.
• Descriptions of procedures to be used.

For small domains, we can try to apply all of our reasoning methods to all of our knowledge, and test for satisfactory solutions. But this is usually impractical, because the search becomes too huge—in both symbolic and connectionist systems. To constrain the extent of mindless search, we must incorporate additional kinds of knowledge—embodying expertise about problem-solving itself and, particularly, about managing the resources that may be available. The spatial metaphor helps us think about such issues by providing us with a superficial unification: if we envision problem-solving as "searching for solutions" in a space-like realm, then it is tempting to analogize between the ideas of similarity and nearness: to think about similar things as being in some sense near or close to one another.

But "near" in what sense? To a mathematician, the most obvious idea would be to imagine the objects under comparison to be like points in some abstract space; then each representation of that space would induce (or reflect) some sort of topology-like structure or relationship among the possible objects being represented. Thus, the languages of many sciences, not merely those of Artificial Intelligence and of psychology, are replete with attempts to portray families of concepts in terms of various sorts of spaces equipped with various measures of similarity. If, for example, you represent things in terms of (allegedly independent) properties then it seems natural to try to assign magnitudes to each, and then to sum the squares of their differences—in effect, representing those objects as vectors in Euclidean space. This further encourages us to formulate the function of knowledge in terms of helping us to decide "which way to go." This is often usefully translated into the popular metaphor of "hill-climbing" because, if we can impose on that space a suitable metrical structure, we may be able to devise iterative ways to find solutions by analogy with the method of hill-climbing or gradient ascent—that is, when any experiment seems more or less successful than another, then we exploit that metrical structure to help us make the next move in the proper "direction." (Later, we shall emphasize that having a sense of direction entails a little more than a sense of proximity; it is not enough just to know metrical distances, we must also respond to other kinds of heuristic differences—and these may be difficult to detect.)

Whenever we design or select a particular representation, that particular choice will bias our dispositions about which objects to consider more or less similar to us (or, to the programs we apply to them) and thus will affect how we apply our knowledge to achieve goals and solve problems. Once we understand the effects of such commitments, we will be better prepared to select and modify those representations to produce more heuristically useful distinctions and confusions. So, let us now examine, from this point of view, some of the representations that have become popular in the field of Artificial Intelligence.

Heuristic Connections of Pure Logic

Why have logic-based formalisms been so widely used in AI research? I see two motives for selecting this type of representation. One virtue of logic is clarity, its lack of ambiguity. Another advantage is the pre-existence of many technical mathematical theories about logic. But logic also has its disadvantages. Logical generalizations apply only to their literal lexical instances, and logical implications apply only to expressions that precisely instantiate their antecedent conditions. No exceptions at all are allowed, no matter how "closely" they match. This permits you to use no near misses, no suggestive clues, no compromises, no analogies, and no metaphors. To shackle yourself so inflexibly is to shoot your own mind in the foot—if you know what I mean.

These limitations of logic begin at the very foundation, with the basic connectives and quantifiers. The trouble is that worldly statements of the form, "For all X, $P(X)$," are never beyond suspicion. To be sure, such a statement can indeed be universally valid inside a mathematical realm—but this is because such realms, themselves, are based on expressions of those very kinds. The use of such formalisms in AI have led most researchers to seek "truth" and universal "validity" to the virtual exclusion of "practical" or "interesting"—as though nothing would do except certainty. Now, that is acceptable in mathematics (wherein we ourselves define the worlds in which we solve problems) but, when it comes to reality, there is little advantage in demanding inferential perfection, when there is no guarantee even that our assumptions will always be correct. Logic theorists seem to have forgotten that any expression like $(\forall X)(PX)$, in actual life—that is, in a world which we find, but don't make—must be seen as only a convenient abbreviation for something more like this:

"For any thing X being considered in the current context, the assertion PX is likely to be useful for achieving goals like G, provided that we apply in conjunction with certain heuristically appropriate inference methods."

In other words, we cannot ask our problem-solving systems to be absolutely perfect, or even consistent; we can only hope that they will grow increasingly better than blind search at generating, justifying, supporting, rejecting, modifying, and developing "evidence" for new hypotheses.

It has become particularly popular, in AI logic programming, to restrict the representation to expressions written in the first order predicate calculus. This practice, which is so pervasive that most students engaged in it don't even know what "first order" means here, facilitates the use of certain types of inference, but at a very high price: that the predicates of such expressions are prohibited from referring in certain ways to one another. This prevents the representation of meta-knowledge, rendering those systems incapable, for example, of describing what the knowledge that they contain can be used for. In effect, it precludes the use of functional descriptions. We need to develop systems for logic that can reason about their own knowledge, and make heuristic adaptations and interpretations of it, by using knowledge about that knowledge—but these limitations of expressiveness make logic unsuitable for such purposes.

Furthermore, it must be obvious that in order to apply our knowledge to commonsense problems, we need to be able to recognize which expressions are similar, in whatever heuristic sense may be appropriate. But this, too, seems technically impractical, at least for the most commonly used logical formalisms—namely, expressions in which absolute quantifiers range over string-like normal forms. For example, in order to use the popular method of "resolution theorem-proving," one usually ends up using expressions that consist of logical disjunctions of separately almost meaningless conjunctions. Consequently, the *natural topology* of any such representation will almost surely be heuristically irrelevant to any real-life problem space. Consider how dissimilar these three expressions seem, when written in conjunctive form:

AVBVCVD   ABVACVADVBCVBDVCD   ABCVABDVACDVBCD

The simplest way to assess the distances or differences between expressions is to compare such superficial factors as the numbers of terms or sub-expressions they have in common. Any such assessment would seem meaningless for expressions like those above. In most situations, however, it would almost surely be useful to recognize that these expressions are symmetric in their arguments, and hence will clearly seem more similar if we re-represent them—for example, by using S_n to mean "n of S's arguments have truth-value T"—so that then they can be written in the form

S_1, S_2, and S_3. Even in mathematics itself, we consider it a great discovery to find a new representation for which the most natural-seeming heuristic connection can be recognized as close to the representation's surface structure. But this is too much to expect in general, so it is usually necessary to gauge the similarity of two expressions by using more complex assessments based, for example, on the number of set-inclusion levels between them, or on the number of available operations required to transform one into the other, or on the basis of the partial ordering suggested by their lattice of common generalizations and instances. This means that making good similarity judgments may itself require the use of other heuristic kinds of knowledge, until eventually—that is, when our problems grow hard enough—we are forced to resort to techniques that exploit knowledge that is not so transparently expressed in any such "mathematically elegant" formulation.

Indeed, we can think about much of Artificial Intelligence research in terms of a tension between solving problems by searching for solutions inside a compact and well-defined problem space (which is feasible only for prototypes)—versus using external systems (that exploit larger amounts of heuristic knowledge) to reduce the complexity of that inner search. Compound systems of that sort need retrieval machinery that can select and extract knowledge which is "relevant" to the problem at hand. Although it is not especially hard to write such programs, it cannot be done in "first order" systems. In my view, this can best be achieved in systems that allow us to use, simultaneously, both object-oriented structure-based descriptions and goal-oriented functional descriptions.

How can we make *logic* more expressive, given that its fundamental quantifiers and connectives are defined so narrowly from the start. This could well be beyond repair, and the most satisfactory replacement might be some sort of object-oriented frame-based language. After all, once we leave the domain of abstract mathematics, and free ourselves from those rigid notations, we can see that some virtues of logic-like reasoning may still remain—for example, in the sorts of deductive chaining we used, and the kinds of substitution procedures we applied to those expressions. The spirit of some of these formal techniques can then be approximated by other, less formal techniques of making chains, like those suggested in chapter 18 of *The Society of Mind*. For example, the mechanisms of defaults and frame-arrays could be used to approximate the formal effects of instantiating generalizations. When we use heuristic chaining, of course, we cannot assume absolute validity of the result, and so, after each reasoning step, we may have to look for more evidence. If we notice exceptions and disparities then, later, we must return again to each, or else remember them as assumptions or problems to be justified or settled at some later time—all things that humans so often do.

Heuristic Connections of Rule-Based Systems

While logical representations have been used in popular research, rule-based representations have been more successful in applications. In these systems, each fragment of knowledge is represented by an *If-Then* rule so that, whenever a description of the current problem-situation precisely matches the rule's antecedent *If* condition, the system performs the action described by that rule's *Then* consequent. What if no antecedent condition applies? Simple: the programmer adds another rule. It is this seeming modularity that made rule-based systems so attractive. You don't have to write complicated programs. Instead, whenever the system fails to perform, or does something wrong, you simply add another rule. This usually works quite well at first—but whenever we try to move beyond the realm of "toy" problems, and start to accumulate more and more rules, we usually get into trouble because each added rule is increasingly likely to interact in unexpected ways with the others. Then what should we ask the program to do, when no antecedent fits perfectly? We can equip the program to select the rule whose antecedent most closely describes the situation—and, again, we're back to "similar." To make any real-world application program resourceful, we must supplement its formal reasoning facilities with matching facilities that are heuristically appropriate for the problem domain it is working in.

What if several rules match equally well? Of course, we could choose the first on the list, or choose one at random, or use some other superficial scheme—but why be so unimaginative? In *The Society of Mind*, we try to regard conflicts as opportunities rather than obstacles—an opening that we can use to exploit other kinds of knowledge. For example, section 3.2 of *The Society of Mind* suggests invoking a *principle of non-compromise*, to discard sets of rules with conflicting antecedents or consequents. The general idea is that whenever two fragments of knowledge disagree, it may be better to ignore them both, and refer to some other, independent agency. In effect this is a managerial approach in which one agency can engage some other body of expertise to help decide which rules to apply. For example, one might turn to case-based reasoning, to ask which method worked best in similar previous situations.

Yet another approach would be to engage a mechanism for inventing a new rule, by trying to combine elements of those rules that almost fit already. Section 8.2 of *The Society of Mind* suggests using K-line representations for this purpose. To do this, we must be immersed in a society-of-agents framework in which each response to a situation involves activating not one, but a variety of interacting processes. In such a system, all the agents activated by several rules can then be left to interact, if only momentarily, both with one another and with the input signals, so as to make a useful self-selection about which of them should remain active. This could be done by combining certain present-day connectionist concepts with other ideas about K-line mechanisms. But we cannot do this until we learn how to design network architectures that can support new forms of internal management and external supervision of developmental staging.

In any case, present-day rule-based systems are still are too limited in ability to express "typical" knowledge. They need better default machinery. They deal with exceptions too passively; they need censors. They need better "ring-closing" mechanisms for retrieving knowledge (see 19.10 of *The Society of Mind*). Above all, we need better ways to connect them with other kinds of representations, so that we can use them in problem-solving organizations that can exploit other kinds of models and search procedures.

Connectionist Networks

Up to this point, we have considered ways to overcome the deficiencies of symbolic systems by augmenting them with connectionist machinery. But this kind of research should go both ways. Connectionist systems have equally crippling limitations, which might be ameliorated by augmentation with the sorts of architectures developed for symbolic applications. Perhaps such extensions and synthesis will recapitulate some aspects of how the primate brain grew over millions of years, by evolving symbolic systems to supervise its primitive connectionist learning mechanisms.

What do we mean by *connectionist*? The usage of that term is still evolving rapidly, but here it refers to attempts to embody knowledge by assigning numerical conductivities or weights to the connections inside a network of nodes. The most common form of such a node is made by combing an analog, nearly linear part that "adds up evidence" with a nonlinear, nearly digital part that "makes a decision" based on a threshold. The most popular such networks today, take the form of multilayer perceptrons—that is, of sequences of layers of such nodes, each sending signals to the next. More complex arrangements are also under study; these can support cyclic internal activities, hence they are potentially more versatile, but harder to understand. What makes such architectures attractive? Mainly, that they appear to be so simple and homogeneous. At least on the surface, they can be seen as ways to represent knowledge without any complex syntax. The entire configuration-state of such a net can be described as nothing more than a simple vector—and the network's input-output characteristics as nothing more than a map from one vector space into another. This makes it easy to reformulate pattern-recognition and learning problems in simple terms—for example, finding the "best" such mapping, etc. Seen in this way, the subject presents a pleasing mathematical simplicity. It is often not mentioned that we still possess little theoretical understanding of the computational complexity of finding such mappings—that is, of how to discover good values for the connection-weights. Most current publications still merely exhibit successful small-scale examples without probing either into assessing the computational difficulty of those problems themselves, or of scaling those results to similar problems of larger size.

However, we now know of quite a few situations in which even such simple systems have been made to compute (and, more important, to learn to compute) interesting functions, particularly in such domains as clustering, classification, and pattern recognition. In some instances, this has occurred without any external supervision; furthermore, some of these systems have also performed acceptably in the presence of incomplete or noisy inputs—and thus correctly recognized patterns that were novel or incomplete. This means that the architectures of those systems must indeed have embodied heuristic connectivities that were appropriate for those particular problem-domains. In such situations, these networks can be useful for the kind of reconstruction-retrieval operations we call *ring-closing*.

But connectionist networks have limitations as well. The next few sections discuss some of these limitations, along with suggestions on how to overcome them by embedding these networks in more advanced architectural schemes.

Limitation of Fragmentation: The Parallel Paradox

In our Epilogue to *Perceptrons*, Papert and I argued as follows:

"It is often argued that the use of distributed representations enables a system to exploit the advantages of parallel processing. But what are the advantages of parallel processing? Suppose that a certain task involves two unrelated parts. To deal with both concurrently, we would have to maintain their representations in two decoupled agencies, both active at the same time. Then, should either of those agencies become involved with two or more sub-tasks, we'd have to deal with each of them with no more than a quarter of the available resources! If that proceeded on and on, the system would become so fragmented that each job would end up with virtually no resources assigned to it. In this regard, distribution may oppose parallelism: the more distributed a system is—that is, the more intimately its parts interact—the fewer different things it can do at the same time. On the other side, the more we do separately in parallel, the less machinery can be assigned to each element of what we do, and that ultimately leads to increasing fragmentation and incompetence. This is not to say that distributed representations and parallel processing are always incompatible. When we simultaneously activate two distributed representations in the same network, they will be forced to interact. In favorable circumstances, those interactions can lead to useful parallel computations, such as the satisfaction of simultaneous constraints. But that will not happen in general; it will occur only when the representations happen to mesh in suitably fortunate ways. Such problems will be especially serious when we try to train distributed systems to deal with problems that require any sort of structural analysis in which the system must represent relationships between substructures of related types— that is, problems that are likely to demand the same structural resources." (See also section 15.11 of *The Society of Mind.*)

For these reasons, it will always be hard for a homogeneous network to perform parallel *high-level* computations—unless we can arrange for it to become divided into effectively disconnected parts. There is no general remedy for this—and the problem is no special peculiarity of connectionist hardware; computers have similar limitations, and the only answer is providing more hardware. More generally, it seems obvious that without adequate memory-buffering, homogeneous networks must remain incapable of recursion, so long as successive "function calls" have to use the same hardware. This is because, without such facilities, either the different calls will side-effect one another, or some of them must be erased, leaving the system unable to execute proper returns or continuations. Again, this may be easily fixed by providing enough short-term memory, for example, in the form of a stack of temporary K-lines.

Limitations of Specialization and Efficiency

Each connectionist net, once trained, can do only what it has learned to do. To make it do something else—for example, to compute a different measure of similarity, or to recognize a different class of patterns—would, in general, require a complete change in the matrix of connection coefficients. Usually, we can change the functionality of a computer much more easily (at least, when the desired functions can each be computed by compact algorithms); this is because a computer's "memory cells" are so much more interchangeable. It is curious how even technically well-informed people tend to forget how computationally massive a fully connected neural network is. It is instructive to compare this with the few hundred rules that drive a typically successful commercial rule-based Expert System.

How connected need networks be? There are several points in *The Society of Mind* which suggest that commonsense reasoning systems may not need to increase in the density of physical connectivity as fast as they increase the complexity and scope of their performances. Chapter 6 argues that knowledge systems must evolve into clumps of specialized agencies, rather than homogeneous networks, because they develop different types of internal representations. When this happens, it will become neither feasible nor practical for any of those agencies to communicate directly with the interior of others. Furthermore, there will be a tendency for newly acquired skills to develop from the relatively few that are already well developed and this, again, will bias the largest scale connections toward evolving into recursively clumped, rather than uniformly connected arrangements. A different tendency to limit connectivities is discussed in section 20.8, which proposes a sparse connection-scheme that can simulate, in real time, the behavior of fully connected nets—in which only a small proportion of agents are simultaneously active. This method, based on a half-century old idea of Calvin Mooers, allows many intermittently active agents to share the same relatively narrow, common connection bus. This might seem, at first, a mere economy, but section 20.9 suggests that this technique could also induce a more heuristically useful tendency, if the separate signals on that bus were to represent meaningful symbols. Finally, chapter 17 suggests other developmental reasons why minds may be virtually forced to grow in relatively discrete stages rather than as homogeneous networks. Our progress in this area may parallel our progress in understanding the stages we see in the growth of every child's thought.

If our minds are assembled of agencies with so little inter-communication, how can those parts cooperate? What keeps them working on related aspects of the same problem? The first answer proposed in *The Society of Mind* is that it is less important for agencies to co-operate than to exploit one another. This is because those agencies tend to become specialized, developing their own internal languages and representations. Consequently, they cannot understand each other's internal operations very well—and each must learn to learn to exploit some of the others for the effects that those others produce—without knowing in any detail how those other effects are produced. For the same kind of reason, there must be other agencies to manage all those specialists, to keep the system from too much fruitless conflict for access to limited resources. Those management agencies themselves cannot deal directly with all the small interior details of what happens inside their subordinates. They must work, instead, with summaries of what those subordinates seem to do. This too, suggests that there must be constraints on internal connectivity: too much detailed information would overwhelm those managers. And this applies recursively to the insides of every large agency. So we argue, in chapter 8 of *The Society of Mind*, that relatively few direct connections are needed except between adjacent "level bands."

All this suggests (but does not prove) that large commonsense reasoning systems will not need to be "fully connected." Instead, the system could consist of localized clumps of expertise. At the lowest levels these would have to be very densely connected, in order to support the sorts of associativity required to learn low-level pattern detecting agents. But as we ascend to higher levels, the individual signals must become increasingly abstract and significant and, accordingly, the density of connection paths between agencies can become increasingly (but only relatively) smaller. Eventually, we should be able to build a sound technical theory about the connection densities required for commonsense thinking, but I don't think that we have the right foundations as yet. The problem is that contemporary theories of computational complexity are still based too much on worst-case analyses, or on coarse statistical assumptions—neither of which suitably represents realistic heuristic conditions. The worst-case theories unduly emphasize the intractable versions of problems which, in their usual forms, present less practical difficulty. The statistical theories tend to uniformly weight all instances, for lack of systematic ways to emphasize the types of situations of most practical interest. But the AI systems of the future, like their human counterparts, will normally prefer to satisfy rather than optimize—and we don't yet have theories that can realistically portray those mundane sorts of requirements.

Limitations of Context, Segmentation, and Parsing

When we see seemingly successful demonstrations of machine learning, in carefully prepared test situations, we must be careful about how we draw more general conclusions. This is because there is a large step between the abilities to recognize objects or patterns (1) when they are isolated and (2) when they appear as components of more complex scenes. In section 6.6 of *Perceptrons* we see that we must be prepared to find that even after training a certain network to recognize a certain type of pattern, we may find it unable to recognize that same pattern when embedded in a more complicated context or environment. (Some reviewers have objected that our proofs of this applied only to simple three-layer networks; however, most of those theorems are quite general, as those critics might see, if they'd take the time to extend those proofs.) The problem is that it is usually easy to make isolated recognitions by detecting the presence of various features, and then computing weighted conjunctions of them. Clearly, this is easy to do, even in three-layer acyclic nets. But in compound scenes, this will not work unless the separate features of all the distinct objects are somehow properly assigned to those correct "objects." For the same kind of reason, we cannot expect neural networks to be generally able to parse the tree-like or embedded structures found in the phrase structure of natural-language.

How could we augment connectionist networks to make them able to do such things as to analyze complex visual scenes, or to extract and assign the referents of linguistic expressions to the appropriate contents of short term memories? This will surely need additional architecture to represent that structural analysis of, for example, a visual scene into objects and their relationships, by protecting each mid-level recognizer from seeing inputs derived from other objects, perhaps by arranging for the object-recognizing agents to compete to assign each feature to itself, while denying it to competitors. This has been done successfully in symbolic systems, and parts have been done in connectionist systems (for example, by Waltz and Pollack) but there remain many conceptual missing links in this area—particularly in regard to how another connectionist system could use the output of one that managed to parse the scene. In any case, we should not expect to see simple solutions to these problems, for it may be no accident that such a large proportion of the primate brain is occupied with such functions.

Limitations of Opacity

Most serious of all is what we might call the problem of *Opacity*: the knowledge embodied inside a network's numerical coefficients is not accessible outside that net. This is not a challenge we should expect our connectionists to easily solve. I suspect it is so intractable that even our own brains have evolved little such capacity over the billions of years it took to evolve from anemone-like reticulae. Instead, I suspect that our societies and hierarchies of sub-systems have evolved ways to evade the problem, by arranging for some of our systems to learn to "model" what some of our other systems do (see *The Society of Mind*, section 6.12). They may do this, partly, by using information obtained from direct channels into the interiors of those other networks, but mostly, I suspect, they do it less directly—so to speak, behavioristically—by making generalizations based on external observations, as though they were like miniature scientists. In effect, some of our agents invent models of others. Regardless of whether these models may be defective, or even entirely wrong (and here I refrain from directing my aim at peculiarly faulty philosophers), it suffices for those models to be useful in enough situations. To be sure, it might be feasible, in principle, for an external system to accurately model a connectionist network from outside, by formulating and testing hypotheses about its internal structure. But of what use would such a model be, if it merely repeated, redundantly? It would not only be simpler, but also more useful for that higher-level agency to assemble only a pragmatic, heuristic model of that other network's activity, based on concepts already available to that observer. (This is evidently the situation in human psychology. The apparent insights we gain from meditation and other forms of self-examination are genuine only infrequently.)

The problem of opacity grows more acute as representations become more distributed—that is, as we move from symbolic to connectionist poles—and it becomes increasingly more difficult for external systems to analyze and reason about the delocalized ingredients of the knowledge inside distributed representations. It also makes it harder to learn, past a certain degree of complexity, because it is hard to assign credit for success, or to formulate new hypotheses (because the old hypotheses themselves are not "formulated"). Thus, distributed learning ultimately limits growth, no matter how convenient it may be in the short term, because "the idea of a thing with no parts provides nothing that we can use as pieces of explanation" (see *The Society of Mind*, section 5.3).

For such reasons, while homogeneous, distributed learning systems may work well to a certain point, they should eventually start to fail when confronted with problems of larger scale—unless we find ways to compensate the accumulation of many weak connections with some opposing mechanism that favors toward internal simplification and localization. Many connectionist writers seem positively to rejoice in the holistic opacity of representations within which even they are unable to discern the significant parts and relationships. But unless a distributed system has enough ability to crystallize its knowledge into lucid representations of its new subconcepts and substructures, its ability to learn will eventually slow down and it will be unable to solve problems beyond a certain degree of complexity. And although this suggests that homogeneous network architectures may not work well past a certain size, this should be bad news only for those ideologically committed to minimal architectures. For all we know at the present time, the scales at which such systems crash are quite large enough for our purposes. Indeed, the *Society of Mind* thesis holds that most of the "agents" that grow in our brains need operate only on scales so small that each by itself seems no more than a toy. But when we combine enough of them—in ways that are not too delocalized—we can make them do almost anything.

In any case, we should not assume that we always can—or always should—avoid the use of opaque schemes. The circumstances of daily life compel us to make decisions based on "adding up the evidence." We frequently find (when we value our time) that, even if we had the means, it wouldn't pay to analyze. Nor does the *Society of Mind* theory of human thinking suggest otherwise; on the contrary it leads us to expect to encounter incomprehensible representations at every level of the mind. A typical agent does little more than exploit other agents' abilities—hence most of our agents accomplish their job knowing virtually nothing of how it is done.

Analogous issues of opacity arise in the symbolic domain. Just as networks sometimes solve problems by using massive combinations of elements each of which has little individual significance, symbolic systems sometimes solve problems by manipulating large expressions with similarly insignificant terms, as when we replace the explicit structure of a composite Boolean function by a locally senseless canonical form. Although this simplifies some computations by making them more homogeneous, it disperses knowledge about the structure and composition of the data—and thus disables our ability to solve harder problems. At both extremes—in representations that are either too distributed or too discrete—we lose the structural knowledge embodied in the form of intermediate-level concepts. That loss may not be evident, as long as our problems are easy to solve, but those intermediate concepts may be indispensable for solving more advanced problems. Comprehending complex situations usually hinges on discovering a good analogy or variation on a theme. But it is virtually impossible to do this with a representation, such as a logical form, a linear sum, or a holographic transformation—each of whose elements seem meaningless because they are either too large or too small—and thus leaving no way to represent significant parts and relationships.

There are many other problems that invite synthesizing symbolic and connectionist architectures. How can we find ways for nodes to "refer" to other nodes, or to represent knowledge about the roles of particular coefficients? To see the difficulty, imagine trying to represent the structure of the Arch in Patrick Winston's thesis—without simply reproducing that topology. Another critical issue is how to enable nets to make comparisons. This problem is more serious than it might seem. Section 23.1 of *The Society of Mind* discusses the importance of "Differences and Goals," and section 23.2 points out that connectionist networks deficient in memory will find it peculiarly difficult to detect differences between patterns. Networks with weak architectures will also find it difficult to detect or represent (invariant) abstractions; this problem was discussed as early as the Pitts-McCulloch paper of 1947. Yet another important problem for memory-weak, bottom-up mechanisms is that of controlling search: In order to solve hard problems, one may have to consider different alternatives, explore their sub-alternatives, and then make comparisons among them— yet still be able to return to the initial situation without forgetting what was accomplished. This kind of activity, which we call "thinking," requires facilities for temporarily storing partial states of the system without confusing those memories. One answer is to provide, along with the required memory, some systems for learning and executing control scripts, as suggested in section 13.5 of *The Society of Mind*. To do this effectively, we must have some *insulationism* to counterbalance our *connectionism*. Smart systems need both of those components, so the symbolic-connectionist antagonism is not a valid technical issue, but only a transient concern in contemporary scientific politics.

Mind-Sculpture

The future work of mind design will not be much like what we do today. Some programmers will continue to use traditional languages and processes. Others programmers will turn toward new kinds of knowledge-based expert systems. But eventually all of this will be incorporated into systems that exploit two new kinds of resources. On one side, we will use huge pre-programmed reservoirs of commonsense knowledge. On the other side, we will have powerful, modular learning machines equipped with no knowledge at all. Then what we know as programming will change its character entirely—to an activity that I envision as more like sculpturing. To program today, we must describe things very carefully, because nowhere is there any margin for error. But once we have modules that know how to learn, we won't have to specify nearly so much—and we'll program on a grander scale, relying on learning to fill in the details.

This doesn't mean, I hasten to add, that things will be simpler than they are now. Instead we'll make our projects more ambitious. Designing an artificial mind will be much like evolving an animal. Imagine yourself at a terminal, assembling various parts of a brain. You'll be specifying the sorts of things that we've only been described heretofore in texts about neuroanatomy. "Here," you'll find yourself thinking, "We'll need two similar networks that can learn to shift time-signals into spatial patterns so that they can be compared by a feature extractor sensitive to a context about this wide." Then you'll have to sketch the architectures of organs that can learn to supply appropriate inputs to those agencies, and draft the outlines of intermediate organs for learning to suitably encode the outputs to suit the needs of other agencies. Section 31.3 of *The Society of Mind* suggests how a genetic system might mold the form of an agency that is predestined to learn to recognize the presence of particular human individuals. A functional sketch of such a design might turn out to involve dozens of different sorts of organs, centers, layers, and pathways. The human brain might have many thousands of such components.

A functional sketch is only the start. Whenever you employ a learning machine, you must specify more than merely the sources of inputs and destinations of outputs. It must also, somehow, be impelled toward the sorts of things you want it to learn—what sorts of hypotheses it should make, how it should compare alternatives, how many examples should be required, and how to decide when enough has been done; when to decide that things have gone wrong, and how to deal with bugs and exceptions. It is all very well for theorists to speak about "spontaneous learning and generalization," but there are too many contingencies in real life for such words to mean anything by themselves. Should that agency be an adventurous risk-taker or a careful, conservative reductionist? One person's intelligence is another's stupidity. And how should that learning machine divide and budget its resources of hardware, time, and memory?

How will we build those grand machines, when so many design constraints are involved? No one will be able to keep track of all the details because, just as a human brain is constituted by interconnecting hundreds of different kinds of highly evolved sub-architectures, so will those new kinds of thinking machines. Each new design will have to be assembled by using libraries of already developed, off-the-shelf sub-systems already known to be able to handle particular kinds of representations and processing—and the designer will be less concerned with what happens inside these units, and more concerned with their interconnections and interrelationships. Because most components will be learning machines, the designer will have to specify, not only what each one will learn, but also which agencies should provide what incentives and rewards for which others. Every such decision about one agency imposes additional constraints and requirements on several others—and, in turn, on how to train those others. And, as in any society, there must be watchers to watch each watcher, lest any one or a few of them get too much control of the rest.

Each agency will need nerve-bundle-like connections to certain other ones, for sending and receiving signals about representations, goals, and constraints—and we'll have to make decisions about the relative size and influence of every such parameter. Consequently, I expect that the future art of brain design will have to be more like sculpturing than like our present craft of programming. It will be much less concerned with the algorithmic details of the sub-machines than with balancing their relationships; perhaps this better resembles politics, sociology, or management than present-day engineering.

Some neural-network advocates might hope that all this will be superfluous. Perhaps, they expect us to find simpler ways. Why not seek to find, instead, how to build one single, huge net that can learn to do all those things by itself. That could, in principle, be done since our own human brains themselves came about as the outcome of one great learning-search. We could regard this as proving that just such a project is feasible—but only by ignoring the facts—the unthinkable scale of that billion year venture, and the octillions of lives of our ancestors. Remember, too, that even so, in all that evolutionary search, not all the problems have yet been solved. What will we do when our sculptures don't work? Consider a few of the wonderful bugs that still afflict even our own grand human brains:

- Obsessive preoccupation with inappropriate goals.
- Inattention and inability to concentrate.
- Bad representations.
- Excessively broad or narrow generalizations.
- Excessive accumulation of useless information.
- Superstition; defective credit assignment schema.
- Unrealistic cost/benefit analyses.
- Unbalanced, fanatical search strategies.
- Formation of defective categorizations.
- Inability to deal with exceptions to rules.

- Improper staging of development, or living in the past.
- Unwillingness to acknowledge loss.
- Depression or maniacal optimism.
- Excessive confusion from cross-coupling.

Seeing that list, one has to wonder, "Can people think?" I suspect there is no simple and magical way to avoid such problems in our new machines; it will require a great deal of research and engineering. I suspect that it is no accident that our human brains themselves contain so many different and specialized brain centers. To suppress the emergence of serious bugs, both those natural systems, and the artificial ones we shall construct, will probably require intricate arrangements of interlocking checks and balances, in which each agency is supervised by several others. Furthermore, each of those other agencies must themselves learn when and how to use the resources available to them. How, for example, should each learning system balance the advantages of immediate gain over those of conservative, long-term growth? When should it favor the accumulating of competence over comprehension? In the large-scale design of our human brains, we still don't yet know much of what all those different organs do, but I'm willing to bet that many of them are largely involved in regulating others so as to keep the system as a whole from frequently falling prey to the sorts of bugs we mentioned above. Until we start building brains ourselves, to learn what bugs are most probable, it may remain hard for us to guess the actual functions of much of that hardware.

There are countless wonders yet to be discovered, in these exciting new fields of research. We can still learn a great many things from experiments, on even the very simplest nets. We'll learn even more from trying to make theories about what we observe in this. And surely, soon, we'll start to prepare for that future art of mind design, by experimenting with societies of nets that embody more structured strategies—and consequently make more progress on the networks that make up our own human minds. And in doing all that, we'll discover how to make symbolic representations that are more adaptable, and connectionist representations that are more expressive.

It is amusing how persistently people express the view that machines based on symbolic representations (as opposed, presumably, to connectionist representations) could never achieve much, or ever be conscious and self-aware. For it is, I maintain, precisely because our brains are still mostly connectionist, that we humans have so little consciousness! And it's also why we're capable of so little functional parallelism of thought—and why we have such limited insight into the nature of our own machinery.

This research was funded over a period of years by the Computer Science Division of the Office of Naval Research.

References

Minsky, Marvin, and Seymour Papert [1988], *Perceptrons*, (2nd edition) MIT Press.

Minsky, Marvin [1987a], *The Society of Mind*, Simon and Schuster.

Minsky, Marvin [1987b], "Connectionist Models and their Prospects," Introduction to Feldman and Waltz Nov. 23.

Minsky, Marvin [1974], "A Framework for Representing Knowledge," Report AIM–306, Artificial Intelligence Laboratory, Massachusetts Institute of Technology, Cambridge, MA.

10

In large human organizations, the members contribute to overall success according to their diverse points of view and diverse capabilities.

So it is with the little agents described in Marvin Minsky's seminal book, The Society of Mind. Intelligence emerges from the mutually compensating abilities of these little agents, no one of which is particularly intelligent by itself. Collectively, they form heterogeneous societies in which the inevitable weaknesses of each individual agent are compensated for by the limited talents of other members of the society.

This chapter introduces Minsky's thinking through a collection of representative excerpts drawn from The Society of Mind. In them, Minsky explains how societies of agents focus attention, solve problems, remember experience, and communicate with one another.

As you read through these excerpts, you may correctly conclude that many key ideas will require a generation or two of graduate students to work out in detail. Reading The Society of Mind is like poking around in a diamond mine, wondering which of the rocks, when polished, will become the most famous gems.

Excerpts from
The Society of Mind

Marvin Minsky

Noncompromise (3.2[†])

To settle arguments, nations develop legal systems, corporations establish policies, and individuals may argue, fight, or compromise—or turn for help to mediators that lie outside themselves. What happens when there are conflict inside minds?

Whenever several agents have to compete for the same resources, they are likely to get into conflicts. If those agents were left to themselves, the conflicts might persist indefinitely, and this would leave those agents paralyzed, unable to accomplish any goal. What happens then? We'll assume that those agents' supervisors, too, are under competitive pressure and likely to grow weak themselves whenever their subordinates are slow in achieving their goals, no matter whether because of conflicts between them, or because of individual incompetence.

> **The Principle of Non-Compromise.** The longer an internal conflict persists among an agent's subordinates, the weaker becomes that agent's status among its own competitors. If such internal problems aren't settled soon, other agents will take control and the agents formerly involved will be "dismissed."

So long as playing-with-blocks goes well, *Play* can maintain its strength and keep control. In the meantime, though, the child may also be growing

---

[†]Section numbers in parenthesis after the section title refer to actual references in *The Society of Mind*.

hungry and sleepy, because other processes are arousing the agents *Eat* and *Sleep*. So long as *Eat* and *Sleep* are not yet strongly activated, *Play* can hold them both at bay. However, any conflict inside *Play* will weaken it and make it easier for *Eat* or *Sleep* to take over. Of course, *Eat* or *Sleep* must conquer in the end, since the longer they wait, the stronger they get.

We see this in our own experience. We all know how easy is it to fight off small distractions when things are going well. But once some trouble starts inside our work, we become increasingly impatient and irritable. Eventually we find it so hard to concentrate that the least disturbance can allow another, different, interest to take control. Now, when any of our agencies loses the power to control what other systems do, that doesn't mean it has to cease its own internal activity. An agency that has lost control can continue to work inside itself—and thus become prepared to seize a later opportunity. However, we're normally unaware of all those other activities proceeding deep inside our minds.

Where does it stop, this process of yielding control to other agencies? Must every mind contain some topmost center of control? Not necessarily. We sometimes settle conflicts by appealing to superiors, but other conflicts never end, and never cease to trouble us.

At first, our principle of non-compromise may seem too extreme. After all, good human supervisors plan ahead to avoid conflicts in the first place and—when they can't—they try to settle quarrels locally before appealing to superiors. But we should not try to find a close analogy between the low-level agents of a single mind and the members of a human community. Those tiny mental agents simply cannot know enough to be able to negotiate with one another, or to find effective ways to adjust to each other's interference. Only larger agencies could be resourceful enough to do such things. Inside an actual child, the agencies responsible for *Building* and *Wrecking* might indeed become versatile enough to negotiate by offering support for one another's goals. "Please, *Wrecker*, wait a moment more till *Builder* adds just one more block: it's worth it for a louder crash!"

B-Brains (6.4)

There *is* one way for a mind to watch itself, and still keep track of what's happening. Divide the brain into two parts, A and B. Connect the A-brain's inputs and outputs to the real world—so it can sense what happens there. But don't connect the B-brain to the outer world at all; instead, connect it so that the A-brain is the B-brain's world!

Now A can see and act upon what happens in the outside world—while B can "see" and influence what happens inside A. What uses could there be for such a B? Here are some A-activities that B might learn to recognize and influence.

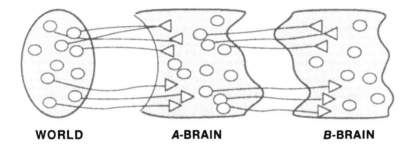

WORLD   **A-BRAIN**   **B-BRAIN**

A seems disordered and confused.	Inhibit that activity.
A appears to be repeating itself.	Make *A* stop. Do something else.
A does something *B* considers good.	Make *A* remember this.
A is occupied with too much detail.	Make *A* take a higher level view.
A is not being specific enough.	Focus *A* on lower-level details.

This two-part arrangement could be a step toward having a more "reflective" mind-society. The *B*-brain could do experiments with the *A*-brain, just as the *A*-brain can experiment with the body, or with the objects and people surrounding it. And just as *A* can attempt to predict and control what happens in the outer world, *B* can try to predict and control what *A* will do. For example, the *B*-brain could supervise how the *A*-brain learns, either by making changes in *A* directly, or by influencing *A*'s own learning processes.

Even though *B* may have no concept of what *A*'s activities mean in relation to the outer world, it is still possible for *B* to be useful to *A*. This is because a *B*-brain could learn to play a role somewhat like that of a counselor, psychologist, or management consultant who can assess a client's mental strategy without having to understand all the details of that client's profession. Without having any idea of what *A*'s goals are, *B* might be able to learn to tell when *A* is not accomplishing them, but only going around in circles, or wandering, confused because certain *A*-agents are repeating the same things over and over again. Then *B* might try some simple remedies, like suppressing some of those *A*-agents. To be sure, this could also result in *B*'s activities becoming nuisances to *A*. For example, if *A* had the goal of adding up a long column of numbers, *B* might start to interfere with this because, from *B*'s point of view, *A* appears to have become trapped in a repetitive loop. This could cause a person accustomed to more variety to find it difficult to concentrate on such a task, and complain of being bored.

To the extent that the *B*-brain knows what is happening in *A*, the entire system could be considered to be partly "self-aware." However, if we connect A and B to "watch" each other too closely, then anything could happen, and the entire system might become unstable. In any case, there is no reason to stop with only two levels; we could connect a C-brain to watch the B-brain, and so on.

Heads in the Clouds (6.9)

What we call a mind is nothing but a heap or collection of different perceptions, united together by certain relations and suppos'd, tho' falsely, to be endow'd with a perfect simplicity and identity.

—DAVID HUME

We'll take the view that nothing can have meaning by itself, but only in relation to whatever other meanings we already know. One might complain that this has the quality of the old question, "Which came first, the chicken or the egg?" If each thing one knows depends on other things one knows, isn't that like castles built on air? What keeps them from all falling down, if none are tied to solid ground? Well, first, there's nothing basically wrong with the idea of a society in which each part lends meaning to the other parts. Some sets of thoughts are much like twisted ropes or woven cloths in which each strand holds others both together and apart. Consider all the music tunes you know. Among them you can surely find two tunes of which, you like each one the more because of how it's similar to or different from the other one. Besides, no human mind remains entirely afloat. Later we'll see how our conceptions of space and time can be based entirely on networks of relationships, yet can still reflect the structure of reality.

If every mind builds somewhat different things inside itself, how can any mind communicate with a different mind? In the end, surely, communication is a matter of degree but it is not always lamentable when different minds don't understand each other perfectly. For then, provided that *some* communication remains, we can still share the richness of each others' thoughts. What good would other people be if we were all identical? In any case, the situation is the same *inside* your mind—since even you, yourself, can never know precisely what *you* mean! How useless any thought would be if, afterward, your mind returned to the selfsame state. But that never happens, because every time we think about a certain thing, our thoughts go off in different ways.

> The secret of what anything means to us depends on how we've connected to other things we know. That's why it's almost always wrong to seek the "real meaning" of anything. A thing with just one meaning has scarcely any meaning at all.

An idea with a single sense can lead you only along one track. Then, if anything goes wrong, it just gets stuck—a thought which sits there in your mind with nowhere to go. That's why, when someone learns something "by rote"—that is, with no sensible connections—we say that they "don't really understand." Rich meaning-networks, however, give you many different ways to go: if you can't solve a problem one way, you can try another. True, too many indiscriminate connections will turn a mind to mush. But well-connected meaning-structures let you turn ideas around in your mind, to consider alternatives and envision things from many perspectives until you find one that works. And that's what we mean by thinking!

Internal Communication (6.12)

If agents can't communicate, how is it that people can—in spite of having such different backgrounds, thoughts, and purposes? The answer is that we overestimate how much we actually communicate. Instead, despite those seemingly important differences, much of what we do is based on common knowledge and experience. So even though we can scarcely speak at all about what happens in our lower-level mental processes, we can exploit their common heritage. Although we can't express what we mean, we can often cite various examples to indicate how to connect structures we're sure must already exist inside the listener's mind. In short, we can often indicate which sorts of thoughts to think, even though we can't express how they operate.

The words and symbols we use to summarize our higher-level goals and plans are not the same as the signals used to control lower-level ones. So when our higher-level agencies attempt to probe into the fine details of the lower-level submachines that they exploit, they cannot understand what's happening. This must be why our language-agencies cannot express such facts from memory. We find it particularly hard to use our language skills to talk about the parts of the mind that learned such skills as balancing, seeing, and remembering, before we started to learn to speak.

"Meaning" itself is relative to size and scale: it makes sense to talk about a meaning only in a system large enough to have many meanings. For smaller systems, that concept seems vacant and superfluous. For example, *Builder's* agents require no sense of meaning to do their work; *Add* merely had to turn on *Get* and *Put*. Then *Get* and *Put* do not need any subtle sense of what those turn-on signals "mean"—because they're wired up to do only what they're wired up to do. In general, the smaller an agency is, the harder it will be for other agencies to comprehend its tiny "language."

> The smaller two languages are, the harder it will be to translate between them. This is not because there are too many meanings, but because there are too few. The fewer things an agent does, the less likely that what another agent does will correspond to

any of those things. And if two agents have nothing in common, no translation is conceivable.

In the more familiar difficulty of translating between human languages, each word has many meanings, and the main problem is to narrow them down to something they share. But in the case of communication between unrelated agents, narrowing down cannot help if the agents have nothing from the start.

Sensing Similarities (11.5)

> *This difficulty [of making definitions] is increased by the necessity of explaining the words in the same language, for there is often only one word for one idea; and though it may be easy to translate words like bright, sweet, salt, bitter, into another language, it is not easy to explain them.*
>
> —SAMUEL JOHNSON

Our ways to think depend in part on how we're raised. But at the start, much more depends upon the wiring in our brains. How do those microscopic features work to influence what happens in our mental worlds? The answer is, *our thoughts are largely shaped by which things seem most similar.* Which colors seem the most alike? Which forms and shapes, which smells and tastes, which timbres, pitches, aches and pains, which feelings and sensations seem most similar? Such judgments have a huge effect at every stage of mental growth—since *what we learn depends on how we classify.*

For example, a child who classified each fire just by the color of its light might learn to be afraid of everything of orange hue. Then we'd complain that the child had "generalized" too much. But if that child classified each flame, instead, by features which were never twice the same, that child would often be burned—and we'd complain that it hadn't generalized enough.

Our genes supply our bodies with many kinds of sensors—external event-detecting agents—each of which sends signals to the nervous system when it detects certain physical conditions. We have sensory agents in our eyes, ears, nose and mouth that discern light, sound, odors, and tastes; we have agents in the skin that sense pressure, touch, vibration, heat, and cold; we have internal agents that sense tensions in our muscles, tendons, and ligaments; and we have many other sensors of which we're normally unaware, such as those that detect the direction of gravity and sense the amounts of various chemicals in different parts of the body.

The agents that sense the colors of light in human eyes are much more complex than the "redness agents" of our toy machine. But this is not the reason that simple machines can't grasp what *Redness* means to us—for neither can the sense-detectors in our human eyes. For, just as there is nothing to say about a single point, there's nothing to be said about an isolated sensory signal. When our *Redness, Touch,* or *Toothache* agents send their signals to our brains, each by itself can only say "I'm here." The rest of what such signals "mean" to us depends on how they're linked to all our other agencies.

In other words, the "qualities" of signals sent to brains depend only on relationships—the same as with the shapeless points of space. This is the problem Dr. Johnson faced, when creating definitions for his dictionary: each separate word like "bitter," "bright," "salt," or "sweet" attempts to speak about a quality of a sensory signal. But all that a separate signal can do is to announce its own activity—perhaps with some expression of intensity. Your *tooth* can't ache it can only send signals; only *you* can ache, once your higher level agencies interpret those signals. Beyond the raw distinctiveness of every separate stimulus, all other aspects of its character or quality—be it of touch, taste, sound, or light—depend entirely on its relationships to the other agents of your mind.

The Functions of Structures (12.5)

Many things that we regard as physical are actually psychological. To see why this is so, let's try to say what we mean by "chair." At first it seems enough to say,

"A chair is a thing with legs and back and seat."

But when we look more carefully at what we recognize as chairs, we find that many of them do not fit this description, because they don't divide into those separate parts. When all is done, there's little we can find in common to all chairs—except for their intended use.

"A chair is something you can sit upon."

But, that too, seems inadequate: it makes it seem as though a chair were as insubstantial as a wish. The solution is that we need to combine at least two different kinds of descriptions. On one side, we need structural descriptions for recognizing chairs when we see them. On the other side we need functional descriptions in order to know what we can *do* with chairs. We can capture more of what we mean by interweaving both ideas. But it's not enough to merely propose a vague association, because in order for it to have some use, we need more intimate details about *how* those chair-parts actually help a person to sit. To catch the proper meaning, we need connections between parts of the chair-structure and the requirements of the human body that those parts are supposed to serve. Our network needs details like these:

Without such knowledge, we might just crawl under the chair or try to wear it on your head. But with that knowledge we can do amazing things,

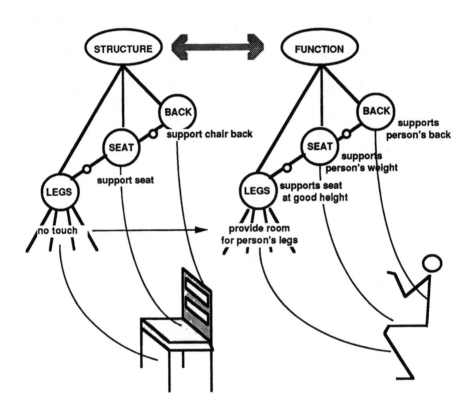

like applying the concept of a chair to see how we could sit on a box, even though it has no legs or back!

Uniframes that include structures like this can be powerful. For example, such knowledge about relations between structure, comfort, and posture could be used to understand when a box could serve as a chair: that is, only when it is of suitable height for a person who does not require a back-rest or room to bend the knees. To be sure, such clever reasoning requires special mental skills with which to re-describe or "re-formulate" the descriptions of both box and chair so that they "match" despite their differences. Until we learn to make old descriptions fit new circumstances, our old knowledge can be applied only to the circumstances in which it was learned. And that would scarcely ever work, since circumstances never repeat themselves perfectly.

Meaning and Definition (12.12)

> **mean'ing. n.** 1. that which exists in the mind, view, or con-
> templation as a settled aim or purpose; that which is meant or
> intended to be done; intent; purpose; aim; object. 2. that which
> is intended to be, or in fact is, conveyed, denoted, signified, or un-
> derstood by acts or language; the sense, signification, or import
> of words; significance; force.
>
> —Webster's Unabridged Dictionary

What is a meaning? Sometimes we're told a definition of a word and
suddenly, we know a way to use that word. But definitions do not often
work so well. Suppose you had to explain what "game" means. You could
start like this:

> **Game.** An activity in which two teams compete to make a ball
> do something that results in a winning score.

This fits a certain range of games—but what of games which just use words,
or keep no scores, or lack the element of competition? We can capture the
nature of more kinds of games by using other definitions, but nothing seems
to catch them all. We simply cannot find much in common to everything
we call a game. Yet one still feels there is a certain unity which underlies
the idea of a game. For example, we feel that we could recognize new
games, and that "game" is more than an arbitrary accumulation.

But now let's turn our attention away from the physical aspects of
games and focus on the *psychological purposes* that games can serve. Then
it is much easier to find some qualities that are common to most adult
games:

> **Game.** An activity that is engaging and diverting, deliberately
> detached from real life.

This second kind of definition treats a game not as a kind of object-thing
but as a process in the mind. At first this might seem somewhat strange,
but really it is nothing new—even our first definition already contained
psychological elements concealed in the words "competing" and "winning."
When seen this way, different kinds of games seem much more similar. This
is because they all serve common purposes—despite the great diversity of
their physical appearances. After all, there is virtually no limit to the
variety of physical objects or structures that could be used to accomplish
the same psychological purpose—in this case, to make an activity diverting
(whatever that might mean). Naturally, then, it would be hard to specify
the range of all possible physical forms of games.

Of course, it is no great surprise to find that "game" has a more
psychological character than does "brick," which we can define in physical
terms without referring to our goals. But most ideas lie in between. We

saw this in the case of "chair," which we cannot describe without referring both to a physical structure and to a psychological function.

Bridge-Definitions (12.13)

At last we're coming close to capturing the meanings of things like chairs and games. We found that structural descriptions are useful, but they always seem too specific. Most chairs have legs, and most games have scores—but there are always exceptions. We also found purposeful descriptions to be useful, but they never seemed specific enough. *"Thing you can sit upon"* is too general to specify a chair, since you can sit on almost anything. *"Diverting activity"* is too broad for game—since there are many other ways to turn our minds from serious things. In general, a single definition rarely works.

> Purposeful definitions are usually too loose.
> *They include many things which we do not intend.*
> Structural definitions are usually too tight.
> *They reject many things that we want to include.*

But we can often capture an idea by squeezing in from several sides at once, to get exactly what we need by using two or more different kinds of descriptions at the same time.

> Our best ideas are often those that bridge between two different worlds!

I don't insist that every definition combine just these particular ingredients of structure and purpose. But that specific mixture does have a peculiar virtue: it helps us bridge between the "ends" we seek and the "means" we have. That is, it helps us connect things we can describe (or, make, find, do, or think) to problems we want to solve. It would be of little use to know that X's "exist," without some way to find and use them.

When we discussed accumulation, we saw that the concepts of "furniture" and "money" have reasonably compact functional definitions but accumulate many structural descriptions. Conversely, the concepts of "square" or "circle" have compact structural definitions, but accumulate endless collections of possible uses.

To learn to use a new or unfamiliar word, you start by taking it to be a sign that there exists, inside some other person's mind, a structure you could use. But no matter how carefully it is explained, you must still rebuild that thought yourself, from materials already in your own mind. It helps to be given a good definition, but still you must mold and shape each new idea to suit your existing skills—hoping to make it work for you the way it seems to work for those from whom you learn.

What people call "meanings" are do not usually correspond to particular and definite structures, but to connections among and across fragments of the great, interlocking networks of connections and constraints among our agencies. Because these networks are constantly growing and changing, meanings are rarely sharp, and we cannot always expect to be able to "define" them in terms of compact sequences of words. Verbal explanations serve only as partial hints; we also have to learn from watching, working, playing—and thinking.

Learning a Script (13.5)

> An expert is one who does not have to think. He knows.
>
> —FRANK LLOYD WRIGHT

What will our portrait-drawing child try next? Some children keep working to improve their person pictures. But most of them go on to put their newfound skills to work at drawing more ambitious scenes in which two or more picture-people interact. This involves wonderful problems about how to depict social interactions and relationships—and these more ambitious projects lead the child away from being concerned with making the pictures of the individual more elaborate and realistic. When this happens, the parent may feel disappointed at what seems to be a lack of progress. But we should try to appreciate the changing character of our children's ambitions and recognize that their new problems may be even more challenging.

This doesn't mean that drawing learning stops. Even as those children cease to make their person pictures more elaborate, the speed at which they draw them keeps increasing, and with seemingly less effort. How and why does this happen? In everyday life, we take it for granted that "practice makes perfect," and that repeating and rehearsing a skill will, somehow, automatically cause it to become faster and more dependable. But when you come to think of it, this really is quite curious. You might expect, instead, that the more you learned, the *slower* you would get—from having more knowledge from which to choose! *How does practice speed things up?*

Perhaps, when we practice skills we can already perform, we engage a special kind of learning, in the course of which the original performance process is replaced or "bridged-across" by new and simpler processes. The "program" below shows the many steps our novice portrait drawer had to take in order to draw each childish body-face. The "script" to the right shows only those steps that actually produce the lines of the drawing; this script has only half as many steps.

The people we call "experts" seem to exercise their special skills with scarcely any thought at all—as though they were simply reading preassembled scripts. Perhaps when we "practice" to improve our skills, we're mainly building simpler scripts that don't engage so many agencies. This

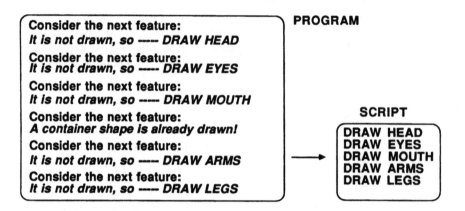

lets us do old things with much less "thought" and gives us more time to think of other things. The less the child had to think of where to put each arm and leg, the more time remains to represent what that picture-person is actually doing.

Parts and Holes (14.7)

As an example of reformulation, we'll represent the concept of a box in the form of a machine that has a goal. We can use this to understand the *Hand-Change* phenomenon. What makes a *Block-Arch* trap a person's arm so that there's no way to escape except to withdraw? One way to explain this is to imagine the arch as made of four potential obstacles—that is, if we include the floor.

An obstacle is an object that interferes with the goal of moving in a certain direction. To be trapped is to be unable to move in any acceptable direction. Why does the *Block-Arch* form a trap? The simplest explanation is that each of its four sides is a separate obstacle that keeps us from escaping in a certain direction. (For our present purposes, we'll regard moving the hand forward or backward as unacceptable.) Therefore we're trapped, since there are only four acceptable directions—up, down, left, or right—and each of them is separately blocked. Psychologically, however, there's something missing in that explanation: it doesn't quite describe our sense of being trapped. When you're caught inside a box, you feel as though something is trying to keep you there. The box seems more than just its separate sides: you don't feel trapped by any particular side. It seems more like a conspiracy in which each obstacle is made more effective

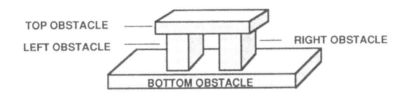

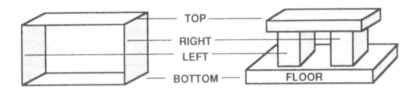

because of how all the other obstacles work together to keep you from going around it. In the next section we'll assemble an agency that represents this active sense of frustration by showing how those obstacles cooperate to keep you in.

In order to represent this concept of trap or enclosure, we'll first need a way to represent the idea of a container. To simplify matters, instead of trying to deal with a genuine, six-sided, three-dimensional boxlike container, we'll consider only a two-dimensional, four-sided rectangle. This will let us continue to use our *Block-Arch* uniframe, together with that extra side to represent the floor.

Why focus so sharply on the concept of a container? Because without that concept, we could scarcely understand the structure of the spatial world. Indeed, every normal child spends a great deal of time learning about space-surrounding shapes—as physical implements for containing, protecting, or imprisoning objects. But the same idea is also important not only physically, but psychologically, as a mental implement for envisioning and understanding other, more complicated structures. This is because the idea of a set of "all possible directions" is one of the great, coherent, cross-realm correspondences that can be used in many different realms of thought.

The Power of Negative Thinking (14.8)

*When life walls us in, our intelligence cuts an opening, for,
though there be no remedy for an unrequited love, one can win
release from suffering, even if only by drawing from the
lessons it has to teach. The intelligence does not recognize in
life any closed situations without an outlet.*

—MARCEL PROUST

How do boxes keep things in? Geometry is a fine tool for understanding shapes, but alone, it can't explain the *Hand-Change* mystery. For that, you also have to know how *moving* works! Suppose that you pushed a car through that *Block-Arch*. Your arm will be imprisoned until you pull it out. How can you comprehend the cause of this? The diagram below depicts an agency that represents the several ways an arm can move inside a rectangle. The top-level agent *Move* has four subagents: *Move-Left*, *Move-Right*, *Move-Up*, and *Move-Down*. (As before, we'll ignore the possibility of moving in and out, in three dimensions). If we connect each of these subagents to the corresponding side of our four-sided box-frame, each agent will be able to test whether the arm can move in the corresponding direction (by seeing whether there is an obstacle there). Then, if every direction is blocked, the arm can't move at all—and that's what we mean by being "trapped."

The "—o" symbol indicates that each box-frame agent is connected to *inhibit* the corresponding subagent of *Move*. An obstacle to the left puts *Move-Left* into a can't-move state. If all four obstacles are present, then all four box-frame agents will be activated; this will inhibit all of *Move's* agents—which will leave *Move* itself in a can't-move state—and we'll know that the trap is complete. However, if we saw a *Topless-Arch*, then the *Move-Up* agent would not be inhibited, and *Move* would not be paralyzed! This suggests an interesting way to find an escape from a *Topless-Arch*. First you *imagine* being trapped inside a box-frame—from which you know there's no escape. Then, since the top block is actually missing, when your vision system looks for actual obstacles, there will be no signal to inhibit the *Move-Up* agent. Accordingly *Move* can activate that agent, and your arm will move upward automatically to escape!

This method has a paradoxical quality. It begins by assuming that escaping is impossible. Then this pessimistic mental act—imagining that one's arm is trapped—leads directly to finding a way out. We usually expect to solve our problems in more positive, goal-directed ways, by comparing what we have with what we wish—and then removing the differences. But here we've done quite the opposite. We compared our plight, not with what we want, but with a situation even worse—the least desirable anti-goal. Yet even that can actually help, by showing how the present situation fails to match that hopeless state. Which strategy is best to use? Both depend on recognizing differences and on knowing which actions affect those differences. The optimistic strategy makes sense when one sees several ways to go—and merely has to choose the best. The pessimistic strategy should be reserved for when one sees no way at all, when things seem really desperate.

The Recursion Principle (15.11)

Let's consider one last time how a mind could juggle non-existent furniture inside an imaginary room. To compare different arrangements, we must somehow maintain at least two different descriptions in the mind at once. Can we store them in different agencies, both active at the same time? That would mean splitting our space-arranging-agency into two different smaller portions, each working on one of those descriptions. On the surface, there's nothing clearly wrong with that. However, if of those smaller agencies became involved with similar jobs then they, in turn, would also have to split in two. And then, we'd have to do each of those jobs with but one quarter of a mind! If we had to divide agencies into smaller and smaller fragments, each job would end up with no mind at all!

At first, this might seem to be an unusual situation. But it really is very common. The best way to solve a hard problem is always to break it into several simpler ones, and break those into even simpler ones. Then we face the same issue of mental fragmentation. Happily, there is another way. We can work on the various parts of a problem in serial order, one after another, using the same agency over and over again. Of course, this takes more time. But it has one absolutely fundamental advantage: each agency can apply its full power to every sub-problem!

> **The Recursion Principle.** When a problem splits into smaller parts, then unless one can apply the mind's full power to each such subjob, one's intellect will get dispersed, and leave less cleverness for each new task.

Indeed, our minds don't usually shatter into helpless fragments when problems split into parts. We *can* imagine how to pack a jewelry-box without forgetting where it will fit into a suitcase. This suggests that we can apply our full space-arranging resources to each problem in turn. But how, then, do we get back to the first problem, after we thought about the other ones, without having to start all over again? To common sense, the answer seems clear: we simply *"remember where we were."* But this means that we must have some way to store, and later re-create, the states of interrupted agencies. Behind the scenes, we need machinery to keep track of all the incomplete accomplishments, to remember what was learned along the way, to compare different results, and to measure progress in order to decide what to do next. All this must go on in accord with larger, sometimes changing plans.

The need to recall our recent states is why our "short term memories" *are* short term memories! In order to do their complex jobs so quickly and effectively, each micro-memory device must be a substantial system of machinery, with many intricate and specialized connections. If so, our brains cannot afford to make too many duplicate copies of that machinery, so we must re-use what we have for different jobs. Each time we reuse a micromemory-device, the information stored inside must be erased—or moved to another, less costly place. But that would also take some time and interrupt the flow of thought. Our short term memories must work too fast to have any time for consciousness.

Closing the Ring (19.10)

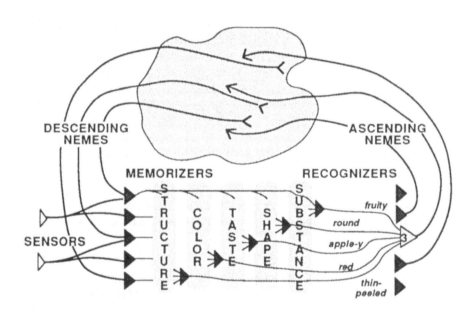

Something amazing happens when you go around a loop like this! Suppose you were to imagine three properties of an apple—for example, its substance, taste, and thin-peeled structure. Then, even if there were no apple on the scene—and even if you had not yet thought of the word "apple"— the recognition-agent on the left will be aroused enough to excite your "apple"—polyneme. (This is because I used the number three for the required sum in the apple polyneme's recognizer instead of demanding that all five properties be present.) That agent can then arouse the K-lines in other agencies, like those for color and shape—and thus evoke your memories of other apple properties! In other words, if you start with enough clues to arouse one of your apple-nemes, it will automatically arouse memories of the other properties and qualities of apples and create a more complete impression, "stimulus," or hallucination of the experience of seeing, feeling, and even of eating an apple. This way, a simple loop machine can reconstruct a larger whole from clues about only certain of its parts!

Many thinkers have assumed that such abilities lie beyond the reach of all machines. Yet here we see that retrieving the whole from a few of its parts requires no magic leap past logic and necessity, but only simple societies of agents that "recognize" when certain requirements are met. If something is red and round and has the right size and shape for an apple, but some other round, red, fruit, such as a tomato or a pomegranate. Any such process leads only to guesses—and frequently these will be wrong. Nonetheless, to think effectively, we often have to turn aside from certainty—to take some chance of being wrong. Our memory systems are powerful *because* they're not constrained to be perfect!

Verbal Expression (22.10)

How easily we people can communicate. We listen and speak without the slightest sense of what's involved! One of us expresses an idea, the other understands it, and neither thinks anything complicated has happened; it seems as natural to talk as it is to walk. Yet both simplicities are illusions. To walk, you must engage a vast array of agencies to move your body down the street. To talk, you must engage a vast array of agencies to build new structures in another person's mind. But *how* do you know just what to say, to affect the other person's agencies?

Let's suppose that Mary wants to tell Jack something. This means that there is a certain structure p, somewhere inside the network of Mary's agencies—and that Mary's language-agency must construct a similar structure inside Jack's mind. To do this, Mary will need to speak words that will activate appropriate activities inside Jack's agencies, then correctly link them together. How can she do that? Here is what we'll call the *"re-duplication"* theory of how we formulate what we say:

> *Mary proceeds, step by step, to construct a new version of p—call it q—inside her own mind.* In doing this, she will apply various memory-control operations to activate certain isonomes and polynemes.

As Mary performs each internal operation, her speech-agency selects certain corresponding verbal expressions—and these cause similar operations to occur inside Jack. As a result, Jack builds a structure similar to q.

To be able to do that, Mary must have learned at least one expressive technique that corresponds to each frequently used mental operation. And Jack must have learned to recognize those expressive techniques—we'll call them *grammar-tactics*—and to use them to activate some corresponding isonomes and polynemes.

To build her new version of p, Mary could employ a goal-achieving scheme: she keeps comparing p with the latest version of q and, whenever she senses a significant difference, she applies some operation to q the removes or reduces that difference. For example, if Mary notices that p has an *Origin* pronome where q lacks one, her memory-control system will focus on p's *Origin*. In this case, if p itself is a motionframe, the usual speech-tactic is to use the word *"from."* Next she must describe the substructure attached to p's *Origin* pronome. If this were a simple polyneme like "Boston," Mary's speech-agency could simply pronounce the corresponding word. But if that pronome is assigned to some more complicated structure, such as an entire frame, Mary's language-agency must interrupt itself to copy *that*. This is expressed, as we have seen, by using words like "who" or "which." In any case, Mary continues this difference-duplication process until she senses no significant discrepancies between q and p. Of course, what Mary finds "significant" depends on what she "wants to say."

This "re-duplication" theory of speech describes only the first stages of how we use language. In later stages, the mental operations we use to construct q are not always immediately applied to pronouncing words. Instead, we learn techniques for storing sequences of grammar-tactics, temporarily; this makes it possible to modify and rearrange our words and sentences before we say them. Learning these arts takes a long time: most children need a decade or more to complete their language systems, and many keep learning, throughout their lives, to sense new sorts of discrepancies and to discover ways to express them.

Creative Expression (22.11)

There is a wonderful capacity that comes along with the ability to "express" ideas. Whatever we may want to say, we probably won't say exactly *that*. But in exchange, there is a chance of saying something else that is both good and new! After all, the "thing we want to say"—the structure p we're trying to describe—is not always a definite, fixed structure that our language-agents can easily read and copy. If p exists at all, it's likely to be a rapidly changing network involving several agencies. If so, then the language-agency may only be able to make guesses and hypotheses about p, and try to confirm or refute them by performing experiments. Even if p were well-defined in the first place, this very process is liable to change it, so that the final version q won't be the same as the original structure p. Sometimes we call this process "thinking in words."

In other words, whether or not what you "meant" to say actually existed before you spoke, your language-agencies are likely either to *reformulate* what did exist, or create something new and different from anything you had before. Whenever you try to express with words any complicated mental state, you're forced to oversimplify—and that can cause both loss and gain. On the losing side, no word description of a mental state can ever be complete; some nuances are always lost. But in exchange, when you're forced to try to separate the essences from accidents, you gain the opportunity to make reformulations. For example, when stuck on a problem, you may "say to yourself" things like, *"Now, let's see—just what was I really trying to accomplish?"* Then, since your language agency knows so little about the actual state of those other agencies, it must answer such questions by making theories about them, and these may well leave you in a state that is simpler, clearer, and better suited to solving your problem.

When we try to explain what we think we know, we're likely to end up with something new. All teachers know how often we understand something for the first time only after trying to explain it to someone else. Our abilities to make language descriptions can engage all our other abilities to think and to solve problems. If speaking involves thinking, then one must ask, *"How much of ordinary thought involves the use of words?"* Surely many of our most effective thinking-methods scarcely engage our language-agencies at all. Perhaps we turn to words only when other methods fail. But then, the use of language can open entirely new worlds of thought. This is because, once we can represent things in terms of strings of words, it becomes possible to use them in a boundless variety of ways to change and rearrange what happens in our other agencies. Of course, we never realize we're doing this; instead we refer tp such activities by names like *paraphrase* or *change of emphasis* as though we weren't changing what we're trying to describe. The crucial thing is that during the moments in which those word-strings are detached from their "meanings," they are no longer subject to the constraints and limitations of other agencies, and the language-systems can do what they want with them. Then we can transmit, from one person's brain to another, the strings of words our grammar-tactics produce, and every individual can gain access to the most successful formulations that others can articulate. This is what we call culture—the conceptual treasures our communities accumulate through history.

Differences and Duplicates (23.2)

It is important for us to be able to notice differences. But this seemingly innocent requirement poses a problem whose importance has never been recognized in psychology. To see the difficulty, let's return to the subject of mental rearrangements. Let's first assume that the problem is to compare two room-arrangement descriptions represented in two different agencies: agency A represents a room that contains a couch and a chair; agency Z represents the same room, but with the couch and chair exchanged.

Now if both agencies are to represent furniture-arrangements in ways that some third agency D can compare, then the "difference-detecting" agency D must receive two sets of inputs that match almost perfectly. Otherwise, every other, irrelevant difference between the outputs of A and Z would appear to D to be differences in those rooms—and D would perceive so many spurious differences that the real ones would be indiscernible!

> **The Duplication Problem.** The states of two different agencies cannot be compared unless those agencies themselves are virtually identical.

But this is only the tip of the iceberg, for it is not enough that the descriptions to be compared emerge from two almost identical agencies. Those agencies must, in turn, receive inputs of near identical character. And for *that* to come about, each of their subagencies must also fulfill that same constraint. The only way to meet all these conditions is for both agencies—*and all the subagencies upon which they depend*—to be identical. *Unless we find another way, we'll need an endless host of duplicated brains!*

This duplication problem comes up all the time. What happens when you hear that *Mary bought John's house*? Must you have separate agencies to keep both Mary and John in your mind at once? Even that would not suffice, for unless both person-representing agencies had similar connections to all your other agencies, those two representations of "persons" would not have similar implications. The same kind of problem must arise when you compare your present situation with some recollection or experience—that is, when you compare how you react to those two different partial states of mind. But to compare those two reactions, what kind of simultaneous machinery would be needed to maintain both momentary personalities? How could a single mind hold room for two—one person old, the other new?

Time-Blinking (23.3)

Fortunately, there is a way to get around the duplication problem entirely. Let's take a cue from how a perfume makes a strong impression first, but then appears to fade away, or how, when you put your hand in water that is very hot or very cold, the sensation is intense at first—but soon will almost disappear entirely. As we say, we "get used to" those sensations. Because *our senses react mainly to how things change in time.* This is true even for the sensors in our eyes—though, normally, we're unaware of it because our eyes are always moving imperceptibly. Most of the sensory agents that inform our brains about the world are sensitive *only* to various sorts of time-changes—and that surely is also true of most of the agents *inside* the brain.

> Any agent that is sensitive to changes in time can also be used to detect differences. For whenever we expose such an agent, first to a situation A and then to a situation B, any output from that agent will signify some difference between A and B.

This suggests a way to solve the duplication problem. Since most agents can be made to serve as difference-agents, *we can compare two descriptions simply by presenting them to the same agency at different times.* This is easily done if that agency is equipped with a pair of high-speed, temporary K-line memories. Then we need only load the two descriptions into those memories and compare them by activating first one and then the other.

> Store the first description in pronome p.
> Store the second description in pronome q.
> Activate p and q in rapid succession.
> Then any changes in the agents' outputs represent differences between A and B!

We can use this trick to implement the scheme we described for escaping from a topless-arch. Suppose that p describes the present situation and q describes a box that permits no escape. Each *Move* agent is designed to detect the appearance of a wall. If we simply "blink" from the present situation to the box frame, one of these agents will announce the appearance of any box wall that was not already apparent in the present situation. Thus, automatically, this scheme will find all the directions that are not closed off. If the outputs of the *Move* agents were connected to cause you to move in the corresponding direction, this agency would lead you to escape!

The method of time-blinking can also be used to simplify our difference-engine scheme for composing verbal expressions, since now the speaker can maintain both p and q inside the selfsame agency. If not for this, each speaker would need what would amount to a duplicate society of mind, in order to simulate the listener's state. Although the method of time-blinking is powerful and efficient, it has some limitations; for example it cannot directly recognize relations among more than two things at a time. I suspect that people share this limitation, too—and this may be why we have relatively few language-forms, like "between" and "middle," for expressing three-way comparisons and relationships.

Several Thoughts at Once (29.2)

To see that we can think in several mental realms at once, consider the role
of the word "give" in this simple sentence:

"Mary gives Jack the kite."

We can see at least three distinct meanings here. First, we could represent
the idea of the kite's motion through physical space by using a *Trans*-frame
whose *Trajectory* begins at Mary's hand and ends at Jack's.

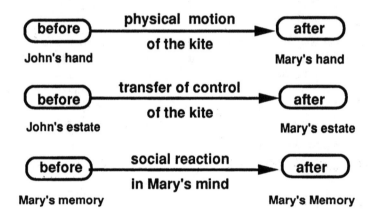

But quite beyond that realm of space, we also find a different significance
in what Mary did—in another realm that we'll call "estates." This involves
a different sense of "give," in which the object need not actually move at
all! Instead, what happens is the transfer of its *ownership*.

Each of us has an "estate"—the collection of possessions we control.
And this "realm of estate" is more important than it might seem, because
it lies between the realms of objects and ideas. In order to carry out our
plans, it is not enough only to know what things or ideas are required,
and how to adapt them to our purposes. We must also be able to take
possession of those objects or ideas, either by right or by might.

> Possession plays essential roles in all our plans, because we can't
> use any materials, tools, or ideas, until we gain control of them.

We can also interpret Mary's act within a social realm, in which we understand that giving gifts involves yet other kinds of relationships. No sooner
do you hear of Mary's gift, than certain parts of your mind becomes concerned with why she was so generous, and how this involved her affections
and obligations.

How can all these different thoughts proceed at the same time, without interfering with one another? I suspect that it is for the same reason that we have no trouble imagining an apple as both round and red at the same time: in that case, the processes for color and shape use agents that do not compete. Similarly, the different processes involved with ideas like "give" may operate in agencies so different they rarely need to compete for the same resources.

Paranomes (29.3)

What enables us to comprehend *"Mary gives Jack the kite"* in so many ways at once? Different meanings don't conflict when they apply to separate realms—but that can't be quite what's happening here, since the physical, social, and mental realms are closely linked in many ways. So now I'll argue just the opposite, that *these meanings are so similar that they don't conflict!* Here is my hypothesis about what holds together all these aspects of our thoughts.

> Many of our higher level conceptual-frames are really parallel arrays of analogous frames, each active in a different realm.

Consider all the different roles played by the *Actor* pronome of our sentence. In the physical realm, the *Origin* of *give* is Mary's hand. In the possessional realm of "give and take," that *Origin* is in Mary's estate—since Mary can only give Jack what she owns. Similarly, in the physical realm, it is the kite itself that moves from Mary's hand to Jack's; however, in the realm of estates, the kite's *ownership* is what "changes hands."

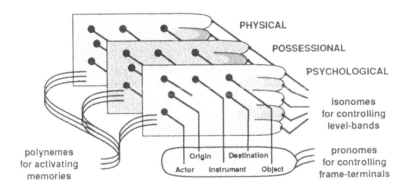

This suggests that certain pronomes can operate in several different realms at once. Let's call them "paranomes" to emphasize their parallel activities. When the language-agency activates some polynemes and paranomes, these agents run cross-wise through the agencies of various realms to arouse several processes and frames at the same time; these correspond to different interpretations, in different realms, of the same phrase or sentence. Then, because each major agency contains its own memory-control system, the agencies within each realm can simultaneously apply their own methods for dealing with the corresponding aspect of the common topic of concern. In this way, a single language-phrase can at the same time evoke different processes involved with social dispositions, spatial images, poetical fancies, musical themes, mathematical structures—or any other assortment of types of thought that don't interfere too much with one another.

This is not to say that all these different modes of thought will proceed independently of one another. Whenever any process gains momentary control over a paranome, many other processes can be affected. For example, one agency's memory-control process might thus cause the agencies in several other realms simultaneously to "blink" on and off their *Origin* and *Destination* paranomes. This would force the agencies active in each of those realms to focus upon whichever types of differences they then discern; then, in between such episodes, each agency can apply its own way of thinking to the corresponding topic, difference, or relationship. By using these cross-connecting polynemes and paranomes, the activity in each realm can proceed sometimes independently, yet at other times influence and be affected by what happens in the other realms.

Cross-Realm Correspondences (29.4)

We often describe the things we like as *"elevated," "lofty,"* or *"heavenly."* Why do we see such things in terms of altitude in space? We often speak of time itself in spatial terms, as though the future were "ahead" of us, while the past remains behind. We think of problems as "obstacles" to go around, and turn to using diagrams to represent things that don't have shapes at all. What enables us to turn so many skills to so many other purposes? These tendencies reflect the systematic "cross-realm correspondences" embodied in our families of polynemes and paranomes.

> At each instant, several realms may be engaged in active processing. Each has separate processes, but must compete for control of the ascending nemes that lead into the language-agency. Which polyneme will play the role of *Origin* in the next sentence-frame? Will it be Mary's physical arm or hand, or Mary's social role as party-guest? It sometimes seems as though the language-agency can focus on only one realm at a time.

This could be one reason why language-scientists find it hard to classify the roles words play in sentence-frames. No sooner does a language agency assign some polynemes and isonomes to a phrase, than various mind-divisions proceed to alter how they're used inside each different realm. Every shift of control from one realm to another affects which particular nemes will be next to influence the language agency. This causes moment-to-moment changes in the apparent meaning of a phrase.

> At one moment, control over language may reside in the realm of thought that is working most successfully; at the next moment, it may be the one experiencing the most difficulty. Each shift in attention affects how the various expressions will be interpreted, and this in turn can affect which realm will next take center stage.

For example, the sentence, *"Mary gives Jack the kite,"* might start by arousing a listener's concern with Mary's social role as party-guest. That would cause the pronomes of a social frame to represent Mary's obligation to bring a present. But then the listener's possession realm might become concerned with Mary's ownership of that gift, or with how she got control of it. This shift from social to possessional concern could then affect the processing of future sentences. For example, it will influence whether a phrase like "Jack's kite" is interpreted to refer to the kite that Jack happens to be holding or to a different kite that Jack happens to own.

Every mental realm accumulates its own abilities, but also discovers, from time to time, how to exploit the skills of other realms. Thus the mind as a whole can learn to exploit the frames developed in the realm of space both for representing events in time, and for thinking about social relationships. Perhaps our chaining skills are the best example of this; no matter which realm or realms they originate in, we eventually learn to apply them to any collection of entities, events, or ideas (in any realm whatever) that we can arrange into sequences. Then chains assume their myriad forms, such as spatial order, psychological causality, or social dominance.

Reference

Minsky, Marvin [1987], this chapter is a collection of excerpts from *The Society of Mind*, Simon and Schuster.

11

It is hard to make a machine intelligent, but it is easy to imagine making a machine that learns to be intelligent by acting like a vast network of simulated neurons. After all, our heads are stuffed with neurons, so they must have a lot to do with our intelligence.

In the 1940s, research on simulated neuron networks was associated with the field of Cybernetics, but for lack of computing power, most of the research focused on relatively simple analog feedback loops of various sorts. Later, in the 1960s, a new generation of neuron-oriented researchers emerged, but again, for lack of computing power, their research was largely limited to the study of individual simulated neurons of a particular sort called Perceptrons. It was not until the 1980s that enough computing power became available to study lots of simulated neurons working together.

Now some answers are beginning to emerge. But importantly, in Poggio and Girosi's work, the answers emerge by a careful mathematical analysis that exploits two simple facts: most networks compute vector-to-vector functions; and most network learning procedures amount to approximating an unknown vector-to-vector function from input-output examples. This enables Poggio and Girosi to draw upon an enormous body of existing mathematics to reach two important conclusions: first, no more than two layers of neurons are needed, in principle; and second, the computation performed by each neuron should be quite different from the sum-and-threshold computation almost universally used by neural-net enthusiasts.

HyperBF: A Powerful Approximation Technique for Learning

Tomaso Poggio
Federico Girosi

Learning an input-output mapping from a set of examples, of the type that many neural networks have been constructed to perform, can be regarded as synthesizing an approximation to a multi-dimensional function. From this point of view, this form of learning is closely related to classical approximation techniques, such as generalized splines and regularization theory. In this chapter, we argue that for multivariate functions, and in the absence of other information, the only choice is to assume smoothness of the mapping to be learned. We then propose an approximation scheme—the HyperBF expansion—that is equivalent to networks with one hidden layer. We show that this technique is equivalent to assuming smoothness of the mapping in the Bayes sense and is equivalent to standard regularization and generalized splines. We characterize the HyperBF expansion and its capabilities of reflecting prior knowledge of the mapping to be learned, such as the type of smoothness and the presence of multiple scales or lower dimensional components. We then discuss Gaussian HyperBF and their interpretation in terms of finding optimal prototypes, represented as the conjunctions of elementary features, and generalizing among them.

Approximation and Learning

Simple forms of learning from examples are equivalent to the approximation of multivariate functions. To illustrate the connection, let us draw an analogy between learning an input-output mapping and a standard approximation problem, surface reconstruction from sparse data points. Learning simply means collecting the *examples*, that is, the input coordinates x_i, y_i and the corresponding output values at those locations, the heights of the surface d_i. *Generalization* means estimating d at locations x, y where there are no examples, that is, no data. This requires interpolating or, more generally, approximating the surface between the data points (interpolation is the limit of approximation when there is no noise in the data). In this sense, learning is a problem of *hypersurface reconstruction* [Poggio & staff 1989; Poggio & Girosi 1989; Omohundro 1987]. The tasks of classification and of learning boolean functions may be regarded in a similar way. They correspond to the problems of approximating a mapping $R^n \to \{0, 1\}$ and a mapping $\{0, 1\}^n \to \{0, 1\}$, respectively.

From this point of view, learning a smooth mapping from examples is clearly ill-posed [Tikhonov & Arsenin 1977], in the sense that the information in the data is not sufficient to reconstruct uniquely the mapping in regions where data are not available. In addition, the data are usually noisy. *A priori* assumptions about the mapping are needed to make the problem well-posed. One of the simplest assumptions is that the mapping is *smooth*: small changes in the inputs cause a small change in the output In the next section we will argue that this is a necessary assumption for approximation in high-dimensional spaces.

Smoothness Is Necessary for Ignorant Multivariate Function Approximation

The approximation of a multivariate function is faced with a fundamental question: *how many samples are needed to achieve a given degree of accuracy* [Stone 1982; Barron & Barron 1988]. It is well known that the answer depends on the dimensionality d and on the degree of smoothness p of the class of functions that have to be approximated [Lorentz 1966, 1986; Stone 1980, 1982, 1985]. This problem—of *sample complexity* —has been extensively studied and some fundamental results have been obtained by Stone [1982]. He considered a class of nonparametric estimation problems, like surface approximation, and computed the optimal rate of convergence ϵ_n, that is, a measure of how accurately a function can be approximated knowing n samples of its graph. Using a local polynomial regression he showed that the optimal rate of convergence $\epsilon_n = n^{-\frac{p}{2p+d}}$, can be achieved by generalizing previous results based on local averages. This means that the number of examples needed to approximate a function reasonably well grows enormously with the dimension d of the space on which it is defined, *and* that this effect is mitigated by a high degree of smoothness p (in fact ϵ_n depends only on the ratio $\frac{d}{p}$). For instance, in the case of a twice differentiable, function of two variables, 8000 examples are needed to obtain $\epsilon_n = 0.05$, but if the function depends on 10 variables the number of examples necessary to obtain the same rate of convergence grows up to 10^9. However, if a function of 10 variables is 10 times differentiable 8000 examples will be enough to obtain $\epsilon_n = 0.05$.

These results provide a powerful justification for assuming that the function to be approximated is very smooth. In fact, when the number of dimensions becomes larger than say 10, and in the absence of any other specific information about the function, one is forced to assume a high degree of smoothness: otherwise the number of examples required will be so large that the approximation task becomes hopeless.

In the next section we describe a natural technique for exploiting assumptions of smoothness.

Regularization, Bayes Theorem, and Smoothness

Techniques that are based on the prior assumption of smoothness to solve approximation problems are well known under the term of standard regularization. Consider the inverse problem of finding the hypersurface values z, given sparse data d. Standard regularization replaces the problem with the variational problem of finding the surface that minimizes a cost functional consisting of two terms [Tikhonov & Arsenin 1977; Morozov 1984; Bertero et al. 1988] (the first to introduce this technique in computer vision was Eric Grimson [1981]). The first term measures the distance between the data and the desired solution z; the second term measures the cost associated with a functional of the solution $\|Pz\|^2$ that embeds the *a priori* information on z. P is usually a differential operator, and thus $\|Pz\|^2$ measures the deviation of z from the specific smoothness assumption embedded in P. In detail, the problem is to find the hypersurface z that minimizes

$$\sum_i (z_i - d_i)^2 + \lambda\|Pz\|^2 \tag{1}$$

where i is a collective index representing the points in feature space where data are available and λ, the regularization parameter, controls the compromise between the degree of smoothness of the solution and its closeness to the data. Therefore λ is directly related to the degree of generalization that is enforced. It is well known that standard regularization provides solutions that are equivalent to generalized splines [Bertero et al. 1988].

The regularization approach can be regarded as a specific application of Bayesian estimation (see Poggio and Girosi [1989]), which is a natural approach, given our previous discussion. Using Bayes theorem one expresses the conditional probability distribution $P_{z/d}(z; d)$ of the hypersurface z given the examples d, in terms of a prior probability $P_z(z)$ that embeds the constraint of smoothness and the conditional probability $P_{d/z}(d; z)$ of

d given z, equivalent to a model of the noise

$$P_{z/d}(z; d) \propto P_z(z) \, P_{d/z}(d; z) \ . \tag{2}$$

The maximum of this posterior probability (the MAP estimate) coincides with standard regularization, that is equation (1), provided that the noise is additive and Gaussian and the prior is a Gaussian distribution of a linear functional of z (see Poggio and Girosi [1989]). Under these conditions, the first term $\sum_i (z_i - d_i)^2$, in the regularization principle equation (1) corresponds to $C(d|z)$, whereas the second term $\|Pz\|^2$, corresponds to the prior $C(z)$ [Geman & Geman 1984; Marroquin et al. 1987].

Note that in practice additional a priori information may be supplied in order to make the learning problem manageable. *Space invariance* or other invariances to appropriate groups of transformations can play a very important role in effectively countering the dimensionality problem (see Poggio [1982]). It is also interesting to observe that there are connections between the formulation in terms of prior probabilities (equation (2)) and formulations in terms of complexity of hypotheses, such as the Minimum Length Principle formulation of Rissanen [1978] (see also Poggio and Girosi [1989]).

From Regularization to HyperBF

The function f to be approximated is regarded as the sum of p components f^m, $m = 1, \ldots, p$, each component having a different prior probability. Therefore the functional $H[f]$ to minimize will contain p stabilizers P^m and will be written as

$$H[f] = \sum_{i=1}^{N} \left(\sum_{m=1}^{p} f^m(\mathbf{x}_i) - y_i \right)^2 + \sum_{m=1}^{p} \lambda_m \|P^m f^m\|^2 \ . \tag{3}$$

Analyzing the structure of the Euler-Lagrange equations associated with equation (3), it can be shown that the function $F(\mathbf{x})$ that minimizes the functional $H[f]$ is a *linear superposition of linear superpositions* of the Green's functions G^m corresponding to the stabilizers P^m, that is

$$F(\mathbf{x}) = \sum_{m=1}^{p} \sum_{i=1}^{N} c_i^m G^m(\mathbf{x}; \mathbf{x}_i^m) + p(\mathbf{x}), \tag{4}$$

where $p(\mathbf{x})$ is a polynomial whose degree depends on the null spaces of an operator associated with the stabilizers. For instance, when $G^m(\mathbf{x})$ are Gaussian a polynomial is not needed though it can always be added. For other Green's functions the theory requires an appropriate $p(\mathbf{x})$, though in many practical cases this is not critical. The simplest case of equation (4) is when $p = 1$. In this case, when the Green's function is radial, that is when $G = G(\|\mathbf{x} - \mathbf{x}_i\|)$ the method corresponds to classical RBF interpolation [Powell 1987; Franke 1982; Micchelli 1986; Broomhead & Lowe 1988; Poggio

& Girosi 1989]. In general the properties of the Green functions G^m depend solely on the nature of the stabilizers P^m. In the radial case, for instance, depending on the stabilizer we can obtain the Gaussian $G(r) = e^{-(\frac{r}{c})^2}$, the well known *thin plate spline* $G(r) = r^2 \ln r$, and other radial functions. We refer to Poggio and Girosi [1989] for other properties concerning the class of allowed Green's functions and the connection with powerful results about radial basis functions obtained by Micchelli [1986] and Powell [1987].

Because the functional $H[f]$ is quadratic and convex the problem of determining the coefficients c_α^m is linear, and it is equivalent to inverting a matrix of size N. When N is large this approach is computationally expensive, and some approximation must be made. We adopt an approximation scheme with fewer centers than examples, as originally suggested by Broomhead and Lowe [1988]. The centers become parameters that are set during the learning step, similar to the coefficients c_α^m [Poggio & Girosi 1989]. An approximated solution $\tilde{F}$ to the variational problem equation (3) is sought of the following form, that we call *HyperBF* expansion

$$\tilde{F}(\mathbf{x}) = \sum_{m=1}^{p} \tilde{f}^m(\mathbf{x}) + p(\mathbf{x}), \tag{5}$$

$$\tilde{f}^m(\mathbf{x}) = \sum_{\alpha=1}^{K_m} c_\alpha^m G^m(\mathbf{x}; \mathbf{t}_\alpha^m) \tag{6}$$

where $K_m < N$. The coefficients c_α^m, and the *centers* $\mathbf{t}_\alpha^m$, are unknown and are computed by minimizing $H[\tilde{F}]$ by a minimization method such as gradient descent, conjugate gradient, or others. Clearly this minimization problem is not convex anymore, and local minima can arise.

The Expansion and the Network

The interpretation of equation (6) is simple: the surface is approximated by the superposition of, say, p sets of Gaussian distributions (if G is Gaussian), each set with a different σ. In the simple case of $p = 1$, $K_1 = N$, each Gaussian is centered at the position of one of the data points.

As observed by Broomhead and Lowe [1988] a superposition of radial functions is equivalent to a simple network, that in the HyperBF case takes the form sketched in figure 1. The interpretation of the network is the following. The centers of the radial functions are somewhat similar to prototypes, because they are points in the multidimensional input space. Each unit computes the euclidean distance of the input from its center, that is, their similarity, and applies to it the radial function. In the case of the Gaussian, a unit will have maximum activity when the new input exactly matches its center. The output of the network is the linear superposition of the activities of all the radial functions in the network. The

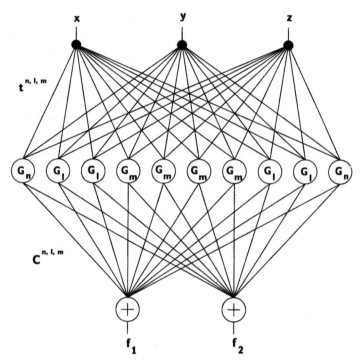

Figure 1. The HyperBF network for the approximation of a multivariate function, shown here for the case $f : R^3 \rightarrow R^2$. The data, a set of points where the value of the function is known, can be considered as examples to be used during learning. The unit G^m evaluates the function $G^m(\|\mathbf{x} - \mathbf{t}_\alpha^m\|)$, that is, the function G^m centered on $\mathbf{t}_\alpha^m$. A fixed, nonlinear, invertible function may be present after the summation. The radial basis functions are in general fewer than the number of *examples*. The parameters that are determined during learning are the coefficients c_α, and the centers $\mathbf{t}_\alpha^m$.

corresponding weights are found during learning by minimizing a measure of the error between the network's prediction and each of the examples. At the same time, the centers of the radial functions are also updated during learning. Moving the centers is equivalent to modifying the corresponding prototypes.

The HyperBF method leads, in particular, to radial basis functions of multiple scales for the reconstruction of the function f. Suppose we know a *priori* that the function to be approximated has components on a number p of scales $\sigma_1, \ldots, \sigma_p$: we can use this information to choose a set of p stabilizers whose Green's functions are, for example, Gaussians of variance $\sigma_1, \ldots, \sigma_p$. We have [Poggio & Girosi 1989]

$$\|P^m f^m\|^2 = \sum_{k=0}^{\infty} a_k^m \int_{R^n} d\mathbf{x} (D^k f^k(\mathbf{x}))^2 \tag{7}$$

where $D^{2k} = \nabla^{2k}$, $D^{2k+1} = \nabla\nabla^{2k}$ and $a_k^m = \frac{\sigma_m^{2k}}{k!2^k}$. As a result, the solution will be a *superposition of superpositions* of Gaussians of different variance. Of course, the Gaussians with large σ should be preset, depending on the nature of the problem, to be fewer and therefore on a sparser grid, than the Gaussians with a small σ.

The HyperBF method yields also non-radial Green's functions—by using appropriate stabilizers—and also Green's functions with a lower dimensionality—by using the associated f^m and P^m in a suitable lower-dimensional subspace. Again this reflects *a priori* information that may be available about the nature of the mapping to be learned. In the latter case the information is that the mapping is of lower dimensionality or has lower dimensional components.

Gradient descent and exclusion principle for HyperBF

We now give the updating rules for the gradient descent algorithm, in the limiting case of $\lambda = 0$ and for radial Green's functions $G^m = G^m(\|\mathbf{x}\|^2)$. The rules are the following

$$c_\alpha^m(t+1) = c_\alpha^m(t) + 2\omega \sum_{i=1}^{N} \Delta_i G^m(\|\mathbf{x}_i - \mathbf{t}_\alpha^m\|^2) \qquad (8)$$

$$\mathbf{t}_\alpha^m(t+1) = \mathbf{t}_\alpha^m(t) - 4\omega c_\alpha^m \sum_{i=1}^{N} \Delta_i G^{m\prime}(\|\mathbf{x}_i - \mathbf{t}_\alpha^m\|^2)(\mathbf{x}_i - \mathbf{t}_\alpha^m) \qquad (9)$$

where ω is a parameter related to the rate of convergence to the fixed point, $\alpha = 1, \ldots, K_m$, $m = 1, \ldots, p$, and $\Delta_i = y_i - \tilde{F}(\mathbf{x}_i)$ is the error between the desired output and the network's output for example i. Other similar, more efficient, iterative methods for minimizing a cost functional could be used in practice. Clearly, because the function $H[\tilde{F}]$ is not convex, local, suboptimal minima could exist. To overcome this problem one could use "stochastic" gradient descent by adding a random term to the gradient descent equations [Wax 1954].

In the gradient descent equations nothing forbids that two or more centers may move towards each other until they coincide. Clearly, this should be avoided *for centers of the same type* (it corresponds to a degeneracy of the solution) in an efficient algorithm. In other words, in equation (4) two identical basis functions with the same center are clearly redundant, but two different basis functions in the same position, for instance two Gaussians with a different scale, may actually make sense. This amounts to a form of an *exclusion principle* for basis units of the same type (the index m in equation (7), see Girosi and Poggio [1989]). A formal way to ensure that centers never overlap is to add to the functional that it is mini-mized the sum of pairwise repulsive interactions among centers of *the same type* only: for instance, among Gaussians with the same σ, of the form $\sum_m \sum_{\alpha \not= \beta} \Psi(\|\mathbf{t}_\alpha^m - \mathbf{t}_\beta^m\|)$, where Ψ is an appropriate repulsive potential, such as $\Psi(r) = \frac{1}{r^2}$.

Equation (9) can be easily modified to reflect this additional term (see Girosi and Poggio [1989]). In practice, it may be sufficient to have a criterion that forbids any two centers to move too close to each other.

Note that an efficient heuristic scheme may want to have the equivalent of *creation and annihilation operators* that *create* basis units in regions of the input space where the network is not performing well, and *annihilate* basis units that are not activated much. This common sense heuristics fits perfectly within the following formal framework: creation of a new unit means moving the center of an existing, remote one, to a useful position; annihilation is equivalent to a 0 value for the associated coefficient c_α^m.

◇ A practical algorithm

The following algorithm can be used to learn the c_α^m and the $\mathbf{t}_\alpha^m$:

- Set the initial value of the centers to a subset of the examples. Al-ternatively, use the k-means algorithm [MacQueen 1967] to find the initial positions $\mathbf{t}_\alpha^m$ of the centers.
- Find the c_α^m with fixed centers by direct methods or by gradient descent (ensured to converge).
- Use the $\mathbf{t}_\alpha^m$ and c_α^m found so far as initial values for the non-convex gradient descent equations with repulsive terms.
- Explore how performance changes by changing incrementally the num-ber of centers.

Gaussian HyperBF

The case of Gaussian basis functions, possibly of different scales and not necessarily radial, is especially interesting. Gaussian functions can be syn-thesized as the product of two-dimensional Gaussian receptive fields, look-ing at a retinotopic map of features, where the coordinates are feature parameters (such as their x, y position). Thus, in the case of Gaussian HyperBF the network's output is the sum of products and therefore repre-sents the logical disjunction of conjunctions, where the disjunction ranges over all the centers. It is especially interesting that this generalization of the simple schemes of *disjunction of conjunctions* is completely equivalent to generalized splines.

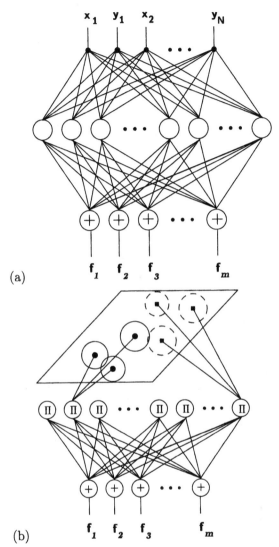

Figure 2. (a) The HyperBF network. (b) Shows a completely equivalent interpretation of (a) for the case of Gaussian radial basis functions. Gaussian functions can be synthesized as the product of one- or two-dimensional Gaussian receptive fields, looking at maps of the features that span the multidimensional input space. The solid circles represent the 2D Gaussians associated with one of the radial basis functions. The dotted circles represent the 2D receptive fields that synthesize another Gaussian radial function. The 2D Gaussian receptive fields transduce parameters of features, represented implicitly as activities in a retinotopic array, and their product computes the radial function without the need of calculating norms and exponentials explicitly (see Poggio and Girosi [1989], and Poggio and Edelman [1989]).

In addition, the Gaussian HyperBF method suggests an intriguing metaphor for a computational strategy that the brain may use. Computation, in the sense of generalization from examples, would be done by superposition of receptive fields in a multidimensional input space. In the case of Gaussian radial basis functions, the multidimensional receptive fields could be synthesized by combining lower dimensional receptive fields, possibly in multiple stages. These units would be somewhat similar to "grandmother" filters, rather than detectors, each representing a prototype (compare Perrett *et al.* [1987]), which in turn results from the conjunction of elementary features.

Discussion

HyperBF have a rather simple structure that seems to capture some of the main lessons that are becoming evident in the fields of statistics and neural networks. In order to clarify it, let us consider a specific, extreme case, in which we consider a HyperBFs network as a classifier: something the formal theory does not strictly allow. Imagine using a HyperBF scheme to classify patterns, such as handwritten digits, in different classes. Assume that the input is a binary 8-bit vector of length N and each of the basis functions is initially centered on the point in the N-dimensional input space that corresponds to one of the training examples (fixed centers case). The system has several outputs, each corresponding to one of the digit classes. Let us consider a series of special cases of HyperBF of increasing generality:

- Each of the units (its center corresponds to an example) is an hypersphere and is connected, with weight 1, to its output class only. Classification is done by reading out the class with maximum output. In this case, the system is performing a Parzen window estimate of the posterior probability and then using a MAP criterion. The Parzen-window approach is similar (and asymptotically equivalent) to the k_n nearest-neighbor estimation, of which the nearest-neighbor rule is a special case. In this special case the network is equivalent to a hypersphere classifier.

- We now replace the hypersphere by a multidimensional Gaussian, that is, an allowed radial basis function. The centers of the radial basis functions may be regarded as representing *templates* against which the input vectors are matched (think, for example, of a radial Gaussian with small σ, centered on its center, which is a point in the n-dimensional space of inputs).

- We may do even better by allowing arbitrary c values between the radial units and the output. The c can then be found by the direct pseudoinverse technique (or by gradient descent) and are guaranteed to be optimal in the l_2 sense.

- We now allow a number of (movable) centers with radial basis functions. This is the Generalized Radial Basis Function (GRBF) scheme [Girosi & Poggio 1989a]. Moving a center is equivalent to modifying the corresponding template. Thus the update equations attempt to develop better templates by modifying, during training, the existing ones. In our example, this means changing the pixel values in the arrays representing the digits. This case is equivalent to generalized splines in many dimensions with free knots.

- Finally the most general network—the HyperBF network—contains radial units of the Gaussian type of different scale (that is, σ), together with non-radial units associated to appropriate stabilizers and units that receive only a subset of the inputs.

This list shows that the HyperBF scheme is an extension of some of the simplest and most efficient approximation and learning algorithms which can be regarded as special cases of it. In addition, it illuminates a few interesting aspects of the HyperBF algorithm, such as its massive parallelism and its use of prototypes. The HyperBF scheme says how to extend look-up tables into a scheme equivalent to generalized splines, which are probably the most powerful approximation method known.

Very recent results [Girosi & Poggio 1989a] suggest that, as one may have expected, the HyperBF scheme is theoretically superior to other neural network schemes from the point of view of approximation theory. It has been recently proved that backpropagation with one hidden layer can approximate arbitrarily well any continuous function on a finite interval [Cybenko 1989; Funahashi 1989], given an unbounded number of units. The same property is valid for Gaussian GRBFs [Girosi & Poggio 1989a] and in fact for most feedforward networks [Stinchcombe & White 1989]. It is, therefore, a rather weak property that does not characterize by itself a good approximation technique. Approximation theory in fact emphasizes the property of *best approximation* that a good approximation scheme has to satisfy. The best approximation property guarantees that in the space of the approximating functions there exists a closest point to the function to be approximated. Regularization techniques satisfy the best approximation property and therefore RBF networks are a best approximation scheme, while backpropagation networks are not [Girosi & Poggio 1989a]. HyperBF with movable centers do not strictly have the property of best approximation either, but have the very important advantage that the centers in the hidden layer can be easily *frozen* (say to a subset of the examples) while still allowing the network to perform satisfactorily (with fixed centers the network has the best approximation property). It is far from obvious how to set in a similar way the weights in the hidden layer of a multilayer perceptron.

It is important to stress that whereas the HyperBF network is appropriate for the approximation of smooth functions, there is no special reason to believe that it is particularly well suited for classification tasks for which the smoothness condition at the heart of the regularization functional underlying HyperBFs is not meaningful. Empirical results suggest that the performance of RBF and GRBFs is good on a few classification tasks [Wolpert 1988; Edelman & Poggio in preparation]. In addition, it is often possible to transform a classification task into the task of learning a smooth transformation, followed by a step that measures distance from a prototype (see Poggio and Edelman [1989]), followed by a threshold. This means that certain classification tasks may be reformulated in a way that is appropriate for the HyperBF approach [Girosi & Poggio 1989].

Conclusions

Let us summarize some of the conclusions suggested by our results:

- Our approximation scheme—and the corresponding network—is a theoretically sound approach to multivariate approximation and learning. It provides a representational scheme which has solid foundations. Most previous neural network techniques can be regarded as special cases of it, or as attempts without a satisfactory theoretical foundation.

- Our learning scheme is quite powerful, compared with more classical schemes and with the many neural network models proposed recently; as shown by the theory, by the related huge body of results on splines, and by initial applications (including previous work by other people).

- Our approach shows clearly the limitations of this class of learning schemes, which attempt to approximate the underlying mapping from a set of examples, and strongly suggests—because of the related results in approximation theory—that these limitations are of a general nature and that, in particular, they are likely to encompass all neural network models proposed. The main limitation has to do with sample complexity and it is likely to be an intrinsic limitation of any learning scheme with weak prior information.

- AI-type machine learning may, in some cases, get around the sample complexity problem by effectively exploiting deep prior information (either common sense knowledge or special domain knowledge).

References

Barron, A. R., and R. L. Barron [1988], "Statistical learning networks: a unifying view," In *Symposium on the Interface: Statistics and Computing Science*, Reston, Virginia.

Bertero, M., T. Poggio, and V. Torre [1988], "Ill-posed problems in early vision," *Proceedings of the IEEE*, vol. 76, pp. 869–889.

Broomhead, D. S., and D. Lowe [1988], "Multivariable functional interpolation and adaptive networks," *Complex Systems*, vol. 2, pp. 321–355.

Cybenko, G. [1989], "Approximation by superposition of a sigmoidal function," *Math. Control Systems Signals*, in press.

Franke, R. [1982], "Scattered data interpolation: tests of some method," *Math. Comp.*, vol. 38, no. 5, pp. 181–200.

Funahashi, K. [1989], "On the approximate realization of continuous mappings by neural networks," *Neural Networks*, vol. 2, pp. 183–192.

Geman, S., and D. Geman [1984], "Stochastic relaxation, Gibbs distributions, and the Bayesian restoration of images," *IEEE Transactions on Pattern Analysis and Machine Intelligence*, vol. PAMI-6 pp. 721–741.

Girosi, F., and T. Poggio [1989], "A theory of networks for approximation and learning: part two," Report AIM–1167, (in preparation), Artificial Intelligence Laboratory, Massachusetts Institute of Technology, Cambridge, MA.

Girosi, F., and T. Poggio [1989a], "Networks and the best approximation property," Report AIM–1164, (in preparation), Artificial Intelligence Laboratory, Massachusetts Institute of Technology.

Grimson, W. E. L. [1981], *From Images to Surfaces*, MIT Press, Cambridge, MA.

Lorentz, G. G. [1966], "Metric entropy and approximation," *Bull. Amer. Math. Soc*, vol. 72, pp. 903–937.

Lorentz, G. G. [1986], *Approximation of Functions*, Chelsea Publishing Co., New York.

This chapter has been written in consultation with Thinking Machines Corporation, Cambridge, Massachusetts, USA. We are grateful to S. Edelman, E. Hildreth, D. Hillis, L. Tucker, and especially to A. Hurlbert for useful discussions and suggestions.

This chapter describes research done within the Artificial Intelligence Laboratory and the Center for Biological Information Processing in the Department of Brain and Cognitive Sciences. Support for this research is provided by a grant from ONR, Cognitive and Neural Sciences Division, by the Artificial Intelligence Center of Hughes Aircraft Corporation, and by the NATO Scientific Affairs Division (0403/87). Support for the Artificial Intelligence Laboratory's artificial intelligence research is provided by the Advanced Research Projects Agency of the Department of Defense under Army contract DACA76–85–C–0010 and in part under Office of Naval Research (ONR) contract N00014–85–K–0124. TP is supported by the Uncas and Ellen Whitaker chair.

MacQueen, J. [1967], " Some methods of classification and analysis of multivariate observations," in *Proc. 5th Berkeley Symposium on Math., Stat., and Prob.*, edited by L. M. LeCam and J. Neyman, p 281, U. California Press, Berkeley, CA.

Marroquin, J. L., S. Mitter, and T. Poggio [1987], "Probabilistic solution of ill-posed problems in computational vision," *J. Amer. Stat. Assoc.*, vol. 82, pp. 76–89.

Micchelli, C. A. [1986], "Interpolation of scattered data: Distance matrices and conditionally positive definite functions," *Constr. Approx.*, vol. 2, pp. 11–22.

Morozov, V. A. [1984], *Methods for solving incorrectly posed problems*, Springer-Verlag, Berlin.

Omohundro, S. [1987], Efficient algorithms with neural network behavior, *Complex Systems*, vol. 1, no. 273.

Perrett, D. I., A. J. Mistlin, and A. J. Chitty [1987], "Visual neurones responsive to faces," *Trends in Neuroscience*, vol. 10, no. 9, pp. 358–364.

Poggio, T. [1982], "Visual algorithms," In *Physical and Biological Processing of Images*, edited by O. J. Braddick and A. C. Sleigh, pp. 128–153, Springer-Verlag, Berlin.

Poggio, T., and S. Edelman [1989], "A network that learns to recognize 3D objects," (submitted for publication).

Poggio, T., and F. Girosi [1989], "A theory of networks for approximation and learning," Report AIM–1140, Artificial Intelligence Laboratory, Massachusetts Institute of Technology.

Poggio, T., and the Staff [1989], "M.I.T. progress in understanding images," In *Proceedings Image Understanding Workshop*, pp. 56–74, Palo Alto, CA. Morgan Kaufmann, San Mateo, CA.

Powell, M. J. D. [1987], "Radial basis functions for multivariable interpolation: a review," in *Algorithms for Approximation*, edited by J. C. Mason and M. G. Cox, Clarendon Press, Oxford.

Rissanen, J. [1978], "Modeling by shortest data description," *Automatica*, vol. 14, pp. 465–471.

Stinchcombe, M., and H. White [1989], "Universal approximation using feedforward networks with non-sigmoid hidden layer activation functions," In *Proceedings of the International Joint Conference on Neural Networks*, pp. I–607, Washington DC. IEEE TAB Neural Network Committee.

Stone, C. J. [1980], "Optimal rates of convergence for nonparametric estimators," *Ann. Stat.*, vol. 8, no. 6, pp. 1348–1360.

Stone, C. J. [1982], "Optimal global rates of convergence for nonparametric regression," *Ann. Stat.*, vol. 10, pp. 1040–1053.

Stone, C. J. [1985], "Additive regression and other nonparametric models," *Ann. Stat.*, vol. 13, pp. 689–705.

Tikhonov, A. N., and V. Y. Arsenin [1977], *Solutions of Ill-posed Problems*, W. H. Winston, Washington, DC.

Wax, N. [1954], *Selected papers on noise and stochastic processes*, Dover Publications, New York.

Wolpert, D. [1988], "Alternative generalizers to neural nets," In *Abstracts of the first annual INNS meeting*, New York, Pergamon Press.

12

Open any textbook on Artificial Intelligence and you will find a chapter on language that shows how a few pattern-matching rules enable toy-world sentences to be transformed into syntax-reflecting parse trees. Thus encouraged, you might suppose that handling real-world sentences is just a matter of a few more rules.

Alas, just a few more rules are inadequate, and many research groups have demonstrated that many thousands are not enough, evoking doubts about whether traditional pattern-matching rules are really the right representation for expressing linguistic competence.

But there is an alternative approach. Instead of an unmanageably large, undifferentiated rule set, Berwick and Fong work with a dozen or so explicitly parameterized modules. Although each module has only a few parameters at most, they combine multiplicatively, explaining the rich variety found in the world's languages.

One of the many advantages of the approach is economy of implementation. You should be able to condition a parsing program to handle your favorite language by selecting the appropriate parameter settings and by supplying the appropriate lexicon. Berwick and Fong have one set of parameter settings that capture the conventions of English. Other sets deal with Spanish, German, and even Warlpiri, an exotic, much studied language, cherished by linguists for its strangeness, spoken only by a few thousand central Australian aborigines.

Principle-Based Parsing: Natural Language Processing for the 1990s

Robert C. Berwick
Sandiway Fong

Introduction: Principle-Based Parsing and Rule-Based Parsing

This chapter describes a new approach to processing natural language, *principle-based parsing*, that has been developed at the MIT Artificial Intelligence Laboratory over the past five years. Principle-based parsing replaces the traditionally large set of rules used to parse sentences on a language by language basis with a much smaller, fixed set of parameterized, universal principles. The principles interact deductively to replace many rules.

We have used this approach to implement a unified parsing scheme that can solve many thorny problems in natural language processing:

- Handle a wide variety of languages, including English, Spanish, German, and even "exotic" language like the Australian aborigine language Warlpiri where words can occur in virtually any order.

- Translate single sentences from one language to another.

- Optimize natural language parsing for use on serial or parallel computers.

This chapter reviews each of these accomplishments.

What is principle-based parsing? Perhaps it is easiest to say what it is *not*. It is not like more traditional parsing that relies on many thousands of individual, language-particular rules, exemplified by augmented transition network systems (ATNs) or most systems based on context-free grammars.

These rule-based parsing systems attempt to describe sentences typolog-
ically by spelling out shallow word surface order and spelling patterns—
passive, dative, and the like.

For instance, consider a "passive" sentence: *The ice-cream was eaten.*
To understand this sentence, at the very least a parser must be able to
analyze *ice-cream* as the object of *eat*—the thing eaten. This is triggered
(in English) by the form of the verb *be* (here, *was*) plus the *en* ending on
the verb *eat*. A typical rule-based parser might capture this left-to-right
pattern in an IF-THEN rule:

> IF: subject filled *be*–Verb+ed No object
> THEN: make the subject the object

Note that this IF-THEN rule directly encodes the left-to-right order of
the English passive pattern, along with all its particular features. It is
appropriate only for English, and only for this particular kind of passive
form.

The basic idea of principle-based parsing is to replace this shallow rule
with a much deeper, smaller, explanatory set of basic principles. In some
ways, this is much like the shift in medical expert systems from a shallow,
descriptivist approach to an explanatory theory based on, for example, a
knowledge of kidney physiology.

The motivation for the shift from rules to principles is the same in
both domains. Rule systems have many problems. They are too inflexible,
too specific, too fragile, too hard to maintain, and too large. As we will
see, principle-based parsing repairs each of these defects:

- What happens when a sentence is only partially well-formed? Sentences like *What do you wonder who likes*, or *John is proud Bill*,
  though hard to understand, do not cause people to collapse like a rule-
  based system. Rather, people understand such sentences uniformly.
  Rule-based language systems have traditionally handled such possibilities by adding weights or more rules that can describe the wrong
  sentences. But this makes the rule set larger still.

- What happens if the rule system is missing a rule that is almost, but
  not quite, like the one that handles passives? Consider the sentence
  The ice-cream got eaten. This is a simple dialect variant, but unless it
  has been preprogrammed into the rule base—often one programmer's
  dialect—the full system will fail on such an example. Of course, once
  the problem is known a system can be patched by adding a new rule,
  but there is no end to the patches, the maintenance problems, and the
  size of the rule system.

- What happens with other languages? The French sentence *faire
  manger la pomme par Jean* ('was eaten the apple by John') is like the
  English passive, but there is no *be* form, and the object can follow *eat*

(*manger*). Thus the entire system must be re-tooled for new dialects and languages, and this in fact has been the traditional approach. In a principle-based approach, we can view such cases as variations on a basic theme. Instead of writing a completely new, specialized IF-THEN rule, we can regard the French (and English) examples as parameterized variants of a set of more primitive, underlying components. The section "Principle-Based Translation," in this chapter and the chapter by Dorr in this volume describe principle-based translation in more detail.

- What happens when the rule set becomes too large? Because rules are fine-grained and language particular, existing rule-based natural language systems use thousands of rules. Because parsing algorithms run as a function of grammar size, an inflated rule size forces poor system performance. Too much effort is expended trying to build special-purpose algorithms or hardware when the real source of the problem is an overly-large rule system. For example, one recent language system developed at Boeing contained many thousands of individual rules just for a portion of English. As a result, even a single sentence could be analyzed in a thousand different ways or more.

A few principles can replace many rules

In contrast, a principle-based approach aims to reconstruct the vocabulary of grammatical theory in such a way that surface and language-particular constructions like passive *follow* from the interactions of a small set of primitive elements. Figure 1 illustrates the difference. The top half of the figure shows a conventional rule-based approach. Each sentence type (a *construction* like passive) is described by a different rule. The bottom half of the figure shows a principle-based approach.

Principles and word meaning building blocks are like atoms in chemistry, or axioms in a logic system. By combining just a few dozen atoms, we can build up a huge number of chemical compounds (sentence rules and word meanings) instead of listing each compound separately. In the language domain, we can replace the surface effect of many rules with longer deductive chains of just a few axioms. Note that one can get the multiplicative effect of $n_1 \times n_2 \times \ldots$ rules by the interaction of $n_1 + n_2 + \ldots$ autonomous modules. Thus, by supplying a dozen or so principles, each with two or three degrees of freedom, we can encode many thousands of rules. By varying the parameters, we can describe different dialects and even different languages. Naturally, no single principle accounts for all the variation we see in a language, just as no single molecule accounts for all chemical compounds and reactions. It is the interaction that matters.

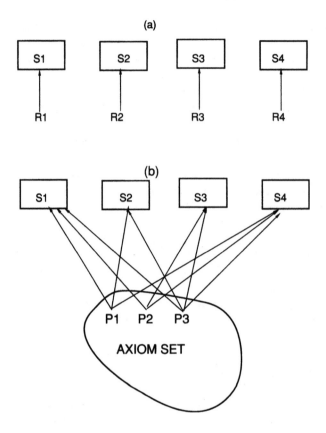

Figure 1. These two figures illustrate the difference between rule-based and principle-based systems. (a) A rule-based system. Each sentence construction type, like passive, is described by a distinct rule. (b) A principle-based system. Sentence types are derived from a smaller basis set of more fundamental principles that deductively interact to yield the effect of constructions like passive. See the section on "Principles and Parameters in Parsing Design" for more details on just how this works.

An outline of things to come

Of course, the principle-based approach raises many questions for parsing. The next three sections of this chapter will answer each of these three key questions in turn:

1   Is principle-based language analysis possible? Can one describe all languages, or even one language, as the interaction of a small, universal set of principles?

2   Can one build parsers that use principles instead of rules?

3   Can one make these parsers computationally efficient?

While we will defer detailed answers to these questions we can offer a glimpse at what's to come now.

Consider first a simple example of how general principles can replace specific rules. One general principle says that action-expressing phrases in a sentence must either *begin* with a verb in some languages, or *end* with a verb in others. This basic description of the tree shapes in a language, dubbed $\overline{X}$ *theory*, gives us part of the variation between languages like English and Spanish on the one hand, and languages like German and Japanese on the other. In English, the verb must come first, with the object after. A second principle, called the *Case Filter*, says that all pronounced nouns like *ice-cream* must receive case, either from an active verb like *ate* or an auxiliary verb like *was*; the adjective-like verb *eaten* does not do the job. Taken together, these two principles plus a few others conspire to push *ice-cream* into its position at the front of a sentence if there is a verb sequence like *was eaten*. There is no explicit passive rule.

The section on principle-based parsing for Warlpiri shows how these principles can be used to build a parser that does not use individual rules. Drawing on research carried out by Michael Kashket [1986], it also shows how the same principles can be made to work with a language that is very different from Romance languages or German, in this case, the Australian aborigine language Warlpiri. Warlpiri is a good test case for the principle-based model because its structure seems at first so different from that of English, German, or Romance languages. This section also briefly describes a related design for a principle-based parser, used by Dorr [this volume] and described in more detail in the section on principle-based translation.

Many principles operate like constraint filters. This lets them handle the problem of partially well-formed sentences. A principle-based parser can accommodate language "mistakes" by constraint relaxation. If a sentence is ill-formed, it is simply because one or another principle fails to hold. In fact, in the principle-based approach, there really is no such thing as an ungrammatical sentence—this notion doesn't even really apply. Every string of sounds is assigned some interpretation. Some of these happen to "pass" all the principles, while some fall short in one area or another.

For example, consider the sentence, *This is the ice-cream that I don't know whether it was eaten by John.* Technically this sentence is ill-formed, and it would break existing language interfaces because they would have no special rule that could apply in such cases. In contrast, a principle-based system would degrade gracefully. In this example, a locality principle that limits the distance between words like *it* and *ice-cream* is at fault, but importantly all other principles hold. In particular, the principle that every sentence has a subject (*it*) and a verb (*eaten*) still holds. Sentence analysis would proceed as before, simply taking note of this violation, which does not impede inference or understanding. No special weights or extra rules are required.

The principle that a sentence needs a subject and object is also parameterized, illustrating how principles can ease the task of language translation. In languages like Spanish and Italian, and under degraded situations in English, the subject need not be expressed. These and other similar, but simple, parameters are what makes English different from Spanish or Italian. Thus our parser does not need special rules to analyze Spanish or another English dialect; it simply sets its parameters to those values required for Spanish, such as "the subject may be missing." Only the dictionary changes from language to language. The section on principle-based translation in this chapter and Dorr's chapter in this volume describe an implemented system, UNITRAN, that adopts this approach.

The final section of this chapter turns to the computational optimization of principle-based parsers, carried out by Sandiway Fong at MIT. Because a principle-based language processor uses several independent constraint modules, it also becomes possible to optimize its performance and test it under a variety of processing assumptions. One can develop an automatic "compiler" (really a source-to-source translation procedure) for such constraint systems, because we expect different dialects and different languages will demand different principle processing topologies for optimal performance. For instance, in a language like English, information often comes at the very beginning of phrases to tell us what the phrase will be like: *the* tells us that we will be describing an object next. But in German or Japanese this information may be delayed until the end of a sentence. Thus different languages, and even different sentences within the same language, might optimally use different processing strategies. Instead of hand-coding these, we would like to automatically, perhaps dynamically, guide the application of constraint modules.

Two general ideas guide principle-based parser design. First, certain modules are logically dependent on others. For example, the locality principle that calculates whether *it* is too far away from *the ice-cream* must use phrases, but phrases are fixed in part by the principle that says whether a verb comes first or last in a phrase. This dependency structure provides a kind of flowchart that is amenable to conventional computer science techniques like dataflow analysis.

Second, as a general condition one should apply the strongest constraints as early as possible while delaying hypothesis-space expanding procedures as long as possible. Well-established techniques exist to impose this ordering among modules by estimating the filtering/expansion power of different principles. Fong calls his resulting design a *principle-ordering parser*. He shows that order-of-magnitude improvement is sometimes possible by optimal ordering.

Principles and Parameters in Parsing Design

To begin, let us answer the first question about principle-based parsing raised earlier: can a small number of principles describe natural language? This is a question about linguistic description, so we rely on linguistic theory to answer it. Currently, we have adopted a variant of the *principles-and-parameters* theory developed at MIT and elsewhere (sometimes called *government-binding* or *GB theory* [Chomsky 1981; Lasnik & Uriagereka, 1988]). Figure 2 shows the topology of the system currently used. It pictures about a dozen modules or *theories*, most of which are described more fully in in the next paragraph. Lines between the modules mark logical dependencies—certain constraints are defined in terms of others.

Let's see just what these principles mean and how they work together to account for passive sentences.

- $\overline{X}$ **theory** describes the basic tree shapes allowed in a language. Roughly, natural languages allow two basic tree forms: function–argument form, as in English where the verb begins a verb phrase, a preposition begins a prepositional phrase, and so forth (*eat the ice-cream, with a spoon*); and argument–function form, as in Japanese and much of German.

- The **Theta Criterion** says that every verb must discharge its thematic arguments—its placeholders that flesh out who did what to whom. Thus a main sentence with *eat* must mention the eater and optionally the thing eaten, whereas *put* must mention the thing that is put somewhere and the location it is put (one can't have *John put the book*).

- The **Case Filter** says that pronounced (*overt*) noun phrases like *ice-cream* must receive Case. What is meant by case? In simplest terms, it is much like what is found in a traditional Latin grammar: the subject noun phrase receives nominative case; the direct object of the verb receives accusative case; the object of a preposition receives oblique case. The pale residue of this *case-marking* system shows up in English in the use of *her* as an object versus *she* as a subject: *Mary likes her*; *She likes Mary*. This is what accounts for the difference between sentences like *It is likely that John will win* versus the (ill-formed) *It is likely John to win*. In the first sentence, *John* receives nominative case from *will*; in the second, there is no tensed verb or verb-like element to give *John* case, and so the sentence violates the case-filter.

- **Binding Theory** spells out how pronouns may be related to their antecedents in certain configurations. For example, compare the sentences,

> *John thinks that he likes ice-cream*
> *He thinks that John likes ice-cream*

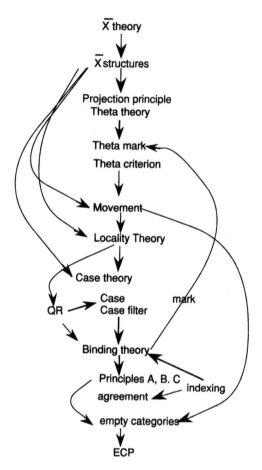

Figure 2. A design for a principle-based parsing system. Each module component varies over a limited parametric range. The joint interaction of all modules
replaces the effects of many particular language rules.

In the first sentence, *John* and *he* may refer to the same person, while in
the second, they cannot.

- **Locality Theory** and the **Empty Category Principle** restrict
  where "silent" noun phrases (*empty categories*) can appear. A silent
  noun phrase is not pronounced, but still needed to understand a sentence. For example, in the sentence below,

  John wants to like ice-cream

there is a silent noun phrase, that we can denote *e*, that acts as the subject
of *to like ice-cream*; just like a pronoun, it refers to *John*:

John wants to e like ice-cream

Empty categories cannot appear too far away from their antecedents (locality) and only in certain configurations (the empty category principle or *ECP*). The first example below shows a violation of locality—the empty category *e* is too far away from *John*—and the second a violation of the ECP. (We will not be concerned in this chapter with exactly how constraints like the ECP are formulated.)

John seems it is certain e to like ice-cream
John was wanted to e like ice-cream

- The **Movement Principle** says basically that any phrase can be moved anywhere. For example, we can change *John likes ice-cream* to *Ice-cream, John likes*. (Of course, this freedom may violate other principles.)

Having covered these basic principles, we can now see in detail how they interact to yield *the ice-cream was eaten*. If we think of the principles as axioms, the passive construction emerges as a theorem. But the deductive chain is much longer than in a simple IF-THEN rule system, where there is a direct, one-step connection between passive sentences and rules. The following sequence outlines the steps:

$\overline{\text{X}}$ theory sets the basic function-argument order of English
↓
was eaten the ice-cream
↓
Eaten is an adjective, and so does not assign case
↓
Ice-cream must receive case
↓
So *ice-cream* moves to subject position
where it receives nominative case
↓
This leaves behind an empty category, linked to *ice-cream*
(so that *eat* can meet the Theta Criterion and
make *ice-cream* the thing eaten)
↓
the ice-cream was eaten e

This may seem like a lot of deductive work for one sentence, but the important point is that the *same* principles combined in different ways yield different sentences, just as the same molecules can combine in different ways to make many different chemical compounds. For example, in the sentence,

It was believed that the ice-cream was eaten

no movement is required because *ice-cream* already receives nominative
case from *that*. (This would show up more clearly if *ice-cream* were replaced
with a pronoun. Then the pronoun would have its nominative form: *It was
believed that he was eaten.*)

Principles and parsing

So far, all that we have done with principles is describe sentences. How
can we use principles to parse sentences—that is, to assign structure to
sentences that shows what the subject and object are, what the thematic
roles are (who did what to whom), and so forth? In some way we must
reproduce the deductions that connect axioms to sentences. Of course, all
we have to start with is the input sentence, a dictionary, and the principles
themselves.

While there are several possible approaches, it is useful to divide the
principles into one of two classes: *generators* and *filters*.

Generators produce or hypothesize possible structures. For example,
consider $\overline{\mathrm{X}}$ Theory. Given a string of words, say, *eat the ice-cream*, $\overline{\mathrm{X}}$ theory would say that *eat* is possibly the beginning of a verb phrase, with *the
ice-cream* as its argument. Similarly, Movement Theory creates possible
structures. Given a valid $\overline{\mathrm{X}}$ structure, Movement Theory can displace various noun phrases like *ice-cream* to create new ones. Binding Theory also
generates new output possibilities from old ones. For example, given the
sentence *John thinks that he likes ice-cream, he* can refer either to *John* or
someone else not mentioned in the sentence, thus generating two candidate
outputs.

Filters weed out possible structures. Most of the remaining boxes
in the module picture are filters—the Case Filter, the Theta Criterion,
the Empty Category Principle, and Locality Theory. For example, if the
structure *John is proud ice-cream* is input to the Case Filter, it would be
filtered out as a violation (it should be *proud of ice-cream*, where *of* assigns
case to *ice-cream*).

Given this generator-filter model, the simplest way to build a parser is
as a cascaded sequence of principle modules, as shown in figure 3(a). (For
reasons of space the figure does not show all the possible principle modules.)
The input sentence, *the ice-cream was eaten*, passes into the first module, in
the figure $\overline{\mathrm{X}}$ Theory, which produces several output possibilities indicated
by multiple arrows (depending on word and structural ambiguities). The
basic point is that these hypotheses are driven from the input in a bottom-
up way. Given a verb, the system posits that a verb phrase must start; if it
is a preposition, then a prepositional phrase must begin, and so on. Note

that this requires access to a dictionary. As usual, these hypotheses are subject to numerous ambiguities (words may be either nouns or verbs, for example), but we will defer these standard problems here. All the usual techniques for efficient bottom-up processing, such as lookahead, can be useful here.

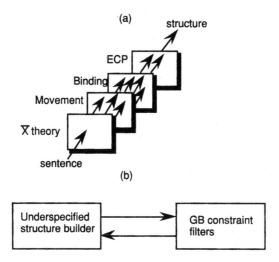

Figure 3. Principles may be classified as *generators* and *filters* and then organized into parsers in a variety of ways. (a) A sequential parser design. The input sentence is successively expanded and collapsed into a series of structural hypotheses. Generators expand the hypothesis space, while filters narrow it down. (b) A coroutine parser design, as used by Dorr in her translation system. Structure-building generators operate in tandem with constraint modules.

Alternatively, such a system could enumerate all possible function-argument structures *before* even looking at the input until it hits upon one that matches the input. Such a straightforwardly hallucinatory approach is known to be fraught with hazards unless special precautions are taken (it may not terminate, for example). For this reason, almost all existing principle-based systems attempt to access the information in the input sentence as quickly as possible, and this will be the case in all the principle-based parsing systems described in the rest of this chapter.

Continuing with our rough conceptual picture, the hypotheses output from the $\overline{X}$ component are fed into the next module down the line, the Movement component, which also expands the number of hypothesized structures. Binding also generates multiple hypotheses. Finally, the ECP whittles down these multiple hypotheses to just one: the output structure *the ice-cream$_i$ was eaten e_i* (the subscript i indicates that the empty category following *eaten* is linked to *ice-cream*). In each step, important information from a dictionary or lexicon may be accessed. For instance, it is the lexicon that says just what thematic roles a verb requires—that *eat* needs an eater and an optional thing eaten. This information must figure in the hypotheses that are generated and filtered.

Because many of the constraints depend on particular structural configurations as inputs the principle modules can only be ordered in certain ways. For instance, case is often assigned only under a particular local structural arrangement—the element receiving case is an immediately adjacent sister to a verb or a preposition. These logical dependencies must be respected in any principle parser design.

As an alternative to the straightforward sequential design it is possible to *coroutine* the operation of filters and generators, alternating between structure-building $\overline{X}$ and movement components, and filters (part (b) of figure 3). This approach has been adopted by Dorr for her translation system (see the "Principle-Based Translation" section). Dorr exploits the structure information in $\overline{X}$ theory to drive an Earley-type parser that is coroutined (operates in tandem) with filtering constraints. Whenever the $\overline{X}$ parse can no longer be extended, filters and some generators are called to weed out underconstrained parsers or propose parsing extensions. See the next section for more details on this coroutine design, and the final section for a more systematic framework in which to evaluate these different architectures.

Having seen how a principle-based parser might work in broad outline, we now review two important principle-based parsers developed over the past three years at the MIT Artificial Intelligence Laboratory: Kashket's Warlpiri parser and Dorr's translation system. The Warlpiri parser will be described first, in the rest of this section while Dorr's parser will be covered in the "Principle-Based Translation" section.

Principle-based parsing for Warlpiri

Warlpiri provides a good testbed for the principle-based parsing approach because it seems on the surface to look very different from English, German, or the Romance languages. Warlpiri word order is quite free. Even so, Kashket [1986] shows that the difference between a parser for Warlpiri and one for English is roughly a parametric difference in case marking: when the verb marks case, as in English, then this tends to fix word order; while if other elements mark case, as in Latin or Warlpiri, or some parts of English, then word order tends to be free. Let's examine how Kashket's model works.

By using a vocabulary other than the *concatenation* and *hierarchy* that are blended in context-free rules we can easily account for the free-word order found in Warlpiri *as well as* that part of English that appears to exhibit fixed-word order (subject-verb-object) and those parts of English that are relatively free (prepositional phrases). One and the same parser will work for both. In contrast, because context-free rules can use only concatenation (linear position) to encode the more basic principles of case marking and case assignment, they ultimately fail to perspicuously describe the range of possibilities seen in natural languages. The result is that a rule-based parser for free-word order languages almost invariably writes out all possible word order sequences, leading to a corresponding increase in grammar size.

Warlpiri and rule-based parsing

To begin, let's consider some variations in a simple Warlpiri sentence. All permutations are legal. (Hyphens are added for readability):

Ngajulu-rlu	ka-rna-rla	punta-rni	kurdu-ku	karli
I	AUX	take-NONpast	child	boomerang

'I am taking the boomerang from the child'

Kurdu-ku	ka-rna-rla	ngajulu-rlu	punta-rni	karli
child	AUX	I	take-NONpast	boomerang

'From the child I am taking the boomerang'

Karli	ka-rna-rla	kurdu-ku	ngajulu-rlu	punta-rni
boomerang	AUX	child	I	take-NONpast

'It is the boomerang I am taking from the child'

(Plus 21 other possibilities)

Although phrase order is free except for the rigid auxiliary verb-like element second position (as in German), phrasal variations lead to different emphasis in topic and focus, as the translations indicate. In contrast, morpheme order is fixed: at the level of words, Warlpiri is in argument-function form, or what is called a *head final* language, with markers *rlu* (ergative), *rni* (tense, nonpast), and *ku* (dative) appearing word final. (The absolutive case marker is null and so does not show up explicitly on *boomerang*. Also, there are basically just two lexical categories: nouns and verbs.)

How could we write a traditional rule system to describe these constructions? Let us consider several possibilities and discuss their deficiencies.

First, aiming at mere string coverage, we could explicitly write out all possible phrasal expansions. (Here, the tags S and O stand for subject and object and we ignore the AUX element, while NP stands for a noun phrase.)

S	→	NP-S NP-O V
S	→	NP-S V NP-O
S	→	NP-O NP-S V
S	→	NP-O V NP-S
S	→	V NP-S NP-O
S	→	V NP-O NP-S

Plainly, this is an unperspicuous grammar that also suffers from computational defects. By explicitly writing out the rules we have missed the basic fact that the phrase order is free. To put the same point another way, the grammar would be almost as simple (almost as small) if we omitted the last rule S→ V NP-O NP-S. And the grammar is large, because it contains more rules, and will thus run more slowly using standard context-free parsing algorithms.

Perhaps more importantly though, this approach ignores the basic and well-known asymmetry between subjects and grammatical functions like direct objects and indirect objects (see Laughren [1987] for discussion). For instance, it is the subject, not the object, that can be empty in constructions such as *I wanted to leave*, which does not have a counterpart *I wanted Bill to leave* meaning I wanted Bill to leave me. This asymmetry leads directly to positing a certain hierarchical structure that explicitly represents the domination of the object by the verb, with the noun phrase subject external to the verb phrase. Thus a better context-free grammar would be something like this:

S	→	NP-S VP
VP	→	V NP-O

But as is plain, this sort of grammar cannot parse the sentence order V NP-S NP-O that is observed in Warlpiri:

punta-rni	ka-rna-rla	Ngajulu-rlu	kurdu-ku	karli
take-NONpast	AUX	I	child	boomerang

'taking am I the boomerang from the child'

To get over this hurdle various proposals have been made: invisible verb phrase nodes, movement rules, and the like. What these rescue operations have in common is some way to break apart the linear phrasal concatenation forced on us by context-free rules.

One could resort to a change in algorithm in order to overcome this hurdle. One such proposal that has been made in the context of a functional unification grammar for Finnish [Kartunnen & Kay 1985] is to say simply that one particular phrasal order is stored and the permutations that actually appear are generated on demand. The base grammar would remain small. As Kartunnen and Kay put it, "the opportunity is to work with a much smaller grammar by embodying the permutation property in the algorithm itself."

As we will see, in effect this is the approach adopted to parse Warlpiri via principles. There is a key distinction. In the Warlpiri system the difference lies not with some special algorithm, but probably where it ought to lie: with the statement of the grammar of Warlpiri. In fact, *nothing special* need be said about the Warlpiri parsing algorithm at all; it does not have to embody some permutation procedure, except implicitly as allowed by the principles of the grammar. Further, the very same parser will work for English as well—crucially, as mentioned, the only changes that have to be stated are the *linguistic* differences between English and Warlpiri, which have to be stated anyway.

Parsing Warlpiri with principles

Kashket's key insight is to apply case marking and case assignment principles for Warlpiri at two autonomous representations. One representation requires precedence-ordered trees and one does not, and this bifurcation allows us to account at the same time for the rigid morpheme order in Warlpiri along with its free word order:

- *Precedence* structure: This level expresses, among other things, precedence relations (one morpheme precedes or follows another).

- *Syntactic* structure: This level expresses hierarchical relations (one phrase dominates another). The phrasal elements bear no precedence relations to one another.

The claim, then, is that phrasal syntax really needs only hierarchical information, not precedence information (as is reflected quite generally in the order-free nature of almost all principle-based predicates for syntax).

Having split apart the representations, Kashket proposes to split apart case marking and case assignment along these very same representational fault lines. It is this division of principles that will allow us to capture the full range of free/fixed word-order phenomena.

Case marking is taken to be an essentially word based (or phonological) process, hence one that logically ought to be represented at the level of precedence structure. Therefore, case marking depends upon precedence information, because this is encoded at the morphemic level. As expected, it is directional, and operates completely locally, under adjacency.

In particular, in Warlpiri case marking is to the left. This makes Warlpiri a head final language at the morpheme level: case markers must appear at the end of words. Let us see how this works in an example.

In the word *ngajulu-rlu*, the ergative case marker *rlu* case marks *ngajulu* (English *I*) to the left, so this word is well-formed; we may imagine it comprising a complete "case phrase" unit ready to be analyzed at the phrasal level, as indicated in figure 4.

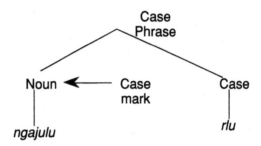

Figure 4. Directional case marking forces fixed internal word order in Warlpiri. The "heads" of Warlpiri words are final, with case marking to the left.

Crucially, in Warlpiri verbs are *not* case markers. We shall see that this forces an essential difference between a so-called "configurational" language like English and "nonconfigurational" languages like Warlpiri. The parser need only know that in English, a verb *is* a case marker, and that in Warlpiri, a verb *is not* a case marker.

Case *assignment* is carried out at the phrasal level under sisterhood, but with one crucial difference: because phrases do not even encode precedence information, case assignment cannot refer to order or adjacency at all and is nondirectional. This is what will allow Warlpiri phrases to be order free.

Let us consider another example to see how this works. Take the word sequence *ngajulu-rlu punta-rni karli* (*I took the boomerang*).[1] This is first parsed as three separate word-level units: *ngajulu-rlu* is a noun-case combination that is case marked as usual to form what Kashket calls a $\overline{\text{C}}$ unit; *punta-rni* is a verb-tense combination that forms what Kashket calls a V unit; while *karli* has a null absolutive marker at its end, so is case-marked (as usual) to form a $\overline{\text{C}}$ phrase. Note that all three words are in argument-function (head final) and well-formed; if, for example, the tense marker had a noun to its left, then such a structure would be rejected.

The verb morpheme unit is now projected into syntax under the usual $\overline{\text{X}}$ format: it contains a node, a $\overline{\text{V}}$ node, and a $\overline{\overline{\text{V}}}$ node. Under Kashket's model, the $\overline{\text{V}}$ node assigns absolutive or dative case (in either direction);

---

[1]The AUX unit will be ignored for these and all remaining examples.

because *karli* is marked for absolutive case, it receives this case no matter whether it is to the left or to the right of *punta-rni*. Similarly, $\overline{\overline{V}}$ case assigns ergative (either to the right or left) Finally, the association between thematic roles and cases is rigid in Warlpiri, so *karli* is identified as the THEME and *ngajulu-rlu* as AGENT:

AGENT   ↔   ERGATIVE
THEME   ↔   ABSOLUTIVE
PATH   ↔   DATIVE

Figure 5 shows the resulting syntactic tree. It is important not to be misled by the order of the subtrees shown in this structure. While one must write the subtrees in some order, in fact the first $\overline{C}$ could have been written to the right of the $\overline{V}$ instead of on the left.

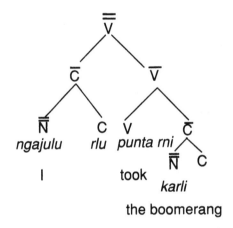

Figure 5. A Warlpiri syntactic structure for *I took the boomerang*. It is important to note that the order of subtrees is not encoded at this level, even though the picture must show some order on the page.

By splitting up case marking and case assignment principles—via adjacency and dominance—and using these principles in parsing, we can account for the difference between Warlpiri and English. In English a verb *is* a case marker, so position matters: the verb case marks subject and object at the morpheme level where linear precedence is encoded. (More precisely, it is the verb's tense that marks the subject's nominative case to the left.) The result is that we usually get the order subject-verb-object in English.

Note that English also exhibits some phrase order freedom: prepositional phrases may appear relatively freely after a verb. Under the current account, that is because case assignment is carried out internally by the preposition. There is no ordering among phrases.

The Warlpiri parser accesses principles, not rules

With this overview behind us, we can now give the details of Kashket's parser, and cover some fine points omitted earlier.

The parser consists of two stages: one for precedence structure and one for syntactic (hierarchical) structure. These two operate in tandem. Input sentences are passed to the precedence-based lexical parser, which breaks words into morphemes and outputs an ordered forest of trees. Every morpheme is also sent to the hierarchical parser, which projects information based on the lexicon and the lexical parser's output and attempts to produce a single hierarchical structure with unordered subtrees. No context-free rules or rules of any kind (in the usual sense) are accessed. The dictionary contains basic syntactic category information as well as *actions* (for a case or tense marker) that say what kind of element the case or tense marker selects (noun or verb), and, in the case of a verb, what arguments it case assigns. Table 1 shows how the actual Warlpiri dictionary transparently encodes the case selection (marking), and assignment actions illustrated earlier; these properties are directly accessed by the parser. (Some of the details are omitted here.)

The lexical parser determines the well-formedness of words according to morphological constraints. Basically, this stage operates on groups of two morphemes at a time. After the first morpheme is input no action can occur. The second input morpheme prompts word construction: the parser looks at the unit immediately to its left to see whether it may be combined (selected) by the case marker. For example, if the case marker is the tense element *rni*, and the unit to the left is not a verb, then the structure is ill-formed, and the two units remain detached; but if the unit to the left is a verb, then combination can occur and a verb node produced, as described earlier. A dictionary is consulted here, as is typical. In addition, if a verb projection (predicate) is being formed, the dictionary will supply case assignment actions to be associated with the projections of the verb, as appropriate. (Note that if there is a null case marker, as with the absolutive, then we assume that morphological analysis supplies a null second morpheme.)

As each word is completely constructed it is fed to the second stage, the phrasal parser. This stage's job is simply to carry out case assignment, in effect "linking" arguments to any predicate and thereby licensing them. Recall that we associate case assignment actions with each V node projection, as retrieved from a dictionary. The phrasal parser will execute *all* applicable actions, globally, *until no more actions apply*, but, plainly, a case marked argument must be present before case assignment can take place. Note that the actions consider all possible directional case assignments, across all subphrases; this permits free phrasal order.

RLA:	actions: data:	SELECT: (OBJECT ((AUXILIARY . SUBJECT))) MORPHEME:. RLA NUMBER: SINGULAR PERSON: 3 AUXILIARY: OBJECT
RNA:	actions: data:	SELECT: (SUBJECT ((AUXILIARY . BASE))) MORPHEME: RNA NUMBER: SINGULAR PERSON 1 AUXILIARY: SUBJECT
KA:	actions: data:	SELECT: (AUXILIARY ((V . +) (N . -))) MORPHEME: KA TENSE: PRESENT AUXILIARY: BASE
RNI:	actions: data:	SELECT (+ ((V. +) (N . -) (CONJUGATION . 2))) ASSIGN: ABSOLUTIVE MORPHEME: RNI TENSE: NONPAST TNS: +
PUNTA:	actions: data:	 MORPHEME: PUNTA THETA-ROLES: (AGENT THEME SOURCE) CONJUGATION: 2 N: - V: +
RLU:	actions: data:	SELECT: (ERGATIVE ((V. -)(N . +))) MARK: ERGATIVE MORPHEME: RLU PERCOLATE: T CASE: ERGATIVE
KU:	actions: data:	SELECT: (DATIVE ((V . -)((N . +))) MARK: DATIVE ASSIGN: DATIVE MORPHEME: KU PERCOLATE: T CASE: DATIVE
NGAJULU	actions: data:	 MORPHEME: NGAJULU NUMBER: SINGULAR PERSON: 1 N: + V: -
KURDU:	actions: data:	 MORPHEME: KURDU N: + V: -
KARLI:	actions: data:	 MORPHEME: KARLI N: + V: -

Table 1. The Warlpiri dictionary directly encodes $\overline{X}$ features, case marking, and case assignment.

Finally, we note that the auxiliary is handled specially: its dictionary entry says that it takes a verb projection as an argument. (The aux-second constraint receives no explanation on this account.)

An example parse

An example parse should make the algorithm clearer. Consider an object-verb-subject-object sentence form, such as *kurdu-ku ka-rna-rla punta-rni ngajulu-rlu karli*. At the word level, nothing happens when the first morpheme *kurdu* is processed. The second morpheme, *ku*, adds a dative case marker, and it selects the noun to its left (a directional, precedence selection), forming a complete word with case as the root of the phrase. The next morphemes comprise the auxiliary and are projected as an auxiliary phrase by a procedure not described here. Third, the verb *take* with its tense *rni* marker is encountered. The tense selects the verb to its left, forming a verb unit, which is passed to the phrasal parser. At the phrasal level the tense marking itself is attached to the A(uxiliary) unit. Also at the phrasal level, the verb unit is projected to a $\overline{\overline{V}}$. Now the morpheme *ngajulu* enters the input and is processed; it is noted as a noun, but no actions can apply to it because it is not yet case marked. The next morpheme, *rlu*, combines to its left with the noun to case mark it ergative and form a $\overline{C}$ phrase; this is passed to the phrasal parser. Figure 6 gives a snapshot of the hierarchical structure built so far, where we have deliberately placed *ngajulu-rlu* to the left of the V projection node to indicate the order-free character of phrasal structure. Note that the tense element *rni* has been removed from the verb (it is attached to the auxiliary unit at this level of representation).

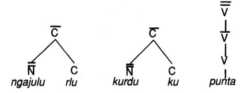

Figure 6. Starting to parse a Warlpiri sentence. The first three words, up through the verb and to the subject that follows it, have been analyzed. This figure represents hierarchical structure, so in fact the tense element *rni*, which is part of the verb at the precedence structure level, does not appear here.

Now any actions attached to the V(erb) projected nodes apply if possible. Because there is an ergative case-marked argument, ergative case assignment applies, linking $\overline{C}$ to the V phrase. Similarly dative assignment is possible and *kurdu-ku* is attached (see figure 7).

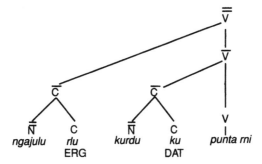

Figure 7. Linking the ergative subject and dative object in a Warlpiri sentence. These actions are forced by the dictionary entries associated with projected verb elements.

Because no more actions apply, *karli* enters the lexical parser; with its null absolute case marker, it is a well-formed word, and is passed as a $\overline{C}$ to the phrasal parser. Once again, a V projection action can now apply to this case marked argument. This action assigns *karli* absolutive case (the THEME of the sentence). Figure 8 shows the final result. "PS" refers to the level of word structure, or precedence structure, while "SS" is hierarchical phrase structure. The figure also shows how the tense marker *rni* is attached as part of the auxiliary or inflection phrase that dominates the entire phrase structure.

Kashket's implemented parser can handle a far wider range of constructions than shown here, including compound nouns. These show a particularly interesting interaction between lexical parsing and phrasal parsing, and indicates the flexibility of a rule-less system. If there is a string of nouns in the form:

Noun Noun Noun Noun ... Case

then there might be some ambiguity as to whether the unmarked nouns get absolutive case. But this does not occur; all the nouns are transmitted the same case at the tail end of the phrase. The reason is that when nouns appear in this kind of a group, they are all part of a *single* intonational phrase, and therefore can be phonologically recognized as a single unit. We may assume this preprocessing to take place prior to or at the time of morpheme processing, as part of speech analysis. In contrast, if compound Nouns appear discontinuously, then they must all be case marked with the same marker, and again there is no parsing ambiguity. In this way, Kashket's system can quite easily accommodate additional information sources that are superimposed on his basic constraints.

Let us summarize why a principle-based approach succeeds where a context-free rule approach fails. Kashket's principled division into two distinct representations, a morphemic level obeying adjacency and linear

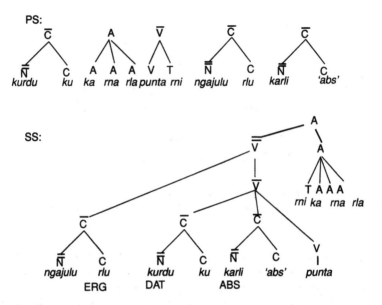

Figure 8. Linking in the Absolutive argument—which is phonologically absent—in the Warlpiri example sentence gives us the THEME of the sentence. This figure shows both the final precedence (PS) and syntactic structures (SS).

precedence, and the phrasal obeying just dominance relations, forces rigid morpheme order and permits free phrase order. At the same time, the case marking/case assignment vocabulary lets us state the difference between languages like English and languages like Warlpiri in a straightforward grammatical way as a difference between which elements case mark and which do not, all without resorting to novel parsing procedures for either languages.

Kashket's parsing algorithm for English and Warlpiri will look exactly the same. Nothing need be said other than what minimally must be said anyway about the difference between the two languages: that verbs case mark in English, but not in Warlpiri. In this way, a uniform principle-based system can significantly advance our understanding of the free-word order/fixed-word order continuum, and show us how one kind of parser can handle many different kinds of languages.

Principle-Based Translation

We next turn to a principle-based parsing for a different domain: language translation. We describe a particular principle-based translation system, implemented by Dorr [1987]. Dorr's system successfully overcomes the difficulties of a rule-based approach. It also illustrates a coroutine design for principle-based parsing, that interleaves generators and filters. (Dorr's chapter in this volume shows how her system handles some of the other difficulties in translation.) We will see how this work on a Spanish example sentence that would ordinarily require a number of complex rules for its description:

¿*Qué vio?*

This short sentence is deceptively simple. It actually shows three interesting phenomena: a null (missing) subject; inversion of the verb; and movement of *qué* to the front of the sentence. A traditional rule-based system would describe each of these explicitly. As we shall see, Dorr's system can describe them all via the same parameters that are required for English.

Dorr's parser works by using a standard context-free parser, the Earley algorithm, on very slightly expanded $\overline{X}$ skeleton tree structures. These skeletons guide the Earley algorithm parser working in tandem with other principles. By modularizing the principles in this way significant computational efficiencies are realized.

Dorr assumes that $\overline{X}$ theory provides the basic phrase configuration possibilities (across all languages). The basic rules,

$$\overline{\overline{X}} \Rightarrow (\text{Specifier}) \ \overline{X}$$
$$\overline{X} \Rightarrow X \ (\text{Complement})$$

are combined with two rules to handle adjuncts,

$$\overline{X} \Rightarrow (\text{Adjunct}) \ \overline{X} \ (\text{Adjunct})$$
$$\overline{\overline{X}} \Rightarrow (\text{Adjunct})\overline{\overline{X}} \ (\text{Adjunct})$$

where parenthesized symbols are optional.

Some terminology is useful here. A *specifier* is simply a word like a determiner that further specifies the properties of a phrase. A *complement* is just what we have been calling the *arguments* of a verb or a preposition. An *adjunct* is an optional phrase that need not be part of a verb's thematic structure.

In addition, Dorr sets a parameter so that adjuncts may occur before or after the specifier and before or after the complement (in a specifier-head-complement language). Finally, if we vary the order of specifier and complement with respect to the head, we have (assuming just one level of recursion) the $2^2 = 4$ possible tree topologies shown in figure 9, where (a) corresponds, for example, to English phrase structure order. What Dorr has done, then, is to partially "compile out" information about skeletal phrase structure possibilities. Note that these skeletons do provide topological information for parsing but do *not* provide any detail about categorial identity or verb selection information—for instance, whether *eat* must take an object or not. However, the system can access online lexical category information—whether a word is a noun or a verb, or its binary feature equivalents. It also knows about a few other parameters in each particular language, and multiplies these into the $\overline{\overline{X}}$ skeletons: choice of specifier, what a possible empty category can be in a particular language. To summarize, the following information is precompiled in Dorr's system:

- The $\overline{\overline{X}}$ order for a language.
- Specifier choice (for example, determiner for $\overline{\overline{N}}$ in Spanish).
- The adjunction possibilities (for example, clitic *le* can adjoin to $\overline{V}$ in Spanish).
- Default values for nonlexical heads (for example, $\overline{\overline{V}}$ complement for I(nflection) in Spanish) (Here, Inflection simply means an element bearing tense, like the auxiliary verb *will* or *would* in English.)

To get the actual context-free rules for Spanish, we simply instantiate the $\overline{\overline{X}}$ template with values for X={N, V, P, A } *at the time parsing occurs* plus two rules for I(nflections) and C(omplementizers), following details that are irrelevant here. For Spanish, the system knows that the choice of specifier for $\overline{\overline{C}}$ may be a wh-phrase like *which* or *what*; and it also knows that if a COMP head is absent, then the complement of C is $\overline{\overline{I}}$. Finally, it knows that a V(erb) and $\overline{\overline{N}}$ are adjunction possibilities. Note that these rules do not form a complete description of Spanish, and are not intended to: they are indeed underconstrained. The entire $\overline{\overline{X}}$ skeleton system multiplies out to on the order of a hundred or so context-free rules.

Dorr's full parser works by using the $\overline{\overline{X}}$ skeleton rules as a driver program coroutined with all remaining principles, as sketched in table 2. The $\overline{\overline{X}}$ component vastly overgenerates; it builds underspecified phrase structure because it does not access details of the thematic roles each verb demands. The actual parser is simply an Earley parser, using the context-free rules given by $\overline{\overline{X}}$ expansion. As each word is processed, the parser uses the standard Earley algorithm PUSH, SCAN, or POP actions until no more actions trigger. It then calls on the remaining principles like the Case Filter or the Theta Criterion. These principles also call on the PUSH, SCAN, and POP actions, but in a much more complicated way. In effect, the skeletal parser has only a vague idea of the actual structure of sentences, which is used just to keep the Earley algorithm's PUSH-SCAN-POP sequence going. By splitting up the computational work in this way, we can vastly reduce the size of the context-free component needed, because we do not multiply out the rules used.

The principle module component has three tasks, accessed on demand: first, it weeds out bad parses (for example, a parse that calls for a complement when the verb does not need one or if bounding conditions are violated); second, it tries out possibilities that the $\overline{\overline{X}}$ skeletal parser does not know about (for example, it can PREDICT that an empty category

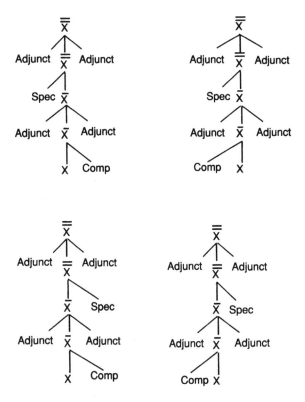

Figure 9. Dorr's $\overline{X}$ theory provides for four basic $\overline{X}$ skeleton structures on which to base further computation.

must be present at a certain point); and third, it tries to extend the Earley parse to a point where skeletal parsing can take over again (for example, by assigning and checking thematic roles, it can get the parse to the point where a phrase is complete, and so the Earley algorithm can execute a POP action).

Table 2 summarizes how work is split between the $\overline{X}$ component and the remaining principles. The overall effect is to implement a back-and-forth flow of information between the Earley parser actions and the filtering constraints and actions. (All parsing possibilities are carried along in parallel, as is typical with the Earley algorithm.)

For each particular language, there will also be a set of parameterized choices in the $\overline{X}$ and constraint modules. For example, Spanish permits $\overline{\overline{N}}$, *wh*-phrase, V(erb), I(nflection), *have*-aux, and *be*-aux as empty categories; while English permits only $\overline{\overline{N}}$ and *wh*-phrase. These are used for predicting an empty category at PUSH time.

To see how this all fits together, consider the simple sentence ¿ *Qué vio?*

ACTION	Earley parser	Principle Constraint Module
PUSH	Expand nonterminal	Predict empty category Check empty category and bounding
SCAN	Traverse terminal	Determine argument structure Perform feature matching
POP	Complete nonterminal	Assign thematic roles Check theta criterion

Table 2. The Earley parser works in tandem with principle-based constraints in Dorr's parsing design. Each standard parser action (start a phrase, scan a token, complete a phrase) runs one or more different constraint checks or structure-building routines.

("What did she/he see"). Figures 10 and 11 show the parsing sequence and final results. There are four final generated trees, labeled (a)–(d), of which just one, (b), is valid. The figure carries this labeling through several steps to show where each tree comes from.

As mentioned, this sentence exhibits three interesting Spanish syntactic phenomena: a null subject; inversion of the verb; and movement of *qué* to the front of the sentence. All of this can be captured *without* explicit rules.

Morphological analysis first reduces this to the actual parsed form *¿Qué ver?*+features past, singular, third person (with the root form for the verb, as is typical). The parse itself then begins.

In step 1 as shown in figure 10, the parser first accesses the $\overline{\overline{X}}$ skeleton for $\overline{\overline{C}}$, which is simply C-spec–C–C-comp (in Spanish), and where C need not be overt. A precompiled parameter particular for Spanish forces selection of $\overline{\overline{I}}$ to be the complement of C, because there is no head present. *Qué* is then scanned (attached) to $\overline{\overline{C}}$ as its (optional) specifier (note once again that this may lead to overgeneration because no conditions are checked at this point to determine whether this attachment is in fact correct).

Next, the expansion of $\overline{\overline{I}}$ has two $\overline{\overline{X}}$ precompiled possibilities, both of which are pursued by the Earley algorithm.

First, $\overline{\overline{I}}$ may be expanded as V–$\overline{\overline{I}}$ (with V filling the adjunct slot of $\overline{\overline{I}}$); let us continue to call this parse (a). (Here, V is one of the adjunction possibilities that has been compiled out beforehand; adjunction is assumed to occur at the $\overline{\overline{X}}$ level.) Second, $\overline{I}$ may be expanded to contain $\overline{\overline{N}}$ in I-spec (parse c, step 1.) At this point, the parser has access to the next word, *ver*, a verb. This rules out any expansion of $\overline{\overline{N}}$ as its usual spec-head-comp sequence. For this parse then, no further $\overline{X}$ actions can occur and the parser consults the principle constraint module.

Moving on to step 2 of the parse, the constraint module determines that the next symbol to operate on for parse (c) is a nonterminal; hence, a PUSH is required. The corresponding action is to predict an empty category. There are two types of empty categories in the system: a *trace*, the position of a moved noun phrase, and *pro*, an empty pronominal. Both are predicted here: there is a possible antecedent that is not too far away, and the subject position (first $\overline{\overline{N}}$ under $\overline{I}$) is still open. (Several principles come into play here, notably bounding; each is checked separately on-line.) We will call these two ongoing possibilities parses (2c) and (2d). (For parse (2c), the binding module links the trace to *qué*; for parse (2d), the system knows that only one special kind of empty category can be placed in the relevant position.) The principle constraint module has nothing to say about parse possibility 1, and parsing is returned to the $\overline{X}$ component.

Finally, still in step 2, the precompiled $\overline{X}$ skeleton notes that I is currently absent, and so adds the (precompiled) complement possibility of $\overline{\overline{V}}$ for parses (2c) and (2d).

We proceed to step 3. The parser next scans *ver*. It can be attached to the V(erb) slot for parse (3a). The constraint module is then called upon: its job is to determine the argument structure for the verb *ver*. The lexical entry for *ver* predicts an $\overline{\overline{N}}$ complement.[2] For parses (c) and (d) this prediction may be realized only as an empty category trace because there is no more input, linked to the antecedent empty category; for parse (a), however, the subject position, known to be (precompiled as) $\overline{\overline{N}}$, is still open, so either two possible empty category types may be predicted here, yielding parses (4a) and a new parse (4b). In all, there are now four parses. (In so doing the parser rules out many possible realizations of the specifier position for I, but we will not cover these here.)

All words are now scanned, so the principle constraint module is now called on to check for any additional actions (step 4). For parses (c) and (d), all that remains is thematic checking: the Theta Condition says that each arguments gets one and only one thematic role. However, both parses (c) and (d) violate this condition because two semantic roles are assigned to the object position: the object is both goal and also, via its antecedent linking, agent. These parses are thrown out.

---

[2]This is actually done in a more principled way, by projection from lexical-conceptual structure, but we ignore this detail here.

For parses (a) and (b), additional actions are possible (steps 5–7). The complement of $\bar{\bar{\text{I}}}$ is precompiled as a $\bar{\bar{\text{V}}}$ (as dictated by a precompiled parameter, not a rule, because I is empty) (step 5). Because there is no word present, this $\bar{\bar{\text{V}}}$ may be expanded (in Spanish) by a precompiled $\bar{\text{X}}$ template as an empty verb (because verbs may be traces), linked to *ver* plus (via online accessed subcategorization facts because of linking to *ver*) an $\bar{\bar{\text{N}}}$ complement (steps 5 and 6, parses (a) and (b)). Finally, the constraint module must again be accessed at this point, because the parser has just predicted an $\bar{\bar{\text{N}}}$ complement. Constraint principles dictate that the $\bar{\bar{\text{N}}}$ may be realized only as an empty category trace in this position, and the results are shown in 7(a) and 7(b). Transliterated, parse (a) means "What saw"; parse (b), "What did she/he see"; parse (c), "What did what see itself"; and parse (d), "What did she/he see herself/himself".

Note that of the remaining two possible parses, (a) and (b), (a) is ruled out by feature checking, because *ver* demands an animate subject. This leaves only parse (b) as valid, "What did she/he see" (with the null subject parameter in Spanish permitting an empty category in subject position). Note that the three syntactic phenomena of null subject, inversion, and movement are covered by filtering principles guiding the $\bar{\text{X}}$ parse, rather than by particular rules.

The Computational Implementation of Principle-Based Parsers

We have now described two different ways to organize a principle-based system for parsing. Kashket's parser operated in a bottom-up, serial fashion; Dorr's coroutined $\bar{\text{X}}$ parsing with constraint filtering. But many other architectures are possible. Are any of these best for all natural languages? For any natural language?

In an attempt to examine parser architecture more systematically, in this section we shall draw on the work of Fong [1989]. In particular, Fong has studied the problem of reordering principles to avoid doing unnecessary work. We will see that although a globally optimal strategy of principle ordering is impossible, it is possible to use standard heuristic techniques for conjunct ordering developed in other domains of AI to reduce parsing time by up to an order of magnitude. Interestingly, this leads to a parser that is dynamically varied, according to the type of sentence it must process—this is in contrast to the usually fixed algorithmic regime of a rule-based system.

The key questions about principle-ordering are these:

- What effect, if any, does principle-ordering have on the amount of work needed to parse a given sentence?

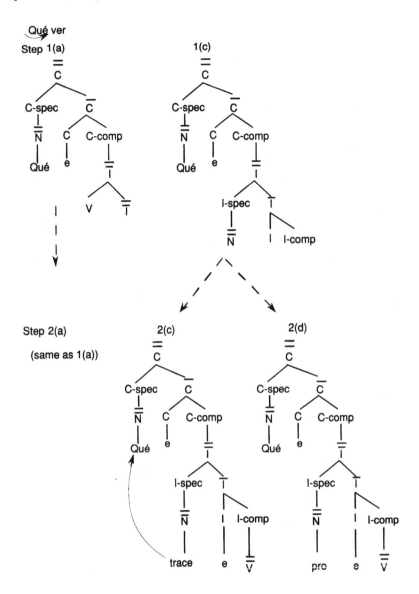

Figure 10. Beginning of the parse of *¿Qué vio?* in Dorr's system. This simple Spanish sentence has four possible parses, but only one is valid. This figure shows parsing steps 1–2. Parsing steps 3–7 are continued onto the next figures. (There are no trees 1(b)–3(b) or 1(d) because possibilities (b) and (d) will arise from the splitting of tree hypotheses in later steps. The *e* nodes stand for absent nodes, not empty categories.)

¿Qué vio?

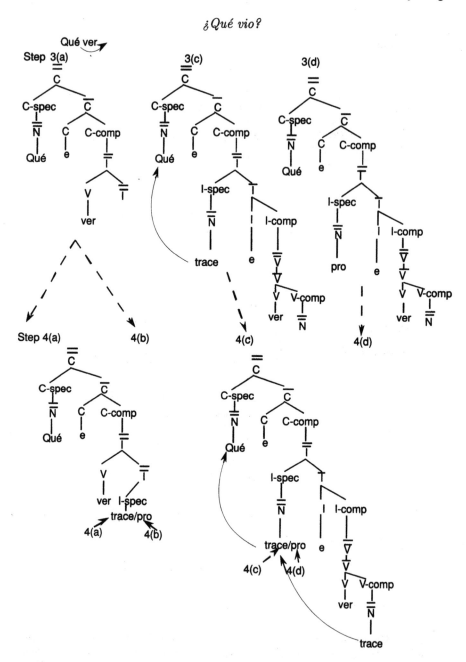

Figure 11. Continuation of the previous parse of ¿Qué vio?, steps 3–4. This simple Spanish sentence has four possible parses, but only one is valid. Parses 4(c) and 4(d) remain the same through the next steps 5–7.

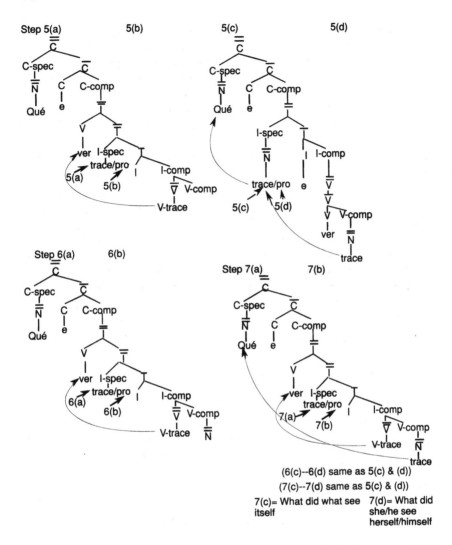

Figure 12. Conclusion of the *¿Qué vio?* parse, steps 5–7. Only parse 7(b) passes all the conditions, corresponding to *What did she/he see?*. Parse 7(a) corresponds to the ill-formed *What saw*. Parses (c)–(d) are the same as they were in step 4, and correspond to the ill-formed sentences *What did what see itself* and *What did she/he see herself/himself*.

- If the effect of principle-ordering is significant, then are some orderings much better than others?
- If so, is it possible to predict (and explain) which ones these are?

A novel, logic-based parser, the Principle-Ordering Parser (POP) has been built by Fong to investigate and demonstrate the effects of principle-ordering. The POP was deliberately constructed in a highly modular fashion to allow for maximum flexibility in exploring alternative orderings of principles. For instance, each principle is represented separately as an atomic parser operation. A structure is deemed to be well-formed only if it passes all parser operations. The scheduling of parser operations is controlled by a dynamic ordering mechanism that attempts to eliminate unnecessary work by eliminating ill-formed structures as quickly as possible. (For comparison purposes, the POP also allows the user to turn off the dynamic ordering mechanism and to parse with a user-specified (fixed) sequence of operations.)

Although it was designed primarily to explore the computational properties of principles for building more efficient parsers, this parser is also designed to be capable of handling a reasonably wide variety of linguistic phenomena. The system faithfully implements most of the principles contained in Lasnik and Uriagereka [1988]. That is, the parser makes the same grammaticality judgments and reports the same violations for ill-formed structures as the reference text. Some additional theory is also drawn from Chomsky [1981, 1986]. Parser operations implement principles from Theta Theory, Case Theory, Binding Theory, Locality theory, and the Empty Category Principle, as described earlier in figure 2.

The principle ordering problem

How important an issue is the principle ordering problem in parsing? An informal experiment was conducted using the parser described in the previous section to provide some indication on the magnitude of the problem. Although we were unable to examine all the possible orderings, it turns out that order-of-magnitude variations in parsing times could be achieved merely by picking a few sample orderings.[3]

Explaining the variation in principle ordering

The variation in parsing times for various principle orderings that was observed can be explained by assuming that overgeneration is the main

---

[3]The parser has about twelve to sixteen modules. Given a set of one dozen operations, there are about 500 million different ways to order these operations. Fortunately, only about half a million of these are actually valid, due to logical dependencies between the various operations. However, this is still far too many to test exhaustively. Instead, only a few well-chosen orderings were tested on a number of sentences from the reference. The procedure involved choosing a default sequence of operations and 'scrambling' the sequence by moving operations as far as possible from their original positions (modulo any logical dependencies between operations).

bottleneck for the parser. That is, in the course of parsing a single sentence, a parser will hypothesize many different structures. Most of these structures, the ill-formed ones in particular, will be accounted for by one or more linguistic filters. A sentence will be deemed acceptable if there exists one or more structures that satisfy every applicable filter. Note that even when parsing *grammatical* sentences overgeneration will produce ill-formed structures that need to be ruled out. Given that our goal is to minimize the amount of work performed during the parsing process, we would expect a parse using an ordering that requires the parser to perform extra work, compared with another ordering, to be slower.

Overgeneration implies that we should order principle filters to eliminate ill-formed structures as quickly as possible. For these structures, applying any parser operation other than one that rules it out may be considered as doing extra, or unnecessary, work (modulo any logical dependencies between principles).

Global optimal ordering is impossible

Because some orderings perform better than others, a natural question to ask is: Does there exist a globally optimal ordering? The existence of such an ordering would have important implications for the design of the control structure of any principle-based parser. The parser has a novel dynamic control structure in the sense that it tries to determine an ordering-efficient strategy for every structure generated. If such a globally optimal ordering could be found, then we can do away with the run-time overhead and parser machinery associated with calculating individual orderings. That is, we could build an ordering-efficient parser simply by hardwiring the optimal ordering into its control structure. Unfortunately, no such ordering can exist.

It is easy to see why this is so. The impossibility of the globally optimal ordering follows directly from the "eliminate unnecessary work" ethic. Computationally speaking, an optimal ordering is one that rules out ill-formed structures at the earliest possible opportunity. A *globally* optimal ordering would be one that always ruled out every possible ill-formed structure without doing any unnecessary work. Consider the following three structures (taken from Lasnik and Uriagereka [1988]):

(a)   *$John_1$ is crucial [$_{CP}$[$_{IP}$ e_1 to see this]]
(b)   *[$_{NP}$$John_1$'s mother][$_{VP}$ likes $himself_1$]
(c)   *$John_1$ seems that he_1 likes e_1

Example (a) violates the Empty Category Principle (ECP). Hence the optimal ordering must invoke the ECP operation before any other operation that it is not dependent on. On the other hand, example (b) violates a

Binding Theory principle. Hence, the optimal ordering must also invoke this principle as early as possible. Given that the two operations are independent, the optimal ordering must order the binding principle before the ECP and vice-versa. Similarly, example (c) demands that a variant of the Case filter must precede the other two operations. Hence a globally optimal ordering is impossible.

Heuristics for principle ordering

While one cannot achieve a globally optimal ordering, it is still possible to apply heuristic strategies that often come close. The principle-ordering problem can be viewed as a limited instance of the well-known conjunct ordering problem [Smith & Genesereth 1985]. Given a set of conjuncts, we are interested in finding all solutions that satisfy all the conjuncts simultaneously. The parsing problem is then to find well-formed structures (solutions) that satisfy all the parser operations (conjuncts) simultaneously. Moreover, we are particularly interested in minimizing the cost of finding these structures by re-ordering the set of parser operations.

This section outlines some of the heuristics used by Fong's parser to determine the minimum cost ordering for a given structure. The parser contains a dynamic ordering mechanism that attempts to compute a minimum cost ordering for every phrase structure generated during the parsing process.

This heuristic mechanism can be subdivided into two distinct phases which are discussed in turn. First, the dynamic ordering mechanism decides which principle is the most likely candidate for eliminating a given structure. Then the parser makes use of this information to reorder parser operation sequences to minimize the total work performed.

Predicting failing filters

Given any structure, the dynamic ordering mechanism attempts to satisfy the "eliminate unnecessary work" ethic by predicting a "failing" filter for that structure. More precisely, it will try to predict the principle that a given structure violates on the basis of the simple structure cues. Because the ordering mechanism cannot know whether a structure is well-formed or not, it assumes that all structures are ill-formed and attempts to predict a failing filter for every structure. In order to minimize the amount of work involved, the types of cues that the dynamic ordering mechanism can test for are deliberately limited. Only inexpensive tests such as whether a category contains certain features are used. Any cues that may require significant computation, such as searching for an antecedent, are considered to be too expensive. Each structure cue is then associated with a list of possible failing filters. (Some examples of the mapping between cues and filters are shown in table 3 below.) The system then chooses one of the possible failing filters based on this mapping.

Structure cue	Possible failing filters
trace	Empty Category Principle, and Case Condition on traces
intransitive	Case Filter
passive	Theta Criterion Case Filter
non-argument	Theta Criterion
+anaphoric	Binding Theory Principle A
+pronominal	Binding Theory Principle B

Table 3. Some of the heuristic cues used for testing which filter will block a given sentence.

The correspondence between each cue and the set of candidate filters may be systematically derived from the definitions of the relevant principles. For example, Principle A of the Binding Theory deals with the conditions under which antecedents for anaphoric items such as *each other* and *himself* must appear. Hence, Principle A can only be a candidate failing filter for structures that contain an item with the +anaphoric feature. Other correspondences may be somewhat less direct. For example, the Case Filter merely states that all overt noun phrases must have abstract Case. Now, in the parser the conditions under which a noun phrase may receive abstract Case are defined by two separate operations, namely, Inherent Case Assignment and Structural Case Assignment. It turns out that an instance where Structural Case Assignment will not assign Case is when a verb that normally assigns Case has passive morphology. Hence, the presence of a passive verb in a given structure may cause an overt noun phrase to fail to receive Case during Structural Case Assignment—which in turn may cause the Case Filter to fail.[4]

---

[4]It is possible to automate the process of finding structure cues simply by inspecting the closure of the definitions of each filter and all dependent operations. One method of deriving cues is to collect the negation of all conditions involving category features. For example, if an operation contains the condition "not (Item has_feature intransitive)", then we can take the presence of an intransitive item as a possible reason for failure of that operation. However, this approach has the potential problem of generating too many cues. Although, it may be relatively inexpensive to test each individual cue, a large number of cues will significantly increase the overhead of the ordering mechanism. Furthermore, it turns out that not all cues are equally useful in predict-

The failing filter mechanism can be seen as an approximation to the Cheapest-first heuristic in conjunct ordering problems. It turns out that if the cheapest conjunct at any given point will reduce the search space rather than expand it, then it can be shown that the optimal ordering must contain that conjunct at that point. Obviously, a failing filter is a "cheapest" operation in the sense that it immediately eliminates one structure from the set of possible structures under consideration.

Although the dynamic ordering mechanism performs well in many of the test cases drawn from the reference text, it is by no means foolproof. There are also many cases where the prediction mechanism triggers an unprofitable re-ordering of the default order of operations. (We will present one example of this in the next section.)

Logical dependencies and reordering

Given a candidate failing filter, the dynamic ordering mechanism has to schedule the sequence of parser operations so that the failing filter is performed as early as possible. Simply moving the failing filter to the front of the operations queue is not a workable approach for two reasons.

First, simply fronting the failing filter may violate logical dependencies between various parser operations. For example, suppose the Case Filter were chosen to be the failing filter. To create the conditions under which the Case Filter can apply, both Case assignment operations, namely, Inherent Case Assignment and Structural Case Assignment, must be applied first. Hence, fronting the Case Filter will also be accompanied by the subsequent fronting of both assignment operations—unless they have already been applied to the structure in question.

Second, the failing filter approach does not take into account the behavior of generator principles. Due to logical dependencies it may be necessary in some situations to invoke a generator operation before a failure filter can be applied. For example, the filter Principle A of the Binding Theory is logically dependent on the generator Free Indexing to generate the possible antecedents for the anaphors in a structure. Consider the possible binders for the anaphor *himself* in *John thought that Bill saw himself* as shown below:

---

ing failure filters. One solution may be to use "weights" to rank the predictive utility of each cue with respect to each filter. Then an adaptive algorithm could be used to "learn" the weighting values, in a manner reminiscent of Samuels [1967]. The failure filter prediction process could then automatically eliminate testing for relatively unimportant cues. This approach is currently being investigated.

(a) *John$_i$ thought that Bill$_j$ saw himself$_i$

(b) John$_i$ thought that Bill$_j$ saw himself$_j$

(c) *John$_i$ thought that Bill$_j$ saw himself$_k$

Only in example (b) is the antecedent close enough to satisfy the locality restrictions imposed by Principle A. Note that Principle A had to be applied a total of three times in the above example in order to show that there is only one possible antecedent for *himself*. This situation arises because of the general tendency of generators to overgenerate. But this characteristic behavior of generators can greatly magnify the extra work that the parser does when the dynamic ordering mechanism picks the wrong failing filter. Consider the ill-formed structure *John seems that he likes e* (a violation of the principle that traces of noun phrases cannot receive Case). If however, Principle B of the Binding Theory is predicted to be the failure filter (on the basis of the structure cue *he*), then Principle B will be applied repeatedly to the possibilities generated by free indexing. On the other hand, if the Case Condition on Traces operation was correctly predicted to be the failing filter, then Free Indexing need not be applied at all. The dynamic ordering mechanism of the parser is designed to be sensitive to the potential problems caused by selecting a candidate failing filter that is logically dependent on many generators.

The utility of principle ordering

From Fong's experiments with the parser we have found that dynamic principle-ordering can provide a significant improvement over any fixed ordering. We have found that speed-ups varying from three- or four-fold to order-of-magnitude improvements are possible in many cases.[5]
    The control structure of the current parser forces linguistic principles to be applied one at a time. Many other machine architectures are certainly possible, and will be explored in future research. For example, we could take advantage of the independence of many principles and apply principles in parallel whenever possible. However, any improvement in parsing performance would come at the expense of violating the minimum (unnecessary) work ethic. Lazy evaluation of principles is yet another alternative. However, principle-ordering would still be an important consideration for efficient processing in this case. Finally, we should also consider principle-ordering from the viewpoint of scalability. The experience with prototypes suggests that as the level of sophistication of the parser increases (both in

---

[5]Obviously the speed-up obtained will depend on the number of principles present in the system and the degree of fine-tuning of the failure filter selection criteria.

terms of the number and complexity of individual principles), the effect of principle-ordering also becomes more pronounced.

References

Abney, S. [1986], "A new model of natural language parsing," unpublished M.S. Thesis, Department of Linguistics and Philosophy, Massachusetts Institute of Technology, Cambridge, MA.

Aho, A., and J. Ullman [1972], *The Theory of Parsing, Translation, and Compiling*, vol. 1, New York, Prentice-Hall.

Chomsky, N. [1981], *Lectures on Government and Binding*, Dordrecht, Foris Publications.

Chomsky, N. [1986], *Knowledge of Language: Its Nature, Origin, and Use*, Prager.

Dorr, B. J. [1987], "UNITRAN: A Principle-Base Approach to Machine Translation," Report AI-TR-1000, Artificial Intelligence Laboratory, Massachusetts Institute of Technology, Cambridge, MA.

Fong, S. [to appear 1989], "Principle-based parsing and Principle-Ordering," Report AIM-1156, Artificial Intelligence Laboratory, Massachusetts Institute of Technology, Cambridge, MA.

Johnson, M. [1988], "Parsing as deduction: the use of knowledge of language." Knowledge as Language," In *The MIT Parsing Volume*, edited by S. Abney, Center for Cognitive Science, Cambridge, MA, pp. 47-69.

Kashket, M. [1986], "Parsing a free-word order language: Warlpiri," *Proc. ACL*, pp. 60–66.

Kartunnen, L., and M. Kay [1985], in *Natural Language Parsing*, edited by Dowty, Kartunnen, and Zwicky, Cambridge University Press, Cambridge, England, pp. 279–306.

Lasnik, H., and J. Uriagereka [1988] *A Course in GB Syntax: Lectures on Binding and Empty Categories*, MIT Press, Cambridge, MA.

Laughren, M. [1987], "The configurationality parameter and Warlpiri," in *Configurationality*, edited by L. Maracz and Pl. Muysken, Dordrecht, Foris Publications.

Samuels, A. L. [1967], "Some Studies in Machine Learning Using the Game of Checkers. II—Recent Progress," *IBM Journal*.

Slocum, J. [1984], "METAL: The LRC machine translation system," ISSCO Tutorial on machine translation, Lugano, Switzerland.

Work on principle-based parsing at the Artificial Intelligence Laboratory has been supported by NSF Grant DCR-85552543 under a Presidential Young Investigator's Award to Professor Robert C. Berwick, by a grant from the Lotus Development Corporation, by the Kapor Family Foundation, and by the IBM Graduate Research Fellowship Program.

Smith, D. E., and M. R. Genesereth [1985], "Ordering Conjunctive Queries," *Artificial Intelligence* vol. 26, pp. 171–215.

Stabler, E. P., Jr. [1989] "The Logical Approach to Syntax: Foundations, Specifications and Implementations of Theories of Government and Binding," *m.s.*, London, Ontario, University of Western Ontario.

Tenney, C. [1986], "A context-free rule system for parsing Japanese," *MIT-Japan Science and Technology Program*, Cambridge, MA.

13

The way thoughts are expressed varies not only at the level of syntax, but also at deeper, more semantic levels. Certain native Spanish speakers might say to you, for example, "the mugger gave him a stab wound," a construction that centers on the result, while native English speakers are more comfortable with, "the mugger stabbed him," a construction that centers on the means. Both the Spanish and the English speakers arguably have the same thought, but they linearize it differently.

Happily, our ability to represent actions and the objects that surround them has matured considerably in the past few years. In particular, the linguists have been on the march, developing a way of describing things in terms of treelike objects that they call lexical conceptual structures.

Dorr's key insight is that the same idea, captured in a lexical conceptual structure, can be composed and decomposed in language-specific ways. When her UNITRAN program translates a thought from Spanish into English, the parsing program described in the previous chapter constructs a lexical conceptual structure out of building blocks in the Spanish lexicon. Then the elements in the lexical conceptual structure are broken up into a different set of chunks, this time based on building blocks in the English lexicon. Once the new, English chunks are identified, production of a natural-sounding English sentence is straightforward. Thus "El asaltante le dio cuchilladas a él" goes in and "The mugger stabbed him" comes out.

Machine Translation: A Principle-Based Approach

Bonnie J. Dorr

This chapter describes UNITRAN, an implemented machine translation system that translates Spanish, English, and German bidirectionally.[1] The primary characteristic of UNITRAN is that it operates *cross-linguistically* (that is, uniformly across all languages), while still accounting for knowledge that is specific to each language. The task of cross-linguistic translation is difficult because there are several types of phenomena within any given language; moreover, the number of ways in which these phenomena can be exhibited is potentially enormous across different source and target languages.

Consider the following translation from English to Spanish:

(1) I stabbed John ⇒ Yo di cuchilladas a Juan
                (I gave knife-wounds to John)

In this example, the source language sentence diverges both syntactically and lexically from the target language sentence. The syntactic divergence shows up in the realization of the verbal object as a noun phrase *John* in English but as the prepositional phrase *a Juan* (literally, *to John*) in Spanish. The lexical divergence shows up in the realization of the main action as the single verb *stab* in English but as the composite form *dar cuchilladas* (literally, *to knife* or *to give knife-wounds*) in Spanish. The

---

[1]The name UNITRAN stands for UNIversal TRANslator; that is, the system serves as the basis for translation across a variety of languages, not just two languages or a family of languages. To date, the system operates only on the three languages mentioned, but plans are currently underway for the addition of Warlpiri, a native aborigine language of Australia.

UNITRAN system partially solves these types of divergences by providing
a principle-based framework within which lexical-semantic information is
abstracted to a level that is distinct from that of syntactic information;
sentences are then translated on the basis of an interaction between these
two levels.

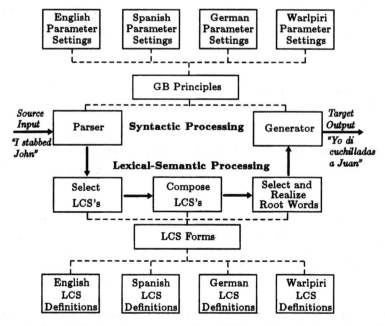

Figure 1. Overall design of UNITRAN, Dorr [1987, 1989a, 1989b, to appear].

The overall design of UNITRAN is shown in figure 1. The syntactic level
of the system is based on a set of linguistic principles, along with their
associated parameters, drawn from *government-binding* (GB) theory (see
Chomsky [1981, 1982]). This level consists of the information necessary to
accept or produce grammatically correct sentences. The lexical-semantic
portion of the system is based on theories of *lexical conceptual structure*
(LCS) (see Jackendoff [1983, 1990], Hale and Laughren [1983], and Hale and
Keyser [1986]). This level consists of the information necessary to provide
an underlying conceptual form (the LCS) and to match this structure to the
appropriate target-language lexical items. The syntactic level of processing
will be discussed briefly in the next section, and the rest of the chapter will
focus on the lexical-semantic level of processing and the types of problems
that are solved within the LCS framework.

What makes the task of principle-based translation difficult is the requirement that the translator process many types of *language-specific* phenomena while still maintaining *language-independent* information about
the source and target languages. For example, it is conceivable that the

system might translate a Spanish sentence incorrectly on the basis of the knowledge it has for translating English sentences. Consider the Spanish sentence (2):

(2) Qué golpeó Juan (What did John hit)

If the translator were to use its syntactic knowledge of English to translate this sentence, it would understand the sentence to mean *what hit john* (that is, the *agent* and *goal* roles would be reversed). Thus, it is crucial that the translator know certain language-specific information (for example, the word-order permitted by a particular language) so that it can provide an appropriate structural realization of this sentence; in addition, the translator must know certain language-independent information (for example, the roles that are introduced by the *hit* action) so that it can assign the appropriate interpretation regardless of how the particular languages structurally realize the sentence.

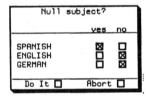

Figure 2. Choosing the null subject setting in UNITRAN.

Given that these two types of knowledge (language-specific and language-independent) are required to fulfill the translation task, one approach to machine translation is to provide a common language-independent representation that acts as a *pivot* between the source and target languages, and to provide a language-specific mapping between this form and the input and output of each language. In the UNITRAN system, the pivot form is the composed LCS that underlies the source and target language sentences. This pivot approach to translation is called *interlingual* because it is based on an underlying form derived on the basis of universal *principles* that hold across all languages. Within this framework, the UNITRAN system handles the distinctions among languages by referring to the settings of *parameters* associated with the universal principles. For example, there is a GB principle that is concerned with the absence or presence of the subject in a sentence. The parameter that is associated with this principle, called the *null subject* parameter, is set to *yes* for Spanish (also, Italian, Hebrew, *etc.*) but *no* for English and German (also French, Warlpiri, *etc.*). This accounts for the possibility of a missing subject in Spanish and the impossibility of a missing subject in English and German.

Setting the null subject parameter in the UNITRAN system is done through a simple menu operation as shown in figure 2. This parameter setting accounts for the word order variation in example (2). Because null subject languages have the property that subjects may freely invert into post-verbal position, the noun phrase *Juan* is taken to be the subject of the Spanish sentence even though it would be taken to be the object in the structurally equivalent English sentence.

Both of the levels shown in figure 1 operate on the basis of language-independent and language-specific knowledge. Within the syntactic level, the language-independent and language-specific information are supplied by the GB principles and parameters, respectively. Within the lexical-semantic level, the language-independent and language-specific information are supplied by a set of general lexical-semantic forms and the associated LCS definitions for each language, respectively. (A more detailed presentation of the LCS descriptions will be provided in the section on lexical conceptual structure in machine translation.) The interface between the syntactic and semantic levels allows the source-language structure to be mapped systematically to the conceptual form, and it allows the target-language structure to be realized systematically from lexical items derived from the conceptual form. This work represents a shift away from complex, language-specific syntactic generation without entirely abandoning syntax. Furthermore, the work moves toward a model that employs a well-defined lexical conceptual representation without relying entirely on semantics. A majority of the approaches to translation do not use this principle-based interlingual strategy, but instead use either a *direct* or a *transfer* strategy as described in the next section.

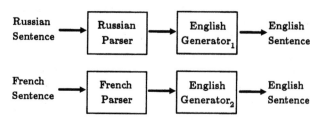

Figure 3. Direct translation approach as embodied by GAT.

Perhaps the most important advance of UNITRAN is that it is able to achieve two crucial machine-translation operations, *lexical selection* and *syntactic realization*, despite the potential for syntactic and lexical divergences. For example, the system is able to select and realize the appropriate target language word *dar* (to give) as the translation of *stab* in (1) despite the fact that *dar* is not the literal translation of *stab*. The execution of these two operations will be described in the section on the design of the LCS component in UNITRAN. The rest of the chapter will provide a framework within which cross-linguistic translation can be achieved in a principle-based fashion. In particular, it will describe the lexical conceptual component of the

UNITRAN system, and it will present a mapping between the semantic and syntactic levels. We will see that the UNITRAN system differs from the systems described in the next section in that it applies cross-linguistically, and it relies on compositionality and lexical-semantics/syntax abstraction in order to provide source-to-target language translations.

Comparison of Interlingual and Non-Interlingual Approaches

This section starts with a description of some non-interlingual approaches and then describes the move toward a syntactic/semantic interlingual approach which led to the current work presented in this chapter.

Early non-interlingual designs

The *direct* translation approach is a word-for-word scheme in which there is a parser and a generator for each source-target language pair (see figure 3). The primary characteristic of such an approach is that it is designed to translate from one specific language to another. This design was used by GAT (the Georgetown Automatic Translation system), which was operational from 1964 to 1976. (See Jordan *et al.* [1976, 1977].) As we have already seen in (2), the direct approach does not work well in the general case because it chooses words that are literal translations without taking word order or other syntactic cues into account.

Later approaches to translation have taken a *transfer* approach in which there is only one parser and one generator for each source and target language. In this approach, there are a set of *transfer* components, one for each source-target language pair (see figure 4). The transfer phase is actually a third translation stage in which one language-specific representation is mapped into another. In contrast to the direct approach to translation, the transfer approach has been somewhat more successful, accommodating a variety of linguistic strategies across different languages. For example, the METAL system (see Slocum [1984]) currently translates from German into Chinese and Spanish, as well as from English into German.

The major disadvantage of the transfer approach is that each parser and generator is based on a large set of language-specific context-free rules. In METAL, the grammar formalism is different for each language. For example, the German parser is based on phrase-structure grammar, augmented by procedures for transformations; by contrast, the English parser employs a modified GPSG approach with no transformations. Regardless of the type of grammar formalism, each parser and generator is nevertheless based on hundreds of rules of a context-free nature. Because the system has no access to universal principles, there is no consistency across the components;

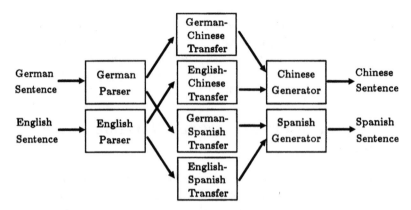

Figure 4. Transfer approach as embodied by METAL.

thus, each module has an independent theoretical and engineering basis. Rather than abstracting principles that are common to all languages into separate modules that can be activated upon translation of any language, each module must independently include all of the information required to translate that language, whether or not the information is universal. For example, agreement information must be encoded into each rule in the METAL system; there is no separate agreement module that can apply to other rules. Furthermore, there is no "rule-sharing"—all rules are language-dependent and cannot apply across several languages.

Figure 5 gives an example of a context-free rule in the METAL system. Essentially, what this rule does is build a syntax tree using the CONSTRuctor part of the rule after it has determined that the constituent tests (the second and third lines) and the TEST portion of the rule are satisfied. The constituent test requires the first element to be word-initial (WI) and the second element to be word-final (WF). The TEST portion of the rule requires that these two constituents agree syntactically. Once these requirements are satisfied, the CONSTRuctor associates a noun with the two constituents NST and N-FLEX. In this example, the parent node (NN) and children (NST and N-FLEX) are built into a syntax tree that corresponds to a noun stem (NST) and its nominal ending (N-FLEX).

	NN	NST	N-FLEX
	0	1	2
	LVL 0	REQ WI	REQ WF
TEST		(INT 1 CL 2 CL)	
CONSTR		(CPX 2 ALO CL)	
		(CPY 2 NU CA)	
		(CPY 1 WI)	

Figure 5. Context-free phrase-structure rule in METAL.

Note that the application of such a rule must be restricted by tests on syntax (positioning and agreement in this example) that are encoded directly in the rule, rather than in independent modules that can account for these constraints globally. In order to account for a wide range of phenomena, hundreds of such rules are required for each language, thereby increasing grammar search time.[2]

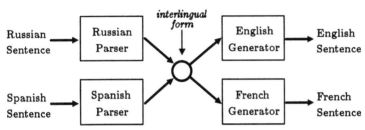

Figure 6. Interlingual translation design as embodied by CETA and Sharp [1985].

The shift toward an interlingual design

The interlingual translation model avoids a detailed language-dependent specification of each source and target language. Instead, the source language is mapped into a form that is independent of any language, and the target-language form is then generated on the basis of parameter values for the selected language. Thus, there are no transfer modules or language-specific rules. The interlingual translation design was used in the CETA (Centre d'Etudes pour la Traduction Automatique) system, which became operational in 1971 (see Hutchins [1978]), and also for a system built by Sharp [1985]. However, the CETA system is not entirely interlingual because there is a transfer component at the lexical level that maps from one language-specific lexical representation to another. Sharp's system, although not rule-based, is also not entirely interlingual because it includes some hard-wired principles that are not user-programmable. The result is that the class of languages that can be translated is limited. The interlingual approach as embodied by CETA and Sharp is illustrated in figure 6.

---

[2]The METAL translation system has approximately 550 phrase-structure rules for each source and target language. According to Bley-Vroman [personal correspondence, 1988], these rules operate at all levels (lexical, morphological, and syntactic), which tends to make the number of rules seem higher than it would be for a purely syntactic processor. Unfortunately, the idiosyncratic choices made in designing the METAL grammar come at a high cost. Because the GPSG formalism is employed, these 550 rules could potentially multiply out to an unmanageable grammar size after meta-rules have applied. For more on the complexity of GPSG, see Ristad [1986].

Note that there are no transfer components, but that there is a separate parser and generator for each source and target language. The interlingual form is assumed to be a form common to all languages.

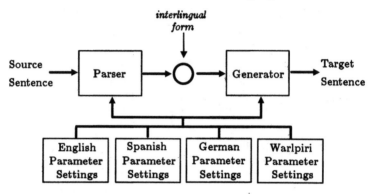

Figure 7. Interlingual approach as embodied by UNITRAN [1987].

One problem with this implementation of the interlingual approach is that the user must supply a parser for each source language and a generator for each target language. In a more uniformly applicable interlingual approach, the design would be slightly different from that of CETA and Sharp: the same parser and generator would be used for all languages. This more closely approximates a true universal approach because the principles that apply across all languages are entirely separate from the language-specific characteristics expressed by parameter settings. This is the approach taken in the syntactic component of the UNITRAN system as shown in figure 7.

Note that the design of the UNITRAN translator allows the operation of the parser and generator to be modified without changing the programs underlying these modules. All of the principles associated with the system have user-modifiable parameter settings; thus, the source-language parser and target-language generator do not need to be modified (or replaced) when new languages are added. The only requirement is that the built-in parser and generator be *programmed* (via parameter settings) to process the source and target languages.

An example of setting a parameter in the UNITRAN system is shown in figure 8. Here, the user specifies the ordering of constituents with respect to a phrase for each language.[3] This parameter, called *constituent order*, is set to *head-initial* for English verbs, but *head-final* for verbs in many other languages including German and Japanese. The *head-initial* parameter

---

[3]This menu enumerates the syntactic categories for each language and allows the user to specify the constituent order associated with each category. Roughly, the spec-initial/spec-final setting corresponds to the positioning of subjects, and the head-initial/head-final setting corresponds to the positioning of objects.

setting forces the object to follow the verb in English (for example, *hit the ball*); by contrast, the *head-final* parameter setting forces the object to precede the verb in German and Japanese (for example, *the ball hit*). In addition to supplying the values for a small set of these parameters, the user must also provide a dictionary for each language, a necessary component in all the approaches discussed here.

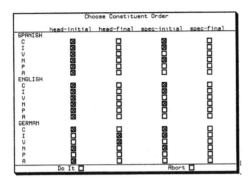

Figure 8. Choosing the constituent order setting in the UNITRAN system.

The work by CETA, Sharp, and the earlier work of Dorr was done almost entirely within the realm of syntax. Other groups that have taken the interlingual approach have operated in the realm of semantics. (See Lytinen and Schank [1982], Lytinen [1985, 1987], Carbonell [1981], Cullingford [1986], Nirenburg [1986], and Nirenburg *et al.* [1987, 1988].) These interlingual approaches are *knowledge-based*, that is, they operate on the basis of a strong underlying model of the current situational context and expectations. Generally, the interlingua can be encoded by means of *primitive* meaning units. For example, in the MOPTRANS system (Lytinen and Schank [1982]), the Spanish word *capturar* is defined as GET-CONTROL in the dictionary. A *specialization* routine determines that *capturar* (= capture) is to be generated as the word *arrest* if the correct context (for example, a police search) has been instantiated.

Several arguments for choosing a semantic-based design over a syntactic-based design for generation systems have prevailed in the past. The first is that the number of rules in a syntactic-based system is potentially enormous: a word may have several word senses, and each word sense would require a myriad of rules specifying the contexts in which the word sense might appear. A second related problem is indexing. Because there are thousands of rules to choose from, Lytinen and Schank [1982] argue that the amount of information the system would have to look for would be enormous, and deciding what information in the sentence was relevant for disambiguating the word in each particular context would be impossible. The third argument for a semantic-based design is that syntactic-based approaches tend to be overly concerned with the form of the input rather than the content. Cullingford [1986] argues that these *grammar-based* approaches do not easily handle deviant input (for example, input that is ungrammatical).

There are several disadvantages to an entirely semantic-based approach. First of all, the claim that rule-based syntactic systems are both too large and too complex to adequately handle natural language translation may be well-grounded, but the semantic-based approach does not combat the problem. In attempting to tackle the problem of word disambiguation, semantic-based systems provide access to a very limited domain of subject matter at the expense of incorporating an incredibly massive amount of knowledge.

An additional drawback to semantic-based approaches is that there is a loss of structure and style in generating the target text from the underlying (interlingual) form; consequently, the output of these systems is a paraphrase, not a translation. Although the *deep contextual meaning* of the input text is preserved, the emphasis or intent of the text is not always fully preserved. The claim is that any other system which attempts to preserve structure and style without the knowledge necessary for text understanding would often produce unreliable translations. However, the loss of structure and style may involve a loss of some of the meaning of the text. Most likely, the speaker chooses a particular structural realization in order to focus on a specific topic or to make a crucial point; the absence of structure preservation might result in a complete misinterpretation of the text.

Finally, another problem with knowledge-based generation systems is that they typically require an involved general inference mechanism in order to arrive at the surface form for a primitive concept. Rather than basing word selection on general lexical principles, complex inferencing routines are applied to conceptual representations. Furthermore, the selection of target-language terms in such systems generally involves searching complex discrimination networks that test selectional restrictions of target language tokens and act accordingly. For example, in Carbonell *et al.* [1981], the sentence *Mary hit John* is represented as:

(3) (event EV001
        (action PROPEL)
        (agent MARY)
        (object JOHN)
        (instrument *UNKNOWN*)
        (force *ABOVE-AVERAGE*)
        (intentionality *POSITIVE*))

In order to translate the above concept into Spanish, the main action (PROPEL) is mapped to the discrimination network shown in figure 9. This

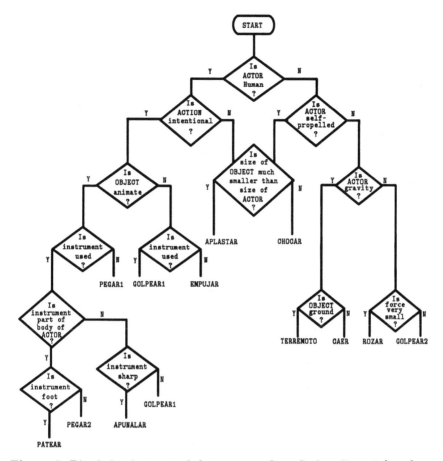

Figure 9. Discrimination network for PROPEL, from Carbonell *et al.* [1981].

network is then used to choose the correct verb.

There are a number of disadvantages associated with the discrimination network approach. First, the network can grow very large as more words are added to the system; the more detailed the network becomes, the more complicated the search for a target-language term becomes. Another problem with the network approach is that generation of compound predicate-argument structures is not accommodated because all the paths lead to a single lexical item (not a *set* of lexical items); thus, composite forms such as *dar cuchilladas* are not accounted for in such a scheme. Finally, the approach is not general enough to apply across several languages because surface forms are not represented as basic units of meaning; consequently, a new network must be hand-written for each language.

A current interlingual approach

The examples in the previous sections provide strong evidence that a suitable representation for conceptual structure is needed. According to Talmy [1983] (following Jackendoff and Gruber), words should be defined in terms of many semantic components that contribute to the overall meaning. This is essentially what has been attempted in some of the existing semantic-based approaches. However, as we have seen, these approaches rely on enormous knowledge-bases that are expensive to access, maintain, and update. Furthermore, these systems are guided almost entirely by general inference, context, and expectations; thus, they do not take advantage of syntactic and lexical-semantic information that aids the realization process.

In the next section, we will see how the UNITRAN system uses a lexical-conceptual scheme that avoids some of the problems of earlier approaches. Rather than basing word selection on knowledge-based information, general inferences, and context tracking, the system matches the underlying conceptual structure of a sentence to the appropriate target-language lexical items, and produces the structural realization of the target-sentence by means of syntactic mappings from these lexical items. The remainder of this chapter will focus on the lexical-semantic module of UNITRAN showing how the lexical conceptual representation offers a partial solution to some of the syntactic and semantic divergences that arise during translation.

Lexical Conceptual Structure in Machine Translation

This section describes the representation underlying the second major component of UNITRAN: the lexical semantic component. The work of Jackendoff [1983, 1990] has been the primary influence on the design of UNITRAN's lexical-semantic component. The representation adopted is *lexical conceptual structure* (henceforth LCS) as formulated by Hale and Laughren [1983] and Hale and Keyser [1986]. Recall example (1) repeated here as (4):

(4) I stabbed John ⇒ Yo di cuchilladas a Juan
           (I gave knife-wounds to John)

Two properties of the LCS representation enable it to provide an appropriate translation for cases such as (4). The first is that the LCS representation is *compositional* in nature. Thus, the LCS representation underlying the *stab* event allows the inherently compositional verb *stab* to be mapped to the overtly compositional form *dar cuchilladas* (literally, *to knife* or *to give knife-wounds*). The second property of the representation is that it provides an abstraction of lexical-semantic information from syntactic information. Thus, the word *John* is syntactically mapped to the phrase *a Juan* (literally, *to John*) without regard to its underlying representation. We will see in the following sections that compositionality and lexical-semantics/syntax abstraction are crucial to the model presented here. Before detailing the design of the LCS component, we will first look at the LCS representation and the mapping between this representation and the syntactic level of description.

The LCS representation

A dictionary of lexical root-word entries is required for each language that is processed by UNITRAN. Each entry has two levels of description: the first is a lexical-semantic representation (the LCS of the lexical word), and the second is a mapping from the LCS representation to the syntactic structure (category and structural positioning of each argument associated with the lexical word). This section presents the LCS representation, and the next section describes the mapping from the LCS to the syntactic structure.

The best way to illustrate the form of the LCS is to present an example. The LCS that describes the *stab* event is:

```
(5) (CAUSE X
        (GO-POSS KNIFE-WOUND
          (TOWARD-POSS (AT-POSS KNIFE-WOUND Z)))
        (WITH-INSTR *HEAD* SHARP-OBJECT))
```

This LCS description provides the meaning "THING X causes a possessional transfer of a knife-wound to THING Z using a sharp object as an instrument."

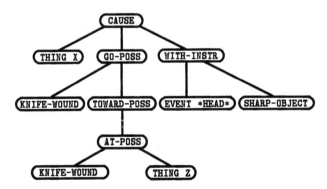

Figure 10. Underlying LCS for stab event.

Figure 10 shows the underlying LCS tree structure generated from (5). Note that the SHARP-OBJECT instrument argument is included in the LCS even though the source language does not realize this argument in (4). Including this argument in the LCS allows flexibility in generating the target-language sentence, which may or may not require this argument to be realized. Thus, it would be possible to generate either *he stabbed the robber*, or *he stabbed the robber with a knife* (*scissors, poker, etc.*). The *HEAD* symbol is a place-holder that points to the overall *stab* event (that is, the *stab* event is performed with a sharp object).

LCS Type	LCS Name
EVENT	CAUSE, LET, GO-POSS, GO-IDENT, GO-TEMP,
	GO-LOC, STAY-POSS, STAY-TEMP
STATE	BE-IDENT, BE-POSS, BE-LOC, BE-TEMP
THING	KNIFE-WOUND, BOOK, PERSON, REFERENT
PROPERTY	TIRED, HUNGRY
PATH	TO-POSS, TO-LOC, FROM-POSS, FROM-LOC,
	TOWARD-POSS, TOWARD-LOC
POSITION	AT-POSS, AT-LOC, IN-LOC, ON-LOC, WITH-INSTR
LOCATION	HERE, THERE
TIME	TOMORROW, 9:00
MANNER	FORCEFULLY, WELL
INTENSIFIER	VERY

Table 1. LCS Types and Names.

Table 1 gives some examples of the lexical primitives used by the system. (Not all of the lexical primitives are listed here; see Dorr [to appear].) In particular, I adopt Jackendoff's notions of EVENT and STATE; these are further specialized into such primitives as CAUSE, GO, BE, STAY, and LET. The specialized primitives are placed into Temporal, Locational, Possessional, Identificational, Circumstantial, Instrumental, Intentional, and Existential fields. For example, the primitive GO-POSS refers to a GO event in the Possessional field (for example, Beth received (= GO-POSS) the doll). If the GO event were placed in the Temporal field, it would become GO-TEMP (for example, the meeting went (= GO-TEMP) from 2:00 to 4:00). One difference between Jackendoff's representation and the one shown here is that the POSITIONS (AT-POSS, AT-LOC, WITH-INSTR, *etc.*) are implemented as two-place predicates; thus, the KNIFE-WOUND argument in figure 10 appears both internally and externally to the AT-POSS LCS node. Although the system uses only a small set of lexical-semantic primitives (approximately 25), this set is quite adequate for defining a potentially large corpus of words due to the compositional nature of LCS's. The advantage of a small set of primitives is that the search space is reduced during the lexical-selection stage of generation. The importance of a small search space will become more apparent later when we look at the lexical selection process during a translation example in the section on stab-dar.

Mapping from LCS to syntactic structure

In order to allow different target-language realizations of the *stab* event, lexical entries must specify certain language-specific syntactic information. This is the nature of the LCS-to-syntax mapping associated with the definition of a word. The LCS-to-syntax mapping is incorporated into a word definition by means of three mechanisms. The first mechanism consists of two markers, :INT and :EXT, that map an LCS argument structure to a predicate-argument structure. A predicate-argument structure is an explicit syntactic representation of hierarchical relations between a predicate and its arguments. In particular, a predicate-argument structure embodies the asymmetry between the external argument position (for example, the subject of a verb) and the internal argument positions (for example, the objects of a verb). According to Rappaport and Levin [1986], language-specific linking rules relate variables in an LCS to positions in a predicate-argument structure. For example, in English the *agent* argument is mapped to a position that is external to the predicate. In UNITRAN, this process is implemented as a single, more general, language-independent linking routine that maps the hierarchically highest argument in the LCS to a syntactically external position, and all other arguments to syntactically internal positions. When this routine is to be overridden by a lexical entry, the language-specific markers :INT and :EXT are used.

The second LCS-to-syntax mechanism is the :CAT marker that provides a syntactic category for an LCS argument. According to Chomsky [1986], there is a language-specific function called CSR (canonical-syntactic representation) which provides a default mapping from the thematic-roles of GB theory to the appropriate syntactic categories. For example, in English the *agent* role is mapped to the category N. In UNITRAN, the CSR function has been implemented as a general language-independent routine that maps an LCS type to a syntactic category (see table 2). When this mapping is to be overridden by a lexical entry, the language-specific marker :CAT is used.

The third LCS-to-syntax mechanism, developed specifically for the UNITRAN system, is the '*' marker; this marker provides a pointer to the position where arguments are explicitly realized in the surface form. Figure 11 shows how the '*' notation is used for the English and Spanish lexical entries that correspond to the *stab* event. Note that the Spanish LCS for *dar* contains a z argument that is realized at the level of TOWARD-POSS, whereas the corresponding argument in the English LCS for *stab* is realized at the

LCS Type	Syntactic Category
EVENT	V
STATE	V
THING	N
PROPERTY	A
PATH	P
POSITION	P
LOCATION	ADV
TIME	ADV
MANNER	ADV
INTENSIFIER	ADV

Table 2. CSR Mapping from LCS Type to Syntactic Category.

lowest level. This accounts for the distinction between the noun phrase *John* and the prepositional phrase *a Juan* in the translation example (4). Also note that the English LCS for *stab* contains a KNIFE-WOUND argument corresponding to the Y argument in the Spanish LCS for *dar*. Because this argument is not associated with a '*' marker in the English entry, it is considered to be *conflated* or "understood" as part of the meaning of the verb *stab*. However, the corresponding Y argument in the Spanish entry is associated with a '*' marker, thus indicating that it must be explicitly realized for the verb *dar*. This corresponds to the distinction between *stab* and *dar cuchilladas* in (4). The *EXTERNAL* symbol used in the LCS definition of *a* is a place-holder for an LCS that will fill this position by means of lexical-semantic composition (to be described in the next section). For example, when the LCS associated with *a* is composed with the LCS associated with *dar*, the Y argument will replace the *EXTERNAL* place-holder in the LCS associated with *a*.

The '*' marker is required for every explicitly realized argument of a lexical entry, whereas the :INT, :EXT, and :CAT markers are used only in cases where the linking and CSR functions need to be overridden. Given this organization of syntactic and semantic information, a target-language syntactic structure can be generated from an underlying LCS structure. The design of the LCS component and the lexical selection and syntactic realization processes that allow syntactic and lexical-semantic decisions to be made will be described in the next section.

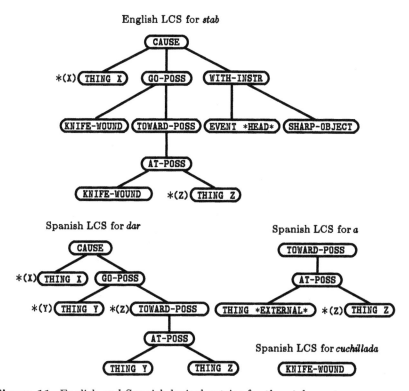

Figure 11. English and Spanish lexical entries for the *stab* event.

Design of the LCS Component in UNITRAN

Figure 12 shows the design of the LCS component of the system as described here and in Dorr [to appear]. Essentially, lexical-semantic processing involves three top-level tasks. The first is the mapping of each word to its corresponding LCS. The second is the composition of the resulting LCS forms into a single LCS that underlies the source- and target-language sentences. The third is the mapping of each node in the composed LCS to an appropriate target-language word, which is then projected to its phrasal (or *maximal*) level and attached according to the positioning requirements of the word that selects it.[4]

We return to our translation example shown in (4), repeated here as (6):

(6) I stabbed John ⇒ Yo di cuchilladas a Juan
          (I gave knife-wounds to John)

---

[4]For discussion of projection to maximal level by the syntactic component of the system, see Dorr [1987]. In a nutshell, X-MAX refers to the XP phrase that contains a word of category X.

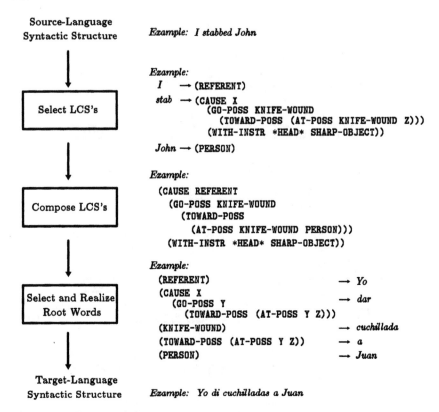

Figure 12. Design of the LCS component in UNITRAN.

The parsing module of the syntactic component supplies a source-language syntactic tree to the LCS component of the system. Figure 13 shows the source-language syntactic tree input for the current example.[5] When this syntactic tree is passed to the LCS component, an LCS is selected for each word (*I*, *stab*, and *John*), and a single underlying LCS is composed by means of the (reversible) LCS-to-syntax mappings described in the last section. For example, the LCS REFERENT is selected for the word *I* and the LCS PERSON is selected for the word *John*; during LCS composition, the REFERENT is mapped by the generalized linking routine to the external position X of *stab*, and the PERSON is mapped by the same routine to the internal position Z of *stab*.

Figure 14 shows the mapping from the syntactic tree to the LCS argument positions in the definition of *stab*; the result of this mapping is the

---

[5]In this case, there is only one possible source-language tree; however, if the structure were ambiguous, other possibilities would be returned. The *e* elements under C and I are syntactic positions for which there is no overt lexical material.

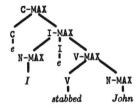

Figure 13. Source-language syntactic tree for *I stabbed John*.

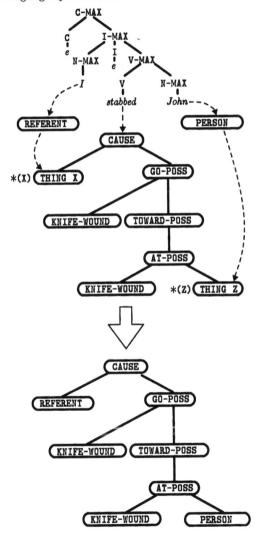

Figure 14. Mapping syntactic tree positions to LCS argument positions: derivation of the composed LCS for the *stab* event.

composed LCS as shown.

Once the LCS has been composed, the third module of the LCS component performs *lexical selection* and *syntactic realization* to produce the final target-language tree and sentence. These two operations are the first and second steps of the procedure applied by this module of the LCS component as shown in figure 15.

1. Lexically select target-language word.
2. Syntactically realize and attach target-language word.
3. Realize arguments of target-language word, if any.

Figure 15. Procedure for lexical selection and syntactic realization.

Note that the third step, argument realization, is actually a recursive call to this procedure: arguments of a target-language word are realized in the same way that the target-language word was realized. We will now examine the lexical selection and syntactic realization steps in more detail, and then go on to show how these steps are applied to the current example.

Lexical selection: Thematic divergence

This section describes the lexical selection task and provides an example showing how the LCS approach handles the problem of thematic divergence during this process. Lexical selection is the task of choosing the target-language words that accurately reflect the meaning of the corresponding source-language words. One of the difficulties of this task is the fact that the equivalent source- and target-language forms are potentially thematically divergent. An example of thematic divergence shows up in the translation of the Spanish word *gustar* to the English word *like*. Although these two verbs are semantically equivalent, their argument structures are not identical: the subject of *like* (*I*) is the *theme* of the action, whereas the subject of *gustar* (*el libro*) is the *agent* of the action. Thus, we have:

(7) Me gusta el libro (The book pleases me) $\Rightarrow$ I like the book

In (7), the subject of the source-language sentence has freely inverted into post-verbal position. Thus, the post-verbal subject is considered to be the external argument of the main verb. Free subject-inversion is a property of *null subject* languages (that is, languages such as Spanish, Italian, Hebrew, *etc.* as described in the introduction section); this property is taken into account during syntactic parsing and generation.

In a purely syntactic-based scheme, the semantics of the verb *gustar* would be lost because the literal translation (*to please*) would be selected

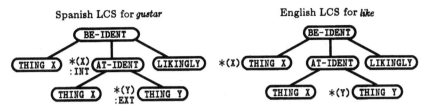

Figure 16. English and Spanish lexical entries for *gustar-like*.

for the target-language verb. In contrast, a semantic-based system would generally be able to make the correct lexical selection, but it might have difficulty with syntactic realization of the target-language arguments because it has no notion of syntactic argument divergence.

In the LCS approach, the underlying conceptual structure for *gustar* and *like* is identical. The only difference is that the syntactic mappings associated with these two verbs are language-specific. Figure 16 shows the LCS definitions underlying *gustar* and *like*. The LCS provides the meaning "THING X is in an identificational state LIKINGLY with respect to THING Y." However, the variables X and Y map to different syntactic positions for English and Spanish. The English version maps the X variable to the external position and the Y variable to the internal position, and the Spanish version interchanges these two positions by means of the :INT and :EXT markers. Thus, the agent of the action becomes the external argument (subject) in Spanish, and the internal argument (object) in English. Furthermore, the level at which these two arguments are to be realized is different: the '*' marker specifies that the level of realization for the internal argument is at the level of AT-IDENT in Spanish, but not in English. This structural divergence shows up during syntactic realization, which will be discussed just below.

Lexical selection of a target-language word involves matching the composed LCS to the appropriate root word in a target-language possibility set. For example, suppose the system is trying to select the appropriate target-language token for the composed LCS that corresponds to the source-language verb *gustar*. Several target words (including *like*, *sleep*, and many others that use the BE-IDENT LCS) are selected as possible lexical possibilities. Each of these possibilities is then examined for a match: not only must the top-level LCS coincide, but all LCS's under the top-level LCS must also coincide. In general, there are two classes of LCS nodes that are taken into consideration during the matching process of lexical selection. The more general nodes (for example, BE-IDENT, GO-POSS, *etc.*) allow the matcher to determine the LCS class of the target-language term; the more specific nodes (for example, LIKINGLY, FORCEFULLY, *etc.*) are used for final convergence on a particular target-language term such as *like* as opposed to *love*, and *force* as opposed to *cause*.

In the current example, the system determines that the *like* LCS is a match because it contains a BE-IDENT event whose arguments coincide with the arguments of the BE-IDENT in the composed LCS. Figure 17 shows the mapping from the source-language syntactic tree to the target-language syntactic tree by means of the composed LCS for example (7).

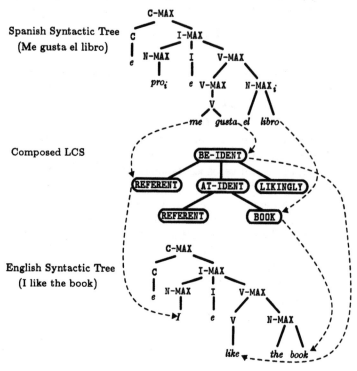

Figure 17. Translation of *Me gusta el libro* as *I like the book*.

Note that, even though the arguments are not syntactically realized in the same way, the lexical selection procedure still succeeds. This is because of the separation between the syntactic description and the conceptual description. LCS descriptions provide the abstraction necessary for lexical selection without regard to syntax. This abstraction is an advance over other approaches because it provides an accurate translation of the source-language terms despite thematic divergences. In the next subsection, we will see how LCS-to-syntax mappings provide the necessary mechanism for syntactic realization without regard to conceptual considerations.

Syntactic realization: Structural and conflational divergence

Syntactic realization is the second step applied by the third module of the LCS component. This step involves mapping an LCS to a syntactic representation using the LCS-to-syntax mapping described previously. Two problems are associated with this task. The first is that source- and target-language forms are potentially structurally divergent, and the second is that source- and target-language terms have potentially divergent argument incorporation characteristics. We will discuss the first of these two problems and return to the second one shortly.

An example of structural divergence is the realization of arguments in the translation of *tener* to *be* as in (8) (the corresponding argument-structures are included):

(8)
Yo tengo hambre (I have hunger)
[v−MAX [v tener] [N−MAX hambre]]
$\Downarrow$
I am hungry
[v−MAX [v be] [A−MAX hungry]]

Here, not only are the predicates *tener* and *be* lexically distinct, but the arguments of these two predicates are structurally divergent: in Spanish, the argument is a noun-phrase, and, in English, the argument is an adjectival-phrase.

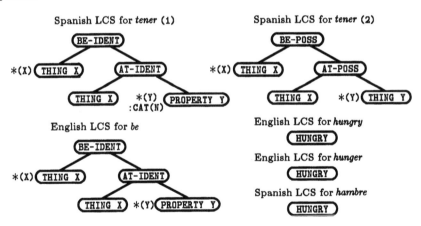

Figure 18. English and Spanish lexical entries for *tener-be*.

Figure 18 shows the LCS definitions used in example (8). The equivalent LCS's for *tener* (1) and *be* provide the meaning "THING X is in an identificational state specified by PROPERTY Y." Note that there is another LCS for the word *tener* (2) that corresponds to a more literal translation (*have*) of the word *tener*.

As for the lexical selection of the appropriate predicate, the same LCS procedure that was used in the *stab-dar* case is used to match the LCS's of

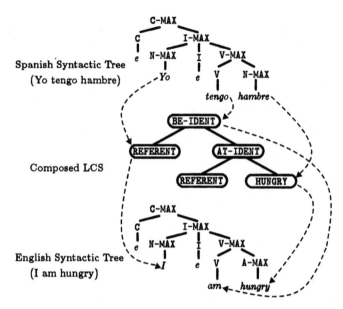

Figure 19. Translation of *Yo tengo hambre* as *I am hungry*.

tener and *be*. However, for structural realization of the PROPERTY argument Y, the system must not only choose the appropriate target-language word, but it must also choose the appropriate syntactic structure (that is, the category that will be projected from the word).

A syntactic-based scheme is inadequate for this example because it would choose the literal translation *hunger* for the source-language word *hambre*. This choice would be semantically awkward, but syntactically correct if the translation were *I have hunger*; however, if the more appropriate predicate *be* were chosen instead of *have*, the translation would be both semantically awkward and syntactically incorrect: *I am hunger*. A semantic-based scheme would make the correct lexical selection (that is, it would probably choose an argument that has a "desire to eat" property associated with it), but it would have no clue as to the syntactic form of the argument.

In the LCS approach, the lexical-selection procedure determines that both *hunger* and *hungry* lexically match the LCS for *hambre* because both are defined as the same LCS HUNGRY, which is a PROPERTY. In order to choose between these two possibilities, the system determines that the internal realization of the predicate *be* is adjectival by applying the CSR function to the type PROPERTY. Because an adjective is selected, the nominal possibility is eliminated, and the adjective *hungry* is chosen. This argument is then projected up to its maximal level (A-MAX). Note that unlike the English definition of *be*, the Spanish definition of *tener* requires a :CAT(N) override for the PROPERTY argument; this is how the argument is realized differently (that is, as N-MAX) for Spanish. Figure 19 shows the mapping from the source-language syntactic tree to the target-language syntactic tree by means of the composed LCS for example (8).

The second problem for structural realization is the potential for a divergence in *conflation* (argument incorporation) between the source- and target-language predicates. According to Talmy [1983], verbs may have a semantic representation that is not entirely exhibited at the level of syntactic structure. For example, the verb *enter* incorporates a *conflated* or "understood" particle *into* as part of its meaning structure; this particle manifests itself in the similar composite predicate *break into*. As it turns out, the Spanish equivalent of *break into* (*forzar*) has an additional conflated argument *entrada* (literally, *entry*); this argument is "understood," but not syntactically realized in English:

Juan forzó la entrada al cuarto (John forced entry to the room)
[v–MAX [v forzar] [N–MAX la entrada] [P–MAX a ···]]

(9)   ⇓

John broke into the room
[v–MAX [v break] [P–MAX into ···]]

Thus, there are three difficult tasks in the translation of *forzar* to *break*: selection of the predicate *break*, suppression (conflation) of the *entry* argument, and realization of the particle *into*.

A syntactic-based scheme has no notion of compositionality and would fail immediately in trying to map *forzar* (literally *force*) to *break* (or *vice versa*). Furthermore, it would have the problem of choosing the appropriate particle, even if it were able to provide the correct structure (a prepositional phrase). On the other hand, a robust semantic-based scheme would have the ability to compose *forzar* and *entrada*, but it would not be able to determine whether the target-language argument was to be left implicit or whether it was to be syntactically realized, because there is no notion of conflation in such a scheme.

The LCS scheme uses compositionality to map *forzar la entrada* to *break*: the LCS for *forzar* contains a CAUSE, and the LCS for *entrada* contains a GO-LOC, both of which combine to match the composite LCS for *break*. Figure 20 shows the LCS definitions used in example (9). The LCS for *break* (1) provides the meaning "THING X goes locationally into THING Y forcefully." The LCS for *forzar* contains the CAUSE portion of this action, and the LCS for *entrada* contains the locational part of this action.

Note that there is another LCS for the word *break* (2) that corresponds to "breaking an object." For the *break into* example, the matching routine of the lexical selection procedure succeeds on the first LCS definition because it is a GO-LOC and (correctly) fails on the second LCS definition because it

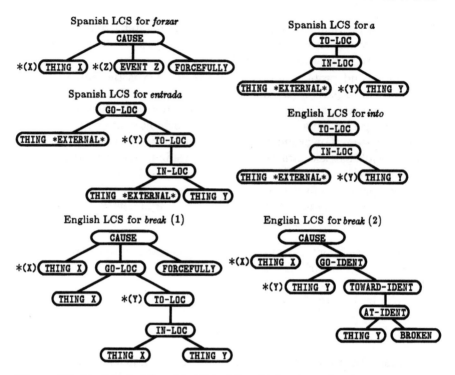

Figure 20. English and Spanish Lexical Entries for *forzar-break*.

is a GO-IDENT. At this point, the structural realization procedure determines that the GO-LOC LCS is not overtly realized for the predicate *break* because it is not associated with a '*' marker. Thus, this argument is left unrealized (fulfilling the conflation task). However, the TO argument *is* marked with a '*' in the LCS-to-syntax mappings of *break*, so the system matches this argument with the TO LCS of *into*, and the phrase *into the room* is realized. Figure 21 shows the mapping from the source-language syntactic tree to the target-language syntactic tree by means of the composed LCS for example (9).

Note that structural realization succeeds even though there are differences in syntactic realization and argument incorporation. This is because the LCS-to-syntax mapping and the compositional nature of LCS's allow syntactic distinctions for conceptually equivalent forms. LCS-to-syntax mappings and compositionality provide an advantage to the LCS approach compared to other approaches because they allow structural and conflational divergences to be accounted for during the syntactic realization portion of the translation process. The next section will show how lexical selection and syntactic realization are applied to the translation example (6) introduced earlier.

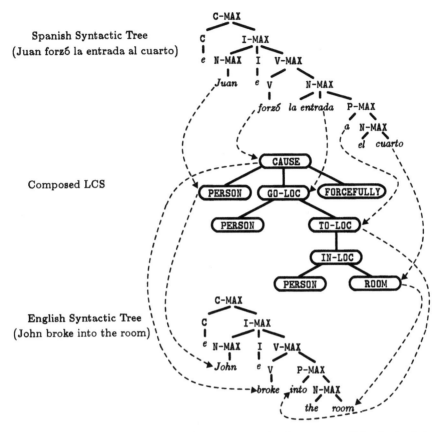

Figure 21. Translation of *Juan forzó la entrada al cuarto* as *John broke into the room*.

Stab-Dar Revisited

We now return to our translation example: *I stabbed John*. Having examined the lexical selection and syntactic realization processes in more detail, we can complete this example. Refer to figure 11 for the LCS definitions underlying the English and Spanish tokens in this sentence. Once the LCS for this sentence has been composed (see figure 14), the lexical selection procedure (step 1 of figure 15) must choose the appropriate Spanish root word by matching the underlying LCS not only at top level, but also at all lower levels. Figure 22 shows how the composed LCS is disassembled into the component LCS definitions associated with target-language words; the argument positions of these LCS definitions map to positions in the syntactic tree that is generated (as shown) for this example.

The list of Spanish root words corresponding to the top-level CAUSE LCS is shown in table 3 (a). Of these root word possibilities, a smaller set

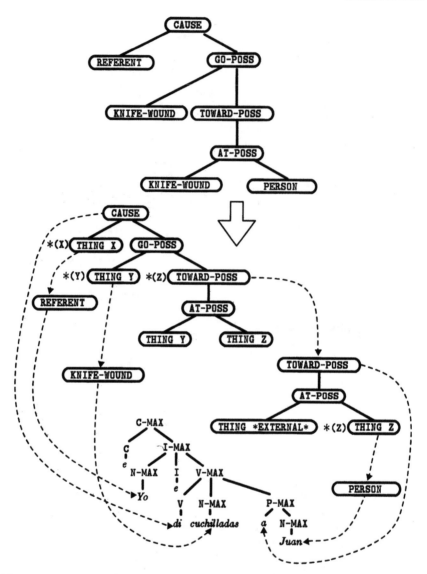

Figure 22. Disassembly of the composed LCS for the *stab* event: mapping LCS argument positions to syntactic tree positions.

matches the LCS GO-POSS at the next level as shown in table 3 (b). Note, for example, that the root word *forzar* (the literal translation of *force*) is eliminated as a possibility at this level because its associated LCS does not contain GO-POSS. Finally, at the next level (that is, the TOWARD-POSS level), only the root word *dar* matches, as shown in table 3 (c). Thus, this root is selected to be the word that will be projected. Note that lexical selection

---

(a) Spanish root words corresponding to the top-level LCS CAUSE:
⟨ROOT-WORD comprar V⟩, ⟨ROOT-WORD contar V⟩,
⟨ROOT-WORD contribuir V⟩,⟨ROOT-WORD cortar V⟩,
⟨ROOT-WORD dar V⟩, ⟨ROOT-WORD decir V⟩,
⟨ROOT-WORD embadurnar V⟩, ⟨ROOT-WORD escribir V⟩,
⟨ROOT-WORD forzar V⟩, ⟨ROOT-WORD matar V⟩,
⟨ROOT-WORD pintarrajear V⟩, ⟨ROOT-WORD recibir V⟩,
⟨ROOT-WORD romper V⟩, ⟨ROOT-WORD vender V⟩

(b) Spanish root words corresponding to the top-level LCS CAUSE
that includes GO-POSS: ⟨ROOT-WORD comprar V⟩,
⟨ROOT-WORD contribuir V⟩, ⟨ROOT-WORD cortar V⟩,
⟨ROOT-WORD dar V⟩, ⟨ROOT-WORD escribir V⟩,
⟨ROOT-WORD recibir V⟩, ⟨ROOT-WORD vender V⟩

(c) Spanish root word corresponding to the LCS GO-POSS that
includes TOWARD-POSS: ⟨ROOT-WORD dar V⟩

Table 3. Spanish Root Word Possibilities for the *stab* Event.

of this root word involves only three iterations of the matcher in a search
space that is reasonably small. Although the compositional nature of the
LCS's allows for a large set of words to be defined, the number of primitives
to search through at each level of the matching process is bounded by the
number of primitives in the system (approximately 25).

Once the appropriate root word is chosen, the CSR function is called,
and CAUSE (which is an EVENT) is realized as a verb phrase (V-MAX). Next,
the system must lexically select the arguments of the root word *dar*. The
'*' marker in the LCS-to-syntax mapping is used to determine the level at
which each argument will be realized. The first argument that gets realized
is the subject of *dar* which is the REFERENT node. The first-person singular
pronominal corresponding to this node is *yo* in Spanish; thus, this root
word is selected to be realized as the subject. The next step is to realize
the objects of *dar*. Note that unlike the *stab* definition, the *dar* definition
requires the Y argument to be overtly realized (see figure 11); thus, the
system performs an "inverse conflation" in order to arrive at the target-
language realization for this example. Because the composed LCS contains
the argument KNIFE-WOUND, this becomes the token that will be overtly realized for the Y variable in the Spanish LCS. Now the lexical selection routine
is called recursively to determine the possible target-language words for the
KNIFE-WOUND argument. As shown in figure 11, the word *cuchillada* is defined
to be a KNIFE-WOUND, so this is the root word chosen to be the direct object
of the main verb. The CSR function is then called to realize KNIFE-WOUND

(which is a THING) as a noun phrase (N-MAX).

Next, the second object of *dar* must be realized. Note that this argument must be realized at the level of TOWARD-POSS (denoted by '*' in figure 11). Because the word *a* is defined as TOWARD-POSS, this word is chosen as the target lexical item. Then the CSR function is called on TOWARD-POSS (which is a PATH) and the argument is realized as a prepositional phrase (P-MAX).

Finally, the lexical selection procedure is called once again to realize the z variable that corresponds to the PERSON argument. This argument is realized as the N-MAX *Juan*, and the Spanish syntactic tree of figure 22 is generated. The final output sentence is produced by reading off the leaves of the syntactic tree.

Limitations and Future Work

Because UNITRAN was deliberately designed to operate on one sentence at a time, there are a number of inherent limitations. For example, the system does not incorporate context or domain knowledge; thus, it cannot use discourse, situational expectations, or domain information in order to generate a sentence. Consequently, there are a number of capabilities found in other systems that cannot be reproduced here including external pronominal reference (see McDonald (MUMBLE) [1983, 1987]), paraphrasing (see Lytinen and Schank (MOPTRANS) [1982]), story telling (see Schank and Abelson (SAM) [1977] and Cullingford [1986]), interactive question-answering (see McKeown (TEXT) [1985]), *etc.* This is not to say that issues of context and domain knowledge should be ignored; on the contrary, these types of knowledge may be the next step in the evolution of the UNITRAN system.

An additional limitation of the LCS approach is the potential for generating several target-language possibilities for a given lexical-semantic primitive. It is possible that the LCS-matching procedure will not adequately cut down the target-language possibilities during the mapping from LCS to lexical items. For example, there are many open-ended classes of words (in particular, proper and common nouns, and certain adjectives and adverbs) that are not distinguishable by their LCS's. This is because LCS's provide an underlying representation of predicates and their arguments; any lexical item that does not exhibit a predicate-argument relationship must be translated by other means. Thus, if the possibility list is still quite large (more than two or three lexical items) after LCS-matching routines have finished the lexical selection process, a direct-mapping routine is used instead for lexicalization. That is, certain lexical-items (*John, book, red, quickly, etc.*) may be selected on the basis of a direct mapping to the surface form. Pustejovsky and Nirenburg [1987] provide an elegant approach to generation of open-class lexical items based on focus information. Because the system described here does not include a model of discourse, the direct-mapping technique is used for such problematic cases.

Another limitation of the system as it stands is that the notion of *aspect* is not represented in the LCS structures. For example, there is no way to establish whether an event is prolonged, repeated, instantaneous, *etc.* Thus, in the *stab* example, there is no way to determine how many times the stabbing action occurred. As it turns out, the Spanish surface realization relies on this missing information. The translation of the repetitive version of *stab* is the surface form *dar cuchilladas* (the plural form of knife-wound), whereas the translation of the non-repetitive version is the surface form *dar una cuchillada* (the singular form of knife-wound). Jackendoff *does* try to include the notion of aspect in some cases. For example, the lexical-semantic token BE-CIRC allows the progressive aspect to be expressed. However, there is no way to determine the appropriate aspect in the general case, so the system arbitrarily chooses a target-language word when such an ambiguity arises. Superimposing a system of aspect such as that of Tenny [1989] could prove to be useful in the future.

Summary

The UNITRAN system is implemented in Common Lisp and is currently running on a Symbolics 3600 series machine. The syntactic component of the system is based on GB theory, and the lexical-semantic component of this system is based on LCS theory. The principles-and-parameters approach provided by the GB-based syntactic component of the system has been shown to be valuable for machine translation because it accounts for several types of surface-syntactic phenomena across diverse languages. The LCS approach has been shown to be valuable for machine translation because it facilitates two crucial translation operations: lexical selection and syntactic realization. Furthermore, because it is compositional in nature, the LCS representation aids in tackling the difficult problems of structural, thematic, and conflational divergence.

We have seen that the definition of a potentially large (theoretically infinite) set of words is supported by the ability to combine the same lexical-semantic primitives in an indefinite number of ways. However, as shown in the last example, the search space for root-word selection is not explosive because there are only a small number of primitives that must be searched at each level of the matching procedure. In addition, LCS descriptions seem to provide the abstraction necessary for selecting appropriate target-language terms with minimal dependence on syntax, and they also provide the necessary mechanism for realizing arguments without regard to conceptual considerations. In particular, lexical entries are divided into two levels of description—lexical-semantic and syntactic—the former used for lexically selecting arguments, and the latter used for syntactically "fitting" these arguments into a predicate-argument structure.

In its description of several approaches to machine translation, this chapter has demonstrated a need for a translator to operate cross-linguistically despite the potential idiosyncrasies for a given language. Two types of knowledge (language-specific and language-independent) have been shown to be crucial for fulfillment of the translation task. Both of these types of knowledge have proven to be useful during syntactic processing and semantic processing.

The approach presented here tries to incorporate some of the more promising syntactic and semantic aspects of existing translation systems. Specifically, the model incorporates structural information for realization and positioning of arguments. Unlike direct-replacement and entirely syntactic-based approaches, however, it avoids non-compositional direct-mapping word selection. In addition, the model has the ability to select target terms on the basis of compositional properties. Unlike many semantic-based approaches, however, it does not rely upon context-dependent routines, and it does not entirely abandon syntactic considerations for selection and realization of root words and their associated arguments.

In summary, this chapter has shown that the UNITRAN system solves a number of traditional problems for machine translation by combining:

1   A principles-and-parameters-based component to handle syntactic variation, and

2   An LCS-based component to handle problems of thematic, structural, and conflational divergence.

References

Bley-Vroman, Robert [1988], personal correspondence.

Carbonell, Jaime G., Richard E. Cullingford, and Anatole V. Gershman [1981], "Steps Toward Knowledge-Based Machine Translation," *IEEE Transactions on Pattern Analysis and Machine Intelligence* PAMI-3:4.

This chapter describes research done at the Artificial Intelligence Laboratory of the Massachusetts Institute of Technology. Support for this research has been provided by NSF Grant DCR-85552543 under a Presidential Young Investigator's Award to Professor Robert C. Berwick. Useful guidance and commentary during this research were provided by Bob Berwick, Michael Brent, Bruce Dawson, Sandiway Fong, and Mike Kashket.

Chomsky, Noam A. [1982], *Lectures on Government and Binding*, Foris Publications, Dordrecht.

Chomsky, Noam A. [1982], *Some Concepts and Consequences of the Theory of Government and Binding*, MIT Press, Cambridge, MA.

Chomsky, Noam A. [1986], *Knowledge of Language: Its Nature, Origin and Use*, MIT Press, Cambridge, MA.

Cullingford, Richard E. [1986], *Natural Language Processing: A Knowledge-Engineering Approach*, Rowman and Littlefield, Totowa, NJ.

Dorr, Bonnie J. [1987], "UNITRAN: A Principle-Based Approach to Machine Translation," AI Technical Report 1000, Master of Science, Department of Electrical Engineering and Computer Science, Massachusetts Institute of Technology, Cambridge, MA.

Dorr, Bonnie J. [1989a], "Lexical Conceptual Structure and Generation in Machine Translation," in *Proceedings of the Eleventh Annual Conference of the Cognitive Science Society*, Ann Arbor, MI.

Dorr, Bonnie J. [1989b], "Conceptual Basis of the Lexicon in Machine Translation," First Annual Workshop on Lexical Acquisition, IJCAI-89, Detroit, MI.

Dorr, Bonnie J. [to appear], "Lexical Conceptual Structure and Machine Translation," Ph.D. dissertation, Department of Electrical Engineering and Computer Science, Massachusetts Institute of Technology, Cambridge, MA.

Hale, Kenneth and M. Laughren [1983], "Warlpiri Dictionary Entries," Warlpiri Lexicon Project, Massachusetts Institute of Technology, Cambridge, MA.

Hale, Kenneth and Jay Keyser [1986], "Some Transitivity Alternations in English," Lexicon Project Working Papers #7, Center for Cognitive Science, Massachusetts Institute of Technology, Cambridge, MA.

Hutchins, W. J. [1978], "Progress in Documentation: Machine Translation and Machine-Aided Translation," in *Journal of Documentation*, 34:2, pp. 119–159.

Jackendoff, Ray S. [1983], *Semantics and Cognition*, MIT Press, Cambridge, MA.

Jackendoff, Ray S. [1990], *Semantic Structures*, MIT Press, Cambridge, MA.

Jordan, S. R., A. F. R. Brown, and F. C. Hutton [1976], "Computerized Russian Translation at ORNL," in *Proceedings of the ASIS Annual Meeting*, San Francisco, CA, p. 163; also in *ASIS Journal*, 28:1, pp. 26–33, 1977.

Lytinen, Steven and Roger Schank [1982], "Representation and Translation" Technical Report 234, Department of Computer Science, Yale University, New Haven, CT.

Lytinen, Steven L. [1985], "Integrating Syntax and Semantics," in *Proceedings of the Conference on Theoretical and Methodological Issues in Machine Translation of Natural Languages*, Colgate University, Hamilton, NY, pp. 167–177.

Lytinen, Steven L. [1987], "Integrating Syntax and Semantics," in *Machine Translation: Theoretical and Methodological Issues*, edited by Sergei Nirenburg, Cambridge University Press, Cambridge, England.

McDonald, David D. [1983], "Natural Language Generation as a Computational Problem," in *Computational Models of Discourse*, edited by Brady, Michael and Robert C. Berwick, MIT Press, Cambridge, MA, pp. 209–265.

McDonald, David D. [1987], "Natural Language Generation: Complexities and Techniques," in *Machine Translation: Theoretical and Methodological Issues*, edited by Sergei Nirenburg, Cambridge University Press, Cambridge, England.

McKeown, Kathleen [1985], *Text Generation: Using Discourse Strategies and Focus Constraints to Generate Natural Language Text*, Cambridge University Press, Cambridge, England.

Nirenburg, Sergei [1986], "Machine Translation," Presented as a Tutorial at the 24th Annual Meeting of the Association for Computational Linguistics, Columbia University, New York City, NY.

Nirenburg, Sergei, Victor Raskin, and Allen B. Tucker [1987], "The Structure of Interlingua in TRANSLATOR," in *Machine Translation: Theoretical and Methodological Issues*, edited by Sergei Nirenburg, Cambridge University Press, Cambridge, England.

Nirenburg, Sergei, Rita McCardell, Eric Nyberg, Scott Huffman, Edward, Kenschaft, and Irene Nirenburg [1988], "Lexical Realization in Natural Language Generation," in *Proceedings of the Second International Conference on Theoretical and Methodological Issues in Machine Translation of Natural Languages*, Carnegie Mellon University, Pittsburgh, PA.

Pustejovsky, James, and Sergei Nirenburg [1987], "Lexical Selection in the Process of Language Generation," in *Proceedings of the 25th Annual Conference of the Association for Computational Linguistics*, Stanford University, Stanford, CA, pp. 201–206.

Rappaport, Malka, and Beth Levin [1986], "What to Do with Theta-Roles," Lexicon Project Working Papers #11, Center for Cognitive Science, Massachusetts Institute of Technology, Cambridge, MA.

Schank, Roger C., and Robert Abelson [1977], *Scripts, Plans, Goals, and Understanding*, Lawrence Erlbaum Associates, Inc., Hillsdale, NJ.

Sharp, Randall M. [1985], "A Model of Grammar Based on Principles of Government and Binding," Master of Science, Department of Computer Science, University of British Columbia.

Slocum, Jonathan [1984], "METAL: The LRC Machine Translation System," Working Paper LRC-84-2, Linguistics Research Center, University of Texas, Austin, TX.

Talmy, Leonard [1983], "How Language Structures Space," in *Spatial Orientation: Theory, Research, and Application*, edited by Pick, Herbert L., Jr., and Linda P. Acredolo, Plenum Press, New York, NY.

Tenny, Carol [1989], "The Aspectual Interface Hypothesis," Lexicon Project Working Paper 31, Center for Cognitive Science at MIT, Cambridge, MA.

14

Explanation-based learning occurs when something useful is retained from an explanation exercise, usually an explanation of how some particular problem can be solved. In one famous example, an integration program learned to integrate faster by explaining to itself why example-evoked transformation sequences worked. In another, an object recognition program learned to recognize cups by explaining to itself why a certain object is a cup using knowledge about bricks, bowls, briefcases, and what cups are for.

If explanation is based on sound theory, as it is in the integration example, then the learning process speeds up future problem solving, but the scope of the learning-augmented theory remains unchanged. No performance errors are introduced, but no new problems can be solved. In contrast, if explanation is based on fragmentary and often defective experience, explanation can be a guide to when that experience can be deployed. Thus one kind of explanation provides speed up; another kind of explanation provides new knowledge.

Experience is not sound theory, however, and wrong things may be learned accidentally, as subsequent failures will likely demonstrate. In this chapter, Winston and Rao describe ways to isolate the facts that cause failures, ways to explain why those facts cause problems, and ways to repair learning mistakes. In particular, their program learns to distinguish pails from cups after learned knowledge about cups leads a recognition program to think pails are cups.

Repairing Learned Knowledge using Experience

Patrick Henry Winston
Satyajit Rao

Becoming an Expert Requires Repair as well as Acquisition

For most of us, in most domains, we get by with simple rulelike knowledge, handling ordinary situations well enough. But if we choose to become an expert in some domain, we begin to see the unusual cases, which we handle by way of an exception-recognizing mechanism or by repairing our original, rulelike knowledge.

In this paper, we show how to repair rulelike knowledge by exploiting situations where the rulelike knowledge leads to incorrect conclusions. Our implemented program learns to distinguish pails from cups after a learned cup recognition rule incorrectly identifies certain pails as cups.

Our work builds on the vast literature on explanation-based learning (see Mitchell *et al.* [1986] for a review). In particular, we build on the ideas in Winston *et al.* [1983], which explained how to acquire rulelike knowledge about what cups look like in the course of explaining how cups achieve their function.

Our Repair Work Builds on Analogy and Explanation

To understand our approach, it is helpful to review the explanation-based analogical reasoning that produces the original rulelike knowledge.

First, note that the *cause* relations in precedents constitutes an implicit AND tree with each node in each AND tree corresponding to a relation and each branch corresponding to a relation-linking *cause* relation.

Glass Precedent

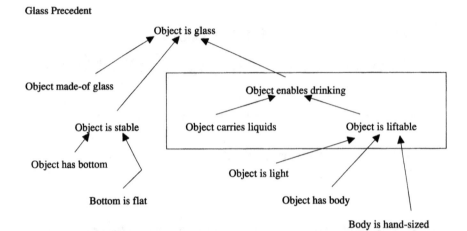

Figure 1. The glass precedent. Precedents include relations that are tied together with *cause* relations, all of which constitute an implied AND tree. The boxed part of the glass precedent helps to bridge a gap in a problem situation shown in the next figure.

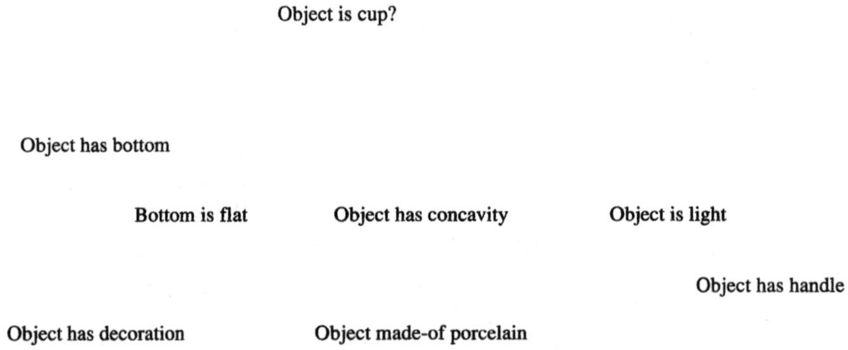

Object is cup?

Object has bottom

Bottom is flat   Object has concavity   Object is light

Object has handle

Object has decoration   Object made-of porcelain

Figure 2. A problem. It contains a relation to be explained, shown with a question mark, and some relations that are known.

Figure 1 shows the *cause* relations in the precedent that describes what it takes to be a glass.

An implicit AND tree can help to bridge the gap in a problem between something that is to be explained and things that are already known. In figure 2 the problem is to show that an unknown object is a cup by connecting the relation, *object is cup?*, to some of the other relations using implicit AND tree fragments from various precedents. In figure 3, the relation, *ob-*

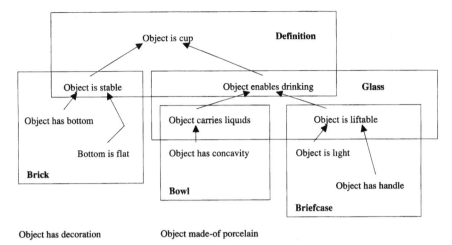

Figure 3. Boxes indicate the origins of the various precedent-supplied AND tree fragments that bridge the gap between the relation to be explained and some of the relations that are known. Only the relevant parts of the precedents are shown.

ject is cup, is connected to some of the other relations using fragments from the brick, glass, bowl, and briefcase precedents along with a functional cup definition expressed itself in the same form as the precedents.

The gap-filling AND tree, consisting of fragments from one or more definitions and precedents, can be retained for future use. Moreover, the leaves of the AND tree in the new chunk of knowledge can be viewed as the *if* conditions in an implicit *if-then* rule. The root of the AND tree can be viewed as the *then* condition. The other nodes can be viewed as *providing* conditions. The *providing* conditions, like the terminal *then* condition, are explained by the *if* conditions.

Here the cup-recognition recollection is viewed as an *if-then* rule:

Cup-recognition Recollection:

If	The object has a bottom
	The bottom is flat
	An object has a concavity
	The object is light weight
	The object has a handle
Then	The object is a cup
Providing	The object is stable
	The object enables drinking
	The object carries liquids
	The object is liftable

Note that although the retained knowledge can be viewed as an *if-then* rule, it is really a full-blown, gap-filling AND tree. We call these retained chunks of AND tree *recollections* to emphasize both that something has been remembered and that there has been an explicit re-collection of knowledge that was formerly distributed implicitly across one or more precedents.

Because we choose to express recollections in the same representation as ordinary situation descriptions and definitions, our analogical reasoning machinery does not care whether the source of a gap-bridging AND tree is a precedent, definition, or an already-learned recollection.

Censors shut off conclusions

Finally, because precedents and precedent combinations involve only plausible explanation, there has to be a way of shutting off conclusions. If there is strong, obvious evidence that indicates one of the providing conditions cannot be true in a particular situation, then the explanation that links the *if* conditions to the *then* condition collapses in that particular situation.

A recollection or precedent is called a *censor* whenever it provides evidence that a providing condition in another recollection or precedent cannot be true. Thus censors are just ordinary recollections or precedents used in a special way.

Explanation-based learning offers more than speedup

Importantly, explanation-based learning based on precedents is particularly useful when the learner has weak or faulty knowledge of how individual precedents can be combined into larger explanations. The reason is that particular problems, often supplied by a knowledgeable teacher, provide heuristic evidence about which precedents can be stuck together usefully. Thus the learning is more than just a speed-up phenomenon.

Cups and Pails Illustrate the Problem

The cup-recognition recollection introduced in the previous section can recognize a variety of cups, including porcelain cups and metal cups. Unfortunately, it also recognizes a variety of pails, including metal pails and wooden pails.

Our general approach to improving the situation involves three desiderata. First, the old recollection should be repaired, rather than a totally new one constructed, on the ground that incremental change is less risky than radical change. Second, the repair procedure should exploit failures on the ground that programs should learn from mistakes. And third, the exploitation procedure should use precedents on the ground that experience is the best guide in the absence of sound theory.

These desiderata lead to the following questions:

- How can a program use failures to *isolate* suspicious relations that should perhaps prevent a recollection from being misapplied?

- How can a program use precedents to *explain* why those now isolated suspicious relations should prevent a recollection from being misapplied?

- How can a program use explanations to *repair* a recollection, preventing further misapplication?

Near-Miss Groups Isolate Suspicious Relations

If a metal pail differs from a porcelain cup only in the position of handle attachment, then we would say that the pail is a near miss. Unfortunately, there are many differences, both relevant and irrelevant: the pail is metal, but the cup is porcelain; the metal pail is gray, but the porcelain cup is white with balloons painted on the side; the metal pail carries oats, but the porcelain cup carries coffee.

The metal pail is a *false-success situation*. Let us assume that our recollection-repair system knows that the metal pail in figure 4c is a false success either because a teacher says so or because an effort to drink from it leads to failure.

Let us also assume that our recollection-repair system knows the wooden pail in figure 4d is also a false success. Both pails differ from the porcelain cup in figure 4a in many ways, and similarly, both pails differ from the tin cup in figure 4b in many ways.

Importantly, however, there are fewer ways in which *both* the metal pail and the wooden pail differ from *both* the porcelain cup and the tin cup: for example, the cups have fixed handles, whereas the pails have hinged handles.

As the Venn diagram in figure 4 shows, all four objects can be used together to separate signallike explanations from noiselike distractions. Because the recollection allows all four objects to be recognized as cups, the antecedent relations in the recollection, viewed as an if-then rule, must lie in the intersection of all the relation sets describing those four objects. Similarly, the relations, if any, that distinguish the true-success situations from the false-success situations must lie in the union of the two relation subsets shown shaded in figure 4.

Because the relations in the true-success set and the false-success set are likely candidates for forming explanations, we say that those relations are *suspicious relations*. Also, we say that the situations used to identify

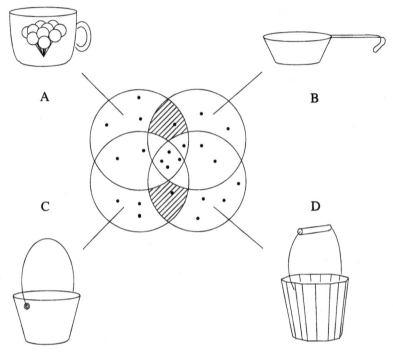

Figure 4. A near-miss group. The dots represent relations. Suspicious relations, the ones in the shaded area, are suspicious because they are in all the true successes but none of the false successes or because they are in all the false successes but none of the true successes.

the suspicious relations constitute a *near-miss group* because they work together as a group to perform like a   single example and a single near miss.

Clearly, the isolation of suspicious relations is just a simple matter of unioning, intersecting, and differencing the relations that appear in the true successes and false successes.

In general, there will be more than one suspicious relation, but the more true successes and false successes we have, the fewer suspicious relations there are likely to be. Note, however, that *isolating* failure-causing relations is not the same as *explaining* failure and *repairing* the flaw.

Suspicious Relation Types Determine Overall Repair Strategy

For suspicious relations that are common to true successes only, there are several possible explanations for how the recollection, viewed as an AND tree, is flawed. For example, a node may involve the wrong relation, a branch corresponding to a particular *cause* relation may be missing, or a chain of two or more branches may have been collapsed into one, eliminating one or more providing conditions that would otherwise be vulnerable to attack by censors. The recollection should be repaired accordingly.

In our example, the relation *handle is fixed* is found in both cups but it is *not* found in either pail. If a program can find a way to include this relation in the rule, then the rule would be more discriminating. It would still recognize the cups, but it would not recognize either pail.

One explanation-free recollection repair would be to include the *handle is fixed* relation in the rule form of the recollection as a new *if* condition:

Repaired Cup-recognition Recollection:

If	The object has a bottom
	The bottom is flat
	An object has a concavity
	The object is light weight
	The object has a handle
	The handle is fixed
Then	The object is a cup
Providing	The object is stable
	The object enables drinking
	The object carries liquids
	The object is liftable

For suspicious relations that are common to false successes only, the failure is the result of not knowing that a providing condition cannot be true. In our example, the relation *handle is hinged* is found in both pails but is *not* found in either cup. If a program can find a way to include this relation in a new censor that attacks one of the providing conditions, that censor would make the rule more discriminating. The rule would still recognize the cups, but it would not recognize either pail.

One explanation-free approach is to manufacture a censor directly out of the *handle is hinged* relation and the *object is not a cup* relation:

New Censor:

If	The handle is hinged
Then	The object is not a cup.

As described, both the cup repair and the censor creation are *ad hoc* because there is no explanation for why the new *if* condition or the new censor should work. We can do better.

The Solution May Be To Explain the True-Success Suspicious Relations, Changing the Recollection

Before showing how we actually handle true-success suspicious relations, we display the result in our cup-and-pail example. Figure 5 shows both the recollection tree of the original, faulty recollection and the recollection tree of the repaired, correct recollection.

Figure 5. A recollection tree before and after repair. The repaired recollection recognizes only cups; it does not recognize pails.

Comparing the recollection trees of the faulty and repaired recollections, you see that the *handle is fixed* relation, which is common to the true successes, now appears in the repaired recollection tree. There are also two other new relations *object is manipulable* and *object is orientable*.

The old recollection was too general because you cannot be sure you can drink from an object just because it carries liquids and is liftable—it has to be orientable by virtue of having a fixed handle. The new recollection still recognizes the cups, but the increased specificity of the recollection prevents it from recognizing the pails.

To make the repair, our program does a breadth-first reexamination of all the relations in the recollection tree, looking for a relation with an explanation that needs replacement. For each relation reexamined, our program looks for a collection of precedents that ties the reexamined relation to at least one of the true-success suspicious relations along with some or all of the relations that lie in the intersection of all the successes.

If such a collection of precedents is found, it is used to replace the subtree beneath the reexamined relation, thus explaining the reexamined relation in a new way.

The new explanation should be as short as possible because the longer the chain of precedent-supplied *cause* relations, the less reliable the conclusion. After all, the contributing precedents supply *cause* relations that are only likely, not certain. Consequently, we initially limit the reexamination effort to the following precedents:

- The precedents originally used to form the recollection. These are included in the expectation that much of the recollection will be unchanged and therefore constructable from the original precedents. These original precedents constitute the initial *top set*.

- Those precedents in which one of the true-success suspicious relations causes something. These precedents constitute the initial *bottom set*.

When our program reexamines a relation, it looks for a way of explaining that relation using all but one of the precedents in the combined top and bottom sets. The exception is the precedent that contained the cause relations that explained the reexamined relation. This precedent is omitted so as to explore the hypothesis that it has provided an incorrect explanation, leading to the recollection's defective behavior.

In the cup-and-pail example, the top set consist of the cup definition along with the brick, glass, bowl, and briefcase precedents. The bottom set consist of all those precedents in which the true-success suspicious relation, *handle is fixed*, causes something.

For our cup-and-pail example, our database contained about 100 miscellaneous precedents, including the brick, glass, bowl, and briefcase precedents, the cup definition, and two other precedents that turn out to be relevant, namely the door and straw precedents.

The *handle is fixed* relation appears in our database in only the door precedent, in which it causes *door is orientable*. Thus the bottom set consists of the door precedent alone.

Accordingly, when our program reexamines the *object is cup* relation, it uses the brick, glass, bowl, briefcase, and door precedents. It does not use the cup definition because the *object is cup* relation is caused by something

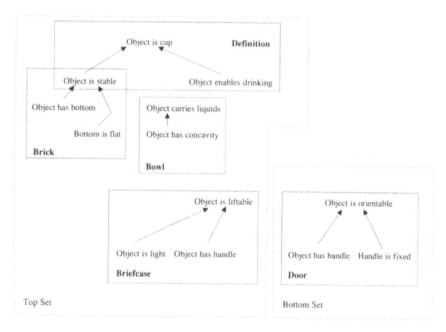

Figure 6. Reexamination fails for the top and bottom sets are not connected to one another. Only the relevant parts of the precedents are shown.

in the cup definition. Our program fails because the top and bottom sets do not connect the reexamined relation, *object is cup*, to the suspicious relation *handle is fixed*.

Similarly, when our program reexamines the *object is stable* relation, it uses the cup definition along with the glass, bowl, briefcase, and door precedents, but fails again. When it reexamines the *object enables drinking* relation, it uses the cup definition along with the brick, bowl, briefcase, and door precedents. Again it fails, because it cannot connect *object enables drinking* to *handle is fixed*, as shown in figure 6.

Our program also fails when it goes on to try reexamining the *object transports liquids* and the *object is liftable* relations. Evidently, more precedents have to be used.

Incorporating true-success suspicious relations may require search

Once our program concludes that more precedents have to be considered, it augments the precedents in either the top or the bottom sets.

To augment the top set, our program identifies new precedents in which there is a relation with two properties: the relation must cause something in an existing top set precedent; and the relation must be caused by something

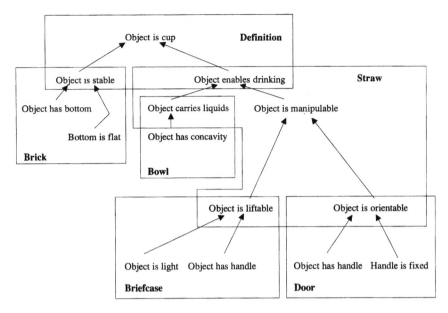

Figure 7. A recollection tree after repair with contributing precedents is shown. Note that the straw precedent, having augmented the bottom set, bridges the gap between the old recollection and the suspicious relation, *handle is fixed*. Now only cups are recognized as cups; pails are not. Only the relevant parts of the precedents are shown.

in the new precedent. Thus the new top-set precedents extend the *cause* chains that lead up through the existing top-set precedents.

Symmetrically, to augment the bottom set, our program identifies new precedents in which there is a relation with two properties: the relation must be explained, in part, by something in an existing bottom set precedent; and the relation must help to explain something in the new precedent. Thus the new bottom-set precedents extend the *cause* relation chains that start down in the existing bottom-set precedents.

To keep the number of precedents as limited as possible, our program augments the set with fewer precedents. In our example, this means augmenting the bottom set because it currently has only one precedent, the door precedent. The straw precedent is added because it contains the relation *straw is orientable*: in the straw precedent, *straw is orientable* causes *straw is manipulable*, and in the door precedent, *handle is fixed* causes *door is orientable*.

Now the reexamination process starts over with the augmented bottom set. As before, reexamination fails on the topmost relation, *object is cup*, and on the first of the relations in the next layer, *object is stable*. However, when our program reexamines the *object enables drinking* relation,

it succeeds in connecting *object enables drinking* with the *handle is fixed*
relation via the definition, the new straw precedent, and the existing door
precedent, as shown in figure 7. Of course, all of the precedents shown in
the figure contain details that are not shown so as to avoid clutter.

Note that the recollection's AND tree is restructured as necessary without reasoning explicitly about wrong or missing nodes and branches. The
restructured AND tree can be viewed as the following if-then rule:

Repaired Cup-recognition rule:

If	The object has a bottom
	The bottom is flat
	An object has a concavity
	The object is light-weight
	The object has a handle
	The handle is fixed
Then	The object is a cup
Providing	The object is stable
	The object enables drinking
	The object carries liquids
	The object is manipulable

Our program tries to explain all true successes

Because we want to incorporate all of the true-success suspicious relations
into the revised recollection tree, our breadth-first reexamination procedure
works top-down. That way, later repairs cannot conflict with the contribution of earlier ones. The reexamination process stops when all true-success
suspicious relations are incorporated into the revised recollection tree.

The Solution May Be To Explain the False-Success Suspicious Relations, Creating a Censor

The repaired recollection tree works on all of our cup-versus-pail problems
because none of the pail descriptions contains a *handle is fixed* relation.
There remains a danger, however, that our problem solver will try hard
to show that a given pail has a fixed handle even though it already knows
that the pail's description contains a *handle is hinged* relation.

Fortunately, however, our system not only repairs recollection trees but
also builds new ones that can serve as censors. In the cup-and-pail example,
the censor constructed, expressed as an *if-then* rule, is quite simple:

Hinged-handle Censor:

If   Handle is hinged
Then   Handle is not fixed

Once this censor is created, our system blocks any attempt to show that a handle is fixed, given that it is hinged. The recollection still recognizes the cups, and fails to recognize the pails, but now the censor blocks useless effort directed at showing that pails have fixed handles.

Censors are created after our repair program has finished explaining the true-success suspicious relations. To create censors, our program does a breadth-first reexamination of all the relations in the repaired recollection tree, looking for precedents that tie the negation of each reexamined relation to a false-success relation. The resulting explanations establish why the false-success suspicious relations should block recognition. These explanations, in turn, permit the creation of new censors.

Initially the precedent set is limited to the following to keep explanations as short as possible:

- Precedents in which the negation of the reexamined relation is caused by something. These precedents constitute the initial *top set*.

- Those precedents in which one of the false-success suspicious relations causes something. These precedents constitute the initial *bottom set*.

Here the idea is to find an explanation for the negation of the reexamined relation that includes at least one of the false-success suspicious relations along with some or all of the relations that lie in the intersection of all the successes. If our program finds such a collection of precedents, it creates a new censor from that collection of precedents.

In the cup-and-pail example, our program reexamines the *object is cup* relation, looking for a chain of precedents that link *object is not a cup* to the suspicious relation, *handle is hinged*. This reexamination must fail because there are no precedents in our database that show that something is not a cup.

Eventually, however, our program's breadth-first reexamination tries to show the *handle is not fixed* relation, given the false-success suspicious relation, *handle is hinged*. At this point, our limited database provides only one precedent, the briefcase, which finds its way into both the top and bottom sets because *handle is hinged* is connected to *handle is not fixed* by a cause relation. This explains the presence of the false-success relation and generates the new censor.

In general, when all false-success suspicious relations are incorporated into the revised recollection tree, the reexamination process stops because everything is completely explained. While false-success suspicious relations remain, the breadth-first reexamination procedure continues.

There Is a Panoply of Heuristic Choices

The keys to our program's operation are the isolation of suspicious relations using near-miss groups and the use of those suspicious relations in reducing the search for an explanation-based repair. In implementing our program, many choices were decided by heuristic arguments, or lacking anything else, plain simplicity. Here are some examples:

- Our program could search for the simplest explanation for a suspicious relation according to, say, the number of precedents involved in the explanation, or the number of links in the causal chains contained in the precedents, or the total number of links in the causal chain leading from the recollection's root, through the precedents, to the suspicious relation. For simplicity, we decided to have our program be content with the first explanation found.

- Our program could terminate when just one suspicious relation has been incorporated into the recollection AND tree or into a new censor. We decided to have our program keep on looking for explanations for the other suspicious relations, within resource limits, so as to learn as much as possible.

- Our program could use smaller initial top sets when trying to explain true-success suspicious relations. We decided to include all of the original precedents to retain as much of the old recollection's AND tree as possible.

- There are many possible give-up conditions. We have our program give up after two rounds of precedent-set expansion on the ground that the more precedents involved, the flimsier the argument.

Many Situations May Contribute to Recollection Repair and Censor Creation

Minimally, only two descriptions are required to learn something as a byproduct of analogical problem solving: an exercise and a precedent. In the cup-recollection repair, many descriptions are involved: there are five precedents held over from the creation of the original recollection, two true-success situations, two false-success situations, two new precedents used to revise the recollection, and one precedent used to create the censor. Evidently, considerable knowledge can be brought to bear, in general:

- Many precedents and previously generated recollections can contribute to the creation of a new recollection.

- Many successes and many near misses may be involved in isolating the suspicious relations.

- Many precedents and previously generated recollections can contribute to a repair or to the creation of a new censor.

- Many cycles of isolation, repair, and censor creation may be needed to correct all problems.

Failure Stimulates a Search for More Detailed Descriptions

Note that it is the job of a benign teacher to be sure that recognition errors can be traced to suspicious relations. If there are no suspicious relations, there are two ways to correct the situation:

- First, although the lack of suspicious relations indicates that there is no common explanation for failure, there may be just a few explanations, each of which is common to a subset of the true successes or the false successes. The problem is to partition situations into groups, inside each of which there is a consistent explanation for failure.
- Second, the lack of suspicious relations may indicate that the situations needs to be described at a finer grain, adding more detail, so that an explicit explanation emerges.

Of these two ways to correct the situation, the more interesting is the one that leads to more detailed description. Typically, AI programs must be supplied from the beginning with all they need to know. Here, however, failure to find an explanation could initiate a search for more information.

Boris Katz has suggested a way of narrowing that search by hypothesizing oversights. Suppose, for example, that we fail to mention that the metal cup in figure 4 has a fixed handle. Then nothing lies in the intersection set, but the cup examples exhibit many relations, including the *handle is fixed*, *object is white*, and *object made-of metal* relations, that are not found in any pail description. Accordingly, we can temporarily assume that these relations are true-success relations, one at a time, looking for a relation that would enable our program to repair the recollection. Once such a relation is found, we can then ask the teacher to affirm that the relation holds in all the true-success situations and holds in none of the false-success situations. In our example, the question posed would be something like "I think the metal cup's handle must be fixed. Is it?"

Generalizing the oversight-hypothesizing approach, if the *handle is fixed* relation appears in some cups, but in none of the ones that happen to be involved in the near miss group, it still makes sense to test them with our procedure rather than asking about random relations.

Near-Miss Groups Solve an Old Problem

In 1970, Winston showed how the notion of what an arch looks like can be learned from samples and near misses. At that time, it was necessary to rank the importance of various relations *a priori* because it was rare that

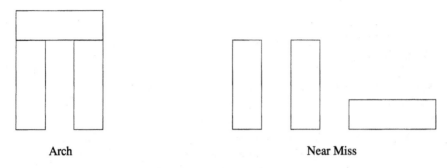

Figure 8. An arch and a near miss. One explanation is that the near miss is
not an arch because it loses the *supported-by* relations between the lintel and
the posts; another is that it is not an arch because it gains a *right-of* relation
between the lintel and both of the posts.

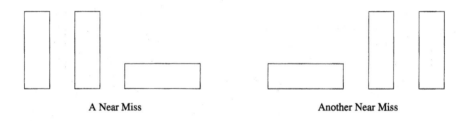

Figure 9. A near-miss group. The only common differences perceived between
each of these and an arch is the lack of *supported-by* relations between the lintel
and the posts.

only one relation would emerge when comparing the current arch model
with a near miss. In figure 8, the near miss can be explained in more than
one way. The ambiguity can be resolved by supplying a second near miss
and treating the two near misses as a near-miss group. Figure 9 illustrates
this.

Related Work

The work in this section is based mainly on early near-miss oriented learning work [Winston 1970] and on more recent work on extracting rules from
Shakespearean plots [Winston 1980, 1982] and on deducing what cups look
like from precedents [Winston et al. 1983]. All of this is described in *Artificial Intelligence, Second Edition* [Winston 1984].

The idea of using differences to focus learning resonates with the difference-based reasoning work of Falkenhainer [1988] in which he uses differences between working devices and nonworking devices, plus domain knowledge, to deduce why the nonworking devices fail.

One defect of the idea described in this paper is that every concept has to have a name, but in many of our experiments, the concepts do not correspond well to English words, forcing us to invent awkward, multiply-hyphenated names. An approach to dealing with this defect is explained in a forthcoming thesis by Rao.

References

Falkenhainer, Brian [1988], "The Utility of Difference-Based Reasoning," *National Conference on Artificial Intelligence*, Saint Paul, Minnesota.

Kratkiewicz, Kendra [1984], "Improving Learned Rules Using Near Miss Groups," B.S. Thesis, Department of Electrical Engineering and Computer Science, Massachusetts Institute of Technology, with Winston, Ms. Kratkiewicz showed that near-miss groups could pull informative differences out of complicated descriptions of historic conflicts.

Mitchell, T. M., R. M. Keller, and S. T. Kedar-Cabelli [1986], "Explanation-based Generalization: A Unifying View," *Machine Learning*, vol. 1, no. 1.

Winston, Patrick Henry [1970], "Learning Structural Descriptions from Examples," Ph.D. Thesis, Massachusetts Institute of Technology. The arch example is introduced, along with the notion of near misses. A shortened version is in *The Psychology of Computer Vision*, edited by Patrick Henry Winston, McGraw-Hill Book Company, New York.

Winston, Patrick Henry [1980], "Learning and Reasoning by Analogy," *Communications of the Association for Computing Machinery*, vol. 23, no. 12.

Winston, Patrick Henry [1982], "Learning New Principles from Precedents and Exercises," *Artificial Intelligence Journal*, vol. 19, no. 3.

Winston, Patrick Henry [1984], *Artificial Intelligence, Second Edition*, Addison-Wesley. Analogical reasoning using precedents is described in detail Chapter 12. Ignore the description of the matcher—there are much better matchers now.

Winston, Patrick Henry, Thomas O. Binford, Boris Katz, and Michael R. Lowry [1983], "Learning Physical Descriptions from Functional Definitions, Examples, and Precedents," *National Conference on Artificial Intelligence*, Washington, DC. Also described in *Artificial Intelligence, Second Edition*, Addison-Wesley, by Patrick Henry Winston, 1984.

15

Today the world is full of simple rule-based and frame-based expert systems. Some companies claim to have hundreds of such systems in daily use. Some government organizations claim to have saved hundreds of millions with one or two. All this seems incredible to many researchers inasmuch as rule-based and frame-based systems mainly embody thin, associational knowledge rather than deep, model-based knowledge.

This chapter is about the deep, model-based alternative, and the creation of systems more deserving of the expert label. Davis and Hamscher use electronic troubleshooting as a research testbed, convincingly demonstrating the advantages of the model-based approach. They observe, for example, that models enable programs to be device independent whereas the rule-based and frame-based systems generally have to be redone for each new device. And importantly, they show that models enable programs to zero in on the difference between desired and actual behavior, thus concentrating on explaining symptoms, rather than wasting time with irrelevancies.

Having divided the troubleshooting problem into hypothesis generation, hypothesis testing, and hypothesis discrimination, Davis and Hamscher introduce many domain-independent principles and explain an extraordinary collection of problem-solving paradigms, including constraint suspension and guided probing. They conclude, however, that much research remains, for the next problem is to create programs that not only use models, but also invent their own models as needed.

Model-Based Reasoning: Troubleshooting

Randall Davis
Walter C. Hamscher

In recent years considerable interest has been generated around the topic of model-based reasoning, particularly its application to diagnosis and troubleshooting. This chapter surveys the current state of the art, reviewing areas that are well understood and exploring areas that present challenging research topics. It begins by describing the nature of the task, exploring what is given and what we are trying to produce. As will become clear, there are considerable advantages to reasoning from a model of structure and behavior, we need representations for both; we review the set of techniques in current use and examine their strengths and weaknesses.

A considerable part of the chapter is devoted to how those representations are used to do model-based diagnosis. We view the fundamental paradigm as the interaction of prediction and observation, and explore it by examining its three fundamental subproblems: *Generating* hypotheses by reasoning from a symptom to a collection of components whose misbehavior may plausibly have caused that symptom; *testing* each hypothesis to see whether it can account for all available observations of device behavior; then *discriminating* among those that survive testing. In any real system these three are likely to be intertwined for reasons of efficiency. We treat them independently to simplify the presentation and because our goal is a knowledge-level analysis—an understanding of what reasoning capabilities arise from the varieties of knowledge available to the program.

The presentation is structured as a sequence of increasingly elaborate examples, starting with the simplest approach and adding successively more knowledge, producing successively more constraints that can be brought to bear. This is useful both as a way of simplifying the presentation and

as a way of making another of the major points of this chapter: While a
wide range of apparently diverse model-based systems have been built for
diagnosis and troubleshooting, they can all be seen as exploring variations
on the basic paradigm outlined here. Their diversity lies primarily in the
varying amounts of and kinds of knowledge they bring to bear at each stage
of the process.

Our survey of this familiar territory leads to a second major conclusion
of the chapter: Diagnostic reasoning from a tractable model is largely well
understood. That is, given a model of structure and behavior of tolerable
complexity, we know how to use it in a variety of ways to produce a diagnosis. Part of the evidence for this is the number of different applications
of that same paradigm in a variety of domains.

There is, by contrast, a rich supply of open research issues in the
modeling process itself. While to some degree we know how to do model-
based reasoning, we do not know how to model complex behavior, how to
create models, and how to select the *right* one for the task at hand. The
last major section of the chapter deals with these topics, exploring the kind
of difficulties that arise and using them to outline some important research
problems.

The Basic Task

The basic paradigm of model-based reasoning for diagnosis can best be
understood as the interaction of observation and prediction (see figure 1).
On one hand we have the actual device, typically some physical artifact
whose behavior we can observe. On the other hand we have a model of that
device that can make predictions about its intended behavior. Observation
indicates what the device is actually doing, prediction indicates what it is
supposed to do. The interesting event is any difference between these two,
a difference termed a *discrepancy*.

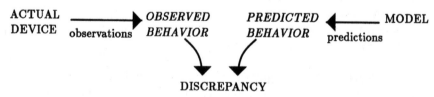

Figure 1. Diagnosis as the interaction of observation and prediction.

A fundamental presumption behind model-based diagnosis is the notion
that if the model is correct, all the discrepancies between observation and
prediction arise from (and can be traced back to) defects in the device.
Simply put, if the model is right, the device must be broken, and the
discrepancies are clues to the character and location of the faults. This is

a useful view of the process that will carry us through the first two thirds of the chapter.

We will eventually see, however, that it is also a simplified view: The assumption that the model is correct is in fact *necessarily wrong in all cases*. It is wrong in ways that are sometimes quite obvious and sometimes quite subtle. Simply put, a model is a model precisely because it is not the device itself and hence must in many ways be only an approximation. There will always be things about the device that the model does not capture.

The good news is that the things the model fails to capture may have no pragmatic consequence. A schematic for a digital circuit will not indicate the color, smell, or coefficient of friction of the plastic used to package the chips, but this typically does not matter. In theory the model is always incomplete, and hence incorrect, in some respects, but it is a demonstration of the power and utility of engineering approximations that models are often pragmatically good enough.

The less good news comes in situations where the approximation is not good enough. In that case we need to ask the more difficult question of how to do model-based reasoning in the face of an incorrect model. What can be done when both the model and the artifact may have defects? We turn to this later in the chapter.

Turning back to the basic problem, the task can be specified slightly more precisely by saying that we are given:

- Observations of the device, typically measurements at its inputs and outputs (because these are often easiest to obtain; in fact measurements at any point will do and are handled identically),

- A description of the device's internal structure, typically a listing of its components and their interconnection, and

- A description of the behavior of each component.

The task is then to determine which of the components could have failed in a way that accounts for all of the discrepancies observed. Figure 2, for example, shows a device made from three multipliers and two adders. We know the values at the five inputs; the value at output F was predicted to be 12 and observed to be 10 (observations are noted in square brackets). The value at G is predicted to be 12 and has not yet been measured. The overall task is to use knowledge about the structure and behavior of the components to determine which ones could have produced the discrepancy at F, a process explored later in detail.

This approach to troubleshooting has been called by a variety of names in addition to model-based, including *reasoning from first principles* because it is based on a few basic principles about causality, and *deep reasoning,* an unfortunate term intended to distinguish it from the associational rules typically used in rule-based expert systems.

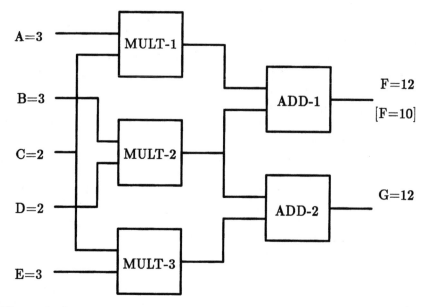

Figure 2. A common example.

Numerous model-based reasoners have been built, exploring a variety of problem domains. The illustrative sample given in table 1 indicates the growth of interest in the area. Some of the earliest work dates from the mid-1970s, with a considerable growth of interest in the mid-1980s. Much of it has been directed to electronic circuits, both analog and digital, but there have also been applications to problems in neurophysiology, hydraulic systems, and other domains. In the remainder of this chapter we use digital circuits as a motivating example, largely because they are a familiar and important application that offers a range of examples from simple to quite complex.

The term *model* has been used widely to refer to a range of different things and is somewhat underdetermined. It is thus useful to review briefly some of the different kinds of models that have been used, to get a sense of the character of the information that models have supplied. As noted, the models used in this chapter contain information about the structure and correct behavior of the components in the device. Work by Patil *et al.* [1981] describes a medical diagnosis system that used models of behavior without structure, models that indicated how one physiological event in the body could lead to another (for example, low blood serum pH causes increased respiration, which causes decreased CO_2 concentration). Traditional circuit diagnosis has often relied on fault models, descriptions of the varieties of component misbehaviors typically encountered. Finally, work by Pan [1984] has attacked the problem of dependent failures by building

INTER	de Kleer [1976]
WATSON	Brown [1976]
ABEL	Patil *et al.* [1981]
SOPHIE	Brown *et al.* [1982]
HT	Davis *et al.* [1982]
LOCALIZE	First *et al.* [1982]
IDS	Pan [1984]
DART	Genesereth [1984]
LES/LOX	Scarl *et al.* [1985]
GDE	de Kleer and Williams [1987]
DEDALE	Dague *et al.* [1987]

Table 1. Sample Model-Based Troubleshooting Systems.

models that capture the behavior of a component when it receives out-of-range inputs and itself begins to malfunction as a result. All of these are varieties of models, so a system built around any one of them could be termed model-based. Within the scope of this chapter we are concerned primarily with models of structure and correct behavior.

Alternative Approaches

Over the years a number of different approaches to diagnosis have been explored. It is useful to consider alternatives to the model-based approach both as a way of setting it in context and as a way of establishing the appropriate circumstances for its use.

One traditional approach has been to use diagnostics, the test programs traditionally used on electronic devices at the end of the manufacturing line, to ensure that the device is capable of doing everything it is supposed to do. A second technique is to build a *fault dictionary* by using simulation and a list of the kind of faults anticipated. The idea here is to simulate the device behavior for every one of the ways in which each individual component can misbehave. Each simulation generates a description of how the entire device would behave if a specific component were broken in a specific way. The overall result is a list of fault/symptom pairs. The list is then inverted so that it is organized by symptom, providing a dictionary that indexes from observed symptom—the surface misbehavior—to one or more underlying faults capable of causing that misbehavior.

Third, we can build programs to do diagnosis by capturing the experience of experts, in the fashion widely used to build rule-based systems that employ empirical associations. Finally, decision trees are a longstanding approach to capturing diagnostic knowledge and offer a way of organizing a set of questions that leads methodically through the process of zeroing in on the faulty component.

Given the diversity of approaches to the problem, why and when does it make sense to use the model-based approach? One way to answer the question is to compare it against the alternatives.

Compared to diagnostics

One problem with traditional diagnostics is that they are misnamed: Diagnostics do not do diagnosis, they do verification. As noted, their job is to ensure that a newly manufactured device will in fact do everything it is supposed to do. There is no misbehavior to diagnose, because there has not been any behavior yet. The fundamental task of verification is to exercise all the intended behaviors and make sure that they are all there. That is a different problem.

Model-based diagnosis, on the other hand, is both diagnostic and *symptom-directed*: It starts with the observed misbehavior and works back toward the underlying components that might be broken. As will become clear, whenever the behavior of a device is reasonably complicated, it is much easier to work from a specific symptom back to an underlying fault than to go exhaustively through all the expected behaviors until we find one that is aberrant.

Fault dictionaries and diagnostics: Prespecified fault models

As we explore in more detail later, the model-based approach also covers a wider class of faults than both fault dictionaries and traditional diagnostics, because both of those require a fixed, preselected class of relatively simple fault models. For fault dictionaries the task is to select a set broad enough to be useful in practice, yet simple enough that the simulation task is tractable. Writers of diagnostics typically have to settle on a small, fixed class of faults in order to create diagnostics that have acceptable coverage (the percent of possible faults actually detected), resolution (how precisely a detected fault can be localized), and efficiency. In the world of digital electronics the most common choices are the faults known as stuck-at-1 (a node in the circuit always exhibits the value 1) and stuck-at-0, largely because these are easily modeled, simulated, analyzed, and turn out to provide good coverage of other types of faults.

Whatever the faults chosen, the important point is that the fault dictionary creator or diagnostic writer must pre-select a set of things that can go wrong and work from just those possibilities. As will become clear, the model-based approach takes a different view, defining a fault as *anything other than the intended behavior*; one consequence of this view is the ability to cover a wider class of possible misbehaviors.

Fault models do offer two useful abilities. First, as we explore in the "Constraint Suspension" section, they can provide an extra degree of specificity to the diagnosis. Where the model-based approach defines a fault by exclusion (anything other than expected behavior), fault models suggest specific misbehaviors that can aid in making the predictions necessary to design further tests.

Second, even though the set of pre-enumerated faults used may be small, it may be adequate for the task at hand. In digital circuits, for example, a large fraction of all faults can be detected (but not diagnosed) by checking just for stuck-ats. Hence two simple fault models turn out to be sufficient for determining that something is wrong (satisfying the verification task); determining the identity and location of the error (diagnosis), however, is more difficult.

Compared to rule-based systems

Traditional rule-based systems have been built by accumulating the experience of expert troubleshooters in the form of empirical associations, rules that associate symptoms with underlying faults and that base those associations on experience with the device, rather than knowledge of structure or behavior. The problem here is the strong device dependence—a new rule set is required for every new device—and the time required to accumulate those rules. To the extent that the knowledge is an encapsulation of experience, a sizable body of experience may be necessary before the patterns emerge.

The issue becomes especially important in dealing with electronic devices, where the design cycle is getting short enough to be comparable to the time required to accumulate a new set of rules. This presents the difficult situation in which the device may be on its way to obsolescence by the time enough experience with it has accumulated to deal with the difficult faults.

The model-based approach is, by contrast, strongly device independent, works from an information source (the design) typically available when the device is first manufactured, and is far more likely to provide methodical coverage. Given a design description for a device, work can begin on diagnosing the device right away. Given a new design description for a different device, work can start on that one just as quickly.

The model-based approach can be less costly to use, because the model needed is often supplied by the description used to design and build the device in the first place. The increasing use of computer aided design and manufacturing also means that those models are increasingly available as explicit descriptions in electronic form, rather than implicit in the head of the designer, or sketched informally on a scattered collection of paper.

The model-based approach is more likely to provide methodical coverage because the model building process supplies a way of systematically enumerating the required knowledge. Systems built from empirical associations capture whatever experience has been encountered to date and offer far less guidance about what may be missing. As a result it is also more difficult to determine the coverage of such a system.

Finally, it may be claimed that rules need not be just empirical associations, they can also be written to take advantage of knowledge about device structure and behavior. But that is just the point: The relevant knowledge concerns structure and behavior. Given that, we ought next to ask what representations are well suited to capturing that information, what representations offer us leverage in thinking about that knowledge. Rules, whether as empirical associations or viewed simply as if/then statements, offer us little or no help in thinking about or representing structure and behavior, or in using such descriptions to do diagnosis. Most fundamentally, they do not even lead us to think in such terms.

In slightly more general terms, the primary question is not whether some existing representation can in some fashion be made to do the task. The primary question is, what is the relevant knowledge, and second, what does that content suggest about appropriate form. We consider such representations in the section on "Describing Structure and Behavior".

Compared to decision trees

Decision trees provide a simple and efficient way to write down the sequence of tests and conclusions needed to guide a diagnosis. But the same simplicity and efficiency that is their strength is also an important weakness: They are a way of writing down the *answer* (a diagnostic strategy), but offer no indication of the knowledge used to create that answer. One consequence is a lack of transparency (the tree provides no indication why the diagnosis is what it is) and difficulty in updating (a small change to the device may mean a major restructuring of the tree). Like rule-based systems they are also device specific and must be recreated anew for each new device.

When not to use the model-based approach

Comparing the model-based approach to its alternatives provides some indication of its strengths and indications for its use. When does it make sense not to use this approach? The answer can be bracketed by examining problems that are too hard and problems that are too easy to be worth trying this way.

Problems that are too difficult are those involving subtle and complicated interactions in the device, interactions whose outcome is too hard to predict with current modeling technology. Consider, for example, a model of a computer that has been found through experience to have unreliable power supplies. The lack of reliability may arise from a sizable collection of interacting factors, like the heating and insulation patterns, air flow, electric and thermal properties of the materials used to build the power supplies, etc. Predicting such behavior from the design description would very likely be pragmatically impossible, yet summarizing and using it once it has been noted is quite easy ("if one of these machines is behaving erratically, it's likely to be the power supply"). We are in effect recognizing here that in some cases it is far easier to *let nature do the experiment*, watch the outcome, and capture the experience in the form of rules, than it would be to predict the result from first principles.

Future advances in modeling and prediction will extend these limits, but the point remains that, given sufficient complexity, it is easier to let nature do the experiment. Reality is sometimes the cheapest simulator.

Problems that are too easy are those in which the device is so simple that we can model its behavior exhaustively and where the set of faults to be considered is well enough known and well enough understood to be reliably pre-enumerated. In that case it may make sense simply to do exhaustive enumeration and create a fault dictionary.

We can thus approach the issue of when to use the model-based approach from two dimensions. First, the structure and behavior of the device should be reasonably well known and simple enough to model, but complex enough that exhaustive simulation is infeasible. Second, the set of possible faults should be difficult to reliably enumerate in advance.

Organization and Vocabulary

The discussion in this chapter uses several basic ideas as organizing principles. First, we view diagnosis in terms of the three stages of hypothesis *generation, test* and *discrimination*. Second, we note that different amounts of knowledge can be brought to bear at each of these stages, producing more or less powerful approaches. Third, the range of programs that can be created by considering different amounts of knowledge at each stage maps out a space of possible program architectures. Finally, and perhaps most interestingly, we claim that this space of architectures captures the current set of programs that have been explored. That is, we can describe all the current model-based systems by characterizing them according to the amount and kind of knowledge they use at each of these three stages.

A number of basic vocabulary terms will facilitate later discussion. By *device* or *system*, we mean the entire artifact, for example, the entire device in figure 2. By *component* we mean any one piece of it, in this case any of the adders or multipliers. (We may choose to represent wires as components as well; this is an issue of modeling choice discussed later.) By *structure* we mean the way things are interconnected, while *behavior* refers to what any one of these components is supposed to do. We use *discrepancy* to mean any of the differences between the behavior the device is supposed to exhibit (for example, $F=12$, predicted by the model) and what it is actually doing ([$F=10$], determined by observation). By *suspect* we mean any component identified in hypothesis generation as able to account for a discrepancy (for example, MULT-1 can account for the discrepancy at F). Finally, by *candidate* we mean a component whose malfunction is consistent with all observations (that is, a suspect that has survived hypothesis testing). When dealing with multiple faults, a candidate may consist of more than one component.

Describing Structure and Behavior

While a number of apparently different approaches to representing structure have been explored, there are several common themes that appear to be widely viewed as good ideas.

- Structure representation should be hierarchical.

Inside any of the boxes in figure 2, for instance, there are more boxes and wires; look inside those and there are more of the same, until we arrive finally at primitive components. A hierarchical description permits hierarchical diagnosis: Work at the highest level initially until specific candidates have been isolated, then explore inside only those components, because there is no need to examine the substructure of components that are not candidates.

- Structure representation should be object centered and isomorphic to the organization of the device.

By *object centered* we mean that there are data objects corresponding to each of the components in the device; attached to each object is a description of its behavior. The representation should be isomorphic in the sense that the topology of interconnections between the objects should match the interconnections in the device. Hence the object associated with MULT-2, for instance, is connected in the LISP sense to the objects for ADD-1 and ADD-2.

One useful consequence of doing this is that it provides a single, unified representation that is both runnable and examinable. It is runnable in the sense that it can be used directly for simulation: If we supply values for the inputs to MULT-1, for instance, the object corresponding to it will discover that it has enough information to predict its output. It will do so, placing the result at its output, where the information will travel via the connections to the next component in line, which may now continue the process.

The same representation is examinable in the sense that it can be inspected to answer questions about device structure. Because it is in part a graph, questions about connectivity can be answered simply by traversing the representation.

- Behavior can be represented by a set of expressions that capture the interrelationships among the values on the terminals of the device.

The behavior of an adder, for example, can be captured with three expressions (see figure 3), indicating that:

- If we know the values at A and B, the value at C is $A+B$ (the solid arrow in figure 3).
- If we know the values at C and A, the value at B is $C-A$ (the dashed arrow).
- If we know the values at C and B, the value at A is $C-B$ (the dotted arrow).

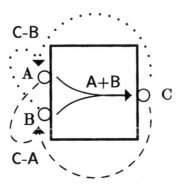

Figure 3. The behavior description of an adder.

While the expressions here are written in algebraic form, the important thing is the knowledge content, not form. Work by Genesereth [1984], for example, has explored the use of predicate calculus as a representation for both behavior and structure.

Interestingly these expressions capture both the causal behavior of the device (the bold arrow), as well as other things we can infer about the device (the other two arrows). The first of these indicates how it works, the other two are useful inferences we can make about what must have been at an input, given observations at other terminals. As we will see, both kinds of information play an important role in supporting diagnosis.

Three Fundamental Tasks

We consider next the three fundamental tasks of diagnosis and examine how each has been attacked in the model-based approach, using a variety of different kinds and amounts of knowledge. We consider each in turn, starting with the common simplifying assumption that there is only a single point of failure; as the discussion proceeds we show how some of the techniques can be extended to cover multiple points of failure.

- **Hypothesis generation:** Given one discrepancy, which of the components in the device might have produced it?
- **Hypothesis testing:** Given a collection of components implicated during hypothesis generation, which of them could have failed so as to account for all available observations of behavior?
- **Hypothesis discrimination:** When, as is almost inevitable, more than one hypothesis survives the testing phase, what additional information should be gathered to discriminate among them?

As noted, for the sake of presentation each of these is discussed independently, even though in most implementations they are interleaved for the sake of efficiency. While interleaving offers useful improvements in speed, it produces no fundamental changes to the paradigm.

Hypothesis generation

The fundamental task here is, given a discrepancy, determine which components might have misbehaved in a way that can produce that discrepancy. Classical AI wisdom tells us that a good generator should be *complete* (that is, capable of producing all the plausible hypotheses); *non-redundant* (that is, capable of generating each hypothesis only once); and *informed* (that is, able to produce few hypotheses that ultimately prove to be incorrect).

In the spirit of proceeding incrementally we consider a sequence of generators from the simplest and least informed, through successively smarter versions that bring additional kinds of knowledge to bear.

The simplest generator, guaranteed to be complete, is one that simply exhaustively enumerates the components in the device. For the device in figure 2, for instance, the generator simply produces each of the five components one by one.

We can improve on this with a succession of observations. For example:

- To be a suspect, a component must have been connected to a discrepancy.

That is, to plausibly explain a discrepancy, the suspect must have in some fashion been involved in it, have contributed to it. Our second generator takes advantage of the insight by traversing the structure description, working from a discrepancy (for example, at F in figure 2) to find all components connected to it. In the current case this provides no improvement, because the connections (wires) leading from F reach every component.

We next observe that:

- Devices often have distinguishable inputs and outputs.

This is clearly true for our adders and multipliers (see figure 4) and can be used to constrain the components considered: We need only consider components that are upstream of the discrepancy. In the current example this reduces the set of suspects to ADD-1, MULT-1, and MULT-2.

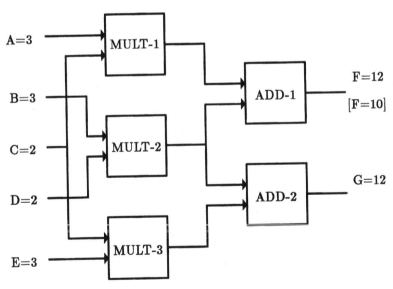

Figure 4. Taking advantage of direction of information flow.

We can be a bit smarter yet, by observing that:

- Not every input to a device influences the output; there is no need to follow irrelevant inputs upstream.

The easiest example of this is an OR gate whose inputs are produced by two independent collections of components further upstream (see figure 5). Given inputs of 1 and 0, the model for the gate makes the obvious prediction at C. If the actual device is observed to be producing 0 there, three possibilities arise. First, the OR gate itself may be broken. Second, the gate may be working but input A is 0 rather than 1 and the problem lies further upstream in that direction, so we should continue tracing that way.

The third possibility, however, is problematic: It is contradictory to believe that the OR gate is working but that the problem lies further upstream of B. No matter what is going on upstream of B, if the OR gate is working, that is not going to account for the observed behavior. As a result we need not consider any components upstream of this point. More generally, the hypothesis generator can use knowledge about component behavior to determine which inputs are irrelevant and avoid tracing back through those.

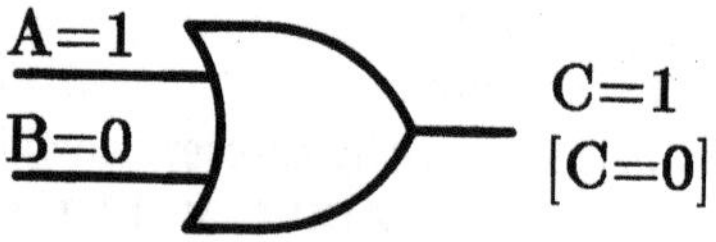

Figure 5. Not every input influences the output.

Finally, we can observe that

- Information from more than one discrepancy can be used to further constrain suspect generation.

When there is more than one discrepancy, we can generate a set of suspects for each, then (assuming a single point of failure) intersect them, possibly reducing the number of suspects generated. Consider figure 6, as an example. Tracing back from the discrepancy at F yields ADD-1, MULT-1, and MULT-2 as candidates; tracing from G yields ADD-2, MULT-1 and MULT-3. Assuming a single point of failure, the suspects lie in the intersection of these two sets.

This scheme is easily elaborated to deal with multiple points of failure by recognizing that the generalization of intersection in this case is set covering: We are trying to find a subset of components that accounts for (covers) all the discrepancies. To deal with the situation in figure 6, for instance, we might select MULT-1 from the first discrepancy and ADD-2 from the second, yielding a hypothesized pair of faults that covers all the discrepancies.

◇ **Machinery**

One brief diversion into mechanism will make clear how to do this kind of reasoning easily and efficiently. The basic insight is to have the simulator

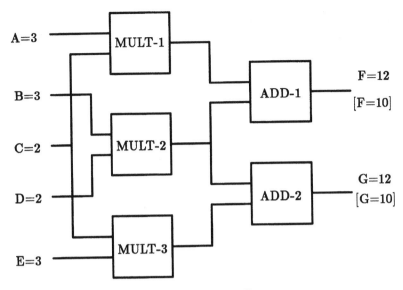

Figure 6. Polybox with discrepancy at F and G.

record *reasons* as well as values. When the simulator predicts 1 at C, for instance, it records both that value and the expression from the behavior model for the component that produced the value (see figure 7). In this case the simulator would indicate that the value at C is 1 and the reason is $E1$.

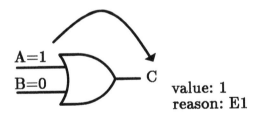

E1: If A=1 then C=1
E2: If B=1 then C=1
E3: If A=0 and B=0 then C=0

Figure 7. Recording reasons as well as values.

This simple mechanism offers an easy way to determine which inputs to a component were relevant to its output, further constraining the search for hypotheses. All we need do is inspect the simulation record to determine what expression was used to predict a value, then inspect that expression to determine which inputs it used.[1] In figure 7, for example, expression *E1* uses only *A*, hence we need never consider hypotheses upstream of *B*.

This is a somewhat simplified but essentially correct view of the machinery in most model-based simulators in use today. The general notion is to have the simulator keep track of dependency records that indicate what information was used to determine each new value; generating candidates can then be done simply by tracing back through the dependencies.

A slightly more elaborate example will demonstrate why this technique can be very useful. Figure 8 shows a collection of gates with arrows indicating the records the simulator has kept as it made its predictions. Given a discrepancy at the output, the task of generating a complete, nonredundant and constrained set of hypotheses becomes simply a process of following the trail of electronic bread crumbs back along the reasons. Part of the overall insight here is that by using a reasonably sophisticated simulator—one that propagates reasons as well as values—the hypothesis generation task becomes relatively simple and straightforward (SOPHIE [Brown *et al.* 1982] provided one of the earliest examples of this approach).

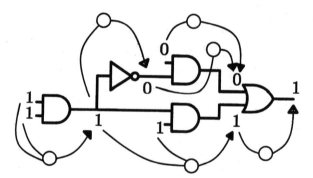

Figure 8. Dependency traces left by the simulator.

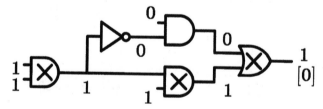

Figure 9. Candidates selected by tracing back through the dependency traces.

---

[1]Alternatively we could simply record which inputs were used. The scheme given is slightly more general, because the reasons can be useful in other ways, for example, as a basis for explanation, and the inputs can be determined from them.

Hypothesis testing: A simple technique

In the second basic task of diagnosis—hypothesis testing—the goal is to test each suspect to see if it can account for *all* the observations made about the device. One simple approach is to use fault-model simulation on the suspects produced by the generator (as for example, in Brown *et al.* [1982] and Pan [1984]). We enumerate all the ways each specified component can malfunction, then simulate the behavior of the entire device on the original set of inputs under the assumption that the candidate is malfunctioning in the way specified. If the overall predicted behavior is inconsistent with the observations, the hypothesis can be discarded; hypotheses accounting correctly for the observations pass the test and are retained. The result is a set of hypotheses specifying how each suspect may be malfunctioning.

One interesting additional inference can be made if we believe that the pre-enumerated list of misbehaviors is *complete*: If none of the misbehaviors hypothesized for a component matches the observations, that component must be working correctly in the current situation and can be exonerated. It may or may not be working perfectly in all circumstances, but it is not causing the current set of discrepancies and we will have to look for the fault elsewhere.

If the misbehavior list is not believed complete, the component cannot be exonerated, because it may be misbehaving in some as yet unknown fashion. In this situation we may end up with two categories of suspects: those for which a hypothesized misbehavior matches the observations and those that may be failing in an unknown way. In that case it may make sense to treat the first category as more likely, falling back on the second only as necessary.

Hypothesis testing: More advanced techniques

Three other slightly more advanced techniques use knowledge about device behavior to test hypothesized candidates, yet do not require a pre-enumerated set of misbehaviors.

◇ Constraint suspension

Constraint suspension [Davis 1984] tests whether a suspect is consistent with all the observed behaviors of the device. The basic idea is to model the behavior of each component as a set of constraints, and test suspects by determining whether it is consistent to believe that only the suspect is malfunctioning. That is, given the known inputs and observed outputs, is it consistent to believe that all components other than the suspect are working correctly?

Consider the standard circuit as an example, in a situation in which the inputs are as shown in figure 10 and where values at both outputs have been measured, yielding a discrepancy at F and the predicted value at G. The behavior of each component is modeled as a set of constraints of the sort shown previously in figure 3; figure 10 shows the entire device with the constraint network sketched in.

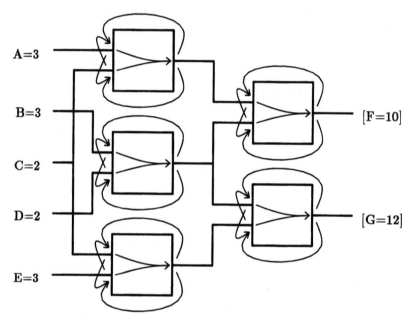

Figure 10. The constraint network view of the device.

This network and set of values is clearly inconsistent. That is, given this set of constraints, if the values shown were inserted at the inputs and outputs, some constraint would soon encounter an inconsistency, that is, attempt to fire and record a value at a node where there was already a different value recorded. Because constraints can propagate either from inputs to outputs or from outputs to inputs, the inconsistency might occur anywhere in the network (at the outputs, the inputs, or an interior node). The important point is that the network would report an inconsistency somewhere.

The traditional approach to handling inconsistencies in constraint networks is to find a value to retract. Here, however, we are sure of the values (the inputs sent in and the outputs measured); we are, however, unsure of the component behaviors. Constraint suspension thus takes the dual view: Rather than looking for a value to retract, it considers which constraint to retract to remove the inconsistency.

To put this back in hypothesis testing terms, recall the basic question stated above: Given the available observations, is it consistent to believe that all components other than the suspect are working correctly? *Working correctly* means the component is behaving as the model predicts; this is simulated by having the corresponding constraint *turned on*. To say something is a suspect, by contrast, is to indicate that we do not know what it is doing, what its behavior is. In that case the most conservative stance is to retract all assumptions about its behavior. This is simulated by suspending its constraint, that is, removing it from the network temporarily. Figure 11 shows the situation when testing the hypothesis that MULT-1 may be at fault.

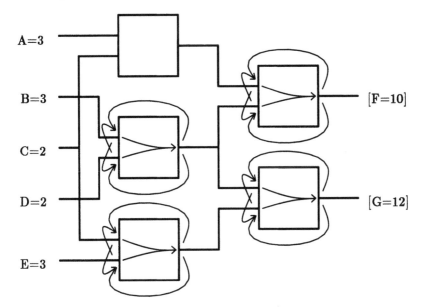

Figure 11. The network with the constraint for MULT-1 suspended.

Hypothesis testing is thus accomplished by suspending the constraint for the suspect, leaving in place the constraints for everything else, then putting in the observed values and allowing the (reduced) constraint network to run to quiescence. If it does so without encountering an inconsistency, we get two interesting pieces of information. First, we know that the current suspect is in fact consistent with all the observations, that is, there is some behavior for it that can account for all the observations. Second, the constraints often propagate values to the terminals of the suspect, supplying information about how it must be misbehaving. For example, the constraint network in figure 11 will eventually determine that MULT-1 is a consistent candidate that could be multiplying 2 and 3 to produce 4. This ability to infer component symptoms is clearly dependent on the ability to propagate *backwards*, in this case inferring the upper input of ADD-1 from its output and lower input.

If the network is still inconsistent even with the suspect's constraint suspended, the current hypothesis can be rejected, exonerating the suspect: There is no set of assignments to the terminals of the suspect consistent with the observed values and the constraints currently in effect. This occurs when testing MULT-2, one of the three suspects produced by hypothesis generation for the situation in figure 10. With only the constraint for MULT-2 suspended, there is no set of assignments to its terminals that is consistent with the inputs and outputs observed. It can thus be rejected.

There are several interesting properties of this technique. First, as noted, it not only indicates whether or not something is a consistent candidate, it can often specify the symptoms at the terminals of that component.

Second, the power of hypothesis testing and its ability to infer symptoms are dependent on the power of the propagation machinery. Current constraint systems are *local* in the sense that they propagate values through one component at a time, at each step solving one equation in one unknown. This style of propagation can stall when it encounters situations requiring more sophisticated algebra (for example, solving two equations with two unknowns). Such situations are relatively common in domains with non-directional components and can arise in domains with directional components in structures that have reconvergent fanout (that is, a signal that branches and then rejoins at the inputs to a component).

The complexity of the algebra required depends on both the vocabulary used in the behavior language and the interconnection topology of the devices; it can quickly grow quite difficult. Some research has attacked the problem by propagating symbolic expressions rather than numbers (for example, Sussman and Steele [1980]) exhaustive enumeration has also been explored where ranges are finite. If propagation does stall, the system will judge the candidate consistent because no contradiction was derived, even though there may in fact be one. Other work, relying on direct symbolic manipulation of expressions (for example, Genesereth [1984] and Scarl *et al.* [1985]) encounters similar problems where their symbolic solution methods are not complete.

Some candidates accepted as a result of stalled propagation are valid; in those cases there is no adverse consequence. Even when an invalid candidate is accepted, however, the only consequence is that the candidate set is larger than it should have been. The diagnosis is thus somewhat less precise, but at least no valid candidate is overlooked.

Third, where many traditional techniques require specifying how a component can fail, the reasoning above simply withdraws any commitment to how it might be behaving. That is an interesting property of model-based reasoning in general, not just the constraint suspension approach: Something is malfunctioning if it is not doing what it is supposed to do, *no matter what else it may be doing.* As a result there is no need to pre-specify how the component might fail, a fault is any behavior that does not match expectations.

It is in that sense that the model-based approach, using a model of correct behavior, covers a broader class of faults than traditional techniques that require pre-specified fault models. Note, for instance, that the device in figure 11 may be misbehaving because the wrong kind of chip was inserted into the socket where the multiplier was supposed to go. In that case there is no simple model for the misbehavior and no plausible way to diagnose it in the traditional fashion. Yet the model-based approach handles this case because it need only observe that the component is not doing what it is supposed to do.

The fault model approach falls short in this case because its models combine both physical and logical plausibility. The model-based approach by contrast deals only with logical plausibility, asking simply whether there is *any* set of values the component might display that can account for all the observations. The technique, by design, does not ask whether that set of values is in fact physically plausible.

As a result it can suggest candidates that, while logically plausible, are in fact physically unrealizable, requiring a second pass to filter them out. This can, however, be an advantage because physical plausibility is technology-specific. A broken wire, for instance, can manifest differently depending on the technology; in TTL logic, for instance, it will appear as a high. Embodying this knowledge separately can both ease the initial construction task and reduce the difficulty of applying model-based reasoning to a new domain.

The traditional use of fault models can also be seen as trading off breadth for specificity: By committing to a pre-specified set of set of possible failures, we can gain in return greater specificity in the diagnosis. In the case of MULT-1, for instance, the model (of correct behavior) approach can say only that the component is multiplying 2 and 3 to get 4, while the fault model approach might indicate as one possibility that the 2-bit of the output is stuck at 0 (turning 6 into 4).

The model-based approach thus supplies a behavioral description of the misbehavior for this specific case, and, by design, says nothing about what the malfunctioning component would do with any other inputs. This permits it to cover a broad variety of possible failures. The fault model approach, on the other hand, pre-commits to a specific set of malfunction mechanisms and as a result can be more specific about what is wrong and can provide the basis for predictions of misbehavior for other inputs (for example, if the 2-bit is stuck at 0, MULT-1 should produce 0 when given inputs of 2 and 1). The tradeoff available thus asks whether we are willing to pre-specify the faults and believe that the list is complete enough; if so fault models might offer useful power.

Finally, we have so far been dealing with the single point of failure assumption. Multiple points of failure are trivial to check using constraint suspension: To check for a pair of failures, for instance, suspend the two corresponding constraints, then proceed as before. Generating multiple fault hypotheses efficiently, however, is somewhat more difficult; no simple extension of constraint suspension offers much leverage on this inherently exponential problem. This issue will resurface when we explore GDE [de Kleer & Williams 1987] later.

◇ Combining generation and test

Two systems—Dart [Genesereth 1984] and GDE [de Kleer & Williams 1987]—integrate hypothesis generation and testing sufficiently that when viewed in terms of generate and test they are best considered systems in which all of the testing knowledge has been integrated into the hypothesis generator.

Dart. The DART system illustrates the use of predicate calculus as a mechanism for model-based reasoning, with structure and behavior represented as axioms. The connection of MULT-1 to ADD-1, for instance, would be represented as

```
CONN(OUT(1, MULT-1), IN(1, ADD-1))
```

indicating that the first (only) output of MULT-1 is connected to the first input of ADD-1. Part of the behavior description of an adder would be

```
IF    ADDER(a) AND VAL(IN(1, a), x) AND VAL(IN(2, a), y)
THEN  VAL(OUT(1, a), x+y)
```

indicating that, if a is an adder with inputs x and y, its output will be x+y.

DART views diagnosis as a form of constrained theory formation. Starting with a set of observations of device misbehavior, the goal is to produce a description of its (faulty) structure. Given only the observations, the task would be the same as designing a device that exhibited the observed behavior. The design description is used to constrain the process by forcing the system to consider only propositions from the design description or their negation. A diagnosis in DART is thus a deduced proposition like

```
(OR (NOT (MULTIPLIER MULT-1)) (NOT (ADDER ADD-1)))
```

indicating which component might be misbehaving.

To arrive at these deductions the system uses a technique called resolution residue, a variation on resolution that works as a direct proof procedure (rather than a refutation method), guided by a number of strategies like unit preference for reducing the number of useless deductions. Details of the process can be found in Genesereth [1984]; at the knowledge level the deductions work much like the dependency tracing mechanism reviewed earlier, except in this case dependencies are deduced as needed (via the behavior descriptions) rather than automatically recorded when doing simulation. DART also uses the same resolution residue mechanism for test generation, providing a certain economy of machinery.

Among the limitations in this approach are the occasional difficulties in expression logic can present. The single point of failure assumption in Genesereth [1984], for example, requires five distinct axioms for a five component device, each stating that if one is broken the other four must be working. Further work in Ginsberg [1986] has demonstrated that reasoning from counterfactuals can produce a notion of minimal faults, at some increase in the complexity of the modeling and inference task.

One of the advantages of logic as a representation and reasoning mechanism is the potential for demonstrating the completeness of the inference procedure. While this can be useful, it does not not imply that the resulting diagnostic process is complete. There are at least two sources of difficulty. First, as noted by de Kleer and Williams [1987], completeness of the inference procedure does not imply completeness of the prediction machinery. As one example, behavior descriptions for analog devices can involve higher-order differential equations; producing exact values for predictions in such devices means solving solutions of such equations, yet no general purpose technique exists.

Second, all of the inference, that is, all of the candidate generation, is done with respect to the device model supplied, and completeness of the inference machinery is quite distinct from the completeness of the model. Simple examples of the problem arise when axioms are accidentally omitted; more subtle instances arise because, as we argue below, the model is necessarily incomplete. Thus while it can be useful to demonstrate completeness of the inference machinery with respect to the model, completeness of the diagnostic process is a distinct issue. Indeed we argue below that the bulk of the work and difficult problems are in the modeling.

GDE.   The GDE system [de Kleer & Williams 1987] provides a single mechanism for generating both single and multiple fault hypotheses, and presents a carefully constructed strategy for measurement selection. At this point we deal with a few of the ideas for hypothesis generation, illustrating the basic notions with a few simple examples; we return to the issue of measurement selection when discussing hypothesis discrimination in section on

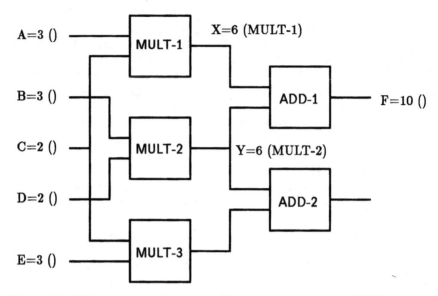

Figure 12. Values and records produced by an assumption-based TMS.

"Hypothesis Discrimination." A detailed picture and additional examples of GDE can be found in de Kleer and Williams [1987].

One important enabling technology for GDE is the use of an assumption-based truth maintenance system (ATMS), that is, one that propagates both values and assumptions. The reasoning begins much like that done previously, with some difference in the record keeping. In figure 12, for example, if we assume that MULT-1 is working, we can use its behavior description to predict the value at X, then record both the value and the set of underlying assumptions (in parentheses). Values that have been measured (in this case inputs and outputs) have no assumptions, indicated by the null set.

A particularly interesting event occurs when there are two contradictory predictions for the same point in the circuit, as in figure 13, which shows the next step in the reasoning. The value at X is also predicted to be 4, this time using the (measured) value at F, the prediction at Y, and the assumption that ADD-1 is working. Note that assumptions accumulate: The prediction $X=4$ carries all the assumptions it relies on.

This is interesting because of the inference that can now be made: If all three assumptions so far were true, (that is, MULT-1 *and* MULT-2 *and* ADD-1 were all working), there is an unavoidable contradiction—two different values at X. Taking the obvious step, we turn that around, inferring that one of the three assumptions must be wrong (that is, one of the three components is not working correctly).

This is the process of constructing *conflicts*: Whenever there are two

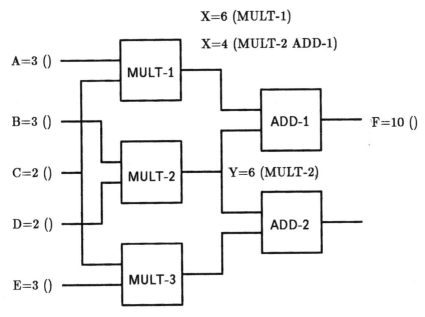

Figure 13. One more step in the propagation.

different predictions for the same place in the circuit, collect all (that is, take the union) of the assumptions underlying the conflicting predictions. The resulting conflict indicates that at least one of the components in it must be malfunctioning.

Continuing the propagation process in figure 13 eventually yields a second conflict as well:

C1:   (MULT-1 MULT-2 ADD-1)
C2:   (MULT-1 MULT-3 ADD-2 ADD-1)

The second step in GDE is to generate a set of candidates that deals with all of the conflicts. MULT-1, for example, is a candidate because it can account for both C1 (one of (MULT-1 MULT-2 ADD-1) must be broken), and C2 (one of (MULT-1 MULT-3 ADD-2 ADD-1) is broken.) Because a single component is capable of accounting for all the conflicts, one of the hypotheses in this case happens to be a single point of failure. ADD-1 is a similar hypothesis; single point of failure hypotheses are produced by intersecting the conflicts.

Accounting for conflicts can be viewed more generally in mathematical terms as set covering: We want a collection of components that covers all the conflicts. Singleton covers like (MULT-1) produce single point of failure hypotheses, multiple point of failure hypotheses are generated by larger set covers like (MULT-2 ADD-2), which takes MULT-2 from the first conflict and ADD-2 from the second.

This process is fairly intuitive, but it can be expensive—computing set covers is in the worst case exponential. One way to reduce the potential impact of this complexity is to use the notion of minimality in both conflicts and hypotheses. The basic intuition is the same in both cases: Any superset of a conflict is also a conflict; any superset of a hypothesis is also a hypothesis. GDE uses this to reduce the amount of work it does by generating and maintaining only minimal conflicts (that is, no subset of one is also a conflict) and minimal hypotheses (that is, no subset of one also covers all the conflicts). By doing this, the system need never examine any non-minimal conflict or hypothesis, saving a substantial amount of work. While the fundamental exponential character of the problem has not changed, the effect has been reduced, enabling the system to handle problems larger than might otherwise have been possible.

The candidate generation part of GDE thus offers an efficient and intuitive mechanism for generating both single and multiple fault hypotheses in a unified approach. The system also offers a degree of mechanism (and hence domain) independence, because the diagnostic process in GDE is separated from the machinery used to predict behavior (the ATMS).

Hypothesis testing via corroborations

It is useful to discuss briefly the notion of corroborations, the situation in which a measured value matches (corroborates) the prediction at that point. Using corroborations to do hypothesis testing is potentially useful, but must be approached with caution. The basic intuition is seductive: Having seen that any component involved in a discrepancy is a suspect, there is unfortunately a great temptation to construct an overly simplistic dual principle—any component involved in a corroboration must be innocent.

Figure 14 illustrates the difficulty in an example that has a discrepancy at F but a corroboration at G, where the observed value matches the predicted value. Straightforward topological tracing back from F yields the usual candidates (ADD-1, MULT-1, MULT-2). We are now, however, tempted to say that because the measurement at G matches the prediction, all components involved in that corroboration (that is, MULT-2, MULT-3, and ADD-2) can be exonerated.

The seductive part is that it works in this case and some others, leading at times to unjustified optimism that it is valid in general. The difficulty is illustrated by the simple counterexample in figure 14, in which ADD-2 has been replaced by a component that computes the maximum of its inputs. Once again there is a conflict at F and a corroboration at G, yet this time

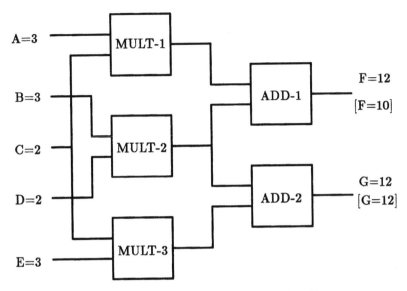

Figure 14. The standard example with a corroboration at G.

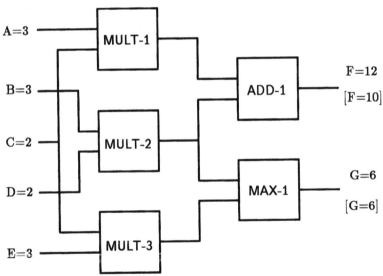

Figure 15. Counterexample showing that corroboration is not valid in general.

the exoneration is incorrect: MULT-2 might in fact be broken, producing 4 as its output.

In general the problem is fault masking, the situation in which a device receives incorrect inputs, yet produces the output that would have been expected with the correct inputs, masking further effects of the fault.

Consider MAX-1 for instance: If it receives incorrect inputs of 6 and 4, it still produces the expected output, 6, that would have resulted from the correct inputs (6 and 6).

Fault masking can arise in several ways. Any component that can be insensitive to one of its inputs (for example, MAX-1) can mask a fault on that input even when working correctly. Multiple points of failure can produce the problem, when one broken component outputs an incorrect value, but a second broken component further downstream masks some of the effects by producing the expected value despite the incorrect input. Finally, even with a single point of failure, the phenomenon of reconvergent fanout can produce fault making.

In figure 16, for example, component B computes the square of its input, component C computes $16-5x$, and ADD-1 is an adder. Component A is supposed to produce 3, which should eventually result in ADD-1 producing 10. If A instead incorrectly produces 2, B, working correctly, will produce 4, while C also working correctly produces 6. The final output at the adder is then the expected 10, despite the single fault present in the circuit. If the signal from A fans out to other places, its error would be manifest elsewhere, yet if we naively trace back from the corroboration at ADD-1 we would incorrectly exonerate A.

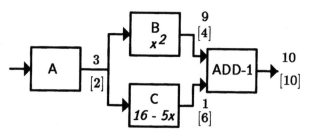

Figure 16. Reconvergent fanout can produce fault masking.

One important reason to be wary about corroborations is thus the number of and subtlety of the phenomena that can cause fault masking and invalidate corroborations as a heuristic.

A second reason is the asymmetry in the consequences of mistakes in hypothesis generation and in hypothesis testing. If the hypothesis generator is overzealous, we may have more hypotheses to test than are logically necessary, but the system will, at worst, be less efficient than it should have been. Overzealous exoneration, on the other hand, can cause the system to arrive at the wrong answer by ruling out a valid candidate. As a result, it may be plausible if desired to be aggressive with respect to hypothesis generation, but it general it is useful to be more cautious about hypothesis testing.

Hypothesis discrimination

Having examined generation and testing, we next consider hypothesis discrimination, where the fundamental problem is how to distinguish among the hypotheses, when, as is almost inevitable, more than one survives testing. Distinguishing among competing hypotheses involves gathering new information about the behavior of the device, either by (i) making additional observations (probing), or (ii) changing the inputs and making observations in that new situation (testing). In both cases the goal is to gain the most information at the least cost.

◊ Probing

In considering probing strategies we proceed as before in steps from the most elementary approach to successively more sophisticated techniques. The simplest approach is to use only structural information to generate the set of all possible probe locations and pick any place that has not been measured previously. Refinements to this include (i) using knowledge about component behavior (ii) using knowledge about expected failure rates, and (iii) trying to find the measurement that will lead to the shortest sequence of probes.

Using Structure And Behavior.   Perhaps the most straightforward and widely used approach is the guided probe. The fundamental idea is to start at the discrepancy and follow it upstream to a component that has an incorrect output but whose inputs are correct. If the component receives valid information but produces a bad result, it must be the culprit. Given the discrepancy in figure 17 at F, for instance, we probe A and Z next, if these are observed to have their predicted values, MAX-1 must be broken. If Z has any value other than 5, we probe upstream at both B and Y to see if they are 1 and 4 respectively, and so forth until we find the culprit.

◊ More sophisticated use of behavior

Note that it was not in fact necessary to probe at A, because a discrepancy there alone could not have produced the observed value 3 at F. The guided probe technique can be extended to use information about component behavior to reduce the probes needed; Breuer [1976], for example, shows how it can be applied to Boolean digital circuits. The reasoning involved is similar to that described earlier for using behavioral information to constrain hypothesis generation.

The guided probe approach is appealing in its simplicity and intuitive clarity. It is also, however, a linear time search, which, with even a little

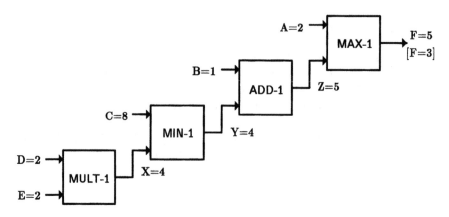

Figure 17. Guided probe example.

cleverness, can be turned into a much more efficient binary search. In the
current example, for instance, simply examining the topology of the device
makes clear that Y is a more effective probe. If the value there is bad, half
the components are exonerated—all those downstream from it. In general
the *half split* probe point can be found by considering for each probe point
the value that would be predicted there given each suspect; the favored
probe is the one that splits the set of current suspects. Figure 18 shows
that Y is the best probe: Y will be 2 if MULT-1 or MIN-1 are broken, and
4 if ADD-1 or MAX-1 are broken; either outcome thus rules out half the
suspects. Ideally, the process of cutting the search space in half can be
continued at each step, producing the traditional binary search, with its
potential increase in speed from linear in the number of suspects to be
discriminated, to logarithmic. The maximal advantage arises in cases like
this with a linear cascade of components, with somewhat less (but still
useful) improvement in other cases.

Using Failure Probabilities. The example above is particularly easy
because one probe is clearly more informative than the others. In more
realistic cases several places may be equally informative. If, for instance,
we apply our methods so far to the example in figure 19, X and Y turn out
to be equally informative.

In the event that MULT-1 and MULT-2 happen to be implemented using
different chips that have different reliability histories, it would make sense
to *play the odds* by probing at the place that has the greatest chance of
having an incorrect value. If MULT-2, for instance, has a much higher *a
priori* likelihood of failure than MULT-1, it would be more efficient in the
long run to try probing at Y first.

While this example uses failure probabilities to help select among
probe points that are indistinguishable using value predictions, the two

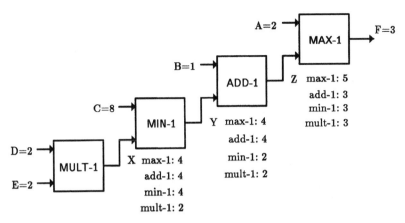

Figure 18. Half split strategy example.

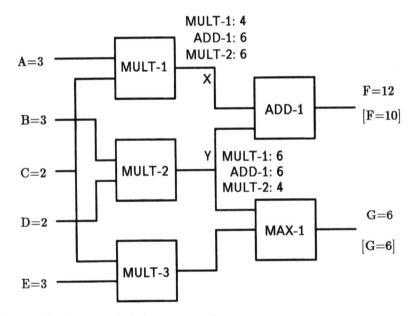

Figure 19. Two equally informative probes.

are independent sources of information. We can in general combine information from predictions (about how discriminating a probe can be) with information from failure probabilities (about how likely that probe will encounter an incorrect value), to yield a measure of how informative a particular probe is likely to be.

Selecting Optimal Probes.   We have thus far used information about predictions and failure probabilities to look only one measurement ahead.

The analysis in the previous section, for instance, considered what single measurement looked best. A more powerful strategy would determine what *sequence* of measurements was likely to be the most effective, because, as with any search problem, the best path is not always clear from a one-step lookahead.

One obvious approach is exhaustive lookahead: The current predictions indicate the potential places to probe first, we can then make new predictions based on the possible outcome of each of those probes, use that information to determine the set of possible places to probe second, make new predictions based on those, etc., continuing until the sequence of hypothesized measurements would identify a unique fault. This is a classic decision tree analysis and as always the difficulty is the size of the search space.

As with any search problem, the challenge is to find a way of estimating the value of a path without having to explore it to the end. The GDE system takes an information theoretic approach, using the notion of minimum entropy as the basis for its evaluation function (see de Kleer and Williams [1987] for details). Part of the difficulty in applying this idea lies in determining the probability that a particular measurement will have a particular value when not every candidate predicts a value at that point. GDE develops a careful approximation and uses it to select a measurement that is, under a reasonable set of assumptions, optimal in the sense that it minimizes the expected total number of probes.

This approach is well-suited to GDE because the assumption-based TMS that it uses maintains a substantial body of context information that includes the values predicted at each point in the device. Hence little additional machinery is needed to generate and keep track of the required information.

◇ Testing

Testing is the second basic technique for hypothesis discrimination. Here the fundamental idea is to select a new set of inputs to the device that will help reduce the suspect set by providing additional information about the behavior of the device. To remain valid, a suspect has to account for both the original symptoms and the behavior observed in response to the new inputs. As with probing, the difficult task is selecting a set of inputs that is particularly informative.

If the set of tests that can be presented to the device is fixed in advance, the problem of selecting an informative test is essentially equivalent to probe selection. For each test, each suspect (ideally) predicts a certain outcome, hence the best test is the one which splits the set of suspects in half.

If, on the other hand, the set of possible tests is unknown or pragmatically infinite, it is necessary to generate an appropriate test. A simple, sub-optimal technique will serve to illustrate the basic idea and difficulties: Design a test for each suspect in turn, that is, find a set of inputs that will give two different outputs depending on the condition of that one component. This will serve to determine whether the fault is in the current suspect or among those remaining.

As an example, assume that AND-gate AND-1 in figure 20 is suspected of malfunctioning, in particular of taking in 1's and sending out 0. We want a set of inputs that will indicate whether that is really how the component is behaving.

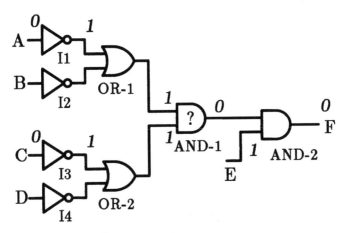

Figure 20. An example of test generation.

To do that we need to get a 1 to both inputs to the gate, then ensure that its output is routed out to where it can be measured. The intuition is straightforward: Work backward from the inputs of AND-1, then forward from the output. We can get a 1 on the upper input by ensuring that OR-1 outputs a 1; this in turn can be ensured if the input to inverter I1 at A is 0. The value at B then does not matter. Similar reasoning from the lower input of AND-1 yields 0 at C. Then in order to ensure that the output of AND-1 can be measured accurately at the device output, we need a 1 at E, the lower input to AND-2. With that input vector it appears that the value at F will determine unambiguously whether AND-1 is malfunctioning in the manner noted.

This style of reasoning is the essence of test generation as traditionally practiced. While the approach is appealing in its intuitive clarity and simplicity, it has important limitations. For our purposes, the most significant limitation is its insensitivity to the presence of other suspects in the device and the resulting insufficient specificity. What if, in the current example,

I1 and I3 also happen to be suspects? The test vector selected will generate a value at F that depends on the state of more than one suspect: If the value is incorrect any of the three components may be to blame.

Stated in this fashion the difficulty immediately suggests one plausible remedy: When routing signals through the device, whenever possible route the signal only through known good components (components that are not suspects). Using this strategy the test generation process would select I2 and I4 to provide the inputs to the OR gates, and end up producing a test that was completely specific, that is, dependent on the condition of only one suspect, AND-1. Work by Shirley and Davis [1983] describes a system that reasons in this fashion and that produces tests that are as informative and specific as possible.

A second substantial problem in testing arises in circuits with reconvergent fanout. If, for example, the lower input of AND-2 had been attached to input D (rather than having its own input E), the value at D would have entered into two different goals: Establishing the lower input to AND-1 and routing the output through AND-2. It is thus a problem of planning in the face of interacting conjunctive subgoals, often resulting in backtracking and potentially involving a considerable amount of search, because test generation is in the worst case NP-complete.

◇ Cost considerations

Underlying the preceding analysis are a number of assumptions about the relative costs of probing, test application, and computation, where the *cost* of an action is typically taken to mean the amount of time it takes to perform.

Analysis aimed at selection of optimal probes is useful only when computation is reasonably cheap compared to the probes themselves. There would, for example, be little point in waiting for a ten-minute computation to determine the optimal probe if all of the measurements are easily made in five minutes. In general the assumption holds true, partly because computation keeps getting cheaper and gets cheaper faster than almost anything else. Probing, by contrast, typically means some sort of physical action (hence is it likely to be slower), and some of those actions may result in losing information (for example, having to move boards to get access to probe points). Hence the assumption is typically valid, but it is important to be explicit about it.

Similarly, generation of distinguishing tests is useful only when the required computation is cheaper than probing or when probing is impossible. As above, there is little point in waiting for a computation to construct an informative test if many measurements that would eliminate suspects could be made in the meantime. Although an adequate working assumption, it is violated occasionally because test generation can be expensive (NP-complete for combinational digital circuits).

Finally, an assumption underlying the preceding discussion is that probes are independent of one another and all have equal cost. This assumption is violated if there are a range of technologies for probing the device, each with its own cost, resolution, and number of resulting observations. A digital logic analyzer, for example, yields detailed observations of several signals simultaneously, but requires much more setup time than a simple voltmeter. Hence the voltmeter may be preferable to the logic analyzer even if it yields less information about the currently outstanding suspects. Similarly, tests may have different setup costs—in fact they may have different setup costs depending upon the order in which they are applied—with analogous consequences. The potentially relevant literature on decision theory is too large to survey here, nevertheless it is important to be aware that subtleties of this kind are likely to arise in real applications.

Interim conclusions

We have discussed a substantial collection of ideas and techniques that form the current basis for model-based diagnosis and troubleshooting. A brief review of the highlights will help set the stage for exploring the open research issues.

- Model-based troubleshooting is based on the comparison of observation and prediction.

Observation indicates what the device is actually doing, prediction describes the intended behavior. Discrepancies between the two provide the starting point for diagnosis. An important part of the diagnostic ability of model-based reasoning is provided by behavior descriptions that capture both the causal behavior of the device (predicting outputs from inputs) and inferences that can be made about its behavior (determining inputs from outputs).

One of the important consequences of the model-based view is the ability to view misbehavior as anything other than what the device is supposed to do. We need not pre-enumerate the kinds of things that might go wrong.

- Model-based troubleshooting is device independent.

Given a new device description, work can begin immediately on troubleshooting the new device. Unlike rule-based approaches, there is no time-consuming accumulation of experience. These systems reason instead from engineering principles applicable to a wide variety of devices.

- Model-based troubleshooting is symptom directed.

It reasons from the observed misbehavior toward the underlying fault. This is particularly important for any device complex enough that the set of correct behaviors is too large to explore exhaustively. In that case it is infeasible to run the device through all its correct behaviors to see which one is not working; we work instead from the information supplied by the symptom. The technique is also familiar, in the sense that it captures some of the intuitions and reasoning that experienced people typically use.

Model-based diagnosis can be understood as a process of hypothesis generation, testing and discrimination. Hypothesis generation works from a single symptom to determine which components might have caused that symptom. The key issue is providing a generator that is both complete and informed. We reviewed three different ways to do that, moving from the simplest version to more sophisticated approaches.

Where hypothesis generation works from a single symptom, the goal in hypothesis testing is to determine which candidates can account for all the observations available about the behavior of the device. We examined four approaches, ranging from straightforward fault simulation, to constraint suspension, DART's use of resolution residue, and the GDE approach.

In hypothesis discrimination the fundamental issue is finding inexpensive ways to gather additional information that will distinguish among the surviving hypotheses. In exploring probing strategies we looked at four ideas that used successively more information, beginning with structure, adding information about behavior, *a priori* failure probabilities, and finally ending with a means of estimating which probe will likely yield the shortest sequence of measurements. A brief review of test generation demonstrated that the traditional technique is indiscriminate in its selection of components to use in constructing a test; considerable advantage can therefore be gained by the simple expedient of using only known good components.

Two important elements of the analysis in this chapter are the view of the basic task as a three step process of generate, test, and discriminate, and the exploration of the character and amount of knowledge that can be brought to bear at each step. Dividing the task into those three steps provides an important form of mental hygiene, making it possible to understand each of these fundamentally different problems on its own terms, without being misled by the common implementation practice of intermingling them for efficiency. Exploring the kinds of knowledge used at each stage offers a sound basis for comparing different variations and understanding how and why one may be more powerful than another.

The combination of these two elements also maps out a sizable space of program architectures. This is valuable because it provides a way of unifying what might otherwise appear to be a diverse collection of systems. We claim in fact that the model-based systems built to date fit comfortably somewhere in that space, that is, all the current systems can be characterized in this framework according to the amount and kind of knowledge they use at each stage.

One overall consequence evident at this stage is that model-based diagnosis is a fairly well-understood process. Part of the evidence for this is the character of the different programs that have been built: The variations in the way they work are minor in comparison with the common core of techniques in use. Additional evidence comes from recent success at recasting much of the reasoning in terms of formal logic. The work by Reiter [1987] and Ginsberg [1986], for instance, provides formal definitions of and proofs for some of the ideas presented in more intuitive form here.

All this has two interesting consequences. First, the technology is ready for application. A body of understanding is in place that is sufficient to attack modest-sized but real problems. Building these applications will no doubt raise additional interesting questions, but there is a sufficient base of knowledge available for us to begin to use it.

Second, the technology is well enough understood that the interesting research agenda now consists of either developing substantial advances beyond the techniques outlined earlier or finding fundamentally different ways to proceed. Interesting applications may result from constructing, tracing, and reasoning about dependencies, but research contributions arise by exploring problems for which the existing techniques are inadequate and finding ways to make substantial advances in them.

We consider next a number of problems that may help spur such results.

The Research Issues

Three categories of research issues seem particularly important and promising at this point in the evolution of the art: Device independence and domain independence, scaling up to more complex behaviors, and selecting the *right* model. The first addresses the question of how broadly we can use the current set of ideas. The case for device independence is easily made, because nothing done so far is specific to the particular device(s) examined, but are the ideas more broadly applicable? What happens if they are applied to devices built with entirely different technologies?

Numerous questions arise in considering scaling up to more complex behaviors. At the most basic level, the question is how to represent and reason about the behavior of more complicated devices, in particular those that have memory and thus can present interesting dynamic behavior. A related question is the power of our predictive engines: How can we improve their performance so that predictions can still be made when dealing with complex devices or complex interaction topologies?

Finally, the question of selecting among models confronts a number of very difficult problems. As will become clear, the difficulties start with acknowledging the apparently simple observation that model-based reasoning is only as good as the models we provide to it. That will lead to an interesting and difficult challenge—the battle between complexity and completeness, where the desire to be complete in diagnosis seems directly contradicted by the impossibility of dealing with an unconstrained problem.

Device independence and domain independence

It appears easy to argue that the technology reviewed so far has a strong degree of device independence—given a new description of a different circuit, the same reasoning process can begin immediately. It is not so obvious, by contrast, what degree of domain independence these techniques exhibit. While there has been a small amount of work done in other domains (for example, neurophysiology, hydraulic systems), the vast majority has been aimed at relatively simple electronic circuits.

At this point an intriguing experiment would be to go out on the edge and apply this in a domain where it is not at all obvious that it will work. It would, for instance, be fun to try thinking about clock repair in this fashion. Not the modern digital kind, though; the interesting challenge would be the old-fashioned gear, wire, and spring-driven models. What would it take to describe the behavior and structure of such a device? Can the techniques reviewed above be used to reason about it? The intent here is to work on a problem that strains the state of the art, to teach us more about representing and reasoning about structure and behavior.

Scaling

In considering whether and how this technology can scale up to larger devices, it is important to recognize that there are at least two independent dimensions—size and complexity—and that size alone is not a particularly difficult issue. If the basic components are simple, it is possible to work with thousands of them without straining the current technology. One current program, for instance, models and diagnoses a system with a few thousand components [First *et al.* 1982]. Each of them is very simple, but nothing new is required to apply the existing ideas to this system of thousands of parts. The model entry task may be sizable, but it is an engineering challenge, not a fundamental advance in representation or reasoning.

More interesting challenges arise when we start to deal with devices with complex behavior. As one common sense example, consider the behavior of a VCR that can be programmed to record two different broadcasts at different times in the future. Even this relatively modest-sized finite state machine can present apparently daunting problems of representing and reasoning about behavior.

As a somewhat more immediately useful example, consider the task of describing the behavior of an ALU (arithmetic/logical unit), using the behavior representation technology available today. If that seems tractable, imagine describing the behavior of a common microprocessor like the 80386. How might we describe what that device can do in a way that makes possible examining and reasoning about it? As long as we are at it, imagine describing the behavior of something genuinely complex, like a disk controller.

Nor is complexity solely the province of large-scale devices. Work at the other end of the scale has demonstrated how complex the behavior of a single transistor can be when coarse abstractions like *switch* or *amplifier* prove to be insufficiently detailed [Dague 1987]. Many of the same issues arise here as well.

What might be done? One approach is to look for a new vocabulary, a new set of abstractions designed to deal with the kinds of complexity encountered. Imagine examining the data sheet for the 80386, making careful note of the vocabulary in use. That data sheet is a form of existence proof: With some degree of success it communicates what this device is supposed to do. The easy speculation is that its success arises in large part because it uses the *right* set of abstractions. The more difficult part is understanding what *right* means—what makes these abstractions effective? What is it that they ignore, what do they emphasize, and why are those effective selections?

Complex behavior also forces the question of the adequacy of our predictive engines. As noted earlier, the simpler local constraint propagators stall when encountering the need to deal with more than one equation in one unknown. Although some effort has been directed toward propagating symbolic expressions, the resulting algebra can be quite complex. One possible approach to the problem would be to guide the algebraic manipulations with some knowledge of the device structure and behavior, similar in spirit to the observation that a physicist guides his mathematics by an understanding of the problem and what he is trying to establish. The question is not how to be good at symbolic manipulation of complex expressions, so much as it is knowing what symbolic manipulation to do to avoid the complexity in the first place.

A third set of challenges arises in dealing with devices with memory. If, as is frequently the case with such devices, we know only the inputs supplied to it initially and the final output that results some time later, hypothesis generation and testing becomes truly indiscriminate. Work reported by Hamscher and Davis [1984] for instance, examined the task of diagnosing a sequential multiplier (a device that multiplies one digit at a time, shifting and adding in much the same way the problem is done by hand). If the multiplier's behavior is modeled using the technology reviewed above, candidate generation becomes indiscriminate—almost every component can account for the misbehavior. This is not a minor consequence of current implementations; the difficulty arises from the basic nature of the problem: If all we know is the input at the beginning and the output at the end, the problem is genuinely underconstrained in much the same way that two equations are insufficient to determine the value of three unknowns.

This is a second place in which new abstractions may prove to be the relevant tool, particularly temporal abstractions. Some early work in this direction has been done and seems promising: Hamscher [1988], for instance, demonstrates how temporal abstractions can be effective for such devices.

One other approach that may prove effective in reasoning about complex devices is the notion of *second principles of misbehavior*. One example is the heuristic that, in a complicated device fault manifestations will be obvious. To illustrate, imagine working with a device that includes a current generation microprocessor, one that happens to be broken in some fashion, and consider the consequences of that fault on the microprocessor's behavior. It is possible, but highly unlikely that the consequences will be subtle: It is unlikely for instance that the device will exhibit only a very small perturbation in its expected behavior for only one of the instructions in its instruction set. It is much more likely that the fault will result in some obviously aberrant behavior every time the device is used. One common form of that aberration is for the device to stop producing any behavior at all, for example, by hitting an illegal instruction and halting.

This is one example of the second principle that complicated devices do not break in subtle ways. It is a *principle* in the sense that it can be explained by (and perhaps eventually derived from) arguments about design. In this case, for instance, the argument is that complex designs often involve re-use of modules, both to simplify the design and reduce cost. Re-use of modules in turn means that any error in such a module will tend to have widespread consequences. In a microprocessor, for instance, a single ALU may be used both for the arithmetic required for an ADD instruction and the arithmetic needed to compute the next instruction address. Any error in that ALU will not only yield incorrect sums (which might be overlooked), it will also introduce instruction sequencing errors that are unlikely to be missed.

Because these principles can be grounded in knowledge about design, they are more than device-specific heuristics and are likely to have widespread applicability. They are also an important addition to the ideas explored thus far, because we are as a field a long way from being able to do such reasoning from a purely first principles approach. Second principles of misbehavior thus offer a way of summarizing what would otherwise be a long and difficult derivation.

One challenge we face is finding more of them; one obvious place to start is with experienced troubleshooters. Whenever a model-based system produces a diagnosis that is logical but strikes a human troubleshooter as inappropriate, there is the standard opportunity to find out what it is that the experienced troubleshooter knows that is still missing from the system. Some of that knowledge may point toward additional second principles of useful breadth and utility.

Modeling is the hard part

The third and possibly most intriguing area of research is brought into focus by acknowledging that all model-based reasoning is only as good as the model. This observation is in some ways obvious and in some ways fairly subtle, but the consequences are interesting and present difficult problems.

To illustrate one version of the problem, note that all of the reasoning techniques reviewed earlier generate predictions by propagating along the pathways shown in the device description, then traced back from the discrepancies along those same pathways to find suspects. The crucial point is twofold: Suspects are found by tracing causal pathways back from a symptom, and all of the reasoning above accepted the device description as given, implicitly assuming that the pathways supplied accurately model causality in the device. Yet this can easily be false.

One commonplace example of this phenomenon is a bridging fault, the event that results when a chip is being soldered in place and enough solder accumulates at two adjacent pins to bridge the gap between them (see figure 21). The result is a connection—a causal pathway—where none was intended.

The possibility of faults of this sort has a particularly interesting consequence. Because candidates are found by tracing back along causal pathways, if the pathways indicated by the device description are different from those in the actual device, the tracing process will lead to the wrong components. Put somewhat more simply, the great virtue of the model-based approach is its ability to reason from the description of structure and behavior, yet the fatal flaw in the model-based approach is that it reasons from the description of structure and behavior, *and that description might not capture the actual causality in the device.*

◇ The model must be wrong

How is it that the model might not be an accurate description of the causality in the device? One possibility is that the device is not supposed to be

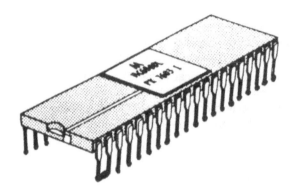

Figure 21. A solder bridge.

that way. The bridge fault is one example of this, another is an error during assembly—the device is simply wired up incorrectly.

A second possibility is unexpected pathways of interaction. In an electronic circuit, a wire is the expected pathway of interaction; that is how components are supposed to affect one another. But there can be other, unexpected, pathways as well: One component may heat up another, two wires carrying high frequency signals may be so close that they affect one another via electromagnetic radiation, etc. The important point is that the design description, by *intent*, only tells us about the pathways of interaction that are supposed to occur. In the device itself other unknown pathways may be operating. The consequences of this are particularly evident in DART's explicit statement that its diagnosis is restricted only to "... propositions from the design description or their negation." Hence the only kinds of diagnoses it can even consider are those stating that some component explicitly mentioned in the design description is malfunctioning.

Third, the model may not match the device because in our routine practice we explicitly decide not to represent a particular level of detail. In a large circuit, for instance, we may choose not to model every individual wire, settling instead for a slightly more coarse-grained model in which components are modeled as connected directly to one another.

But most importantly, it is in principle necessarily true that the model be different from the device. It is the fundamental nature of all models, all representations, that is at issue here: There is no such thing as an assumption-free representation. Every model, every representation contains simplifying assumptions. That is what models are, so in some ways this is perfectly obvious.

The perhaps less obvious part is the unavoidable impact this has on model-based reasoning. As noted, the fundamental idea behind the technique is the idea that, if the model is correct, then all the discrepancies between observation and prediction arise from, and can be traced back along causal pathways to, defects in the device. But the model is, inevitably and in principle, *never* correct.

To be more precise, the model is never *completely* correct. When it is a good enough approximation, the techniques described earlier are successful. But the inevitability of incorrectness in theory and the pragmatic reality of it in practice mean that this issue is real and crucial to the robustness of the systems we build. We need to understand both what effect it has on the systems we build and how to deal with it.

◊ **Consequence: Complexity versus completeness**

One of the most important effects of the phenomenon is an inevitable tension between complexity and completeness. To be complete, diagnostic reasoning would have to consider all the things that may possibly go wrong, along every *possible* pathway of interaction. But such reasoning would be indiscriminate, implicating every component—there would always be some (perhaps convoluted) pathway by which that component might have caused the problem. Yet if we make any simplifying assumptions, that is, omit any pathway, there will be entire classes of faults that the system will never be able to diagnose.

There is a fundamental problem here. If we make any simplifying assumptions we run the risk of being incomplete, because the simplifying assumption might be the one that encompasses the actual fault. Yet without some simplifying assumptions the reasoning drowns in complexity.

While this arises in a particularly immediate fashion here, it appears to be a fundamental issue for problem solving in general. Any time we set out to solve a problem, we need to make simplifying assumptions about the world in order to get started, yet sometimes those assumptions are wrong. Thus any techniques that can help us to select, organize and manage the assumptions that will be of potentially broad utility.

◊ **Consequence: Model selection is fundamental**

Perhaps the most interesting implication of this line of argument is the significance of the problem of model selection. Because there are no assumption-free representations, one strategy would be to assemble a collection of them, each embodying a different set of assumptions, along with a body of knowledge about how to select carefully from among them. No one of them or any simple combination of them provides a complete representation, but progress might be made by selecting carefully from among them, attempting to make enough assumptions to keep the problem tractable, yet making a few as possible to reduce the chance of not being able to see the actual problem.

It is likely as well that the choice will not only have to be judicious, but repeated and dynamic as well, changing views on the fly as understanding of the problem evolves. One support for this approach is the observation that experienced engineers do something like this. We need to understand what it is they know and how they reason about model selection.

The problem seems to lie at the heart of engineering problem solving: Perhaps the most basic, most important decision made in starting to solve a problem is deciding *how to think about it*. What is it that suggests modeling something as an analog device, a digital device, or a hydraulic device? How do we know what is relevant? How does the process begin? The problem seems difficult but particularly intriguing.

Three speculations suggest possible approaches to the problem. First, we might review the difficulties mentioned above that are encountered when using models, and reformulate them as heuristics for model design [Hamscher 1988]. The difficulty presented by reconvergent fanout (that is, causing local propagation to stall) can, for instance, be reduced to some degree by selecting module boundaries to encapsulate the fanout. Similarly, judicious selection of module boundaries can help reduce hidden state, the problem that makes diagnosis underconstrained in the case of the sequential multiplier. A set of such heuristics would assist in the design of models that reduce or avoid some of the problems encountered above.

A second speculation explores the problem of deciding how to model something by suggesting that different pathways of interaction define different kinds of models, different representations, which can then be layered to provide a sequence of successively more complex views [Davis 1984]. A wire, for instance, is one pathway of interaction, it defines the traditional schematic. If heat is the relevant pathway, that defines a different representation of the device, one in which *distance* is defined in terms of how easily one device heats another. Electromagnetic radiation is a third pathway that defines yet another kind of model and another distance metric.

These multiple different kinds of models are then organized from simplest to more complex (defining *simplicity* is itself an open issue), so that the system starts by using the simplest and falls back on more complex models only as necessary. The technique has been used to diagnose a bridging fault successfully, demonstrating that multiple models using different representations and different definitions of distance can be used to reduce complexity without permanently losing completeness [Davis 1984].

A third speculation begins with the observation that every model is defined by a set of simplifying assumptions. We might collect the set of all the simplifying assumptions routinely made and consider the space of models that are generated by it. For example, figure 22 shows three differ-

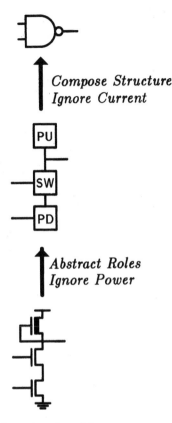

Figure 22. A simple hierarchy of models.

ent models of a NAND gate, beginning with the traditional transistor level model at the bottom.

Assuming that power can be ignored, then abstracting away from the specific subcomponents to the roles they play, produces the intermediate level representation in the middle. Two further simplifying assumptions—that current can be ignored and that all the subcomponents can be encompassed by a single box, yield the traditional representation at the top. Hence these two pairs of assumptions yield two successively simpler models of the device.

But these are not the only models those assumptions can generate. The simple trick of changing the order in which the assumptions are made produces an entire lattice of different models (see figure 23).

Some of them are admittedly rather obscure, but there are in fact (perhaps obscure) circumstances under which every one of them will be the *right* way to think about the device. One reason why some faults are so difficult to diagnose may be precisely because the *right* model in that case is a particularly unusual set of assumptions. Even faults as commonplace as

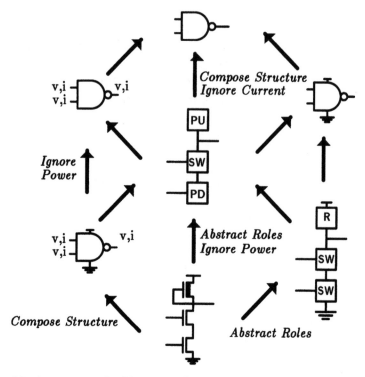

Figure 23. A more complex hierarchy of models.

bridges illustrate the issue: Part of the reason they are especially difficult to diagnose is that they require examining a less familiar representation—the physical layout of the chips. While the fault is *simple* in that representation (two adjacent pins), it can appear on the functional diagram as a connection between two widely separated points.

This is, of course, still speculation. Given that the lattice in figure 23 was generated simply by changing the order of the assumptions, there is no particularly compelling reason to believe that it will work well. Nor have we answered the second half of the question: How to select from among the models, and how to know which to choose next when one of them begins to fail. This is only a beginning, but it may be worth further consideration.

Summary

We began this survey by viewing model-based diagnostic reasoning as the interaction of prediction and observation, and saw that one useful consequence was the chance to view misbehavior as anything other than what the device is supposed to do. Model-based reasoning thus covers a broader collection of faults than traditional approaches to diagnosis. A second virtue of the technique is its device independence, enabling us to begin reasoning about a system as soon as its structure and behavior description is available.

In examining how to represent structure, we noted the utility of descriptions that were hierarchic, object-centered, and topologically identical to the device being modeled. In examining behavior we noted the widespread use of constraint-like descriptions that allow both simulating the actual behavior of the device and making inferences about what the values at inputs must have been.

We explored diagnostic reasoning by viewing it in the three phases of hypothesis generation, test, and discrimination. This view allowed exploration of each of these fundamentally different problems on its own terms, made clear the common core of techniques that are in use, and offered evidence for the claim that model-based systems to date fit into the space of architectures characterized by the amount and kind of knowledge they use at each stage. The view also supports the claim that the process is reasonably well understood: Building a dependency-tracing model-based reasoner is now a fairly routine process.

Finally, we examined three major open research issues. We explored the question of domain independence, leading to the suggestion of trying these techniques on devices from widely different domains, to extend our ability to describe structure and behavior. We examined the difficulties in scaling up to devices with considerably more complex behavior, speculated about the possibility of finding a new vocabulary of effective abstractions, and touched on the difficulty of producing predictions in the face of complex behavior. And we emphasized the fundamental role and fundamental difficulty of model selection as the central problem in both extending the reach of these programs and ensuring their robustness.

Many people contributed useful suggestions aiding both the research and writing of this chapter, including Johan de Kleer, Mike Genesereth, Paul Resnick, Mark Shirley, Howard Shrobe, Reid Simmons, Jeff Van Baalen, Dan Weld, Brian Williams, and Peng Wu.

This chapter describes research done at the Artificial Intelligence Laboratory of the Massachusetts Institute of Technology. Support for the laboratory's artificial intelligence research has been provided in part by the Digital Equipment Corporation, in part by the Advanced Research Projects Agency of the Department of Defense under Office of Naval Research contract N00014-85-K-0124, and in part by Wang Corporation. The views and conclusions contained in this document are those of the authors, and should not be interpreted as representing the policies, either expressed or implied, of the Digital Equipment Corporation or of the Department of Defense.

References

Breuer, M. A., and A. Friedman [1976], *A Diagnosis and Reliable Design of Digital Systems*, Computer Science Press, Rockville, MD.

Brown, A. L., "Qualitative Knowledge, Causal Reasoning, and the Localization of Failures," Report AI-TR-362, Artificial Intelligence Laboratory, Massachusetts Institute of Technology, Cambridge, MA, 1976.

Brown, J. S., R. R. Burton, and J. de Kleer, "Pedagogical, Natural Language, and Knowledge Engineering Techniques in SOPHIE I, II, and III," in *Intelligent Tutoring Systems*, edited by D. Sleeman, and J. S. Brown, Academic Press, New York, pp. 227–282, 1982.

Dague, P., O. Raiman, and P. Deves, "Troubleshooting: When Modeling is the Difficulty," *Proceedings of AAAI-87*, Seattle, WA, pp. 600–605, 1987.

Davis R., H. Shrobe, W. Hamscher, K. Wieckert, M. Shirley, and S. Polit, "Diagnosis Based on Structure and Function," *Proceedings of AAAI-82*, Pittsburgh, PA, pp 137–142, 1982.

Davis, R, "Diagnostic Reasoning Based on Structure and Behavior," *Artificial Intelligence* vol. 24, no. 3, pp. 347–410, 1984.

de Kleer, J., "Local Methods for Localizing Faults in Electronic Circuits," Report AIM-394 (out of print), Artificial Intelligence Laboratory, Massachusetts Institute of Technology, Cambridge, MA, 1976.

de Kleer, J., and B. C. Williams, "Diagnosing Multiple Faults," *Artificial Intelligence*, vol. 32, no. 1, pp. 97–130, 1987.

First, M. B., B. J. Weimer, S. McLinden, and R. A. Miller "LOCALIZE: Computer-Assisted Localization of Peripheral Nervous System Lesions," *Computers and Biomedical Research*, vol. 15, no. 6, pp. 525–543, 1982.

Genesereth, M. R., "The Use of Design Descriptions in Automated Diagnosis," *Artificial Intelligence*, vol. 24, no. 3, pp. 411–436, 1984.

Ginsberg, M., "Counterfactuals," *Artificial Intelligence*, vol. 30, no. 1, pp. 35–80, 1986.

Hamscher, W., and R. Davis, "Candidate Generation for Devices with State: An Inherently Underconstrained Problem," *Proceedings of AAAI-84*, Austin, TX, pp. 142–147, 1984.

Hamscher, W., and R. Davis, "Issues in Model Based Troubleshooting," Report AIM-893, Artificial Intelligence Laboratory, Massachusetts Institute of Technology, Cambridge, MA, 1987.

Hamscher, W., "Representations for Model Based Troubleshooting," available from the author, 1988.

Pan, J., "Qualitative Reasoning with Deep-level Mechanism Models for Diagnoses of Mechanism Failures," *Proceedings of CAIA-84*, Denver, CO, pp. 295–301, IEEE, 1984.

Patil, R., P. Szolovits, and W. Schwartz, "Causal understanding of patient illness in medical diagnosis," *Proceedings of IJCAI-81*, Vancouver, BC, pp. 893–899, 1981.

Reiter, R., "A Theory of Diagnosis from First Principles," *Artificial Intelligence*, vol. 32, no. 1, pp. 57–96, 1987.

Scarl, E., J. R. Jamieson, and C. I. Delaune, "A Fault Detection and Isolation Method Applied to Liquid Oxygen Loading for the Space Shuttle," *Proceedings of IJCAI-85*, Los Angeles, CA, pp. 414–416, 1985.

Shirley, M. H., and R. Davis, "Generating Distinguishing Tests based on Hierarchical Models and Symptom Information," *IEEE International Conference on Computer Design*, 1983.

Sussman, G. J., and G. L. Steele, "Constraints: A Language for Expressing Almost-Hierarchical Descriptions," *Artificial Intelligence*, vol. 14, no. 1, pp. 1–40, 1980.

16

What is innovative invention and how might a computer do it? To answer these questions, Williams has developed a collection of programs that have invented fluid-level regulators like those used in ancient lamps and that have improved the design of VLSI circuits like those used in modern computers.

Williams' approach centers on representation, especially the representation of what devices do and how devices interact. One of Williams' programs uses suitably represented knowledge to create a large network of constraint-enforcing elements, all stuck together via their interaction variables. Such a network constitutes what he calls the interaction topology. Next, another program searches for a path in the interaction topology that properly connects the input-output variables that specify the behavior of the desired device. Finally, still another program translates the elements along the discovered path into physical components.

Invention from First Principles: An Overview

Brian C. Williams

"Discoveries and inventions arise from the observation of little things."

—ALEXANDER GRAHAM BELL

One hallmark of intelligence is the ability to create. In this chapter we explore one aspect of creativity—the process of invention. Invention involves much more than applying accumulated design experience to routine problems. A robust approach to invention—one that captures a designer's ability to exploit fundamentally new technologies and to handle extraordinary design situations—requires the ability to construct novel artifacts from basic physical principles, in the absence of adequate prior experience. A central question we address is:

> How might a designer use his understanding of basic physical principles to develop innovative devices?

Throughout this chapter we use the term *invention* to highlight our specific focus within design on the process of innovation from basic physical principles (as opposed, for example, to design solely from libraries of design fragments). And we use *inventor* to refer to the expert designer who is particularly skillful at constructing novel devices.

Innovation is a complex process that researchers are only beginning to explore [Murthy & Addanki 1987; Ulrich 1988; Williams 1989; Joskowicz & Addanki 1989]. This chapter focuses on the invention of analog devices whose desired behavior is described by qualitative state diagrams

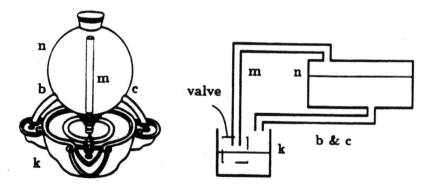

Figure 1. Philon's lamp, taken from Mayr [1970] (left), and a schematic description highlighting the lamp's components and interconnection (right). Letters denote corresponding parts in the two diagrams. The open pan at the bottom, k, is the lamp, which holds a floating wick. The upper, spherical vessel, n, holds a supply of oil, used to restore the oil level in the pan. Pipe m allows air flow into vessel n, while b and c are capillary tubes that allow oil to flow from n to pan k, without letting air to flow up through them. The end of pipe b and the oil surface of k act like a valve, opening or closing off airflow through b.

[deKleer 1984; Forbus 1984; Williams 1984; Kuipers 1986],[1] and whose physical structure is described by a network of primitive components, such as containers, pipes, and valves. The theory presented captures several key aspects of the design process used to construct innovative devices like the ancient oil lamp shown in figure 1.[2]

This lamp consists of a wick floating in a pan of oil, plus a clever mechanism for automatically refilling the pan as oil is consumed:

> Assume the storage vessel n is full of oil, and the height of oil in the pan k is sufficient to just cover the opening of the vertical pipe m. As the wick burns, consuming oil, the oil level in the pan k goes down. When an air gap appears between the end of pipe m and the surface of the oil in k, air flows through m into the storage vessel n. This allows oil to flow out of n, through pipes b and c, and into pan k, thus restoring the oil level in k. When

---

[1] A qualitative state diagram describes the movement of quantities between distinct intervals of interest, such as a digital circuit's voltage moving between intervals denoting logic 1 and 0, and the movement of components between interesting regions of their state space, such as a transistor moving between regions where it is saturated, unsaturated or cutoff.

[2] In our design approach we model the pipe end and fluid surface as a primitive component—a type of valve. Our theory currently does not capture the detailed geometric reasoning necessary to invent it.

the oil rises enough to cover the lower end of pipe m, air cannot enter the storage vessel n to replace oil leaving. Thus the outflow through b and c stops.

Our theory, called *Interaction-based Invention*, is based on the following insights:

- One way a device is innovative is if it works in a way noticeably different from those seen before.

- To identify noticeably different ways of producing a desired behavior, the inventor focuses on the topology of interactions between quantities that a device produces (see figure 2).

- Invention involves constructing a graph of interactions (called an *interaction topology*) that both produces the desired behavior and makes evident a network of physical components that implements those interactions (see figure 3).

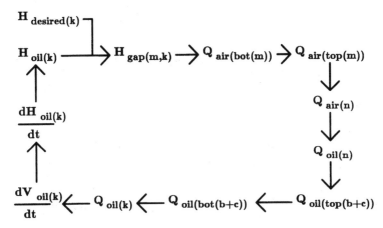

Figure 2. Philon's oil lamp is innovative in the way it works. One such innovation is that the sequence of interactions used by the lamp to produce the desired behavior is one of the first that was consciously designed to contain a feedback loop. Another innovation is the use of air flow into the supply vessel, $Q_{air(n)}$, to control its oil outflow, $Q_{oil(n)}$. These innovations are conveyed by the graph shown above. Each edge denotes a set of state variables that interact as a result of some component or connection. The letters b, c, k, m, and n correspond to components labeled in figure 1. $H_{desired(k)}$ and $H_{oil(k)}$ are the desired and current levels of oil in pan k; $H_{gap(m,k)}$ is the height of the air gap between the oil surface of k and the lower end of pipe m; $Q_{air(top(m))}$ and $Q_{air(bot(m))}$ are air flow through the top and bottom of pipe m, $Q_{air(n)}$ is air flow into and $Q_{oil(n)}$ is oil flow out of storage vessel n; $Q_{oil(top(b+c))}$ and $Q_{oil(bot(b+c))}$ are oil flow through pipes b and c; $Q_{oil(k)}$ is oil flow into pan k, and $V_{oil(k)}$ is the volume of oil in k.

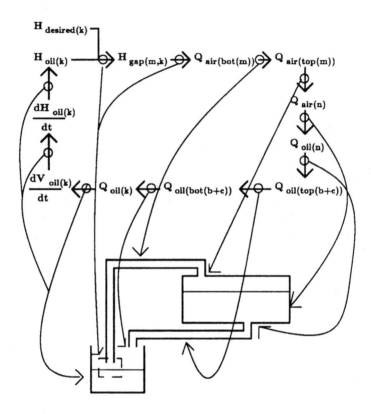

Figure 3. Interaction-based Invention applied to Philon's lamp. The desired behavior of the lamp is to restore its oil level, that is to raise or lower $H_{oil(k)}$ until it is equivalent to $H_{desired}$. Interaction-based invention accomplishes this by constructing a topology of interactions that relates $H_{oil(k)}$, $H_{desired}$, and $dH_{oil(k)}/dt$ in the desired manner (see the upper half of this figure). The topology is built from interactions each of which is producible by a single component or structural connection. Thus the selection of interactions used to build the topology determine the components and connections of the physical structure. In the figure, each arrow from the interaction topology to physical structure denotes the component or connection that produces a specific interaction.

These insights were gained by exploring the *art of invention from a historical perspective*. It is likely, during ancient times, that innovative devices were developed primarily from a basic knowledge of physics. At that time little else was known; a body of design experience had not yet been accumulated.[3] We claim that this process of constructing innovative devices from

---

[3]We do not claim that all early designs arose from basic principles. For example, in some instances it is likely that a device was designed using a direct analogy

fundamental principles of physics is also a crucial component of modern invention. Thus understanding how past innovations arose is an important means of shedding light on modern invention. To this end, our theory of interaction-based invention is based on insights derived from case studies of historically significant devices, invented in ancient (300 BC) and recent times (the 1970's). The former is a set of Arabian fluid regulators, and the latter is a progression of high performance, MOS memory buffers. The resulting insights have allowed us to capture key aspects of the process by which innovative devices first emerge from basic principles of physics, and then evolve over time into sophisticated high performance devices. While we have used the case studies to provide clues about the salient features of the design process, their purpose is not to argue for the psychological validity of our theory. Ultimately, computational grounds provide the true test of the theory.

To test our theory we have implemented a program, called the Interaction-Based Invention System (*IBIS*), which has been demonstrated by walking it through the design of simple electrical and hydro-mechanical devices, similar to the ancient fluid devices shown earlier.

The objective of this chapter is to highlight the underlying motivation, insights, and key contributions of our approach. A detailed technical exposition is presented in Williams [1989].

Why Invention?

Why is a theory of invention important? We claim that such a theory is central both to understanding artificial intelligence and to developing a robust automation of the design process. First, with respect to artificial intelligence, invention strikes at the heart of two key aspects of intelligence—tool building and creativity. The former is the ability, not only to explain physical phenomena, but to put these phenomena to use by constructing tools. In our case, the phenomena are described as basic laws of physics and the tools constructed are hydro-mechanical or electrical devices. An important aspect of the second—creativity—is a facility to construct non-obvious solutions, to a task, which are qualitatively different from those seen before. In our case the task is design, the solutions are physical devices, and the qualitative differences are a type of design innovation where devices work in noticeably different ways.

In addition, our theory of invention unifies and substantially contributes to many areas of reasoning that are at the center of artificial intelligence research. These include, but are not limited to, qualitative, causal,

---

to a naturally occurring object, rather than basic principles. But in many cases a device, such as Philon's lamp, has no obvious analogue. Thus, it is plausible that these devices were designed largely from basic principles.

temporal, algebraic, and *constructive* reasoning.[4] These types of reasoning are fundamental, not only to invention, but scientific and commonsense reasoning tasks in general, such as diagnosis, planning, and theory formation. The specific contributions made to each area are highlighted later in this chapter.

Next consider our claim that capturing the process of invention is at the heart of developing a robust approach to design—that is, that both design from fundamental principles and the process of innovation are central. To achieve the desired generality, a robust approach might have to consider the behavior of any possible device structure, in our case any configuration of primitive components. Evaluating the behavior of any such configuration requires reasoning from fundamental principles—physical laws that describe the behavior of primitive components and connections, and mathematical axioms that describe how these behaviors compose. We call reasoning from this set of physical laws and mathematical axioms *design from first principles*. In our approach the laws are those of physical systems dynamics [Shearer *et al.* 1971; Rosenberg & Karnopp 1983], and circuit theory [Bose & Stevens 1965], and the axioms are those of a qualitative algebra that we call $Q1$.

But these principles are not enough. A naive design approach quickly becomes overwhelmed by the number of possibilities that result from the generality of the first principles. Thus a robust approach must capture the process of innovation—an expert designer's facility at picking out noticeably different solutions from this enormous space.

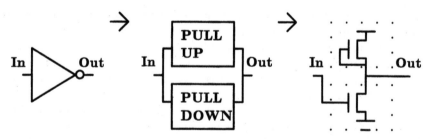

Figure 4. Example of library design applied to constructing an inverter.

Existing design approaches are inadequate exactly because they cannot invent. To see this consider the state of the art in design research. The predominant approach explored in the artificial intelligence design community [McDermott 1977; Ressler 1984; Mitchell *et al.* 1983; Mitchell *et al.* 1985; Mittal *et al.* 1986; Murthy & Addanki 1987; Roylance 1980]

---

[4]Constructive reasoning is a type of terminological reasoning we have developed for building interaction topologies. Terminological reasoning involves reasoning from the definitions of concepts, and is one focus of the knowledge representation community [Brachman & Levesque 1985].

and the computer-aided design community [Johannsen 1979; Sisskind *et al.* 1982; Matson 1985] is library design.[5] These appear under labels such as routine design, hierarchical refinement, configuration, or silicon compilation. The basic idea is, given a desired behavior, a design schema is looked up in the library that matches this behavior. For example, suppose we want to design an inverter (see the left side of figure 4).

Then the library is consulted, for example, deriving a schema which uses a pullup and pulldown subcircuit (see the middle of figure 4).

This schema is then refined by successively instantiating schemas from the library, until a design is constructed that consists only of primitive components, in this case MOS transistors (see the right side of figure 4). The schemas serve the purpose of restricting the possible configurations of components, and precompiling their composite behavior. This helps the efficiency of the design system, but at a substantial expense to its generality.

Consider the question—how close are we to a theory of invention? Library design systems are users, but not *producers* of innovations. They have no ability to use first principles, or to focus their application on constructing innovative devices. While it is conceivable that these systems could stumble across a novel design, they have not been embodied with the abilities that allow skilled designers to consistently come up with innovations. Thus, very little progress has been made in this earlier work towards a theory of invention.

Yet such a theory is important, even for apparently routine design tasks. Existing automated design systems often fail on these problems, because they cannot meet the minimum performance constraints. For example, the design system fails to design an inverter whose output rises and falls fast enough.

From a practical standpoint, this inadequacy cannot be overcome by manually augmenting the design libraries with innovations developed by human designers. It is not feasible to anticipate the set of all innovations required—the continual desire for higher performance and rapid technology shifts provides an extraordinary demand for new innovations. Meeting these demands requires a tremendous effort that occupies a significant component of a designer's time.

Instead, to alleviate this burden from the designer, a design system's routine design techniques must be augmented with the ability to innovate when required, by exploiting new technologies and existing technologies in novel ways. An important way to accomplish this is to reason from the fundamental principles of physics that characterize these technologies. Thus, for technologies that rapidly change, *being a competent designer means being able to invent.*

---

[5]Two recent exceptions are Joskowicz and Addanki [1989] and Ulrich [1988] which reason at or close to the level of first principles.

Structuring a Theory of Invention

How do we account for inventions like Philon's lamp? In the preceding section we argued that a designer can achieve the desired generality by reasoning from first principles, but that the resulting set of options presented can be overwhelming. An inventor is distinguished not so much by the fundamental principles he knows, but by the way he uses them and how he guides the search for a new device in an overwhelming space of possibilities.

To avoid being overwhelmed the inventor must use every element available to focus the search for innovative devices. We know from artificial intelligence that three basic elements of problem solving are the *search strategies, representations, and basic operations* used. To be successful, each of these elements must be used to increase the inventor's ability to focus.

Artificial intelligence has developed some well known insights that provide guidelines for selecting appropriate representations, operations, and search strategies for invention. Some examples are:

- A representation should make qualitative differences between solutions explicit.
- A representation should be as abstract as possible, while capturing the salient features of a solution.
- The basic operations performed by a problem solver should allow it to take the biggest steps possible through the search space, without sacrificing generality.
- A solution can be arrived at quickly by constructing a coarse solution in an approximate search space and then refining it.
- An incorrect solution can be refined by pinpointing the cause of failure and debugging it.

Each of these insights provides an important starting point. To date, however, little has been known, for example, about the specific qualitative differences, abstractions, operations, approximate spaces, and debugging techniques that are suitable for a particular category of problem solving tasks.

We believe that our concept of a topology of interactions, and our perspective of design as building interaction topologies provides a key to determining these specific elements for invention. The next two sections elaborate on these two points. The remaining sections highlight the major contributions of our theory in terms of the strategies, representations, and operations it contains.

What Makes a Device Innovative

To gain insight into how to focus the search for innovations, we begin by examining the distinguishing features of the devices we would like to invent. Consider the problem, faced by ancient inventors, of building a water clock (see figure 5).[6] The key to developing a water clock is to produce a steady flow of water that can be accumulated to measure time. A device that produces this steady flow is called a fluid regulator. A common way to implement a fluid regulator is to put a hole at the base of a container. The flow out of this hole is then made constant by maintaining a constant height of water in the container. Inventors of the era knew about many of the properties of fluids (due in part to Archimedes), as well as simple devices such as containers, pipes, valves, floats, scales, and linkages. The problem then becomes, how can we maintain a constant height of water in a container using these simple devices and principles?

Fluid Regulator

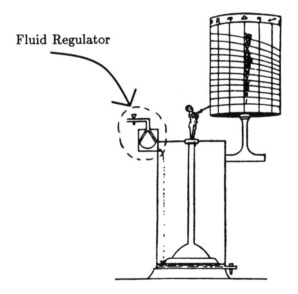

Figure 5. Ktesibios' water clock with fluid regulator, developed by Ktesibios of Alexandria in the third century BC (the figure is adapted from Mayr [1970]). The fluid regulator provides a constant flow of fluid into the large container, causing its fluid level to increase at a constant rate. A float rises with the fluid, and a figurine attached to the top of the float points to the corresponding time.

---

[6]The examples of feedback control used in this section are taken from *The Origins of Feedback Control* by Otto Mayr [1970]. This book has provided a valuable source of inspiration in exploring the evolutionary design process.

The Egyptians and Arabs came up with many solutions to this and similar problems. We consider two of the most innovative designs. Figure 6 shows a device (developed by Heron of Alexandria in the first century AD) that maintains a constant fluid height by weighing the contents of the container. The device consists of a cup k, whose height of fluid is being regulated, a large vase n, that supplies fluid, together with a scale, weight, linkage, valve, and pipe that regulate the fluid level. The valve is formed by using a disk d, attached to the linkage l, to open and close the end of the pipe b, inside the vase. The device maintains a constant fluid level as follows:

> If the fluid level in the cup is too low, then the cup will be too light, and the weight at the end of the scale will move downward. Through a set of linkages this opens the valve inside the vase, allowing fluid to flow into the cup. As a result the cup's height of fluid and weight increases. Eventually the fluid reaches the desired height, at which point the scale tips, closing the valve.

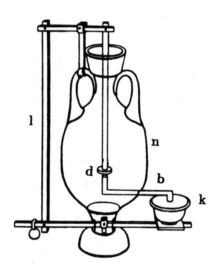

Figure 6. Heron's weight regulator.

A second design for a fluid regulator, by Philon of Byzantium, was shown earlier in figure 1, and is a clever means of maintaining a constant height of oil in a lamp. How this device works is summarized in figure 1.

An important component of what makes these devices innovative is that they work in a way that is qualitatively different from preceding inventions of the time. But what do we mean by *working qualitatively differently?* In fact what do we mean by *how something works?*

One of the major perspectives taken in our research is the notion that *how a device "works" is captured by the sequence of interactions between variables that achieve the desired behavior.* We call this sequence an *interaction topology*. These interactions are traced in the explanations for the behavior of the above two fluid regulators and are depicted graphically in figure 7.

The devices are *qualitatively different* in part because the paths traced by the interactions are different from their predecessors: that is, the *connectivity of the interactions* is different. Both devices are considered innovative for their time because they use the difference between existing and desired fluid height to control the rate that fluid flows into the container. The sequence of comparison followed by adjustment (that is, feedback control) had not appeared in earlier designs. Graphically, they are the first devices that are explicitly designed so that their interaction topologies contain a loop.

The particular path of interactions used to relate height and rate of inflow is also innovative in each case. Heron measures the fluid height indirectly through container weight, which is then used to control the rate of water inflow through a mechanical linkage. For Philon's lamp the innovative component of the path is the interactions used to control flow of oil into the lamp. Earlier designs controlled this flow directly through a valve. Philon's lamp controls this flow indirectly—using oil height to control air flow into the closed oil container; which in turn controls the flow of oil into the lamp by exploiting conservation of flow for a closed container. The devices are distinguished by differences in their topology of interactions.

In some domains, such as digital electronics, a device's interaction topology is reflected in its physical structure. However, this is not the case for our focus—continuous analog systems. Thus a distinct representation is required. A diagram of a device's physical structure (such as figure 1 or figure 6), is not a vivid representation of the device's innovative aspects. That is, it takes a while to extract from the diagram how a device works. Part of the problem is that the physical structure of a device often does not make apparent the complex set of interactions it produces. For example, a single container of fluid produces a set of interactions interrelating pressures, fluid flows, fluid heights, fluid density, and gravity. Thus to understand the devices above we must first make the set of interactions explicit (see figure 8). Similarly, to search for innovations during design, the primary focus should be on the interaction topology, rather than physical structure.

Also because the set of interactions produced by each component of a device is often complex, many interactions may be produced that are extraneous or parasitic to the desired behavior of the overall device. We need to focus, during analysis or design, on the interactions relevant to producing the desired behavior (see figure 8, highlighted interactions). In

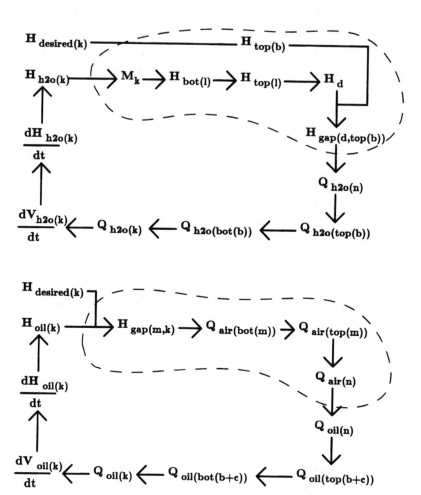

Figure 7. Graphs of interactions between quantities traced by explanations of how ancient fluid devices work. The upper graph is that for Heron's weight regulator and the lower is that for Philon's lamp (repeated from figure 2). In the upper graph M_k is the mass of the cup (including water). As before, H, V, and Q are height, volume, and flow. The topology of these interactions highlights qualitative differences between how the two devices work. Although both graphs contain a feedback loop, the sequence of variables related are different. In this figure differences between the two topologies are highlighted by dashed circles. Note that these graphs are simplified versions of the interaction topologies required to understand each device's behavior in detail.

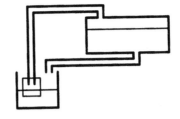

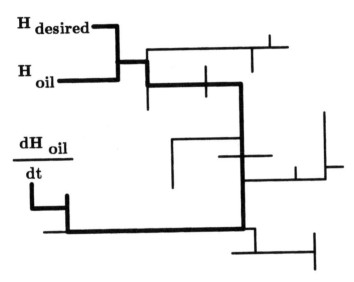

Figure 8. To understand how a device works we must make explicit the topology of interactions, and also identify those interactions that impact the device's desired behavior (the highlighted interactions).

more complex devices an interaction may play several roles during different periods of a device's behavior. We need to separate out these different roles.

During this discussion our primary focus has been on the connectivity of interactions. But this is only part of the picture. To capture how a device works an interaction topology must also include a qualitative description of *how* the variables interact. These descriptions highlight features of the interactions necessary to achieve the device's desired behavior. We elaborate upon the interaction representation later in this chapter.

It is much easier to understand what is innovative about the devices above after reading the explanations of how each works, *because the explanations make the topology of relevant interactions more explicit.* The explanations do not need to use quantitative information; a qualitative description of interactions is often sufficient to understand a device's operation, and suppresses substantial irrelevant details. A representation for interactions must capture this qualitative information at the right level of abstraction. Next, consider how these observations impact our perspective on invention.

Interaction-based Invention

We claim that the topology of interactions is an appropriate central focus of invention because we believe that the notion of how a device *works* is best thought of as constructing a set of interactions between quantities and then modulating these interactions over time. Thus, to identify fundamentally different ways of producing a desired behavior, we focus on the topologies of time-varying interactions between quantities. The representation we have developed for this purpose is called an *Interaction Topology*.

This viewpoint significantly impacts our perspective on invention:

> The process of invention involves constructing a topology of interactions that both produces the desired behavior and makes evident a topology of physical devices that implements those interactions. [7]

We call this approach *Interaction-based Invention*, and its implementation the Interaction-Based Invention System (IBIS).

The major stages of interaction-based invention are highlighted in figure 9. IBIS starts with a desired behavior and produces a device structure. Desired behavior is represented as a qualitative state diagram, where each arc describes a quantity shifting from one value or interval to another. The state diagram at the top of figure 9 describes the behavior of Philon's lamp. The left arc says to *raise the height of fluid in the lamp to the desired level*, and the right arc says *when the desired level is reached hold it there*.

Device structure is represented as a network of primitive components and connections. No restrictions are placed on the domain of the components; for example, during this research we have worked with networks of both hydro-mechanical and electrical components. This representation of structure is sufficient to capture many types of innovations, such as those highlighted earlier for Heron's float regulator and Philon's lamp. But some types cannot be captured, such as those involving the detailed geometry of a device. For example, an additional aspect of Philon's lamp that makes it innovative is that the surface of the oil is used to close off the mouth of a pipe, thus acting like a valve. This innovation can be encapsulated

---

[7]This approach builds an interaction topology and transforms it to a physical structure. For more complex tasks the design process involves transformations between different types of interaction topologies as well as transformations between interaction topologies and physical structure.

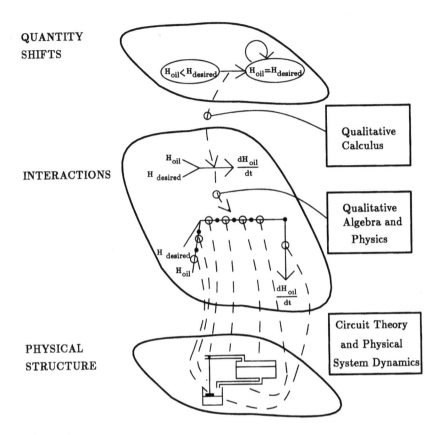

Figure 9. An account for the invention of a device similar to Philon's lamp according to interaction-based invention. Boxes to the right indicate the types of first principles used at the different stages of interaction-based invention.

into a primitive component, and then IBIS will be able to incorporate it into a design, but it cannot invent that element. To model this aspect of Philon's lamp using standard components we use a valve, mechanical linkage and float. The additional components used are one open and one closed container, and two pipes.

IBIS first turns this diagram into a set of one or more desired interactions that produce the specified quantity shifts. These interactions are described by equations in a new hybrid qualitative/quantitative algebra called $Q1$. For this example the desired interaction is *change the height of fluid in the lamp in the direction of the difference between the desired level and the current height.*

IBIS then constructs a detailed topology of interactions that produces the desired interaction and makes augmentations to device structure evident. By *make evident* we mean that each interaction in this topology is producible by a single connection or component. The producible interactions are identified using basic laws of physics—for hydro-mechanical systems the laws of physical system dynamics [Shearer *et al.* 1971; Rosenberg & Karnopp 1983], and for electrical systems the laws of circuit theory [Bose & Stevens 1965]. The end result of the invention process is the detailed topology of interactions and the physical structure that implements it, in this case Philon's lamp.

The first stage of the process, going from state diagrams to interactions, is roughly analogous to finite state machine synthesis [Hill & Peterson 1974], and is described in Williams [1989]. The second stage—constructing a detailed interaction topology—is much more difficult, and is the focus of the remainder of this chapter.

Strategies for Invention

Our goal is a theory that embodies the broad spectrum of invention—a process that begins with a knowledge of first principles alone, and results in a set of successively more sophisticated devices.

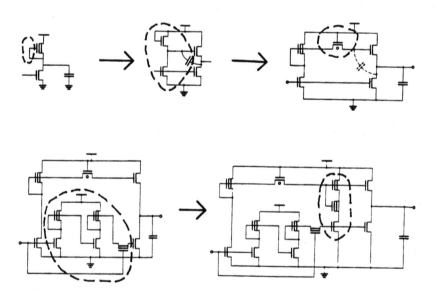

Figure 10. A sequence of high performance MOS memory buffer designs provides an example of evolutionary design through successive innovations. Dashed circles indicate modifications made at each step.

To this end, we have identified two complementary design strategies, which we call *visualizing potential interactions* and *design by stress*. The first is our theory of how innovative devices, like Philon's lamp and Heron's float regulator, might be derived directly from first principles alone. The second is a way of evolving simple devices to more sophisticated ones, by selectively applying the first strategy where innovation is crucial. The source of motivation for this second strategy is a progression of successively more complex and higher performance MOS memory buffers (see figure 10), developed during the 1970's.

The first strategy has been the primary focus of our recent research, and is described extensively in Williams [1989]. The second strategy is currently under development, and will be described more extensively in a future document.

Visualizing potential interactions

The first strategy proposes a way that simple devices emerge from first principles by using the interaction topology to focus on innovative alternative solutions. The conjecture is that *new innovative devices are constructed in a manner similar to how existing inventions are understood.*

Earlier we observed that, to understand how a device works, we first visualize all the interactions produced by every component and every connection in the device, and then identify those interactions that contribute to the desired behavior (see figure 8). Analogously, to invent a device, we use our first principles to visualize *all* possible interactions producible by each type of component and each type of connection available in the current technology, and *all ways* that these interactions can be connected. The result is a graph, which we call a *topology of potential interactions*. Constructing a new device involves identifying the interactions in this topology that produce a desired interaction. These interactions trace a path through the topology between variables in the desired interaction. For example, figure 11 shows a topology of potential interactions for hydro-mechanical components available in ancient times, together with a path relating fluid height change to height difference. The interactions along the path correspond to those produced by Philon's lamp. A more detailed diagram of these interactions was shown in figure 3.

Alternative solutions are proposed by identifying different paths through the potential interaction topology. These paths result in devices with distinct interaction topologies, and thus correspond to innovative alternatives. For example, figure 12 shows paths for three solutions that are explored in Williams [1989]. Each corresponds roughly to a novel fluid regulation device developed in ancient times.

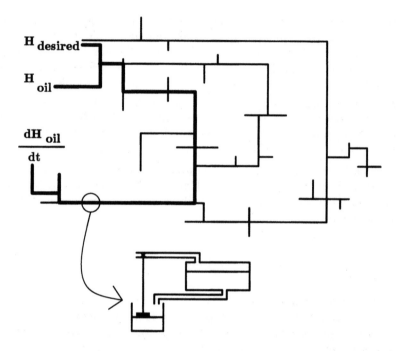

Figure 11. The topology of interactions for a new device is identified by tracing a path through the topology of potential interactions for the available technology.

The fact that the topology of potential interactions embodies the first principles for a technology, and highlights innovative alternatives, strengthens our claim that we are doing innovative design from first principles.

In addition, what is important about the topology of potential interactions is that it represents which quantities interact, but suppresses the behavior of the interactions. This provides an abstraction of the interaction space that preserves some of the space's most constraining features, yet is easy to search. Consider the two parts of this claim.

Part of the difficulty of constructing an interaction topology is that primitive components produce a complex set of interactions between several variables—only a few which we want to relate. For example, a graph of the interactions produced by a container are shown in figure 13.

In addition, variables are decomposed into a variety of exclusive types (for example, flow Q, height H, volume V, and mass M), and a component rarely produces an interaction directly between the types of variables we want to relate. For example, in Philon's lamp we want to relate height difference to change in height, but there is no simple component that relates these variables directly. As a result of these two factors—complex

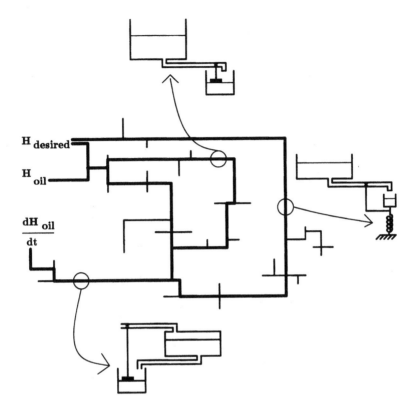

Figure 12. Distinct paths through the topology of potential interactions correspond to innovative alternatives.

interactions and typed variables—it is difficult to construct an interaction topology that relates the right variables, without producing destructive interactions with other variables. The topology of potential interactions preserves features responsible for this difficulty by representing which variables interact.

There are two features of the topology of potential interactions that makes it simple to search: it represents interactions produced by classes of components and connections, rather than explicitly enumerating the interactions of individual components, and it suppresses the behavior of interactions, by representing which variables interact but not how they interact. By representing classes the topology of potential interactions stays small—the number of classes and the number of interactions for each class is relatively small. Also by searching first for interaction topologies that relate a set of variables without worrying about how they interact, the search process becomes one of tracing paths through potential interactions—a fast operation for such a small graph.

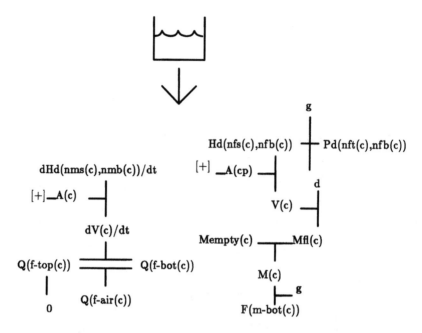

Figure 13. A container's interactions demonstrates the complexity of the interactions that a primitive component can produce, and the variety of variables that are interrelated. The variables in the figure are pressure difference (Pd), height (H), height difference (Hd), area (A), volume (V), mass (M), force (F), fluid flow (Q), fluid density (d), and gravity (g).

Returning to the design task, once the potential interactions are visualized, and a suitable interaction topology is identified two steps remain: it must be shown that these interactions produce the desired behavior, and a physical structure must be identified that produces those interactions.

First consider verifying that the desired behavior is entailed by the behaviors of the interactions in the proposed topology. As we discuss in the next section, each interaction is described in a qualitative algebra, called $Q1$. To verify the behavior, equations corresponding to the individual interactions are combined into a single equation, which is shown to be a specialization of an equation describing the desired behavior. These manipulations are performed by a symbolic algebra system called Minima, and is described in a later section.

Next consider how the interaction topology is mapped to a physical structure. Each interaction traced in the potential interaction topology is producible by a particular type of component or connection. Thus, each interaction along a path is created by instantiating a component or connection of the corresponding type.

This step is depicted in figure 3 by downward arrows. For example, the three interactions on the right side of the figure ($Q_{air(top(n))} \rightarrow$ $Q_{oil(bottom(n))} \rightarrow Q_{oil(top(b\&c))} \rightarrow Q_{oil(bottom(b\&c))}$) are created by introducing a container (n), a connection between fluid ports ($p1$ and $p2$) of two, yet to be specified, components and a pipe ($b\&c$), respectively. This produces three relevant interactions—$Q_{air(top(n))} \rightarrow Q_{oil(bottom(n))}, Q_{p1} \rightarrow Q_{p2}$ and $Q_{oil(top(b\&c))} \rightarrow Q_{oil(bottom(b\&c))}$—that are not interconnected.

Next, constraints are placed on the structure that connect together these distinct interactions into a topology. Pairs of interactions are connected by making them share a variable. For example, the first two interactions above are connected by making variables $Q_{oil(bottom(n))}$ and Q_{p1} be the same. This is accomplished by making port $p1$ be $bottom(n)$. Similarly the second and third interactions are connected by making port $p2$ be the top of pipe $b\&c$. Thus, making Q_{p2} and $Q_{oil(bottom(b\&c))}$ be the same. The net effect of connecting these three interactions is to connect the top of pipe $b\&c$ to the bottom of container n. Connecting together interactions is performed by an equality and terminological reasoning system called Iota. By using this approach to introduce and connect all the interactions together, a structure is produced corresponding to Philon's lamp (bottom of figure 3.[8]

Design by stress

Complex devices are rarely developed from first principles in a single step. Rather, simple devices are proposed and then evolved through a progression of focused design changes, continuously spurred on by the need for higher performance. A sequence of design changes made to MOS memory buffers during the 1970's was shown earlier in figure 10. Each change is marked by an innovation—an alteration to a device's interaction topology, which results in a novel change to how the device works. Each alteration is the result of focusing innovative design strategies on critical points of a device. At each stage in this process the inventor stresses a leading edge design by optimizing it for higher performance until it breaks. The inventor then uses the insights gained about the cause of failure to find ways to improve the design. This involves identifying changes to the structure of existing interactions and points where new interactions are required. These modifications are made by strengthening, weakening, adding, or eliminating interactions during windows of time, and are performed, when necessary, by reasoning from first principles (for example, by using the strategy of visualizing potential interactions). The effect of design by stress is to hill climb towards sophisticated, high performance devices through a sequence of simpler innovations.

---

[8]Note a proposed topology may fail either because it produces an incorrect behavior, or because it requires a physical structure that can not be constructed. In this event the topology is refined–see Williams [1989] for details.

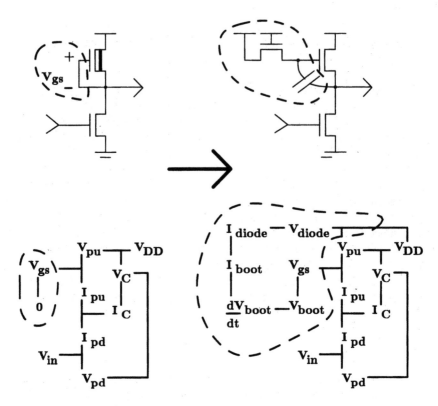

Figure 14. Each step in the evolution involves an innovation, consisting of a change to the interaction topology.

For example, consider the first step in the evolution of the MOS memory buffer, shown in the upper half of figure 14. The memory buffer is a digital inverter that quickly raises and lowers the voltage on a large output capacitance C_{out}. For the purpose of this example, we assume that the capacitance on the output is 1 pF, and the output voltage must be raised or lowered within 5 ns. A logic 1 is represented by a high voltage (close to the supply voltage V_{dd}), and a logic 0 is represented by a low voltage (close to the ground voltage V_{gnd}). To invert, the output V_{out} goes to high whenever the input V_{in} is low, and low when the input is high. V_{out} is raised and lowered by pouring electrical charge into or draining charge out of C_{out}, similar to the way in which the fluid level is raised and lowered in Philon and Heron's devices.

Suppose the initial design proposed is a ratioed inverter (upper left corner of figure 14). This consists of a pulldown—a transistor that, whenever V_{in} is high, turns on and drains current from C_{out}—and a pullup—a transistor that pours current into C_{out} whenever the pulldown is off.

First the design is evaluated to determine whether or not it meets the specification, and if not the necessary modifications to behavior are identified. For example, suppose it is determined, by back of an envelope calculations, that the output rises in 10 ns. The output is supposed to rise within 5 ns, and thus fails to meet the specification. Bringing the design in line with the specification involves shortening the output rise time, between when V_{in} reaches "0" and V_{out} reaches "1".

Next modifications to the inverter's interaction topology are proposed that produce the desired changes to behavior (increasing rise time). To do this we must first determine how the inverter raises V_{out}; that is, how the inverter's interactions produce this behavior. The inverter works as follows: Initially V_{in} is high, and V_{out} is low. The pullup and pulldown transistors are on, and all the current flowing through the pullup is flowing through the pulldown. When V_{in} goes low, the pulldown turns off, and the current through the pullup is redirected into C_{out}. Current into C_{out} charges it up, causing V_{out} to rise. Current continues to flow through the pullup until its voltage $V_{d,s}$ becomes zero, at which point V_{out} stops rising.

Next working backward through this explanation, we identify changes to quantities that increase V_{out}'s rise time. The rise time is shortened by increasing V_{out}'s derivative. This is accomplished by making C_{out} charge faster—supplying more current to it—or by decreasing the amount of charge required—by decreasing C_{out}'s capacitance. The pulldown is off; thus, all the current is supplied by the pullup, and can be increased by making it conduct better. The amount of current supplied by the pullup is proportional to $S(V_{g,s} - V_t)$; thus, the current can be increased by increasing S or $V_{g,s}$, or decreasing V_t.[8]

The next step is to change one or more of these quantities in the directions identified. Some of these quantities, such as S and V_t are independent parameters of the device that can be changed directly without changing any interactions. For example, S is the aspect ratio of the pullup transistor, and is modified by changing the transistor's dimensions (width and length). V_t is the threshold voltage where a transistor turns on, and is altered by changing parameters of the fabrication process. These independent parameters can be changed to improve rise time, for example, by using traditional optimization techniques.

Suppose, however, that this optimization is insufficient, then a second possibility is to change the structure of the inverter's interaction topology.

---

[8]The process of identifying quantities to be changed is roughly analogous to DQ analysis [Weld 1988; Forbus 1984]; there are two primary differences. First the process is abductive, rather than deductive—we are interested in identifying changes to quantities that produce a desired effect, rather than determining the effects of some change. Second, as we see below our primary interest is in producing these changes through alterations to a device's interaction topology, as opposed to changes in the values of independent parameters.

More specifically we consider changing the inverter's dependent quantities, such as the pullup $V_{g,s}$ or the capacitor current, by changing interactions that directly effect them. For example, $V_{g,s}$ can be changed by modifying the interaction $V_{g,s} = 0$, imposed by the wire connecting the pullup's gate and source (the wire and its corresponding interaction are circled in the upper and lower left corners of figure 14). To increase rise time, the desired change is to make $V_{g,s}$ positive during the time window while V_{out} is rising, which is achieved if $V_{g,s}$ is positive while V_{in} is low. This is the modification made during the first step of the MOS buffer evolution (see figure 10). Note that a variety of alternative changes are possible, which modify interactions highlighted by the graph in the lower left corner of figure 14).

After one or more proposed changes is selected, they are implemented by removing some existing interactions and introducing others. In our example, the interaction $V_{g,s} = 0$ is removed by eliminating the wire between the pullup's gate and source. The desired interaction "$V_{g,s}$ on the pullup is positive when V_{in} is logic 0" is achieved by introducing the interactions circled in the lower right corner of figure 14, and the corresponding physical structure in the upper right corner. This addition is called bootstrapping in electrical engineering circles, and works as follows: Intuitively the addition connects a "battery" between the pullup's gate and source that produces a constant, positive voltage when V_{in} is low (logic 0). Using the fact that voltage across a capacitor is proportional to charge, the battery is implemented by connecting a capacitor (C_{boot}) between gate and source, charging up the capacitor while V_{in} is high, and then holding the charge constant when V_{in} is low. C_{boot} is charged up, and then held constant using a transistor connected in a way that makes it behave like a diode. Consider how this "diode" works. Assuming that the voltage across C_{boot} is too low, then when V_{in} is high, and thus V_{out} is low, current flows through the diode into C_{boot}. The diode turns off (current stops flowing) when the voltage across it reaches zero, leaving the voltage across C_{boot} positive and constant. C_{boot}'s voltage remains constant while V_{in} falls and V_{out} rises, since the voltage across the diode becomes negative and the diode stays off.

The above example demonstrates the major stages of design by stress:

1   Compare a proposed device's behavior with the specification and list discrepancies (such as the rise time is too slow).

2   Determine modifications, first optimizing independent parameters (such as W, L and V_t), and then if neccessary proposing changes to interactions (such as changing "$V_{g,s} = 0$" to "$V_{g,s}$ is positive when V_{in} is logic 0").

3   Implement these changes by deleting and adding interactions and their corresponding physical structure.

The remaining steps in the MOS buffer progress (see figure 10) can be accounted for through a similar design by stress process.

When coupled with library design, the two strategies outlined in this section span both ends of the design spectrum, from the early exploration of simple inventions in a new domain to high performance design in an established technology. The first strategy—visualizing potential interactions—uses only knowledge of first principles and thus is appropriate when first exploring a domain. In contrast, traditional library design relies on knowledge developed from past explorations in a domain. Thus, it is more appropriate for exploration of a mature field, where more is known, but the designs are also more complex due to extreme performance constraints. Design by stress provides a bridge between the other two approaches. Using only first principles a complex device can evolve by successively pushing a simpler device for performance and enhancing it. In an established domain, past experience and simple design strategies, such as library design, can be used to construct most of the design efficiently, while only using more innovative techniques at critical points. This results in a graceful integration of routine and innovative design techniques.

Representing Interaction Topologies

Thus far we have presented interaction topologies pictorially as graphs, in order to convey in simple images the basic intuitions behind interaction-based invention. While it is important to highlight connectivity of interactions, as we pointed out earlier, this is insufficient to capture how a device works. A far more sophisticated representation is required. A crucial element of focusing the invention process is capturing the topology of interactions at the right level of abstraction—that is, capturing only the salient features of the interaction topology with respect to how a device works. Developing a representation that captures this level of abstraction is a central concern of our research.

Producing a set of quantity shifts in a continuous system is a subtle process, often requiring a complex topology of interactions. Quantity shifts do not occur instantaneously. Either a quantity is nudged in a particular direction and it is carried to its destination by momentum, or it is pushed to its destination by a sustained influence. This is quite different from the sequence of discrete, instantaneous actions used in many artificial intelligence planning approaches [Fikes & Nilsson 1971; Sacerdoti 1975; Allen & Koomen 1983: Simmons 1983] or digital finite state machine design [Hill & Peterson 1974]. Furthermore, these influences are often not easily relinquished. Instead the device must orchestrate a set of competing influences that combine to move a quantity in a particular direction, and then bring it to a stop at the desired destination. A device's behavior changes over time by strengthening, weakening, adding, or eliminating interactions during windows of time.

The interaction topology representation, and the invention approach, must capture these aspects of continuous behavior. To be a good representation it must make it possible to express *all and only* the salient properties of interactions—properties necessary to account for how the desired quantity shifts are produced. This is absolutely crucial—given the difficulty of designing from first principles, any superfluous details introduced by the representation may overwhelm the design system.

Researchers are aware that capturing these salient properties requires representing qualitative, causal, and temporal aspects of interactions [Rieger & Grinberg 1977; deKleer & Brown 1984; Forbus 1984; Williams 1984; Iwasaki & Simon 1986; Kuipers 1986; Weld 1988]. For example, the explanation of Philon's lamp included the sentence "when an air gap appears between the end of pipe m, and the surface of the oil in k, air flows through m ..." This describes an interaction between the quantities height difference $H_{gap(m,k)}$ and air flow $Q_{air(bot(m))}$; the qualitative aspect is that height difference and flow are positive; the temporal aspect is that this interaction holds until the oil reaches the desired level, and the causal aspect is that height difference causes flow.

Although a useful starting point, current representations for capturing how devices work are inadequate. Overcoming these inadequacies requires a new perspective with respect to qualitative, temporal, and causal representations, and their integration. Our research makes three notable contributions along this front:

- **Q1.** Existing qualitative representations over-abstract—they are too weak to capture the relevant constraints between quantities imposed by interactions. Avoiding over-abstraction requires a representation that allows the abstraction of each interaction to be selected along a qualitative/quantitative spectrum. We propose such a representation based on a hybrid qualitative/quantitative algebra, called Q1.

- **Concise Histories.** Existing temporal representations of behavior impose a total ordering on events (for example, the situational calculus) are too restrictive to capture only the salient properties of dynamic interactions—they introduce too many irrelevant temporal orderings and events. Our solution, called *concise histories*, is to use a compact description of dynamically changing interactions to identify only those events and temporal orderings that impact how a device produces its desired behavior.

- **Causal Dominance.** Due to the pervasiveness of feedback, the set of interactions that contribute to device behavior is often exceedingly complex. Nevertheless, inventors are able to construct causal accounts of these feedback systems that are relatively simple, yet are sufficient for tasks like design debugging. How then are these accounts constructed, and what aspects of device behavior do they ignore? Existing theories of causality neither explicate or correctly predict these causal accounts. We have developed a theory, called *causal dominance*, which proposes that causal accounts are constructed by tracing paths through an interaction topology along the paths of dominant signal flow. The net effect is to break each feedback loop at its weakest point. These accounts are used when altering an invention to identify quantities and interactions that have the greatest impact on device behavior.

The qualitative algebra $Q1$ is used by the visualize potential interactions strategy to describe the behavior of the individual interactions in an interaction topology, and the desired interactions that this topology is constructed to achieve. A formalization of $Q1$ appears in Williams [1988]. The second two representations—concise histories and causal dominance—are used by the design-by-stress strategy, to describe the contribution of a device's interaction topology to its time-varying behavior (for example, an inverter's output rising and falling). This description is used to pinpoint which interactions in a topology to change, in order to eliminate undesirable aspects of the temporal behavior. The use of concise histories and causal dominance to eliminate irrelevant temporal orderings and to identify dominant influences is crucial to pinpointing these interactions. Early versions of these representations and their use are presented in more detail in Williams [1986, 1984]. A more detailed exposition of how these two representations are used in interaction-based invention is forthcoming.

An Inventor's Procedural Skills

The phrase *design from first principles* indicates the importance of first principles as a foundation for achieving a robust and domain independent theory of invention. However, this does not imply that all first principles are explicitly manipulated by the design strategies. Typically the first principles focus one level of granularity below basic operations required for invention.

To make IBIS efficient, many of these principles are embodied in a set of *procedural skills*. These skills are an efficient set of procedures, such as algebraic manipulation, that raise the granularity of first principles to operations of interest for invention—without sacrificing robustness. For interaction-based invention these include operations for constructing interaction topologies and their corresponding physical structure, determining the composite behavior of a topology, and comparing it to the interactions desired. These skills facilitate IBIS' efficiency by placing it in the role of coordinator—using the strategies to decide which interactions and structures to add—while using the procedural skills to handle the details of performing and evaluating the additions. The skills necessary to build interaction topologies use a sophisticated combination of qualitative, constructive, causal, and temporal reasoning; drawing substantially upon and requiring significant advances in the corresponding areas of artificial intelligence. The following are three of the most notable skills developed for our theory of invention:

- **Minima.** Determining whether an interaction topology produces the desired interactions requires operations for combining and comparing interactions. Given that interactions are described as qualitative equations, this requires skills for qualitative algebraic manipulation. These skills are embodied in a powerful symbolic algebra system, called *Minima*, for the Q1 algebra. The existence of this system refutes the claims sometimes heard in the qualitative reasoning community that qualitative algebras can never be made powerful enough to do interesting tasks [Struss 1988], such as verification or design.

- **Iota.** To construct an interaction topology, interactions are *joined* together by sharing a variable between them. Sharing a variable may impose additional constraints on physical structure; for example, two pipes can share pressure by connecting them together. We refer to this process of joining together interactions as *constructive reasoning*. Determining the constraints on structure involves reasoning about the relationships between classes of variables, and parts of physical structure the variables depend on. These are the types of relationships manipulated by traditional knowledge representation systems. All of IBIS' constructive reasoning skills are embodied in a simple, complete, and efficient knowledge representation system, called *Iota*. Over the last decade researchers (for example, Brachman and Schmolze [1985], Patel-Schneider [1984], and Vilain [1985]) in the knowledge representation community have found that there is a computational cliff that most knowledge representation systems fall off because computing subsumption and classifying concepts is NP-hard for even extremely impoverished knowledge representation languages [Brachman & Levesque 1984]. Thus, Iota's completeness, efficiency, and adequacy for interaction-based invention provides an important counter example.

- **Episode-based Prediction.** A domain independent analysis technique has been developed that constructs concise histories—a topology of dynamically changing interactions unraveled over time—to describe how a device produces its time-varying behavior. This technique captures important components of an inventor's skill at explaining how a device works in response to changing inputs. This plays a crucial role during design by stress, when identifying points in an interaction topology where innovative changes are required.

The first two procedural skills support the design strategy of visualizing potential interactions. Recall that a candidate topology is identified by tracing the topology of potential interactions. Once a candidate is identified, Iota is used to determine what constraints this topology imposes on physical structure, and whether these constraints are consistent. Minima is then used to determine whether the topology produces the desired interactions. The remaining skill—episode-based prediction—is used during the design by stress strategy to construct a concise history of the dynamic changes in a device's interactions. Recall that this history is traced when pinpointing interactions causing deficiencies in a device's temporal behavior.

The procedural skills, coupled with the design strategies, interaction topology representation, and first principles are the basic elements that enable IBIS to focus the process of invention, without sacrificing robustness. An overview of all of these components is given in figure 15.

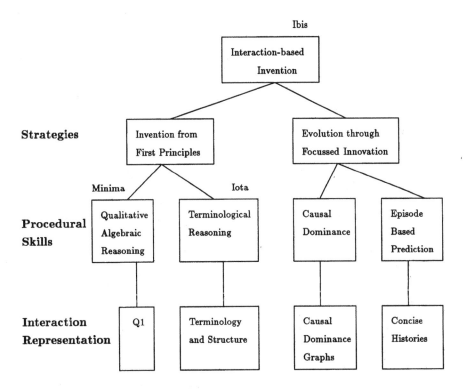

Figure 15. Major components of Interaction-based Invention.

Conclusion

In this chapter we outlined a theory of invention from fundamental principles of physics based on topologies of interaction. We began by arguing that the existing approach of routine, library design is often inadequate to achieve the high performance required of modern devices. Overcoming this inadequacy requires a theory of invention—identifying innovative alternatives by reasoning from first principles.

We also argued, as a research strategy, for viewing the art of invention from a historical perspective. That is, we gain insight into design from first principles by examining devices developed at a time when little design experience had been accumulated, and thus when it is plausible that first principles were relied on heavily.

Using these case studies we characterized one type of innovation—that a device is innovative if it works in a way noticeably different from those seen before. We claimed that the topology of interactions is an appropriate central focus of invention because we believe that the notion of how a device *works* is best thought of as constructing a set of interactions between quantities and then modulating these interactions over time. Thus, to identify fundamentally different ways of producing a desired behavior, we focus on differences between alternative topologies of interactions between quantities. A representation we have developed to capture the qualitative, time-varying character of these interactions we call an interaction topology.

Using this perspective of innovation we proposed a design approach, called interaction-based invention, which involves constructing a topology of interactions that both produces the desired behavior and makes evident a topology of physical components that implements those interactions.

The remainder of the chapter highlighted key elements of the design strategies, procedural skills, first principles, and interaction topology representation that constitute our theory of invention. Most notable are the two design strategies—visualizing potential interactions and design by stress. Together these strategies map out crucial components of the design spectrum, which begins with the invention of simple devices from first principles alone, and carries forward to the evolution of complex, high performance devices.

I would like to thank my advisor Randy Davis, and thesis committee Tomás Lozano Pérez and Patrick Winston for extensive advice throughout this research project. I would also like to thank Daniel Bobrow, Brian Falkenhainer, Dan Weld, Leah Williams, Jeff Van Baalen, Johan de Kleer, and Mark Shirley for fruitful discussions and comments on earlier drafts.

Research described in this chapter was pursued at the Artificial Intelligence Laboratory of the Massachusetts Institute of Technology and at the System's

References

Allen, J., and J. Koomen [1983], "Planning Using a Temporal World Model," *Proceedings of the Eighth IJCAI*, pp. 741-747.

Brachman, R. J., and H. J. Levesque [1984], "The Tractability of Subsumption in Frame-Based Description Languages," *Proceedings of the National Conference on Artificial Intelligence.*

Brachman, R. J., and H. J. Levesque [1985], *Readings in Knowledge Representation*, Morgan Kaufman Publishers, Inc., Los Altos, CA.

Brachman, R. J., and J. G. Schmolze [1985], "An Overview of the KL-ONE Knowledge Representation System," *Cognitive Science*, vol. 9, pp. 171-216.

Bose, A. G., and K. N. Stevens [1965], *Introductory Network Theory*, Harper and Row, New York.

deKleer, J., and J. S. Brown [1984], "A Qualitative Physics Based on Confluences," *Artificial Intelligence*, vol. 24, no. 1-3, pp. 7-84.

Fikes, R. and N. Nilsson [1971], "STRIPS: A New Approach to the Application of Theorem Proving to Problem Solving," *Artificial Intelligence*, vol. 2, no. 3.

Forbus, K. [1984], "Qualitative Process Theory," *Artificial Intelligence*, vol. 24, no. 1-3.

Hill, F. J., and G. R. Peterson [1974], *Introduction to Switching Theory and Logical Design*, Wiley, New York.

Iwasaki, Y., and H. A. Simon [1986], "Causality in Device Behavior," *Artificial Intelligence*, vol. 29.

Johannsen, D. [1981], "Bristle Blocks: A Silicon Compiler," *Proceedings of the 16th Design Automation Conference.*

Joskowicz, L., and S. Addanki [1989], Innovative Design of Kinematic Pairs," Report RC14507, IBM Research Division, T.J.Watson Research Center, Yorktown Heights, N.Y.

Kuipers, B. [1986], "Qualitative Simulation," *Artificial Intelligence*, vol. 29.

Matson, M. [1985], "Macromodeling and Optimization of Digital MOS VLSI Circuits," VLSI Memo 85-231, Massachusetts Institute of Technology, Cambridge, MA.

Mayr, O. [1970], *The Origins of Feedback Control*, MIT Press, Cambridge, MA.

McDermott, D. [1977], "Flexibility and Efficiency in a Computer Program for Designing Circuits," Report AI-TR-402, Artificial Intelligence Laboratory, Massachusetts Institute of Technology, Cambridge, MA.

Science Laboratory of the Xerox Palo Alto Research Center. Support for the MIT Artificial Intelligence Laboratory's artificial intelligence research is provided in part by the Advanced Research Projects Agency of the Department of Defense under Office of Naval Research Contract numbers N0014-80-C-0505 and N00014-80-C-0622.

Mitchell, T., S. Mahadevan, and L. I. Steinberg [1985], "LEAP: A Learning Apprentice for VLSI Design," *Proc. of the Ninth International Joint Conference on Artificial Intelligence*, pp. 573-80.

Mitchell, T. M., L. I. Steinberg, S. Kedar-Cabelli, V. E. Kelly, J. Shulman, and T. Weinrich [1983], "An Intelligent Aid for Circuit Redesign," in *Proceedings of the National Conference on Artificial Intelligence*.

Mittal, S., C. M. Dym, and M. Morjaria [1986], "PRIDE: An Expert System for the Design of Paper Handling Systems," *Computer*.

Murthy, S. S., and S. Addanki [1987], "PROMPT: An Innovative Design Tool," *Proceedings of the 6th National Conference on Artificial Intelligence*, pp. 637-42.

Patel-Schneider, P. F. [1984], "Small can be Beautiful in Knowledge Representation," *Proceedings of the IEEE Workshop on Principles of Knowledge-Based Systems*, Denver, CO, pp. 11-16.

Ressler, A. [1974], "A Circuit Grammar for Operational Amplifier Design," Report AI-TR-807, Artificial Intelligence Laboratory, Massachusetts Institute of Technology, Cambridge, MA.

Rieger, C., and M. Grinberg [1977], "Representation and Procedural Simulation of Causality in Physical Mechanisms," *Proceedings of the fifth IJCAI*, Cambridge, MA, pp. 250-256.

Rosenberg, R. C., and D. C. Karnopp [1983], *Introduction to Physical System Dynamics*, McGraw-Hill Book Co., New York.

Roylance, G. [1980], "A Simple Model of Circuit Design," Report AI-TR-703, Artificial Intelligence Laboratory, Massachusetts Institute of Technology, Cambridge, MA.

Sacerdoti, E. [1975] "The Nonlinear Nature of Plans," *Proceedings of the Fourth IJCAI*, pp. 206-214.

Shearer, J. L., A. T. Murphy, and H. H. Richardson [1971], *Introduction to System Dynamics*, Addison-Wesley, Reading, MA.

Simmons, R. [1983], "Representing and Reasoning About Change in Geologic Interpretation," Report AI-TR-749, Artificial Intelligence Laboratory, Massachusetts Institute of Technology, Cambridge, MA.

Struss, P. [1988], "Mathematical Aspects of Qualitative Reasoning," *Artificial Intelligence in Engineering*.

Siskind, J., J. Southard, and K. Crouch [1982], "Generating Custom High Performance VLSI Designs from Succinct Algorithmic Descriptions," *Proceedings of the Conference on Advanced Research in VLSI*.

Ulrich, K. [1988], "Computation and Pre-Parametric Design," Report AI-TR-1043, Artificial Intelligence Laboratory, Massachusetts Institute of Technology, Cambridge, MA.

Vilain, M. [1985], "The Restricted Language Architecture of a Hybrid Representation System," *Proceedings of the Ninth International Joint Conference on Artificial Intelligence*, pp. 547-51.

Weld, D. [1988], "Comparative Analysis," *Artificial Intelligence*, vol. 36, no. 3, pp. 333-374.

Williams, B. C. [1984], "Qualitative Analysis of MOS Circuits," *Artificial Intelligence*, vol. 24, no. 1-3, pp. 281-346.

Williams, B. C. [1986], "Doing Time: Putting Qualitative Reasoning on Firmer Ground," *Proceedings of the National Conference on Artificial Intelligence*, pp. 105-112.

Williams, B. C. [1988], "MINIMA: A Symbolic Approach to Qualitative Reasoning," *Proceedings of the National Conference on Artificial Intelligence*.

Williams, B. C. [1989], "Invention from First Principles via Topologies of Interaction," Report AI-TR-1127, Artificial Intelligence Laboratory, Massachusetts Institute of Technology, Cambridge, MA.

17

Why are theorem-proving steps that are obvious to human mathematicians far from obvious to reasoning programs? To address this question, McAllester has developed a new theorem prover with many remarkable properties, including impressive performance: acting in verification mode, it has verified sophisticated mathematical proofs that contain about the amount of detail supplied in mathematical textbooks.

One key to McAllester's success is his idea of focus objects, which are specified in the proof to be verified. His verifier classifies those focus objects and then applies type-specific lemmas to them. Thus the focus objects direct his verifier's attention in a way that is somewhat reminiscent of the way good sketches direct human attention.

Mathematical Knowledge Representation

David A. McAllester

This chapter describes Ontic, an interactive system for developing and verifying mathematics. Ontic's verification mechanism is capable of automatically finding and applying information from a library containing hundreds of mathematical facts. Starting with only the axioms of Zermelo-Fraenkel set theory, the Ontic system has been used to build a data base of definitions and lemmas leading to a proof of the Stone representation theorem for Boolean lattices. The Ontic system has been used to explore issues in knowledge representation, automated deduction, and the automatic use of large data bases.

The Ontic Proof-Verification System

Pure mathematics is a good domain for basic research in automated reasoning. The formal verification of deep mathematical results from a foundational system such as set theory presents a severe challenge for current automated reasoning technology. Consider a formal verification, starting with the axioms of set theory, that every Riemannian manifold can be embedded in a Euclidean space. Consider the proof of the independence of the continuum hypothesis. No automated inference system can be expected to find complete foundational proofs of theorems such as these without human assistance. The amount of human assistance needed provides a measure of the power of the automated reasoning techniques used. It should be possible to demonstrate progress in the area of automated reasoning by demonstrating a reduction in the amount of human assistance needed to machine verify deep mathematical proofs.

Some may feel that it is not possible, at this point in time, to formally verify deep conceptual theorems of mathematics starting with only the axioms of set theory. However, considerable success in verifying such arguments has already been achieved. Starting with the axioms of Zermelo-Fraenkel set theory, including Zorn's lemma as a version of the axiom of choice, the Ontic system has been used to verify a proof of the Stone representation theorem for Boolean lattices. This theorem involves an ultra-filter construction and is similar in complexity to the Tychonoff theorem in topology which states that an arbitrary product of compact spaces is compact.

When evaluating theorem proving mechanisms for verification one should distinguish foundational and non-foundational verification systems. Foundational systems such as the Boyer-Moore prover [Boyer & Moore 1979], EKL [Ketonen 1984], and nuPRL [Constable *et al.* 1986] are based on a single foundational logic which is extended via definitions and theorems. A theorem proving system is non-foundational if it allows the human user to add domain specific axioms without justification. Systems based on resolution theorem proving are typically non-foundational. The Ontic system is a foundational verification system based on Zermelo-Fraenkel set theory.

There are several reasons that foundational verification provides a better framework for evaluating theorem proving mechanisms than does non-foundational verification. First, foundational verification of a given benchmark theorem is more difficult than verification of the same theorem from unjustified axioms. Thus foundational verification provides a more demanding test of the theorem proving mechanisms. Second, foundational verification, as opposed to non-foundational verification, provides a more objective way of evaluating the performance of theorem proving techniques; when unjustified axioms can be introduced by the user it is not clear how much work is being done by the theorem prover and how much is being done by the introduction of axioms. Finally, in foundational verification one is forced to deal with the conceptual problems of representation and implementation; in a foundational system all mathematical objects must ultimately be implemented in terms of the primitive notions, for example, sets. Reasoning techniques which are effective for reasoning about multiple levels of representation may be useful in verifying computer systems with multiple levels of implementation.

The Ontic theorem prover is based on object-oriented inference. Object-oriented inference is a forward chaining inference process applied to a large lemma library and guided by a set of *focus objects*. The focus objects are terms in the sense of first order predicate calculus; they are expressions which denote objects. It is well known that unrestricted forward chaining starting with a large lemma library, leads to a combinatorial explosion. However, the Ontic theorem prover is guided by the focus objects; the inference process is restricted to statements that are, in a technical sense, about the focus objects, and inference is guaranteed to terminate quickly. In verifying an argument the user specifies the set of focus objects. For example, the user may tell the system to consider an arbitrary lattice L, an arbitrary subset S of L, and an arbitrary member x of S.

Object-oriented inference operates in a context consisting of three things: a lemma library, a set of focus objects, and set of suppositions about the focus objects. Figure 1 gives a block diagram of the object-oriented inference mechanisms used in the Ontic system. The four basic forward chaining inference mechanisms shown in figure 1 are described in detail in McAllester [1987]. In a given context the four forward chaining inference mechanisms terminate after generating a set of formulas about the focus objects called "obvious truths."

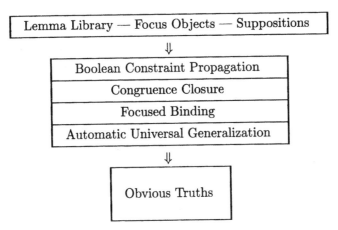

Figure 1. A block diagram of object-oriented inference.

The formal language used by the Ontic system is organized around types. In the Ontic language there is no distinction between types, classes, sorts, and predicates of one argument. For an object x and type τ the phrases "τ contains x," "x is an instance of τ," and "τ is true of x" all mean the same thing. The word type is used, as opposed to the word class or predicate, because Ontic types are similar to types in computer programming languages; functions take typed arguments and there is a distinguished class of well-typed expressions.

Most of the axioms of Zermelo-Fraenkel set theory are instances of naive comprehension; they state when a formula can be used to define a set. In Ontic any formula can be used to define a type and certain types can then be *reified* as sets. More specifically, if τ is a *syntactically small* type expression then the expression

<code>(the-set-of-all τ)</code>

denotes the set of all instances of the type τ. Any syntactically small type expression can be converted to a set in this way and most of the axioms of set theory are incorporated in the definition of a syntactically small type expression. Thus the human user need never explicitly invoke axioms of set theory—he simply converts types to sets as needed.

The formulas of the Ontic language are organized around types. The formula (IS x τ) is true just in case x denotes an instance of the type τ. Formulas of the form (IS x τ) are the *only* atomic formulas in the Ontic language; all predication is expressed with types. To say that x is less than than y, for example, one uses the formula (IS x (LESS-THAN y)) where the symbol LESS-THAN is a type generator.

Types play a central role in the focused binding inference mechanism. The Ontic system *classifies* focus objects by identifying a set of types which hold for each focus object. The focused binding mechanism then invokes lemmas that apply to the focus objects by virtue of their types.

The Ontic system provides an interactive environment for developing and checking arguments. The result of an interaction with the system is a machine readable argument that establishes some lemma. The interactive Ontic environment is described in McAllester [1987] and will not be described here; here we deal only with the textual representations of machine readable arguments.

The textual representation of an argument is an *argument expression*. Figure 2 shows both an English argument (taken from Gratzer's textbook on lattice theory [1978, p. 24]) and a corresponding Ontic argument expression. Note that the Ontic argument expression, like the English argument, does not make any explicit references to definitions or lemmas.

One way of measuring the performance of a verification system is to compare the length of a previously published natural language argument with the length of a corresponding machine readable proof. The ratio of the length of a machine readable proof to the length of the corresponding natural language argument is called the *expansion factor* for that proof. The English argument in figure 2 contains 75 words and mathematical symbols, while the Ontic proof contains 73 symbols, yielding a word count expansion factor of about one.

One can argue that the expansion factor measured for the proof of figure 2 is too low because the Ontic interpreter was allowed to use pre-proven lemmas. But all of the lemmas used by the Ontic interpreter in proving this theorem are of general interest and have in fact been used in several different contexts. Furthermore, all of lemmas used in this example have simple one or two line proofs; even without the preproven lemmas, the proof shown in figure 2 would not be much longer.

A complete listing of a mathematical development that ends with a proof of the Stone representation theorem for Boolean lattices is presented

Lemma: If P is a partial order in which every subset has a least upper bound then every subset also has a greatest lower bound.

Proof: Let P be a poset in which $\bigvee S$ exists for all $S \subseteq P$. For $H \subseteq P$, let K be the set of all lower bounds of H. By hypothesis $\bigvee K$ exists; set $a = \bigvee K$. If $h \in H$, then $h \geq k$ for all $k \in K$; therefore $h \geq a$ and $a \in K$. Thus a is the greatest member of K, that is $a = \bigwedge H$.

```
(IN-CONTEXT ((LET-BE P POSET)
             (SUPPOSE (FORALL ((S (SUBSET-OF (U-SET P))))
                      (EXISTS (LEAST-UPPER-BOUND-OF S P))))
             (LET-BE H (SUBSET-OF (U-SET P)))
             (PUSH-GOAL
               (EXISTS (GREATEST-LOWER-BOUND-OF H P)))); #1
  (IN-CONTEXT
      ((LET-BE K (THE-SET-OF-ALL (LOWER-BOUND-OF H P)))
       (LET-BE a (THE (LEAST-UPPER-BOUND-OF K P))))
    (IN-CONTEXT ((PUSH-GOAL (IS a (LOWER-BOUND-OF H P)))); #2
      (IN-CONTEXT ((SUPPOSE (EXISTS (MEMBER-OF H)))
                   (LET-BE h0 (MEMBER-OF H)))
        (IN-CONTEXT
            ((PUSH-GOAL (IS h0 (UPPER-BOUND-OF K P)))); #3
          (IN-CONTEXT
              ((SUPPOSE (EXISTS (MEMBER-OF K)))
               (LET-BE k0 (MEMBER-OF K)))
            (NOTE-GOAL)); #3
          (NOTE-GOAL))); #3
        (NOTE-GOAL)); #2
      (NOTE-GOAL))); #1
```

Figure 2. Least upper bounds yield greatest lower bounds.

Lemma	Predicate Count Expansion Factor	Word Count Expansion Factor
If arbitrary least upper bounds exist then arbitary greatest lower bounds also exist.	0.9	1.0
Every filter is contained in an ultrafilter.	1.3	1.2
If F is an ultrafilter and $x \vee y \in F$ then $x \in F$ or $y \in F$.	2.1	2.7
Every Boolean algebra is isomorphic to a field of sets.	2.0	1.7

Table 1. Various measurements of the expansion factor.

in McAllester [1987]. This development gives a large number of examples of Ontic argument expressions. Table 1 shows two different kinds of expansion factor measurements made on four different arguments. Both the previously published English argument and the corresponding Ontic argument expression for each test case can be found in McAllester [1987].

Ontic as a Cognitive Model

One can attempt to evaluate Ontic as a model of human mathematical cognition by comparing the formal "proofs" that are acceptable to the Ontic system with the natural language proofs that are acceptable to people. There are some clear differences between Ontic proofs and natural arguments. In certain cases the Ontic system can verify proof steps that are not obvious to people; we say that Ontic exhibits superhuman performance. In other cases there are statements which are obvious to people but which require multistep proofs in the Ontic system; we say that Ontic exhibits subhuman performance. The superhuman performance and much of the subhuman performance indicate ways in which the Ontic system might be modified to yield a better cognitive model.

Ontic's congruence closure mechanism provides a clear example of superhuman performance. The Ontic system can use its congruence closure mechanism to "see" that in a distributive lattice complements are unique. This fact is not obvious to people. The Ontic proof of the Stone representation theorem relies on proofs of a series of lattice theoretic identities which were obvious to the Ontic system but not to human mathematicians. These identities included de Morgan's laws which were proven from the algebraic axioms for a Boolean lattice.

It is possible to modify the Ontic system in a way that eliminates superhuman behavior while preserving most of the inferential power of the system. Unlike the current Ontic system, the modified version has a straightforward implementation on a very fast parallel architecture. The elimination of superhuman behavior and the provision for a highly parallel implementation yield a more plausible cognitive model.

Of course, Ontic also exhibits subhuman performance. Some cases of subhuman performance in the proof of the Stone representation theorem can be traced to weaknesses in the lemma library. A more significant set of examples of subhuman performance involves mathematical induction. Although the Ontic system can be used to verify induction arguments, the expansion factor is large. In natural mathematics induction arguments are often unstated and unnoticed even though people understand the arguments and agree to their validity. For example, consider a graph where the nodes of the graph are colored such that any two nodes with an arc between them have the same color. Clearly if nodes n and m have different colors then there is no path between them in the graph. To verify this fact with the Ontic system would require an induction on the length of paths. There are many other examples from both mathematics and common sense where induction arguments seem to be done at a subconscious level.

Future experimentation will certainly turn up additional ways in which the Ontic system exhibits subhuman performance. Hopefully, examples of subhuman performance will lead to the discovery of additional inference mechanisms that bring the system closer to human ability in verifying natural arguments.

Superhuman performance

Congruence closure accounts for all the examples of superhuman performance of the Ontic system. The Ontic proof of the Stone representation theorem contains six examples of superhuman performance based on congruence closure [McAllester 1987]. All of these examples involve reasoning about lattice identities.

```
(IN-CONTEXT ((LET-BE B BOOLEAN-LATTICE)
             (LET-BE X (IN-U-SET B))
             (LET-BE Y (IN-U-SET B))
             (LET-BE CX (COMPLEMENT X B))
             (LET-BE CY (COMPLEMENT Y B))
             (LET-BE M (MEET X Y B))
             (LET-BE J (JOIN CX CY B)))
    (NOTE (IS J (COMPLEMENT-OF M B))))
```

Let x^* and y^* be the complements of x and y respectively. Let m be the meet of x and y and let j be the join of x^* and y^*. We must show that m and j are compliments, that is, that $m \wedge j = 0$ and $m \vee j = 1$. This can be done as follows.

$$
\begin{aligned}
m \wedge (x^* \vee y^*) \quad &= (m \wedge x^*) \vee (m \wedge y^*) && \text{By distributivity of } \wedge \text{ over } \vee. \\
&= ((x \wedge x^*) \wedge y) \vee ((y \wedge y^*) \wedge x) && \text{By assoc. and comm. of } \wedge. \\
&= (0 \wedge y) \vee (0 \wedge x) && \text{By definition of complement.} \\
&= 0 && \text{By algebraic properties of 0.}
\end{aligned}
$$

$$
\begin{aligned}
(x \wedge y) \vee j \quad &= (x \vee j) \wedge (y \vee j) && \text{By distributivity of } \vee \text{ over } \wedge. \\
&= (y^* \vee (x^* \vee x)) \wedge (x^* \vee (y^* \vee y)) && \text{By assoc. and comm. of } \vee. \\
&= (y^* \vee 1) \vee (x^* \vee 1) && \text{By definition of complement.} \\
&= 1 && \text{By algebraic properties of 1.}
\end{aligned}
$$

Figure 3. An example of a superhuman Ontic proof and a corresponding natural argument.

One example of a superhuman Ontic proof is the proof of de Morgan's laws for complemented distributive lattices. De Morgan's laws are straightforward if one assumes that Boolean operations have their standard meaning as operators on sets, or equivalently, if Boolean operations have their standard meaning as operations on truth functions. However, until one has proven the Stone representation theorem, one must consider the possibility that there exist pathological complemented distributive lattices in which the Boolean operations cannot be viewed as operations on sets or as truth functions. The superhuman Ontic proof of de Morgan's laws and an analysis of that proof are shown in figure 3.

The Ontic proof of the Stone representation theorem relies on a proof that for any elements x and y of a complemented distributive lattice the following are equivalent:

1    $x \leq y$
2    $y^* \leq x^*$
3    $x \wedge y^* = 0$
4    $x^* \vee y = 1$

The Ontic proof of the equivalence of these four facts is done by showing that $1 \Rightarrow 2 \Rightarrow 3 \Rightarrow 4 \Rightarrow 1$. This is done in a context where the uniqueness of complements and de Morgan's laws have already been established. For each implication there is a set of four focus objects which makes the implication obvious to the Ontic system. The proof of each implication shows superhuman performance involving congruence closure.

A very fast parallel architecture

This section proposes an architecture for massively parallel computation and argues that, unlike Boolean constraint propagation, congruence closure is difficult to implement on this architecture[1]. People make truth judgments about obvious statements in about a second. Although the computation performed by neurons is not well understood, it is clear that neurons run very slowly. It seems likely that neurons would require one to ten milliseconds to compute the logical **and** of two Boolean signals. If people are computing truth judgments with Boolean circuitry, and if the gate delay for neuronal hardware is on the order of one to ten milliseconds, then people make truth judgments about obvious statements in 100 to 1000 gate delays. Computing complex truth judgments in only 100 to 1000 gate delays requires massive parallelism.

Consider a finite state machine where the state of the machine at time i is given by an n-bit bit vector D_i. The state transition table of the

---

[1] It is easy to show that Boolean constraint propagation is polynomial time complete and thus "unparallelizable;" the worst case running time on a parallel machine is linear in the size of the graph. In many cases however, a parallel implementation would run much faster than a serial implementation; a parallel implementation runs in time proportional to the longest single inference chain while a serial implementation runs in time proportional to the total number of inferences.

machine can be given by a Boolean circuit Φ of n inputs and n outputs where the state transitions of the machine are governed by the equation

$$D_{i+1} = \Phi(D_i).$$

To make the finite state machine run quickly the Boolean circuit Φ should have low depth, say ten gates. If Φ has depth ten then a state transition can be computed in ten gate delays. However, the bit vector defining the state of the machine can be very large: millions or tens of millions of bits, and the circuit Φ can involve millions or tens of millions of gates.

It seems possible to compile an Ontic graph into a Boolean circuit governing a finite state machine. More specifically, a labeling of an Ontic graph could be encoded in the state bit vector of the machine. The basic inference operations on graph labels could be incorporated into a Boolean circuit Φ governing state transitions. Two bits are needed for each formula node to represent the three possible labeling states of the node: true, false, and unknown. Boolean constraints on formula nodes could be compiled directly in the structure of the Boolean circuit Φ. Every node in an Ontic graph is also associated with a color label. The color label for a given node in the graph could be represented with a set of bits in the machine's state vector. The Boolean circuit governing state transitions could be designed in such a way that if an equation node became true then the color labels of the equated nodes at time $i + 1$ would each be set to the maximum of the two labels at time i. In this way the color labels could be made to respect the truth of equality formulas. With the exception of congruence closure, all of the inference techniques used in the Ontic system seem to be amenable to a massively parallel implementation in a low-depth Boolean circuit governing a finite state machine.

Ontic's implementation of congruence closure uses a hash table to map color tuples to colors. In order to implement a hash table one needs to be able to compute memory addresses for a random access memory. The use of a hash table seems incompatible with an implementation based on a low depth Boolean circuit governing a large finite state machine.

Congruence closure can be replaced with substitution constraints as described in the next section. Substitution constraints are Boolean constraints involving equality formulas; such constraints can be compiled directly into a low-depth Boolean circuit governing a finite state machine.

Substitution constraints

Substitution constraints provide an alternative to congruence closure for reasoning about equality. Substitution constraints rely on Boolean constraint propagation's ability to handle certain equality inferences. Boolean constraint propagation ensures a simple relationship between the truth of equality formulas and the color labels encoding equivalence. Boolean constraint propagation, however, does not automatically handle the substitution of equals for equals; in the Ontic system substitution is handled by congruence closure. On the other hand, Boolean constraint propagation can be made to handle substitution by adding certain Boolean constraints which I will call substitution constraints. Boolean constraint propagation with substitution constraints is weaker than congruence closure in that it generates fewer obvious truths in a given context.

As a simple example of a substitution constraint consider a term $f(c)$ which consists of an operator f applied to a specific argument c. We can assume that the operator f is defined on objects of a certain type τ and that c is an instance of τ. Suppose that g is a generic individual of type τ. To ensure that inheritance works properly one can add the Boolean constraint

$$g = c \; \Rightarrow \; f(g) = f(c).$$

Now if the system ever generates a binding $g \mapsto c$ then g and c will get the same color label and Boolean constraint propagation will ensure that the equation $g = c$ gets labeled true and thus, by the above substitution constraint, the equation $f(g) = f(c)$ will be labeled true. Independent of congruence closure, if $f(g)$ has the same color label as $f(c)$ then certain facts about $f(g)$ can be inherited by $f(c)$. For example, if $f(g)$ is known to be an instance of a type σ then $f(c)$ will also be known to be an instance of the type σ. Thus the above Boolean constraint allows the binding $g \mapsto c$ to cause c to inherit facts that are stated in terms of g.

Substitution constraints can be used to perform inferences based on the substitution of equals for equals. Suppose that c is known to be equal to b and consider the terms $f(c)$ and $f(b)$. Furthermore assume the graph structure underlying Boolean constraint propagation includes the following substitution constraints

$$g = c \; \Rightarrow \; f(g) = f(c)$$
$$g = b \; \Rightarrow \; f(g) = f(b).$$

Now suppose that the system focuses on c and generates the binding $g \mapsto c$. Because c and b are known to be equal, the nodes for g, c, and b will all get the same color label. Thus the equations $g = c$ and $g = b$ will become true. Thus both the equations $f(g) = f(c)$ and $f(g) = f(b)$ will become true and the nodes for $f(g)$, $f(c)$ and $f(b)$ will all get the same color label. Thus focusing on c causes the system to deduce that $f(c)$ equals $f(b)$. This scheme for handling substitution of equals for equals via substitution constraints can be suitably generalized to handle operators of more than one argument.

Superhuman performance re-examined

The scheme for equality inference based substitution constraints is not as powerful as the full congruence closure mechanism. More specifically, when using substitution constraints, the substitution of equals for equals can only be done when the substituted expressions are equal to some focus object. An analysis of examples of superhuman performance indicates that substitution for non-focus objects plays a central role in these examples.

Even the weaker scheme based on substitution constraints could prove that complements are unique in a single inference step if the system focused on x, y_1, y_2, $y_2 \vee x$, $y_1 \wedge x$, $y_2 \wedge x$, and $y_2 \vee x$ all at the same time. However, it seems that people have a hard time focusing on seven objects simultaneously. The ability of the Ontic system to focus on a large number of objects simultaneously is perhaps another source of superhuman performance.

Subhuman performance

The clearest examples of subhuman behavior on the part of the Ontic system involve mathematical induction. Many common sense inferences appear to involve induction. I mentioned the colored graph problem earlier. Here are other examples:

- Consider a chess board. The white pawns start on the second rank and never move backward. Therefore no white pawn can ever appear on the first rank. A formal proof of this statement requires induction on the number of steps in the game.

- Consider two containers for holding marbles. Initially each container is empty. Marbles are then placed in the containers in pairs; one marble from each pair is placed in each container. No matter how many times this is done, assuming the containers do not overflow, there will be the same number of marbles in each container. A formal proof of this statement requires an induction on the number of marbles placed in the containers.

- Consider Rubic's cube. Suppose the cube starts in a solved position and is scrambled by some number of rotations of faces of the cube. There exists a set of steps that unscrambles the cube. A formal proof of this statement requires an induction on the number of rotations used to scramble the cube.

- Consider a mouse running in a maze. Suppose the maze is arranged inside a box such that there are no openings in the walls of the box and the mouse cannot jump over the walls. No matter how long the mouse runs, and no matter where it goes inside the maze, the mouse will not get outside the box. This statement can be formally proved by induction on the number of "moves" the mouse makes in the box.

In each of the above examples the conclusion is obvious to people. In each example, if the concepts involved were approximated by mathematically precise notions then any mathematician would accept the conclusion as obvious and would not ask for further proof.

Ontic has to deal with induction proofs explicitly: one must explicitly formulate the induction hypothesis and explicitly verify the induction step. For example, consider verifying that white pawns in a game of chess cannot get to the first rank. This fact can be verified using the following induction principle for natural numbers.

```
(DEFTYPE SET-OF-NATNUMS
  (LAMBDA ((S SET))
    (IS-EVERY (MEMBER-OF S) NATURAL-NUMBER)))

(LEMMA
  (FORALL ((S SET-OF-NATNUMS))
    (⇒ (AND (IS ZERO (MEMBER-OF S))
            (FORALL ((N (MEMBER-OF S)))
              (IS (SUCCESSOR N) (MEMBER-OF S))))
       (IS-EVERY NATURAL-NUMBER (MEMBER-OF S)))))
```

The above induction principle says that if a set S contains zero and is closed under successor then it contains all numbers. The set S represents an induction hypothesis; S is the set of numbers which satisfy the hypothesis. In the chess example one must prove that white pawns never end up on the first rank.

```
(FORALL ((G CHESS-GAME)
         (N NATURAL-NUMBER))
  (IS-EVERY (WHITE-PAWN-ON-BOARD G (SUCCESSOR N))
            (WHITE-PAWN-ON-BOARD G N)))

(FORALL ((G CHESS-GAME)
         (N NATURAL-NUMBER)
         (P (WHITE-PAWN-ON-BOARD G (SUCCESSOR N))))
  (IS (RANK-OF P G (SUCCESSOR N))
      (GREATER-OR-EQUAL-TO (RANK-OF P G N))))

(FORALL ((P (WHITE-PAWN-ON-BOARD G ZERO)))
  (IS (RANK-OF P G ZERO)
      (EQUAL-TO TWO)))
```

Figure 4. Statements which follow from the rules of chess.

More formally, let an instance of the type CHESS-GAME be a particular game of chess, that is, a particular sequence of moves. If G is a chess game and N is a number then (WHITE-PAWN-ON-BOARD G N) denotes the type whose instances are the white pawns which are on the chess board after the Nth move of the game G. We let (RANK-OF P G N) be the rank occupied by the pawn P immediately after the Nth move of the game G. Figure 4 contains statements which follow from the rules of chess. An Ontic proof that pawns never get to the first rank is given in figure 5. The goals in the proof are numbered and the NOTE-GOAL steps are labeled with the number of the goal being noted. The proof uses the facts listed in figure 4 together with simple facts about the ordering of natural numbers.

The proof starts by considering an arbitrary chess game G. The proof shows that the following induction hypothesis holds for any number N.

```
(FORALL ((P (WHITE-PAWN-ON-BOARD G N)))
  (IS (RANK-OF P G N)
      (GREATER-OR-EQUAL-TO TWO)))
```

The induction principle for natural numbers states that if a set of numbers contains zero and is closed under successor then it contains all numbers. If the induction hypothesis is $\Phi(N)$ then one should consider the set of all N such that $\Phi(N)$. For the above induction hypothesis one should consider the following set.

```
(THE-SET-OF-ALL
  (LAMBDA ((N NATURAL-NUMBER))
    (FORALL ((P (WHITE-PAWN-ON-BOARD G N)))
      (IS (RANK-OF P G N)
          (GREATER-OR-EQUAL-TO TWO)))))
```

The Ontic proof in figure 5 focuses on the set representing the induction hypothesis. It then proceeds to prove the base case and induction step. The base case uses the fact that the rank of a white pawn at time zero equals two and every number is greater than or equal to itself. In order to apply the fact that every number is greater than or equal to itself one must focus on the number two. The induction step uses the fact that the rank of the pawn at time n is greater or equal to two and the rank of the pawn at time $n + 1$ is greater or equal to the rank at time n. To invoke the transitivity of the ordering on natural numbers one must focus on the three numbers given by the rank of pawn at times n and $n + 1$ together with the number two.

The proof shown in figure 5 is clearly much longer than a natural language argument which simply states that white pawns never get to the first rank. This example indicates that without additional theorem proving mechanisms the Ontic system will exhibit a large expansion factor on many induction proofs.

One possible mechanism for reducing the expansion factor in induction proofs would be a backward chaining procedure (a tactic) for automatically generating proofs such as the one shown in the figure 5. It would be easy to automatically convert the induction hypothesis into a set of numbers and automatically focus on that set of numbers. Furthermore one could automatically attempt to prove the base and induction cases of the argument. As figure 5 shows, however, proving the base and induction cases with the Ontic system may require focusing on additional objects. In the

```
(IN-CONTEXT ((LET-BE G CHESS-GAME)
            (LET-BE HYP-SATISFIERS
              (THE-SET-OF-ALL
                (LAMBDA ((N NATNUM))
                  (FORALL ((P (WHITE-PAWN-ON-BOARD G N)))
                    (IS (RANK-OF P G N)
                        (GREATER-OR-EQUAL-TO TWO))))))))
   (PUSH-GOAL ; #1
    (IS-EVERY NATURAL-NUMBER
              (MEMBER-OF HYP-SATISFIERS))))
  (IN-CONTEXT ((PUSH-GOAL ; #2
               (IS ZERO (MEMBER-OF HYP-SATISFIERS))))
   (IN-CONTEXT ((LET-BE ZEROVAR ZERO))
    (IN-CONTEXT ((SUPPOSE
                  (EXISTS-SOME (WHITE-PAWN-ON-BOARD G ZERO)))
                 (LET-BE P (WHITE-PAWN-ON-BOARD G ZERO))
                 (LET-BE TWOVAR TWO))
     (NOTE-GOAL)) ; #2
    (NOTE-GOAL))) ; #2
  (IN-CONTEXT ((PUSH-GOAL ; #3
               (FORALL ((N (MEMBER-OF HYP-SATISFIERS)))
                 (IS (SUCCESSOR N) (MEMBER-OF HYP-SATISFIERS))))
              (LET-BE SATISFIER (MEMBER-OF HYP-SATISFIERS))
              (LET-BE NEXT-SATISFIER (SUCC SATISFIER)))
   (IN-CONTEXT
    ((PUSH-GOAL ; #4
      (FORALL ((P (WHITE-PAWN-ON-BOARD G NEXT-SATISFIER)))
        (IS (RANK-OF P G NEXT-SATISFIER)
            (GREATER-OR-EQUAL-TO TWO)))))
    (IN-CONTEXT ((SUPPOSE
                  (EXISTS-SOME
                    (WHITE-PAWN-ON-BOARD G NEXT-SATISFIER)))
                 (LET-BE P (WHITE-PAWN-ON-BOARD G NEXT-SATISFIER))
                 (LET-BE R1 (RANK-OF P G SATISFIER))
                 (LET-BE R2 (RANK-OF P G NEXT-SATISFIER))
                 (LET-BE TWOVAR TWO))
     (NOTE-GOAL)) ; #4
    (NOTE-GOAL)) ; #4
   (NOTE-GOAL)) ; #3
  (IN-CONTEXT ((LET-BE N (MEMBER-OF HYP-SATISFIERS)))
   (NOTE (IS HYP-SATISFIERS SET-OF-NATNUM)))
  (NOTE-GOAL)) ; #1
```

Figure 5. The proof that white pawns never get to the first rank.

base case of figure 5 the user focuses on an arbitrary white pawn and the number two. In the induction case the user focuses on the rank of the pawn at two different times. It seems that it might be difficult to automatically generate these additional focus objects.

Several automated inference systems include inference mechanisms for handling mathematical induction [Boyer & Moore 1979; Huet & Hullot 1983; Ketonen 1984]. Research is needed to determine if these, or other, induction mechanisms can be incorporated into the Ontic system. These inference mechanisms are all backward chaining; the induction hypothesis is taken from the goal statement. It would be interesting to see if some forward chaining induction mechanism could be found that was more in the spirit of Ontic's forward chaining inference techniques.

It might be possible to construct a forward chaining induction mechanism as part of Ontic's classification process. Recall that classification involves assigning a set of types to each focus object. Consider a focus object $r(n)$ that involves an arbitrary number n and consider a type τ. It may be possible to prove that the focus object $r(n)$ is an instance of the type τ via induction on the number n. More specifically, the system could show that $r(0)$ is an instance of τ and that if $r(n)$ is an instance of τ then $r(n + 1)$ is an instance of τ. In the chess example the focus object $r(n)$ would be (RANK-OF P G N) where P is an arbitrary instance of (WHITE-PAWN-ON-BOARD G N). In the chess example the system would classify the object (RANK-OF P G N) to be an instance of the type (GREATER-OR-EQUAL-TO TWO). This example shows that classification could be made more powerful by incorporating an induction mechanism.

The above examples show that special inference mechanisms for induction are needed in the Ontic system. Hopefully an induction mechanism can be found which allows the above examples to be machine verified at a human, or near-human, level of detail.

Applications

There are two ways of evaluating the ideas used in the Ontic system. First, one can attempt to evaluate the utility of the ideas in constructing useful systems. Second, one can attempt to evaluate the extent to which Ontic's inference mechanisms provide a plausible model of human mathematical cognition. This chapter addresses the first evaluation technique by presenting a list of potential applications of automated inference systems. These applications represent directions for future research; the limitations of Ontic's object-oriented inference techniques in these applications are not currently understood and future research may uncover other inference techniques that make these applications practical.

One potential application for automated inference systems is simply the verification of mathematical arguments; an author could increase his confidence in the correctness of a proof using machine verification. The time required to "debug" the formal representation of proofs in the Ontic system seems to make this application impractical at the current time. However, as the inference power of the system is increased, and the lemma library is made larger, machine verification of new mathematics could become practical.

Automated inference mechanisms are needed in the construction of interactive knowledge bases. The Ontic system is able to automatically use information from a lemma library. An Ontic system based on a lemma library that contained the contents of a mathematical textbook could answer certain questions about the contents of that book. Such an interactive textbook would be valuable in education. If the system could be made to run with a very large lemma library, a library containing the contents of many textbooks, one could construct an interactive mathematical encyclopedia. An interactive encyclopedia could be used by professional mathematicians to answer questions and verify arguments in domains that were not familiar to the human user.

Automated inference systems might also be useful in constructing interactive documentation systems. A computer operating system, for example, is usually associated with a large amount of documentation. One could translate this documentation into first order axioms that serve as a lemma library underlying an inference system. One would then have a device for answering questions about the documented system. The problem of answering questions about engineered devices seems similar to, but possibly more difficult than, the problem of answering questions about the material in a mathematical textbook.

Ontic's object-oriented inference mechanism could be applied to program verification. Ontic's type system is similar to the type systems of strongly typed programming languages. With sufficiently expressive types there is no distinction between type checking and verification; any verification problem for a computer program can be phrased as a type-checking problem. Ontic's object-oriented inference mechanisms are organized around types. It would be interesting to explore the application of Ontic's object-oriented inference mechanisms to program verification where verification is viewed as a form of type-checking.

Another possible application for Ontic's inference mechanisms is common sense reasoning. In his naive physics manifesto Hayes proposed writing down first order axioms that express common sense knowledge about the physical world [Hayes 1985]. One might object to Hayes' proposal on the grounds that first order inference is intractable. It is clear, however, that certain limited inferences can be done quickly. It would be interesting to explore the application of Ontic's inference mechanisms to reasoning about common sense situations. Another objection to Hayes' proposal is that much, if not most, common sense reasoning is heuristic: the conclusions are not strictly implied by the given information. The heuristic nature of common sense reasoning does present a challenge to researchers attempting to build such systems and the integration of heuristic and mathematically sound reasoning seems like an important area for future research.

The following two sections explore particular potential applications in more detail.

Interactive knowledge bases

Ontic's object-oriented inference mechanisms are designed to access a large lemma library automatically. By placing various kinds of information in the knowledge base underlying an Ontic-like system one could construct interactive mathematical textbooks, interactive mathematical encyclopedias, and interactive technical documentation libraries.

Access to information in Ontic's lemma library is controlled via types: the inference mechanism accesses only those portions of the lemma library that concern types that apply to the given focus objects. For example, when reasoning about graphs the system automatically ignores facts about differentiable manifolds. Thus the lemma library could include information about a large number of different subjects and still be used effectively.

There are several ways one could use an interactive mathematical encyclopedia. First, the encyclopedia could be used to answer questions about areas of mathematics that are unfamiliar to the user. Second, the encyclopedia could verify a user's argument. This would be especially useful when the human user is unfamiliar with the subject matter of his own argument. Finally, a mathematician who develops a new concept could ask the system if that concept has already been defined under some other name.

Recognizing user-defined concepts is particularly difficult; there may be a defined concept in the encyclopedia which is "essentially the same" as a user-defined concept but the two definitions are technically different. For example, consider the concept of an equivalence relation. An equivalence relation can be defined as a relation, that is, a set of pairs, which is symmetric, transitive, and reflexive. Alternatively, an equivalence relation can be defined as a partition of a set into equivalence classes. These two definitions seem to define the same concept and yet the two classes are technically distinct: a partition is different from a set of pairs. Yet these two objects are in some sense the same; I will say they are *iso-ontic*.[2] There are many examples of iso-onticities. For example, a function f of two arguments defines a Curried function f' such that for all arguments x and y, the application $f'(x)$ yields a function such that $f(x, y) = f'(x)(y)$. The function f is iso-ontic to its Curried version f'. Another example is the definition of a topological space. A topological space can be defined as a pair of a set s and a higher-order predicate p such that for any subset u of s, $p(u)$ is true if and only if u is open. Alternatively, a topological space

---

[2]The term iso-ontic means "same being," or more loosely, equi-existent. For example, in any situation where an equivalence relation exists a partition also exists. This is different from the term isomorphic which means "same shape."

can be defined simply as a family of sets. An interactive knowledge base should recognize that these two definitions are equivalent; if a user defines a topological space in a way that is formally different from the definition in the knowledge base, the system should still recognize the user's definition as a simple variant of the notion of a topological space, even though instances of the user's definition are unambiguously distinct objects from instances of the knowledge-base definition. Intuitively, a family of sets is iso-ontic to a certain set together with a higher-order predicate on subsets of that set.

Iso-onticity is not the same as isomorphism under the technical sense of isomorphism used by mathematicians. Intuitively, two objects x and y are isomorphic if there exists a bijection between the "points" of the objects that "carries" the structure of x exactly onto the structure of y. If x and y are isomorphic then they must both have the same structure, for example, they are both groups or both topological spaces or both differentiable manifolds. Iso-onticity, on the other hand, is a relationship that holds between objects of completely different structure, for example, a family of disjoint sets (a partition) and a set of pairs (an equivalence relation). Although iso-onticity is not the same as isomorphism, it is possible to give a completely general formal definition of iso-onticity (for details see chapter 18). It seems likely that this notion of iso-onticity between terms can be used in some way to recognize when two type expressions are "equivalent," that is, they are technically different versions of the single concept of a topological space. The definition of equivalence for types can presumably be based on some combination of the notions of isomorphism and iso-onticity for terms. Ideally, the technical notion of equivalent types should agree with human intuitions about equivalent definitions.

Software verification

Type checking has proved to be a practical way of finding certain errors in computer programs. Currently available type checking systems use a weak vocabulary of types—there is no way to treat an arbitrary predicate as a data type. If the type vocabulary is made richer then stronger "semantic" properties of programs can be expressed as type constraints. In fact, if any predicate on data structures can be expressed as a type then any semantic specification for a computer program can be expressed as type restrictions. For example, if iteration is replaced by recursion then a programmer can provide loop invariants simply by placing type restrictions on the arguments of recursive functions.

If arbitrary predicates on data structures can be expressed as types then type checking requires theorem proving. One might argue that, because theorem proving is intractable, one should not use fully expressive type systems. This criticism carries little weight, however, if one is willing to allow type checking to fail. A failure to type check simply means that the system failed to prove the program correct; it does not mean that the program is wrong. Because Ontic's object-oriented theorem proving mechanisms are guaranteed to terminate quickly, a type checking system based on Ontic's theorem proving mechanisms could also be made to terminate quickly. One could give rules of obviousness for type checking that are analogous to Ontic's rules. These rules of obviousness would define the the notion of an obviously well-typed program. A programmer could be required to make sure that all his programs are obviously well typed. A correct program that is not obviously well-typed could be made obviously well-typed in one of two different ways. First, one could weaken the type restrictions on certain procedures. This corresponds to using a weaker type vocabulary such as the ones currently in use. Second, new lemmas could be asserted in the lemma library so that a the well-typedness of the procedure is obvious in the presence of these new lemmas.

Type checking has already been demonstrated to be practical for certain restricted type vocabularies. It seems likely that type checking using more expressive types would be equally practical in the sense that all programs that are well-typed under existing systems would correspond to obviously well-typed programs in the more expressive setting. In a more expressive setting, however, a programmer would be free to experiment with stronger type restrictions and with the statement of lemmas about stronger types that make his programs obviously well typed. In this more expressive setting the distinction between type checking and program verification would be eliminated and a programmer could select any degree of verification in the continuum between type checking and the full-blown verification of arbitrary loop invariants.

Sources of Ontic's Strengths

The Ontic system has many features not found in previous systems. Ideally, each new feature would be introduced and evaluated independent of the other features. For example, the uniform elimination of predicates in favor of types and type generators could be evaluated in a more traditional first-order framework, one independent of the axioms of set theory. Unfortunately, an independent evaluation of each individual new feature would be quite time consuming and would not properly account for synergistic interactions between various features. For example, the encoding of the set-theoretic axioms into a syntactic notion of smallness would be more cumbersome in a system that did not already have a rich type vocabulary. Although it is difficult to independently evaluate each individual feature of Ontic, it is possible to enumerate the novel features and to gain some intuition about the importance of each feature in the overall usefulness of the system. The Ontic system includes the following features.

- The Ontic formal language is organized around a rich vocabulary of types. The variety of ways types can be constructed interacts with the variety of ways types can be used resulting in the concise representation of a large variety of statements. Types can be constructed as λ-predicates, applications of type generators, or with the special type-constructor RANGE-TYPE. Types can be used to make formulas of the form (IS s τ), to restrict the range of quantifiers, to form a definite description term involving the THE, to form sets using the operator THE-SET-OF-ALL, or to express simple implications using the type-combinator macro IS-EVERY.

- Most of the axioms of Zermelo-Fraenkel set theory are incorporated into the syntactic definition of a small type expression and a small function expression; type and function expressions which are syntactically small can be *reified* using the operators THE-SET-OF-ALL and THE-RULE respectively.

- Ontic provides a high-level proof language in which proof correctness is specified by a technical notion of an obviously correct step. The notion of obviousness is specified by inference rules called rules of obviousness.

- The high-level proof language allows for the explicit specification of certain terms, called focus objects, and the rules of obviousness are defined in terms of these focus objects. Thus we say that the high-level proof language and the rules of obviousness are both object-oriented.

- Ontic automatically finds and applies information from a large lemma library. It is possible to construct a decision procedure for the rules of obviousness that is capable of efficiently using all of the lemmas in a large lemma library when determining if a given statement is obvious.

- All Ontic variables include a type as part of their syntactic structure. This allows variables to play the role of Skolem witnesses for existential statements. It also allows variables to be used as generic individuals in the semantic modulation implementation. It further allows typed variables to act as arbitrary values in the universal generalization rule of obviousness; in universal generalization typed variables play the role of the Skolem constants in a resolution refutation proof that result from the negation of a universally quantified goal formula.

- Ontic's implementation of the decision procedure for the notion of obviousness is based on a semantic network style label-propagation technique. This mechanism allows a given node in the network structure to be re-used in many different contexts. The cost of label-propagation is also amortized over different contexts.

- Ontic's implementation of the rules of obviousness that involve focus is based on a semantic network style inheritance mechanism called semantic modulation. Semantic modulation avoids the construction of highly context-specific network structure by varying, or modulating, the semantic interpretation of fixed network structure. This is done by varying the semantic interpretation of certain variables called generic individuals. By allowing increased sharing of network structure and network labels, semantic modulation increases the effectiveness of the amortization of label-propagation over different contexts.

As of this writing it is not clear which of the above features are most responsible for the effectiveness of the Ontic system. It seems likely that all of the features contribute in some way. Future systems may incorporate new features such as new rules of obviousness, automatic type-checking, or tactics for automatically finding high-level proofs. In any case, I believe that progress in knowledge representation and machine reasoning is inevitable.

References

Bledsoe, W. W. [1977], "Non-resolution theorem Proving," *Artificial Intelligence*, vol. 9, pp. 1-35.

Boyer, Robert S., and J. Struther Moore [1979], "A Computational Logic," *ACM Monograph Series*.

Hayes, Patrick [1985], "The Second Naive Physics Manifesto," in *Formal Theories of the Commonsense World*, edited by J. Hobbs, and R. Moore, Ablex Publishers.

Huet, Gerard, and Jean-Marie Hullot [1982], "Proofs by Induction in Equational Theories with Constructors," *JCSS*, vol. 25, pp. 239-366.

Gratzer, George [1978], *General Lattice Theory*, Academic Press.

Ketonen, Jussi [1984], "EKL—A Mathematically Oriented Proof Checker," *Proceedings of the 7th International Conference on Automated Deduction*, Lecture Note in Computer Science, pp. 65-79.

Constable, R. L., S. F. Allen, H. M. Bromely, W. R. Cleaveland, J. F. Cremer, R. W. Harper, D. J. Howe, T. K. Knoblock, N. P. Mendler, P. Panangaden, J. T. Sasaki, and S. F. Smith [1986], *Implementing Mathematics with the Nuprl Development System*, Prentice Hall.

McAllester, David A. [1983], "Symmetric Set Theory, A General Theory of Isomorphism, Abstraction, and Representation," Report AIM-710, Artificial Intelligence Laboratory, Massachusetts Institute of Technology, Cambridge.

McAllester, David, A. [1987], "Ontic: A Knowledge Representation System for Mathematics," Report AI-TR-979, Artificial Intelligence Laboratory, Massachusetts Institute of Technology, Cambridge, MA.

McAllester, David, A. [1989], *Ontic: A Knowledge Representation System for Mathematics*, MIT Press, Cambridge, MA.

McAllester, David, A. [1990], "Three Universal Relations," *Artificial Intelligence at MIT: Expanding Frontiers*, edited by Patrick H. Winston with Sarah A. Shellard, MIT Press, Cambridge, MA, Ch. 18, pp. 474–485.

18

When a mathematician says that two mathematical objects are the same, he sometimes means that the two objects are isomorphic, indicating that there are two objects that behave in exactly the same way, and he sometimes means that the two objects are iso-ontic, indicating that there is really just one object viewed in two ways. In this chapter, McAllester carefully teases these two relations apart, makes both more precise by defining them in terms of symmetric set theory, and introduces the essential-property relation along the way. His ultimate purpose is to understand the nature of inference and to use that understanding to make more powerful inferencing programs.

Three Universal Relations

David A. McAllester

Consider a hypothetical automated encyclopedia of mathematics. A user of this encyclopedia wants to get information about a certain kind of mathematical object that he or she has been calling foo spaces. Because foo spaces are fairly simple it seems likely that they have already been well studied and are described somewhere in the mathematical encyclopedia. Although the user does not know the standard mathematical name for a foo space, the user can define foo spaces in terms of more basic concepts. The user states the definition of a foo space in a machine-readable language as a pair of a domain (a set) and a family of subsets of that domain such that the union of all sets in the family is the entire domain and the family of subsets is closed under arbitrary union and finite intersection. It should be clear to any human mathematician that foo spaces are the same as topological spaces and have a long history in mathematics. Unfortunately, in the automated encyclopedia a topological space is defined to be a family of sets that is closed under arbitrary union and finite intersection. From a purely formal perspective, based on these two formal definitions, a foo space is not a topological space and a topological space is not a foo space. More specifically, let F be the foo space $\langle D, X \rangle$ where D is the domain of F and X is the family of subsets of D. Under the encyclopedia's definitions, the family X is a topological space but the pair $\langle D, X \rangle$ is definitely not a topological space because it is not a family of sets. It does not matter that D can be expressed as the simple union of all sets in X; it is still the case that a pair is different from a family of sets and thus foo spaces are not topological spaces. The encyclopedia tells the user that it has no information about foo spaces.

There is clearly some inadequacy in the automated encyclopedia described above; it should have recognized a foo space as simply an alternative way of defining a topological space. The same problem arises in virtually all mathematical concepts—definitions that are really "the same" are technically quite different. As another example consider the definition of a group. A group can be defined as an algebra with one binary operation satisfying certain non-equational conditions, or it can be defined as an algebra with a binary operation, a unary operation (inverse) and a constant (the identity) satisfying certain equations. These two definitions result in technically disjoint classes of objects.

Can an automated reasoning system search for equivalences between technically distinct definitions, such as the equivalence between foo spaces and topological spaces, or the equivalence between a group as an algebra with one operation and a group as an algebra with two operations and a constant? The first step in answering this question is to find some formal characterization of when two definitions are "the same." It is tempting to try to characterize these equivalences in terms of the well known notion of isomorphism. Unfortunately, there is no standard notion of isomorphism under which a foo space is isomorphic to a topological space. Two distinct topological spaces can be homeomorphic, the standard notion of isomorphism for topological spaces, but there is no way a topological space can be homeomorphic to an object that is not a topological space. Similarly an algebra with one operation can not be isomorphic, in the standard sense for algebras, with an algebra that has two operations and a constant.

If an automated mathematical encyclopedia can not use some standard notion of isomorphism to identify equivalences between definitions, perhaps it can use a more general category-theoretic notion of isomorphism. The basic challenge in formulating a category theoretic approach to equivalence between definitions is to define a single notion of equivalence that can be used for arbitrary mathematical definitions. The mathematical definitions that appear in textbooks and journals are not usually explicitly associated with categories. Even if a user of an automated encyclopedia explicitly associates a category with every defined concept, it is not clear that an association of a single category with each concept is sufficient for all purposes. For example, consider the two standard definitions of a lattice. A lattice can be defined as either a partially ordered set with least upper bounds and greatest lower bounds, or as an algebra satisfying certain equations. It is not clear what category should be associated with the concept of a partial order, or whether the categories associated with partial orders and with algebras are useful in recognizing the equivalence between the order-theoretic and the algebraic definitions of a lattice. As another example, consider an equivalence relation defined as a relation, that is, a set of pairs, and defined as a partition into equivalence classes, that is, a family of sets. Again, it is not clear what category should be associated with the set of pairs definition

and what category should be associated with the equivalence class partition
definition. Even if these concepts are associated with categories, it is not
clear if a single association of categories with these concepts is appropriate
for all possible equivalences. For many particular examples of equivalences
between definitions, and perhaps even for the examples discussed so far, it is
possible to associate each concept with some particular category such that
some form of category theoretic equivalence is apparent. However, defining
particular categories for exhibiting particular equivalences is quite different
from providing a *general* definition of equivalence that can be applied to
arbitrary pairs of mathematical concepts. One would like a general theory
of equivalence that can be applied unambiguously to the examples given so
far, and an unbounded number of other examples. In each case the general
theory should determine unambiguously, at least in principle, whether or
not any two given mathematical definitions are equivalent. The lack of any
objective way of associating a category with arbitrary definitions, such as
the definition of a partial order, partition, or equivalence relation, seems to
be a major obstacle to any category-theoretic approach.

This chapter takes a set-theoretic approach to the problem of recognizing equivalences between mathematical definitions. All of the mathematical
definitions discussed have simple unambiguous set-theoretic formulations.
For each mathematical definition, the objects which are instances of that
definition, for example, the topological spaces, are particular elements of
the set-theoretic universe. Thus each definition corresponds to an unambiguous class of sets. Thus, any unambiguous notion of equivalence between classes of sets yields an unambiguous notion of equivalence between
mathematical definitions.

The equivalence between the definition of a foo space and the definition of a topological space is an example of a general form of equivalence
that I will call iso-onticity. The formal definition of iso-onticity given below states iso-onticity as a relationship between particular mathematical
objects rather than between mathematical definitions—we say that a particular foo space is iso-ontic to a particular topological space. The concept
of iso-onticity can be applied to arbitrary mathematical objects—any two
mathematical objects either are or are not iso-ontic to each other. Because
the concept of iso-onticity applies to arbitrary mathematical objects, iso-
onticity will be called a *universal relation*, that is, a relation that is defined
on all objects.

But before formally defining iso-onticity, it is illuminating to consider
two other universal relations: isomorphism and essential properties. Intuitively, isomorphism corresponds to the notion of type identity. Consider
two pennies which have just been minted by the same machine. These
two pennies are physically identical for all macroscopic purposes (we might
say that they are *type identical* as physical objects). Similarly we could
consider two cans of Diet Pepsi, or two copies of the "same" book. In

each case the two objects are (for all practical purposes) physically identical. A more exact case of type identicality is given by two gaseous carbon dioxide molecules; it seems that any two such molecules in their ground energy state are truly type identical (isomorphic). In fact the notion of isomorphism seems to be universal; any object whatsoever could have a doppelgänger in some parallel universe. An object is always isomorphic to its doppelgänger.

It is important to distinguish isomorphism from iso-onticity. Isomorphic objects (type identical objects) are doppelgängers (like identical pennies) which are usually "materially" disjoint. On the other hand iso-ontic objects are just different "views" of "the same thing," like an equivalence relation and a partition, or the various equivalent representations of the state of a LISP processor.

The final universal relation discussed here is the notion of an *essential property*. The term essential property is *not* being used here in its standard philosophical sense. However, I have not been able to find a better term for the notion I wish to discuss. To understand this notion of essential property consider an array as a computer data structure. An array can be treated as a function. For an array A and an index value i we can let $A[i]$ denote the value of the array at the ith index location. Intuitively, the value of $A[i]$ is not a property of the index i itself but rather it is a property of the array A. This situation can be contrasted with the projection function **first** defined on mathematical pairs. For any pair $\langle x, y \rangle$, $\mathbf{first}(\langle x, y \rangle)$ equals x. It seems clear that x is a property of the pair $\langle x, y \rangle$. For any pair z we say that $\mathbf{first}(z)$ is an *essential property* of z, while for an index value i, $A[i]$ need not be an essential property of the index i. A third example concerns electronic circuits. A circuit has a physical layout and a circuit topology (the topology is the way in which the components are electrically connected). The distance (in inches) between the input coupling capacitor and the output coupling capacitor is a property of the physical layout but is not a property of the circuit topology.

While the three basic universal relations discussed above seem to be based on certain natural intuitions, it is far from clear how one should go about making these notions mathematically precise. For example, it is tempting to say that y is a property of x just in case there is some function f such that $f(x)$ equals y. But this is clearly wrong because there is always a mathematical function (a set of pairs) mapping x to y.

It turns out that the notions of isomorphism, essential property, and iso-onticity can be cleanly and precisely defined in terms of a set-theoretic mathematical ontology, as shown in the next section.

Symmetric Set Theory

The notion of isomorphism, essential property, and iso-onticity can be precisely defined in terms of a set-theoretic universe with class-many ur-elements, that is, class-many objects that are considered as distinct points without internal structure. I am not concerned with the particular first order axioms of Zermelo-Fraenkel set theory—I prefer to consider a particular "intended model" of these axioms. An intended model can be defined up to isomorphism with a few simple axioms.

A set-theoretic universe is a pair $\langle U, \in \rangle$ where U is some domain and $\in$ is a binary membership relation on U (I assume that the domain U is a set; no meta-theoretic distinction is made here between sets and classes). The relation $\in$ associates each element x of U with some particular subset of U, denoted as **mems**(x).

> *Definition*:   If x is an element of U, **mems**(x) is defined to be the subset of U given by: $\{y \text{ in } U\colon y \in x\}$. If **mems**$(x)$ is empty then x will be called a *point*. For non-points x we say that x *represents* the subset **mems**(x).

To understand the significance of the axioms of symmetric set theory it is important to distinguish elements of U from the sets that those elements represent. In particular if x is a non-point *element* of U, then **mems**(x) is a *subset* of U. A particular element of U can often be thought of as representing a set of sets. For example if **mems**(x) is $\{p, z\}$ and **mems**(z) is $\{r, s\}$, then one can think of x as representing $\{p, \{r, s\}\}$. Thus the universe $\langle U, \in \rangle$ can contain representations for tuples, sets of tuples (for example, relations and functions), vector spaces, and topological manifolds. The following axioms specify a particular universe of sets up to isomorphism.

> *Axiom One, Extensionality*:   There are no two distinct non-point elements x and y of U such that **mems**(x) equals **mems**(y).

> *Axiom Two, Strong Replacement*:   A subset C of U is represented by an element of U if and only if it has fewer members than U, that is, just in case $|C| < |U|$.

> *Axiom Three, Strong Foundation*:   There is no infinitely decreasing sequence of elements of U, that is, there is no infinite sequence $x_1, x_2, x_3, \ldots$ where $x_{i+1} \in x_i$ for all i.

> *Axiom Four, Infinity*:   There exists a *represented* infinite subset of U. Or equivalently, U must be uncountably infinite.

> *Axiom Five, Union*:   The union over any represented family of sets is represented. Equivalently, for any family F of subsets of U, if each member of F is smaller than U and the family F itself

has fewer members than U, then the union of all members of F is also smaller than U.

Axiom Six, Power Set: The power set of any represented set is represented. Equivalently, for any subset C of U, if C is smaller than U then there must be more elements of U than there are subsets of C.

Axiom Seven, The Large Base Axiom: The set of all points is not represented. Equivalently, there are as many points in $\langle U, \in \rangle$ as there are elements of U.

Axiom Eight, The No Large Cardinal Axiom: There does not exist any model of axioms one through seven whose domain has cardinality smaller than the cardinality of U.

Axiom eight is not necessary for the theory of universal relations but has the advantage of completely specifying the intended set theoretic universe up to isomorphism. Intuitively, the above axioms specify that the intended universe is isomorphic to the universe of all sets that can be built from a strongly inaccessible number of points (ur-elements) and that have rank less than any strongly inaccessible cardinal.

Three Universal Relations

Isomorphism is the universal relation most directly definable in symmetric set theory. Intuitively two objects are isomorphic just in case they have the same shape, or in other words, just in case they are the same "modulo the identity of their points." For example, the set $\{p, \{p, q\}\}$ is isomorphic to the set $\{r, \{r, s\}\}$. This notion can be made precise by the following definitions.

Definition: For any element x of U, the expression **hmems**(x) will denote the set which includes x, all elements of x, all elements of elements of x, etc. (**hmems**(x) is the set of all things "under" x). The expression $\langle$**hmems**$(x), \in \rangle$ will denote the first order structure derived by restricting the relation $\in$ to **hmems**(x).

Definition: Two objects x and y in $\langle U, \in \rangle$ are *isomorphic* just in case the sub-universes $\langle$**hmems**$(x), \in \rangle$ and $\langle$**hmems**$(y), \in \rangle$ are isomorphic as first order structures.

It turns out that when point-based algebraic structures and topologies are represented as sets the above universal notion of isomorphism provides the standard notions of isomorphism for these objects. For example, consider two "algebras" $\langle D, f \rangle$ and $\langle D', f' \rangle$ where D and D' are sets and f and f' are functions from D to D and D' to D' respectively. Under the standard notion of isomorphism for algebras, these two algebras are isomorphic if there exists a bijection ρ from D to D' such that for any element d of D we have that $f'(\rho(d))$ equals $\rho(f(d))$. These two algebras have standard representations as sets. For example, $\langle D, f \rangle$ is the set $\{D, \{D, f\}\}$ where D is a set and f is a set of pairs of elements of D. Provided that D and D' are sets of points, the reader can check that the algebras $\langle D, f \rangle$ and $\langle D', f' \rangle$ are isomorphic in the standard way for algebras if and only if they are isomorphic in the sense of the above definition. A similar analysis holds for the notion of homeomorphic topological spaces whose domains are sets of points.

The notion of isomorphism can be better understood in terms of the symmetries, or automorphisms, of the universe as a whole. A symmetry (automorphism) of the universe $\langle U, \in \rangle$ is a bijection ρ from U to itself such that for any two elements x and y of U, $\rho(x) \in \rho(y)$ just in case $x \in y$ (a symmetry of $\langle U, \in \rangle$ is an isomorphism of $\langle U, \in \rangle$ with itself). The next lemma completely characterizes all symmetries of any universe $\langle U, \in \rangle$ satisfying axioms one through three. The set of points in a universe $\langle U, \in \rangle$ can be thought of as a *base* for that universe upon which all other elements of U are built. It turns out that the symmetries $\langle U, \in \rangle$ exactly correspond to the permutations of the base of $\langle U, \in \rangle$ (a permutation of the base of $\langle U, \in \rangle$ is a one-to-one and onto mapping of the points in $\langle U, \in \rangle$ to themselves).

> *Global Symmetry Lemma:* Any permutation of the points in $\langle U, \in \rangle$ has a unique extension to a full symmetry (automorphism) of $\langle U, \in \rangle$. Thus there is a natural one-to-one correspondence between the symmetries of $\langle U, \in \rangle$ and the permutations of the "base" of $\langle U, \in \rangle$.

The following lemma is fundamental for the notion of isomorphism. This lemma justifies the intuition that isomorphic objects are truly indistinguishable. (It is interesting to note that the following lemma depends on axiom seven, the large base axiom).

> *The Fundamental Isomorphism Lemma:* Two objects x and y are isomorphic just in case there exists a symmetry (automorphism) of $\langle U, \in \rangle$ which carries x to y.

The second universal relation is the notion of essential property. To understand the notion of an essential property in the context of symmetric set theory it is useful to consider some examples. Suppose x is the set $\{p, \{p, q\}\}$ where p and q are points. We could define p as "the element of z which is also an element of an element of X." Thus p is a "definable" property of the set $\{p, \{p, q\}\}$ (the set $\{p, \{p, q\}\}$ is a standard representation for the *pair* $\langle p, q \rangle$). On the other hand consider the set of points $\{p, q, r\}$. There is "no difference" between the points p and q as elements of the set $\{p, q, r\}$. In fact p is not a definable property of the set $\{p, q, r\}$. The sense in which p is a property of $\{p, \{p, q\}\}$ but not a property of $\{p, q, r\}$ is captured by the following definition.

Definition: We say that y is *individuated* by x just in case every symmetry of $\langle U, \in \rangle$ which leaves x fixed also leaves y fixed.

Again consider the set $\{p, q, r\}$. It is easy to show that there is a symmetry of $\langle U, \in \rangle$ which moves p to q, q to r, and r to p. This symmetry leaves the set $\{p, q, r\}$ fixed while moving the point p. Thus, the point p is not individuated in the context of the set $\{p, q, r\}$. This notion of individuation seems to be related to the category theoretic notion of a "natural transformation." It is easily shown in symmetric set theory that there is no individuated linear bijection between a point-based vector space and its dual.

The notion of individuation can be further clarified by the following notion of an essential function (the notion of an essential function is somewhat related to the notion of a generic embedding between abstract data types [O'Dunlaing & Yap 1982]).

Definition: An *essential function* is a function f from U to U which commutes with symmetries of the universe $\langle U, \in \rangle$, that is, for any symmetry ρ of the universe and any object x, $f\left(\rho\left(x\right)\right)$ equals $\rho\left(f(x)\right)$.

For any essential function f, if x is isomorphic to y then $f(x)$ must be isomorphic to $f(y)$. In some sense an essential function is one which can be defined *purely* in terms of its arguments, that is, the function itself does not carry information. It is easy to see that an array function A is not essential, $A[i]$ need not be isomorphic to $A[j]$ even when i and j are isomorphic. The following lemma relates essential functions and the notion of individuation.

Essential Property Lemma: An object y is individuated by an object x just in case there exists an *essential* function f such that y equals $f(x)$.

We can now define the notion of an essential property in the obvious way.

Definition: We say that y is an *essential property* of x just in case y is individuated by x, or equivalently, just in case there exists an essential function mapping x to y.

Essential properties can be more deeply understood by relating them to the points which objects are "made of."

Definition: For any non-point object x, we let **points**(x) denote the set of all points which are either elements of x, elements of elements of x, *etc.* For a point p, **points**(p) denotes the singleton set containing p.

Essential Property Point Lemma: If y is an essential property of x then **points**(y) must be a subset of **points**(x).

The above lemma says that an essential function cannot introduce points (an essential function cannot "know" which point it should introduce).

The third universal relation is iso-onticity. Two things are iso-ontic just in case each is definable in terms of the other. For example, an equivalence relation, as a set of pairs, is iso-ontic to a partition into equivalence classes, that is, a set of sets. A Topological space defined as a pair of a set and a set of subsets of that set, is iso-ontic to the same space considered as a simple set of sets.

> *Definition*:   Two objects x and y are iso-ontic just in case each is an essential property of the other.

If x and y are iso-ontic then **points**(x) must equal **points**(y). Furthermore, if x and y are iso-ontic then any essential property of x is also an essential property of y and vice versa (for example, every property of an equivalence relation can be expressed as a property of the induced partition into equivalence classes).

Eliminating Arbitrariness in Set-Theoretic Definitions

When using set-theoretic foundations one usually takes the ordered pair of x and y to be some particular set, such as $\{x, \{x, y\}\}$. However this seems somewhat arbitrary; why not represent the pair $\langle x, y \rangle$ as $\{\{x\}, \{x, y\}\}$ or $\{y, \{y, x\}\}$? (This sort of set-theoretic arbitrariness is discussed at great length in Benacerraf [1965].) However the set-theoretic representation of a pair is not *completely* arbitrary; the pair $\langle x, y \rangle$ could not in general be represented by the simple set $\{x, y\}$. So what is the essence of the pair $\langle x, y \rangle$ such that some set-theoretic representations "work" while others do not?

The universal relations defined in the previous section provide a way of specifying the notion of an ordered pair without making any commitment about particular set-theoretic representations. More specifically we can specify the notion of a pair by assuming the existence of three *essential* functions, **pair**, **first**, and **second** (the notion of an essential function can be easily generalized to n-ary functions). We further require that these *essential* functions satisfy the following equations for all objects x and y.

$$\textbf{first}\,(\textbf{pair}(x, y)) = x$$
$$\textbf{second}\,(\textbf{pair}(x, y)) = y.$$

Given that the functions **pair**, **first**, and **second** are *essential* it is possible to prove that **pair**(x, y) must be *iso-ontic* to $\{x, \{x, y\}\}$. However the set-theoretic nature of the functions need not be specified and thus one is not committed to any particular set theoretic representation for **pair**(x, y).

The essential function **pair** should be contrasted to an array A of two arguments. We have specified that **pair** be an essential function so that

pair(x, y) is an essential property of x and y. However, a two dimensional array function A need not be essential, and in particular $A[i, j]$ can be arbitrary (it need not be an essential property of i and j).

This approach to specifying the notion of a pair is similar to modern techniques for algebraically specifying programs and data structures (for example, Guttag and Horning [1980], and Burstall and Goguen [1977]). The major innovation of the above approach involves the semantics of the equations. Previous approaches have interpreted equational specifications over sorted algebras [Goguen *et al.* 1977]. However, sorted algebras do not provide an adequate theoretical bases for saying that x and y are essential properties of **pair**(x, y), or that **pair**(x, y) is iso-ontic to the set $\{x, \{x, y\}\}$.

Discussion

It seems clear that human mathematicians make use of some universal notion of isomorphism, essential property, and iso-onticity. The purpose of this chapter is to provide a precise mathematical theory of these universal relations, in the expectation that such a theory will be useful in guiding the construction of general purpose inferencing techniques, and shed light on the general nature of inference.

Iso-onticity is perhaps the easiest of the universal relation to justify on pragmatic grounds. Intuitively, it seems that one should be able to contract the space of possible mathematical concepts by collapsing any two iso-ontic concepts into a single concept. By reducing the number of concepts that can be asked about, the collapsing of iso-ontic mathematical concepts reduces the number of distinct statements that can be formulated. A reduction in the number of statements should make theorem-proving search processes more efficient. It seems likely that the concepts of isomorphism and iso-onticity can also be justified in terms of improved efficiency for automated inference.

References

Benacerraf, Paul [1965], "What Numbers Could Not Be," *The Philosophical Review*, vol. LXXIV, no. 1, pp. 47–73.

Burstall, R. M., and J. A. Goguen, "Putting Theories Together to Make Specifications," *IJCAI–77*, pp. 1045–1058.

Goguen, J. A., J. W. Thatcher, E. G. Wagner, and J. B. Wright [1977], "Initial Algebra Semantics," *JACM*, vol. 24, pp. 68–95.

Guttag, J., and J. J. Horning [1980], "Formal Specification as a Design Tool," *Seventh Annual ACM Symposium on Principles of Programming Languages*, Las Vegas, pp. 251–261.

O'Dunlaing, Colm, and Chee K. Yap [1982], "Generic Transformations of Data Structures," 23rd Annual Symposium on the Foundations of Computer Science, pp. 186–195.

Part III

Creating Hardware
and Software Revolutions

Traditionally, AI researchers voraciously consume incredible amounts of
hardware power and eagerly adopt the best in software ideas. Accordingly,
many AI research laboratories have been attractive, inspirational homes
for people who dream about new computing concepts. Today, these people
concentrate on issues raised by parallel computing:

- In the first chapter of Part III, Knight explains a way of executing
  existing programs in parallel, without rewriting them, by using taglike
  bits to detect interprocess interference and by rerunning potentially
  damaged processes.
- Dally shows that the right way to wire together parallel computers
  usually is with low-dimensional networks, like tori, rather than with
  high-dimensional networks, like binary n-cubes, given equal wiring
  density.
- Dally then describes his J-machine, a highly parallel computer design
  in which each processor has hardware to deal with messages efficiently
  and in which the operating system enables tasks to be created, suspended, resumed, and destroyed with only a few instructions rather
  than hundreds or thousands.
- Hewitt and Agha demonstrate that languages based on Hewitt's inherently parallel Actor model have much in common with languages
  championed by researchers in the Japanese Fifth Generation Computer Project.
- Finally, Hewitt explains his view that cooperative procedures provide
  an informative perspective on how human organizations work and
  vice versa, especially when the focus is concurrency, asynchrony, or
  negotiation.

19

Today you can run your favorite programs faster if you rewrite them in a new language for a parallel computer. But can you build a machine that will run your favorite programs ten times faster than a fast workstation without rewriting? Knight believes you can, but only with an armamentarium of ideas that range from language implementation through computer architecture to circuit design.

At the language level, the subject of this chapter, the problem has been side-effect interaction, which occurs whenever one procedure writes into a location that is read by another. Traditionally, the problem is avoided by forbidding side effects, handicapping programmers, or by demanding that programmers know about possible interactions and explicitly control them.

Knight's idea is that most programs are almost functional in that side effects occur only occasionally. This means that programs can be broken up by a compiler into chunks that terminate with a side effect. Each chunk can run in parallel with others as long as no logically earlier chunk writes into its memory. The hardware assigned to each chunk watches for such external writes and reruns the chunk whenever such an external write occurs.

In contrast to other approaches, this one does not require the programmer to make explicit decomposition annotations; it does not even require the programmer to understand how his program will be decomposed; and it certainly introduces no risk of incorrect operation. But if a programmer does want to work hard to condition a program for parallelism, he sees monotonic improvement as he reduces the number of side effects.

An Architecture for Mostly Functional Languages

Tom Knight

This chapter describes a new computer architecture, characterized by its ability to execute several portions of a program in parallel, while giving the appearance to the programmer that the program is being executed sequentially. This automatic extraction of parallelism makes the architecture attractive because we can exploit the existing programming tools, languages, and algorithms which have been developed over the past several decades of computer science research, while we gradually endeavor to improve them for the parallel environment. Not all of the benefits of parallel execution will be attained with this architecture, but the ability to extract even modest amounts of parallel execution from existing programs may be worth the effort. We will also discuss how the architecture can be extended, as algorithms are improved, to provide some explicit and modular programmer control over the parallelism.

Functional Languages

Many parallel architecture papers start by defining the programming model they support as strictly functional. Computer architects find that the strictly functional approach makes their task easier, because the order in which computation is performed, once the basic dependencies are satisfied, is irrelevant. Building highly parallel machines which execute strictly functional languages then becomes quite straightforward. Strictly functional languages certainly have advantages [Backus 1978], including the relative ease of proving their correctness and the ease of thinking and reasoning about certain simple kinds of programs.

Functional languages have problems

Unfortunately, there is a class of algorithms for which the strictly functional programming style appears to be inadequate. The problems are rooted in the difficulty in interfacing a strictly functional program to a non-functional outside environment. It is impossible to program a task such as an operating system, for instance, in the unmodified strictly functional style. Clever modifications of the strict functional style have been proposed which cure this defect. For example, McCarthy's AMB operator, which returns whichever of two inputs are ready first, appears to be adequate to solve this and similar problems. Several equivalent operators have been proposed [Henderson 1980].

However, the introduction of such non-functional operators into the programming language destroys many of its advantages. Architects can no longer ignore the order of execution of functions. Proving program correctness again becomes a very much more difficult task. Users also find that programming with such operators is tedious and error prone. In particular, as shown by Agha [1985], the presence of such an operator allows the definition of a new data type, the cell, which can be side effected just as normal memory locations in non-functional languages. Thus, the introduction of the the AMB operator, while adequate to solve the lack of side effect problem, re-introduces many of the problems which the functional language advocates are attempting to avoid.

As Minsky says, "It appears we have a choice: we can either define weak systems, such as purely functional languages, about which we can prove theorems, or we can define strong systems which we can prove little about."

Functional languages can be hard to program

Much more serious, in my mind, than any of the theoretical difficulties of strictly functional languages, is the difficulty programmers face in implementing certain types of programs. It is often more natural to think about an algorithm in terms of the internal state of a set of objects (see, for example, chapter 3 of Abelson and Sussman [1985]). This object oriented viewpoint in programming language design is incompatible with the strictly functional approach to computation. The same algorithms can be implemented in either style, and both systems are surely universal—but the fact that programmers find one representation for programs easier to think about, easier to design, and easier to debug is, in itself, a powerful motivation for a programming language to provide that representation.

If this were merely a representation issue, there would be hope that suitable compiler technology could eventually lead to a programming language which provides support for side effects, but which compiles into purely functional operations. As we saw above, however, in the general case this is not possible.

An Alternative—Mostly Functional Languages

Side effects cause problems. Architects find it difficult to build parallel architectures for supporting them. Verification software finds such programs difficult to reason about; and programming styles, with an abundance of side effects, are difficult to understand, modify, and maintain.

Instead of completely eliminating side effects, we propose that their use be severely curtailed. Most side effects in conventional programming languages like Fortran are gratuitous. They are not solving difficult multitasking communications problems; nor are they improving the large scale modularity or clarity of the program. Instead, they are used for trivial purposes such as updating a loop index variable.

Elimination of these unnecessary side effects can make code more readable, more maintainable, and, as we will argue later in this chapter, faster to execute.

The Multi-Lisp Approach

These issues motivate Halstead's Multi-Lisp [1985], a parallel variant of Scheme. Multi-Lisp has three basic primitives which distinguish it from conventional Lisp:

- The *future* primitive allows an encapsulated value to be evaluated, while simultaneously returning to its caller a promise for that value. The caller can continue to compute with this returned object, incorporating it into data structures, and passing it to other functions. Only when the value is examined is it necessary for the parallel computation of its value to complete.

- The *pcall* primitive allows the parallel evaluation of arguments to a function. Halstead shows in his paper that pcall can be implemented as a simple macro which expands into a sequence of futures. It can be thought of as syntactic sugar for a stylized use of futures.

- The *delay* primitive allows a programmer to specify that a particular computation be delayed until the result is needed. Similar in some respects to a future, delay returns a promise to compute the value, but does not begin computation of a value until the result is needed. Thus the delay primitive is not a source of parallelism in the language. It is a way of providing lazy evaluation semantics to the programmer.

Both *delay* and *future* result in an order of execution different from applicative order computation. In the absence of side effects, both will result in the same value as the equivalent program without the primitives, because they affect only the order in which the computation is performed. (This is not strictly true for *delay* because its careful use can allow otherwise non-terminating programs to return a value.)

In the presence of side effects, it is difficult to predict the behavior of a future, because its value may be computed in parallel with other computations.

While the value of a delay is deterministic, because it does not introduce additional parallelism, its time of computation is dependent on when its value is first examined. This can be very non-intuitive and difficult to think about while writing programs.

Halstead implements the future and delay primitives by returning to the caller an object of data-type *future*. This object contains a pointer to a slot, which will eventually contain the value returned by the promised computation. The future may be stored in data structures and passed as a value. Computations which attempt to reference the value of the future prior to its computation are suspended. When the promised computation completes, the returned value is stored in the specified slot, and the future becomes determined. This allows any pending suspended procedures waiting for this value to run, and any further references to the future will simply return the now computed value.

Future as a Declaration

The use of future or delay can be thought of as a declaration. They declare that either the computation done within the scope of the delay or future has no side effects, or that, if it does, the order in which those side effects are done, relative to other computations, is irrelevant. We also guarantee with such a declaration that no free or shared variable referenced by the computation is side effected by some *other* parallel-executing portion of the program.

Like all declarations, the use of future or delay is a very strong assertion. In a way similar to type declarations, their use is difficult to check automatically, is error prone, has a significant performance impact if omitted, and may function correctly for many test cases, but fail unexpectedly on others.

Advocates of strong type checking in compiled languages have attempted for years to build compilers capable of proving the type correctness of programs. We believe that they have failed. All languages sophisticated enough for serious programming require at least some dynamic checks for type safety at execution time. These checks are implemented as additional instructions on conventional architectures, or as part of the normal instruction execution sequence on more recent architectures [Moon 1985]. One alternative, declaring the types and relying on the word of the programmer, while leading to good performance on conventional architectures, is dangerous, error-prone, and inappropriate for sophisticated modern programming environments.

Just as hardware has provided important runtime support for type checking, we propose the use of hardware in the runtime checking of future declarations.

Dynamic Side Effect Checks

In our implementation of Lisp, we do not use explicit language extensions such as future and pcall. Instead, we will assume that each evaluation is encapsulated in a future and that each call can freely evaluate its arguments in parallel. Our approach is to detect and correct those cases in which this assumption is unjustified.

Our compiler transforms the program into sequences of compiled primitive instructions, called *transaction blocks*. Each transaction block has the following characteristics:

- Each block is independent of previous execution, except for the contents of main memory. In particular, no registers or other internal bits in the processor are shared across blocks.
- Each block contains exactly one side-effecting store into main memory, occurring at the end of the block.

Each transaction block is, from the standpoint of the memory system, a strictly functional program, consisting of register loads and register-to-register instructions, followed by a single side effecting store into main memory.

Each of these blocks can be executed independently, potentially on several different processors. Except for the relative timing of the single side-effect at the end of each block, there is no interaction between blocks. However, the order in which we execute the single side effect per block is critical. These side effects must be executed in a well defined order: the order specified in the program. Further, the execution of a side effect can potentially modify a location which some other block has already read.

These two tasks—execution of the side effects in order, and enforcing the dependencies of later blocks on earlier side effects—require special hardware.

Each processor is free to execute its block at will, up until the final side effect. Upon reaching the side effect, execution halts. Because this program is functional, this partial execution cannot affect other processors. A *block counter* is maintained, similar in purpose to a normal program counter. The block counter's job is to keep track of which block is next allowed to perform its side effect. As the block counter reaches each block in turn,

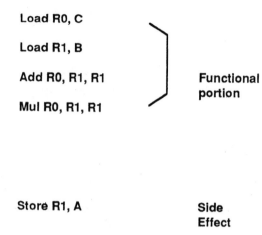

Figure 1. A transaction block.

the block is allowed to actually perform the side effect specified by its final instruction. This process is called *confirming* the block. Confirming a block modifies the contents of main memory. Other blocks, not yet confirmed, may already have referenced the location which has just been modified. If they have, then the data upon which they are computing is now invalid.

But the program which they are executing is functional—it has not modified main memory. We are free to abandon the partially executed block, and to attempt re-executing it a second time. This process of abandoning a partially executed block is called *aborting* the block (see figure 2).

In order to detect when a block needs to be aborted, we need to keep track of which memory locations it has referenced. A *dependency list*, is maintained, containing the addresses of all locations in main memory which have been referenced during execution of a block. When a processor executes a load instruction, it adds the address being loaded to the executing block's dependency list.

When a block is confirmed, the address it is side effecting is broadcast to all other executing processors. Each processor checks its dependency list to determine if the block it is executing has referenced the modified location. If it has, the block is aborted and re-executed.

Eventually, a given block will be reached by the block counter, and it will be allowed to complete and perform its side-effect. The block counter advances to the next block, and if the block is ready, we confirm that block in the following cycle. Ideally, we will confirm a block per clock cycle. If the confirmation of one block aborts the execution of successor blocks, however, the performance will be limited by the time it takes the aborted block to re-execute its program.

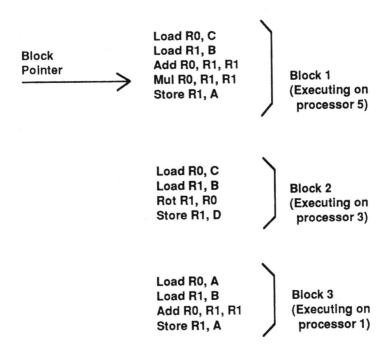

Figure 2. Several Transaction Blocks executing in parallel. the third block will abort when the first commits, because it has referenced the variable A, which has been side effected.

The performance improvement resulting from this technique depends on two factors: the average block length, and the frequency of aborts. The longer the block, the fewer confirms are necessary to execute a given program. The more frequent the aborts, the more the block counter must await a sequential computation before confirming the next block.

We can see now the influence of reducing the number of side effects in the source program: as the number of side effects is reduced, the length of the blocks increases. Because the blocks are longer, fewer blocks need be executed to perform a computation. Because the block execution is sequential, at a rate limited to a maximum of one per clock cycle, this limits the performance of the architecture. There is probably a maximum desirable block length, because as the block size increases, the length of the dependency list, and thus the likelihood of a side effect from another block influencing the computation goes up. We are currently studying these issues in simulation, but have no results as yet.

The Order of Block Execution

Because we are simulating the behavior of a uniprocessor by using parallel hardware, there is a defined order in which the blocks must be confirmed. We want to start execution of a given block early enough so that its results are ready by the time that block is reached by the block counter. But starting execution of a block earlier is potentially bad, because it will reference data which is older than necessary, and because the processor being used to execute it may be needed to execute a block which must be confirmed sooner.

These observations lead to the following block execution strategy:

1   Start executing blocks downward and to the left in the call tree.
2   Start executing blocks which branch downward and to the right from a node in the call tree.
3   If additional processors are required for (1) or (2), abort execution of the farthest right branches of the call tree, and reclaim their processors.

Heuristic (1) is very similar to instruction pre-fetching on conventional pipelined architectures. Because we are executing this block, we will next need to execute its successor.

Heuristic (2) depends on the fact that parallel execution of evaluations from the same level of the call tree are often independent, and can often be executed without conflicting side effects.

Heuristic (3) is a simple consequence of the fact that we must finish execution of the bottom left portion of the call tree prior to executing the right portion of the call tree. Thus, it is better to use the processors executing blocks to the right for more immediate needs.

These heuristics give us a very good handle on the difficult problem of resource allocation in the multiprocessor environment.

Treatment of Conditionals

The presence of conditionals in the language, however, makes the tidy resource allocation scheme described above much more difficult. Because we do not know which of the two paths a conditional will follow until the data computation is confirmed, we must start blocks executing down both branches, or risk delaying execution waiting for a block on the path not followed. Fortunately, we are free to start executing down both paths, because until we confirm a block, it performs no side effects. The blocks started along the unfollowed branch of a conditional are simply abandoned without confirming their side effects.

Allocation of processor resources in the presence of conditionals is substantially more difficult, because we cannot, except heuristically, predict which of two paths is more worthwhile for expending processor resources.

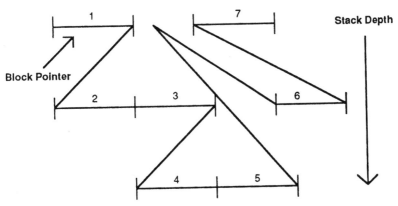

Figure 3. The call tree of a process provides heuristic data to guide the block starting process. Here, we want to start execution of blocks 2 and 3, while the clock counter is at block 1, because these are the next sequential blocks. We also want to start execution of block 6, because it is unlikely that confirming blocks 1-5 will side effect data which block 6 depends on.

Loop Compilation

Loops are a special case of conditional execution. As with most parallel processors, there is an advantage in knowing the high level semantics of a loop construct. Rather than attempting to execute repetitive copies of the same block, incrementing the loop index as a setup for the next pass, it is far preferable to know that a loop is required, and that the loop is, for example, indexing over a set of array values from 0 to 100. We can then execute 101 copies of the loop block, each with a unique value of the loop index. The unpalatable alternative is to rely on the side effect detection hardware to notice that the loop index is changed in each block iteration, resulting in an abort of the next block on every loop iteration.

Unlike most of the parallel proposals for executing loops, however, the architecture we propose can also handle the hard case where the execution of the loop body modifies the loop control parameters, perhaps in a very indirect or conditional way.

Predicted Values

The way we deal with both conditional execution and with loop iteration involves *prediction* of the future value of a variable. In a sense, the dependency list maintenance already described is a form of value prediction: we predict that the value we are depending upon will not change by the time the executing block commits.

We can extend this idea to predicting the future value of variables which we know are likely to be modified from their current value prior to executing the block. One application of this technique is to the problem of loop iterations. Instead of relying on the current value of the loop index as the predicted value for the next iteration, we really want to predict the future value—predicting a different future value for each parallel body block we start.

Similarly, we can implement conditionals by predicting the value of the predicated result slot—predicting that it is true in one arm of the conditional, and that it is false in the other. The predicate is then evaluated, and when it confirms, it side effects the predicate result slot, aborting one of the two branches. When aborting the execution of conditional blocks, we must abandon execution of the block rather than update the variable and retry, as we would in normal block execution.

The Proposed Hardware

The hardware proposed for implementing this scheme is a shared memory multiprocessor, with each processor containing two fully associative caches (see figure 4). The first of these caches, the *dependency cache*, usually holds read data, copied from main memory. This cache also watches bus transactions in a way similar to the snoopy cache coherency protocol [Goodman 1983]. A second cache, the *confirm cache*, holds only data written by this processor, but not yet confirmed.

Each main memory location, therefore, can have two entries in a processor's caches, one in the dependency cache, and one in the confirm cache. This is because we must maintain a knowledge of what data the processor's current computation has depended upon, in the dependency cache, while also allowing the processor to tentatively update its version of memory, in the confirm cache. For processor reads, priority is always given to the contents of the confirm cache if there is an entry in both caches, because we want the processor to see its own modifications to memory, prior to them being confirmed.

The Dependency Cache

The dependency cache performs three functions:

1   It acts as a normal read data cache for main memory data.
2   It stores block dependency information.
3   It holds predicted values of variables associated with this block.

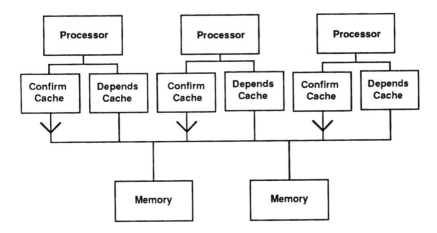

Figure 4. The processors share a common memory bus, and thus each cache writes to main memory. The *depends cache* acts as a normal data read cache, but also implements the dependency list and predicted value features. The *confirm cache* is used to allow processors to locally side effect their version of main memory, without those changes being visible to other processors prior to their block confirmation.

Figure 5 shows a state transition diagram for the dependency cache. There are six states shown in the cache state diagram: Invalid, Valid, Depends, Predicted/Valid, Predicted/Invalid and Predicted/Abandon.

- Invalid is the state associated with an empty cache line.
- Valid is the state representing that the cache holds a correct copy of main memory data
- Depends indicates that the cache holds correct data, and that the ongoing block computation is depending on the continued correctness of this assumption.
- Predicted/Valid indicates that the block is predicting that, when it is ready to confirm, the value held in this cache location will continue to be equal to the value in main memory. This state indicates that the held value is now equal to main memory. This state differs from Depends only in the action taken when a bus cycle modifies this memory location.
- Predicted/Invalid indicates that the block is predicting that, when it is ready to confirm, the value held in this cache location will be equal to the value in main memory. The contents of main memory currently differ from the value held in the cache.
- Predicted/Abandon indicates that the block execution is conditional on the eventual contents of memory being side effected to be equal to

that held in the cache. If it is side effected to some other value, the block will be aborted and not restarted (abandoned).

At the start of each block execution, the dependency cache is initialized (see figure 5). This results in setting all locations to either the `invalid` or `valid` states. Cache entries which are currently `Valid`, `Depends`, or `Predicted/Valid` are forced to the `Valid` state. All others are forced to the `Invalid` state.

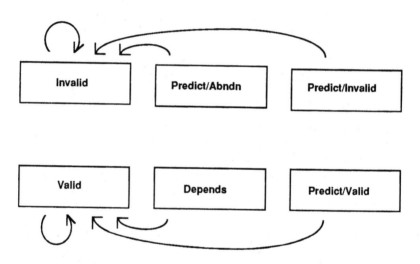

Figure 5. Response to initializing the cache when starting a new block.

Each time the processor loads a data item into a register from the depends cache, the state of the cache line is potentially modified (see figure 6). If the cache entry for the location is the `Invalid` state, a memory bus read request is performed, a new cache line allocated, the data stored in the depends cache, and the line state is set to `Depends`. If the cache line is already `Valid`, then the state is simply set to `Depends`. In all other states, the data is provided from the cache, and the state of the entry is unmodified.

A cache miss is allowed to replace any entry in the cache which is in the `Invalid` or `Valid` states, but must not modify other entries. We require this because the dependencies are being maintained by these states. This implies that the cache must be fully associative, otherwise a conflict over the limited number of sets available for a given location would make it impossible to store the dependency information.

A Predict-Value request from the processor stores a predicted future value for a memory location into the depends cache (see figure 7). The cache initiates a main memory read cycle for the same location. If the location

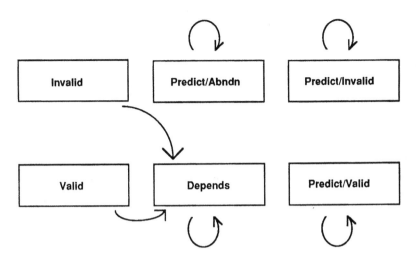

Figure 6. Response to processor load request.

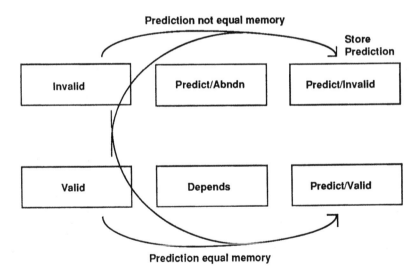

Figure 7. Response to processor predict operation.

contains the predicted value, the cache state is set to `Predicted/Valid`. If the values disagree, the cache state is set to `Predicted/Invalid`.

A Predict-Abandon request from the processor stores a predicted future value of a predicate into the depends cache, and forces the cache line to the `Predict/Abandon` state (see figure 8).

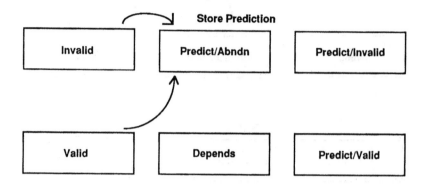

Figure 8. Response to processor predict/abandon request.

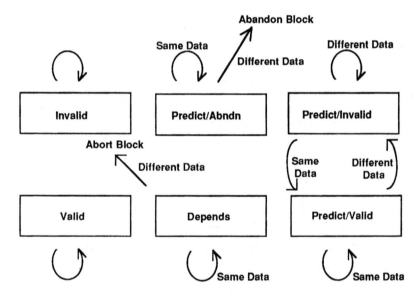

Figure 9. Response to a bus write.

A bus write cycle, taken by some other processor, can potentially modify a location in main memory which is held in the depends cache (see figure 9). Because there is a shared memory bus connecting all of the caches, each cache can monitor all of these writes. For Invalid cache entries, nothing is done. For Valid entries, the newly written data is copied into the cache, and the cache maintains validity.

For Depended entries, the cache is updated, and if the new contents differs from the old contents, the running block on the cache's associated processor is aborted and then restarted. This is the key mechanism for enforcing inter-block sequential consistency.

Bus writes to locations which are `Predict/Valid` or `Predict/Invalid` are compared with the contents of the depends cache. If the values agree, the cache state is set to `Predict/Valid`. If they disagree, the state is set to `Predict/Invalid`.

Bus writes to locations which are `Predict/Abandon` are compared with the contents of the depends cache. If they agree, no change occurs. If they disagree, the associated processor is aborted, and the block currently executing is permanently abandoned.

The Confirm Cache

The confirm cache consists of a fully associative cache which holds only side-effected data. When the block is initialized, the confirm cache is emptied by invalidating all its entries. When the processor performs a side-effecting write, the write data is held in the confirm cache, but not written immediately into main memory. There, it is visible to the processor which performed the side-effect, but to no other processors. The confirm cache has priority over the depends cache in providing read data to the processor. If both hold the contents of a location, the data is provided by the confirm cache. This allows a processor to modify a location, and to have those modifications visible during further computation within the block.

Confirming

When the block counter reaches a block associated with a particular processor, and the block has completed execution, it is time to confirm that block. One final memory consistency check is performed. The load dependencies are necessarily satisfied, because if they were not, then the block would have been aborted. But the predicted-value dependencies may not be satisfied. We check these dependencies by testing if there are any entries in the depends cache which are in the `Predicted/Invalid` state. Any entry in that state indicates a memory location whose value was predicted to be one thing, and whose actual memory contents are another. We must re-execute this block with the now-current value.

After performing this final consistency check, the side effects associated with this block may be performed. This operation consists of sweeping the confirm cache, and writing back to memory any modified entries. The write-back of these entries may, of course, force other processors to abort partially or completely executed blocks, if they have depended on the old values of these locations.

One consequence of using this cache strategy for implementing the dependency checking is that each block can perform multiple side-effects, and those side-effects will be visible only to the executing block until the block is confirmed. This relaxes the old requirements of exactly one terminal side-effect per transaction block, and allows the compiler flexibility in choosing the optimal block size independent of how many side-effects are present within the block.

Another important feature of using the cache as a dependency tracking mechanism is that when a transaction aborts, the valid entries in the cache remain, so that the re-execution of the block will usually achieve an almost 100% cache hit rate, reducing memory bus traffic and improving processor speed.

Consing Is Not a Side Effect

The Lisp operation *cons*, although it performs a write into main memory, is not a side-effect. We are guaranteed that no one else has a pointer to the location being written, and thus no one can be affected by its change. In the block execution architecture, this can be implemented by providing each processor with an independent free pointer. Consing and other local memory allocating writes done within a block are performed using the free pointer. The value of the pointer is saved when the block is entered, and abort resets the pointer to its entry value, automatically reclaiming the allocated storage. During a confirm, the free pointer's value is updated. All of these free pointer manipulations happen automatically if it is treated simply as another variable whose value can be loaded and side-effected. Writes of data into newly consed locations need not be confirmed. They can be best handled with a write-through technique in the depends cache. It is important that the depends cache not contain stale copies of data which has been written with a cons write operation.

Introduction of Explicit Parallelism

The addition of one primitive to the processor instruction set allows the re-introduction of explicit, programmer visible parallelism into the language supported by this architecture. The primitive performs a load operation without adding the location being loaded to the dependency list. In the depends cache, it returns valid data if present, and reads memory if necessary to produce valid data. It never changes the state of the cache to Depends.

With this primitive, it is possible to express algorithms which compute results based on potentially stale data. In those cases where this is acceptable from an algorithmic point of view, then parallel execution with no inter-block dependencies can be supported. One example is the Gauss-Jacobi parallel iterative matrix solution technique, as contrasted with the sequential Gauss-Seidel technique.

Future Work

The independence of blocks is a strong assumption. Many situations arise, particularly in the area of argument passing and value returning, where it is awkward to require values to be passed in memory. There seems to be a requirement for a way to chain blocks together in a such a way that the aborting of one block forces the aborting of a selection of dependent blocks. Some complex issues also surround the correct execution of conditionals.

There are dozens of parameters, such as the desirable block size, and the number of side effects per block, whose range of appropriate values must be established. There are alternative hardware implementations, involving, for example, dependency hash tables rather than fully associative caches, whose effectiveness must be studied. The strategies for allocating processor resources appear to be quite complex, when, for example, it is allowable to abandon a partially executed block to work on one closer to being confirmed.

While we currently believe that this work will lead to an architecture which can achieve factors of 10 to 100 times the performance of uniprocessors on unmodified Lisp programs, we have no proof, even in simulation. With modified programming techniques, eliminating gratuitous side effects, we may be able to achieve even higher speedups.

Relationship to Other Work

The intentionally evocative terminology of transactions, confirms, and aborts in this chapter was chosen to reflect the close analogy of this technique to work in the database field. In particular, the work by Kung and Robinson [1981] on optimistic concurrency is very similar, except for the inter-block ordering constraint. Taking the analogy of main memory as a database seriously, may lead to other interesting ideas involving, for example, nested transactions. Similarly, the idea of supporting database transactions with dependency caches also looks like an attractive direction for further research.

The idea of splitting programs up into functional blocks terminating in side effects also occurs in the program proof literature, as in Crocker's [1977] work.

If one views the blocks of this scheme as very complex instructions, then this architecture devolves to a pipelined architecture for executing those instruction, and the interlocks to prevent inter-instruction dependency violations.

Morris Katz [1986] has independently arrived at a similar programming methodology, but has concentrated on software implementations of the dependency tracking mechanisms.

Summary

This chapter presents some provocative ideas on how one might use a small amount of hardware in the memory subsystem of a shared memory multiprocessor to enforce correctness of execution of parallel blocks of side effecting code. While the programs are being executed in a multi-processor environment, the programmer need not be aware of this fact. The architecture is capable of executing unmodified lisp code at a speedup dependent on the frequency of side effects. As the frequency of side effects is reduced, the effective execution rate will increase. Many issues remain in the design of an architecture for these mostly functional languages.

References

Backus, J. [1978], "Can Programming be Liberated from the von Neumann Style? A Functional Style and its Algebra of Programs," *Communications of the ACM*, vol. 21, no. 8, pp. 613-641.

Henderson, Peter [1980], "Is it Reasonable to Implement a Complete Programming System in a Purely Functional Style?" Technical memo PMM/94, The University of Newcastle upon Tyne, Computing Laboratory.

Agha, Gul A. [1985], "Actors: A Model of Concurrent Computation in Distributed Systems," Report AIM–844, Artificial Intelligence Laboratory, Massachusetts Institute of Technology, Cambridge, MA.

Abelson, Harold, and Gerald Jay Sussman [1985], *Structure and Interpretation of Computer Programs*, MIT Press, Cambridge, MA.

Halstead, Bert [1985], "Multilisp: A Language for Concurrent Symbolic Computation," *ACM Transactions on Programming Languages and Systems*.

Moon, David A. [1985], "The Architecture of the Symbolics 3600," *The 12th Annual International Symposium on Computer Architecture*, pp. 76-83.

These ideas are a direct result of discussion with many students and faculty at the Massachusetts Institute of Technology and with many employees of Symbolics. Todd Matson, Ramin Zabih, David Chapman, Bruce Edwards, Alan Bawden, David Moon, Scott Wills, Daniel Weinreb, and David Gifford have been especially helpful. Thanks also to Jeanne Speckman for drawing the figures.

Goodman, James R. [1983], "Using Cache Memory to reduce Processor Memory Traffic," *The 10th Annual International Symposium on Computer Architecture*, pp. 123-131.

Kung, H. T., and J. T. Robinson [1981], "On optimistic Methods of Concurrency Control," *ACM Transactions on Database Systems*, vol. 6, no. 2.

Crocker, Steven [1977], "State Deltas: Formalism for Representing Segments of Computation," USC-ISI Technical Report ISI RR-77-61.

Katz, Morris J. [1986], "Paratran, A Transparent, Transaction Based Runtime Mechanism for Parallel Execution of Scheme," M.S. Thesis, Department of Electrical Engineering and Computer Science Department, Massachusetts Institute of Technology.

20

Historically, many world-class computer architects have been
inspired by the challenges AI research creates. Conversely,
many world-class AI researchers have been attracted to the
places where unique hardware offers unique research opportunities. This produces a short feedback loop between inventors and consumers, often with dramatic results. At MIT
this short feedback loop led to such innovations as the Lisp
Machine in the 1970s and the massively parallel Connection
Machine in the 1980s.

Today, the AI-encouraged reach for more and better
computing continues with special emphasis on the issue of
interprocessor communication networks. Progress in VLSI
fabrication technology enables us to build computers with
hundreds of thousands of processors, but to keep those processors busy, in all but a few special cases, they have to
be able to communicate with each other over low-latency,
high-throughput networks. Thus high-performance communication networks are the key to building machines that will
eventually make today's supercomputers look as quaint as
the PDP-10s of early AI look to us today.

In this chapter, Dally explains his views on how to
design such high-performance communication networks. In
particular, he shows, with an analysis confirmed by experiment, that low-dimensional networks (for example, tori)
have lower latency and higher hot-spot throughput than
high-dimensional networks (for example, binary n-cubes),
given equal wiring density.

Performance Analysis of k-ary n-cube Interconnection Networks

William J. Dally

The critical component of a concurrent computer is its communication network. Many algorithms are communication rather than processing limited. Fine-grain concurrent programs execute as few as ten instructions in response to a message [Dally 1987a]. To efficiently execute such programs the communication network must have a latency no greater than about 10 instruction times, and a throughput sufficient to permit a large fraction of the nodes to transmit simultaneously. Low-latency communication is also critical to support code sharing and garbage collection across nodes.

As the grain size of concurrent computers continues to decrease, communication latency becomes a more important factor. The diameter of the machine grows, messages are sent more frequently, and fewer instructions are executed in response to each message. Low latency is more difficult to achieve in a fine-grain machine because the available wiring space grows more slowly than the expected traffic. Because the machine must be constructed in three dimensions, the bisection area grows only as $N^{\frac{2}{3}}$ while traffic grows at least as fast as N, the number of nodes.

VLSI systems are wire limited. The cost of these systems is predominantly that of connecting devices, and the performance is limited by the delay of these interconnections. Thus, to achieve the required performance, the network must make efficient use of the available wire. The topology of the network must map into the three physical dimensions so that messages are not required to *double back* on themselves, and in a way that allows messages to use all of the available bandwidth along their path.

This chapter considers the problem of constructing *wire-efficient* communication networks, networks that give the optimum performance for a given wire density. We compare networks holding wire bisection, the number of wires crossing a cut that evenly divides the machine, constant. Thus we compare low dimensional networks with wide communication channels against high dimensional networks with narrow channels. We investigate the class of k-ary n-cube interconnection networks and show that low-dimensional networks out perform high-dimensional networks with the same bisection width.

The remainder of this chapter describes the design of wire-efficient communication networks. The next section describes the assumptions on which this chapter is based: The family of k-ary n-cube networks; we restrict our attention to k-ary n-cubes because it is the dimension of the network that is important, not the details of its topology; *wormhole routing* [Seitz et al. 1985], is introduced, a low-latency routing technique; network cost is determined primarily by wire density which we will measure in terms of bisection width. The idea of *bisection width* is introduced, and along with a discussion of delay models for network channels. A performance model of these networks is derived in the Performance Analysis section. Expressions are given for network latency as a function of traffic that agree closely with experimental results. Under the assumption of constant wire density, it is shown that low-dimensional networks achieve lower latency and better hot-spot throughput than do high-dimensional networks.

Preliminaries

k-ary n-cubes

Many different network topologies have been proposed for use in concurrent computers: trees [Browning 1985; Leiserson 1985; Sequin 1979], Benes networks [1965], Batcher sorting networks [1968], shuffle exchange networks [Stone 1971], *Omega* networks [Lawrie 1975], *indirect* binary n-cube or *flip* networks [Batcher 1976; Siegel 1979], and direct binary n-cubes [Seitz 1984; Pease 1977; Sullivan & Bashkow 1977]. The binary n-cube is a special case of the family of k-ary n-cubes, cubes with n dimensions and k nodes in each dimension.

Most concurrent computers have been built using networks that are either k-ary n-cubes or are isomorphic to k-ary n-cubes: rings, meshes, tori, direct and indirect binary n-cubes, and Omega networks. Thus, in this chapter we restrict our attention to k-ary n-cube networks. We refer to n as the *dimension* of the cube and k as the *radix*. Dimension, radix, and number of nodes are related by the equation

$$N = k^n, \quad \left(k = \sqrt[n]{N}, \quad n = \log_k N \right). \tag{1}$$

Again, it is the dimension of the network that is important, not the details of its topology.

A node in a k-ary n-cube can be identified by an n-digit radix k address, $a_0, \ldots, a_{n-1}$. The ith digit of the address, a_i, represents the nodes position in the ith dimension. Each node can forward messages to its upper neighbor in each dimension, i, with address, $a_0, \ldots, a_i + 1 (\text{mod} k), \ldots, a_{n-1}$.

In this chapter we assume that our k-ary n-cube are unidirectional for simplicity. We will see that our results do not change appreciably for bidirectional networks. For an actual machine, however, there are many compelling reasons to make our networks bidirectional. Most importantly, bidirectional networks allow us to exploit locality of communication. If an object, A, sends a message to an object, B, there is a high probability of B sending a message back to A. In a bidirectional network, a round trip from A to B can be made short by placing A and B close together. In a unidirectional network, a round trip will always involve completely circling the machine in at least one dimension.

Figures 1–3 show three k-ary n-cube networks in order of decreasing dimension. Figure 1 shows a binary 6-cube (64 nodes). A 3-ary 4-cube (81 nodes) is shown in figure 2. An 8-ary 2-cube (64 nodes), or torus, is shown in figure 3. Each line in figure 1 represents two communication channels, one in each direction, while each line in figures 2 and 3 represents a single communication channel.

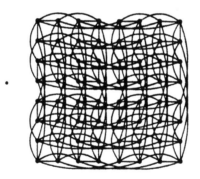

Figure 1. A binary 6-cube embedded in the plane.

Wormhole routing

In this chapter we consider networks that use *wormhole* [Seitz *et al.* 1985] rather than *store-and-forward* [Tanenbaum 1981] routing. Instead of storing a packet completely in a node and then transmitting it to the next node, wormhole routing operates by advancing the head of a packet directly from incoming to outgoing channels. Only a few flow control digits (flits) are buffered at each node. A *flit* is the smallest unit of information that a queue or channel can accept or refuse.

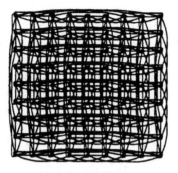

Figure 2. A ternary 4-cube embedded in the plane.

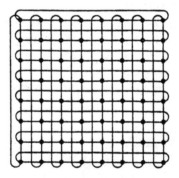

Figure 3. An 8-ary 2-cube (torus).

As soon as a node examines the header flit(s) of a message, it selects the next channel on the route and begins forwarding flits down that channel. As flits are forwarded, the message becomes spread out across the channels between the source and destination. It is possible for the first flit of a message to arrive at the destination node before the last flit of the message has left the source. Because most flits contain no routing information, the flits in a message must remain in contiguous channels of the network and cannot be interleaved with the flits of other messages. When the header flit of a message is blocked, all of the flits of a message stop advancing and block the progress of any other message requiring the channels they occupy.

A method similar to wormhole routing, called *virtual cut-through*, is described in [Kermani & Kleinrock 1979]. Virtual cut-through differs from wormhole routing in that it buffers messages when they block, removing them from the network. With wormhole routing, blocked messages remain in the network. Figure 4 illustrates the advantage of wormhole routing. There are two components of latency, distance and message aspect ratio. The distance, D, is the number of *hops* required to get from the source

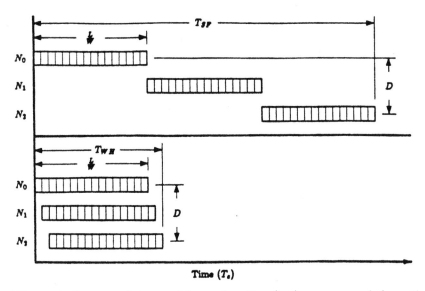

Figure 4. Latency of store-and-forward routing (top) versus wormhole routing (bottom).

to the destination. The message aspect ratio (message length, L, normalized to the channel width, W) is the number of channel cycles required to transmit the message across one channel. The top half of the figure shows store-and-forward routing. The message is is entirely transmitted from node N_0 to node N_1, then from N_1 to N_2 and so on. With store-and-forward routing, latency is the product of D, and $\frac{L}{W}$.

$$T_{SF} = T_c \left(D \times \frac{L}{W} \right). \tag{2}$$

The bottom half of figure 4 shows wormhole routing. As soon as a flit arrives at a node, it is forwarded to the next node. With wormhole routing latency is reduced to the sum of D and $\frac{L}{W}$.

$$T_{WH} = T_c \left(D + \frac{L}{W} \right). \tag{3}$$

In both of these equations, T_c is the channel cycle time, the amount of time required to perform a transaction on a channel.

VLSI complexity

VLSI computing systems [Mead & Conway 1980] are wire-limited; the complexity of what can be constructed is limited by wire density, the speed at which a machine can run is limited by wire delay, and the majority of power consumed by a machine is used to drive wires. Thus, machines must be organized both logically and physically to keep wires short by exploiting locality wherever possible. The VLSI architect must organize a computing system so that its form (physical organization) fits its function (logical organization).

Networks have traditionally been analyzed under the assumption of constant channel bandwidth. Under this assumption each channel is one bit wide ($W = 1$) and has unit delay ($T_c = 1$). The constant bandwidth assumption favors networks with high dimensionality (for example, binary n-cubes) over low-dimensional networks (for example, tori). This assumption, however, is not consistent with the properties of VLSI technology. Networks with many dimensions require more and longer wires than do low-dimensional networks. Thus, high-dimensional networks cost more and run more slowly than low-dimensional networks. A realistic comparison of network topology must take both wire density and wire length into account.

To account for wire density, we will use bisection width [Thompson 1980] as a measure of network cost. The bisection width of a network is the minimum number of wires cut when the network is divided into two equal halves. Rather than comparing networks with constant channel width, W, we will compare networks with constant bisection width. Thus, we will compare low-dimensional networks with large W with high-dimensional networks with small W.

The delay of a wire depends on its length, l. For short wires, the delay, t_s, is limited by charging the capacitance of the wire and varies logarithmically with wire length.

$$t_s = \tau_{\text{inv}} e \log_e Kl, \tag{4}$$

where τ_{inv} is the inverter delay, and K is a constant depending on capacitance ratios. For long wires, delay, t_l, is limited by the speed of light.

$$t_l = \frac{l\sqrt{\epsilon_r}}{c} \tag{5}$$

In this chapter we will consider three delay models: constant delay, T_c independent of length, logarithmic delay, $T_c \propto \log l$, and linear delay, $T_c \propto l$. Our main result, that latency is minimized by low-dimensional networks, is supported by all three models.

Performance Analysis

In this section we compare the performance of unidirectional k-ary n-cube interconnection networks using the following assumptions:

- Networks must be embedded into the plane. If a three-dimensional packaging technology becomes available, the comparison changes only slightly.

- Nodes are placed systematically by embedding $\frac{n}{2}$ logical dimensions in each of the two physical dimensions. We assume that both n and k are even integers. The long end-around connections shown in figure 3 can be avoided by folding the network as shown in figure 5.

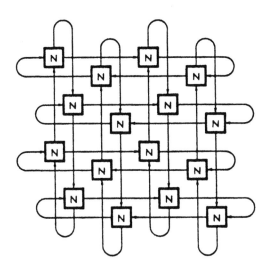

Figure 5. A folded torus system.

- For networks with the same number of nodes, *wire density is held constant*. Each network is constructed with the same bisection width, B, the total number of wires crossing the midpoint of the network. To keep the bisection width constant, we vary the width, W, of the communication channels. We normalize to the bisection width of a bit-serial ($W = 1$) binary n-cube.
- The networks use *wormhole* routing.
- Channel delay, T_c, is a function of wire length, l. We begin by considering channel delay to be constant. Later, the comparison is performed for both logarithmic and linear wire delays; $T_c \propto \log l$ and $T_c \propto l$.

When k is even, the channels crossing the midpoint of the network are all in the highest dimension. For each of the $\sqrt{N}$ rows of the network, there are $k^{(\frac{n}{2}-1)}$ of these channels in each direction for a total of $2\sqrt{N}k^{(\frac{n}{2}-1)}$ channels. Thus, the bisection width, B, of a k-ary n-cube with W-bit wide communication channels is

$$B(k,n) = 2W\sqrt{N}k^{(\frac{n}{2}-1)} = \frac{2WN}{k}. \qquad (6)$$

For a binary n-cube, $k = 2$, the bisection width is $B(2,n) = WN$. We set B equal to N to normalize to a binary n-cube with unit width channels,

$W = 1$. The channel width, $W(k, n)$, of a k-ary n-cube with the same bisection width, B, follows from (6):

$$\frac{2W(k,n)N}{k} = N,$$

$$W(k,n) = \frac{k}{2}. \tag{7}$$

The peak wire density is greater than the bisection width in networks with $n > 2$ because the lower dimensions contribute to wire density. The maximum density, however, is bounded by

$$D_{\max} = 2W\sqrt{N} \sum_{i=0}^{\frac{n}{2}-1} k^i = k\sqrt{N} \sum_{i=0}^{\frac{n}{2}-1} k^i = k\sqrt{N} \left(\frac{k^{\frac{n}{2}} - 1}{k - 1} \right)$$

$$= k\sqrt{N} \left(\frac{\sqrt{N} - 1}{k - 1} \right) < \left(\frac{k}{k - 1} \right) B. \tag{8}$$

A plot of wire density as a function of position for one row of a binary 20-cube is shown in figure 6. The density is very low at the edges of the cube and quite dense near the center. The peak density for the row is 1364 at position 341. Compare this density with the bisection width of the row, which is 1024. In contrast, a two-dimensional torus has a wire density of 1024 independent of position. One advantage of high-radix networks is that they have a very uniform wire density. They make full use of available area.

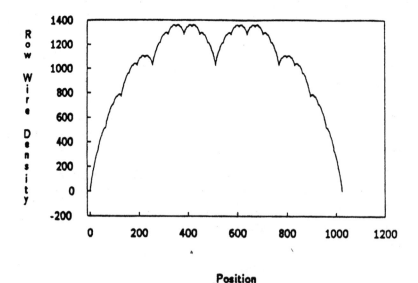

Figure 6. Wire density versus position for one row of a binary 20-cube.

Each processing node connects to $2n$ channels (n input and n output) each of which is $\frac{k}{2}$ bits wide. Thus, the number of pins per processing node is

$$N_p = nk . \qquad (9)$$

A plot of pin density as a function of dimension for $N = 256$, 16K and 1M nodes[3] is shown in figure 7. Low-dimensional networks have the disadvantage of requiring many pins per processing node. A two-dimensional network with 1M nodes (not shown) requires 2048 pins and is clearly unrealizable. However, the number of pins decreases very rapidly as the dimension, n, increases. Even for 1M nodes, a dimension 4 node has only 128 pins. All of the configurations that give low latency also give a reasonable pin count.

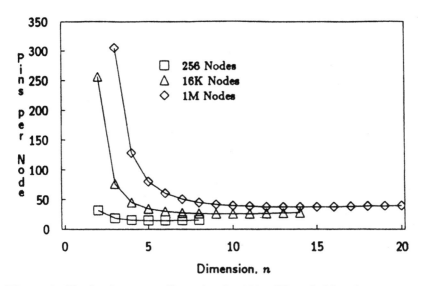

Figure 7. Pin density versus dimension for 256, 16K, and 1M nodes.

Latency

Latency, T_l, is the sum of the latency due to the network and the latency due to the processing node,

$$T_l = T_{net} + T_{node} . \qquad (10)$$

In this chapter we are concerned only with T_{net}. Techniques to reduce T_{node} are described in [Dally 1987a] and [Dally et al. 1987].

If we select two processing nodes, P_i, P_j, at random, the average number of channels that must be traversed to send a message from P_i to P_j is

---

[3] $1K = 1024$ and, $1M = 1K \times 1K = 1048576$.

given by

$$D = \left(\frac{k-1}{2}\right) n .$$ (11)

The average latency of a k-ary n-cube is calculated by substituting (7) and (11), into (3)

$$T_{\text{net}} = T_c \left(\left(\frac{k-1}{2}\right) n + \frac{2L}{k} \right) .$$ (12)

Figure 8 shows the average network latency, T_{net}, as a function of dimension, n, for k-ary n-cubes with 2^8 (256), 2^{14} (16K), and 2^{20} (1M) nodes[4]. The leftmost data point in this figure corresponds to a torus ($n = 2$) and the rightmost data point corresponds to a binary n-cube ($k = 2$). This figure assumes constant wire delay, T_c, and a message length, L, of 150 bits. This choice of message length was based on the analysis of a number of fine-grain concurrent programs [Dally 1987a]. Although constant wire delay is unrealistic, this figure illustrates that even ignoring the dependence of wire delay on wire length, low-dimensional networks achieve lower latency than high-dimensional networks.

The latency of the tori on the left side of figure 8 is limited almost entirely by distance. The latency of the binary n-cubes on the right side of the graph is limited almost entirely by aspect ratio. With bit serial channels, these cubes take 150 cycles to transmit their messages across a single channel.

In an application that exploits locality of communication, the distance between communicating objects is reduced. In such a situation, the latency of the low-dimensional networks, dominated by distance, (the left side of figure 8) is reduced. High-dimensional networks, on the other hand, cannot take advantage of locality. Their latency, because it is dominated by message length, will remain high.

In applications that send short messages, the component of latency due to message length is reduced resulting in lower latency for high-dimensional networks (the right side of figure 8).

For the three cases shown in figure 8, minimum latencies are achieved for $n = 2$, 4, and 5 respectively. In general the lowest latency is achieved when the component of latency due to distance, D, and the component due to message length, $\frac{L}{W}$, are approximately equal $D \approx \frac{L}{W}$. The following assertion makes this statement more precise.

Assertion: Minimum latency, T_{net}, occurs at a dimension, $n \leq n_x$, where n_x is the dimension for which $D = \frac{L}{W}$.

---

[4] For the sake of comparison we allow radix to take on non-integer values. For some of the dimensions considered, there is no integer radix, k, that gives the correct number of nodes. In fact, this limitation can be overcome by constructing a *mixed-radix cube* [Bhuyan & Agrawal 1984].

Proof: Differentiating (12) with respect to n gives

$$\frac{\partial T_{\text{net}}}{\partial n} = \frac{k - 1 - k \log k}{2} + \frac{2L \log^2 k}{k \log N} . \tag{13}$$

For $n = n_x$, substituting $D = \frac{L}{W}$ into (7) and (11) gives

$$4L = nk(k - 1) = \frac{k(k - 1) \log N}{\log k} . \tag{14}$$

Substituting into the derivative (13) gives

$$\left.\frac{\partial T_{\text{net}}}{\partial n}\right|_{n=n_x} = \frac{k - 1 - k \log k}{2} + \frac{(k - 1) \log k}{2} = \frac{k - 1 - \log k}{2} . \tag{15}$$

For all $k \geq 2$, $\left.\frac{\partial T_{\text{net}}}{\partial n}\right|_{n=n_x} \geq 0$. The derivative is monotonically increasing for $n \leq n_x$. Thus, the minimum latency $\left(\frac{\partial T_{\text{net}}}{\partial n} = 0\right)$ occurs for $n < n_x$.

Empirically, for all networks with $N < 2^{20}$ and integral valued k and n the minimum latency occurs when k and n are chosen so that $|D - \frac{L}{W}|$ is minimized.

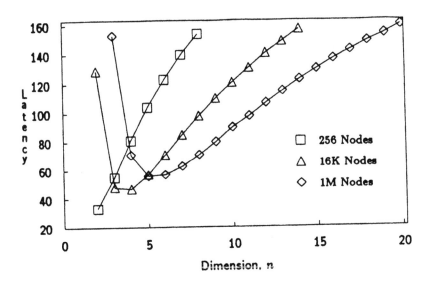

Figure 8. Latency versus dimension for 256, 16K, and 1M nodes, constant delay.

The longest wire in the system becomes a bottleneck that determines the rate at which each channel operates, T_c. The length of this wire is given by

$$l = k^{\frac{n}{2}-1} . \tag{16}$$

If the wires are sufficiently short, delay depends logarithmically on wire length. If the channels are longer, they become limited by the speed of light, and delay depends linearly on channel length. Substituting (16) into (4) and (5) gives

$$T_c \propto \begin{cases} 1 + \log_e l = 1 + \left(\frac{n}{2} - 1\right) \log_e k & \text{logarithmic delay} \\ l = k^{\frac{n}{2}-1} & \text{linear delay.} \end{cases} \quad (17)$$

We substitute (17) into (12) to get the network latency for these two cases:

$$T_l \propto \begin{cases} \left(1 + \left(\frac{n}{2} - 1\right) \log_e k\right) \left(\left(\frac{k-1}{2}\right) n + \frac{2L}{k}\right) & \text{logarithmic delay} \\ \left(k^{\frac{n}{2}-1}\right) \left(\left(\frac{k-1}{2}\right) n + \frac{2L}{k}\right) & \text{linear delay.} \end{cases}$$

$$(18)$$

Figure 9 shows the average network latency as a function of dimension for k-ary n-cubes with 2^8 (256), 2^{14} (16K), and 2^{20} (1M) nodes, assuming logarithmic wire delay and a message length, L, of 150. Figure 10 shows the same data assuming linear wire delays. In both figures, the leftmost data point corresponds to a torus ($n = 2$) and the rightmost data point corresponds to a binary n-cube ($k = 2$).

In the linear delay case, figure 10, a torus ($n = 2$) always gives the lowest latency. This is because a torus offers the highest bandwidth channels and the most direct physical route between two processing nodes. Under the linear delay assumption, latency is determined solely by bandwidth and by the physical distance traversed. There is no advantage in having long channels.

Under the logarithmic delay assumption, figure 9, a torus has the lowest latency for small networks ($N = 256$). For the larger networks, the lowest latency is achieved with slightly higher dimensions. With $N = 16K$, the lowest latency occurs when n is three[5]. With $N = 1M$, the lowest latency is achieved when n is 5. It is interesting that assuming constant wire delay does not change this result much. Recall that under the (unrealistic) constant wire delay assumption, figure 9, the minimum latencies are achieved with dimensions of 2, 4, and 5 respectively.

The results shown in figures 8 through 10 were derived by comparing networks under the assumption of constant wire cost to a binary n-cube with $W = 1$. For small networks it is possible to construct binary n-cubes with wider channels, and for large networks (for example, $1M$ nodes) it may not be possible to construct a binary n-cube at all. The available wiring area grows as $N^{\frac{1}{3}}$ while the bisection width of a binary n-cube grows as N. In the case of small networks, the comparison against binary n-cubes with wide channels can be performed by expressing message length in terms of the binary n-cube's channel width, in effect decreasing the message length for purposes of comparison. The net result is the same:

---

[5] In an actual machine the dimension n would be restricted to be an even integer.

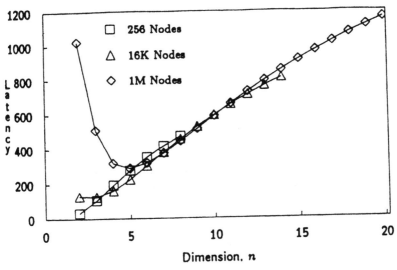

Figure 9. Latency versus dimension for 256, 16K, and 1M nodes, logarithmic delay.

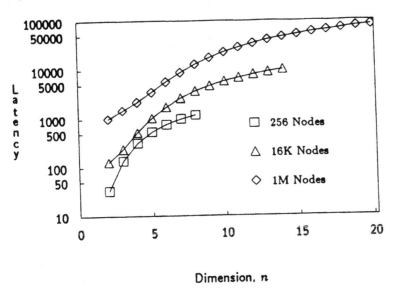

Figure 10. Latency versus dimension for 256, 16K, and 1M nodes, linear delay.

lower-dimensional networks give lower latency. Even if we perform the 256 node comparison against a binary n-cube with $W = 16$, the torus gives the lowest latency under the logarithmic delay model, and a dimension 3 network gives minimum latency under the constant delay model. For large networks, the available wire is less than assumed, so the effective message length should be increased, making low-dimensional networks look even more favorable.

In this comparison we have assumed that only a single bit of information is in transit on each wire of the network at a given time. Under this assumption, the delay between nodes, T_c, is equal to the period of each node, T_p. In a network with long wires, however, it is possible to have several bits in transit at once. In this case, the channel delay, T_c, is a function of wire length, while the channel period, $T_p < T_c$, remains constant. Similarly, in a network with very short wires we may allow a bit to ripple through several channels before sending the next bit. In this case, $T_p > T_c$. Separating the coefficients, T_c and T_p, (3) becomes

$$T_{\text{net}} = \left(T_c D + T_p \frac{L}{W} \right). \tag{19}$$

The net effect of allowing $T_c \neq T_p$ is the same as changing the length, L, by a factor of $\frac{T_p}{T_c}$ and does not change our results significantly.

When wire cost is considered, low-dimensional networks (for example, tori) offer lower latency than high-dimensional networks (for example, binary n-cubes). Tori outperform binary n-cubes because they better match form to function. The logical and physical graphs of the torus are identical; Thus, messages always travel the minimum distance from source to destination. In a binary n-cube, on the other hand, the fit between form and function is not as good. A message in a binary n-cube embedded into the plane may have to traverse considerably more than the minimum distance between its source and destination.

Throughput

Throughput, another important metric of network performance, is defined as the total number of messages the network can handle per unit time. One method of estimating throughput is to calculate the capacity of a network, the total number of messages that can be in the network at once. Typically the maximum throughput of a network is some fraction of its capacity. The network capacity per node is the total bandwidth out of each node divided by the average number of channels traversed by each message. For k-ary n-cubes, the bandwidth out of each node is nW, and the average number of channels traversed is given by (11), so the network capacity per node, Γ, is given by

$$\Gamma \propto \frac{nW}{D} \propto \frac{n\left(\frac{k}{2}\right)}{\left(\frac{k-1}{2}\right)n} \approx 1. \tag{20}$$

The network capacity is independent of dimension. For a constant wire density, there is a constant network capacity.

Throughput will be less than capacity because contention causes some channels to block. This contention also increases network latency. To simplify the analysis of this contention, we make the following assumptions:

- Messages are routed using e-cube routing (in order of decreasing dimension) [Dally & Seitz 1987]. That is a message at node $a_0, \ldots, a_{n-1}$ destined for node $b_0, \ldots, b_{n-1}$ is first routed in dimension $n-1$ until it reaches node $a_0, \ldots, a_{n-2}, b_{n-1}$. The message is then routed in dimension $n-2$ until it reaches node $a_0, \ldots, a_{n-3}, b_{n-2}, b_{n-1}$, and so on. As shown in figure 11, this assumption allows us to consider the contention in each dimension separately.

- The traffic from each node is generated by a Poisson process with arrival rate $\lambda \frac{\text{bits}}{\text{cycle}}$.

- Message destinations are uniformly distributed and independent.

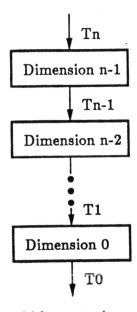

Figure 11. Contention model for a network.

The arrival rate of $\lambda \frac{\text{bits}}{\text{cycle}}$ corresponds to $\lambda_E = \frac{\lambda}{L} \frac{\text{messages}}{\text{cycle}}$. At the destination, each flit is serviced as soon as it arrives, so the service time at the sink is $T_0 = \frac{L}{W} = \frac{2L}{k}$. Starting with T_0 we will calculate the service time seen entering each preceding dimension.

For convenience, we will define the quantities in equation (21) as illustrated in figure 12:

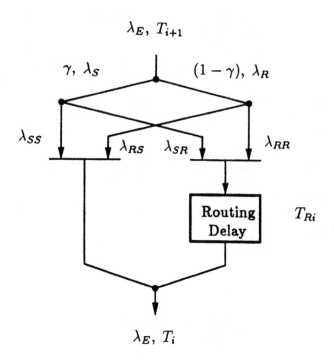

Figure 12. Contention model for a single dimension.

$\gamma = \frac{1}{k}$

probability that a message *skips*—does not route in—a dimension,

$\lambda_S = \gamma\lambda_E$

rate of traffic that skips the previous dimension, $i+1$, $\left(\frac{messages}{cycle}\right)$,

$\lambda_R = (1-\gamma)\lambda_E$

rate of traffic that routes in the previous dimension, $i+1$, $\left(\frac{messages}{cycle}\right)$,

$\lambda_{SS} = \gamma^2\lambda_E$

rate of traffic that skips both the previous dimension, $i+1$, and the current dimension, i, $\left(\frac{messages}{cycle}\right)$,

$\lambda_{SR} = \gamma(1-\gamma)\lambda_E$

rate of traffic that skips the previous dimension, $i+1$, and routes in the current dimension, i, $\left(\frac{messages}{cycle}\right)$,

$\lambda_{RS} = \gamma(1-\gamma)\lambda_E$

rate of traffic that routes in the previous dimension, $i+1$, and skips the current dimension, i, $\left(\frac{messages}{cycle}\right)$,

$\lambda_{RR} = (1-\gamma)^2\lambda_E$

rate of traffic that routes in both the previous dimension, $i+1$, and the current dimension, i,$\left(\frac{messages}{cycle}\right)$.

(21)

Consider a single dimension, i, of the network as shown in figure 12. All messages incur a latency due to contention on entering the dimension. Those messages that are routed incur an additional latency, T_{Ri}, due to contention during routing. The rate λ_E message stream entering the dimension is composed of two components: a rate λ_S stream that skipped the previous $(i + 1^{\text{st}})$ dimension, and a rate λ_R stream that was routed in the previous dimension. These two streams are in turn split into components that will skip the ith dimension (λ_{SS} and λ_{RS}) and components that will be routed in the ith dimension (λ_{SR} and λ_{RR}). The entering latency seen by one component (say λ_{SS}) is given by multiplying the probability of a collision (in this case $\lambda_{RS}T_i$) by the expected latency due to a collision, (in this case $\frac{T_i}{2}$). The components that require routing must also add the latency due to contention during routing, T_{Ri}. Adding up the four components with appropriate weights gives the following equation for T_{i+1}.

$$T_{i+1} = T_i + (1 - \gamma)T_{Ri} + \gamma(1 - \gamma)^3\lambda_E(T_i + T_{Ri})^2 + \gamma^3(1 - \gamma)\lambda_E T_i^2. \quad (22)$$

The first term of (22) is the latency seen entering the next dimension. The second term accounts for the routing latency, T_{Ri}, incurred by messages routing in this dimension (λ_{SR} and λ_{RR}). The entering latency due to contention when the two routing streams merge is given by the third term. The final term gives the entering latency for the messages that skip the dimension.

For large k, *gamma* is small and the latency is approximated by $T_{i+1} \approx T_i + T_{Ri}$. For $k = 2$ (binary n-cubes), $T_{Ri} = 0$; thus, $T_{i+1} = T_i + \frac{\lambda_E T_i}{8}$.

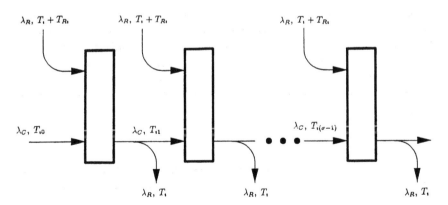

Figure 13. Contention model for routing latency.

To calculate the routing latency, T_{Ri}, we use the model shown in figure 13. Messages enter the dimension with rate λ_R, route through a number of stages, denoted by boxes, and exit the dimension. The latency due to contention in the stages sums to T_{Ri}. Given that a message is to be routed in a dimension, the expected number of channels traversed by the message is $\frac{k}{2}$, one entering channel and $\sigma = \frac{k-2}{2}$ continuing channels. Thus, the *average* message rate on channels continuing in the dimension is $\lambda_C = \sigma \lambda_R$.

Using the average message rate to calculate latency is an approximation. The symmetry of the network assures that the traffic on physical channels is uniform. However, using virtual channels and e-cube routing [Dally & Seitz 1987] results in logical channels that form a spiral. Traffic on the jth channel of this spiral is given by $\lambda_{Cj} = \left(j - \frac{i^2+i}{2k} \right) \lambda_R$. Using the uniform physical message rate results in a slightly pessimistic estimate of latency because contention for the physical channel occurs on flit boundaries while contention for the logical channel occurs on message boundaries.

To compute, T_{Ri}, we work backwards from the output. The service time in the last continuing channel in dimension i is $T_{i(\sigma-1)} = T_i$. Once we know the service time for the jth channel, T_{ij}, the additional service time due to contention at the $j - 1^{\text{st}}$ channel is given by multiplying the probability of a collision, $\lambda_R T_{i0}$, by the expected waiting time for a collision, $\frac{T_{i0}}{2}$. Repeating this calculation σ times gives us T_{i0}.

$$T_{i(j-1)} = T_{ij} + \frac{\lambda_R T_{i0}^2}{2},$$

$$T_{i0} = T_i + \frac{\sigma \lambda_R T_{i0}^2}{2} = T_i + \frac{\lambda_C T_{i0}^2}{2}, \tag{23}$$

$$= \frac{1 - \sqrt{1 - 2\lambda_C T_i}}{\lambda_C}.$$

Equation (23) is valid only when $\lambda_C < \frac{T_i}{2}$. If the message rate is higher than this limit, there is no steady-state solution and latency becomes infinite. There are two solutions to (23). Here we consider only the smaller of the two latencies. The larger solution corresponds to a state that is not encountered during normal operation of a network.

To calculate T_{Ri} we also need to consider the possibility of a collision on the entering channel.

$$T_{Ri} = T_{i0} \left(1 + \frac{\lambda_C T_{i0}}{2} \right) - T_i. \tag{24}$$

If sufficient queueing is added to each network node, the service times do not increase, only the latency and equations (24) and (22) become.

$$T_{Ri} = \left(\frac{T_i}{1 - \frac{\lambda_C T_0}{2}} \right) \left(1 + \frac{\lambda_C T_0}{2} \right) - T_i, \tag{25}$$

$$T_{i+1} = T_i + (1 - \gamma)T_{Ri} + \left(\gamma(1 - \gamma)^3 + \gamma^3(1 - \gamma) \right) \lambda_E T_0. \tag{26}$$

To be effective, the total queueing between the source and destination should be greater than the expected increase in latency due to blocking.

Two flits of queueing per stage is sufficient when $\lambda < 0.3$ and $L < 200$. Longer messages result in a longer service time, T_0, and require additional queueing. The analysis here is pessimistic in that it assumes no queueing. Using equation (22), we can determine:

1   The maximum throughput of the network, and
2   How network latency increases with traffic.

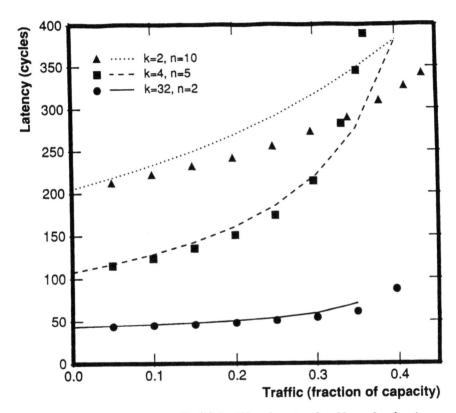

Figure 14. Latency versus traffic (λ) for 1K node networks: 32-ary 2-cube, 4-ary 5-cube, and binary 10-cube, L=200bits. Solid line is predicted latency, points are measurements taken from a simulator.

Figures 14 and 15 show how latency increases as a function of applied traffic for 1K node and 4K node k-ary n-cubes. The vertical axis shows latency in cycles. The horizontal axis is traffic per node, λ, in bits/cycle. The figures compare measurements from a network simulator (points) to the latency predicted by (24) (lines). The simulation agrees with the prediction within a few percent until the network approaches saturation.

For 1K networks, a 32-ary 2-cube always gives the lowest latency. For 4K networks, a 16-ary 3-cube gives the lowest latency when $\lambda < 0.2$.

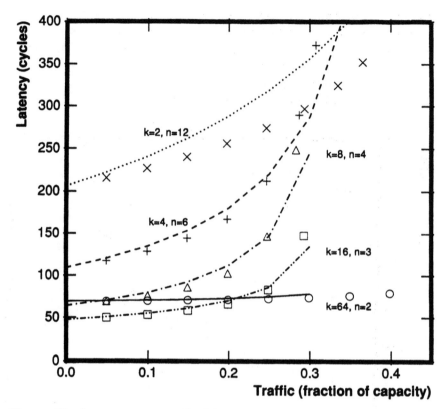

Figure 15. Latency versus traffic (λ) for 4K node networks: 64-ary 2-cube, 16-ary 3-cube, 8-ary 4-cube, 4-ary 6-cube, and binary 12-cube, L=200 bits. Solid line is predicted latency, points are measurements taken from a simulator.

Because latency increases more slowly for 2-dimensional networks, a 64-ary 2-cube gives the lowest latency when $\lambda > 0.2$.

At the left side of each graph ($\lambda = 0$), latency is given by (12). As traffic is applied to the network latency increases slowly due to contention in the network until saturation is reached. Saturation occurs when λ is between 0.3 and 0.5 depending on the network topology. Networks should be designed to operate on the flat portion of the curve ($\lambda < 0.25$). When the network saturates, throughput levels off as shown in figures 16 and 17. These figures show how much traffic is delivered (vertical axis) when the nodes attempt to inject a given amount of traffic (horizontal axis). The curve is linear (actual = attempted) until saturation is reached. From this point on, actual traffic is constant. This plateau occurs because:

1   The network is source queued.

2   Messages that encounter contention are blocked rather than aborted.

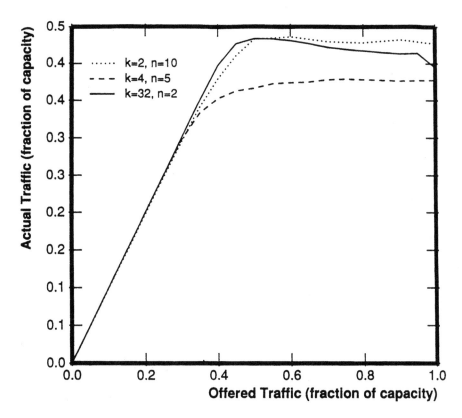

Figure 16. Actual traffic versus attempted traffic for 1K node networks: 32-ary 2-cube, 4-ary 5-cube, and binary 10-cube, L=200 bits.

In networks where contention is resolved by dropping messages, throughput usually decreases beyond saturation.

To find the maximum throughput of the network, the source service time, T_0, is set equal to the reciprocal of the message rate, λ_E, and equations (22), (23), and (24) are solved for λ_E. At this operating point the network can accept no more traffic. Messages are being offered as fast as the network can deliver them. The maximum throughput as a fraction of capacity for k-ary n-cubes with 1K node is tabulated in table 1 and with 4K node in table 2. Also shown is the total latency for L = 200bit messages at several message rates. The table shows that the additional latency due to blocking is significantly reduced as dimension is decreased.

In networks of constant bisection width, the latency of low-dimensional networks increases more slowly with applied traffic than the latency of high-dimensional networks. At $\lambda = 0.2$, the 32-ary 2-cube has $\approx \frac{1}{5}$ the latency of the binary 10-cube. At this point, the additional latency due to contention

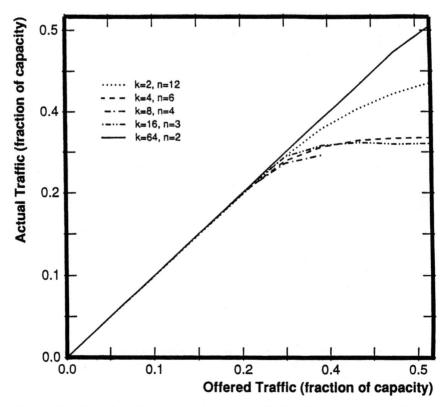

Figure 17. Actual traffic versus attempted traffic for 4K node networks: 64-ary 2-cube, 16-ary 3-cube, 8-ary 4-cube, 4-ary 6-cube, and binary 12-cube, L=200 bits.

Dimension	2	5	10
radix	32	4	2
Max Throughput	0.36	0.41	0.43
Latency $\lambda = 0.1$	46.1	128.0	233.0
Latency $\lambda = 0.2$	50.5	161.0	269.0
Latency $\lambda = 0.3$	59.3	221.0	317.0

Table 1. Maximum Throughput as a Fraction of Capacity and Blocking Latency in Cycles for 1K Node networks.

in the 32-ary 2-cube is $7T_c$ compared to $64T_c$ in the binary 10-cube.

Low-dimensional networks handle contention better because they use fewer channels of higher bandwidth and thus get better queueing perfor-

Dimension	2	3	4	6	12
radix	64	16	8	4	2
Max Throughput	0.35	0.31	0.31	0.36	0.41
Latency $\lambda = 0.1$	70.7	55.2	79.9	135.0	241.0
Latency $\lambda = 0.2$	73.1	70.3	112.0	181.0	288.0
Latency $\lambda = 0.3$	78.6	135.0	245.0	287.0	357.0

Table 2. Maximum Throughput as a Fraction of Capacity and Blocking Latency in Cycles for 4K Node networks.

mance. The shorter service times, $\frac{L}{W}$, of these networks results in both a lower probability of collision, and a lower expected waiting time in the event of a collision. Thus the blocking latency at each node is reduced quadratically as k is increased. Low-dimensional networks require more hops, $D = \frac{n(k-1)}{2}$, and have a higher rate on the continuing channels, λ_C. However, messages travel on the continuing channels more frequently than on the entering channels, thus most contention is with the lower rate channels. Having fewer channels of higher bandwidth also improves hot-spot throughput as described below.

Hot spot throughput

In many situations traffic is not uniform, but rather is concentrated into *hot spots*. A *hot spot* is a pair of nodes that accounts for a disproportionately large portion of the total network traffic. As described by Pfister and Norton [1985] for a shared-memory computer, hot-spot traffic can degrade performance of the entire network by causing congestion.

The *hot-spot throughput* of a network is the maximum rate at which messages can be sent from one specific node, P_i, to another specific node, P_j. For a k-ary n-cube with deterministic routing, the hot-spot throughput, Θ_{HS}, is just the bandwidth of a single channel, W. Thus, under the assumption of constant wire cost we have

$$\Theta_{HS} = W = k - 1. \tag{27}$$

Low-dimensional networks have greater channel bandwidth and thus have greater hot-spot throughput than do high-dimensional networks. Low-dimensional networks operate better under non-uniform loads because they do more resource sharing. In an interconnection network the resources are wires. In a high-dimensional network, wires are assigned to particular dimensions and cannot be shared between dimensions. For example, in a binary n-cube it is possible for a wire to be saturated while a physically adjacent wire assigned to a different dimension remains idle. In a torus all physically adjacent wires are combined into a single channel that is shared by all messages that must traverse the physical distance spanned by the channel.

Conclusion

Under the assumption of constant wire bisection, low-dimensional networks with wide channels provide lower latency, less contention, and higher hot-spot throughput than high-dimensional networks with narrow channels. Minimum network latency is achieved when the network radix, k, and dimension, n, are chosen to make the components of latency due to distance, D, and aspect ratio, $\frac{L}{W}$ approximately equal. The minimum latency occurs at a very low dimension, two, for up to 1024 nodes.

Low dimensional networks reduce contention because having a few high-bandwidth channels results in more resource sharing and thus better queueing performance than having many low-bandwidth channels. While network capacity and worst-case blocking latency are independent of dimension, low-dimensional networks have a higher maximum throughput and lower average blocking latency than do high-dimensional networks. Improved resource sharing also gives low-dimensional networks higher hot-spot throughput than high-dimensional networks.

The results of this chapter have all rested on the assumption of constant channel delay, independent of channel length. The main result, that low-dimensional networks give minimum latency, however, does not change appreciably when logarithmic or linear delay models are considered. In choosing a delay model one must consider how the delay of a switching node compares to the delay of a wire. Current VLSI routing chips [Dally & Seitz 1986] have delays of tens of nanoseconds, enough time to drive several meters of wire. For such systems a constant delay model is adequate. As chips get faster and systems get larger, however, a linear delay model will more accurately reflect system performance.

Fat-tree networks have been shown to be universal in the sense that they can *efficiently* simulate any other network of the same volume [Leiserson 1985]. However, the analysis of these networks has not considered latency. k-ary n-cubes with appropriately chosen radix and dimension are also universal in this sense. A detailed proof is beyond the scope of this chapter. Intuitively, one cannot do any better than to fill each of the three physical dimensions with wires and place switches at every point of intersection. Any point-to-point network can be embedded into such a 3-D mesh with no more than a constant increase in wiring length.

This chapter has considered only *direct* networks [Seitz 1984]. The results do not apply to *indirect* networks. The depth and the switch degree of an indirect network are analogous to the dimension and radix of a direct network. However, the bisection width of an indirect network is independent of switch degree. Because indirect networks do not exploit locality it is not possible to trade off diameter for bandwidth. When wire density is the limiting resource, a high-bandwidth direct network is preferable to an indirect network.

The low-dimensional k-ary n-cube provides a very general communication media for digital systems. These networks have been developed primarily for message-passing concurrent computers. They could also be used in place of a bus or indirect network in a shared-memory concurrent computer, in place of a bus to connect the components of a sequential computer, or to connect subsystems of a special purpose digital system. With VLSI communication chips the cost of implementing a network node is comparable to the cost of interfacing to a shared bus, and the performance of the network is considerably greater than the performance of a bus.

The networks described here have been demonstrated in the laboratory and incorporated into commercial multiprocessors. The Torus Routing Chip (TRC) is a VLSI chip designed to implement low-dimensional k-ary n-cube interconnection networks [Dally & Seitz 1986]. The TRC performs wormhole routing in arbitrary k-ary n-cube interconnection networks. A single TRC provides 8-bit data channels in two dimensions and can be cascaded to add more dimensions or wider data channels. A TRC network can deliver a 150-bit message in a 1024 node 32-ary 2-cube with an average latency of $7.5\mu s$, an order of magnitude better performance than would be achieved by a binary n-cube with bit-serial channels. A new routing chip, the Network Design Frame (NDF), improves this latency to $\approx 1\mu s$ [Dally & Song 1987]. The Ametek 2010 uses a 16-ary 2-cube (without end around connections) for its interconnection network [Ametek 1987].

Now that the latency of communication networks has been reduced to a few microseconds the latency of the processing nodes, T_{node}, dominates the overall latency. To efficiently make use of a low-latency communication network we need a processing node that interprets messages with very little overhead. The design of such a *message-driven processor* is currently underway [Dally 1987a; Dally et al. 1987].

The real challenge in concurrent computing is software. The development of concurrent software is strongly influenced by available concurrent hardware. We hope that by providing machines with higher performance internode communication we will encourage concurrency to be exploited at a finer grain size in both system and application software.

I thank Chuck Seitz of Caltech for his many helpful suggestions during the early stages of this research.

The research described in this chapter was supported in part by the Defense Advanced Research Projects Agency under contracts N00014-80-C-0622

References

Ametek Corporation [1987], Ametek 2010 product announcement.

Batcher, K. E. [1968], "Sorting Networks and Their Applications," *Proceedings AFIPS FJCC*, vol. 32, pp. 307-314.

Batcher, K. E. [1976], "The Flip Network in STARAN," *Proceedings, International Conference on Parallel Processing*, pp. 65-71.

Benes, V. E. [1965], *Mathematical Theory of Connecting Networks and Telephone Traffic*, Academic, New York.

Bhuyan, L. N., and D. P. Agrawal [1984], "Generalized Hypercube and Hyperbus Structures for a Computer Network," *IEEE Transactions on Computers*, vol. C-33, no. 4, pp. 323-333.

Browning, Sally [1985], *The Tree Machine: A Highly Concurrent Computing Environment*, Department of Computer Science, California Institute of Technology, Technical Report 3760.

Dally, William J. [1987a], *A VLSI Architecture for Concurrent Data Structures*, Kluwer, Hingham, MA.

Dally, William J. [1987b], "Wire Efficient VLSI Multiprocessor Communication Networks," *Proceedings Stanford Conference on Advanced Research in VLSI*, edited by Paul Losleben, MIT Press, Cambridge, MA, pp. 391-415.

Dally, William J. [1987c], "Architecture of a Message-Driven Processor," *Proceedings of the 14th ACM/IEEE Symposium on Computer Architecture*, pp. 189-196.

Dally, William J., and Charles L. Seitz [1987], *Deadlock-Free Message Routing in Multiprocessor Interconnection Networks, IEEE Transactions on Computers*, vol. C-36, no. 5, pp. 547-553.

Dally, William J., and Charles L. Seitz [1986], "The Torus Routing Chip," *J. Distributed Systems*, vol. 1, no. 3, pp. 187-196.

Dally, William J., and Paul Song [1987], "Design of a Self-Timed VLSI Multicomputer Communication Controller," To appear in *Proc. IEEE International Conference on Computer Design*.

Kermani, Parviz, and Leonard Kleinrock [1979], "Virtual Cut-Through: A New Computer Communication Switching Technique," *Computer Networks*, vol 3., pp. 267-286.

Lawrie, H. Duncan [1975], "Alignment and Access of Data in an Array Processor," *IEEE Transactions on Computers*, vol. C-24, no. 12, pp. 1145-1155.

Leiserson, Charles L. [1985], "Fat Trees: Universal Networks for Hardware-Efficient Supercomputing," *IEEE Transactions on Computers*, vol. C-34, no. 10, pp. 892-901.

---

and N00014-85-K-0124 and in part by a National Science Foundation Presidential Young Investigator Award with matching funds from General Electric Corporation.

Mead, Carver A., and Lynn A. Conway [1980], *Introduction to VLSI Systems,* Addison-Wesley, Reading, Mass.

Pease, M. C., III [1977], "The Indirect Binary n-Cube Microprocessor Array," *IEEE Transactions on Computers,* vol. C-26, no. 5, pp. 458-473.

Pfister, G. F., and V. A. Norton [1985], "Hot Spot Contention and Combining in Multistage Interconnection Networks," *IEEE Transactions on Computers,* vol. C-34, no. 10, pp. 943-948.

Seitz, Charles L. [1984], "Concurrent VLSI Architectures," *IEEE Transactions on Computers,* vol. C-33, no. 12, pp. 1247-1265.

Seitz, Charles L., *et al.* [1985], *The Hypercube Communications Chip,* Department of Computer Science, California Institute of Technology, Display File 5182:DF:85.

Sequin, Carlo, H. [1979], "Single Chip Computers, The New VLSI Building Block," *Caltech Conference on VLSI,* edited by C. L. Seitz, pp. 435-452.

Siegel, Howard Jay [1979], "Interconnection Networks for SIMD Machines," *IEEE Computer,* vol. 12, no. 6, pp. 57-65.

Stone, H. S. [1971], "Parallel Processing with the Perfect Shuffle," *IEEE Transactions on Computers,* vol. C-20, no. 2, pp. 153-161.

Sullivan, H., and T. R. Bashkow [1977], "A Large Scale Homogeneous Machine," *Proc. 4th Annual Symposium on Computer Architecture,* pp. 105-124.

Tanenbaum, A. S. [1981], *Computer Networks,* Prentice Hall, Englewood Cliffs, NJ.

Thompson, C. D. [1980], *A Complexity Theory of VLSI,* Department of Computer Science, Carnegie-Mellon University, Technical Report CMU-CS-80-140.

21

In this chapter, Dally explains his J-machine, so named to encourage thinking of processors as low-cost components used in large quantities just as jellybeans are low-cost, high-consumption candies.

The J-machine design reflects the view that effective parallelism requires the division of big problems into many small tasks accomplished with about twenty instructions each. This view leads directly to conclusions that affect many hardware and software components. For example, the processors must be connected via a low-latency, high-throughput interprocessor communication network of the sort Dally advocates in the previous chapter; the processors must be able to initiate and receive messages quickly; and the operating system must be such that tasks can be created, suspended, resumed, and destroyed by executing only a few instructions, not hundreds or thousands as in conventional operating systems.

Specifically, the J-machine design uses a high-speed 3-D mesh network to connect up to 65,536 36-bit processors, each of which has 4K of 36-bit memory, and each of which has the required hardware to deal with messages efficiently. Each processor has little memory by conventional standards because the important parameter is how much memory each processor can access quickly, not how much memory there is per processor. Given the J-machine's fast network and global virtual address space, each processor has quick access to the entire memory in the machine, which is a quarter of a gigabyte in the full 65,536 processor version.

The J-Machine System

William J. Dally

The J-Machine is a distributed-memory, MIMD, concurrent computer. In concert with its operating system kernel, JOSS, the J-Machine provides low-overhead system services to support actor programming systems. The combined hardware/software system efficiently implements two abstractions: object and task. An object is a named collection of data. All data in the system: program data, code, and contexts are objects. The object namespace is global—an object can be referenced from any node of the machine. Tasks are procedure activations that may operate on the state of objects. To support fine-grain concurrent programming systems, the system is designed to handle small objects (eight words) and small tasks (twenty instructions).

The J-Machine is not specialized to actor systems; instead, it provides primitive mechanisms for communication, synchronization, and translation. Communication mechanisms are provided that permit a node to send a message to any other node in the machine in $< 2\mu s$. No processing resources on intermediate nodes are consumed and buffer memory is automatically allocated on the receiving node. The synchronization mechanisms schedule and dispatch a task in $< 1\mu s$ on message arrival and suspend tasks that attempt to reference data that is not yet available. The translation mechanism maintains bindings between arbitrary names and values. It is used to perform address translation to support a global virtual address space. These mechanisms have been selected to be both general and amenable to efficient hardware implementation. They efficiently support many parallel models of computation including actors [Agha 1986], dataflow [Dennis 1980], and communicating processes [Hoare 1978].

The hardware is an ensemble of up to 65,536 message-driven processors (MDPs) [Dally *et al.* 1987]. This limit is set by the addressability of the router and the bandwidth of the network. Each node contains a 36-bit processor, 4K 36-bit words of memory, and a communications controller (router). The nodes are connected by a high-speed, three-dimensional mesh network. Each network channel has a bandwidth of 360Mbits/s. The first medium-scale prototype will be a 4096-node system.

This design was chosen to make the most efficient use of available chip and board area. Packaging a small amount of memory on each node gives us an extremely high memory bandwidth (3Gbits/s per chip or 200Tbits/s in a fully populated system). Memory consumes most of the chip area; from one point of view, the system is a memory with processors added to each node to improve bandwidth for local operations. The fast communication and global address space prevent the small local memories from limiting programmability or performance. The 3-D network gives the highest throughput and lowest latency for a given wire density [Dally 1987b; Dally to appear]. It allows the processing nodes to be packed densely and results in uniformly short wires.

The J-Machine project is driven by the following goals:

- To identify and implement simple hardware mechanisms for communication, synchronization, and naming suitable for supporting a broad range of concurrent programming models.

- To reduce the overhead associated with these mechanisms to a few instruction times so that fine-grain programs may be efficiently executed.

- To design an area-efficient machine: one that maximizes performance for a given amount of chip and wiring area.

Grain size

The J-Machine is a fine-grain concurrent computer in that it is:

1   Designed to efficiently support fine-grain programs.
2   Composed of fine-grain processing nodes [Dally 1988b].

The *grain size* of a program refers to the size of the tasks and messages that make up the program. Coarse-grain programs have a few long ($\approx 10^5$ instruction) tasks, while fine-grain programs have many short (≈ 20 instruction) tasks. With more tasks that can execute at a given time—namely more concurrency—fine-grain programs (in the absence of overhead) result in faster solutions than coarse-grain programs.

The *grain size* of a machine refers to the physical size and the amount of memory in one processing node. A coarse-grain processing node requires hundreds of chips (several boards) and has $\approx 10^7$ bytes of memory while fine-grain node fits on a single chip and has $\approx 10^4$ bytes of memory. Fine-grain nodes cost less and have less memory than coarse-grain nodes, however, because so little silicon area is required to build a fast processor, they need not have slower processors than coarse-grain nodes.

Background

The J-Machine builds on previous work in the design of message-passing and shared memory machines. Like the Caltech Cosmic Cube [Seitz 1985], the Intel [Intel Scientific Computers 1985], and the N-CUBE [Palmer 1986], each node of the J-Machine has a local memory and communicates with other nodes by passing messages. Because of its low overhead, the J-Machine can exploit concurrency at a much finer grain than these early message passing computers. Delivering a message and dispatching a task in response to the message arrival takes $< 3\mu s$ on the J-Machine as opposed to 5ms on an IPSC. Like the BBN Butterfly [BBN Advanced Computers 1986] and the IBM RP3 [Pfister 1985] the J-Machine provides a global virtual address space. The same IDs (virtual addresses) are used to reference on and off node objects. Like the InMOS transputer [Inmos 1984] and the Caltech MOSAIC [Lutz *et al.* 1984] a J-Machine node is a single chip processing element integrating a processor, memory, and a communication unit.

The J-Machine is unique in that it extends these previous efforts with efficient primitive mechanisms for communication, synchronization, and naming.

Summary

The remainder of this chapter describes the J-Machine and the JOSS operating system kernel. The "System Architecture" section gives an overview of the system describing how the network, processor, and operating system layers work together to provide services. The network is described in the section called "The Network." The topology, performance, and router design are discussed. "The Message Driven Processor" section deals with the message driven processor and the mechanisms it provides for concurrency. The operating system is briefly described in section called "The Jellybean Operating System."

System Architecture

The J-Machine system is layered as shown in figure 1. A hardware layer provides primitive mechanisms. A software layer, the JOSS kernel, uses these primitives to build system services in two stages. First, local services

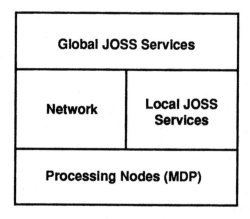

Figure 1. The J-Machine System. The hardware layer consists of a number of MDPs connected by a network. The operating system kernel running on each node provides local services. Global services are provided by exchanging messages with other nodes.

are provided on each node. Second, global services are built on top of these local services by passing messages between the nodes.

The hardware layer consists of an ensemble of (up to 64K) MDP-based processing nodes connected by a three-dimensional mesh network. The network delivers messages between nodes. All routing and flow-control are handled in the network. The network consists of a communication controller or router on each node, and wires connecting these routers to their neighbors in each of the three physical dimensions.

Each node contains a memory, a processor, and a communication controller. The communication controller is logically part of the network but physically part of the node. The 4K-word by 36-bit memory is used to store objects and system tables. Each word of the memory contains a 32-bit data item and a 4-bit tag. In addition to the usual uses of tags to support dynamic typing and garbage collection, special tags are provided to synchronize on data presence and to indicate if an address is local or remote. Memory accesses to write messages or read code are made a row (144bits) at a time to improve memory bandwidth. A part of the memory can be mapped as a set associative cache. This cache is used to implement the processor's translation mechanism.

The processor is message driven. It executes user and system code in response to messages arriving over the network. A conventional processor is instruction-driven in that it fetches an instruction from memory and dispatches a control sequence to execute the instruction. A message-driven processor receives a message from the network and dispatches a control sequence to execute the task specified by the message. The MDP uses an instruction sequence to *execute* a message. Hardware mechanisms for communication, synchronization, and translation are provided to accelerate the dispatch operation and the subsequent task execution.

To support communication over the network, the MDP provides a SEND instruction and performs automatic buffering of arriving messages. To synchronize execution with arriving messages, a primitive dispatch operation is provided that eliminates scheduling overhead. To synchronize on data, tags are provided to support futures. A general translation mechanism uses a set associative cache in the node memory to maintain arbitrary bindings.

The software layer is implemented by the JOSS kernel [Totty 1988] which provides services for allocating memory and processor resources to objects and tasks. The first level of JOSS provides memory management and multitasking on each node independently. Objects are allocated locally as memory segments and assigned a unique name. A binding is maintained between the object name (its ID or virtual address) and the base and length of its segment. Each node allocates names from a different partition of the global name space so the local object name is also its global name.

The second level of JOSS extends services globally across the network. A distributed global name table is maintained that contains bindings of object names to node addresses (node numbers). Remote objects are referenced by translating the object name to a node number and sending a message containing the object name to the node. At the node, the name is translated into a local segment descriptor. Objects are free to migrate from node to node. The global name table keeps track of the object's current location.

To handle large objects, JOSS provides support for *distributed objects* [Dally 1987a]. A distributed object is a collection of objects distributed over many nodes that share a common name. JOSS translates distributed object names to the location of the nearest *constituent object*.

The JOSS task manager schedules tasks in response to message arrival. It makes heavy use of the MDP synchronization mechanisms. The MDP dispatch mechanism is used to create tasks in response to message arrival. Tasks that terminate without suspending require no further services. If a task suspends awaiting a message, a context object is created to hold its state. When the message to restart the task arrives, its context is reloaded to resume the task.

To see how the system functions together, consider the example shown in figure 2. In figure 2a, a task executing in Context 37 on Node 124 sends a Sum message to an object, point1. This message requests that the object sum its two fields x and y. The sending node translates the object name for point1 (a unique 32-bit pattern) into a node address, Node 262 (a 16-bit integer), using the MDP translation mechanism. A sequence of MDP

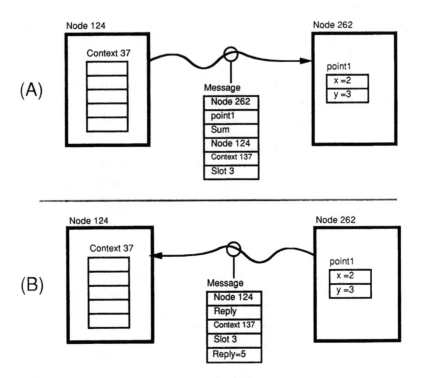

Figure 2. (a) A task executing in Context 37 on Node 124 sends a message to object **point1** requesting that it perform the **Sum** method. (b) A reply message is returned to Context 37.

SEND instructions is then used to inject the message into the network. The message includes:

1   The node address of **point1** (Node 262).
2   The object name of **point1**.
3   The message name or selector, Sum.
4   A continuation (the node and ID of the sender's context and the slot into which the reply should be stored).

The sending task continues to execute until it needs the result of the **Sum** message.

The network delivers the injected message to Node 262. At this node, the MDP buffering mechanism allocates storage for the message and sequences the message off the network into the node's memory. When the node completes its current task (and any other tasks ahead in the queue), the MDP dispatch mechanism creates a new task in response to the message. This task translates the ID of **point1** into a segment descriptor for the object, adds the x and y fields of the object together, and uses a sequence of SEND instructions to inject a message containing the sum into the network. As shown in figure 2b, this message contains the:

1   Node address of the sender's context.
2   ID of the sender's context.
3   Context slot awaiting the reply.
4   Result.

This task then terminates.

The network delivers the reply message to Node 124 where it is buffered and eventually dispatched to create a task. This task translates the ID for Context 37 into a segment descriptor. The reply value is stored into the specified slot of this context. The sending task is then resumed by loading its context from this segment.

The round trip delay for this example message send and reply is $\approx 5\mu s$. The difficulty in building a concurrent system the scale of the J-machine is not developing the mechanisms conceptually. It is implementing them efficiently so the overhead of accessing remote nodes is made small enough to permit the execution of fine-grain programs.

In the following sections we will examine the implementation of each component of the J-Machine system.

The Network

The J-Machine network has a 3-D mesh topology as shown in figure 3. Each node is located by a three coordinate address (x, y, and z). A node is connected to its six neighbors (if they exist) that have addresses differing in only one coordinate by ±1. All connections are bidirectional channels. Each channel requires 15 wires to carry 9-data bits, one tail bit, and five control lines [Dally & Song 1987]. Addressing is provided to support up to a 32 × 32 × 64 cube of 65536 nodes. The prototype will be built as a 16 × 16 × 16 cube of 4096 nodes. For a machine, such as the J-Machine where wire density is a limiting factor, this topology has been shown to give the lowest latency and highest throughput for a given wire density [Dally 1987b; Dally to appear].

The network topology is not visible to the programmer. The latency of sending a message from any node, i, to any other node, j, is sufficiently low that the programmer sees the network as a complete connection. Zero load network latency is given by

$$T = T_d D + T_c \frac{L}{W}. \tag{1}$$

Where D is the distance (number of hops) the message must travel, L is the length of the message in bits, and W is the width of the channel in

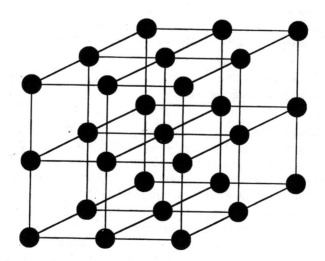

Figure 3. The J-Machine Network is a 3-D mesh or k-ary 3-cube (a 3× 3×3 mesh is shown here). Messages injected into the network at any node are routed to the destination node specified in the head of the message. All routing and flow control is performed in the network.

bits. The network is expected to have a propagation delay per stage, T_d, of 50ns and a channel cycle time, T_c of 25ns. With these times, a six word (L =216 bit) message traversing half the network diameter ($D = 24$) has a latency of 1800ns [Dally *to appear*]. An average message travels one third of the network diameter for a latency of 1350ns.

The network provides all end to end message delivery services. The sending node injects a message containing the absolute address of the destination node. The network determines the route of the message, and sequences each flit (flow-control digit) of the message over the route. Flow control is performed as required to resolve contention and match channel rates.

There is no acknowledgment, error detection, or error correction on the network channels. The network wires are all short, contained within a single physical cabinet, and operated at low impedance. The error rate of a network channel is no higher than that of a properly terminated signal in a conventional CPU.

The J-Machine network uses e-cube routing, a deterministic routing algorithm. Messages are routed one dimension at a time as illustrated in figure 4. At the sending node, the source address is subtracted from the absolute destination address to yield a relative destination address. The three coordinates of the relative destination address are contained in the three leading flits of the message. Routing is performed according to

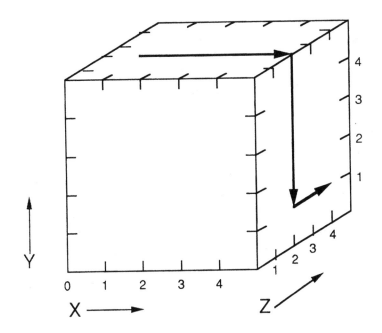

Figure 4. The J-Machine Network performs e-cube or destination tag routing. Messages are routed in each dimension in turn to the proper coordinate in that dimension. In this figure a message is routed from (1,5,2) to (5,1,4) routing first in x, then y, then z.

the relative address one coordinate at a time. After each hop the leading coordinate is adjusted to reflect the current position of the head of the message. When this coordinate reaches zero, routing is complete in that dimension. The coordinate is then stripped off and routing begins in the next dimension.

In figure 4, the relative address is (4,-4,2). The message is first routed four hops in the positive x direction. When the relative address reaches (0,-4,2) at node (5,5,2) the message is at the proper x coordinate. The x address is stripped off the message header and the message is routed four hops in the negative y direction to bring it to the proper y coordinate at (5,1,2). Two hops in the positive z direction brings the message to its destination.

To support system services operating at different priorities, two logical networks are provided, one for each priority level. The two logical networks have completely separate buffers and control state, but share the same set of physical channels between nodes. Each level does see the presence of the other except when performance degrades because a physical channel is being shared. If one network becomes completely congested, the other

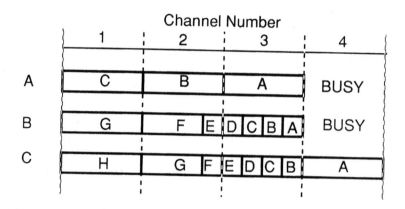

Figure 5. The J-Machine Network performs blocking flow control with four stages of queueing per node. (a) Message arrives at busy channel. (b) Message becomes compressed by queueing. (c) Channel is available; message continues advancing.

network still functions normally [Dally & Song 1987].

The network performs blocking flow control to resolve contention as shown in figure 5. When a message requires use of a channel that is busy, it is blocked. The head of the message stops and begins filling the current channel's four-stage queue. When the four stages of queueing are full, the blockage propagates back to the preceding channel. Finally, when the channel becomes available, the message continues to advance toward its destination. This flow control is performed in a manner that is provably deadlock free [Dally & Seitz 1987].

While logical channels are allocated on a message by message basis, the bidirectional wires between two nodes (shared by four logical channels) are allocated to messages at different priorities and/or traveling in opposite directions on a flit-by-flit basis. Thus contention for the bidirectional channel slows messages without blocking them.

The internal structure of a network router is illustrated in figure 6. The router consists of three levels. At the highest level, two completely separate priority routers interact only by competing for access to the physical communication channel (figure 6a). Each priority consists of six dimension routers that handle routing in the positive and negative x,y, and z dimensions (figure 6b). As described above, a message routes in a single dimension until it reaches the proper coordinate. The message then enters the next dimension in sequence.

Each dimension router (figure 6c) consists of an input switch, a comparator checker, and an output controller. Messages entering the dimen-

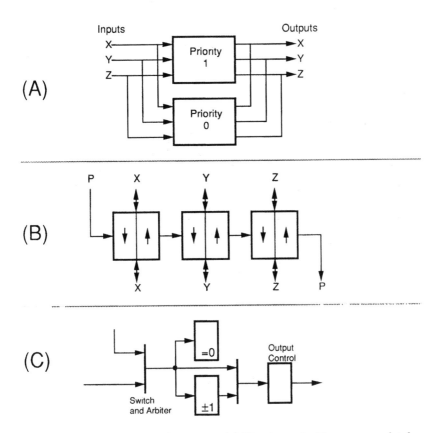

Figure 6. Block diagram of a router. (a) The two priorities are completely separate except where they share the physical channels. (b) Each priority contains three dimension data paths. (c) Each dimension data path performs switching and flow control for one dimension of routing.

sion compete with messages continuing in the dimension at a 2 to 1 switch. Once one message is granted this switch, the other input is locked out for the duration of the message. Once a message passes the input switch, it is compared to the node coordinate. If the head flit does not match the node coordinate the message continues in the current direction. Otherwise the head flit is stripped and the message is routed to the next dimension. Small output buffers are provided on both outputs. Once the head flit of the message has set up the route, subsequent flits follow from the input switch directly to the output buffer, bypassing the decrementer. Figure 7 shows a prototype routing chip that implements two dimensions of the logic shown in figure 6.

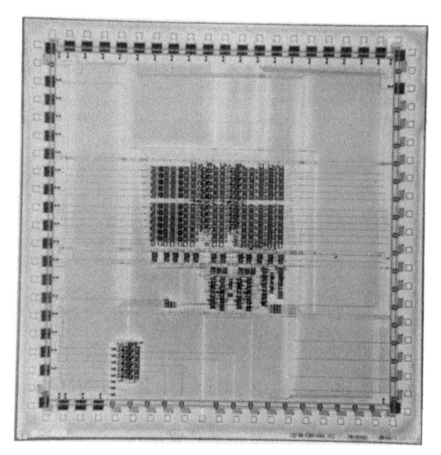

Figure 7. Photomicrograph of the network design frame, a prototype of the J-Machine router.

The Message-Driven Processor

The message-driven processor (MDP) is a 36-bit single-chip microcomputer specialized to operate efficiently in a multicomputer [Dally *et al.* 1987; Dally *et al.* 1988]. The MDP chip includes the processor, a 4K-word by 36-bit memory, and a router (figure 8). An on-chip memory controller with ECC permits local memory to be expanded up to 1M-words by adding external DRAM chips.

Other machines have combined processor, memory, and communications on a single chip [Inmos 1984; Lutz *et al.* 1984; Palmer 1986]. The MDP extends this work by providing fast, primitive mechanisms for synchronization, communication, and translation (naming) that allow the processor to efficiently support many parallel models of computation. A fast network is of little use if very large overheads are required to initiate and

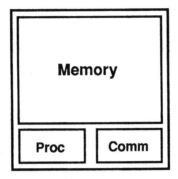

Figure 8. The Message-Driven Processor chip incorporates a 36-bit processor, a 4K-word × 36-bit memory, and a router (described above).

receive messages at the processing nodes. The MDP's mechanisms reduce the overhead of interacting with other processors over the network to levels that make fine-grain parallelism efficient.

The following mechanisms are provided:

- **Communication Mechanisms**
  - A SEND instruction injects messages into the network.
  - Messages arriving from the network are automatically buffered in a circular queue.

- **Synchronization Mechanisms**
  - A dispatch mechanism creates and schedules a task (thread of control and addressing environment) to handle each arriving message.
  - Tags for *futures* [Baker & Hewitt 1977] synchronize tasks based on data dependencies.

- **Translation**
  - ENTER and XLATE (translate) instructions make bindings between arbitrary 36-bit key and data values (ENTER) and retrieve a value given the corresponding key (XLATE).
  - Segmented memory management provides relocation and protection for data objects stored in a node's memory.

The processor is *message driven* in the sense that processing is performed in response to messages (via the dispatch mechanism). There is no receive instruction. A task is created for each arriving message to handle that message. A computation is advanced (driven) by the messages carrying tasks about the network.

User architecture

This section gives a brief overview of the user architecture. For a complete description, the user should consult [Dally *et al.* 1988].

◇ Processor state

Figure 9 shows the register set of the MDP. There are three copies of most registers. One copy holds the state of the task being executed in response to the most recent priority zero message, a second set handles priority one tasks, and the third set holds the state of the background task that executes when the node is awaiting a message. The three register sets enable the MDP to task switch between priorities without saving or restoring state.

Each priority contains four general registers, R0–R3, that can be used to hold arbitrary data. The register set is kept small to minimize the time required to save state when suspending a task. Also, the on-chip memory can be accessed in a single clock cycle. Fast local memory eliminates many of the advantages of large register sets.

Four segment registers, A0–A3, hold segment descriptors for the current addressing environment of a task. Each descriptor contains the base of the segment in local memory and its length. If the i-bit of a descriptor is set, the segment is invalid. The r-bit indicates if the segment is relocatable. The i and r bits are used to invalidate relocatable segments when the heap is compacted. The four ID registers, ID0–ID3, hold the names (virtual addresses) of the segments. The MDP translation mechanism is used to convert segment names into segment descriptors.

The instruction pointer, IP, locates the current instruction in the code segment (A0). Included in the IP are three status bits, U, F, and A . If the U (unchecked) bit is set, no type checking is performed. The F bit indicates when the machine can handle faults. A fault occurring when the F bit is set results in an unrecoverable double fault. If the A (absolute) bit is set, the IP is used as an absolute address and not as an offset into the code segment. These bits are included in the IP so the control state of the machine can be saved or restored by storing or loading a single register.

The FIP, FIR, and FOP registers are used for fault handling. When a fault or system call occurs, these registers are loaded from the current machine state. The fault handler examines the registers to correct the fault and returns from the fault by moving FIP into IP.

The QBM and QHL registers determine the memory allocated to the message queue, and the current state of the queue. The TBM register determines the memory allocated to the translation buffer.

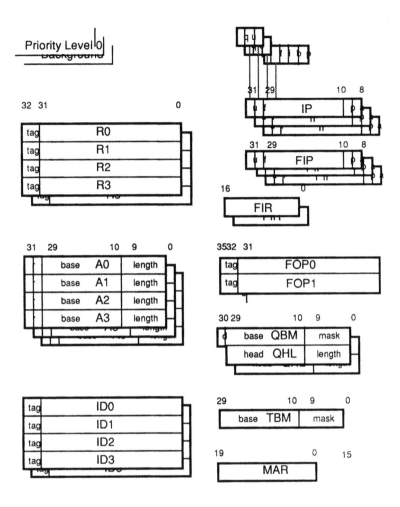

Figure 9. The MDP machine state contains three register sets, one for each of two message priorities and one for background execution.

◇ **Instruction set**

The MDP uses three address instructions as shown in figure 10. Two of the operands are restricted to be general registers (R0-R3). The remaining operand can be any register, or a memory location specified by a displacement or index into one of the segments. This instruction format was selected to give good code density—important with a small local memory—while permitting efficient access to variables stored in memory.

A synopsis of the instruction set is shown in figure 11. In addition to the usual instructions for data movement, arithmetic, and control, the

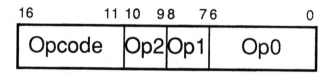

Figure 10. The MDP instruction format. Instructions are three address with two of the operands restricted to the general registers.

MDP provides instructions for sending messages over the network and for performing associative translations. If the U bit is clear, all instructions are type checked, the figure shows the admissible types for each instruction. This run-time type checking in combination with fast fault handling efficiently supports both dynamic typing and suspension of tasks when undetermined futures are touched.

Send instruction

The MDP injects messages into the network using a send instruction that transmits one or two words (at most one from memory) and optionally terminates the message. The first word of the message is interpreted by the network as an absolute node address (in x,y format) and is stripped off before delivery. The remainder of the message is transmitted without modification. A typical message send is shown in figure 12. The first instruction sends the absolute address of the destination node (contained in R0). The second instruction sends two words of data (from R1 and R2). The final instruction sends two additional words of data, one from R3, and one from memory. The use of the SENDE instruction marks the end of the message and causes it to be transmitted into the network. In a Concurrent Smalltalk message [Dally & Chien 1988], the first word is a message header, the second specifies the receiver, the third word is the selector, subsequent words contain arguments, and the final word is a continuation. This sequence executes in 4 clock cycles (200ns).

A first-in-first-out (FIFO) buffer is used to match the speed of message transmission to the network as shown in figure 13. In some cases, the MDP cannot send message words as fast as the network can transmit them. Without a buffer, *bubbles* (absence of words) would be injected into the network pipeline degrading performance. The SEND instruction loads one or two words into the buffer. When the message is complete or the eight-word buffer is full, the contents of the buffer are launched into the network.

Early in the design of the MDP we considered making a message send a single instruction that took a message template, filled in the template

Mnemonic	Operands	Name	Op	Modes	Types
General Movement and Type Instructions					
READ	Src,Rd	Move Word	$01	R,A,m,i,c	All but CFUT
WRITE	Rs,Dst	Move Word	$02	m	All
READR	Src,Rd	Read Register	$03	Register	All but CFUT
WRITER	Rs,Dst	Write Register	$04	Register	All
RTAG	Src,Rd	Read Tag	$05	R,A,m,i,c	All but CFUT
WTAG	Rs,Src,Rd	Write Tag	$06	R,A,m,i,c	All,Int
LDIP	Src	Load IP	$07	R,A,m,i,c	Ip
LDIPR	Src	Load IP from Register	$08	Register	Ip
CHECK	Rs,Src,Rd	Check Tag	$09	R,A,m,i,c	All,Int
Arithmetic and Logic Instructions					
CARRY	Rs,Src,Rd	Carry from Add	$0A	R,A,m,i,c	Int,Int
ADD	Rs,Src,Rd	Add	$0B	R,A,m,i,c	Int,Int
SUB	Rs,Src,Rd	Subtract	$0C	R,A,m,i,c	Int,Int
MULH	Rs,Src,Rd	Multiply High	$0E	R,A,m,i,c	Int,Int
MUL	Rs,Src,Rd	Multiply	$0F	R,A,m,i,c	Int,Int
ASH	Rs,Src,Rd	Arithmetic Shift	$10	R,A,m,i,c	Int,Int
LSH	Rs,Src,Rd	Logical Shift	$11	R,A,m,i,c	Int,Int
ROT	Rs,Src,Rd	Rotate	$12	R,A,m,i,c	Int,Int
AND	Rs,Src,Rd	And	$18	R,A,m,i,c	Int,Int or Bool,Bool
OR	Rs,Src,Rd	Or	$19	R,A,m,i,c	Int,Int or Bool,Bool
XOR	Rs,Src,Rd	Xor	$1A	R,A,m,i,c	Int,Int or Bool,Bool
FFB	Src,Rd	Find First Bit	$1B	R,A,m,i,c	Int
NOT	Src,Rd	Not	$1C	R,A,m,i,c	Int or Bool
NEG	Src,Rd	Negate	$1D	R,A,m,i,c	Int
LT	Rs,Src,Rd	Less Than	$20	R,A,m,i,c	Int,Int or Bool,Bool
LE	Rs,Src,Rd	Less Than or Equal	$21	R,A,m,i,c	Int,Int or Bool,Bool
GE	Rs,Src,Rd	Greater Than or Equal	$22	R,A,m,i,c	Int,Int or Bool,Bool
GT	Rs,Src,Rd	Greater Than	$23	R,A,m,i,c	Int,Int or Bool,Bool
EQUAL	Rs,Src,Rd	Equal	$24	R,A,m,i,c	Int,Int or Bool,Bool or Sym,Sym
NEQUAL	Rs,Src,Rd	Not Equal	$25	R,A,m,i,c	Int,Int or Bool,Bool or Sym,Sym
EQ	Rs,Src,Rd	Pointer Equal	$26	R,A,m,i,c	All but CFut or Fut
NEQ	Rs,Src,Rd	Pointer not Equal	$27	R,A,m,i,c	All but CFut or Fut
Network Instructions					
SEND	Src,P	Send	$34	R,A,m,i,c	All but CFut
SENDE	Src,P	Send and End	$35	R,A,m,i,c	All but CFut
SEND2	Src,Rs,P	Send 2	$36	R,A,m,i,c	All but CFut
SEND2E	Src,Rs,P	Send 2 and End	$37	R,A,m,i,c	All but CFut
Associative Lookup Table Instructions					
XLATE	Rs,Dst,C	Associative Lookup	$28	R,A	All but CFut
ENTER	Src,Rs	Associative Enter	$29	R	All but CFut,All but CFut
PROBE	Rs,Dst	Probe Associative Cache	$2D	R	All but CFut
Special Instructions					
NOP		NOP	$00		
INVAL		Invalidate	$2A		
SUSPEND		Suspend	$30		
CALL	Src	System Call	$31	R,A,m,i	Int
Branches					
BR	Src	Branch	$38	R,i	Int
BNIL	Rs,Src	Branch if NIL	$3A	R,i	All but CFut,Int
BNNIL	Rs,Src	Branch if Non-NIL	$3B	R,i	All but CFut,Int
BF	Rs,Src	Branch if False	$3C	R,i	Bool,Int
BT	Rs,Src	Branch if True	$3D	R,i	Bool,Int
BZ	Rs,Src	Branch if Zero	$3E	R,i	Int,Int
BNZ	Rs,Src	Branch if NonZero	$3F	R,i	Int,Int

Figure 11. The MDP instruction set. Instructions are included to inject messages into the network and to enter and retrieve translations.

```
SEND    R0          ; send net address
SEND2   R1,R2       ; header and receiver
SEND2E  R3,[3,A3]   ; selector and continuation - end msg.
```

Figure 12. MDP assembly code to send a 4 word message uses three variants of the SEND instruction.

using the current addressing environment, and transmitted the message. Each template entry specified one word of the message as being either a constant, the contents of a data register, or a memory reference offset from an address register (like an operand descriptor). The template approach was abandoned in favor of the simpler one or two operand SEND instruction because the template did not significantly reduce code space or execution time. A two operand SEND instruction results in code that is nearly as dense as a template and can be implemented using the same control logic used for arithmetic and logical instructions.

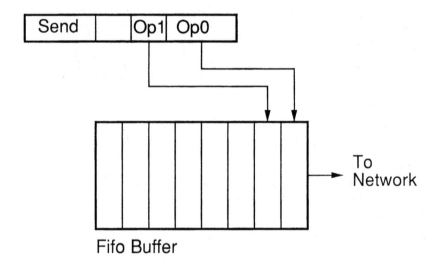

Figure 13. A FIFO buffer is used to match network speed. The SEND instruction loads message words into the buffer. When the message is complete or the buffer is full, the message is *launched*.

Previous concurrent computers have used direct-memory access or I/O channels to inject messages into the network. First an instruction sequence composed a message in memory. Direct-memory access registers or channel command words were then set up to initiate sending. Finally, the direct-memory access controller transferred the words from the memory into the network. This approach to message sending is too slow for two reasons. First, the entire message must be transferred across the memory interface twice, once to compose it in memory and a second time to transfer it into the network. Second, for very short messages, the time required to set up the direct-memory access control registers or I/O channel command words often exceeds the time to simply send the message into the network.

Message reception

The MDP maintains two message/scheduling queues (one for each priority level) in its on-chip memory. The queues are implemented as circular buffers. As shown in figure 14a, the QBM (queue base and mask) register determines the location of this queue. The QHL (queue head and length) register holds the present state of the queue.

As messages arrive over the network, they are buffered in the appropriate queue. To improve memory bandwidth, messages are enqueued by rows (figure 14b). Incoming message words are accumulated in a row buffer until the row buffer is filled or the message is complete. The row buffer is then written to memory. The head and length fields of the QHL register are added together to form the address of the queue tail and this address is *wrapped* by masking with the QBM register as shown in figure 14c. After the row is written, the queue length is incremented by four.

It is important that the queue have sufficient performance to accept words from the network at the same rate at which they arrive. Otherwise, messages would backup into the network causing congestion. The queue row buffers in combination with hardware update of queue pointers allow enqueuing to proceed using one memory cycle for each four words received. Thus a program can execute in parallel with message reception with little loss of memory bandwidth.

Providing hardware support for allocation of memory in a circular buffer on a multicomputer is analogous to the support provided for allocation of memory in push-down stacks on a uniprocessor. Each message stored in the MDP message queue represents a method activation much as each stack frame allocated on a push-down stack represents a procedure activation.

An alternative queue organization, considered early in the MDP project, allocated storage from the heap for each incoming message. This eliminated the need to copy messages when a method suspended for intermediate results. However, the cost of allocating and reclaiming storage for each message proved to be prohibitive. Instead, we settled on the preallocated circular buffer. When a method suspends for intermediate results, message arguments are copied into a context object. The overhead of this copying is small because the context must be created anyway to specify

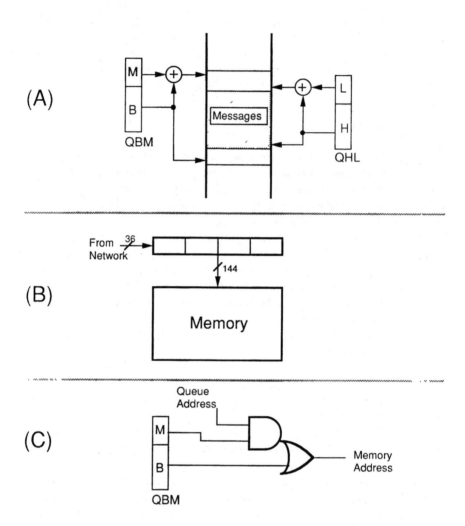

Figure 14. Message reception: (a) The QBM and QHL registers maintain a circular buffer message queue in local memory for each priority level. (b) Messages are enqueued a row (4-words) at a time to improve memory bandwidth. (c) Addresses are wrapped by masking with QBM.

a continuation and to hold live variables. The fixed buffer also provides a convenient layering. Priority zero messages are sent when the memory allocator runs out of room and priority one messages are sent when the priority zero queue fills.

Dispatch

Each message in the queues of an MDP represents a task that is ready to run. When the message reaches the head of the queue, a task is created to handle the message. At any time, the MDP is executing the task associated with the first message in the highest priority non-empty queue. If both queues are empty, the MDP is idle—namely, executing a background task. Sending a message implicitly schedules a task on the destination node. This simple two-priority scheduling mechanism removes the overhead associated with a software scheduler. More sophisticated scheduling policies may be implemented on top of this substrate.

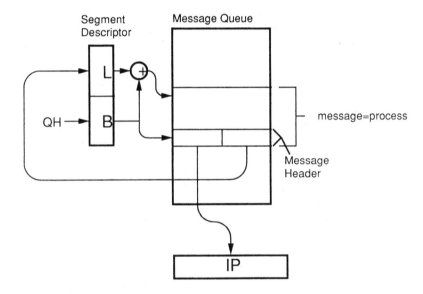

Figure 15. Message dispatch. In one clock cycle, a new task is created by (1) setting the IP to change the thread of control and (2) creating a message segment to provide the initial addressing environment.

Messages become *active* either by arriving while the node is idle or executing at a lower priority, or by being at the head of a queue when the preceding message *suspends* execution. When a message becomes active a task is created to handle it. Task creation, changing the thread of control and creating a new addressing environment, are performed in one clock cycle as shown in figure 15. Every message header contains a message *opcode* and the message *length*. The message opcode is loaded into the IP to start a new thread of control. The length field is used along with the queue head to create a message segment descriptor in **A3** that represents the initial addressing environment for the task. The message handler code may open additional segments by translating object IDs in the message into segment descriptors.

No state is saved when a task is created. If a task is preempting lower priority execution, it executes in a separate set of registers. If a task, A, becomes active when an earlier task, B, at the same priority suspends, B is responsible for saving its live state before suspending.

The dispatch mechanism is used directly to process messages requiring low latency (for example, combining and forwarding). Other messages (for example, remote procedure call) specify a handler that locates the required method (using the translation mechanism described below) and then transfers control to it.

For example, a remote procedure call message is handled by the call handler code as shown in figure 16. The execution of this handler is depicted in figure 17. The first instruction gets the method ID (offset 1 into the message segment reference by A3). The next instruction translates this method ID into a segment descriptor for the method and places this descriptor in A0. If the translate faults, because the method is not resident or the descriptor is not in the translation cache, the fault handler *fixes* the problem and reschedules the message. If the translation succeeds, the final instruction transfers control to the method. The method code may then read in arguments from the message queue. The argument object identifiers are translated to physical memory base/length pairs using the translate instruction. If the method needs space to store local state, it may create a context object. When the method has finished execution, or when it needs to wait for a reply, it executes a SUSPEND instruction passing control to the next message.

```
MOVE    [1,A3],R0       ; get method id
XLATE   R0,A0           ; translate to segment descriptor
LDIP    INITIAL_IP      ; transfer control to method
```

Figure 16. MDP assembly code for the CALL message.

An early version of the MDP had a fixed set of message handlers in microcode. An analysis of these handlers showed that their performance was limited by memory accesses. Thus there was little advantage in using microcode. The microcode was eliminated, the handlers were recoded in assembly language, and the *message opcode* was defined to be the physical address of the handler routine. This approach simplifies the control structure of the machine and gives us flexibility to redefine message handlers to fix bugs, for instrumentation (for example, to count the number of sends), and to implement new message types.

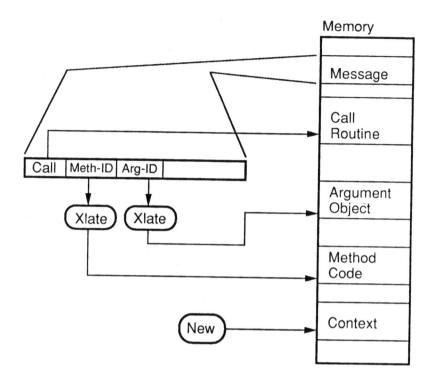

Figure 17. The CALL message invokes a method by translating the method identifier to find the code, creating a context (if necessary) to hold local state, and translating argument identifiers to locate arguments.

Synchronization with tags

Every register and memory location in the MDP includes a 4-bit tag that indicates the type of data occupying the location. The MDP uses tags for synchronization on data availability in addition to their conventional uses for dynamic typing and run-time type checking. Two tags are provided for synchronization: future, and c-future. A future tag is used to identify a named placeholder for data that is not yet available [Baker & Hewitt 1977]. Applying a strict operator to a future causes a fault. A future can, however, be copied without faulting. A c-future tag identifies a cell awaiting data. Applying any operator to a c-future causes a fault. As they are unnamed placeholders, they cannot be copied.

The c-future tag is used to suspend a task if it attempts to access data that has not yet arrived from a remote node. When a task sends a message requesting a reply, it marks the cell that will hold the reply as a c-future. Any attempt to reference the reply before it is available will fault and suspend the task. When the reply arrives, it overwrites the c-future and resumes the task if it was suspended. For example, when the task executing in Context 37 in figure 2 sends the Sum message, it marks Slot 3 of its context as a c-future. The reply message overwrites Slot 3 to indicate data presence.

The future tag is used to implement named futures as in Multilisp [Halstead 1986]. Futures are more general than c-futures in that they can be copied. However, they are much more expensive than c-futures. A memory area and a name must be allocated for each future generated.

Translation

The MDP is an experiment in unifying shared-memory and message-passing parallel computers. Shared-memory machines provide a uniform global name space (address space) that allows processing elements to access data regardless of its location. Message-passing machines perform communication and synchronization via node-to-node messages. These two concepts are not mutually exclusive. The MDP provides a virtual addressing mechanism intended to support a global name space while using an execution mechanism based on message passing.

The MDP implements a global virtual address space using a general translation mechanism. The MDP memory allows both indexed and set-associative access. By building comparators into the column multiplexer of the on-chip RAM, we are able to provide set-associative access with only a small increase in the size of the RAM's peripheral circuitry.

The translation mechanism is exposed to the programmer with the ENTER and XLATE instructions. ENTER Ra,Rb associates the contents of Ra (the key) with the contents of Rb (the data). The association is made on the full 36 bits of the key so that tags may be used to distinguish different keys. XLATE Ra,Ab looks up the data associated with the contents of Ra and stores this data in Ab. The instruction faults if the lookup *misses* or if the data is not a segment descriptor. XLATE Ra,Rb can be used to lookup other types of data. This mechanism is used by our system code to cache ID to segment descriptor (virtual to physical) translations, to cache ID to node number (virtual to physical) translations, and to cache class/selector to segment descriptor (method lookup) translations.

Tags are an integral part of our addressing mechanism. An ID may translate into a segment descriptor for a local object, or a node address for a global object. The tag allows us to distinguish these two cases and a fault provides an efficient mechanism for the test. Tags also allow us to distinguish an ID key from a class/selector key with the same bit pattern.

Most computers provide a set associative cache to accelerate translations. We have taken this mechanism and exposed it in a pair of instruc-

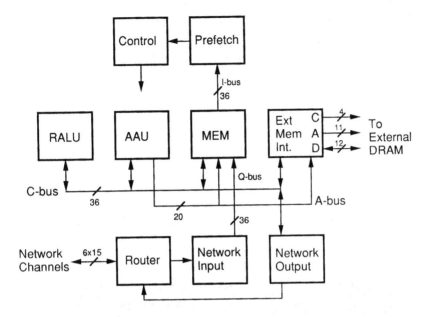

Figure 18. MDP block diagram.

tions that a systems programmer can use for any translation. Providing this general mechanism gives us the freedom to experiment with different address translation mechanisms and different uses of translation. We pay very little for this flexibility because performance is limited by the number of memory accesses that must be performed.

Micro architecture

The MDP consists of eight major subsystems as shown in Figure 17.

- **Control and Prefetch.** The controller interprets an instruction sequence and monitors the state of the queues and network to generate state sequences that control the operation of the remaining blocks.

- **RALU.** The general registers and ALU. The standard arithmetic, logical and comparison instructions are performed in this block.

- **AAU.** The address arithmetic unit generates all memory addresses for data read and write, instruction fetches, network enqueuing, and task dispatch.

- **Memory.** The memory block is a 4K × 36-bit static read/write memory. It includes input row buffers for enqueuing network data, one output row buffer for reading instructions, and comparators for implementing set associative access.

- **External Memory Interface.** This subsystem generates timing signals, multiplexed addresses, and error detection and correction to interface standard dynamic memory components to the MDP.
- **Network Input.** The network input module accepts data from the network, formats the 9-bit flits into 36-bit words, assembles words into the queue row buffers, and signals the control module to run an enqueue cycle to write the row buffer to memory.
- **Network Output.** The network output contains a FIFO send buffer, and logic to sequence messages into the network.
- **Router.** The router is described in The Network section. It handles routing and flow control to deliver messages across the network.

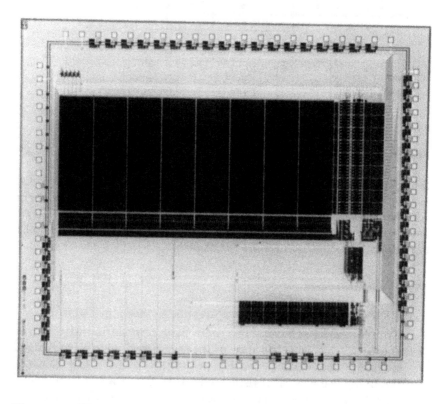

Figure 19. Photomicrograph of an MDP memory test chip.

An MDP memory test chip was implemented to test the feasibility of implementing row buffers and comparators in the peripheral circuitry of a memory [Hassoun 1988]. The chip, shown in figure 19, is a 1K-word × 37-bit (36 + parity) dynamic read/write memory organized as 256 rows of 148 bits. It is implemented in a 2μ double-metal CMOS technology. The circuitry at the bottom of the memory array includes one row buffer and the comparator and multiplexer circuitry required for set-associative access. This circuitry requires less than 10% of the total array area.

The Jellybean Operating System

JOSS is an operating system for the J-Machine that is designed to efficiently support fine-grain concurrent computation where tasks are very short (20 instructions), and data objects are very small (8 words) [Totty 1988]. It is also tailored for an environment where local computation is inexpensive. Communication bandwidth and memory capacity are the limiting resources.

JOSS consists of a collection of system calls, fault handlers, message handlers, and remote-procedure call (RPC) code. System calls and fault handlers are similar to their counterparts in sequential systems. A message handler is a physically addressed system routine that is executed each time a particular type of message is received.

Abstractions

All JOSS abstractions are constructed from objects. System objects that are handled specially include the following:

- A *Method* is an object containing code. The system performs hierarchical distribution of methods and caches methods locally on each node.
- A *Context* is an object containing the state of a task. The system provides special allocation and deallocation of contexts to speed task creation and provides services for suspending and resuming contexts.
- A *Class* is an object that defines the properties of a specific class (or type) of object.

All computation takes place by sending messages between objects. Consider, for example, sending the message increment to the object counter. The *class* of counter is accessed to look up a *method* to be executed in response to an increment message. A task is then created to execute the code in this method. If the task must suspend its execution to await a message, it saves its state in a *context* object before relinquishing the processor.

Global object namespace

Most message-passing multicomputers have a separate memory address space on each node. Nodes interact only by sending messages between processes [Su *et al.* 1985]. A partitioned address space makes it difficult to construct distributed data structures [Dally 1987a], limits the size of a processes address space to the memory size of a node, and requires entire processes to be relocated to balance memory use. Also, because storage on remote nodes cannot be directly accessed, these machines replicate the operating system and application code on each node.

JOSS overcomes these limitations by providing a global object namespace. All data and code are stored in objects. Each object is assigned a unique global ID. Given an object ID, a task on any node can reference the corresponding object. Objects are free to migrate between nodes. Accesses to objects are bounds checked and protected. The system supports distributed objects [Dally & Chien 1988]. Large distributed objects are implemented as a collection of small constituent objects accessed via a single ID. A one to many translation service prevents the single ID from becoming a bottleneck.

A global object namespace provides many of the advantages of a shared memory multicomputer while retaining the scalability of a message-passing machine. Distributed data structures are easily constructed by linking together objects on different nodes using IDs. Processes have an address space limited only by the size of an ID. Also, code need not be replicated on each node because it can be referenced through its ID.

To support this global object space, JOSS provides (1) services to allocate and deallocate objects, and (2) services to translate object names (IDs) into object locations. Both functions are layered with one component providing the service locally within a node and a second component extending the service across the network.

Objects are created locally by allocating a contiguous region of memory off the top of the heap and assigning a unique name (ID) to the object. The global ID space is partitioned so that nodes may assign unique global IDs autonomously. Object creation is extended across the network by providing a NEW message that creates an object of a specified class on a remote node and returns its ID.

Objects are deleted by marking. Their storage is reclaimed by a compactor that copies objects down in memory to fill unused holes. As segments are relocated during compaction, the local translation table is updated and all segment registers are invalidated. Compaction is very fast because local memory is small and fast and because the operation is completely local—no communication is required.

Given an object ID, an object is located in two steps. First, a distributed global name table is accessed to find the node on which the object is resident. A message is then sent to the node where the ID is translated into a segment descriptor for the object. The segment descriptor for an object is strictly local information. Thus, each node may relocate objects locally without interacting with any other nodes.

Accessing the global name table involves a message send. To avoid this indirection, nodes may maintain hints as to the present location of a remote object. The global name table must be consulted, however, if the hint becomes stale or is discarded to free up space.

In a fine-grain multicomputer, segment-based memory management is preferred to paging because fine-grain relocation and protection is required. The ability to compact all of memory in a few milliseconds eliminates concerns over external fragmentation. Internal fragmentation is an issue. Objects are small and must be protected and relocated individually. To support fine-grain computation, a paging system would either have to have a very small page size (8 words), or sacrifice protection by packing unrelated objects into the same page.

Task management

To make use of a machine with tens of thousands of processing nodes one must divide the problem at hand into many small tasks. A typical fine-grain task executes only 20 instructions before exiting or suspending to await a message. Conventional operating systems are poorly suited to manage such fine-grain tasks. They require thousands of instructions to create a task, and hundreds of instructions to context switch between tasks.

JOSS provides a set of low-overhead task management services that efficiently support fine-grain tasks. Using the hardware task scheduling and dispatching mechanisms of the MDP, creating a task, suspending a task, resuming a task, and destroying a task each require fewer than ten instructions. This inexpensive task management is provided without sacrificing protection. Each task executes in its own addressing environment.

Context allocation is much faster than object allocation. Fixed size contexts are allocated off a list of free contexts. After waiting for all pending replies, the context storage and name are recycled by appending them to the list of free contexts. A strict request/reply protocol insures that there are no dangling references to a recycled context name.

Low overhead task switching in JOSS depends on three features of the design.

1   The MDP dispatch mechanism to eliminates scheduler overhead.
2   Contexts to hold the state of a task are allocated quickly.
3   The small MDP register set limits the state to be saved on suspension to five words.

Input/output

No special support is provided in JOSS for input and output. I/O devices are considered to be non-relocatable objects. These I/O objects respond to messages to transfer information in and out of the system. I/O devices are protected by restricting distribution of their object names. A disk object, for example, may be protected by allowing it to be referenced only through file objects.

Conclusion

The J-Machine is a general purpose parallel computer. It provides general mechanisms for communication, synchronization, and translation rather than hardwiring mechanisms for a specific model of computation. These mechanisms efficiently support many proposed models of computation. Using these mechanisms, the overhead of creating a task on a remote node is reduced to a few microseconds. This low overhead permits concurrency to be exploited at a fine-grain size.

The J-Machine provides a substrate on which actor systems can be built. Creating an actor on a remote node, sending a message to an actor to request a service, and dispatching an actor to execute a script in response to a message can all be performed with a few microseconds overhead. The global address space of the machine can be used to name actors and continuations.

The J-Machine is designed to make efficient use of silicon and wiring area. Each message driven processing node is a *jellybean* part. It can be fabricated in the same technology used to manufacture existing commodity semiconductor parts such as DRAMs. The network is designed to make efficient use of wires so the machine can be packaged densely—with processing nodes consuming most of the volume. There are no large wiring channels.

At the time of this writing (November 1989) the logical design of the J-Machine is complete. Message-level, instruction-level, register-transfer-level, and logic-level simulators have been built to test the J-Machine design and these simulators have been validated on a large test suite of programs. Prototype versions of the operating system and CST compiler are operational. The logic design is currently being sized to meet performance goals. We expect to complete this sizing by the end of 1989, have working chips by summer 1990, and have a prototype J-Machine system running by the end of 1990.

The following MIT students and staff have contributed to the work described here: Linda Chao, Andrew Chien, Stuart Fiske, Soha Hassoun, Waldemar Horwat, Michael Larivee, Rich Lethin, John Keen, Peter Nuth, Paul Song, Brian Totty, Michael Noakes, and Scott Wills. I thank Tom Knight, Gerry Sussman, Steve Ward, Dave Gifford, Tom Leighton, and Carl Hewitt of MIT, Chuck Seitz and Bill Athas of Caltech, and Paul Carrick, Greg Fyler, Mark Vestrich, Justin Rattner, and George Cox of Intel Corporation for many valuable suggestions,

References

Agha, Gul A. [1986], *Actors: A Model of Concurrent Computation in Distributed Systems*, MIT Press, Cambridge, MA.

Ametek Computer Research Division [1987], *Series 2010 Product Description.*

Athas, W. C., and C. L. Seitz [1986], "Cantor Language Report," Report 5232–TR–86, Department of Computer Science, California Institute of Technology.

Baker, H., and C. Hewitt [1977], "The Incremental Garbage Collection of Processes," *ACM Conference on AI and Programming Languages*, Rochester, New York, pp. 55-59.

BBN Advanced Computers, Inc. [1986], "Butterfly Parallel Processor Overview," BBN Report no. 6148.

Dally, William J. [1987a], *A VLSI Architecture for Concurrent Data Structures*, Kluwer, Hingham, MA.

Dally, William J. [1987b], "Wire Efficient VLSI Multiprocessor Communication Networks," *Proceedings Stanford Conference on Advanced Research in VLSI*, edited by Paul Losleben, MIT Press, Cambridge, MA, pp. 391-415.

Dally, William J. [1987c], "Concurrent Computer Architecture," *Proceedings of Symposium on Parallel Computations and Their Impact on Mechanics.*

Dally, William J. *et al.* [1987], "Architecture of a Message-Driven Processor," *Proceedings of the 14th ACM/IEEE Symposium on Computer Architecture*, pp. 189-196.

Dally, William J., and Charles L. Seitz [1986], "The Torus Routing Chip," *J. Distributed Systems*, vol. 1, no. 3, pp. 187-196.

Dally, William J., and Charles l. Seitz [1987], " Deadlock-Free Message Routing in Multiprocessor Interconnection Networks," *IEEE Transactions on Computers*, vol. C-36, no. 5, pp. 547-553.

Dally, William J., and Paul Song [1987], "Design of a Self-Timed VLSI Multicomputer Communication Controller," *Proceedings International Conference on Computer Design, ICCD-87*, pp. 230-234.

Dally, William J. [1988a], "Concurrent Data Structures," Chapter 7 in *Message-Passing Concurrent Computers: Their Architecture and Programming*, C. L. Seitz *et. al.*, Addison-Wesley, Reading, MA, publication expected.

Dally, W.J. [1988b], "Fine-Grain Concurrent Computers," *Proceedings 3rd Symposium on Hypercube Concurrent Computers and Applications*, ACM.

comments, and advice.

The research described in this chapter was supported in part by the Defense Advanced Research Projects Agency under contracts N00014-87-K-0825 and N00014-85-K-0124 and in part by a National Science Foundation Presidential Young Investigator Award with matching funds from General Electric Corporation and International Business Machines Corporation.

Dally, William J. [to appear], "Performance Analysis of k-ary n-cube Interconnection Networks," *IEEE Transactions on Computers.*

Dally, William J. *et al.* [1988], "Message-Driven Processor Architecture, Version 11," Report AIM-1069, Artificial Intelligence Laboratory, Massachusetts Institute of Technology, Cambridge, MA.

Dally, W.J., and A. A. Chien [1988], "Object Oriented Concurrent Programming in CST," *Proc.* 3rd *Symposium on Hypercube Concurrent Computers and Applications*, ACM.

Dennis, Jack B. [1980], "Data Flow Supercomputers," *IEEE Computer*, vol. 13, no. 11, pp. 48-56,.

Flaig, Charles, M. [1987], "VLSI Mesh Routing Systems," Report 5241:TR:87, Department of Computer Science, California Institute of Technology.

Halstead, Robert H. [1986], "Parallel Symbolic Computation," *IEEE Computer*, vol. 19, no. 8, pp. 35-43.

Hassoun, S. [1988], "Memory Design for a Message-Driven Processor," MIT VLSI Memo.

Hoare, C.A.R. [1987], "Communicating Sequential Processes," *Comm. ACM*, vol. 21, no. 8, pp. 666-677.

Inmos Limited [1984], "IMS T424 Reference Manual," Order No. 72 TRN 006 00, Bristol, United Kingdom.

Intel Scientific Computers [1985], "iPSC User's Guide," Order No. 175455-001, Santa Clara, CA.

Kermani, Parviz, and Leonard Kleinrock [1979], "Virtual Cut-Through: A New Computer Communication Switching Technique," *Computer Networks*, vol. 3., pp. 267-286.

Knight, Tom, and Alex Krymm [1987], "Self Terminating Low-Voltage Swing CMOS Output Driver," *Proceedings Custom Integrated Circuits Conference.*

Ligtenberg, Adriaan [1987], Presentation at *Princeton Workshop on Algorithm, Architecture, and Technology Issues in Models of Concurrent Computation.*

Lutz, C., *et. al.* [1984], "Design of the Mosaic Element," *Proceedings MIT Conference on Advanced Research in VLSI*, Artech Books, pp. 1-10.

Mead, Carver A., and Lynn A. Conway [1980], *Introduction to VLSI Systems*, Addison-Wesley, Reading, Massachusetts.

Palmer, John F. [1986], "The NCUBE Family of Parallel Supercomputers," *Proceedings IEEE International Conference on Computer Design, ICCD-86*, p. 107.

Pfister, G. F. *et. al.* [1985], "The IBM Research Parallel Processor Prototype (RP3): Introduction and Architecture," *Proceedings International Conference on Parallel Processing, ICPP*, pp. 764-771.

Seitz, Charles L. [1980], "System Timing," reprinted in *Introduction to VLSI Systems*, C. A. Mead and L. A. Conway, Addison-Wesley, Ch. 7.

Seitz, Charles L., *et al.* [1985], "The Hypercube Communications Chip," Display File 5182:DF:85, Department of Computer Science, California Institute of Technology.

Seitz, Charles L. [1985], "The Cosmic Cube," *Comm. ACM*, vol. 28, no. 1, pp. 22-33.

Seitz, Charles L., William C. Athas, William J. Dally [1988], Reese Faucette, Alain J. Martin, Sven Mattisson, Craig S. Steele, and Wen-King Su, *Message-Passing Concurrent Computers: Their Architecture and Programming,*
Addison-Wesley, publication expected 1988.

Su, Wen-King, Reese Faucette, and Charles L. Seitz [1985], "C Programmer's Guide to the Cosmic Cube," Report 5203:TR:85, Department of Computer Science, California Institute of Technology.

Totty, Brian [1988], "An Operating Environment for the Jellybean Machine," Report AIM-1070, Artificial Intelligence Laboratory, Massachusetts Institute of Technology, Cambridge, MA.

22

During the past ten years, there have been many designs for parallel computers, yet there are only a few ideas about how to exploit the latent power in those designs. One approach, long among Hewitt's research foci, involves Actors. Another approach, popular in the Japanese Fifth Generation Computer Project, centers on Flat Guarded Horn Clauses. On the surface, these approaches seem quite different, for Actors have their roots in message passing, while Flat Guarded Horn Clauses were inspired by logic programming in general and Prolog in particular. Nevertheless, Hewitt and Agha demonstrate that the Actor Formalism and Flat Guarded Horn Clauses have much in common. This suggests that one of them might be used to implement the other and raises the question of which way around is more efficient.

Guarded Horn Clause Languages: Are they Deductive and Logical?

Carl Hewitt
Gul Agha

A family of concurrent logic languages using a notation based on Horn clauses has been defined. These languages include *Parlog* [Clark & Gregory 1986], *Concurrent Prolog* [Shapiro 1987], and *Guarded Horn Clauses* [Ueda 1986]. A Horn clause consists of an atomic formula called the *head*, and a set of atomic formulae, called the *body*, with a "$\Leftarrow$" between the head and the body, and "&"s between the atomic formulae in the body, for example,

$$H \Leftarrow B_1 \ \& \ \ldots \ \& \ B_n$$

where an atomic formula has the usual meaning of predicate symbol applied to some functions. A Horn clause is taken to be universally quantified over all the variables that occur in the terms of its atomic formulae,

$$(\forall X, Y, Z)\, H \Leftarrow B_1 \ \& \ \ldots \ \& \ B_n$$

where X, Y, and Z are the variables occurring in H and the B_i.

Strictly speaking, a *guarded* Horn clause, $H : - G_1, \ldots, G_m | B_1, \ldots, B_n$ is not really a Horn clause since it involves the *commit* operator "|". Here, as before, H is the *head* and $B_1, \ldots, B_n$ is the *body*. In addition, $G_1, \ldots, G_m$ are the *guards*. The procedural interpretation is that if all atoms in the guard succeed, then a system is *committed* to the clause in the sense that no other clause will be tried for proving the goal in question; thus, that goal will succeed if and only if all the atoms in the body succeed. For example, in Guarded Horn Clause, (*GHC*) the recursive part of a quicksort could be written as follows [Ueda 1986]:

```
qsort([Pivot | Xs], Ys0, Ys2) :- true |
        part(Xs, Pivot, Small, Large),
```

```
qsort(Small, Ys0, [Pivot | Ys1]),
qsort(Large, Ys1, Ys2).
```

where **part** partitions the Xs into Small and Large sublists containing elements that are smaller and larger than the pivot, respectively.

In addition, these languages have *flat* versions which disallow recursion in a guard. In other words, only system predicates such as $N > 0$, as opposed to user-defined predicates, are allowed in guards. Thus, in Flat GHC (*FGHC*) there is no unification of variables in a goal with non-variables during head or guard evaluation. This means that variable occurrences in heads and guards have what is called "input mode." Flatness further simplifies evaluation and allows efficient implementation.

We will use *FGHC* notation for our examples but the discussion applies equally well to other guarded Horn clause languages (*GHCLs*).

Alternative Interpretations

In this section, we consider some alternative interpretations of *FGHC*. Later on, we will consider some alternative approaches to base-level implementation languages. Just as we did above, the developers of *FGHC* have traditionally given a *backward chaining* interpretation in which the head of a clause H is considered as a goal to be satisfied, the guards G1, G2, ..., Gm as preconditions that must be satisfied before subgoals can be processed, and B1, B2, ..., Bn as subgoals that must be proved to establish H. In backward chaining, the system hypothesizes a conclusion and uses the rules provided to find the hypothesis supporting facts.

However, it may be more natural to interpret *FGHC* in terms of constraint-driven or directed *forward chaining*, in which the head H of a clause is interpreted as a constraint to be satisfied, the guards G1, G2, ..., Gm as preconditions that must be satisfied before other constraints can be processed, and B1, B2, ..., Bn are interpreted as further constraints propagated from H.[1] In forward chaining, the system uses known facts to deduce new ones. In *GHCLs*, facts are represented by clauses.

The forward-chaining interpretation fits GHCLs better because GHCLs do *not* actually search for alternative ways to satisfy a goal. Instead, they just elaborate one possible solution to the constraints imposed by H. In *GHCLs*, once a guard is satisfied, the system is committed to that clause, and even if the clause fails to yield a value that contributes to an overall solution, no other clause will be tried. By contrast, *Prolog backtracks*, that

---

[1] We use the term constraint-driven in a very restricted sense. *GHCLs* are not constraint-oriented languages with the same generality as [Steele 1980]. The term *directed* is appropriate since the "goal" clause constrains which new facts are to be used in deriving other facts.

is, it undoes some variable bindings and tries to find other values for them that can satisfy the entire set of clauses.

The forward chaining interpretation of *GHCLs* can also be seen to have a *message-passing* interpretation, whereby given a clause

```
H :- G1, G2, ..., Gm | B1, B2, ..., Bn
```

the head H matches incoming messages, the guard atoms G1, ..., Gm must all be satisfied before the clause can commit, and the body atoms B1, ..., Bn all send messages after the clause commits. Under this interpretation, *GHCLs* are very similar to actor languages.

For each guarded Horn clause, there is a corresponding Horn clause obtained by ignoring the commit operator, and this Horn clause has a legitimate declarative reading in logic. Nevertheless, the relationship between the Horn clause logical semantics and computations of *GHCLs'* programs remains to be characterized.

Arrival Order Nondeterminism

The execution of *GHCLs* involves an exponentially increasing number of assumptions about the order in which messages arrive. We can illustrate this issue with a simple example, a bank account that responds to Deposit, Withdraw and BalanceQuery messages. This account can be represented by a variable, say Acct1Messages.

```
account(Acct1Messages, 100, Clark)
```

which means that the unification variable Acct1Messages is the message stream for an account with balance 100 and owner Clark. The implementation of a shared account would consist of a clause for each kind of message that might be processed by a bank account. Thus a withdrawal message might be handled in *FGHC* using two clauses, one for the case where there is enough money in the account to cover the request and the second for the case where there is not. Note that [Head | Tail] represents a list with head Head and tail Tail, and [ ] denotes the empty list. The clauses may look something like this:

```
account([withdraw(Amount, Response) | MoreMessages],
              Balance, Owner) :-
  /* withdraw Amount into the account */
  )=(Balance, Amount) |
          /* Balance is greater than request */
```

```
    plus(Balance, NewBalance, Amount),
     /* Bind NewBalance */
    Response =
      withdrawalReceipt(Amount, Owner, NewBalance),
   /* Bind Response to a receipt */
  account(MoreMessages, NewBalance, Owner).
   /* ask account to process MoreMessages */
   /*   with Balance NewBalance         */
account([withdraw(Amount, Response) | MoreMessages],
              Balance, Owner) :-
 /* withdraw Amount from the account */
 ⟨(Balance, Amount) |
  /* Balance is less than request */
    Response = OverDraftNotice(Amount, Owner, Balance),
     /* Bind Response to an overdraft notice */
    account(MoreMessages, Balance, Owner).
    /* ask account to process MoreMessages */
    /*   keeping the same Balance and Owner */
```

If two users named Ueda and Shapiro need to share common access to Clark's account, then a stream merge must be explicitly declared. The following expressions declare the variables `UedaAcct1Messages` and `ShapiroAcct1Messages` such that when these two message streams are merged, the result is `Acct1Messages`:

```
merge(UedaMessages, ShapiroMessages, Acct1Messages)

UedaMessages = [UedaAcct1Messages | MoreUedaMessages]

ShapiroMessages = [ShapiroAcct1Messages |
                   MoreShapiroMessages]
```

where the implementation of `merge` uses a standard technique for stream merges described in Shapiro [1987]. Now Ueda and Shapiro can concurrently communicate with the account using their respective message streams. If Ueda attempts to withdraw 70 using

```
UedaAcct1Messages = [withdraw(70, UedaResponse)]
```

while concurrently Shapiro attempts to withdraw 80 using

```
ShapiroAcct1Messages = [withdraw(80, ShapiroResponse)]
```

then one of them is going to get an overdraft notice.

Let us try to state the possibilities in a logical framework. Let T_0 be the theory which is derived from the Horn clauses that are obtained by ignoring the commit operators in the above expressions. In order to logically derive from T_0 the values of UedaResponse and ShapiroResponse, some additional assumptions must be made. Making these assumptions, we can obtain new theories T_1 and T_2 by taking the union of T_0 and, respectively, the first assumption or the second assumption below:

```
{Acct1Messages = [withdraw(70, UedaResponse),
                  withdraw(80, ShapiroResponse)]}
{Acct1Messages = [withdraw(80, ShapiroResponse),
                  withdraw(70, UedaResponse)]}
```

The assumptions made to derive T_1 and T_2 are called *arrival order assumptions*. The requirement for such assumptions is an inherent characteristic of concurrent systems, where it is often the case that subsequent behavior can be critically affected by the order of arrival of communications.

Now in T_1, we can deduce

```
UedaResponse = withdrawalReceipt(70, Clark, 30)

ShapiroResponse = OverDraftNotice(80, Clark, 30)
```

which states that Ueda gets his money while Shapiro gets an overdraft notice, whereas in T_2, we can deduce

```
ShapiroResponse = withdrawalReceipt(80, Clark, 20)

UedaResponse = OverDraftNotice(70, Clark, 20)
```

which states that Ueda instead gets an overdraft notice while Shapiro gets his money.

The above discussion can be formalized in a metatheory which records the assumptions that need to be made in order to account for possible *FGHC* computations. We define a relation $\prec_c$ to represent the notion of an *immediate computational extension* of a theory.

$$(T_0 \prec_c T) \Leftrightarrow \{(T \equiv T_1) \vee (T \equiv T_2)\}.$$

More generally a notion *computational extension*, $(\prec_c^*)$ can be defined simply as the transitive closure of $\prec_c$ relation. In other words, a computational extension is a theory which includes assumptions that cannot be inferred from a logical reading of a given set of axioms but have instead been added by the computational system.

Because arrival order assumptions represent interleavings of messages (or, alternately the order in which the constraints are propagated), the number of these assumptions may grow exponentially with time. The need for these assumptions is not dependent on whether one is using a backward chaining or a forward chaining interpretation of *FGHC*. Furthermore, the *computationally extends* relation does not provide a basis for choosing between the possibilities and therefore does not serve as an adequate logical semantics for *FGHC*.

Notice that the two theories have contradictory assumptions. Because a logical deductive system cannot allow two contradictory statements to be inferred from the same set of facts, it is our conjecture that there is no logical deductive system such that the computations of a *GHCL* program correspond exactly to the provable theorems.

The computational extension of a theory is equivalent to augmenting the original theory with a set of axioms specifying the order in which constraints are to be processed, or in the message-passing interpretation, the order in which messages arrive. The computational system provides this extension.

In the context of *GHCLs*, an *event* is the binding of the head and the guards of a clause (that is, a commitment). The *activation order* is the link between events caused by constraint propagation (or alternately, goal reduction). The *arrival order* is the order of messages on a stream; in the case of shared streams, such as the one in Clark's account in the example above, this order is determined by the merge. The order of events in any concurrent system is a partial order obtained by the transitive closure of the arrival and activation orders.

Early work in actor semantics showed that the laws of parallel processing [Hewitt & Baker 1977] imply realizability of events in a concurrent system in a global time [Clinger 1981]. Global time is a retroactive construct and dependent on the frame of reference; it is constrained by the fact that it may not violate the transitive closure of arrival and activation orders. This limitation also applies to computational extensions. In actor semantics, a history consistent with the initial configuration is obtained by the transitive closure of the *possible transition* relation [Agha 1986].

Complete Merges

The merge described above need not be *complete*.[2] If Ueda keeps sending messages, Shapiro's message may never be received. The assumption that communications sent will eventually be received is similar to the notion that a function when called will actually be invoked. The *guarantee of*

---

[2]Complete merges are often called *fair* in literature. We prefer to use the term "complete" because it is more in accord with standard mathematical terminology. The term *complete merge* is more appropriate because there are a number of other definitions of *fairness*.

delivery of communications in actor systems means that such merges are complete.

The guarantee of delivery simplifies reasoning about programs. For example, it can allow us to reason about convergence in the computation of a function despite the possible presence of other diverging invocations of the function. In practical terms, the guarantee implies that a continuously functioning operating system can be brought down gracefully [Agha 1986]

One consequence of the guarantee of delivery is *unbounded nondeterminism* in the results of the execution of a program. For example, a program can be written which will produce one of an infinite number of integers and which is nevertheless guaranteed to stop. Unbounded nondeterminism cannot be modeled by choice-point nondeterminism with a finite number of choices at any given time. This limitation is a simple consequence of Konig's lemma.

For example, using (nondeterministic) Turing machines, it is impossible to specify a program which may have one of an infinite number of possible results and which is nevertheless guaranteed to halt. In a model of concurrency which assumes the guarantee of delivery (or complete merges), it is possible to write such programs.

The usual interpretation of *GHCLs* is based on choice-point nondeterminism between clauses that match a given set of constraints. Using this interpretation, a complete merge cannot be defined. Shapiro [1987] provides two possible implementations of complete merge in *Concurrent Prolog*. However, these implementations assume that the underlying Concurrent Prolog machine is "weakly stable," a property which in turn cannot be defined in *Concurrent Prolog*.

Unbounded nondeterminism has been handled in actor semantics by defining a potentially infinite transition relation, called the *subsequent transition* [Agha 1986]. The subsequent transition relates a given configuration to the first configuration along any path (defined by the possibility relation) in which all communications pending in the given configuration have been processed. Such a relation can also provide an operational model of *GHCLs* with complete merges.

Comparison with Actors

We briefly compare programming in *FGHC* with programming in a core actor language. While the actor metaphor differs considerably, both the code and its execution have a rather similar functionality. The difference is that actors have the characteristics of object-based languages, whereas object-based languages have to be simulated on top of a language such as *FGHC*.

We provide the code for the shared account discussed above in an actor base-level implementation language named *Acore* [Manning 1986], an expression-oriented actor language based on the actor execution model in [Agha 1986]. Each actor has a number of message handlers (indicated by => below); one of these handlers will be applicable to the incoming communication. Note that there is or-concurrency between the message handlers and and-concurrency between different commands within a handler. There is also and-concurrency in the selection of a *pending communication* which is to be processed "next," where the notion of "next" is relative to a frame of reference.[3]

History-sensitive behavior in actors is captured by the concept of *replacement behavior*. The replacement process is fully pipelined to provide maximal concurrency. In *Acore*, if the replacement behavior can be denoted by a change in the parameters of the same behavior definition, a *"ready"* command is used. The command provides new values for the parameters. As soon as these values have been determined, the actor is ready to accept the next message.

The code for a communication handler to process withdrawals in an account is as follows:[4]

```
(DefName Account
 (Behavior [balance owner]
  [(Withdraw[amount])
  (If ()= balance amount)
      Withdraw amount requested
   (Then
    (Let {[newBalance = (− balance amount)]}
    let   newBalance be balance less withdrawal
    (Ready [balance = newBalance])
     Account is ready for the next message
    (Return (WithdrawalReceipt amount owner newBalance))))
   (Else
    (Ready)
    Account is ready for the next message
    (Complain (OverDraftNotice amount owner balance))))))))
```

The interactions corresponding to those discussed above for *FGHC* are as follows:

```
(DefName Acct1 (Account 1000 Clark))
```

---

[3] A pending communication is a communication which has been sent but not processed.

[4] A communication handler is also called a "method" in object-oriented languages.

declares a new identifier named `Acct1` and binds it to a new account with balance 100 and owner `Clark`. Again suppose that two users named Ueda and Shapiro need to share access to Clark's account. The following commands give them the ability to communicate with `Acct1`:

```
(Send Ueda Acct1)
(Send Shapiro Acct1)
```

Now if Ueda attempts to withdraw 70 from `Acct1` using the command (`Withdraw Acct1 70`), while concurrently Shapiro attempts to withdraw 80, then the operation of the account will be serialized so that one of them will get a withdrawal receipt and the other an overdraft complaint.

Conclusions

Code and interactions in *FGHC* are very similar in structure and results to those in actor base-level implementation languages, as the above example shows in detail. This is rather surprising and confirms the fact that a *GHCL* such as *FGHC* has the requisite structure and functionality to serve as a base-level implementation interface between concurrent hardware and software, much in the same way as actor languages can.

   The closeness of *FGHC* to actor core languages raises the issue of how their semantics are related. A denotational semantics for actor languages based on system configurations has been defined. Actor Theory provides a meaning for the scripts of actor programming languages, obtained recursively by analyzing the script as a system of communicating actors [Theriault 1983; Agha 1986]. On the other hand, to our knowledge no formal semantics has yet been proposed for *FGHC*. It is true that some types of reasoning about *FGHC* can be carried out using a declarative reading of the programs. Such reasoning is in fact similar in structure to the concept of *serializer induction* in actors which permits the inference of static properties of a program.

   Another interesting issue is the relative efficiency of implementing the two languages. Because *FGHC* is based on the use of unification variables to implement local changes, it may well be that actor-based systems are more efficient than *FGHC*. Furthermore, it appears that *FGHC* can be implemented using actors with the same efficiency as any other implementation method.

   The base-level language of the classic von Neumann architecture provides instructions to perform a sequence of fetch-compute-store cycles. This implies that von Neumann architectures and their programming languages such as COBOL and FORTRAN are both inherently sequential; and in fact, as we all know, they fit together very well. Unfortunately, the enormously long sequences of fetch-compute-store cycles imply a tremendous traffic between the processor and memory, and so the link between them becomes a chief limitation on the speed of execution. One of the objectives of new base-level languages, or to use Shapiro's terminology, high-level machine languages, is to break this bottleneck.

A number of base-level languages have been proposed besides *GHCLs* and actor languages. Some of these languages, such as vector and array processing languages—which provide the model for machines like the Cray—are only slight extensions of the basic von Neumann model. Others, such as the *SIMD* languages, are quite special purpose, though elegant and powerful for those applications that can fully use them. Actor languages and guarded Horn clause languages, on the other hand, are general purpose base-level languages for implementing concurrent systems. Research on the relationship between these two kinds of languages should continue to be fruitful.

References

Agha, G. [1986], *Actors: A Model of Concurrent Computation in Distributed Systems*, MIT Press, Cambridge, MA.

Clark, K. J., and S. Gregory [1986], "Parlog: parallel programming in logic," *ACM TOPLAS*, vol. 8, no. 1, pp. 1-49.

Clinger, W. D. [1981], *Foundations of Actor Semantics*, Report AI-TR-633, Artificial Intelligence Laboratory, Massachusetts Institute of Technology, Cambridge, MA.

Hewitt, C., and H. Baker [1977], "Laws for communicating parallel processes," *Congress Proceedings, IFIP*, pp. 987-992.

Manning, Carl R. [1986], "Acore: an actor core language reference manual," Internal Memo, MIT Message Passing Semantics Group Design Note: 7.

Shapiro, E. [1987], "A subset of concurrent prolog and its interpreter," in *Concurrent Prolog: Collected Papers*, MIT Press, Cambridge, MA, pp. 27-83.

Steele, G. L. [1980], "The Definition and Implementation of a Computer Programming Language Based on Constraints," Report AI-TR-595, Artificial Intelligence Laboratory, Massachusetts Institute of Technology, Cambridge, MA.

The first author's work has been supported by DARPA under ONR contract number N00014-85-K-0124. The second author's work has been supported in part by DARPA under ONR contract number N00014-86-K-0310.

The authors have benefitted from discussions with Joseph Goguen. In particular, the standard backward-chaining interpretation in the Alternative Interpretations section has benefitted from a write-up by Goguen.

Theriault, D. [1983], "Issues in the Design and Implementation of Act2," Report AI-TR-728, Artificial Intelligence Laboratory, Massachusetts Institute of Technology, Cambridge, MA.

Ueda, K. [1986], *Guarded Horn Clauses*, Ph.D. Thesis, University of Tokyo.

23

Groups of people working together effectively exhibit enviable characteristics. Individuals work concurrently and largely asynchronously. No individual needs to have a good understanding of how others do their job. As a group, they operate continuously in spite of individual failures, and they cope with inconsistent information. Somehow differences are resolved through negotiation.

Inspired by these characteristics, Hewitt has made them the cornerstones of what he calls open systems. In this chapter, he turns the research around and uses the characteristics of open systems, made more precise by their transit through computer science, to take a fresh view of organizational work. The ultimate objective is the development of better ideas for harnessing human and computer systems together.

Organizations are Open Systems

Carl E. Hewitt

In this chapter, we discuss the nature of organizational work from an open systems perspective. Coping with the conflicting, inconsistent, and partial information is one of the major challenges in organizational information systems. Negotiation is the organizational activity of human and computer systems for generating, sound, relevant, and reliable information as a basis of action-taking. Within negotiation, logical reasoning takes place within relatively small, coherent modules called microtheories. In general the microtheories will be inconsistent with one another. Negotiation makes use of debate and negotiation to deal with conflicts and inconsistencies between microtheories.

Organizations

Organizational work can take place in an automobile with a mobile telephone, in the anteroom of a lecture hall, or at a networked personal computer. There is no special place where organizational work takes place. Of course, the situation including place, time, and participants can materially affect the work. All organizational work takes place within a particular concrete situation. The point that we want to make here is that there is no *special* place where organizational work has to take place.

Later, we discuss how organizational work is situated in *particular concrete* space and time, and how the situation provides an important part of the context in which the work is done.

We will take *organizational work* to be information processing which is done to coordinate all the work that an organization does with the exception of direct manipulation of physical objects. The organizations in which organizational work takes place are "going concerns" in the sense of Everett Hughes [1971]. For example, it includes the processing of beliefs, goals, and mutual commitments as well as the development and management of responsibilities, policies, tasks, transactions, projects, and procedures. However, the processes just mentioned are involved in most kinds of work. Organizational work is specialized by excluding *robotics*. Robotics involves information processing directly involved in physical production, transformation, transportation, servicing, or consumption of physical objects.

Organizational work is situated social action in the sense that it is the action produced by participants at particular times and places. However, we need to extend the usual notion of situated social actions to encompass the social actions of computer systems in their interactions with other computer systems as well as the interactions of computer systems with human participants.

Open Systems

Organizations are inherently open systems because of the requirement to communicate with operational divisions as well as the external world in the task of coordinating the work of the organization. In all nontrivial cases, the communication necessary for coordination takes place asynchronously. Unplanned dynamic adaptation and accommodation is required in organizational information systems to meet the unplanned changing needs of coordination, because the execution of any plan requires articulation, change, and adjustment.

Open systems deal with large quantities of diverse information and exploit massive concurrency. They can be characterized by the following fundamental characteristics:

- **Concurrency.** Open systems are composed of numerous components such as workstations, databases, and networks. To handle the simultaneous influx of information from many outside sources, these components must process information concurrently.

- **Asynchrony.** There are two sources of asynchrony in open systems. First, because the behavior of the environment is not necessarily predictable by the system itself, new information may enter the system at any time requiring it to operate asynchronously with the outside world. Second, the components are physically separated; distance prohibits them from acting synchronously. Any attempt to clock all the components synchronously would result in an enormous performance degradation because the clocks would have to be slowed down by orders of magnitude in order to maintain synchronization.

- **Decentralized Control.** In an open system, a centralized decision maker would become a serious bottleneck. Furthermore, because of communications asynchrony and unreliability, a controlling agent could never have complete, up-to-date information on the state of the system. Therefore, control must be distributed throughout the system so local decisions can be made close to where they are needed.
- **Inconsistent Information.** Information from outside the system or even from different parts of the same system may turn out to be inconsistent. Therefore, decisions must be made by the components of an open system by considering whatever evidence is currently available.
- **Arms-Length Relationships.** The components of an open system have *arms-length relationships*. The internal operation, organization, and state of one computational agent may be unknown and unavailable to another agent for reasons of privacy or outage of communications. Information should be passed by explicit communication between agents to conserve energy and maintain security. This ensures that each component can be kept simple because it only needs to keep track of its own state and its interfaces to other agents.
- **Continuous Operation.** Open systems must be reliable. They must be designed so that failures of individual components can be accommodated by operating components while the failed components are repaired or replaced.

Concurrency

The underlying concurrent basis of operation enables negotiation to react dynamically to asynchronous input and in many cases makes the results indeterminate.

Asynchronous input

Concurrent systems differ from Turing Machines in that they allow asynchronous communication from the external environment to affect ongoing operations. Sequential systems deal with this problem as a kind of "interrupt" in which they "switch tasks." Organizational information systems rarely have all the material at hand needed to make an important decision. Information which is known in advance to be required arrives asynchronously as the decision making proceeds and is often incomplete. Unanticipated information can arrive at any time in the process and affect the outcome even though it arrives quite late. For instance, an unanticipated story in the *Wall Street Journal* the morning of a corporate board meeting to give final approval to a merger has been known to kill or delay a deal.

Indeterminacy

Concurrent systems are inherently indeterminate. The indeterminacy of concurrent systems does not stem from invoking a random element such as flipping a coin. Instead, it results from the indeterminate arrival order of inputs to system components.

In general, it is not possible to know ahead of time that a concurrent system will make a decision by a certain time. For example, a jury might not return a verdict and the judge might have to declare a mistrial.[1]

Conflicting Information and Contradictory Beliefs

Conflicting sources of information and inconsistent beliefs are a staple of life in organizational information systems. This partly results from dealing with differing external organizations that retain their own autonomy and belief structures.

Inconsistencies inevitably result from the measurements and observations made on complicated physical systems. Higher level abstractions are used to attempt to construct a consistent description of parts of the environment in which the organization operates. For example, a firm's earnings might be labeled "provisional" and then "subject to audit." But even after being published in the annual report, they might later have to be "restated." In this case, "provisional," "subject to audit," and "restated" are attempts to construct a consistent description from conflicting information about earnings.

Whatever consistency exists among the beliefs within an organization, is *constructed* and *negotiated* by the participants. In the case of reported earnings, the chief executive officer, finance department, board of directors, and regulatory authorities play important roles in constructing and negotiating the financial reports.

Any belief concerning an organization or its environment is subject to internal and external challenges. Organizations must efficiently take action and make decisions in the face of conflicting information and contradictory beliefs. How they do so is a fundamental consideration in the foundations of organizational information systems.

Conflicting information and contradictory beliefs are engendered by the enormous interconnectivity and interdependence of knowledge that comes from multiple sources and viewpoints. This interconnectivity makes it impossible to separate knowledge of the organization's affairs into independent modules. The knowledge of any physical aspect has extensive

---

[1] Agha [1986] provides an excellent exposition of the nature of a mathematical model of concurrent computation and its differences with classical nondeterministic Turing Machine based theories.

spatiotemporal, causal, terminological, evidential, and *communicative* connections with other aspects of the organization's affairs. The interconnectivity generates an enormous network of knowledge which is inherently inconsistent because of the multiple sources of actors making contributions at different times and places.

By way of example, suppose that in the middle of 1990 an organization undertakes to consider its knowledge of sales currently in progress for that year for the New England region. In such a situation, there is an enormous amount of information about other pieces of information. The following considerations show a small part of the enormous interconnectivity of knowledge:

- **Spatiotemporal interconnectivity.** The organization has a great deal of knowledge about the history of sales in the New England region in the first few months of 1990, including how the sales were generated and recorded. In addition, it has sales projections of what will happen in the remainder of the year.

- **Causal interconnectivity.** The marketing department believes that increased advertising is causing sales to go up. On the other hand, the sales department believes that the increased sales commissions are the real reason that sales are increasing.

- **Terminological interconnectivity.** Some of the sales are really barter agreements with uncertain cash value. Do the barter agreements qualify as sales?

- **Evidential interconnectivity.** The accounting department fears that sales might really not be increasing because many of the products could be returned because of a new 30 day free trial offer. It does not believe that the evidence presented shows that sales are increasing.

- **Communicative interconnectivity.** The organization consists of a community of actors operating concurrently, asynchronously, and nondeterministically. The asynchronous communications engender interconnectivity that defies any complete description of the global state of the organization at any particular point in time.

Conflicting information and contradictory beliefs are an inherent part of organization work that must be explicitly addressed in any foundation for organizational information systems.

Negotiation

Negotiation is the organizational activity of humans and computers for generating sound, relevant, and reliable information as a basis for decision and action within the constraints of allowable resources [Davis 1971]. It provides an arena in which beliefs and proposals can be gathered, analyzed, and debated. Part of negotiation is to provide a record of the decision-making process which can later be referenced.

Negotiation is inherently reflective in that beliefs, goals, plans, requests, commitments, etc. exist as objects that can be explicitly mentioned and manipulated in the ongoing process.

Negotiation does not make external decisions or take external actions *per se*. Instead, it is the process that informs the decision-making process. Each instance of negotiation begins with *preconceptions* handed down through traditions and culture that constitute the initial process but which are open to future testing and evolution. Decision-making criteria, such as preferences in predicted outcomes, are included in this knowledge base. For example, increased profitability is preferable to decreased profitability. Also, increased market share is preferable to decreased market share. Conflicts between these preferences can be negotiated [Strauss 1978]. In addition, preferences can arise as a result of conflict. Negotiating conflict can bring the negotiating process itself into question as part of the evaluative criteria of how to proceed—which can itself change the quality of conflict among the participants [Gerson 1976].

Changing the price of a product can affect both its profitability and market share in conflicting ways, as shown in figure 1.

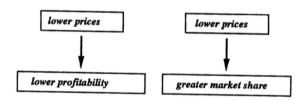

Figure 1. Conflicting effects of lowering prices.

Market research and internal cost analysis can help model the effects of lower prices on profitability and market share. The sales and financial divisions can have very different views on the subject. They need to organize their respective positions, including counterarguments to opposing views. The cost effectiveness of generating new information by market research and new product development can be considered using negotiation.

All this activity takes place within a context that sets the time frame for the decision-making process. Sometimes the time frames can be very short, and, at the same time, the decision could be very important to the organization. Consider the sudden appearance of a new product which is drastically undercutting prices and demands a quick decision whether or not to cut prices. It is extremely common for a "case" to occur in negotiation that has to be settled promptly but which has implications for more general issues. A company may develop a general vacation policy because a request by a particular employee for certain vacation privileges has to be granted or refused [March & Simon 1958]. Negotiation takes place within action-taking and decision-making situations. It occurs at a particular place and time within a community of actors (both human and computer) that communicate with one another in a historical context involving information gathering, discussion, and debate.

Rationale

The *rationale* is the record of the decision-making and action-taking process, including which organization is responsible for dealing with problems, responses, and questions for the decision made or the action taken. This is one way in which responsibility is assessed for the decisions and actions taken.

The record can include justifications for various courses of action such as:

- **Predicted beneficial results.** Better targeted advertising will increase sales.

- **Policies guiding conduct.** Products may not be returned for credit more than 30 days after sale.

- **Reasons tied to specific institutional roles or processes.** A corporation may not be able to enter the computer business because of a consent decree that it has signed.

- **Precedent.** The organization might always have taken Patriot's day as a holiday. Precedent may seem like a weak rationale. However, deciding according to precedent in the absence of strong alternatives has the consequences of predictability, stability, and improvement in the general coherence between decided cases.

Negotiation is an inherently self-reflective process in that the process by which information is gathered, organized, compared, and presented is subject to evaluation, debate, and evolution within the organization. Thus the debate is not just about whether or not to lower prices, but also about the beliefs used in the decision and the process used by the organization to decide whether or not to lower them.

Cooperation

Negotiation is not a magical way for an organization to make "correct" decisions. Instead, negotiation is concerned with the reasonableness with which information is gathered, organized, compared, and presented. It addresses the question "How can the decision-making process be improved?"

instead of "What is the right decision?" Efforts to find the basis for "correct" decision making before the organization goes to work are fruitless. Attempting to critique a particular course of action to be chosen by an organization would involve us in the very *same* activities that are embodied in negotiation.

In general, negotiation will involve cooperation among the participant actors in the organization. The participants' investment in the process of information gathering, evaluation, debate, and presentation helps to produce the consensus. Every participant knows that their views need to be put forth in order to be considered and balanced against the others. In general, those actors whose authority and responsibility is most affected by the choice of action must at least give their passive cooperation. Pre-existing organizational precedents and traditions are influential in the exact way a choice of action is made. Even if the course of action taken is not the participants' first choice, the execution of the decision can be tailored to reflect the views and concerns that have been uncovered in negotiation. Also, recompense can often be offered to disgruntled parties by making allowances in other concurrent decision making within the organization.

Task performance assessment

Assessing how well the task was performed or how the performance might be improved can be quite problematical. Each performance is unique. It must be assessed in terms of quality of analysis, planning, and execution, as well as the appropriate balance of these activities. Performance assessment is subject to severe limitations in available knowledge about realistic alternatives because of unknown interactions between details in a performance. For example, the timing of an advertising campaign can affect the results of sales.

Microtheories as Tools in Negotiation

A microtheory is a relatively small, idealized, mathematical model that embodies a model of some physical system. A microtheory should be internally consistent and clearly demarcated. Any modification of a microtheory is a new microtheory. Special relativity, evolution by natural selection, a spread sheet model of a company's projected sales, and a Spice simulation of an integrated circuit are examples of microtheories. Microtheories are simple because they have simple axiomatizations. The physical system being modeled may be enormously complicated. We expect that computer systems will require hundreds of thousands of microtheories in order to participate effectively in organizational work.

In general, negotiation deals with *conflicting* microtheories that cannot always be measured against one another in a pointwise fashion. In negotiation, debate is conducted between rival microtheories which are compared with one another without assuming that there is a fixed common standard of reference. We do not assume the existence of a global axiomatic theory of the world which gradually becomes more complete as more microtheories are debugged and introduced. Instead, we propose to deal with each problematical concrete situation, using negotiation and debate among the available overlapping and possibly conflicting microtheories that are adapted to the situation at hand. For many purposes in negotiation, it is preferable to work with microtheories which are small and oversimplified, rather than large and full of caveats and conditions [Star 1983].

Logical deduction is a powerful tool for working *within* a microtheory. The strengths of logical deduction include:

- **Well understood.** Logical deduction is a very well understood and characterized process. Rigorous model theories exist for many logics, including the predicate calculus, intuitionistic logics, and modal logics.

- **Validity locally decidable.** An important goal of logical proofs is that that their correctness should be mechanically decidable from the proof inscription. In this way, the situation of proof creation can be distinct from the subsequent situations of proof-checking. In order to be algorithmic, the proof checking process cannot require making any observations or consulting any external sources of information. Consequently, all of the premises of each proof step as to place, time, objects, etc. must be explicit. In effect, a *situational closure* must be taken for each deductive step. Proof checking proceeds in a closed world in which the axioms and rules of deductive inference have been laid out explicitly beforehand. Ray Reiter has developed closure axioms that justify the default rules used in relational data bases as logical deductions. Similarly, the circumscription technique proposed by John McCarthy is a closure operator on sets of axioms which results in stronger, more complete axiom sets.

- **Belief constraining.** Logical deduction deals with issues about logically entailed relationships among beliefs. If an actor believes P and (P implies Q), then it is constrained to believe Q. Similarly, if an actor believes (P implies Q) and entertains the goal of believing Q, then it can entertain the goal of believing P. Examples below illustrate how both of these techniques can be valuable in evolving and managing belief structures.

Let's consider a simple concrete example to illustrate the use of logical deduction in organizational decision making. Commercial enterprises sometimes put their merchandise "on sale" to increase sales. Often this is done

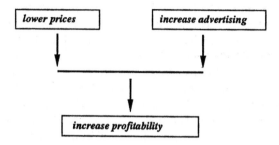

Figure 2. Profitable-sale microtheory.

by cutting prices and increasing advertising. Consider the microtheory shown in figure 2 which we will call `profitable-sale`.

We will use the above deduction rule as a *microtheory* to explore how deduction can be used in organizational decision making. Microtheories are simply very small, partial, logical theories. They are kept small and partial to avoid the problems of entanglement by interconnectivity discussed above.

We take a very general view of deduction. Deductive proofs are tree structures in which a computer can mechanically decide whether or not a step is valid just by inspecting the premises and conclusion of the deduction.

A microtheory should be internally consistent. Ideally, there should even be good arguments for its consistency. If an inconsistency is discovered in a microtheory, then a repair can be attempted. Sometimes the repair attempt will fail in the face of well-justified contrary beliefs. This can be dealt with by splitting the microtheory into more specialized microtheories.

Contradictory knowledge

Microtheories are often inconsistent with one another. The financial department might argue that lowering prices brings in less revenue than would be lost by the expense of increased advertising, therefore profitability could very well decrease. We could express this model in the microtheory shown in figure 3 which we will call `unprofitable-sale`.

Our second microtheory directly contradicts the first. Proofs are not convincing in a contradictory knowledge base in which we can prove both that the profitability will increase and that it will decrease. Therefore, we confine logical deduction to within microtheories that are presumed to be consistent, and use negotiation to mediate contradictory microtheories.

Counterarguments

The tree-structured, locally decidable character of logical deductive proof cannot take audiences into account. The `profitable-sale` microtheory

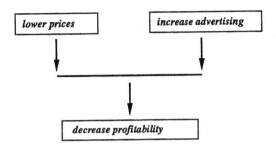

Figure 3. Unprofitable-sale microtheory.

cannot take into account the counterargument of the **unprofitable-sale** microtheory. We will use extradeductive techniques such as negotiation and debate to deal with the inconsistencies and conflicts between microtheories.

The microtheory might in fact be a *meta* microtheory that has as part of its content axioms about other microtheories as in the work of Richard Weyhrauch. Such meta-microtheories can be very useful. Negotiation often involves debate between multiple, conflicting meta-microtheories [Wimsatt 1985]. The meta-microtheories arise in the course of debate about the reasonableness and applicability of previously introduced microtheories. Often the meta-microtheories are also inconsistent with one another.

For example, the microtheory shown in figure 4 takes into account the limited inventory as well as the decreased profitability and increased profitability microtheories to conclude that the sale would be of low profitability because of the limited inventory. On the other hand, the meta-microtheory in figure 4 concludes that desirable inventory clearance would take place as a result of the sale.

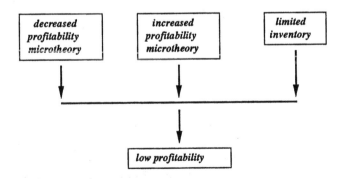

Figure 4. Limited-inventory microtheory.

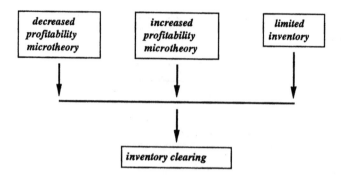

Figure 5. Inventory-clearance microtheory.

Context

The validity of a deductive proof is supposed to be timeless and acontextual. If it is valid at all, then it is supposed to be valid for all times and places. The timeless and acontextual character of logical deduction is a tremendous advantage in separating the proof creation situation from the proof checking context. However, applicability of an empirical deductive rule, such as the `profitable-sale` rule, is problematical in many situations. For example, the rule might be challenged on the grounds that the conditions under which it worked in the past no longer hold because the market is saturated. To meet this constraint, we take the extradeductive step of dynamically adapting rules to the context at hand. Challenges to the applicability of the deductive rule may need to be entertained and debated [Gasser 1984]. For example, the `profitable-sale` rule might need to be further adapted by specifying that the increased advertising be presented to appeal to new customer needs which are not saturated. Operations like these contribute episodic precedents, which are material for the synthesis of new microtheories.

Indeterminacy

Decisions need to be made on the basis of the arrival order of communications. The arrival order may not be determined by complete knowledge of system state, structure, and inputs. Consequently, the arrival order may not be able to be deduced. For example, decisions on whether or not to honor a withdrawal request for an account depend on the arrival order of withdrawals and deposits. The order of arrival of communications can drastically affect overall outcomes.

Description versus action

Deduction can only *describe* possible actions and their possible effects, it cannot be used to take action. Suppose that an organization wants to decide how to increase sales on March 1, 1990. The optimistic sales rule can be instantiated as shown in figure 6.

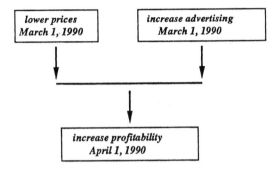

Figure 6. Optimistic sales rule.

However, the above deduction does not take any action. Instead, it raises useful questions depending on the viewpoint from which it is considered. Considered from a viewpoint after March 1, 1990, it raises questions of the history of what happened. Logical deductions are useful in drawing further conclusions about the relationship of historical beliefs. On the other hand, considered from a viewpoint before March 1, 1990, it raises questions about predicting the future. Deductions can be very useful in analyzing the logical relations among the beliefs about the future.

The validity of a deduction is supposed to be decided mechanically, solely from the premises and conclusion. In this way, the situation of proof checking can be separated from the situation of proof generation so that proof generation and proof checking can take place in completely separate situations. In addition, the proof is supposed to be checkable solely from the text of the proof. In this way, proofs can be checked by multiple actors at different times and places adding to the confidence in the deductions. The requirements on proof means that the validity of the above deductions is independent of whether they are made after March 1, 1990 and thus concern the past, or are made before March 1, 1990 and concern the future.

Logical reasoning can be used before the happening to *predict* what might happen. It can be used after the happening to *analyze* what did happen. In either case, logical proof does not control the action taken.

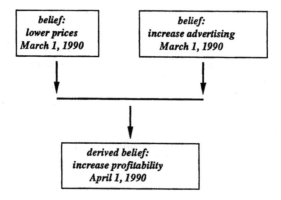

Figure 7. Belief in increased profitability.

Constraints among beliefs

Deduction is a powerful tool for propagating constraints among the beliefs and goals of a microtheory. For example, the belief that prices are lower and that advertising is increased on March 1, 1990 can be used to derive the belief that profitability is increased on April 1, 1990. This is shown in figure 7.

Furthermore, the goal of increased profitability on March 1, 1990 can be used to derive the subgoals of lowering prices and increasing advertising. This is shown in figure 8.

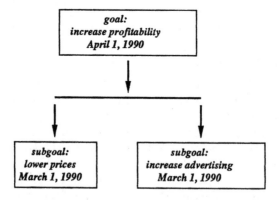

Figure 8. Deriving subgoals on price and advertising.

New beliefs and subgoals derived by deduction in microtheories are useful to actor communities in conducting debates about the results and applicability of microtheories such as the `profitable-sale` and `unprofitable-sale`

microtheories.   Decisions can then be made based on the results of the
debates.

Recommendations and policy

Deduction can be used to derive recommendations and to draw conclusions
from policies, as shown in figure 9.

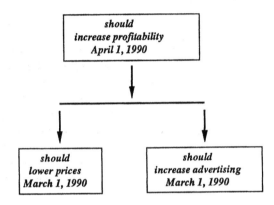

Figure 9. Deriving recommendations and conclusions.

However, the recommendations and implications of policy that are produced by deduction do not by themselves determine actions. In general,
just as beliefs will be contradictory, recommendations for action will be
in conflict. This is shown in figure 10. The inconsistency among the microtheories results in inconsistent recommendations based on them.

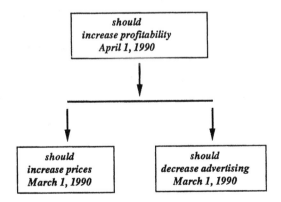

Figure 10. Conflicting recommendations for action.

Conclusions

Foundations for organizational information systems are still in a primitive state. The enterprise is inherently interdisciplinary and requires contributions from anthropology, artificial intelligence, cognitive science, computer science, economics, management science, philosophy of science, psychology, and sociology. It also needs research on indicators and models, and on needs and organizational factors. Foundations are needed in which to describe their function, structure, and principles of operation, and which can serve as the basis for managing, evolving, and designing better organizational information systems.

The effort to find the basis for decisions before the organization goes to work is meaningless. It is to forget the very purpose for which the organizational decision-making processes have been fashioned. Negotiation plays a central role in the operation of any organizational information system. Negotiation allows for the the consideration of multiple inconsistent microtheories. Logical deduction plays a role in analyzing the constraints among beliefs and goals within microtheories. Negotiation is manifested by situated action at the particular time and place that a choice of action is made. Negotiation specifically includes the social actions of computer systems.

The contrast between correct decision making and the actual organizational processes does not make sense. Negotiation has a systematicity of its own. It serves to test constantly whether the organization has come to see new differences or similarities. Negotiation process is a situated process: the outside socio-physical world interacts with the organizational processes at particular places and times of the process that results in a particular decision. In general, the decision is not determined by these interactions. Nor can it be said that the result of negotiation is too uncertain to obtain satisfactory choices in organizational course of action. The compulsion of adherence to negotiation is clear; any fundamental breakdown directly impairs the organization.

Negotiation is the only kind of system which will work when parts of the organization do not agree completely and represent different responsibilities. The meaning of the words in the rules, policies, and goals change to receive the meaning which organization gives to them in negotiation.

Many of the ideas in this chapter have been developed jointly with the members of the MIT Message Passing Semantics Group and the Tremont Research Institute. Fanya Montalvo, Elihu M. Gerson, and Susan Leigh Star contributed important ideas and helped with the organization. The negotiation task analysis example was developed jointly with David Kirsh. Tom Reinhardt greatly helped with the presentation. The ideas in this chapter are related to previous work in distributed artificial intelligence. In particular, we build on the work of Corkhill and Lesser [1981] and Corkhill [1979]. The approach here

References

Agha, G. [1986], *Actors: A Model of Concurrent Computation in Distributed Systems*, MIT Press, Cambridge, MA.

Becker, Howard S. [1960], "Notes on the Concept of Commitment," *American Journal of Sociology*, vol. 66, pp. 32–40.

Corkill, Daniel D. [1979], "Hierarchical planning in a distributed environment," in *Proceedings of the Sixth International Joint Conference on Artificial Intelligence*, pp. 168–175.

Davis, Kenneth C. [1971], *Discretionary Justice*, University of Illinois Press.

Davis, R., and R. Smith, [1981], "Negotiation as a Metaphor for Distributed Problem Solving," Report AI-TR-624, Artificial Intelligence Laboratory, Massachusetts Institute of Technology, Cambridge, MA.

Gasser, Leslie George [1984], "The Social Dynamics of Routine Computer Use in Complex Organizations," Ph.D. Thesis, University of California at Irvine.

Gerson, Elihu M. [1976], "On the Quality of Life," *American Sociological Review*, vol. 41, pp. 793–806.

Hughes, Everett C. [1971], "Going Concerns: the Study of American Institutions," in *The Sociological Eye: Selected Papers*, Aldine-Atherton.

Lesser, Victor, and Daniel D. Corkill [1981], "Functionally accurate, cooperative distributed systems," *IEEE Transactions on Systems, Man, and Cybernetics*, vol. SMC-11, no. 1, pp. 81–96.

March, and Simon [1958], *Organizations*, John Wiley and Sons, New York, NY.

Star, S. L. [1983], "Simplification in Scientific Work: An Example from Neuroscience Research," *Social Studies of Science*, vol. 13, no. 2, pp. 205–228.

Strauss, Anselm [1978], *Negotiations*, Jossey-Bass.

Wimsatt, William [1985], "False Models as Means to Truer Theories," in *Systematics Symposium on Neutral Models in Biology*, Chicago, IL.

---

differs from Davis and Smith [1981] in that organizational mechanisms are emphasized instead of market mechanisms.

This chapter describes research done at the Artificial Intelligence Laboratory of the Massachusetts Institute of Technology. Major support for the research reported in this chapter was provided by the System Development Foundation. Major support for other related work in the Artificial Intelligence Laboratory is provided, in part, by the Advanced Research Projects Agency of the Department of Defense under Office of Naval Research contract N0014-80-C-0505. I would like to thank Carl York, and Charles Smith for their support and encouragement.

Bibliography

Abarbanel, R. M. [1984], "Protein Structural Knowledge Engineering," Ph.D. Thesis, University of California, San Francisco.

Abelson, H., M. Halfant, J. Katzenelson, and G. J. Sussman [1988], "The Lisp Experience," *Annual Review of Computer Science*, vol 3., Annual Reviews, Palo Alto, pp. 167–195.

Abelson, H., and G. J. Sussman [1987], "The Dynamicist's Workbench I: Automatic Preparation of Numerical Experiments," Report AIM–955, Artificial Intelligence Laboratory, Massachusetts Institute of Technology, Cambridge, MA. pp. 116–121, Detroit, MI.

Abelson, Harold, and Gerald Jay Sussman [1985], *Structure and Interpretation of Computer Programs*, MIT Press, Cambridge, MA.

Abney, S. [1986], "A new model of natural language parsing," unpublished M.S. Thesis, Department of Linguistics and Philosophy, Massachusetts Institute of Technology, Cambridge, MA.

Abramowitz, M., and I. Stegun [1965], *Handbook of Mathematical Functions*, Dover Publications.

Agha, Gul A. [1986], *Actors: A Model of Concurrent Computation in Distributed Systems*, MIT Press, Cambridge, MA.

Aho, A., and J. Ullman [1972], *The Theory of Parsing, Translation, and Compiling*, vol. 1, New York, Prentice-Hall.

Akmajian A., and F. Heny [1975], *An Introduction to the Principles of Transformational SyntaxF*, MIT Press, Cambridge, MA.

Alberts, B. M. (chairman) [1988], *Report of the Committee on Mapping and Sequencing the Human Genome,* Natl. Research Council for Natl./Academy of Sciences, Natl. Acad. Press, Washington, DC.

Allen, J., and J. Koomen [1983], "Planning Using a Temporal World Model," *Proceedings of the Eighth IJCAI*

Ametek Computer Research Division [1987], *Series 2010 Product Description.*

Applegate, J., M. Douglas, Y. Gürsel, P. Hunter, C. Seitz, G. J. Sussman [1985], "A digital orrery," *IEEE Trans. on Computers.*

Athas, W. C., and C. L. Seitz [1986], "Cantor Language Report," Report 5232–TR–86, Department of Computer Science, California Institute of Technology.

Atkins, B. T., J. Kegl, and B. Levin [1986], "Explicit and Implicit Information in Dictionaries," Lexicon Project Working Papers 12, Center for Cognitive Science, MIT, Cambridge, MA.

Attardi, G., and M. Simi [1981], "Semantics of Inheritance and Attributions in the Description System Omega," *Proceedings of IJCAI 81*, Vancouver, BC, Canada.

BBN Advanced Computers, Inc. [1986], "Butterfly Parallel Processor Overview," BBN Report no. 6148.

Baase, S. [1978], *Computer Algorithms*, Addison-Wesley.

Backus, J. [1978], "Can Programming be Liberated from the von Neumann Style? A Functional Style and its Algebra of Programs," *Communications of the ACM*, vol. 21, no. 8, pp. 613-641.

Baker, H., and C. Hewitt [1977], "The Incremental Garbage Collection of Processes," *ACM Conference on AI and Programming Languages*, Rochester, New York, pp. 55-59.

Barber, G. [1982], "Office Semantics," Ph.D. Thesis, Artificial Intelligence Laboratory, Massachusetts Institute of Technology, Cambridge, MA.

Barron, A. R., and R. L. Barron [1988], "Statistical learning networks: a unifying view," In *Symposium on the Interface: Statistics and Computing Science*, Reston, Virginia.

Batcher, K. E. [1968], "Sorting Networks and Their Applications," *Proceedings AFIPS FJCC,* vol. 32, pp. 307-314.

Batcher, K. E. [1976], "The Flip Network in STARAN," *Proceedings, International Conference on Parallel Processing,* pp. 65-71.

Bathe, K. [1982], *Finite Element Procedures in Engineering Analysis*, Prentice Hall.

Battini, C., M. Lenzerini, and S. B. Navathe [1986], "A Comparative Analysis of Methodologies for Database Schema Integration," *ACM Computing Survey* vol. 18, no. 4, pp. 323-364.

Becker, Howard S. [1960], "Notes on the Concept of Commitment," *American Journal of Sociology*, vol. 66, pp. 32–40.

Belletti, A., and L. Rizzi [1988], "Psych-Verbs and Θ-Theory," *Natural Language and Linguistic Theory*, vol. 6, pp. 291-352.

Benacerraf, Paul [1965], "What Numbers Could Not Be," *The Philosophical Review*, vol. LXXIV, no. 1, pp. 47–73.

Benes, V. E. [1965], *Mathematical Theory of Connecting Networks and Telephone Traffic*, Academic, New York.

Bertero, M., T. Poggio, and V. Torre [1988], "Ill-posed problems in early vision," *Proceedings of the IEEE*, vol. 76, pp. 869–889.

Bhuyan, L. N., and D. P. Agrawal [1984], "Generalized Hypercube and Hyperbus Structures for a Computer Network," *IEEE Transactions on Computers*, vol. C-33, no. 4, pp. 323-333.

Biggerstaff, T. [1989], "Design recovery for maintenance and reuse," *IEEE Computer*, vol. 22, no. 7, pp. 36–49.

Birnbaum, L., M. Flowers, R. McGuire [1980], "Towards an AI Model of Argumentation," in *Proceedings of AAAI*, pp. 313-315, Stanford, CA.

Bledsoe, W. W. [1977], "Non-resolution theorem Proving," *Artificial Intelligence*, vol. 9, pp. 1-35.

Bley-Vroman, Robert [1988], personal correspondence.

Bobrow, D., D. Fogelsong, and M. Miller [1987], "Definition Groups: Making Sources into First-Class Objects," in [Wegner & Shriver 1987] pp. 129-146.

Boehm, B. W. [1988], "A Spiral Model of Software Development and Enhancement," *IEEE Computer*, pp. 61-72.

Bose, A. G., and K. N. Stevens [1965], *Introductory Network Theory*, Harper and Row, New York.

Boyer, Robert S., and J. Struther Moore [1979], "A Computational Logic," *ACM Monograph Series*.

Brachman, R. J., and H. J. Levesque [1984], "The Tractability of Subsumption in Frame-Based Description Languages," *Proceedings of the National Conference on Artificial Intelligence*.

Brachman, R. J., and H. J. Levesque [1985], *Readings in Knowledge Representation*, Morgan Kaufman Publishers, Inc., Los Altos, CA.

Brachman, R. J., and J. G. Schmolze [1985], "An Overview of the KL-ONE Knowledge Representation System," *Cognitive Science*,

Bradley, M., T. Smith, R. Lathrop, D. Livingston, and T. Webster [1987], "Consensus Topography in the ATP Binding Site of the Simian Virus 40 and Polyomavirus Large Tumor Antigens," *Proc. Natl. Acad. Sciences USA*, vol. 84, pp. 4026–4030.

Breuer, M. A., and A. Friedman [1976], *A Diagnosis and Reliable Design of Digital Systems*, Computer Science Press, Rockville, MD.

Brodie, M., and J. Mylopoulos [1986], *On Knowledge Base Management Systems*, Springer-Verlag, New York.

Broomhead, D. S., and D. Lowe [1988], "Multivariable functional interpolation and adaptive networks," *Complex Systems*, vol. 2, pp. 321–355.

Brotsky, D. C. [1984], "An algorithm for parsing flow graphs," M.S. Thesis, Report AI-TR-704, Artificial Intelligence Laboratory, Massachusetts Institute of Technology, Cambridge, MA.

Brown, A. L. [1976], "Qualitative Knowledge, Causal Reasoning, and the Localization of Failures," Report AI-TR-362, Artificial Intelligence Laboratory, Massachusetts Institute of Technology, Cambridge, MA.

Brown, J. S., R. R. Burton, and J. de Kleer [1982], "Pedagogical, Natural Language, and Knowledge Engineering Techniques in SOPHIE I, II, and III," in *Intelligent Tutoring Systems*, edited by D. Sleeman, and J. S. Brown, Academic Press, New York, pp. 227–282.

Browning, Sally [1985], *The Tree Machine: A Highly Concurrent Computing Environment*, Department of Computer Science, California Institute of Technology, Technical Report 3760.

Brownstein, S. C., and M. Weiner [1985], "How to Prepare for the Graduate Record Examination," Barron's Educational Series, Inc., Woodbury, N.Y.

Burstall, R. M., and J. A. Goguen [1977], "Putting Theories Together to Make Specifications," *IJCAI-77*, pp. 1045–1058.

Carbonell, Jaime G., Richard E. Cullingford, and Anatole V. Gershman [1981], "Steps Toward Knowledge-Based Machine Translation," *IEEE Transactions on Pattern Analysis and Machine Intelligence* PAMI-3:4.

Chapman, D. [1985], "Planning for Conjunctive Goals," Report AI-TR-802, Artificial Intelligence Laboratory, Massachusetts Institute of Technology, Cambridge, MA.

Chomsky, N. [1957], *A Theory of Syntactic Structures*, Moulton & Co.

Chomsky, N. [1981], *Lectures on Government and Binding*, Dordrecht, Foris Publications.

Chomsky, Noam A. [1982], *Lectures on Government and Binding*, Foris Publications, Dordrecht.

Chomsky, Noam A. [1982], *Some Concepts and Consequences of the Theory of Government and Binding*, MIT Press, Cambridge, MA.

Chomsky, Noam A. [1986], *Knowledge of Language: Its Nature, Origin and Use*, MIT Press, Cambridge, MA.

Clark, K. B., W. B. Chew, and T. Fujimoto [1987], "Product Development in the World Auto Industry: Strategy, Organization and Performance," Working Paper, Harvard Business School 1987.

Clark, K. J., and S. Gregory [1986], "Parlog: parallel programming in logic," *ACM TOPLAS*, vol. 8, no. 1, pp. 1-49.

Clinger, W. D. [1981], *Foundations of Actor Semantics*, Report AI-TR-633, Artificial Intelligence Laboratory, Massachusetts Institute of Technology, Cambridge, MA.

Cohen, F. E., R. M. Abarbanel, I. D. Kuntz, and R. J. Fletterick [1986], "Turn Prediction in Proteins Using a Pattern-Matching Approach," *Biochemistry*, vol. 25, pp. 266–275.

Cohen, F. E., and I. D. Kuntz [1989], "Tertiary Structure Predictions," in *Prediction of Protein Structure and the Principles of Protein Conformation*, edited by G. D. Fasman, Plenum Press, New York, pp. 647-706.

Collins, J. F., and A. F. Coulson [1984], "Applications of Parallel Processing Algorithms for DNA Sequence Analysis," *Nucl. Acids Res.*, vol. 12, pp. 181–192.

Conklin, J., and M. L. Begeman [1988], "gIBIS: A Hypertext Tool for Exploratory Policy Discussion," *Proceedings of Computer Supported Cooperative Work*, Portland, Oregon.

Constable, R. L., S. F. Allen, H. M. Bromely, W. R. Cleaveland, J. F. Cremer, R. W. Harper, D. J. Howe, T. K. Knoblock, N. P. Mendler, P. Panangaden, J. T. Sasaki, and S. F. Smith [1986], *Implementing Mathematics with the Nuprl Development System*, Prentice Hall.

Corkill, Daniel D. [1979], "Hierarchical planning in a distributed environment," in *Proceedings of the Sixth International Joint Conference on Artificial Intelligence*, pp. 168–175.

Crandall, S. H. [1986], *Engineering Analysis*, Robert E. Krieger Publishing Co.

Crocker, Steven [1977], "State Deltas: Formalism for Representing Segments of Computation," USC-ISI Technical Report ISI RR-77-61.

Cullingford, Richard E. [1986], *Natural Language Processing: A Knowledge-Engineering Approach*, Rowman and Littlefield, Totowa, NJ.

Cutkosky, M. R., and J. M. Tenenbaum [1987], "CAD/CAM Integration Through Concurrent Product and Process Design," *Proceedings of the ASME Winter Annual Meeting*, PED vol. 25.

Cybenko, G. [1989], "Approximation by superposition of a sigmoidal function," *Math. Control Systems Signals*, in press.

Czuchry, A. J., and D. R. Harris [1988], "KBRA: A New Paradigm for Requirements Engineering," *IEEE Expert*, vol. 3, no. 4, pp. 21-35.

Dague, P., O. Raiman, and P. Deves [1987], "Troubleshooting: When Modeling is the Difficulty," *Proceedings of AAAI-87*, Seattle, WA, pp. 600–605.

Dahlquist, G., and A. Bjork [1974], *Numerical Methods*, Prentice-Hall.

Dally, W. J., and A. A. Chien [1988], "Object Oriented Concurrent Programming in CST," *Proc. 3rd Symposium on Hypercube Concurrent Computers and Applications*, ACM.

Dally, W. J. [1988b], "Fine-Grain Concurrent Computers," *Proceedings 3rd Symposium on Hypercube Concurrent Computers and Applications*, ACM.

Dally, William J. [1988a], "Concurrent Data Structures," Chapter 7 in *Message-Passing Concurrent Computers: Their Architecture and Programming*, C. L. Seitz et al., Addison-Wesley, Reading, MA, publication expected.

Dally, William J. et al. [1987], "Architecture of a Message-Driven Processor," *Proceedings of the 14th ACM/IEEE Symposium on Computer Architecture*, pp. 189-196.

Dally, William J. et al. [1988], "Message-Driven Processor Architecture, Version 11," Report AIM-1069, Artificial Intelligence Laboratory, Massachusetts Institute of Technology, Cambridge, MA.

Dally, William J., and Charles L. Seitz [1986], "The Torus Routing Chip," *J. Distributed Systems*, vol. 1, no. 3, pp. 187-196.

Dally, William J., and Charles l. Seitz [1987], " Deadlock-Free Message Routing in Multiprocessor Interconnection Networks," *IEEE Transactions on Computers*, vol. C-36, no. 5, pp. 547-553.

Dally, William J., and Paul Song [1987], "Design of a Self-Timed VLSI Multicomputer Communication Controller," *Proceedings International Conference on Computer Design, ICCD-87*, pp. 230-234.

Dally, William J. [1987a], *A VLSI Architecture for Concurrent Data Structures*, Kluwer, Hingham, MA.

Dally, William J. [1987b], "Wire Efficient VLSI Multiprocessor Communication Networks," *Proceedings Stanford Conference on Advanced Research in VLSI*, edited by Paul Losleben, MIT Press, Cambridge, MA, pp. 391-415.

Dally, William J. [1987c], "Concurrent Computer Architecture," *Proceedings of Symposium on Parallel Computations and Their Impact on Mechanics*.

Dally, William J. [1987d], "Architecture of a Message-Driven Processor," *Proceedings of the 14th ACM/IEEE Symposium on Computer Architecture*, pp. 189-196.

Dally, William J. [to appear], "Performance Analysis of k-ary n-cube Interconnection Networks," *IEEE Transactions on Computers*.

Davis R., H. Shrobe, W. Hamscher, K. Wieckert, M. Shirley, and S. Polit [1982], "Diagnosis Based on Structure and Function," *Proceedings of AAAI-82*, Pittsburgh, PA, pp 137–142.

Davis, Kenneth C. [1971], *Discretionary Justice*, University of Illinois Press.

Davis, R., and R. Smith, [1981], "Negotiation as a Metaphor for Distributed Problem Solving," Report AI-TR-624, Artificial Intelligence Laboratory, Massachusetts Institute of Technology, Cambridge, MA.

Davis, R. [1984], "Diagnostic Reasoning Based on Structure and Behavior," *Artificial Intelligence* vol. 24, no. 3, pp. 347–410.

deKleer, J., and J. S. Brown [1984], "A Qualitative Physics Based on Conflu- ences," *Artificial Intelligence,*

de Kleer, J., and B. C. Williams [1987], "Diagnosing Multiple Faults," *Artificial Intelligence*, vol. 32, no. 1, pp. 97–130.

de Kleer, J. [1976], "Local Methods for Localizing Faults in Electronic Cir- cuits," Report AIM-394 (out of print), Artificial Intelligence Laboratory, Massachusetts Institute of Technology, Cambridge, MA.

Dennis, Jack B. [1980], "Data Flow Supercomputers," *IEEE Computer*, vol. 13, no. 11, pp. 48-56,.

Dertouzos, M. L., R. K. Lester, and R. M. Solow [1989], *Made in America*, MIT Press Cambridge, MA.

Doolittle, R. F., M. W. Hunkapillar, L. E. Hood, S. G. Devare, K. C. Rob- bins, S. A. Aaronson, and H. N. Antoniades [1983], "Simian Sarcoma Virus *onc* Gene, v-*sis,* Is Derived from the Gene (or Genes) Encoding a Platelet- Derived Growth Factor," *Science,* vol. 221, pp. 275–277.

Dorr, Bonnie J. [1987], "UNITRAN: A Principle-Base Approach to Machine Translation," Report AI-TR-1000, Artificial Intelligence Laboratory, Mas- sachusetts Institute of Technology, Cambridge, MA.

Dorr, Bonnie J. [1989a], "Lexical Conceptual Structure and Generation in Ma- chine Translation," in *Proceedings of the Eleventh Annual Conference of the Cognitive Science Society*, Ann Arbor, MI.

Dorr, Bonnie J. [1989b], "Conceptual Basis of the Lexicon in Machine Trans- lation," First Annual Workshop on Lexical Acquisition, IJCAI-89, Detroit, MI.

Dorr, Bonnie J. [to appear], "Lexical Conceptual Structure and Machine Trans- lation," Ph.D. Thesis, Department of Electrical Engineering and Computer Science, Massachusetts Institute of Technology, Cambridge, MA.

Doyle, J. [1980], *A Model for Deliberation, Action, and Introspection*, Report AI- TR-581, Artificial Intelligence Laboratory, Massachusetts Institute of Tech- nology, Cambridge, MA.

Doyle, R. J. [1984], "Hypothesizing and Refining Causal Models," Report AIM- 811, Massachusetts Institute of Technology, Artificial Intelligence Labora- tory, Cambridge, MA.

Drescher, G. L. [1989], "A Mechanism for Early Piagetian Learning," Ph.D. The- sis, Massachusetts Institute of Technology, Cambridge.

Duda, R. O., P. E. Hart, and N. Nilsson [1976], "Subjective Bayesian Methods for Rule-based Inference System," in Webber and Nilsson [1981], pp. 192-199.

Ehrig, H., M. Nagl, G. Rozenberg, and A. Rosenfeld, (editors) [1986], *Graph- Grammars and Their Application to Computer Science*, Springer-Verlag, New York. Lecture Notes In Computer Science Series, vol. 291.

Eppinger, S. D., C. F. Fine, and K. T. Ulrich [1989], *Interdisciplinary Product De- sign Education*, Working Paper 3013-89-MS, Sloan School of Management, Massachusetts Institute of Technology, Cambridge, MA.

Farmer, J., and N. Packard [1986], "The Immune System, Adaptation, and Ma- chine Learning," *Physica*, vol. 22D, pp. 187–204.

Feinberg, M. [1980], "Chemical oscillations, multiple equilibria, and reaction net- work structure," in *Dynamics and Modelling of Reactive Systems*, edited by

W. Stewart, W. H. Ray and C. Conley, Academic Press, New York, pp. 59–130.

Feynman, R. [1982], "Simulating Physics with Computers," *International Journal of Theoretical Physics*, vol. 21, pp. 468-488.

Figge, J., T. Webster, T. Smith, and E. Paucha [1988], "Prediction of Similar Transforming Region in Simian Virus 40 Large T, Adenovirus E1A, and myc Oncoproteins," *J. Virology*, vol. 62, no. 5, pp. 1814–1818.

Figge, J., and T. Smith [1988], "Cell-Division Sequence Motif," *Nature*, vol. 334, p. 109.

Fikes, R., and N. Nilsson [1971], "STRIPS: A New Approach to the Application of Theorem Proving to Problem Solving," *Artificial Intelligence*,

Finger, Susan, and John Dixon [1989], "A Review of Research in Mechanical Engineering Design," *Research in Engineering Design*, vol. 1, no. 1. vol. 29.

First, M. B., B. J. Weimer, S. McLinden, and R. A. Miller [1982], "LOCALIZE: Computer-Assisted Localization of Peripheral Nervous System Lesions," *Computers and Biomedical Research*, vol. 15, no. 6, pp. 525–543.

Flaig, Charles, M. [1987], "VLSI Mesh Routing Systems," Report 5241:TR:87, Department of Computer Science, California Institute of Technology.

Fong, S. [1989], "Principle-based parsing and Principle-Ordering," Report AIM-1156, Artificial Intelligence Laboratory, Massachusetts Institute of Technology, Cambridge, MA (to appear).

Forbus, K. [1984], "Qualitative Process Theory," *Artificial Intelligence*,

Fox, G. C., and P. C. Messina [1987], "Advanced Computer Architectures," *Scientific American*, vol. 267 no. 4. vol. 24, no. 1-3, pp. 7-84.

Franceschini, V. [1983], "Two models of truncated Navier-Stokes equations on a two-dimensional torus," *Phys. Fluids*, vol. 26, no. 2, pp. 433–447.

Frank, B., B. Katz, and J. Palmucci [1989], "Reviewing the Voyager Information System," Research Report, Jet Propulsion Laboratory, Pasadena, CA.

Franke, R. [1982], "Scattered data interpolation: tests of some method," *Math. Comp.*, vol. 38, no. 5, pp. 181–200.

Friedland, P., and L. Kedes [1985], "Discovering the Secrets of DNA," *Computer*, vol. 18, no. 11, pp. 49–69.

Friedrichs, M., and P. Wolynes [1989], "Toward Protein Tertiary Structure Recognition by Means of Associative Memory Hamiltonians," *Science*, vol. 246, pp. 371–373.

Funahashi, K. [1989], "On the approximate realization of continuous mappings by neural networks," *Neural Networks*, vol. 2, pp. 183–192.

Gascuel, O., and A. Danchin [1986], "Protein Export in Prokaryotes and Eukaryotes: Indications of a Difference in the Mechanism of Exportation," *J. Mol. Evol.*, vol. 24, pp. 130-142.

Gasser, Leslie George [1984], "The Social Dynamics of Routine Computer Use in Complex Organizations," Ph.D. Thesis, University of California at Irvine.

Gaulding, J., and B. Katz [1989], "Using Word-Knowledge Reasoning for Question Answering," in *The Society of Text*, edited by E. Barrett, MIT Press, Cambridge, MA.

Gelernter, H. [1963], "Realization of a geometry theorem proving machine," *Proc. Int. Conf. on Information Processing*, Paris: Unesco House, pp. 273-282, 1959; also in *Computers and Thought*, edited by E. Feigenbaum, and J. Feldman, McGraw-Hill, New York, pp. 134–152.

Geman, S., and D. Geman [1984], "Stochastic relaxation, Gibbs distributions, and the Bayesian restoration of images," *IEEE Transactions on Pattern Analysis and Machine Intelligence*, vol. PAMI-6 pp. 721–741.

Genesereth, M. R. [1984], "The Use of Design Descriptions in Automated Diagnosis," *Artificial Intelligence*, vol. 24, no. 3, pp. 411–436.

Gerson, Elihu M. [1976], "On the Quality of Life," *American Sociological Review*, vol. 41, pp. 793–806.

Ginsberg, M. [1986], "Counterfactuals," *Artificial Intelligence*, vol. 30, no. 1, pp. 35–80.

Girosi, F., and T. Poggio [1989a], "Networks and the best approximation property," Report AIM–1164, Artificial Intelligence Laboratory, Massachusetts Institute of Technology.

Girosi, F., and T. Poggio [1989b], "A theory of networks for approximation and learning: part two," Report AIM–1167, Artificial Intelligence Laboratory, Massachusetts Institute of Technology, Cambridge, MA.

Goguen, J. A., J. W. Thatcher, E. G. Wagner, and J. B. Wright [1977], "Initial Algebra Semantics," *JACM*, vol. 24, pp. 68-95.

Goldsborough, M. D., D. DiSilvestre, G. F. Temple, A. T. Lorincz [1989], "Nucleotide Sequence of Human Papilloma Virus Type 31: A Cervical Neoplasia-Associated Virus," *J. Virology*, vol. 171, pp. 306–311.

Goldstein, I., and D. Bobrow [1981], "Layered Networks as a Tool for Software Development," *Proceedings of 7th IJCAI*, University of British Columbia, Vancouver, BC, Canada, pp. 913-919.

Goodman, James R. [1983], "Using Cache Memory to reduce Processor Memory Traffic," *The 10th Annual International Symposium on Computer Architecture*, pp. 123-131.

Gratzer, George [1978], *General Lattice Theory*, Academic Press.

Green, C., and D. R. Barstow [1978], "On program synthesis knowledge," *Artificial Intelligence*, vol. 10, no. 3, pp. 241–279, 1978. Reprinted in Rich and Waters [1986].

Grimshaw, J. [1990], *Argument Structure*, MIT Press, Cambridge, MA.

Grimson, W. E. L. [1981], *From Images to Surfaces*, MIT Press, Cambridge, MA.

Guckenheimer, J., and P. Holmes [1983], *Nonlinear Oscillations, Dynamical Systems, and Bifurcations of Vector Fields*, Springer-Verlag.

Guttag, J., and J. J. Horning [1980], "Formal Specification as a Design Tool," *Seventh Annual ACM Symposium on Principles of Programming Languages*, Las Vegas, pp. 251–261.

Hénon, M. [1969], "Numerical Study of Quadratic Area-Preserving Mappings," *Quarterly Journal of Applied Mathematics*, vol. 27.

Hale, Kenneth and Jay Keyser [1986], "Some Transitivity Alternations in English," Lexicon Project Working Papers #7, Center for Cognitive Science, Massachusetts Institute of Technology, Cambridge, MA.

Hale, Kenneth and M. Laughren [1983], "Warlpiri Dictionary Entries," Warlpiri Lexicon Project, Massachusetts Institute of Technology, Cambridge, MA.

Halfant, M., and G. J. Sussman [1988], "Abstraction in Numerical Methods," Report AIM–997, *Proceedings of ACM Conference on Lisp and Functional Programming*.

Hall, R. J. [1988], "Learning by Failing to Explain: Using Partial Explanations to Learn in Incomplete or Intractable Domains," *Machine Learning*, vol. 3, pp. 45–77.

Halstead, Bert [1985], "Multilisp: A Language for Concurrent Symbolic Computation," *ACM Transactions on Programming Languages and Systems*.

Halstead, Robert H. [1986], "Parallel Symbolic Computation," *IEEE Computer*, vol. 19, no. 8, pp. 35-43.

Hamscher, W., and R. Davis [1984], "Candidate Generation for Devices with State: An Inherently Underconstrained Problem," *Proceedings of AAAI-84*, Austin, TX, pp. 142–147.

Hamscher, W., and R. Davis [1987], "Issues in Model Based Troubleshooting," Report AIM-893, Artificial Intelligence Laboratory, Massachusetts Institute of Technology, Cambridge, MA, 1987.

Hamscher, W. [1988], "Representations for Model Based Troubleshooting," available from the author.

Harig, Herbert [1976], *Estimating Stamping Dies*, Harig Educational Systems, Philadelphia, PA.

Hassoun, S. [1988], "Memory Design for a Message-Driven Processor," Report VLSI Memo, Artificial Intelligence Laboratory, Massachusetts Institute of Technology.

Hayes, Patrick [1985], "The Second Naive Physics Manifesto," in *Formal Theories of the Commonsense World*, edited by J. Hobbs, and R. Moore, Ablex Publishers.

Hayes, R. H., S. C. Wheelwright, and K. B. Clark [1988], *Dynamic Manufacturing*, The Free Press, New York.

Hayes-Roth, B., *et al.* [1986], "PROTEAN: Deriving Protein Structure from Constraints," in *Proc. Fifth Natl. Conf. on Artificial Intelligence*, pp. 904–909.

Henderson, Peter [1980], "Is it Reasonable to Implement a Complete Programming System in a Purely Functional Style?" Technical memo PMM/94, The University of Newcastle upon Tyne, Computing Laboratory.

Hewitt, C., and H. Baker [1977], "Laws for communicating parallel processes," *Congress Proceedings, IFIP*, pp. 987-992.

Hewitt, C. [1986], "Offices Are Open Systems," *Proceedings of ACM Conference on Office Information Systems*, Providence, RI.

Hill, F. J., and G. R. Peterson [1974], *Introduction to Switching Theory and Logical Design*, Wiley, New York.

Hillis, W. D. [1986], *The Connection Machine*, MIT Press, Cambridge, MA.

Hoare, C.A.R. [1987], "Communicating Sequential Processes," *Comm. ACM*, vol. 21, no. 8, pp. 666-677. vol. 29.

Holland, J., K. Holyoak, R. Nisbett, and P. Thagard [1986], *Induction: Processes of Inference, Learning, and Discovery*, MIT Press, Cambridge, MA, USA.

Holley, L. H., and M. Karplus [1989], "Protein Structure Prediction With a Neural Network," *Proc. Natl. Acad. Sciences USA*, vol. 86, pp. 152–156.

Hsu, C. S., W. H. Cheng, and H. C. Yee [1977], "Steady-state response of a nonlinear system under impulsive parametric excitation," *Journal of Sound and Vibration*, vol. 50, no. 1, pp. 95–116.

Hsu, C. S. [1980], "A theory of index for point mapping dynamical systems," *Journal of Applied Mechanics*, vol. 47, pp. 185–190.

Huet, Gerard, and Jean-Marie Hullot [1982], "Proofs by Induction in Equational Theories with Constructors," *JCSS*, vol. 25, pp. 239-366.

Huff, K. E., and V. R Lesser [1988], "A plan-based intelligent assistant that supports the process of programming," *ACM SIGSOFT Software Engineering Notes*, vol. 13, no. 5, pp. 97-106; also *Proc. ACM SIGSOFT 3rd Symp. on Software Development Environments*, Boston, MA.

Hughes, Everett C. [1971], "Going Concerns: the Study of American Institutions," in *The Sociological Eye: Selected Papers*, Aldine-Atherton.

Hunter, L. E. [1989], *Knowledge Acquisition Planning: Gaining Expertise Through Experience*, Ph.D. Thesis, Yale University.

Hut, P., and G. J. Sussman [1987], "Advanced Computing for Science," *Scientific American*, vol. 257, no. 4.

Hutchins, W. J. [1978], "Progress in Documentation: Machine Translation and Machine-Aided Translation," in *Journal of Documentation*, 34:2, pp. 119–159.

IEEE [1988], Special issues on expert-system software, *IEEE Software*, vol. 5, no. 6, and *IEEE Expert*, vol. 3, no. 4.

Inmos Limited [1984], "IMS T424 Reference Manual," Order No. 72 TRN 006 00, Bristol, United Kingdom.

Intel Scientific Computers [1985], "iPSC User's Guide," Order No. 175455-001, Santa Clara, CA.

Iwasaki, Y., and H. A. Simon [1986], "Causality in Device Behavior," *Artificial Intelligence*,

Jackendoff, Ray S. [1983], *Semantics and Cognition*, MIT Press, Cambridge, MA.

Jackendoff, Ray S. [1990], *Semantic Structures*, MIT Press, Cambridge, MA.

Johannsen, D. [1981], "Bristle Blocks: A Silicon Compiler," *Proceedings of the 16th Design Automation Conference*.

Johnson, M. [1988], "Parsing as deduction: the use of knowledge of language." Knowledge as Language," In *The MIT Parsing Volume*, edited by S. Abney, Center for Cognitive Science, Cambridge, MA, pp. 47-69. vol. 36, no. 3, pp. 333-374.

Johnson, W. L. [1986], *Intention-Based Diagnosis of Novice Programming Errors*, Morgan Kaufmann, Los Altos, CA.

Jordan, S. R., A. F. R. Brown, and F. C. Hutton [1976], "Computerized Russian Translation at ORNL," in *Proceedings of the ASIS Annual Meeting*, San Francisco, CA, p. 163; also in *ASIS Journal*, 28:1, pp. 26–33, 1977.

Joskowicz, L., and S. Addanki [1989], Innovative Design of Kinematic Pairs," Report RC14507, IBM Research Division, T.J.Watson Research Center, Yorktown Heights, N.Y.

Karp, P., and P. Friedland [1989], "Coordinating the Use of Qualitative and Quantitative Knowledge in Declarative Device Modeling," in *Artificial Intelligence, Modeling and Simulation*, edited by, Widman, L. E., D. H. Helman, and K. Loparo, John Wiley and Sons, 1988.

Kratkiewicz, Kendra [1984], "Improving Learned Rules Using Near Miss Groups," B.S. Thesis, Department of Electrical Engineering and Computer Science, Massachusetts Institute of Technology.

Kartunnen, L., and M. Kay [1985], in *Natural Language Parsing*, edited by Dowty, Kartunnen, and Zwicky, Cambridge University Press, Cambridge, England, pp. 279–306.

Kashket, M. [1986], "Parsing a free-word order language: Warlpiri," *Proc. ACL*, pp. 60–66.

Katz, B., and B. Levin [1988], "Exploiting Lexical Regularities in Designing Natural Language Systems," *Proceedings of the 12th International Conference on Computational Linguistics, COLING '88*, Budapest.

Katz, B., and P. H. Winston [1982], "A Two-way Natural Language Interface," in *Integrated Interactive Computing Systems*, edited by P. Degano and E. Sandewall, North-Holland, Amsterdam.

Katz, B., and R. Brooks [1987], "Understanding Natural Language for Spacecraft Sequencing," *JBIS*, vol. 40, no. 10.

Katz, B. [1980], "A Three-step Procedure for Language Generation," Report AIM-599, Massachusetts Institute of Technology, Artificial Intelligence Laboratory, Cambridge, MA.

Katz, Morris J. [1986], "Paratran, A Transparent, Transaction Based Runtime Mechanism for Parallel Execution of Scheme," M.S. Thesis, Department of Electrical Engineering and Computer Science Department, Massachusetts Institute of Technology.

Katz, R. H., M. Anwarrudin, and E. Chang [1986], "Organizaing a Design Data/-base Across Time," in [Brodie & Mylopoulos 1986].

Kermani, Parviz, and Leonard Kleinrock [1979], "Virtual Cut-Through: A New Computer Communication Switching Technique," *Computer Networks*, vol. 3, pp. 267-286.

Ketonen, Jussi [1984], "EKL—A Mathematically Oriented Proof Checker," *Proceedings of the 7th International Conference on Automated Deduction*, Lecture Note in Computer Science, pp. 65-79.

Kinoshita, H., and H. Nakai [1984], "Motions of the Perihelions of Neptune and Pluto," *Celestial Mechanics*, vol. 34.

Knight, Tom, and Alex Krymm [1987], "Self Terminating Low-Voltage Swing CMOS Output Driver," *Proceedings Custom Integrated Circuits Conference*.

Knuth, D. E. [1968], "Semantics of context-free languages," *Mathematical Systems Theory*, vol. 2, no. 2, pp. 127–145.

Koile, K., and C. Overton [1989], "A Qualitative Model for Gene Expression," *Proc. 1989 Summer Computer Simulation Conf.*, Soc. for Computer Simulation.

Kolata, G. [1986], "Trying to Crack the Second Half of the Genetic Code," *Science*, vol. 233, pp. 1037-1039.

Kolodner, J. [1988], (Editor) *Proceedings of a Workship on Case-Based Reasoning*, Clearwater Beach, FL.

Kornfeld, B. [1982], "Concepts in Parallel Problem Solving," Ph.D. Thesis Artificial Intelligence Laboratory, Massachusetts Institute of Technology, Cambridge, MA.

Kuipers, B. [1986], "Qualitative Simulation," *Artificial Intelligence,*

Kung, H. T., and J. T. Robinson [1981], "On optimistic Methods of Concurrency Control," *ACM Transactions on Database Systems*, vol. 6, no. 2.

Kuper, R. I. [1988], "Automated techniques for the localization of software bugs," M.S. Thesis Report AIM-1053, Artificial Intelligence Laboratory, Massachusetts Institute of Technology, Cambridge, MA.

Lai, K., T. Malone, and K. C. Yu [1989], "Object Lens: A Spreadsheet for Cooperative Work," *ACM Transaction on Office Information Systems*, vol. 6, pp. 332-353.

Laidler, K. [1987], *Chemical Kinetics* (3rd edition), Harper and Row, New York.

Lander, E., J. Mesirov, and W. Taylor [1988], "Study of Protein Sequence Comparison Metrics on the Connection Machine CM-2," *Proc. Supercomputing 1988.*

Lasnik, H., and J. Uriagereka [1988] *A Course in GB Syntax: Lectures on Binding and Empty Categories*, MIT Press, Cambridge, MA.

Lathrop, R. H., R. J. Hall, and R. S. Kirk [1987], "Functional Abstraction From Structure in VLSI Simulation Models," in *Proc. 24th Design Automation Conf.*, Miami Beach, FL, pp. 822–828.

Lathrop, R. H., T. A. Webster, and T. F. Smith [1987], "ARIADNE: Pattern-Directed Inference and Hierarchical Abstraction in Protein Structure Recognition," *Comm. of the ACM*, vol. 30, no. 11, pp. 909–921.

Lathrop, R. H. [1990], *Efficient Methods For Massively Parallel Symbolic Induction: Algorithms and Implementation*, Ph.D. Thesis, Massachusetts Institute of Technology, Cambridge (in preparation).

Laughren, M. [1987], "The configurationality parameter and Warlpiri," in *Configurationality*, edited by L. Maracz and Pl. Muysken, Dordrecht, Foris Publications.

Lawrie, H. Duncan [1975], "Alignment and Access of Data in an Array Processor," *IEEE Transactions on Computers*, vol. C-24, no. 12, pp. 1145-1155.

Lee, J., and T. Malone [1988], "How Can Groups Communicate When They Use Different Languages?" *Proceedings of ACM Conference on Office Information Systems*, Palo Alto, CA.

Lee, J. [1989a], "A Qualitative Decision Management System: An Overview," Report AIM–1191, Artificial Intelligence Laboratory, Massachusetts Institute of Technology, Cambridge, MA (to appear).

Lee, J. [1989b], "Task-Embedded Knowledge Acquisition through a Task-Specific Language," *Proceedings of IJCAI Knowledge Acquisition Workshop*, Detroit, MI.

Leiserson, Charles L. [1985], "Fat Trees: Universal Networks for Hardware-Efficient Supercomputing," *IEEE Transactions on Computers*, vol. C-34, no. 10, pp. 892-901.

Lesser, Victor, and Daniel D. Corkill [1981], "Functionally accurate, cooperative distributed systems," *IEEE Transactions on Systems, Man, and Cybernetics*, vol. SMC-11, no. 1, pp. 81–96.

Letovsky, S. [1988], "Plan analysis of programs," Ph.D. Thesis, Research report, Yale University, Computer Science Deptment.

Levin, B. [1985], "Introduction," in *Lexical Semantics in Review*, edited by B. Levin, Lexicon Project Working Papers 1, Center for Cognitive Science, MIT, Cambridge, MA.

Ligtenberg, Adriaan [1987], Presentation at *Princeton Workshop on Algorithm, Architecture, and Technology Issues in Models of Concurrent Computation*.

Lorentz, G. G. [1966], "Metric entropy and approximation," *Bull. Amer. Math. Soc*, vol. 72, pp. 903–937.

Lorentz, G. G. [1986], *Approximation of Functions*, Chelsea Publishing Co., New York.

Lowe, D. [1986], "SYNVIEW: The Design of a System for Cooperative Structuring of Information," *Proceedings of Computer Supported Cooperative Work*, Austin, TX.

Lukey, F. J. [1980], "Understanding and debugging programs," *International Journal of Man-Machine Studies*, vol. 12, pp. 189–202.

Lutz, C., et al. [1984], "Design of the Mosaic Element," *Proceedings MIT Conference on Advanced Research in VLSI*, Artech Books, pp. 1-10.

Lutz, R. [1989], "Chart parsing of flowgraphs," *Proceedings 11th Int. Joint Conf. Artificial Intelligence,*

Lytinen, Steven L. [1985], "Integrating Syntax and Semantics," in *Proceedings of the Conference on Theoretical and Methodological Issues in Machine Translation of Natural Languages*, Colgate University, Hamilton, NY, pp. 167–177. Also in *Machine Translation: Theoretical and Methodological Issues*, edited by Sergei Nirenburg [1987], Cambridge University Press, Cambridge, England .

Lytinen, Steven and Roger Schank [1982], "Representation and Translation" Technical Report 234, Department of Computer Science, Yale University, New Haven, CT.

MacKay, R. [1982], *Renormalization in Area-Preserving Maps*, Ph.D. thesis, Princeton University.

MacQueen, J. [1967], " Some methods of classification and analysis of multivariate observations," in *Proc. 5th Berkeley Symposium on Math., Stat., and Prob.*, edited by L. M. LeCam and J. Neyman, p 281, U. California Press, Berkeley, CA.

Malone, T., K. C. Yu, and J. Lee [1989], "What Good Are Semi-Structured Objects?" Sloan Working Paper, 3064-89-MS, Massachusetts Institute of Technology, Cambridge, MA.

Mann, R. W., and S. A. Coons [1965], "Computer-Aided Design," *McGraw-Hill Yearbook Science and Technology*, McGraw-Hill.

Manning, Carl R. [1986], "Acore: an actor core language reference manual," Internal Memo, MIT Message Passing Semantics Group Design Note: 7.

March, and Simon [1958], *Organizations*, John Wiley and Sons, New York, NY.

Marroquin, J. L., S. Mitter, and T. Poggio [1987], "Probabilistic solution of ill-posed problems in computational vision," *J. Amer. Stat. Assoc.*, vol. 82, pp. 76–89. vol. 9, pp. 171-216.

Maryanski, F. J., and T. L. Booth [1977], "Inference of Finite-State Probabilistic Grammars," *IEEE Trans. on Computers,* C-26, no. 6, pp. 521–536.

Matson, M. [1985], "Macromodeling and Optimization of Digital MOS VLSI Circuits," VLSI Memo 85-231, Massachusetts Institute of Technology, Cambridge, MA.

Mayr, O. [1970], *The Origins of Feedback Control,* MIT Press, Cambridge, MA.

McAllester, David A. [1983], "Symmetric Set Theory, A General Theory of Isomorphism, Abstraction, and Representation," Report AIM-710, Artificial Intelligence Laboratory, Massachusetts Institute of Technology, Cambridge.

McAllester, David, A. [1989], *Ontic: A Knowledge Representation System for Mathematics,* MIT Press, Cambridge, MA.

McAllester, David, A. [1990], "Three Universal Relations," *Artificial Intelligence at MIT: Expanding Frontiers,* edited by Patrick H. Winston with Sarah A. Shellard, Vol. 1, Ch. 18, MIT Press, Cambridge, MA.

McCormick, B., T. Desanti, and M. Brown (editors) [1987], "Visualization in Scientific Computing," *Computer Graphics,* vol. 21, no. 6.

McDermott, D. [1977], "Flexibility and Efficiency in a Computer Program for Designing Circuits," Report AI-TR-402, Artificial Intelligence Laboratory, Massachusetts Institute of Technology, Cambridge, MA.

McDonald, David D. [1983], "Natural Language Generation as a Computational Problem," in *Computational Models of Discourse,* edited by Brady, Michael and Robert C. Berwick, MIT Press, Cambridge, MA, pp. 209–265.

McDonald, David D. [1987], "Natural Language Generation: Complexities and Techniques," in *Machine Translation: Theoretical and Methodological Issues,* edited by Sergei Nirenburg, Cambridge University Press, Cambridge, England.

McKeown, Kathleen [1985], *Text Generation: Using Discourse Strategies and Focus Constraints to Generate Natural Language Text,* Cambridge University Press, Cambridge, England.

McLaughlin, W. I. [1987], "Automated Sequencing," *Spaceflight,* vol. 29, no. 1.

McLaughlin, W. I. [1988], "Computers and Language," *Spaceflight,* vol. 30, no. 8.

Mead, Carver A., and Lynn A. Conway [1980], *Introduction to VLSI Systems,* Addison-Wesley, Reading, Massachusetts.

Mead, Carver A., and Lynn A. Conway [1980], *Introduction to VLSI Systems,* Addison-Wesley, Reading, Mass.

Micchelli, C. A. [1986], "Interpolation of scattered data: Distance matrices and conditionally positive definite functions," *Constr. Approx.,* vol. 2, pp. 11–22.

Michalski, R. S., J. G. Carbonell, and T. Mitchell (editors) [1986], *Machine Learning* vol 2, Morgan Kauffman, Los Altos, CA.

Michalski, R. S., J. G. Carbonell, and T. M. Mitchell [1983], (editors), *Machine Learning: An Artificial Intelligence Approach,* (first in a series), Tioga Press, Palo Alto, CA.

Minsky, Marvin, [1986], *The Society of Mind,* Simon and Schuster.

Minsky, Marvin [1987b], "Connectionist Models and their Prospects," Introduction to Feldman and Waltz Nov. 23.

Minsky, Marvin [1974], "A Framework for Representing Knowledge," Report AIM–306, Artificial Intelligence Laboratory, Massachusetts Institute of Technology, Cambridge, MA.

Minsky, Marvin, and Seymour Papert [1988], *Perceptrons*, (2nd edition) MIT Press.

Mitchell, T., S. Mahadevan, and L. I. Steinberg [1985], "LEAP: A Learning Apprentice for VLSI Design," *Proc. of the Ninth International Joint Conference on Artificial Intelligence*, pp. 573–80.

Mitchell, T. M., L. I. Steinberg, S. Kedar-Cabelli, V. E. Kelly, J. Shulman, and T. Weinrich [1983], "An Intelligent Aid for Circuit Redesign," in *Proceedings of the National Conference on Artificial Intelligence*.

Mitchell, T. M. [1977], "Version Spaces: A Candidate Elimination Approach to Rule Learning," *Proc. Fifth Intl. Joint Conf. on Artificial Intelligence*, Cambridge, MA, pp. 305–310.

Mittal, S., C. M. Dym, and M. Morjaria [1986], "PRIDE: An Expert System for the Design of Paper Handling Systems," *Computer*.

Moon, David A. [1985], "The Architecture of the Symbolics 3600," *The 12th Annual International Symposium on Computer Architecture*, pp. 76-83.

Morozov, V. A. [1984], *Methods for solving incorrectly posed problems*, Springer-Verlag, Berlin.

Munster, Gregory A. [1989], *Analyzing the Costs of Product Quality*, M.S. Thesis, Sloan School of Management, Massachusetts Institute of Technology, Cambridge, MA.

Murray, W. R. [1985], "Heuristic and formal methods in automatic program debugging," *Proceedings 9th Int. Joint Conf. Artificial Intelligence*, pp. 15–19, Los Angeles, CA.

Murthy, S. S., and S. Addanki [1987], "PROMPT: An Innovative Design Tool," *Proceedings of the 6th National Conference on Artificial Intelligence*, pp. 637-42. pp. 547-51.

Nevins, A. J. [1974], "Plane Geometry theorem Proving using Forward Chaining," Report AIM–303, Artificial Intelligence Laboratory, Massachusetts Institute of Technology, Cambridge, MA.

Nirenburg, Sergei [1986], "Machine Translation," Presented as a Tutorial at the 24th Annual Meeting of the Association for Computational Linguistics, Columbia University, New York City, NY.

Nirenburg, Sergei, Rita McCardell, Eric Nyberg, Scott Huffman, Edward, Kenschaft, and Irene Nirenburg [1988], "Lexical Realization in Natural Language Generation," in *Proceedings of the Second International Conference on Theoretical and Methodological Issues in Machine Translation of Natural Languages*, Carnegie Mellon University, Pittsburgh, PA.

Nirenburg, Sergei, Victor Raskin, and Allen B. Tucker [1987], "The Structure of Interlingua in TRANSLATOR," in *Machine Translation: Theoretical and Methodological Issues*, edited by Sergei Nirenburg, Cambridge University Press, Cambridge, England.

Novak, G. [1977], "Representations of Knowledge in a Program for Solving Physics Problems," *Proc. 5th IJCAI*, Cambridge, MA, pp. 286–291.

O'Dunlaing, Colm, and Chee K. Yap [1982], "Generic Transformations of Data Structures," *23rd Annual Symposium on the Foundations of Computer Science*, pp. 186–195.

Omohundro, S. [1987], Efficient algorithms with neural network behavior, *Complex Systems*, vol. 1, no. 273.

Palmer, John F. [1986], "The NCUBE Family of Parallel Supercomputers," *Proceedings IEEE International Conference on Computer Design, ICCD-86*, p. 107.

Pan, J. [1984], "Qualitative Reasoning with Deep-level Mechanism Models for Diagnoses of Mechanism Failures," *Proceedings of CAIA-84*, Denver, CO, pp. 295–301, IEEE.

Patel-Schneider, P. F. [1984], "Small can be Beautiful in Knowledge Representation," *Proceedings of the IEEE Workshop on Principles of Knowledge-Based Systems*, Denver, CO, pp. 11-16.

Patil, R., P. Szolovits, and W. Schwartz [1981], "Causal understanding of patient illness in medical diagnosis," *Proceedings of IJCAI-81*, Vancouver, BC, pp. 893–899.

Pear, J. [1987], "On the Connection between the complexity and Credibility of Inferred Models," *Int. J. General Systems*, vol. 4, pp. 255-264.

Pease, M. C., III [1977], "The Indirect Binary n-Cube Microprocessor Array," *IEEE Transactions on Computers*, vol. C-26, no. 5, pp. 458-473.

Pentland, A., and J. Kuo [1989], "The Artist at the Interface," *Media Lab Vision Science Technical Report*, vol. 114, Massachusetts Institute of Technology, Cambridge, MA.

Perrett, D. I., A. J. Mistlin, and A. J. Chitty [1987], "Visual neurones responsive to faces," *Trends in Neuroscience*, vol. 10, no. 9, pp. 358–364.

Pesetsky, D. [1987], "Binding Problems with Experiencer Verbs," *Linguistic Inquiry* vol. 18, pp. 126-140.

Pfister, G. F. *et al.* [1985], "The IBM Research Parallel Processor Prototype (RP3): Introduction and Architecture", *Proceedings International Conference on Parallel Processing, ICPP*, pp. 764–771.

Pfister, G. F., and V. A. Norton [1985], "Hot Spot Contention and Combining in Multistage Interconnection Networks," *IEEE Transactions on Computers*, vol. C-34, no. 10, pp. 943-948.

Poggio, T., and F. Girosi [1989], "A theory of networks for approximation and learning," Report AIM–1140, Artificial Intelligence Laboratory, Massachusetts Institute of Technology.

Poggio, T., and S. Edelman [1989], "A network that learns to recognize 3D objects," (submitted for publication).

Poggio, T., and The Staff [1989], "M.I.T. progress in understanding images," In *Proceedings Image Understanding Workshop*, pp. 56–74, Palo Alto, CA. Morgan Kaufmann, San Mateo, CA.

Poggio, T. [1982], "Visual algorithms," In *Physical and Biological Processing of Images*, edited by O. J. Braddick and A. C. Sleigh, pp. 128–153, Springer–Verlag, Berlin.

Port, Otis [1989], "The Best-Engineered Part is No Part at All," *Business Week*.

Postal, P. [1971], *Cross-Over Phenomena*, Holt, Rinehart, and Winston, NY.

Powell, M. J. D. [1987], "Radial basis functions for multivariable interpolation: a review," in *Algorithms for Approximation*, edited by J. C. Mason and M. G. Cox, Clarendon Press, Oxford.

Press, W. H., B. P. Flannery, S. A. Teukolsky [1986], and W. T. Vetterling , *Numerical Recipes: The Art of Scientific Computing*, Cambridge University Press.

Pustejovsky, James, and Sergei Nirenburg [1987], "Lexical Selection in the Process of Language Generation," in *Proceedings of the 25th Annual Conference of the Association for Computational Linguistics*, Stanford University, Stanford, CA, pp. 201–206.

Qian, N., and T. Sejnowski [1988], "Predicting the Secondary Structure of Globular Proteins Using Neural Network Models," *J. Mol. Biol.*, vol. 202, pp. 865–884.

Quinlan, J. R. [1983], "Inferno: A Cautious Appropach to Uncertain Inference," *The Computer Journal*, vol. 26, no. 3, pp. 255-267.

Quirk, R., S. Greenbaum, G. Leech, and J. Svartvik [1985], *A Comprehensive Grammar of the English Language*, Longman, London.

Ralph, W., T. Webster, and T. Smith [1987], "A Modified Chou and Fasman Protein Structure Algorithm," *CABIOS,* vol. 3, pp. 211-216. *PRSTRC* program available from MBCRR, Dana Farber Cancer Institute, 44 Binney St., Boston, MA.

Rappaport, Malka, and Beth Levin [1986], "What to Do with Theta-Roles," Lexicon Project Working Papers #11, Center for Cognitive Science, Massachusetts Institute of Technology, Cambridge, MA.

Rees, J., and W. Clinger *et al.* [1986], *Revised Report on the Algorithmic Language Scheme*, ACM SIGPLAN Notices, vol. 21, no. 12, pp. 37-79, 1986; also, Report AIM-848a, Artificial Intelligence Laboratory, Massachusetts Institute of Technology, Cambridge, MA.

Reiter, R. [1987], "A Theory of Diagnosis from First Principles," *Artificial Intelligence*, vol. 32, no. 1, pp. 57-96.

Ressler, A. [1974], "A Circuit Grammar for Operational Amplifier Design," Report AI-TR-807, Artificial Intelligence Laboratory, Massachusetts Institute of Technology, Cambridge, MA.

Reubenstein, H. B., and R. C. Waters [1989], "The Requirements Apprentice: An Initial Scenario" *Proc. 5th Int. Workshop on Software Specs. and Design.*

Rich, C., and R. C. Waters, [1988], "The Programmer's Apprentice: A research overview," *IEEE Computer*, vol. 21, no. 11, pp. 10–25. Reprinted in *Artificial Intelligence and Software Engineering*, edited by D. Partridge, Ablex, Norwood, NJ, 1989.

Rich, C., and R. C. Waters, [1990], *The Programmer's Apprentice*, Addison-Wesley, Reading, MA; and ACM Press, Baltimore, MD.

Rich, C., and R. C. Waters [1987], "The Programmer's Apprentice: A program design scenario," AIM-933A, Artificial Intelligence Laboratory, Massachusetts Institute of Technology, Cambridge, MA.

Rich, C., and R. C. Waters [1988], "Automatic programming: Myths and

Rich, C., and R. C. Waters (editors) [1986], *Readings in Artificial Intelligence and Software Engineering.* Morgan Kaufmann, Los Altos, CA.

Rich, C. [1981], "A formal representation for plans in the Programmer's Apprentice," *Proc. 7th Int. Joint Conf. Artificial Intelligence*, pp. 1044–1052, Vancouver, BC, Canada. Reprinted in Rich and Waters [1986].

Rich, C. [1985], "The layered architecture of a system for reasoning about programs," *Proc. 9th Int. Joint Conf. Artificial Intelligence*, pp. 540–546, Los Angeles, CA.

Richardson, J. [1981], "The Anatomy and Taxonomy of Protein Structure," *Advances in Protein Chemistry*, vol. 34, pp. 167–339.

Rieger, C., and M. Grinberg [1977], "Representation and Procedural Simulation of Causality in Physical Mechanisms," *Proceedings of the fifth IJCAI*, Cambridge, MA, pp. 250-256.

Rissanen, J. [1978], "Modeling by shortest data description," *Automatica*, vol. 14, pp. 465–471. vol. 2, no. 3.

Rosenberg, R. C., and D. C. Karnopp [1983], *Introduction to Physical System Dynamics*, McGraw-Hill Book Co., New York.

Roylance, G. L. [1987], "Expressing mathematical subroutines constructively," Report AIM–999, 1987. To appear in proceedings of *ACM Conference on Lisp and Functional Programming*, 1988.

Roylance, G. [1980], "A Simple Model of Circuit Design," Report AI-TR-703, Artificial Intelligence Laboratory, Massachusetts Institute of Technology, Cambridge, MA.

Sacerdoti, E. [1975] "The Nonlinear Nature of Plans," *Proceedings of the Fourth IJCAI*,

Sacerdoti, E. [1975], *A Structure for Plans and Behavior*, American Elsevier, New York, NY.

Sacks, E. P. [1987a], "Hierarchical reasoning about inequalities," AAAI, pp. 649–654.

Sacks, E. P. [1987b], "Piecewise linear reasoning," AAAI, pp. 655–659.

Sacks, E. P. [1988], "Automatic Qualitative Analysis of Ordinary Differential Equations Using Piecewise Linear Approximations," Report TR–416, Laboratory for Computer Science.

Samuels, A. L. [1967], "Some Studies in Machine Learning Using the Game of Checkers. II—Recent Progress," *IBM Journal*.

Sanchez-Pescador, R., M. Power, P. Barr K. Steimer, M. Stempien, S. Brown-Shimer, W. Gee, A. Renard, A. Randolph, J. Levy, D. Dina, and P. Lucie [1985], "Nucleotide Sequence and Expression of an AIDS-Associated Retrovirus (ARV-2)," *Science*, vol. 227, pp. 484–492.

Sankoff, D., and J. B. Kruskal [1983], (editors) *Time Warps, String Edits, and Macromolecules: The Theory and Practice of Sequence Comparison*, Addison–Wesley, Reading, MA.

Scarl, E., J. R. Jamieson, and C. I. Delaune [1985], "A Fault Detection and Isolation Method Applied to Liquid Oxygen Loading for the Space Shuttle," *Proceedings of IJCAI-85*, Los Angeles, CA, pp. 414–416.

Schank, Roger C., and Robert Abelson [1977], *Scripts, Plans, Goals, and Understanding*, Lawrence Erlbaum Associates, Inc., Hillsdale, NJ.

Schmenner, Roger W. [1987], *Production/Operations Management: Concepts and Situations*, Science Research Associates, Chicago.

Searls, D. B. [1988], "Representing Genetic Information with Formal Grammars," in *Proc. of the Seventh Natl. Conf. on Artificial Intelligence,* pp. 386–391.

Seitz, Charles L., William C. Athas, William J. Dally [1988], Reese Faucette, Alain J. Martin, Sven Mattisson, Craig S. Steele, and Wen-King Su, *Message-Passing Concurrent Computers: Their Architecture and Programming,* Addison-Wesley, publication expected 1988.

Seitz, Charles L., *et al.* [1985], "The Hypercube Communications Chip," Display File 5182:DF:85, Department of Computer Science, California Institute of Technology.

Seitz, Charles L. [1980], "System Timing" reprinted in *Introduction to VLSI Systems,* C. A. Mead and L. A. Conway, Addison-Wesley, Ch. 7.

Seitz, Charles L. [1984], "Concurrent VLSI Architectures," *IEEE Transactions on Computers,* vol. C-33, no. 12, pp. 1247-1265.

Seitz, Charles L. [1985], "The Cosmic Cube", *Comm. ACM,* vol. 28, no. 1, pp. 22-33.

Sequin, Carlo, H. [1979], "Single Chip Computers, The New VLSI Building Block," *Caltech Conference on VLSI,* edited by C. L. Seitz, pp. 435-452.

Shafer, G., and Logan, R. [1987], "Implementing Dempster's rule for hierarchical Evidence," *Artificial Intelligence* vol. 33, no. 3, pp. 271-98

Shafer, G. [1976], *A Mathematical Theory of Evidence,* Princeton University Press, Princeton, NJ.

Shapiro, E. [1987], "A subset of concurrent prolog and its interpreter," in *Concurrent Prolog: Collected Papers,* MIT Press, Cambridge, MA, pp. 27-83.

Sharp, Randall M. [1985], "A Model of Grammar Based on Principles of Government and Binding," Master of Science, Department of Computer Science, University of British Columbia.

Shearer, J. L., A. T. Murphy, and H. H. Richardson [1971], *Introduction to System Dynamics,* Addison-Wesley, Reading, MA.

Shirley, M. H., and R. Davis [1983], "Generating Distinguishing Tests based on Hierarchical Models and Symptom Information," *IEEE International Conference on Computer Design.* pp. 741-747.

Shriver, B., and P. Wegner [1987], *Research Directions in Object-Oriented Programming,* MIT Press, Cambridge, MA.

Siegel, Howard Jay [1979], "Interconnection Networks for SIMD Machines," *IEEE Computer,* vol. 12, no. 6, pp. 57-65.

Simmons, R. [1983], "Representing and Reasoning About Change in Geologic Interpretation," Report AI-TR-749, Artificial Intelligence Laboratory, Massachusetts Institute of Technology, Cambridge, MA.

Siskind, J., J. Southard, and K. Crouch [1982], "Generating Custom High Performance VLSI Designs from Succinct Algorithmic Descriptions," *Proceedings of the Conference on Advanced Research in VLSI.*

Slocum, J. [1984], "METAL: The LRC machine translation system," ISSCO Tutorial on machine translation, Lugano, Switzerland. Also Working Paper LRC-84-2, Linguistics Research Center, University of Texas, Austin, TX.

Smith, D. E., and M. R. Genesereth [1985], "Ordering Conjunctive Queries," *Artificial Intelligence* vol. 26, pp. 171–215.

Smith, R. F., and T. F. Smith [1990], "Automatic Generation of Primary Sequence Patterns from Sets of Related Protein Sequences," *Proc. Natl. Acad. Sci. USA,* in press.

Smith, T. F., and M. S. Waterman [1981], "Identification of Common Molecular Subsequences," *J. Mol. Biol.,* vol. 147, pp. 195–197.

Soloway, E., and K. Ehrlich [1984], "Empirical studies of programming knowledge," *IEEE Trans. on Software Engineering,* vol. 10, no. 5, pp. 595–609. Reprinted in Rich and Waters [1986].

Soloway, E., and K. Ehrlich [1984], "Empirical studies of programming knowledge," *IEEE Trans. on Software Engineering,* vol. 10, no. 5, pp. 595–609. Reprinted in *Readings in Artificial Intelligence and Software Engineering,* edited by C. Rich and R. C. Waters, Morgan Kaufmann, 1986.

Stabler, E. P., Jr. [1989] "The Logical Approach to Syntax: Foundations, Specifications and Implementations of Theories of Government and Binding," *m.s.,* London, Ontario, University of Western Ontario.

Star, S. L. [1983], "Simplification in Scientific Work: An Example from Neuroscience Research," *Social Studies of Science,* vol. 13, no. 2, pp. 205–228.

Steele, G. L. [1980], "The Definition and Implementation of a Computer Programming Language Based on Constraints," Report AI-TR-595, Artificial Intelligence Laboratory, Massachusetts Institute of Technology, Cambridge, MA.

Steele, G. L. [1984], *Common LISP: The Manual,* Digital Press, Billerica, MA.

Stinchcombe, M., and H. White [1989], "Universal approximation using feedforward networks with non-sigmoid hidden layer activation functions," In *Proceedings of the International Joint Conference on Neural Networks,* pp. I–607, Washington DC. IEEE TAB Neural Network Committee.

Stone, C. J. [1980], "Optimal rates of convergence for nonparametric estimators," *Ann. Stat.,* vol. 8, no. 6, pp. 1348–1360.

Stone, C. J. [1982], "Optimal global rates of convergence for nonparametric regression," *Ann. Stat.,* vol. 10, pp. 1040–1053.

Stone, C. J. [1985], "Additive regression and other nonparametric models," *Ann. Stat.,* vol. 13, pp. 689–705.

Stone, H. S. [1971], "Parallel Processing with the Perfect Shuffle," *IEEE Transactions on Computers,* vol. C-20, no. 2, pp. 153-161.

Strauss, Anselm [1978], *Negotiations,* Jossey-Bass.

Struss, P. [1988], "Mathematical Aspects of Qualitative Reasoning," *Artificial Intelligence in Engineering.*

Su, Wen-King, Reese Faucette, and Charles L. Seitz [1985], "C Programmer's Guide to the Cosmic Cube," Report 5203:TR:85, Department of Computer Science, California Institute of Technology.

Sullivan, H., and T. R. Bashkow [1977], "A Large Scale Homogeneous Machine," *Proc. 4th Annual Symposium on Computer Architecture,* pp. 105-124.

Sussman, G. J., and G. L. Steele [1980], "Constraints: A Language for Expressing Almost-Hierarchical Descriptions," *Artificial Intelligence,* vol. 14, no. 1, pp. 1–40.

Sussman, G. J., and J. Wisdom [1988], "Numerical evidence that the motion of Pluto is chaotic," *Science*, (to appear). Also available as Report AIM–1039, Artificial Intelligence Laboratory, Massachusetts Institute of Technology, Cambridge, MA.

Sussman, G. J., and R. M. Stallman [1975], "Heuristic techniques in computer-aided circuit analysis," *IEEE Trans. on Circuits and Systems*, CAS-22, pp. 857–865.

Sussman, G. [1975], *A Computational Model of Skill Acquisition*, American Elsevier, New York, NY.

Swets, J. A. [1986a], "Indices of Discrimination or Diagnostic Accuracy: Their ROCs and Implied Models," *Psychological Bull.*, vol. 99, no. 1, pp. 100–117.

Swets, J. A. [1986b], "Form of Empirical ROCs in Discrimination and Diagnostic Tasks: Implications for Theory and Measurement of Performance," *Psychological Bull.*, vol. 99, no. 2.

Talmy, Leonard [1983], "How Language Structures Space," in *Spatial Orientation: Theory, Research, and Application*, edited by Pick, Herbert L., Jr., and Linda P. Acredolo, Plenum Press, New York, NY.

Tambe, M., D. Kapl, A. Gupta, C. Forgy, B. Milnes, A. Newell [1988], "Soar/-PSM-E: Investigating Match Parallelism in a Learning Production System," *Proc. Parallel Programming Environments Applications Languages and Systems*.

Tanenbaum, A. S. [1981], *Computer Networks*, Prentice Hall, Englewood Cliffs, NJ.

Taylor, W. [1987], "Identification of Protein Sequence Homology by Consensus Template Alignment," *J. Mol. Biol.*, vol. 188, pp. 233-258.

Tenney, C. [1986], "A context-free rule system for parsing Japanese," *MIT-Japan Science and Technology Program*, Cambridge, MA.

Tenny, Carol [1989], "The Aspectual Interface Hypothesis," Lexicon Project Working Paper 31, Center for Cognitive Science at MIT, Cambridge, MA.

Theriault, D. [1983], "Issues in the Design and Implementation of Act2," Report AI-TR-728, Artificial Intelligence Laboratory, Massachusetts Institute of Technology, Cambridge, MA.

Thinking Machines Corp. [1988], *Paris Reference Manual*, Cambridge, MA.

Thompson, C. D. [1980], *A Complexity Theory of VLSI*, Department of Computer Science, Carnegie-Mellon University, Technical Report CMU-CS-80-140.

Thompson, J. M. T., and H. B. Stewart [1986], *Nonlinear Dynamics and Chaos*, Wiley.

Thompson, J. M. T. [1983], "Complex dynamics of compliant offshore structures," *Proc. Royal Soc. London A*, vol. 387, pp. 407–427.

Tikhonov, A. N., and V. Y. Arsenin [1977], *Solutions of Ill-posed Problems*, W. H. Winston, Washington, DC.

Totty, Brian [1988], "An Operating Environment for the Jellybean Machine," Report AIM-1070, Artificial Intelligence Laboratory, Massachusetts Institute of Technology, Cambridge, MA.

Toulmin, S. [1969], *The Uses of Argument*, Cambridge University Press, Cambridge, England.

Ueda, K. [1986], *Guarded Horn Clauses*, Ph.D. Thesis, University of Tokyo.

Ulrich, K. T. [1988], "Computation and Pre-Parametric Design," Report AI-TR-1043, Artificial Intelligence Laboratory, Massachusetts Institute of Technology, Cambridge, MA.

Ulrich, K. T. [1989], "Achieving Multiple Goals in Conceptual Design," in *Intelligent CAD* edited by Yoshikawa and Gossard, North-Holland.

Valiant, L. G. [1984], "A Theory of the Learnable," *Comm. of the ACM*, vol. 27, no. 11, pp. 1134–1142.

Van Oosten, J. [1980], "Subjects, Topics and Agents: Evidence from Property-factoring," *Proceedings of the Berkeley Linguistics Society 6*, Berkeley, CA.

Vilain, M. [1985], "The Restricted Language Architecture of a Hybrid Representation System," *Proceedings of the Ninth International Joint Conference on Artificial Intelligence*.

Voelcker, H. B., A. A. G. Requicha, and R. W. Conway [1988], "Computer Applications in Manufacturing," *Ann. Rev. Comput. Sci.*, vol. 3, pp. 349-87.

Waltz, David A. [1985], "Generating semantic descriptions from drawings of scenes with shadows," in *The Psychology of Computer Vision*, edited by P. H. Winston, McGraw-Hill, New York.

Waterman, M. S. [1984], "General Methods of Sequence Comparison," *Bull. of Math. Biol.*, vol. 46, pp. 473-500.

Waters, R. C. [1985], "The Programmer's Apprentice: A session with KBEmacs, *IEEE Trans. on Software Engineering*, vol. 11, no. 11, pp. 1296–1320. Reprinted in Rich and Waters [1986].

Waters, R. C. [1988a], "Program translation via abstraction and reimplementation," *IEEE Trans. on Software Engineering*, vol. 14, no. 8.

Waters, R. C. [1988b], "Using obviously Synchronizable series expressions instead of loops," *Proc. 1988 IEEE Int. Conf. on Computer Languages*, Miami, FL.

Wax, N. [1954], *Selected papers on noise and stochastic processes*, Dover Publications, New York.

Webber, B., and N. Nilsson [1981], *Readings in Artificial Intelligence*, Tioga Publishing Company, Palo Alto, CA.

Webster, T. A., R. H. Lathrop P. H. Winston, and T. F. Smith [1989b], "Predicted Common Structural Motif in DNA-directed and RNA-directed DNA Polymerases," (submitted).

Webster, T. A., R. H. Lathrop, and T. F. Smith [1987], "Prediction of a Common Structural Domain in Aminoacyl-tRNA Synthetases Through Use of a New Pattern-Directed Inference System," *Biochemistry*, vol. 26, pp. 6950–6957.

Webster, T. A., R. H. Lathrop, and T. F. Smith [1988], "Pattern Descriptors and the Unidentified Reading Frame 6 Human mtDNA Dinucleotide-Binding Site" *Proteins*, vol. 3, no. 2, pp. 97–101.

Webster, T. A., R. Patarca R. H. Lathrop, and T. F. Smith [1989a], "Potential Structural Motifs in Reverse Transcriptases," *Mol. Biol. Evol.*, vol. 6, no. 3, pp. 317-320.

Weld, D. [1988], "Comparative Analysis," *Artificial Intelligence*,

Whitney, Daniel E. [1988], "Manufacturing by Design," *Harvard Business Review*.

Williams, B. C. [1984], "Qualitative Analysis of MOS Circuits," *Artificial Intelligence.*

Williams, B. C. [1986], "Doing Time: Putting Qualitative Reasoning on Firmer Ground," *Proceedings of the National Conference on Artificial Intelligence,*

Williams, B. C. [1988], "MINIMA: A Symbolic Approach to Qualitative Reasoning," *Proceedings of the National Conference on Artificial Intelligence.* vol. 24, no. 1-3.

Williams, B. C. [1989], "Invention from First Principles via Topologies of Interaction," Report AI-TR-1127, Artificial Intelligence Laboratory, Massachusetts Institute of Technology, Cambridge, MA. pp. 206-214.

Wills, L. M. [1987], "Automated program recognition," M.S. Thesis, Report AI-TR-904, Artificial Intelligence Laboratory, Massachusetts Institute of Technology, Cambridge, MA.

Wills, L. M. [1990], "Automated Program Recognition: A Feasibility Demonstration," *Artificial Intelligence*, North-Holland, Amsterdam,

Wimsatt, William [1985], "False Models as Means to Truer Theories," in *Systematics Symposium on Neutral Models in Biology*, Chicago, IL. vol. 24, no. 1-3, pp. 281-346.

Wing, J. M. [1988], "A study of 12 specifications of the library problem," *IEEE Software*, pp. 66–76.

Winston, Patrick Henry [1970], "Learning Structural Descriptions from Examples," Ph.D. Thesis, Massachusetts Institute of Technology.

Winston, Patrick Henry (editor) *The Psychology of Computer Vision*, edited by Patrick Henry Winston, McGraw-Hill Book Company, New York.

Winston, Patrick Henry [1980], "Learning and Reasoning by Analogy," *Communications of the Association for Computing Machinery*, vol. 23, no. 12.

Winston, Patrick Henry [1982], "Learning New Principles from Precedents and Exercises," *Artificial Intelligence*, vol. 19, no. 3.

Winston, Patrick Henry [1984], *Artificial Intelligence, Second Edition*, Addison-Wesley, Reading, MA.

Winston, Patrick Henry [1986], "Learning by Augmenting Rules and Accumulating Censors," in Michalski *et al.* [1986].

Winston, Patrick Henry, Thomas O. Binford, Boris Katz, and Michael R. Lowry [1983], "Learning Physical Descriptions from Functional Definitions, Examples, and Precedents," *National Conference on Artificial Intelligence*, Washington, DC.

Winston, P. H., T. O. Binford, B. Katz, and M. Lowry [1983], "Learning Physical Descriptions from Functional Descriptions, Examples, and Precedents," in *Proc. of the Natl. Conf. on Artificial Intelligence*, (Washington, DC., August 22-26, 1983), William Kaufman, Los Altos, CA, 1983, pp. 433-439.

Witkin, Andrew P. [1983], "Scale-Space Filtering," *IJCAI.*

Wolpert, D. [1988], "Alternative generalizers to neural nets," In *Abstracts of the first annual INNS meeting*, New York, Pergamon Press.

Wong, S., A. Wahl, P. Yuan, N. Arai B. Pearson, K. Arai, D. Korn, M. Hunkapillar, T. Wang [1988], "Human DNA Polymerase α Gene Expression is Cell Proliferation Dependent and its Primary Sequence is Similar to Both

Prokaryotic and Eukaryotic Replicative DNA Polymerases," *EMBO J.*, vol. 7, pp. 37–47.

Woods, W. A. [1985], "What's in a Link: Foundations for Semantic Networks," in *Readings in Knowledge Representation*, edited by R. J. Brachman and H. J. Levesque, Morgan Kaufmann Publishers, Los Altos.

Yip, K. [1987], "Extracting qualitative dynamics from numerical experiments," AAAI.

Yip, K. [1988], "Generating global behaviors using deep knowledge of local dynamics," AAAI.

Zahn, C. T. [1971], "Graph-theoretical methods for detecting and describing Gestalt clusters", IEEE, *Trans. on Computers*, vol. C-20.

Zhang, X., D. Waltz, and J. Mesirov [1989], "Protein Structure Prediction by a Data-level Parallel Algorithm," *Proc. Supercomputing 1989*, Nov. 13–17, Reno, NV, USA, pp. 215–223.

Zhao, F. [1987], *An O(N) Algorithm for three-dimensional N-body Simulations*, Report TR–995, Artificial Intelligence Laboratory, Massachusetts Institute of Technology, Cambridge, MA.

Index

S

Contributions

1 **Intelligence in Scientific Computing** by Harold Abelson, Michael Eisenberg, Matthew Halfant, Jacob Katzenelson, Elisha Sacks, Gerald Jay Sussman, Jack Wisdom, and Kenneth Yip, appeared in *Communications of the ACM* [1989] vol. 32, no. 5, pp. 546–562. Copyright ©1989 ACM, reprinted with permission.

2 **Abstraction in Numerical Methods** by Matthew Halfant and Gerald Jay Sussman, appeared in *ACM Lisp and Function Program Communication* [1988], Utah. Copyright ©1988 ACM, reprinted with permission.

3 **Intelligent Tools for Mechanical Design** by Karl T. Ulrich, appeared in *Artificial Intelligence at MIT: Expanding Frontiers*, edited by Patrick H. Winston with Sarah A. Shellard [1990] vol. 1, ch. 3, pp. 52–69, MIT Press, Cambridge, MA. Copyright ©1990 MIT Press.

4 **ARIEL: A Massively Parallel Symbolic Learning Assistant for Protein Structure and Function** by Richard H. Lathrop, Teresa A. Webster, Temple F. Smith, and Patrick H. Winston, appeared in *Artificial Intelligence at MIT: Expanding Frontiers*, edited by Patrick H. Winston with Sarah A. Shellard [1990] vol. 1, ch. 4, pp. 70–103, MIT Press, Cambridge, MA. Copyright ©1990 Richard H. Lathrop.

5 **SIBYL: A Qualitative Decision Management System** by Jintae Lee appeared in *Artificial Intelligence at MIT: Expanding Frontiers*, edited by Patrick H. Winston with Sarah A. Shellard [1990] vol. 1, ch. 5, pp. 104–133, MIT Press, Cambridge, MA. Copyright ©1990 Jintae Lee.

6 **Using English for Indexing and Retrieving** by Boris Katz appeared in *Artificial Intelligence at MIT: Expanding Frontiers*, edited by Patrick H. Winston with Sarah A. Shellard [1990] vol. 1, ch. 6, pp. 134–165, MIT Press, Cambridge, MA. Copyright ©1990 Boris Katz.

7 **The Programmer's Apprentice** by Charles Rich and Richard C. Waters, was first published in *IEEE Computer* [1988], vol. 21, no. 11, pp. 10–25. Copyright ©1988 IEEE, reprinted with permission.

16 **Invention From First Principles: An Overview** by Brian Williams, appeared in *Artificial Intelligence at MIT: Expanding Frontiers*, edited by Patrick H. Winston with Sarah A. Shellard [1990] vol. 1, ch. 16, pp. 430–463, MIT Press, Cambridge, MA. Copyright ©1990 Brian Williams.

17 **Mathematical Knowledge Representation** by David Allen McAllester, is a series of extracts taken from *Ontic: A Knowledge Representation System for Mathematics*, by David A. McAllester [1989] MIT Press, Cambridge, MA. Copyright ©1989 MIT Press, reprinted with permission.

18 **Three Universal Relations** by David Allen McAllester, appeared in *Artificial Intelligence at MIT: Expanding Frontiers*, edited by Patrick H. Winston with Sarah A. Shellard [1990] vol. 1, ch. 18, pp. 486–497, MIT Press, Cambridge, MA. Copyright ©1990 MIT Press.

19 **An Architecture for Mostly Functional Languages** by Tom Knight, appeared in *Proceedings of the Lisp and Functional Programming Conference* [1986]. Copyright ©1986 ACM, reprinted with permission.

20 **Performance Analysis of k-ary n-cube Interconnection Networks** by William J. Dally, is a revision of a paper first published in *Proceedings of the 1987 Stanford Conference on Advanced Research in VLSI, IEEE Transactions on Computers*. Copyright ©1987 IEEE, reprinted with permission.

21 **The J-Machine System** by William J. Dally, appeared in *Artificial Intelligence at MIT: Expanding Frontiers*, edited by Patrick H. Winston with Sarah A. Shellard [1990] vol. 1, ch. 21, pp. 520–547, MIT Press, Cambridge, MA. Copyright ©1990 MIT Press.

22 **Guarded Horn Clause Languages: Are They Deductive and Logical?** by Carl Hewitt and Gul Agha, appeared in *International Conference on Fifth Generation Computer Systems* [1988] ICOT, Tokyo. Copyright ©1988 Carl Hewitt and Gul Agha, reprinted with permission.

23 **Organizations are Open Systems** by Carl Hewitt, appeared in *ACM Transactions on Office Information Systems* [1986] vol. 4, no. 3. Copyright ©1986 ACM, reprinted with permission.

24   **A Robust Layered Control System for a Mobile Robot** by Rodney A. Brooks, is a substantially revised version of a paper first published in *IEEE Journal of Robotics and Automation* [1986], vol. RA-2 no. 1. Copyright ©1986 IEEE, reprinted with permission.

25   **A Robot that Walks: Emergent Behaviors from a Carefully Evolved Network** by Rodney A. Brooks, appeared in *Neural Computation 1:2* [1989], pp. 253-262, MIT Press. Copyright ©1989 MIT Press, reprinted with permission.

26   **Task-Level Planning of Pick-and-Place Robot Motions** by Tomás Lozano-Pérez, Joseph L. Jones, Emmanuel Mazer, and Patrick A. O'Donnell, appeared in *IEEE Computer* [1989], vol 22, no 3. Copyright ©1989 IEEE, reprinted with permission.

27   **Automatic Synthesis of Fine-Motion Strategies for Robots** by Tomás Lozano-Pérez, Matthew T. Mason, and Russell H. Taylor, appeared in *International Journal of Robotics Research* [1984], vol. 3, no 1. Copyright ©1984 MIT Press, reprinted with permission.

28   **Using Associative Content-Addressable Memories to Control Robots** by Christopher G. Atkeson and David J. Reinkensmeyer, appeared in *Artificial Intelligence at MIT: Expanding Frontiers*, edited by Patrick H. Winston with Sarah A. Shellard [1990], vol. 2, ch. 28, pp. 102–127, MIT Press, Cambridge, MA. Copyright ©1990 Christopher G. Atkeson and David J. Reinkensmeyer.

29   **Preshaping Command Inputs to Reduce System Vibration** by Neil C. Singer and Warren P. Seering, appeared in *ASME Journal of Dynamic Systems, Measurement, and Control* [1990], vol. 112, no. 1. Copyright ©1990 ASME, reprinted with permission.

30   **Legged Robots** by Marc H. Raibert, is revised version of a paper first published in *Communications of the ACM* [1986], vol. 29, no. 6. Copyright ©1986 ACM, reprinted with permission.

31   **Biped Gymnastics** by Jessica K. Hodgins and Marc H. Raibert, appeared in *International Journal of Robotics Research* [1990], vol.8, no. 2. Copyright ©1990 MIT Press, reprinted with permission.

32   **Using an Articulated Hand to Manipulate Objects** by Kenneth Salisbury, David Brock, and Patrick O'Donnell, appeared in *Proceeding of the SDF Benchmark Symposium on Robotics Research* [1987], Santa Cruz, CA. Copyright ©1987 MIT Press, reprinted with permission.

33 **An Experimental Whole-Arm Manipulator** by Kenneth Salisbury, Brian Eberman, Michael Levin, and William Townsend, appeared in *Robotics Research: The Fifth International Symposium* [1989], Tokyo, Japan. Copyright ©1990 MIT Press, reprinted with permission.

34 **Calibrating Closed Kinematic Chains** by David J. Bennett and John M. Hollerbach, appeared in *Artificial Intelligence at MIT: Expanding Frontiers*, edited by Patrick H. Winston with Sarah A. Shellard [1990], vol. 2, ch. 34, pp. 250–267, MIT Press, Cambridge, MA. Copyright ©1990 MIT Press.

35 **Identifying the Kinematics of Robots** by David J. Bennett and John M. Hollerbach, appeared in *Artificial Intelligence at MIT: Expanding Frontiers*, edited by Patrick H. Winston with Sarah A. Shellard [1990], vol. 2, ch. 35, pp. 268–285, MIT Press, Cambridge, MA. Copyright ©1990 MIT Press.

36 **Object Recognition by Constrained Search** by W. Eric L. Grimson, appeared in *Machine Vision—Acquiring and Interpreting the 3D Scene* edited by Herbert Freeman, Academic Press [1990]. Copyright ©1990 Academic Press, reprinted with permission.

37 **On the Recognition of Parameterized 2D Objects** by W. Eric L. Grimson, is a revised version of a paper first published in *International Journal of Computer Vision* [1988], vol. 3, pp. 353–372. Copyright ©1988 Kluwer Academic Publishers, reprinted with permission.

38 **Aligning Pictorial Descriptions** by Shimon Ullman, appeared in *Cognition* [1989], vol. 32, no. 3, pp. 193-254. Copyright ©1989 North-Holland Publishers, reprinted with permission.

39 **Maximizing Rigidity: Recovery of 3-D Structure from Motion** by Shimon Ullman appeared in *Perception* [1984], vol. 13, pp. 255-274. Copyright ©1984 Pion Publishers, reprinted with permission.

40 **Direct Methods for Recovering Motion** by Berthold K. P. Horn and E. J. Weldon Jr., appeared in *International Journal of Computer Vision* [1988], no. 2, pp. 51-76, Kluwer Academic Publishers. Copyright ©1988 Kluwer Academic Publishers, reprinted with permission.

41 **Computational Vision and Regularization Theory** by Tomaso Poggio, Vincent Torre, and Christof Koch, appeared in *Nature* [1985],

vol. 317, no. 26. Copyright ©1985 Macmillan Journals, reprinted with permission.

42 **The MIT Vision Machine** by T. Poggio, J. Little, E. Gamble, W. Gillett, D. Geiger, D. Weinshall, M. Villalba, N. Larson, T. Cass, H. Bülthoff, M. Drumheller, P. Oppenheimer, W. Yang, A. Hurlbert, D. Beymer, and P. O'Donnell, appeared in *Proceedings of the Image Understanding Workshop* [1988], edited by L. Bauman, SAI Corp., McLean,VA. Copyright ©1988 Morgan Kaufmann Publishers, reprinted with permission.

43 **Parallel Networks for Machine Vision** by Berthold K. P. Horn, appeared in *Artificial Intelligence at MIT: Expanding Frontiers*, edited by Patrick H. Winston with Sarah A. Shellard [1990], vol. 2, ch. 43, pp. 530–573, MIT Press, Cambridge, MA. Copyright ©1990 MIT Press.

Artificial Intelligence

Patrick Henry Winston and J. Michael Brady, founding editors. J. Michael Brady, Daniel G. Bobrow, and Randall Davis, current editors.

Artificial Intelligence: An MIT Perspective, Volume I: Expert Problem Solving, Natural Language Understanding, Intelligent Computer Coaches, Representation and Learning, edited by Patrick Henry Winston and Richard Henry Brown, 1979.

Artificial Intelligence: An MIT Perspective, Volume II: Understanding Vision, Manipulation, Computer Design, Symbol Manipulation, edited by Patrick Henry Winston and Richard Henry Brown, 1979.

NETL: A System for Representing and Using Real-World Knowledge, Scott Fahlman, 1979.

The Interpretation of Visual Motion, by Shimon Ullman, 1979.

A Theory of Syntactic Recognition for Natural Language, Mitchell P. Marcus, 1980.

Turtle Geometry: The Computer as a Medium for Exploring Mathematics, Harold Abelson and Andrea di Sessa, 1981.

From Images to Surfaces: A Computational Study of the Human Visual System, William Eric Leifur Grimson, 1981.

Robot Manipulators: Mathematics, Programming, and Control, Richard P. Paul, 1981.

Computational Models of Discourse, edited by Michael Brady and Robert C. Berwick, 1982.

Robot Motion: Planning and Control, edited by Michael Brady, John M. Hollerbach, Timothy Johnson, Tomás Lozano-Pérez, and Matthew T. Mason, 1982.

In-Depth Understanding: A Computer Model of Integrated Processing for Narrative Comprehension, Michael G. Dyer, 1983.

Robotic Research: The First International Symposium, edited by Hideo Hanufusa and Hirochika Inoue, 1985.

Robot Hands and the Mechanics of Manipulation, Matthew T. Mason and J. Kenneth Salisbury, Jr., 1985.

The Acquisition of Syntactic Knowledge, Robert C. Berwick, 1985.

The Connection Machine, W. Daniel Hillis, 1985.

Legged Robots that Balance, Marc H. Raibert, 1986.

Robotics Research: The Third International Symposium, edited by O. D. Faugeras and Georges Giralt, 1986.

Machine Interpretation of Line Drawings, Kokichi Sugihara, 1986.

ACTORS: A Model of Concurrent Computation in Distributed Systems, Gul A. Agha, 1986.

Knowledge-Based Tutoring: The GUIDON Program, William Clancey, 1987.

AI in the 1980's and Beyond: An MIT Survey, edited by W. Eric L. Grimson and Ramesh S. Patil, 1987.

Visual Reconstruction, Andrew Blake and Andrew Zisserman, 1987.

Reasoning about Change: Time and Causation from the Standpoint of Artificial Intelligence, Yoav Shoham, 1988.

Model-Based Control of a Robot Manipulator Chae H. An, Christopher G. Atkeson, and John M. Hollerbach, 1988.

A Robot Ping-Pong Player: Experiment in Real-Time Intelligent Control, Russell L. Andersson, 1988.

Robotics Research: The Fourth International Symposium, edited by Robert C. Bolles and Bernard Roth, 1988.

The Paralation Model: Architecture-Independent Parallel Programming, Gary Sabot, 1988.

Concurrent System for Knowledge Processing: An Actor Perspective, edited by Carl Hewitt and Gul Agha, 1989.

Solid Shape, Jan J. Koenderink, 1989.

Automated Deduction in Nonclassical Logics: Efficient Matrix Proof Methods for Modal and Intuitionistic Logics, Lincoln Wallen, 1989.

3D Model Recognition from Stereoscopic Cues, edited by John E. W. Mayhew and John P. Frisby, 1989.

Shape and Shading, edited by Berthold K. P. Horn and Michael J. Brooks, 1989.

Artificial Intelligence at MIT: Expanding Frontiers, edited by Patrick Henry Winston with Sarah Alexandra Shellard, 1990.

The MIT Press, with Peter Denning, general consulting editor, and Brian Randell, European consulting editor, publishes computer science books in the following series:

ACM Doctoral Dissertation Award and Distinguished Dissertation Series

Artificial Intelligence, Michael Brady, Daniel Bobrow, and Randall Davis, editors

Charles Babbage Institute Reprint Series for the History of Computing, Martin Campbell-Kelly, editor

Computer Systems, Herb Schwetman, editor

Exploring with Logo, E. Paul Goldenberg, editor

Foundations of Computing, Michael Garey and Albert Meyer, editors

History of Computing I, Bernard Cohen and William Aspray, editors

Information Systems, Michael Lesk, editor

Logic Programming, Ehud Shapiro, editor; Fernando Pereira, Koichi Furukawa, and D. H. D. Warren, associate editors

The MIT Electrical Engineering and Computer Science Series

Research Monographs in Parallel and Distributed processing, Christopher Jesshope and David Klappholz, editors

Scientific Computation, Dennis Gannon, editor

CPSIA information can be obtained
at www.ICGtesting.com
Printed in the USA
FFHW011116271219
57296414-62781FF